DUMBARTON OAKS STUDIES

XXXIV

Codex Parisinus Graecus 1115
and Its Archetype

Codex Parisinus Graecus 1115
and Its Archetype

Alexander Alexakis

Dumbarton Oaks Research Library and Collection

Washington, D.C.

© 1996 Dumbarton Oaks
Trustees for Harvard University
Washington, D.C.

Library of Congress Cataloging-in-Publication Data

Alexakis, Alexander.
    Codex Parisinus Graecus 1115 and its archetype / Alexander
Alexakis.
        p.   cm.—(Dumbarton Oaks studies ; 34)
    Includes bibliographical references and indexes.
    ISBN 0-88402-234-X (alk. paper)
    1. Codex Parisinus Graecus 1115.   2. Councils and synods.
Ecumenical.   3. Council of Nicaea (2nd : 787)   4. Manuscripts, Greek
(Medieval and modern).   5. Icons—Cult.   I. Title.   II. Series.
BR203.A54   1996
262'.514—dc20   96-3603
                                                                       CIP

CONTENTS

Preface   ix
List of Abbreviations   xii
List of Manuscripts Cited   xvii
List of Illustrations   xviii

I. The Use of Florilegia in Church Councils   1

1. Introduction   1
2. The Florilegia of the Council of Ephesus (431)   6
3. The Florilegium of the Council of Chalcedon (451)   8
4. The Florilegia of the Council of Constantinople II (553)   10
5. The Lateran Council of 649   16
6. The Florilegia of the Council of Constantinople III (680/81)   21
7. The Iconoclastic Florilegia of the Synods of Hiereia (754) and St. Sophia (815)   31
8. The Florilegia of the Roman Synods of 731 and 769   37
9. Conclusions   41

II. Codex Parisinus Graecus 1115   43

1. Introduction   43
2. Bibliographic Survey   43
3. The Additional Part of Codex P and the Epistles Related to the Council of Ephesus   53
4. The *Collectio Epistularum* from the Fourth, Fifth, and Sixth Ecumenical Councils   55
     Fourth Ecumenical Council   55
     Fifth Ecumenical Council   55
     Sixth Ecumenical Council   57
5. Dogmatic Texts in the Form of Ἐρωταποκρίσεις: *Hodegos* (parts I and II), *Testimonia e scriptura,* and *De dogmatum solutione*   57
6. The Parts from the *Doctrina Patrum*   58
7. The Florilegium on the Procession of the Holy Spirit   71
8. The Collection of *Miscellanea:* (a) *Historica et canonica,* (b) *Canonica et dogmatica*   85

III. The Iconophile Florilegium of Parisinus Graecus 1115   92

1. Introduction   92
2. The *Adversus Iconoclastas*   93
3. Restoring the Initial Extent of the Iconophile Florilegium of 770: P and the Iconophile Florilegia of M and V   100
   The Two Letters of Pope Gregory II to Leo III   108
   The *Adversus Constantinum Caballinum* and the Νουθεσία γέροντος περὶ τῶν ἁγίων εἰκόνων   110
4. The Original of P, M, and V (= F) and Other Florilegia   116
   The Florilegium of the Roman Councils of 731 and 769   116
   The *Doctrina Patrum*   123
   The Florilegia of John of Damascus   125
   Conclusions   134
5. F and the Acts of Nicaea II (787)   137
   Introduction   137
   PVM and the Quotations of Nicaea II   141
   Conclusions   214
6. F and Works Later than Nicaea II   222

IV. On the Use of Florilegia by the Seventh Ecumenical Council, Nicaea II, 787   227

V. The Archetype of Codex Parisinus Graecus 1115, the *Liber de Fide Trinitatis* (*Libellus*) of Nicholas of Cotrone, and the Treatise *Contra Errores Graecorum* of Thomas Aquinas   234

1. The Treatise *Contra Errores Graecorum* of Thomas Aquinas and the *Libellus* of Nicholas of Cotrone   234
2. The *Libellus* and the Archetype of Paris. gr. 1115   240

VI. Conclusions   254

1. The Nature of the Archetype of Paris. gr. 1115   254
2. The Availability of Greek Books in Rome until the Ninth Century   257

Appendices

I. List of Contents of Parisinus Graecus 1115 (fols. 235ᵛ–283ᵛ not included) ... 261

II. List of Contents of Folios 235ᵛ–283ᵛ of Parisinus Graecus 1115 (Iconophile Florilegium) ... 313

III. List of Contents of the Iconophile Florilegium of Mosquensis Historici Musei 265 (Vladimir 197) (M) (fols. 142–241) ... 335

IV. List of Contents of the Iconophile Florilegium of Venetus Marcianus Graecus 573 (V) (fols. 2–26) ... 343

V. Concordance of Appendices II–IV and Other Iconophile Florilegia ... 352

VI. Possible Stemma of Iconophile Florilegia ... 360

Addenda ... 361
Bibliography ... 363
General Index ... 379
Index of Proper Names ... 387
Index of Works Cited ... 393
Index of Manuscripts Cited ... 416
Index of Modern Authors ... 419

PREFACE

This book began as a doctoral dissertation planned in December 1988 at an Oxford pub, during a semi-official tutorial with Professor Cyril Mango. It was a period when five of his graduate students used to gather together after his Monday lectures on Byzantine Constantinople and discuss with him the problems we had in mind. In the course of these discussions Professor Mango suggested the subject of this book to me: "You know, there is a manuscript whose colophon contains detailed information concerning the manuscript itself and its archetype. Some people accept this information at face value, others disagree with them. You would possibly like to prove who's right." This was the beginning, and in the course of my research the initial question had to be broken down into many particular problems stemming, on many occasions, from what other researchers had written on codex Parisinus graecus 1115. The results, however, were rewarding, and from the colophon the research extended to the entire manuscript and to its archetype. During the two and a half years of research at Oxford, the initial findings concerning the use of florilegia by the ecumenical councils, and in particular by the seventh ecumenical council, were followed by discoveries on the beginning of the *Filioque* controversy, until Thomas Aquinas entered the picture. For that period the help and support of Professor Mango were invaluable, and the final shape of my dissertation owes much to his guidance. I also had considerable help from Prof. J. Howard-Johnston and my colleagues at that time, Prof. Ioannes Polemis—who is always present in my mind as the "person with the right answers to the right questions" that saved me weeks of research—Dr. Stefanos Efthymiades, Professor Claudia Rapp, and from Father J. Munitiz, Master of Campion Hall, Oxford, to all of whom I would like to extend my grateful thanks.

My subsequent work at Dumbarton Oaks brought me into contact with many people who took the trouble to read my dissertation and suggested improvements and changes to many parts of it. Among them, Professor E. Chrysos of the University of Ioannina offered me advice and references (especially to German bibliography) that helped me bridge the gap that separates a dissertation from a book proper. The reader will easily find how much this book owes to his erudite suggestions. Professor S. Gero's criticism and objections helped me focus on particular weaknesses of my study.

In this brief account of my indebtedness I wish to include Professor

A. Markopoulos of the University of Crete and Dr. Sebastian Brock of the University of Oxford for their eagerness to provide me with last-minute information on new editions and articles related to the subject of this book. I am also gratefully indebted to the Rev. Professor Henry Chadwick for his support, advice, and encouragement for the last three years. Dr. Michael Kakouros helped me from Paris when an *in situ* examination of the manuscript was impossible for me to carry out. I must also underscore the fact that much of the inspiration for the work I have put into this book came from endless hours spent in the mid-1980s discussing the manifold aspects of Byzantine Christianity with my friend Demetrios Kalomoirakes. The technical part of my work also owes much to the knowledge imparted to me by the excellent educational system of pre-1980 Greece and to Mr. Zacharias Androulakes, my private tutor in classics, who put that knowledge into order in 1977–78.

Dumbarton Oaks and its Byzantine Library would not have been the best possible environment for the writing of this book without the presence of Dr. Irene Vaslef and Mr. Mark Zapatka, who many times provided me with rare books and articles through interlibrary loans. I would like to conclude the list of my colleagues in scholarship with my heartfelt thanks to Victoria Erhart and Dr. Eric McGeer, who read parts of the book and corrected my English. I am enormously thankful to the people who read the entire manuscript and suggested a number of changes: the two anonymous readers whose detailed corrections and suggestions have contributed much to the improvement of this work; Dr. Alice-Mary Talbot; the copy-editor, Dr. Frances Kianka; the proofreader, Dr. Leslie MacCoull, and the industrious staff of the Dumbarton Oaks Publishing Service: Glenn Ruby, Robin Surratt and Matthew Rieck. Of course I alone am responsible for any mistakes and inaccuracies.

I am also grateful to Mr. Vassilis Gregoropoulos and Dr. George Mastorakis for the help and inspiration I received from them in the form of letters and taped music. Finally, I cannot conclude this small list without mentioning my wife, Georgia, who took great pains to secure a peaceful and inspiring environment for my work and had the patience to wait for me during my long periods of mental absence and during my endless peregrinations in the realms of scholarly hypotheses. Any expression of thankfulness toward her fails to match her contribution.

I hope that the readers will find this book not that much user-unfriendly and to that effect I add here some warnings. The names of the Byzantine and Latin authors (of which there are dozens) are given in their Latin form (according to the standards set out by the *Clavis Patrum Grae-*

corum) when listed along with their works in catalogues and in the Appendices; otherwise, I have adopted their English transliteration. For the passages that I discuss in the course of this study I usually retain the spelling and the punctuation of the manuscript(s) and omit the iota subscript. However, in the Appendices and when the text is taken from a printed edition this rule is not applied. I am aware that a careful reader will find many inconsistencies, especially with my use of the indication (sic) which I kept only for the cases of misspellings I personally considered as "frappantes." To this and to other criticisms I can only respond with a small phrase written by an anonymous 12th-century scribe at the end of the colophon of codex Parisinus graecus 633: Σύγγνωτέ μοι, παρακαλῶ, εἴ τι ἐσφάλην ἀπό τε ὀξείας, βαρείας, ἀποστρόφου, δασείας τε καὶ ψιλῆς καὶ ὁ Θεὸς σώσει ὑμᾶς πάντας.

LIST OF ABBREVIATIONS

AASS	*Acta Sanctorum Bollandiana* (Brussels, 1643 ff)
AB	*Analecta Bollandiana*
AbhMünch- Philos.- hist.Kl.	Abhandlungen der Bayerischen Akademie der Wissenschaften, München, Philosophisch-historische Klasse
ACO	*Acta Conciliorum Oecumenicorum,* 4 vols. in 27 parts, ed. E. Schwartz (Berlin, 1914–40); J. Straub (1971); R. Riedinger, *Series Secunda* (Berlin, 1984–92)
AHC	*Annuarium Historiae Conciliorum*
Alexander, *Nicephorus*	P. J. Alexander, *The Patriarch Nicephorus of Constantinople: Ecclesiastical Policy and Image Worship in the Byzantine Empire* (Oxford, 1958)
BCH	*Bulletin de correspondance hellénique*
Beck, *KThL*	H.-G. Beck, *Kirche und theologische Literatur im byzantinischen Reich* (Munich, 1959)
BHG	*Bibliotheca Hagiographica Graeca,* 3rd ed., ed. F. Halkin, 3 vols., SubsHag 8a (Brussels, 1957)
BZ	*Byzantinische Zeitschrift*
CCSA	*Corpus Christianorum Series Apocryphorum* (Turnhout, 1983 ff)
CCSG	*Corpus Christianorum Series Graeca* (Turnhout, 1976 ff)
CCSL	*Corpus Christianorum Series Latina* (Turnhout, 1953 ff)
CEG	*Contra errores Graecorum = Sancti Thomae de Aquino Opera omnia iussu Leonis XIII P.M. edita.* Tomus XL, *Contra errores Graecorum,* ed. H. F. Dondaine (Rome, 1969)
CFHB	*Corpus Fontium Historiae Byzantinae* (Berlin, etc., 1967 ff)
CPG	*Clavis Patrum Graecorum,* ed. M. Geerard, vols. II–IV (Turnhout, 1974–80)
CPL	*Clavis Patrum Latinorum,* 2nd ed., ed. E. Dekkers (Steenbrugge, 1961)
CSCO	*Corpus Scriptorum Christianorum Orientalium* (Louvain, 1903 ff)
CSEL	*Corpus Scriptorum Ecclesiasticorum Latinorum* (Vienna, 1866 ff)
Diekamp, *Doctrina Patrum*	F. Diekamp, *Doctrina Patrum de incarnatione Verbi: Ein griechisches Florilegium aus der Wende des siebenten und achten Jahrhunderts* (Münster, 1907, reedited with additions by E. Chrysos and B. Phanourgakis, Münster, 1981)

DOP	*Dumbarton Oaks Papers*
DOS	Dumbarton Oaks Studies
DSp	*Dictionnaire de spiritualité ascétique et mystique*
DTC	*Dictionnaire de théologie catholique*
EO	*Échos d'Orient*
GCS	*Die griechischen christlichen Schriftsteller der ersten [drei] Jahrhunderte*
Gero, Constantine V	S. Gero, *Byzantine Iconoclasm during the Reign of Constantine V: With Particular Attention to the Oriental Sources*, CSCO 384, Subsidia 52 (Louvain, 1977)
Gero, *Leo III*	S. Gero, *Byzantine Iconoclasm during the Reign of Leo III: With particular Attention to the Oriental Sources*, CSCO 346, Subsidia 41 (Louvain, 1973)
Gill, *Quae supersunt*	J. Gill (ed.), *Concilium Florentinum Series B: Quae supersunt auctorum graecorum Concilii Florentini*, Pars I, vol. V, fasc. 1–2, (Rome, 1953)
GOTR	*Greek Orthodox Theological Review*
Gouillard, "Origines"	J. Gouillard, "Aux origines de l'Iconoclasme: Le témoignage de Grégoire II?" *TM* 3 (1968), 243–307
Gregory of Nazianzus: Bernardi, *Discours 1–3*	*Grégoire de Nazianze, Discours 1–3*, ed. J. Bernardi, *SC* 247 (Paris, 1978)
Bernardi, *Discours 4–5*	*Grégoire de Nazianze, Discours 4–5, contre Julien*, ed. J. Bernardi, *SC* 309 (Paris, 1983)
Mossay, *Discours 20–23*	*Grégoire de Nazianze, Discours 20–23*, ed. J. Mossay, *SC* 247 (Paris, 1978)
Mossay, *Discours 24–26*	*Grégoire de Nazianze, Discours 24–26*, ed. J. Mossay, *SC* 284 (Paris, 1981)
Gallay, *Discours 27–31*	*Grégoire de Nazianze, Discours 27–31*, ed. P. Gallay, *SC* 250 (Paris, 1978)
Moreschini, *Discours 32–37*	*Grégoire de Nazianze, Discours 32–37*, ed. C. Moreschini, *SC* 318 (Paris, 1985)
Moreschini, *Discours 38–41*	*Grégoire de Nazianze, Discours 38–41*, ed. C. Moreschini, *SC* 358 (Paris, 1990)
Bernardi, *Discours 42–43*	*Grégoire de Nazianze, Discours 42–43*, ed. J. Bernardi, *SC* 384 (Paris, 1992)

Grumel,   V. Grumel, *Les regestes des Actes du Patriarchat de*
   Regestes   *Constantinople*, vol. I, fasc. 2–3, 2nd ed. revised by J.
                 Darrouzès (Paris, 1989)

Hadrian I,   *Hadrianum*, ed. K. Hampe, *MGH, Epistulae 5, Karolini Aevi* 3
   Hadrianum   (Berlin, 1899), 5–57

HSCPh   *Harvard Studies in Classical Philology*

HTR   *Harvard Theological Review*

Hussey, *The*   J. M. Hussey, *The Orthodox Church in the Byzantine Empire*
   Orthodox   (Oxford, 1986)
   Church

JE   P. Jaffé, *Regesta Pontificum Romanorum ab Condita Ecclesia ad*
                 Annum post Christum Natum MCXCVIII, 2nd ed. G.
                 Wattenbach (Leipzig, 1885–88)

JÖB   *Jahrbuch der Österreichischen Byzantinistik*

JTS   *Journal of Theological Studies*

Kotter,   B. Kotter, ed., *Die Schriften des Johannes von Damaskos*, vol.
   Schriften III   III, *Contra Imaginum Calumniatores Orationes Tres, PTS* 17
                 (Berlin-New York, 1975)

Lampe   G.W.H. Lampe, *A Patristic Greek Lexicon* (Oxford, 1961–68)

Liber   *Liber Pontificalis*, ed. L. Duchesne, 2 vols. (Paris, 1886–92)
   Pontificalis

Mango,   C. Mango, "The Availability of Books in the Byzantine
   "Availability"   Empire, A.D. 750–850," in *Byzantine Books and Bookmen: A*
                 Dumbarton Oaks Colloquium (Washington, D.C., 1975),
                 29–45

Mansi   J. D. Mansi, *Sacrorum Conciliorum Nova et Amplissima*
                 Collectio, 31 vols. (Florence-Venice, 1759–98)

Melioranskij,   B. M. Melioranskij, *Georgij Kiprianin i Ioann Ierusalimlianin,*
   Georgij   *dva maloizviestnych bortsa za pravoslavie v VIII viekie* (St.
                 Petersburg, 1901)

MGH   *Monumenta Germaniae Historica* (Hanover, 1826 ff)

Migne   See *PG, PL*

Munitiz,   J. Munitiz, "Le *Parisinus Graecus 1115:* Description et
   "Parisinus"   arrière-plan historique," *Scriptorium* 36 (1982), 51–67

OCA   *Orientalia Christiana Analecta*

OCP   *Orientalia Christiana Periodica*

ODB   *The Oxford Dictionary of Byzantium*, ed. A. Kazhdan et al., 3
                 vols. (New York-Oxford, 1991)

PG   *Patrologiae Cursus Completus, Series Graeca*, ed. J. P. Migne
                 (Paris, 1857–66)

PL   *Patrologiae Cursus Completus, Series Latina*, ed. J. P. Migne
                 (Paris, 1844–55)

PLP   *Prosopographisches Lexikon der Palaiologenzeit*, ed. E. Trapp et
                 al. (Vienna, 1977–94)

PO	*Patrologia Orientalis,* ed. R. Graffin and F. Nau (Paris, 1903 ff)
Ps.-Dionysius Areopagita: *Corpus Dionysiacum,* I	*De divinis nominibus,* ed. B. R. Suchla, *Corpus Dionysiacum,* I. *Pseudo-Dionysius Areopagita De divinis nominibus, PTS* 33 (Berlin-New York, 1990)
Corpus Dionysiacum, II	*De coelesti hierarchia, De ecclesiastica hierarchia, De mystica theologia, Epistulae,* ed. G. Heil and A. M. Ritter, *Corpus Dionysiacum,* II, *PTS* 36 (Berlin-New York, 1991)
PTS	*Patristische Texte und Studien* (Berlin, 1964 ff)
RAC	*Reallexikon für Antike und Christentum,* ed. Th. Clauser (Stuttgart, 1950 ff)
RBibl	*Revue biblique*
REB	*Revue des études byzantines*
RevSR	*Revue des sciences religieuses*
RHE	*Revue d'histoire ecclésiastique*
ROC	*Revue de l'Orient chrétien*
RSPhTh	*Revue des sciences philosophiques et théologiques*
Sansterre, *Les moines grecs*	J. M. Sansterre, *Les moines grecs à Rome aux époques byzantine et carolingienne (milieux du VIᵉ siècle–fin du XIᵉ siècle)* (Brussels, 1983)
SBMünch-Philos.-hist.Kl.	Sitzungsberichte der Bayerischen Akademie der Wissenschaften, München, Philosophisch-historische Klasse
SBWien	Sitzungsberichte der Kaiserlichen (österreichischen) Akademie der Wissenschaften, Wien, Philosophisch-historische Klasse
SC	*Sources chrétiennes* (Paris, 1924 ff)
ST	*Studi e testi* (Rome, 1900 ff)
SubsHag	Subsidia Hagiographica, Société des Bollandistes
Thümmel, *Frühgeschichte*	H. G. Thümmel, *Die Frühgeschichte der ostkirchlichen Bilderlehre (Texte und Untersuchungen zur Zeit vor dem Bilderstreit), TU* 139 (Berlin, 1992)
TLG	*Thesaurus Linguae Graecae* (located at the Univ. of California at Irvine)
TM	*Travaux et mémoires* (Paris, 1965 ff)
TU	*Texte und Untersuchungen zur Geschichte der altchristlichen Literatur. Archiv für die griechisch-christlichen Schriftsteller der ersten drei Jahrhunderte* (Leipzig-Berlin, 1882 ff)
Uthemann, "Ein Beitrag"	K.-H. Uthemann, "Ein Beitrag zur Geschichte der Union des Konzils von Lyon (1274): Bemerkungen zum Codex Parisinus gr. 1115 (Med. Reg. 2951)," *AHC* 13 (1981), 27–49

Van den Ven,   P. van den Ven, "La patristique et l'hagiographie au concile
  "Patristique"   de Nicée de 787," *Byzantion* 25–27 (1955–57), 325–62

Wallach,   L. Wallach, *Diplomatic Studies in Latin and Greek Documents
  Diplomatic   from the Carolingian Age* (Ithaca-London, 1977)
  Studies

ZKG   *Zeitschrift für Kirchengeschichte*

LIST OF MANUSCRIPTS CITED

Ar	Londiniensis Musei Britannici Arundelianus 529
B	Mediolanensis Bibliothecae Nationalis Brerae, AF.X.47
Ba	Vaticanus graecus 1255
C	Vaticanus graecus 2013
D	Vaticanus Pii II graecus 23
Fa	Parisinus graecus 582
M	Mosquensis Historici Musei 265 (Vladimir 197)
Ma	Venetus Marcianus graecus 166
N	Vaticanus graecus 511 (fols. 66ᵛ–69ᵛ)
Na	Vaticanus graecus 660
O	Vaticanus Ottobonianus graecus 27
Oa	Vaticanus Ottobonianus graecus 14
P or Parisinus	Parisinus graecus 1115
S	Scorialensis graecus 449 (Ψ.II.14)
T	Taurinensis Bibliothecae Nationalis 110
V	Venetus Marcianus graecus 573
Va	Vaticanus graecus 836
W	Vindobonensis historicus graecus 29
X	Vaticanus graecus 834
Y	Vaticanus graecus 1181

LIST OF ILLUSTRATIONS

1 Paris. gr. 1115, fol. 1. Written by a fourteenth-century scribe on an additional sheet of paper; the older numberings are present on the upper margin. (photo: courtesy Bibliothèque Nationale, Paris)

2 Paris. gr. 1115, fol. 2. Written by the same scribe who wrote fol. 1. (photo: courtesy Bibliothèque Nationale, Paris)

3 Paris. gr. 1115, fol. 8ᵛ. The upper nine lines are written by scribe X1 (see p. 53), and the remainder by Leo Cinnamus. (photo: courtesy Bibliothèque Nationale, Paris)

4 Paris. gr. 1115, fol. 208. Note the Greek *Filioque* on lines 21 and 22. (photo: courtesy Bibliothèque Nationale, Paris)

5–6 Paris. gr. 1115, fols. 224ᵛ–225. The opening lines of the *Chronographiae* of Julius Sextus Africanus start at line 35 (see pp. 86–87). (photo: courtesy Bibliothèque Nationale, Paris)

7 Paris. gr. 1115, fol. 235ᵛ. The beginning of the frontispiece of the Iconophile florilegium (*Adversus Iconoclastas*). (photo: courtesy Bibliothèque Nationale, Paris)

8 Paris. gr. 1115, fol. 283ᵛ. The end of the Iconophile florilegium with the anathemas against the Iconoclast bishops of Hiereia. (photo: courtesy Bibliothèque Nationale, Paris)

9 Paris. gr. 1115, fol. 306ᵛ. The colophon of the manuscript; a note by a later hand is on the lower part of the page. (photo: courtesy Bibliothèque Nationale, Paris)

10 Codex Venetus Marc. gr. 573, fols. 3ᵛ–4. (photo: courtesy the Biblioteca Marciana, Venice)

11 Codex Mosquensis Hist. Musei 265, fol. 209. (photo: courtesy the Historical Museum, Moscow)

Codex Parisinus Graecus 1115
and Its Archetype

CHAPTER I

The Use of Florilegia in Church Councils

1. Introduction

This study deals with codex Parisinus graecus 1115 (Parisinus or P), a manuscript written, according to its colophon, in 1276, and with its archetype that is dated, according to the same colophon, to the year 759/60 or 774/75. P contains a number of Greek patristic florilegia relating to church councils,[1] and other ecclesiastical literature including sections from the recorded acts of the ecumenical councils. On fol. 4ᵛ, F. Combefis had written that in this manuscript "multa . . . continentur quibus illustrari possunt concilia III, IV, V, VI, et VII." Accordingly, all the editors of the *Acta Conciliorum Oecumenicorum* have taken Parisinus into account for the critical editions of the existing minutes of the councils. Since we now have in printed form the acts of all the ecumenical councils from Ephesus (431) to Constantinople III (680/81), including the Lateran Council of 649, many of the problems concerning the relationship of P to all these councils have been resolved.[2]

However, its relationship to the acts of the seventh ecumenical council (Nicaea II, 787) remains unclear. Although Parisinus preserves parts of the acts of all the councils from Ephesus to Constantinople III (again including the Lateran Council), the only thing in P that is related to the seventh ecu-

---

[1] There is already ample literature on the subject. See, for example, C. Hefele and H. Leclercq, *Histoire des conciles* (Paris, 1907 ff), vol. II.1, 302–5, 309 and n. 1; vol. II.2, 730–31; vol. III.1, 84–89, 91, 105–6, 434–51, etc.; J. de Ghellinck, *Patristique et moyen âge*, vol. II (Brussels-Paris, 1947), 291–92; Van den Ven, "Patristique," 325–31; M. Richard, "Les florilèges diphysites du Vᵉ et du VIᵉ siècle," in *Das Konzil von Chalkedon, Geschichte und Gegenwart*, ed. A. Grillmeier and H. Bacht (Würzburg, 1951), 721–48. On the subject of florilegia in general, see M. Richard, "Florilèges spirituels grecs," *DSp*, vol. 5, cols. 475–512; "Florilegium" by H. Chadwick, *RAC* 7 (1969), cols. 1131–60 (includes further bibliography); and *ODB*, 793–94. The most recent and comprehensive study of florilegia for the period between 451 and ca. 730 is found in A. Grillmeier, *Jesus der Christus im Glauben der Kirche*, vol. II.1 (Freiburg-Basel-Vienna, 1985), 58–88.

[2] See *ACO* I,1,1 p. VII; I,1,4 pp. XXVI, XXVIII; I,1,7 p. VIII ff; I,4 p. 73; II,1,1 p. VIIII; II,1,2 p. VI; II,4 p. XXXXVI (X/X1); IV,1 pp. V, XXIV ff, XXX.141–208 (Π). *ACO* IV,3,1 (= *Index Generalis Tomorum I–IIII* by R. Schieffer, 1974), p. 36; *ACO Ser. II*, vol. I, p. XI ff; II,1 p. VIII n. 5, pp. X–XI, XIII.

menical council is an Iconophile florilegium that contains a large number of Iconophile quotations. Some of these quotations can also be found in the acts of the seventh ecumenical council, but P alone preserves many more than Nicaea II does. In addition, as far as the quotations shared by the acts and P are concerned, the two transmissions present very similar (if not identical) texts. This raises a question that has puzzled many scholars during the last three centuries: was the archetype of P copied from the acts of the seventh ecumenical council (Nicaea II) or not?[3]

Where this question is concerned, matters become even more complicated. If one reviews the florilegia that appear in the acts of the Council of Ephesus (431) or those of the Lateran Council (649), and other councils in between, it seems that: (a) these florilegia were prepared in advance, and (b) their use had superseded that of books containing the entire works from which the fragments of the florilegia had been taken. It is possible that the first deviation from this practice was that of Constantinople III. At this council, in addition to florilegia, books were used to check the textual accuracy of the fragments included in some monothelete and dyothelete anthologies. According to Van den Ven, the first exception to the practice of using florilegia occurs during the fourth and fifth sessions of Nicaea II in 787. Van den Ven, in his brief recapitulation of the use of florilegia, made the absolute claim that: "Le concile de 787 n'a fait usage d'aucun florilège, fût-il de S. Jean Damascène."[4] His statement alleges a noteworthy exception to an uninterrupted tradition of at least three centuries, a tradition that was also followed during the centuries after the council of 787. Van den Ven's opinion may, at first sight, seem justified: in the acts of Nicaea II, it is evident that passages from patristic works and other Iconophile *testimonia* were read out from books presented to the assembly by various clerics, and not from a florilegium or florilegia. And if this is so, the archetype of Parisinus must have been copied from the acts of Nicaea II. Can this truly be the case?

To obtain a more accurate idea about what happened at Nicaea in 787, it is useful to try to establish the role that florilegia played in conciliar procedures, that is, how the major church councils used them, their possible relationship to preexisting florilegia, and the significance that they acquired from council to council.[5]

---

[3] Of course, this is the simplest formulation of the question. For more details see Chapter III below.

[4] Van den Ven, "Patristique," 360.

[5] It is self-evident that the florilegia included in the acts of the various councils are just the tip of the iceberg compared to the scores of anthologies that circulated before and after each council. Here I focus on the conciliar florilegia, taking the rest of them into account only

Along the same lines, and in connection with Nicaea II and P in particular, one may recall that three[6] synods dealing with the veneration of images had taken place before 787, one in Jerusalem (ca. 764) and two in Rome (731 and 769). Their proceedings have not been preserved, but we have explicit references to some of the patristic quotations supporting the veneration of icons that were presented during their sessions.[7] The contribution of the work carried out by these synods to the 787 council is still unknown. The same is also true for the relationships among the various Iconophile florilegia that were compiled before Nicaea II and the quotations that were cited there.

This brief discussion of the historical role that florilegia have played will first scrutinize the external characteristics of "conciliar" florilegia in the strict sense, that is, the small or large groups of pieces extracted from patristic and other theological works and presented to the participants at a council in order to support a dogmatic thesis. It will then examine their possible relationship to other florilegia and their contribution to the course of events and discussions recorded in the proceedings of the councils.

Before any actual appearance of a florilegium among the texts of the acts of a council, one finds an unsuccessful attempt to use patristic authority favoring a dogmatic thesis. In 383, Orthodox Christians and Arians came into conflict once again, and the emperor, Theodosius, attempted to ease the friction by summoning a synod in which all the foremost heretics would participate and discuss dogmatic issues. A certain Sissinius, *anagnostes* of the Novatian church, suggested referring to the written authority of the church fathers rather than engaging in an oral confrontation. But his plan, although approved by Patriarch Nectarius and the emperor, failed because of disagreement among representatives of the various Arian sects on the value of patristic *testimonia*.[8]

However, 170 years later, during the third session of the fifth ecumenical council (Constantinople II), the following statement closed the recitation of the *confessio fidei* drawn up by the participants:

---

to the extent that they relate to and predate the conciliar ones. For bibliography see above, note 1, especially Richard, "Florilèges diphysites," and Grillmeier, *Jesus der Christus.*

[6] Four if one takes into account the Iconoclastic Council of Hiereia (754).

[7] See Pope Hadrian I's letter of the year 793 to Charles the Great, commonly known as the *Hadrianum*, 11, 15, 19, 31–32, 36, 41, 47, 51, and 54.

[8] Mansi III 643 ff. This event is thoroughly described in the church histories of Sozomen and Socrates. See Sozomen, *Kirchengeschichte*, ed. J. Bidez, *GCS* 50 (Berlin, 1960), 314.17–315.26; Socrates, *Historia ecclesiastica*, *PG* 67, 584A–588A. Also Hefele-Leclercq, *Histoire*, II, 1, 63–64. Other unsuccessful attempts are related by Richard, "Florilèges diphysites," 721.

. . . πάντα μὲν τὰ συμφωνοῦντα τοῖς παρὰ τῶν μνημονευθεισῶν ἁγίων τεσ-
σάρων συνόδων περὶ τῆς ὀρθῆς πίστεως ὁρισθεῖσι δεχόμεθα . . . πρὸς τούτοις δὲ ἀκολουθοῦμεν ἐν ἅπασι καὶ τοῖς ἁγίοις πατράσι καὶ διδασκάλοις
τῆς ἐκκλησίας, Ἀθανασίῳ, Ἱλαρίῳ, Βασιλείῳ, Γρηγορίῳ τῷ Θεολόγῳ καὶ
Γρηγορίῳ τῷ Νύσσης, Ἀμβροσίῳ, Αὐγουστίνῳ, Θεοφίλῳ, Ἰωάννῃ τῷ
Κωνσταντινουπόλεως, Κυρίλλῳ, Λέοντι, Πρόκλῳ, καὶ δεχόμεθα πάντα τὰ
παρ᾽ αὐτῶν περὶ τῆς ὀρθῆς πίστεως καὶ εἰς κατάκρισιν τῶν αἱρετικῶν ἐκ-
τεθέντα. δεχόμεθα δὲ καὶ τοὺς ἄλλους ἁγίους καὶ ὀρθοδόξους πατέρας,
τοὺς ἐν τῇ ἁγίᾳ τοῦ Θεοῦ ἐκκλησίᾳ τὴν ὀρθὴν πίστιν ἀδιαβλήτως μέχρι
τέλους κηρύξαντας.[9]

What had prompted this shift of the church from the rejection of 383 to the
complete acceptance of patristic authority in disputes over the true faith, an
acceptance that indirectly authorized the use of florilegia?[10]

Of course, as will be shown later, the use of florilegia was finally adopted
on condition that the quotations extracted from the works of the recognized
orthodox (ἔγκριτοι, ἔκκριτοι) fathers should not be altered, falsified, or
taken out of context. This was an essential precaution taken to ensure that
the extracts assembled in a florilegium had the same textual value as the
original works themselves and therefore expressed the true opinion of
their authors.[11]

It has often been stressed that one of the main characteristics of the
Christian church was its persistent and strict adherence to traditional doctrine. What was to be defined as orthodox tradition was based on the authority of holy scripture in the first instance and, furthermore, on "the
authority of a Scripture properly interpreted, that is, interpreted according
to the spiritual sense and in harmony with patristic exegesis."[12]

In the history of the Christian church, next to the apostles come their
successors, the holy teachers, "the divinely guided fathers of the Catholic
Church."[13] Consequently, their work was of a significance almost equal to

---

[9] *ACO* IV,1, 37.17–18, 23–31 (Latin text). The Greek text cited here is taken from the acts
of the Lateran Council of 649, *ACO Ser. II*, vol. I, 254.31–256.3.

[10] From this point of view, it is no accident that this text appears in the acts of the Lateran
Council (649) right before the citation of the very extended florilegia of the fifth *actio*. *ACO Ser.
II*, vol. I, 254.26–256.8.

[11] For a brief discussion of the textual accuracy of the 5th- and 6th-century florilegia, see
M. Richard, "Notes sur les florilèges dogmatiques du Vᵉ et du VIᵉ siècle," in *Actes du VIᵉ Congrès
International d'Études Byzantines,* vol. I (Paris, 1950), 307–18, and idem, "Florilèges diphysites,"
728–32.

[12] See J. Pelikan, *The Spirit of Eastern Christendom* (600–1700), vol. II of *The Christian Tradition: A History of the Development of Doctrine* (Chicago, 1974), 19.

[13] Maximus Confessor, *Opuscula theologica et polemica; Spiritualis tomus ac dogmaticus* (*CPG*
7697.15), *PG* 91, 160.

that of holy scripture. Therefore, whenever a doctrinal issue emerged within the church, the appeal to this tradition was one of the basic weapons in the hands of both opposing parties. The words ταῦτα ἐκ τῶν πατέρων καὶ τῶν ἁγίων οἰκουμενικῶν συνόδων παρελάβομεν[14] were constantly uttered not only by orthodox believers but also by heretics as the usual *coda* to their arguments. In such confrontations heretics were usually declared to be Christians who supplemented, subtracted, or distorted the words of scripture and the fathers.[15] After the fifth century, as the age of the great fathers of the church slowly passed, a canon of orthodox authors was established with its official authorization in the fragment of the acts of the fifth ecumenical council quoted above.

This doctrinal conservatism also had a very strong impact on the transmission of the texts of scripture, of the fathers, and of the acts of the councils. In any doctrinal dispute, the *ipsissima verba* of the fathers had the power to overwhelm the novelties (καινοφωνίαι) of heretics. As a result, the codices (βίβλοι) containing works of the fathers became more and more important, and particular care was taken to transcribe them accurately and preserve a text identical, if possible, to the original.[16] In this respect dogmatic correctness was intertwined with philological accuracy.

However, since the citation of an extensive treatise was inappropriate for the needs of a conciliar session, the extraction of the crucial passages from the work in question was soon adopted for reasons of convenience.[17] The books of the fathers had to be reduced to collections of extracts, and,

---

[14] Cf. a similar formulation in the *Epistula Agathonis papae ad Constantinum IV imp.* (*CPG* 9417), *ACO Ser. II*, vol. II,1, 58.21–23: τί περιέχει ἡ δύναμις τῆς ἀποστολικῆς ἡμῶν πίστεως, διὰ βραχέων δηλοποιήσωμεν, ἣν καὶ παρελάβομεν διὰ τῆς ἀποστολικῆς παραδόσεως τῶν τε ἀποστολικῶν ἀρχιερέων καὶ τῶν ἁγίων πέντε οἰκουμενικῶν συνόδων.

[15] See, for example, *ACO Ser. II*, vol. II,1, 242.3–6. For more about these practices, see W. Speyer, *Die literarische Fälschung im heidnischen und christlichen Altertum. Ein Versuch ihrer Deutung* (Munich, 1971), 260–77. The fact that the orthodox were also involved in textual manipulation is fully discussed (ibid., 277–303).

[16] Even in the 9th century, Theodore of Studios, in his *Poenae monasteriales*, did not forget to order a specific penance for the scribes of his monastery who did not perform their task diligently (*PG* 99, 1740B–C): νδ´ Εἴ τις μὴ φιλοκάλως κρατεῖ τὸ τετράδιον, καὶ τίθησι τὸ ἀφ᾽ οὗ γράφει βιβλίον, καὶ σκέπει ἐν καιρῷ ἑκάτερα, καὶ παρατηρεῖται τά τε ἀντίστοιχα καὶ τοὺς τόνους καὶ τὰς στιγμάς, ἀνὰ μετανοίας λ´ καὶ ρ´ . . . νς´ Εἴ τις πλέον τῶν γεγραμμένων ἀναγνώσει ἐξ οὗ γράφει βιβλίου, ξηροφαγείτω.

[17] This practice should not be connected exclusively with the councils because florilegia are first found in dogmatic treatises of the 3rd century; see Richard, "Florilèges diphysites," 721–22. M. Tetz, in "Zum Streit zwischen Orthodoxie und Häresie an der Wende zum 4. u. 5. Jahrhunderts," *Evangelische Theologie* 20 (1961), 360–61, gives credit to St. Basil for the introduction of this new literary genre of theological proof in his *De Spiritu Sancto*, chap. 29, *PG* 32, 200B–209C.

although initially there was no particular objection to this practice,[18] the falsification of the quoted passages and their presentation out of context soon compelled close scrutiny of the quotations presented at the sixth ecumenical council (Constantinople III), where, as will be seen, textual criticism played a significant role.

2. The Florilegia of the Council of Ephesus (431) (*ACO* I,1,2, 39–45, *CPG* 8675.9; *ACO* I,1.7, 89–95, *CPG* 8721)[19]

In the extensive corpus of the acts of the third ecumenical council, two florilegia were presented. That of the first session (22 June 431) played a complementary role to the citation of the correspondence between Cyril, Pope Celestine, and Nestorius. It was recited after Theodotus bishop of Ancyra and Acacius of Melitene had testified against Nestorius. This florilegium comprised sixteen fragments taken from twelve works by ten authors,[20] but was not very carefully prepared. Precise references are not given, and the three Cappadocian fathers are represented by only a single passage each, cited without any further indication of their provenance (Gregory of Nazianzus, *Epistula* 101; Basil of Caesarea, *De Spiritu Sancto;* and Gregory of

---

[18] See, for example, the ceremonial announcement of the recitation of the extracts in the Lateran Council of 649 by Pope Martin I, *ACO Ser.* II, vol. I, 252.20–22: οὗ χάριν τὰς ἱερὰς αὐτῶν βίβλους ἐνεχθῆναι προστάσσομεν, μᾶλλον δὲ τὰς ἀναλεγείσας ἡμῖν ἐξ αὐτῶν εὐσεβεῖς περὶ Χριστοῦ τοῦ Θεοῦ μαρτυρίας.

[19] On the existence, or rather nonexistence, of any minutes of the second ecumenical council, Constantinople I in 381, see E. Chrysos, "Die Akten des Konzils von Konstantinopel I (381)," in *Romanitas—Christianitas: Untersuchungen zur Geschichte und Literatur der römischen Kaiserzeit (Festschrift Johannes Straub)* (Berlin, 1982), 426–35.

[20] The florilegium consisted of excerpts from the following works:

1–3. Petrus Alex., *De deitate* (fragmenta) (3 fragments) *CPG* 1635.1, 2, and 3
   4. Athanasius Alex., *Oratio I contra Arianos*, *CPG* 2093, *PG* 26, 393A–396A
5–6. Idem, *Epistula ad Epictetum*, *CPG* 2095, *PG* 26, 1053B–C and 1061A–B (2 fragments)
   7. Timotheus Apollinarista, *Epistula ad Prosdocium*, *CPG* 3726, ed. H. Lietzmann, *Apollinaris von Laodicea und seine Schule*, TU 1 (Tübingen, 1904), 284
   8. Scripta Apollinaristica Incerta, *Fragmentum* 186, *CPG* 3741.2, Lietzmann, *Apollinaris*, 318
   9. Theophilus Alex., *Epistulae festales, Epistula quinta*, *CPG* 2582, *PG* 65, 60
  10. Idem, *Epistula sexta*, *CPG* 2583, *PG* 65, 60
  11. Cyprianus Episcopus Carthaginensis, *De opere et eleemosynis*, *CPL* 47, *CSEL* 3.1 (Vienna, 1868), 371.1–10 (Latin version)
  12. Ambrosius Episcopus Mediol., *De fide*, 1.94, *CPL* 150, *PL* 16, 573B, *CSEL* 78, 40.61–41.70 (Latin version)
  13. Idem, *De fide*, 2.77–78, *PL* 16, 600B, *CSEL* 78, 84.30–85.43 (Latin version)
  14. Gregorius Naz., *Epistula* 101, *CPG* 3032, *SC* 208, 40–46
  15. Basilius Caes., *De Spiritu Sancto*, *CPG* 2839, *SC* 17bis, 308.12–19
  16. Gregorius Nyss., *Oratio I de beatitudinibus*, *CPG* 3161, *PG* 44, 1201B–C.

Nyssa, *Oratio I de beatitudinibus*). There is also one fragment falsely attributed to Pseudo-Julius the Pope (= Timotheus Apollinarista, *Epistula ad Prosdocium*), and another to Pope Felix (= *Fragmentum Apollinaristicum* 186). Some extracts, such as those from the fifth and sixth *Epistulae festales* of Theophilus of Alexandria, have survived thanks in large part to this florilegium.

This anthology was followed by another collection of twenty-five quotations taken from some *quaternia* (τετράδες) that contained works of Nestorius.[21] Then came the recitation of the letter of Capreolus bishop of Carthage to the council.

The same florilegium was repeated one month later (22 July 431) at the opening of the sixth session after the citation of a *horos* or ὑπόμνημα[22] composed by the participants. It is also worth noting that the purpose of this florilegium was to demonstrate the sense in which the Nicene creed should be interpreted.[23] This second anthology included four fragments in addition to the sixteen cited in the first session.[24] The Nestorian florilegium was also appended.[25] There had been no specific discussion of the contents

---

[21] *ACO* I,1,2, 45–52. The compiler had perused eleven sermons of Nestorius from which the fragments were taken:

1. *Sermo I, CPG* 5690 = fragment XIII
2. *Sermo II, CPG* 5691 = XVI
3. *Sermo III, CPG* 5692 = XXI, XXII
4. *Sermo V, CPG* 5694 = XII, XVII–XX
5. *Sermo VIII, CPG* 5697 = V, X
6. *Sermo IX, CPG* 5698 = VII, VIII, XIV, XV
7. *Sermo X, CPG* 5699 = I, IX, XXIII, XXIV
8. *Sermo XI, CPG* 5700 = II, III
9. *Sermo XIV, CPG* 5703 = IV, XXV
10. *Sermo XV, CPG* 5704 = VI
11. *Sermo XVI, CPG* 5705 = XII

[22] *ACO* I,1,7, 88.33–95.18.

[23] Ibid., 89.14–20:

Τῇ μὲν οὖν ἁγίᾳ ταύτῃ πίστει πάντας συντίθεσθαι προσήκει. . . . ἐπειδὴ δέ τινες προσποιοῦνται μὲν ὁμολογεῖν αὐτὴν καὶ συντίθεσθαι, παρερμηνεύουσι δὲ τῶν ἐννοιῶν τὴν δύναμιν ἐπὶ τὸ αὐτοῖς δοκοῦν καὶ σοφίζονται τὴν ἀλήθειαν. . . . ἐδέησεν ἀναγκαίως ἁγίων πατέρων καὶ ὀρθοδόξων παραθέσθαι χρήσεις πληροφορῆσαι δυναμένας τίνα τε τρόπον νενοήκασιν αὐτὴν καὶ κυρῆξαι τεθαρρήκασιν, ὥστε δηλονότι καὶ πάντας τοὺς ὀρθήν . . . ἔχοντας πίστιν οὕτω καὶ νοεῖν καὶ ἑρμηνεύειν καὶ κηρύττειν αὐτήν.

[24] Fragments 17–20 (*ACO* 1,1,7, 94.16–95.18):

17. Atticus CPolitanus, *Homilia in nativitatem (syriace), CPG* 5650
18. Amphilochius Iconiensis, *Fragmentum iii* (e libro deperdito *De generationi domini secundum carnem*), *CPG* 3245.3b
19. Idem, ibid., *CPG* 3245.3c
20. Atticus CPolitanus, *Fragmentum, CPG* 5657.

[25] *ACO* I,1,7, 106.9–111.29.

of the orthodox and Nestorian florilegia, and the main dogmatic work of the council had been carried out through the vast correspondence exchanged among its most eminent participants.[26]

According to the words of Peter,[27] the πριμικήριος νοταρίων,[28] the quotations were extracted from copies of patristic books. One should note, however, that many of the fragments had already appeared in earlier literature, namely, in the *Oratio ad Dominas* written in 430 (*CPG* 5220), and in the *Apologia xii capitulorum contra Orientales* (*CPG* 5221) of early 431, both by Cyril of Alexandria.[29] The least we can assume is that these two works provided the basic guidelines for the compilers of the conciliar florilegia, unless Cyril of Alexandria himself procured the books or the florilegium itself.

3. The Florilegium of the Council of Chalcedon (451) (*ACO* II,1,3, 114 [473] – 116 [475], *CPG* 9021)

The fourth ecumenical council did not rely on a particular florilegium, and the main bulk of its work had been carried out by letters, *libelli,* and discussions of the recorded trial of Eutyches and the acts of the "Robber" Council of Ephesus in 449 (*Latrocinium*).[30] It is characteristic that even the florilegium that accompanied the famous Tome of Pope Leo I (*CPG* [8922]) was omitted when the letter was solemnly read during the second session.[31]

However, a florilegium can be found at the end of the *Adlocutio ad Marci-*

---

[26] See *CPG* [8620]–[8793].

[27] *ACO* I,1,2. 39.1–3: Ἐπειδὴ μετὰ χεῖρας ἔχομεν καὶ βιβλία τῶν ἁγιωτάτων καὶ ὁσιωτάτων πατέρων καὶ ἐπισκόπων καὶ διαφόρων μαρτύρων, ἐπελεξάμεθα δὲ ἐκ τούτων ὀλίγα κεφάλαια, εἰ παρίσταται, ἀναγνωσόμεθα.

[28] For this office see below, note 59.

[29] The correspondence between the florilegia of the acts and the *Oratio ad Dominas* (= A) and the *Apologia* (= B) is as follows (numbers refer to the two lists in notes 20 and 24 above):

2. *ACO* I,1,2, 39.14–21 = B *ACO* I,1,7, 36.32–37.2
4. *ACO* I,1,2, 40.5–7 = B *ACO* I,1,7, 37.4–5
5. *ACO* I,1,2, 40.14–23 = B *ACO* I,1,7, 37.6–15
7. *ACO* I,1,2, 41.1–6 = B *ACO* I,1,7, 45.20–25
8. *ACO* I,1,2, 41.7–13 = B *ACO* I,1,7, 45.26–31
15. *ACO* I,1,2, 44.9–14 = B *ACO* I,1,7, 64.15–20
16. *ACO* I,1,2, 44.15–45.2 = B *ACO* I,1,7, 64.1–14
17. *ACO* I,1,7, 94.16–24 = A *ACO* I,1,5, 66.22–30
18. *ACO* I,1,7, 95.1–3 = B *ACO* I,1,7, 37.21–23.

[30] See *CPG* 9000–9020. Basic bibliography: E. Schwartz, *Der Prozeß des Eutyches,* SBMünch-Philos.-hist.Kl., Abt. 5 (Munich, 1929); G. May, "Das Lehrverfahren gegen Eutyches im November des Jahres 448," *AHC* 21 (1989), 1–61.

[31] *ACO* II,1,2, p. [277] 81.20–22. For this florilegium see E. Schwartz, *Codex Vaticanus graecus 1431,* in AbhMünchPhilos.-hist.Kl. (Munich, 1927), 137–41; also Richard, "Florilèges diphysites," 725–26. It is preserved only in Greek in *ACO* II,1,1, 20.7–25.6.

anum imp. aug. (CPG 9021) with quotations supporting the conformity of Pope Leo to orthodox doctrine. Like that of the third ecumenical council, it is a small florilegium of sixteen extracts from the writings of Ambrose of Milan, Amphilochius of Iconium, Antiochus of Ptolemais, Athanasius of Alexandria, Atticus of Constantinople, Basil of Caesarea, Cyril of Alexandria, Gregory of Nazianzus, John Chrysostom, and Proclus of Constantinople. Compared to the florilegia of Ephesus, it appears to be more accurate, and the indications of the provenance of the quotations are more precise,[32] although the small fragment from Antiochus of Ptolemais is simply quoted under the name of the author.[33] Moreover, the quotations from the works of preeminent fathers such as Basil and Gregory of Nyssa make up a larger proportion of the florilegium.[34] The authority of their writings and their significance in matters of orthodox doctrine have acquired a higher status.

It is clear that this florilegium constitutes a limited selection of quotations already existing in the florilegium of the *Eranistes II (CPG* 6217) of Theodoret of Cyrus, written in about 447/8.[35] It therefore follows that the participants in the Council of Chalcedon did not use any florilegia. On the unique occasion when a florilegium was employed, it was not part of the proceedings proper, but came as an appendix to the *Adlocutio* that marked the closing of the council. However, this absence of florilegia is easily explained. The main sessions of the council (*Actiones* I and III, *CPG* 9000 and 9002 respectively) had been devoted to the examination of the acts of the "Robber" Council of Ephesus in 449. So the main issue was not dogma

[32] E.g., *ACO* II,1,3, 115 [474].16: Τοῦ μακαρίου Ἀττικοῦ ἐκ τῆς πρὸς Εὐψύχιον ἐπιστολῆς.

[33] See *CPG* 4296 nota.

[34] There are only two minor authors, Antiochus of Ptolemais and Atticus of Constantinople, represented in this florilegium. The rest are all among the names of the "canon" cited above, p. 4.

[35] See *ACO* II,1,3, p. XIIII, where the authorship of the *Adlocutio* and the florilegium is attributed to Theodoret of Cyrus. The florilegium can be found ibid., 114 [473]–116 [475]. The list below includes the place the passage occupies in the *Eranistes* of Theodoret (references are to the new edition by G. H. Ettlinger, *Theodoret of Cyrus, Eranistes* [Oxford, 1975]).

1. Basilius Caes., *Adversus Eunomium I, CPG* 2837, *PG* 29, 552c–553A; *Eranistes*, 166.12–17 (= *Oratio II, Inconfusus* no. 39)

2. Ambrosius Mediol., *De fide, CPL* 150, *CSEL* 78, 84.32–34; *Eranistes*, 163.24–26 (= *Orat. II* no. 31 with many variants)

3. Gregorius Naz., *Epistula* 101, *CPG* 3032, *SC* 208, 44.19; *Eranistes*, 166.24–167.2 (= *Orat. II* no. 41)

4. Idem, *Oratio* 30, *CPG* 3010.30, *PG* 36, 113B; *Eranistes*, 168.10–13 (= *Orat. II* no. 46)

5. Athanasius Alex., *Oratio II contra Arianos, CPG* 2093, *PG* 26, 296B; *Eranistes*, 159.10–17 (= *Orat. II* no. 22)

6. Amphilochius Iconiensis, *Fragmentum xii* (ex *Oratione in illud: Quia pater maior me est* [Ioh. 14, 28]), *CPG* 3245.12, *PG* 39, 109A–B; *Eranistes*, 170.16–20 (= *Orat. II* no. 54), also *Eranistes,*

but whether Dioskoros had properly followed the established procedural rules during the conciliar proceedings at Ephesus.

4. The Florilegia of the Council of Constantinople II (553)

Unfortunately the Greek acts of Constantinople II, except for some small fragments, are no longer extant.[36] All we possess today is the Latin text, which can also be of great help for this study.[37]

The fifth ecumenical council relied extensively on written material, and a large part of its proceedings was based on the recitation of extracts from letters and dogmatic works. A brief survey of the work recorded in the Latin acts provides the following information.

The first session (*CPG* 9355) opened with the *Epistula ad synodum de Theodoro Mopsuesteno* of Emperor Justinian (*CPG* 6887), which set the tone and main directives for the council's participants.[38] It was followed by the *Epistula Eutychii ad Vigilium papam* (*CPG* 6937) together with the pope's reply, the *Epistula Vigilii papae ad Eutychium* (*CPG* [9350]). The second and third sessions (*CPG* 9356–57) were devoted to introductory discussions;[39] and the

---

107.5–12 (= *Orat. I, Immutabilis* no. 56, with many variants)

7. Antiochus Episcopus Ptolemaidis, *Homilia de nativitate* (fragmentum), *CPG* 4296 nota; *Eranistes*, 177.27–28 (= *Orat. II* no. 78)

8. Flavianus I Antioch., *Fragmentum ex homilia in Theophania*, *CPG* 3435.6, *PG* 83, 204C; *Eranistes*, 177.5–9 (= *Orat. II* no. 76)

9. Iohannes Chrys., *In Iohannem homilia* 11.2, *CPG* 4425, *PG* 59, 80.8–18; *Eranistes*, 175.17–20 (= *Orat. II* no. 70)

10. Atticus CPolitanus, *Epistula ad Eupsychium*, *CPG* 5655; *Eranistes*, 181.25–182.6 (= *Orat. II* no. 86)

11. Proclus CPolitanus, unidentified

12. Cyrillus Alex., (*Ep.* 4) *Ad Nestorium*, *CPG* 5304, *ACO* I,1,1, 27.1 ff; *Eranistes*, 182.7–11 (= *Orat. II* no. 87)

13. Idem, (*Ep.* 39) *Ad Iohannem Antiochenum* (*de pace*), *CPG* 5339, *ACO* I,1,4, 18.26 ff; *Eranistes*, 182.18–20 (= *Orat. II* no. 89)

14. Idem, (*Ep.* 45) *Ad Successum episc. Diocaesareae*, *CPG* 5345, *ACO* I,1,6, 153.16 ff; *Eranistes*, 182.21–26 (= *Orat. II* no. 90)

15. Idem = 13, *ACO* I,1,4, 17.14 ff; *Eranistes*, 182.12–17 (= *Orat. II* no. 88)

16. Iohannes Chrys., *In Matthaeum homilia* 2.2, *CPG* 4424, *PG* 57, 26.22–27; *Eranistes*, 175.26–30 (= *Orat. II* no. 71).

It is worth noting that this florilegium has nothing in common with that appended to the Tome of Leo, apart from quotation no. 2 in the list above, which is also found in a longer passage in *ACO* II,1,1, 22.19–21. This is to be expected: the *Adlocutio* was meant to defend the orthodoxy of the Tome; therefore its author (Theodoret) could not use passages that were *sub judice*.

[36] The problem is thoroughly discussed by E. Chrysos, Ἡ Ἐκκλησιαστικὴ πολιτικὴ τοῦ Ἰουστινιανοῦ (Thessalonike, 1969), 145–99.

[37] Ibid., 105–30.

[38] For the significance of this *epistula*, see ibid. 110–11.

[39] Ibid., 113–19.

dogmatic work began in the fourth session (13 May 553) (*CPG* 9358). A carefully prepared florilegium, comprised exclusively of seventy-one extracts from the works of Theodore of Mopsuestia, was read out.[40] In this anthology the emphasis was on the heretical deviations expressed in certain passages of Theodore's works.[41] Its purpose was to demonstrate clearly the dogmatic deviations and novelties that would warrant his condemnation and anathematization.

It is obvious from the minutes that the florilegium had been prepared in advance.[42] This conclusion can also be corroborated by at least one contemporary source, which allows one to attribute its compilation to clerics in

[40] The following works were represented in this anthology:
1. *Contra Apollinarium* (*CPG* 3858)
2. *Commentarii in Iohannem* (*CPG* 3843)
3. *Fragmenta in Actus Apostolorum* (*CPG* 3844)
4. *De incarnatione* (*CPG* 3856.2a)
5. *Fragmenta in Lucam* (*CPG* 3842)
6. *Expositio in Psalmos* (*CPG* 3833)
7. *Commentarius in XII prophetas minores* (*CPG* 3834)
8. *Expositio Symboli* (*CPG* 3871g) (spurious)
9. *Fragmenta in epistulam ad Hebraeos* (*CPG* 3848)
10. *Homiliae catecheticae* (*Liber ad baptizandos*) (*CPG* 3852)
11. *Fragmenta in Matthaeum* (*CPG* 3840)
12. *Fragmenta in Genesim* (*CPG* 3827)
13. *Fragmenta in Iob* (*CPG* 3835)
14. *Fragmenta in Canticum* (*CPG* 3837).

In some cases the extracts from these works are presented with some introductory explanations. Cf. *ACO* IV,1, 51.18-19: "Eiusdem Theodori ex libro quartodecimo de incarnatione, ubi dicit quod imago erat Christus dei verbi et sicut imago imperialis adorabatur ab hominibus"; also ibid., 50, 65, 66, etc. The Latin version of some of the fragments listed above (nos. 1, 4, 10, 11, 14) is preserved thanks mainly to this florilegium.

[41] The intense discussion concerning the authorship of the extracts in the anthology is not pertinent to this study, and only the basic bibliography is given here. The attribution of many fragments to Theodore is doubted by R. Devreesse, "Par quelles voies nous sont parvenus les commentaires de Théodore de Mopsueste?" *RBibl* 39 (1930), 362-77; idem, *Essai sur Théodore de Mopsueste*, *ST* 141 (Vatican City, 1948), 243-58; M. Richard, "La tradition des fragments du traité Περὶ τῆς ἐνανθρωπήσεως de Théodore de Mopsueste," *Le Muséon* 56 (1943), 55-75; idem, "Les traités de Cyrille d'Alexandrie contre Diodore et Théodore et les fragments dogmatiques de Diodore de Tarse," *Mélanges Félix Grat*, I (Paris, 1946), 99-116; and by others. The attribution is supported by J. M. Vosté, "L'oeuvre exégétique de Théodore de Mopsueste au IIe concile de Constantinople," *RBibl* 38 (1929), 382-95; and F. Sullivan, *The Christology of Theodore of Mopsuestia*, Analecta Gregoriana 82 (Rome, 1956), 35-159. See also Chrysos, Ἐκκλησιαστικὴ πολιτική, 120-21.

[42] This is evident from the following passage: at a certain moment during this session, the reading of the extracts of Theodore was spontaneously interrupted by the indignant members of the assembly who started uttering anathemas and curses against Theodore. After they had calmed down, Calonymus the *diaconus et notarius* took up the recitation, reading *ex eadem charta* (*ACO* IV,1, 56.11-17).

the entourage of Justinian, if not to the emperor himself.[43] Modern research has also indicated that there is a common source behind all the "Theodorean" florilegia.[44] In addition, it has been suggested that this archetypal anthology was already in existence within the first decade after Theodore's death in 428.[45]

Another interesting point concerning this florilegium has to do with its presentation: we may assume that all the participants were well aware of its immediate source. Still, before its recitation, the *notarii* offered it to the assembly with the following words: "Habemus prae manibus scripta quae ex Theodori codicibus collegistis[46] [sc. some of the participants]." The short phrase "scripta quae ex Theodori florilegio [Iustinianus] collegit" would have sounded more sincere to the assembly. In any case, this is a small indication of how even the details of the entire conciliar procedure were arranged *before* the beginning of any transaction. The session closed with the announcement of the agenda for the next session in which a florilegium was to be read that would give the appropriate *testimonia* for the refutation and condemnation of the teachings of Theodore.[47]

What had been announced in the fourth session was carried out in detail during the fifth (17 May 553) (*CPG* 9359). Diodorus the *archidiaconus et primicerius notariorum* was the person who orchestrated the procedure by recalling what had been said in the previous sessions and announcing the passages to be cited, as well as the issues remaining to be resolved.[48]

---

[43] Most of the fragments had also been included in the first *Constitutum* of Pope Vigilius (*CPG* [9363]). The *Constitutum* was written just one day after the fourth session (14 May 553), but Vigilius states that he extracted the fragments from a manuscript that had been sent to him by Justinian a few days before Easter. The Latin translation of the fragments is the same in both the acts and the *Constitutum;* it therefore follows that Justinian himself had also provided this florilegium to the assembly. See O. Günter, *Collectio Avellana, Epistulae imperatorum, pontificum, aliorum inde ab a. 367 usque ad a. 553, CSEL* 35 (Bonn, 1895–98), p. LXXI ff (comparison of florilegia), and 235.13–15; 236.20–23 (provenance of the quotations in the *Constitutum*); also Chrysos, Ἐκκλησιαστικὴ πολιτική, 122–23.

[44] Richard, "La tradition," 74; Sullivan, *Christology,* 44–52.

[45] Sullivan, *Christology,* 51–52.

[46] *ACO* IV,1, 43.27–28.

[47] *ACO* IV,1, 72.23–29:

... sancta synodous dixit: Multitudo lectarum blasphemiarum quas contra magnum Deum ... immo magis contra suam animam Theodorus Mopsuestenus evomuit. unde oportebat nos quidem nihil aliud expectantes et per synodicam sententiam anathemati eum subicere. verumtamen licet manifesta sint *quae sancti patres et leges imperiales et historiarum conscriptores* contra eum dixerunt, tamen, quia oportet in examinatione quae contra eum procedit, nihil praetermitti subtilitatis, alio die etiam cetera audiamus.

[48] *ACO* IV,1, 73, 96, 101, 115, 137, etc.

The first part of the fifth session was occupied by a somewhat extensive florilegium of twenty-eight quotations.[49] All of them criticized the teachings of Theodore of Mopsuestia found in the extracts read out in the preceding session.[50]

The council then turned to some secondary issues, namely, the objection that Cyril of Alexandria had expressed a positive opinion about Theodore and that Gregory of Nazianzus had corresponded with him. Any dispute on these subjects was to be resolved by the presentation of the extracts in question from the relevant works or letters.[51]

On the basis of much lengthier documentation, an answer was given to the question whether heretics should be anathematized *post mortem*. That florilegium included fragments from the works of the Greek church fathers

---

[49] The fragments were taken from the following works or documents:

1. Cyrillus Alex., *Libri contra Diodorum et Theodorum* (*CPG* 5229) (9 fragments)
2. *Libelli Armeniorum ad Proclum*
3. Proclus CPolitanus, (*Ep.* 2) *Tomus ad Armenios* (*CPG* 5897) (2 fragments)
4. Cyrillus Alex., (*Ep.* 70) *Ad Lamponem presb. Alexandrinum* (*CPG* 5370)
5. Idem, (*Ep.* 68) *Ad Acacium Melitenum* (*CPG* 5368)
6. Idem, (*Ep.* 74) *Ad Rabbulam Edessenum* (*CPG* 5374)
7. Idem, (*Ep.* 55) *Ad Anastasium, Alexandrum . . . ceterosque monachos Orientales* (*CPG* 5355) (2 fragments)
8. Rabbulas Edessenus, *Epistula ad Cyrillum Alex.* (*CPG* 6494)
9. Hesychius Hierosolym., *Historia ecclesiastica* (*CPG* 6582)
10. *Lex Theodosii et Valentiniani*
11. *Lex Theodosii et Valentiniani . . . imperatorum adversus Nestorium et Theodorum et eos qui similia eis sapiunt*
12. Theophilus Alex., *Epistula ad Porphyrium episcopum Antiochenum* (*CPG* 2605) (2 fragments)
13. Gregorius Nyss., *Epistula ad Theophilum* (*CPG* 3167)
14. Theodoretus Episcopus Cyri, *Pro Diodoro et Theodoro* (*CPG* 6220) (4 fragments)
15. Idem, (*Ep.* 16) *Ad Irenaeum digamum* (*CPG* 6240).

Items 10 and 11 on the list appear here with some alterations that disfavor Theodore (see Devreesse, *Essai*, 235–36).

[50] See Chrysos, Ἐκκλησιαστικὴ πολιτική, 123–24. For the history of the collection of these extracts, which also dates prior to 440, see L. Abramowski, "The Controversy over Diodore and Theodore in the Interim between the Two Councils of Ephesus," in *Formula and Context: Studies in Early Christian Thought,* Variorum (Hampshire, 1992), originally published in German in *ZKG* 67 (1955–56), 252–87.

[51] *ACO* IV,1, 96–100. The examined passages belonged to the (1) *Libri contra Diodorum et Theodorum* of Cyril of Alexandria (*CPG* 5229) and (2) epistles 162, 122, 77, 163, 152, and 183 of Gregory of Nazianzus (*CPG* 3032). In the first case, it was demonstrated that the words "bono Theodoro" were used by Cyril in an ironic sense against Theodore. As for the letters, it turned out that their recipient was not Theodore of Mopsuestia but his namesake, the bishop of Tyana. (For these letters see, however, the observations of E. Schwartz in *ACO* II,5, pp. xx–xxi.)

and Augustine and from the acts of a local synod in Africa.[52] The extracts
from the works of Augustine and the acts of the synod at Carthage were
offered by Sextilianus, bishop of Tunis, as a contribution of the church of
Carthage to the council.[53] However, some of these quotations had already
been used by Justinian in two of his works.[54] This is undoubtedly another
instance of a prearranged action in the course of the conciliar procedure.[55]
The session came to an end with the recitation of extracts from works of
Theodoret of Cyrus.[56]

[52] *ACO* IV.1, 101–30. In support of the positive answer, fragments from the following
works were quoted and discussed:
1. Cyrillus Alex., *Libri contra Diodorum et Theodorum* (*CPG* 5229) (3 fragments)
2. Idem, (*Epistula* 55) (*CPG* 5355)
3. Augustinus Hippon., *Epistula CLXXXV, De correctione Donatistarum liber* (*CPL* 262)
4. *Gesta collationis Carthaginensis III 187* (Mansi IV 220c–d)
5. Augustinus Hippon., *Epistula ad Catholicos de secta Donatistarum* (*CPL* 334)
6. Idem, *Contra Cresconium* (*CPL* 335) (2 fragments)
7. Cyrillus Alex., (*Ep.* 67) *Ad Iohannem et synodum Antiochenum* (*CPG* 5367) (3 fragments)
8. Idem, (*Ep.* 69) *Ad Acacium Melitenum* (*CPG* 5369)
9. Idem, (*Ep.* 71) *Ad Theodosium imperatorem* (*CPG* 5371)
10. Idem, *Liber contra Synousiastas* (fragmenta) (*CPG* 5230.2)
11. Idem, (*Ep.* 72) *Ad Proclum CPolitanum* (*CPG* 5372) (2 fragments)
12. Proclus CPolitanus, (*Ep.* 2) *Tomus ad Armenios* (*CPG* 5897)
13. Idem, (*Ep.* 3) *Ad Iohannem Antiochenum* (*CPG* 5900)
14. Basilius Caes., *Epistula 244* (*ad Patrophilum ep. Aegearum*) (*CPG* 2900)
15. Gregorius Nyss., *Ad Theophilum adversus Apollinaristas* (*CPG* 3143)
16. *Gesta Synodi Mopsuestenae* (17 July 550) (*CPG* 9340).
[53] *ACO* IV,1, 102.7–16.
[54] Part of the *De correctione* of Augustine can also be found in Justinian's *Epistula contra tria
capitula* (*CPG* 6882), written in 549–550, and in his *Confessio fidei* (*CPG* 6885), dating from June
551, ed. E. Schwartz, *Drei dogmatische Schriften Iustinians*, in AbhMünch–Philos.-hist.Kl., N.F. 18
(Munich, 1939), 68.11–17 and 108.30–33 respectively. Compare also *ACO* IV,1, 102.11–13 with
Schwartz, *Drei Schriften*, 68.20–22, 108.33–35.
[55] For further discussion see Chrysos, Ἐκκλησιαστικὴ πολιτική, 124.
[56] Fragments were excerpted from the following works:
1. *Impugnatio xii anathematismorum Cyrilli* (*CPG* 6214, [8660]) (6 fragments)
2. *Epistula ad eos qui in Euphratesia et Osroena . . . et Cilicia vitam monasticam degunt* (*CPG* 6276)
3. *Ex sermone Chalcedone contra Cyrillum habito* (*CPG* 6226)
4. *Ex alio sermone ibidem contra Cyrillum habito* (*CPG* 6227)
5. *Ex sermone ibidem, cum essent abituri, habito* (*CPG* 6228)
6. (*Ep.* 162) *Ad Andream Samosatenum* (*CPG* 6255)
7. (*Ep.* 172) *Ad Nestorium* (*CPG* 6270)
8. (*Ep.* 171) *Ad Iohannem Antiochenum* (*CPG* 6266)
9. (*Ep.* 180) *Ad Iohannem Antiochenum cum mortuus esset Cyrillus* (*CPG* 6287)
10. *Ex allocutione Antiochiae dicta* (*CPG* 6229)
11. *Ex alia allocutione ibidem dicta* (*CPG* 6230).
This anthology is the unique source for the Latin text of some of these quotations (nos.
10, 11, etc.).

The sixth session of the council (*CPG* 9360), relying on equally extensive and well-prepared literature, dealt with the *Epistula Ibae ad Marim Persam* (*CPG* 6500). After a painstaking comparison with lengthy excerpts from the acts of the Councils of Ephesus and Chalcedon, this letter was condemned as heretical.[57] The seventh session (*CPG* 9361) included the recitation of the letters of Pope Vigilius. Finally, the council closed on 2 June 553 with a *Sententia Synodica* and fourteen canons issued in the eighth session (*CPG* 9362).

This was the first ecumenical council in which florilegia played such an important role. Just a brief glance at its recorded acts is enough to form the impression that almost everything had been prearranged, and that florilegia marked the starting and concluding points on every subject. There were some basic questions—the so-called Three Chapters—to be dealt with: that of the orthodoxy of Theodore of Mopsuestia, and to some extent of a work of Theodoret of Cyrus,[58] and of the letter of Ibas of Edessa to Maris. Another issue related to Theodore of Mopsuestia concerned the possibility of an anathematization *post mortem* of individuals who had been proved to be heretics. Other, less important, questions were also addressed. For every subject a more or less extensive florilegium had been prepared, though the extracts had been taken from a small number of authors.

Also noteworthy is the important role of Diodorus, the *primicerius notariorum*.[59] He appears at the most significant moments of the debate and, in many cases, suggests to the assembly the next move, but it is evident that his proposals are usually dictated by what is to follow. The *Sancta Synodus* always accepts his motions and the citations go on.[60] In some other cases the same role is undertaken by the collective *Sancta Synodus*.[61]

---

[57] *ACO* IV,1, 147–81.

[58] Namely, of the *Libri V contra Cyrillum* (*CPG* 6215).

[59] On this office see J. Darrouzès, *Recherches sur les ὀφφίκια de l'Église byzantine*, Archives de l'Orient Chrétien 11 (Paris, 1970), 356 ff.

[60] See, for example, *ACO* IV,1, 101.2-4: "Diodorus archidiaconus et primicerius reverentissimorum notariorum dixit: Sunt nobis prae manibus quae electa sunt ad praesentem quaestionem pertinentia eo quod oportet haereticos et post mortem condemnari."

[61] Ibid., 97, 100–101, 130, 137–38, etc. Chrysos, Ἐκκλησιαστικὴ πολιτική, 106–10, suggested that these words are used to denote one (or more) of the four patriarchs who constituted the collective body that presided over the work of the council. However, another explanation for the presence of these words in the acts of almost every council is provided by Aetios *diakonos notarios* who kept the minutes of the trial of Eutyches: *ACO* II,1,1, 170.34–171.2:

Ἀέτιος διάκονος καὶ νοτάριος εἶπεν· Ἐν τοῖς τοιούτοις ἁγιωτάτοις συνεδρίοις συμβαίνει πολλάκις ἕνα τῶν παρόντων θεοφιλεστάτων ἐπισκόπων εἰπεῖν τι καὶ τὸ παρὰ τοῦ ἑνὸς λεγόμενον ὡς παρὰ πάντων ὁμοῦ ἐκφωνούμενον καὶ γράφεται καὶ νοεῖται. τοῦτο ἐξ ἀρχῆς παρηκολούθησεν· ἀμέλει ἑνὸς λέγοντος γράφομεν ἡ ἁγία σύνοδος εἶπεν. εἰ τοίνυν εὑρεθείη νῦν εἷς ἢ δεύτερος εἰπών, ὡς καὶ κατέθεντο οἱ θεοφιλέστατοι καὶ συνεφώνησαν καὶ ἐπεβόησεν τότε ὁ ἁγιώ-

There were also some seemingly spontaneous interventions of individual participants either to offer some additional information about the subject under debate[62] or to give new *testimonia* in support of what had already been said or read.[63] We have seen, however, that these interventions were somehow "stage-managed." This is the reason why, when seen in their context, they contributed to the homogeneous result one reads in the edited text.

After an examination of the acts, it becomes evident that part, if not all, of the proceedings recorded in the minutes had been carefully prearranged. In addition, the council followed a basic guideline which for the fourth, fifth, and sixth sessions was provided by florilegia that had been prepared in advance.

5. The Lateran Council of 649[64]

A procedure almost identical to that of the fifth ecumenical council can be observed throughout the Lateran Council of 649. It took five sessions to complete its work (5, 8, 17, 19, and 31 Oct. 649, *CPG* 9398–9402). The first session began with the recitation of the *Allocutio Martini Papae* (*CPG* 9398.2) and of the *Epistula Mauri Ravennatensis episcopi* (*CPG* 9398.3),[65] which outlined the problems to be dealt with by the council. In the second session, seven documents (ἀναφοραί) were read out, bringing forward accusations against the monothelete innovations introduced by Cyrus of Alexandria, Sergius, and Pyrrhus of Constantinople.[66] One of the documents concluded with a small florilegium of four extracts from Ambrose of Milan and two from Augustine.[67] The second session closed with the announcement of the

---

τατος κλῆρος, ἀξιοῦμεν μηδ' ὅλως τὴν φωνὴν ταύτην ἐκβληθῆναι ἢ παρατρωθῆναι τῶν ὑπομνημάτων, ἐπειδήπερ φαίνονται πάντες οἱ ἁγιώτατοι ἐπίσκοποι ὑπογράψαντες.

[62] *ACO* IV,1, 99.29–100.21.

[63] Ibid., 102.6–16.

[64] Text edited by R. Riedinger, *ACO Ser. II*, vol. I. E. Caspar's, "Die Lateransynode von 649," *ZKG* 51 (1932), 75–137, and the discussion of Pope Martin I in idem, *Geschichte des Papsttums*, vol. II, (Tübingen, 1933), 553–86 are still the basic studies for this synod. Some of his conclusions, however, have been superseded by the new findings of Riedinger (references below).

[65] *ACO Ser. II*, vol. I, 10–21, and 22.30–24.34.

[66] For a list of these documents, see *CPG* 9399.

[67] The document in question is the *Epistula Probi et universorum episcoporum concilii proconsularis* (*CPG* 9399.6). The fragments were extracted from the *De fide* (*CPL* 150) of Ambrose and the *Contra sermonem Arianorum* (*CPL* 702) and *Epistula* 140 (*CPL* 262) of Augustine, *ACO Ser. II*, vol. I, 80.7–90.34.

forthcoming reading of the heretical texts that way meant to expose their disagreement with the patristic and conciliar *horoi*.[68]

Consequently, a florilegium of eleven quotations extracted from the writings of Theodore of Pharan, who first introduced (προαρξάμενος) the monothelete novelty, was cited at the beginning of the third session.[69] They were refuted immediately by Pope Martin I himself, who concluded by opposing to the formulations of Theodore another small florilegium of six extracts from the works of orthodox church fathers (one each from Cyril of Alexandria, Gregory of Nazianzus, and Basil, two from Pseudo-Dionysius, and one from the fourth ecumenical council). The reading of heretical quotations then continued, with excerpts from Cyrus of Alexandria, Sergius of Constantinople, Themistius, Emperor Heraclius, and others. In one instance a falsified extract from Pseudo-Dionysius (*Epistula ad Gaium*) included in the *Epistula Sergii CPolitani ad Cyrum Alexandrinum* (*CPG* 9400.3) had to be collated with the original text of this letter to prove the falsification.[70]

Two more monothelete quotations of Paul of Constantinople were read out at the beginning of the fourth session,[71] and thus the list of the heretical authors and works was completed. The first part of the proceedings was finished, and the process continued with the recitation of the orthodox quotations, starting with the *Symbola* of the first three ecumenical councils and the *Definitiones* of the Councils of Chalcedon and Constantinople II.[72]

Following upon the conciliar quotations came the *testimonia* (χρήσεις) of the orthodox fathers featured in the massive florilegium that constitutes a considerable part of the final session of this council. Pope Martin I introduced the recitation of this florilegium with the following words:

. . . δι᾽ ὑπομονῆς τρέχωμεν τὸν προκείμενον ἡμῖν ἀγῶνα, ἀφορῶντες εἰς αὐτὸν τὸν τῆς πίστεως ἀρχηγὸν καὶ τελειωτὴν Ἰησοῦν, ὃς ἐπὶ τῆς προκειμένης ἡμῖν δι᾽ αὐτὸν ὑποθέσεως τὸ πνεῦμα τῆς αὐτοῦ κατὰ φύσιν ἀληθείας

---

[68] Ἀλλ᾽ ἤδη καιρὸς ὑπάρχει καὶ τὴν ἑκάστου τῶν αἰτιαθέντων προσώπων εἰς μέσον ἡμῖν ἀχθῆναι καὶ ἐξετασθῆναι κανονικῶς συγγραφήν, ὅπως τὸ ἀπᾷδον αὐτῆς καὶ ἀπονεῦον πρὸς τὰς τῶν πατρικῶν καὶ συνοδικῶν ὅρων ὁμολογίας ἐν τάξει κατίδωμεν. *ACO Ser. II*, vol. I, 108.10–13.

[69] The fragments belonged to two works of Theodore of Pharan: (1) *Sermo ad Sergium* (*CPG* 7601/9400.1) and (2) *De interpretationibus* (*CPG* 7602/9400.1). For a new edition of these texts, see R. Riedinger, *Lateinische Übersetzungen griechischer Häretikertexte des siebenten Jahrhunderts*, SBWien 352 (Vienna, 1979), 9–62.

[70] *ACO Ser. II*, vol. I, 140.

[71] *Epistula Pauli CPolitani ad Theodorum papam* (*CPG* 7620) and the *Typus* (*CPG* 7621), attributed in the acts to Emperor Constans II but actually a work of the same Paul (see *CPG* 9401.2). *ACO Ser. II*, vol. I, 196.31–204.8 and 206.31–210.15 respectively.

[72] Ibid., 218.1–234.5; see also *CPG* 9401.

χαρίσεται λαλοῦν ἐν ἡμῖν καὶ φθεγγόμενον τὰ μεγαλεῖα τῆς πίστεως διὰ τῆς διδασκαλίας τῶν ἁγίων πατέρων, οὓς ἐγγράφως οἱ δι᾽ ἐναντίας ἐσυκοφάντησαν, εἰπόντες ἐκεῖνα διδάσκειν αὐτοὺς ἅπερ αὐτοὶ διὰ τῆς καινοτομίας ἐδίδαξαν. οὗ χάριν τὰς ἱερὰς αὐτῶν βίβλους ἐνεχθῆναι προστάσσομεν, μᾶλλον δὲ τὰς ἀναλεγείσας ἡμῖν ἐξ αὐτῶν εὐσεβεῖς περὶ Χριστοῦ τοῦ Θεοῦ μαρτυρίας· . . . [73]

At this point one of the participants, Leontius of Neapolis, suggested that the synodal definition of Constantinople II, which proclaims the acceptance of the patristic works and dogmas by all Christians, should be publicly heard before the recitation of the extracts. When this was done, the florilegium was read out.

It was the most extensive florilegium ever to appear among the documents of a council, including as it did 123 quotations, extracted from fifty-eight works of twenty-six authors. The extracts were divided into four parts, each bearing a relevant title: (a) Περὶ ἐνεργειῶν φυσικῶν (34), (b) Περὶ θελημάτων φυσικῶν (10), (c) Περὶ τῶν φυσικῶν Χριστοῦ τοῦ Θεοῦ ἡμῶν θελημάτων (44), (d) Περὶ τῶν φυσικῶν Χριστοῦ τοῦ θεοῦ ἡμῶν ἐνεργειῶν (35).[74] This florilegium was coupled with another less extensive one comprising forty-two monothelete quotations (33 χρήσεις τῶν συγχεόντων αἱρετικῶν plus 9 χρήσεις τῶν διαιρούντων αἱρετικῶν) before the council closed with the issuance of twenty canons.[75]

The procedure hardly differed in its rough outline from that followed during the fifth ecumenical council, but was totally different from another point of view. This point has been revealed through the detailed study of both the Greek and the Latin versions of the acts by R. Riedinger, the modern editor. His investigation led him to conclude that the Greek text of this council was the original one[76] and served as the basis of the Latin translation.[77]

---

[73] *ACO*, ibid., 252.15–22.

[74] Ibid., 258.1–314.13.

[75] Ibid., 320.21–334.35, 338.31–341.8, 368–86. I omit the list of authors and works of both florilegia because this information is conveniently given in the *apparatus fontium* of the modern edition. Even the *CPG* numbers of the works can be found at the end of the volume (*ACO Ser. II*, vol. I, 459–67). Another list of the names of the authors in these two anthologies is given in *CPG* 9404.2 and 9404.3. It is worth noting that of all the 123 quotations, only 27 were extracted from four Latin fathers: Ambrose of Milan (14), Augustine (6), Leo I (6), and Hilary (1).

[76] In the acts, however, care had been taken that the Greek text would appear as the translation of the Latin original. *ACO Ser. II*, vol. I, 54.35–37: the Greek abbots, presbyters, and monks conclude their *Libellus* (*CPG* 9399.2) by saying: παρακαλοῦμεν τὴν ὑμετέραν ἁγιωσύνην, ἄχρι μιᾶς κεραίας σὺν ἀκριβείᾳ πάσῃ, πρὸς τὴν Ἑλλάδα μεθερμηνευθῆναι φωνὴν τὰ νῦν παρὰ τῆς ὑμετέρας ἁγιωσύνης πραττόμενά τε καὶ ἐκφωνούμενα. See also Sansterre, *Les moines grecs*, 74 n. 144.

[77] Before this unexpected discovery, Caspar had already observed the preponderance of the Greek element in this council ("Lateransynode," 120) and suggested that the Greek monks

Riedinger has suggested that the entire text was originally conceived and written in Greek as a "text [of conciliar acts] written before [the actual council took place]" (*vorgegebenes Textbuch*). This council was meant to convene some years before 649, during the papacy of Theodore (24 Nov. 642–14 May 649), but was finally canceled because of that pope's death.[78] What appear to be the minutes of a council presided over by his successor, Pope Martin I, was in fact a text that "nicht in freien Diskussionen und in einer Konzilsaula, sondern an römischen Archiven und über Schreibpulten formuliert wurde," and therefore one should assume that "jedes seiner Worte wohlüberlegt ist."[79]

Moreover, even the Latin translation of this text had been made by the Byzantine monks who came to Rome together with Maximus the Confessor.[80] Equally amazing is the fact that Martin I, who appears to have spoken so many times during the sessions of this council and explained very delicate theological issues, did not know Greek and, apart from that, had very little understanding of the theological substance, the arguments, and the problems that were supposedly discussed at this council.[81]

In these circumstances, the examination of the florilegia of the Lateran Council and their contribution to the supposed proceedings of the fifth session becomes a minor issue for the present study. However, a few words on the texts and the provenance of the florilegia are necessary. J. Pierres attributed to Maximus the Confessor the authorship of canons 10 and 11 of the Lateran Council. He also proved that the Greek version of these canons was the original, and not the Latin one.[82] Moreover, he pointed out that a total of twenty-seven orthodox and heretical quotations out of those cited during the fifth session had already appeared in the *Tomus spiritualis* (*CPG* 7697.15)

in Rome made the first draft of the canons of the synod in Greek and then translated them into Latin (ibid., 86–120). F. X. Murphy and P. Sherwood did not fail to notice that "Le discours final de Maxime d'Aquilée est parfois plus intelligible dans la version grecque que dans la latine," in *Constantinople II et Constantinople III*, vol. III of *Histoire des conciles oecuméniques* (Paris, 1974), 178.

[78] R. Riedinger, "Griechische Konzilsakten auf dem Wege ins lateinische Mittelalter," *AHC* 9 (1977), 256; also idem, "Die Lateransynode von 649 und Maximos der Bekenner," in *Maximus Confessor*, Actes du Symposium sur Maxime le Confesseur, Fribourg, 2–5 septembre 1980, ed. F. Heinzer and Chr. Schönborn (Fribourg, 1982), 119.

[79] Riedinger, "Griechische Konzilsakten," 257.

[80] R. Riedinger, "Die Lateranakten von 649, ein Werk der Byzantiner um Maximus Homologetes," ΔΩΡΗΜΑ ΕΙΣ Ι. ΚΑΡΑΓΙΑΝΝΟΠΟΥΛΟ (= *BYZANTINA* 13.1 [1985]), 519–20, 522.

[81] Riedinger, "Griechische Konzilsakten," 255–56. A more detailed recapitulation of the work of Riedinger can be found in Sansterre, *Les moines grecs,* 117–19, with further bibliography.

[82] J. Pierres, *S. Maximus Confessor, princeps apologetarum synodi Lateranensis,* Diss. Pont. Univ. Greg. (Rome, 1940), 12*–14*.

of Maximus the Confessor.[83] The major part of the remaining quotations should be attributed to the work of Maximus the Confessor and his followers, although the Latin monks in Rome may have contributed the modest number of quotations that were extracted from Latin fathers.[84] Therefore, the contribution of the papal *scrinium* and the library cannot be confirmed on this occasion, despite the frequent mentions of it made by Theophylactus, the *primicerius notariorum*.[85]

It is very difficult to explain the entire situation in purely philological terms, but, in light of the evidence presented by Riedinger, the Lateran Council of 649 (if indeed the pope and his bishops gathered in the Lateran Palace),[86] appears to have been a stage-managed performance. Riedinger suggested that, as a "Realitätsanspruch," Pope Martin I demanded that the acts be read to him and his bishops in a Latin translation, before they put their signature to them.[87]

The inadequacy of a purely philological interpretation of this phenomenon becomes more evident with the realization that Martin I was never

[83] Ibid., 30*–51*; see also Riedinger, *Übersetzungen*, 13 and n. 8.

[84] See Sansterre, *Les moines grecs*, 119 and n. 55.

[85] So also C. Mango, "La culture grecque et l'Occident au VIIIᵉ siècle," *Settimane di Studio del Centro Italiano di Studi sull'Alto Medioevo 20* (Spoleto, 1972), *I problemi dell'Occidente nel secolo VIII* (Spoleto, 1973), 713.

[86] See also Riedinger, "Die Lateransynode und Maximos," 120.

[87] Ibid., 120; idem, "Griechische Konzilsakten," 256. This conclusion seems to agree with the Greek life of Pope Martin I (ed. P. Peeters, "Une Vie grecque du pape S. Martin I," *AB* 51 [1933]), according to which it was Maximus the Confessor who incited Martin I to summon a council in order to condemn the Monotheletes: καταλαβὼν ὁ ὅσιος Μάξιμος ὁ ὁμολογητής . . . τὴν Ῥώμην . . . παρασκευάζει Μαρτῖνον τὸν ἁγιώτατον πάπαν Ῥώμης συναγεῖραι σύνοδον καὶ ἀναθέματι καθυποβαλεῖν τοὺς τῶν μονοθελητῶν δογμάτων εἰσηγητὰς (ibid., 254). The next passage gives a brief description of the events of the council, ascribing to the pope and his bishops the role of observers:

Συγκροτηθείσης οὖν τῆς συνόδου . . . εἰσελθόντες οἱ ἐπίσκοποι καὶ οἱ ἡγούμενοι καὶ οἱ μονάζοντες πάσης τῆς ἀνατολικῆς χώρας ἀνεδίδαξαν διά τε λιβέλλων καὶ λόγου τὰ τῆς δυσσεβεστάτης αἱρέσεως. . . . Ταῦτα ἀκούσας ὁ ἁγιώτατος Μαρτῖνος, καὶ ἀναγνωσθέντων τινῶν ἐπιστολῶν παρὰ τῶν σταλέντων ἐν τῇ Ῥώμῃ, σημαινόντων τὸ αὐτῶν ἀσεβὲς φρόνημα ἀπεκηρύχθησαν τῆς καθολικῆς ἐκκλησίας, καίτοι (leg. καὶ ἔτι) καὶ οἱ ὁμόφρονες αὐτῶν· καὶ ἐξέθεντο ὅρον εὐσεβείας, ἀνατρέψαντες καὶ ἀναθεματίσαντες τὴν αἵρεσιν τῶν μονοθελητῶν (ibid., 254–55). The anti-dyothelete Syriac *vita* of Maximus the Confessor is less clear on the subject, but still accuses Maximus of having "ensnared" Pope Martin so that he accepted Maximus' doctrine (see S. Brock, "An Early Syriac Life of Maximus the Confessor," *AB* 91 [1973], 318, 327). Other sources also give credit to Maximus for the convocation of the Lateran Council (see R. Devreesse, "La vie de S. Maxime le Confesseur et ses recensions," *AB* 46 [1928], 18, 44 ff). For a more elaborate theory on the way the Lateran Council was conducted, see P. Conte, *Il Sinodo Lateranense dell'ottobre 649* (Rome-Vatican City, 1989), 142–48. An extensive review of the sources that refer to or mention the Lateran Council can be found ibid., 169 ff.

accused of staging a council. The authority of the Lateran Council of 649 has never been disputed within this context as well.[88] Later, in 653, when Martin I was taken as a prisoner to Constantinople, he was accused only of having accepted the papal throne without obtaining imperial approval of his election through the exarch of Ravenna, and of having given support to Olympius, the exarch of Ravenna, who rebelled in 649.[89] According to Riedinger:

> Seinen Anklägern dürfte bekannt gewesen sein, daß nicht er der geistige Urheber der Synode war, man zog ihn dafür jedenfalls nicht zur Rechenschaft. Er büßte, weil er sich gegen den Willen des Kaisers zum Papste hatte wählen lassen, um mit dieser Autorität seinen Namen unter ein Dokument setzen zu können, das zu dieser Zeit einen Angriff auf die kaiserliche Religionspolitik, also Hochverrat, bedeutete.[90]

It must be noted that the study of the texts common to the acts of Nicaea II and codex Parisinus graecus 1115 offers some evidence that parts of that council had also been staged, but, to my knowledge, no one has ever criticized Tarasius for off-stage manipulation of the proceedings. An attempt at an interpretation of this phenomenon is presented in Chapter IV below.

6. The Florilegia of the Council of Constantinople III (680/81)

If we accept that a formal pattern of conciliar procedure was established by the fifth ecumenical council in 553 and the acts of the Lateran Council of 649, it is easy to observe that a similar pattern was repeated, with some variations, at the Council of Constantinople in 680/81. In its eighteen sessions spread over a period of ten months (7 Nov. 680–16 Sept. 681),[91] the problem of Monotheletism was debated for the second time after 649, and once again florilegia played a prominent role.

[88] See also the *Relatio motionis inter Maximum et principes* of Anastasius Apocrisiarius (*CPG* 7736), wherein a brief altercation between Maximus and a certain official called Demosthenes is recorded. Demosthenes contends that the Lateran Council has never been ratified because the pope was deposed, and Maximus retorts that Martin was not deposed but persecuted. *PG* 90, 128D: Ἐν δὲ τῷ κινεῖσθαι περὶ τῆς συνόδου Ῥώμης λόγον, κράζει ὁ Δημοσθένης· Οὐ κεκύρωται ἡ σύνοδος τοῦ συγκροτήσαντος ταύτην καθαιρεθέντος. Καὶ λέγει ὁ τοῦ Θεοῦ δοῦλος [sc. Maximus the Confessor]· Οὐ καθηρέθη, ἀλλ᾽ ἐδιώχθη.

[89] Cf. Peeters, "Une Vie grecque," 258–59: Καὶ πολλὰ διαλεχθέντες τυραννικῶς καὶ ὑβριστικῶς, παραστήσαντές τε κατηγόρους ψευδεῖς ἐσυκοφάντουν ὡς τυραννίδα ἐργασάμενον . . . Τρωΐλος ὁ πατρίκιος μετὰ κραυγῆς εἶπεν· "Μὴ ἀγάγῃς ἡμῖν ὧδε λόγους περὶ πίστεως· περὶ ἀνταρσίας νῦν ἐρωτᾶ σε.

[90] Riedinger, "Griechische Konzilsakten," 256; same position in idem, "Die Lateransynode und Maximos," 120.

[91] *CPG* 9420–37; Mansi XI, 207–694. Recent edition for the first eleven sessions: *ACO, Ser. II*, vol. II,1; the remaining seven sessions ibid., vol. II,2.

It is also worth noting that Macarius of Antioch and his disciple Stephen the monk, the defenders of Monotheletism, were present during the most controversial parts of the proceedings of this council.[92] These two, following the current tactics of textual falsification, obliged the orthodox party to resort to basic principles of textual criticism.

Because this council, in the words of G. Bardy "fut vraiment le concile des antiquaires et des paléographes," where "on n'y parle que de manuscrits interpolés, de lettres fictives, d'actes supposés," and "on collationne des textes; on fouille les archives; on vérifie des signatures,"[93] and so on, a more detailed survey of its proceedings is appropriate.[94]

The council was summoned by two letters of Emperor Constantine IV. In the *Sacra Constantini IV imperatoris ad Domnum papam* (*CPG* 9416) of 12 August 678, the emperor asked the pope to send to Constantinople up to twelve western bishops and no more than four representatives of each of the four Greek monasteries in Rome. He also requested the shipment of books that might contribute to a solution of the monothelete issue.[95] Two years later, in his *Sacra ad Georgium CPolitanum* (*CPG* 9419, 10 Sept. 680), he announced the official convocation of the council to the patriarch of Constantinople.[96]

In the first session of the council (7 Nov. 680, *CPG* 9420), Theodore and George, the presbyters, John the deacon, and other legates of Pope Agathon took up the role of prosecutors. They brought the indictment of the heresy of Monotheletism against Sergius, Paul, Pyrrhus, and Peter, the former patriarchs of Constantinople, Cyrus of Alexandria, and Theodore of Pharan, and asked to be informed of the origins of the heresy.[97]

---

[92] Not that this practice is unprecedented; see, for example, the first *actio* of the fourth ecumenical council (*CPG* 9000, *ACO* II,1,1, pp. 55–196), where Dioskoros of Alexandria is also present in the place of the accused, but in this particular council it was the presence of the heretics and their activity that dictated the course the procedure finally followed.

[93] G. Bardy, "Faux et fraudes littéraires dans l'antiquité chrétienne," *RHE* 32 (1936), 290 ff.

[94] Similar surveys have already been presented by Murphy and Sherwood in *Constantinople II, III*, 198–219, and Riedinger *ACO Ser.* II, vol. II,2, pp. x–xix. Riedinger has covered almost every aspect that is of interest here.

[95] *ACO Ser. II*, vol. II,1, 6.7–8.4 (*CPG* 9416).

[96] Ibid., 10.11–12.25 (*CPG* 9419).

[97] Ibid., 20.27–22.5:

. . . φαμὲν δή, Σέργιος, Παῦλος, Πύρρος καὶ Πέτρος, οὐ μὴν ἀλλὰ καὶ Κῦρος, ὁ τῆς Ἀλεξανδρέων πόλεως γενόμενος πρόεδρος, ἔτι δὲ καὶ Θεόδωρος ὁ γενόμενος ἐπίσκοπος . . . Φαράν, καί τινες ἕτεροι τούτοις ἐξακολουθήσαντες, . . . ἓν θέλημα ἐπὶ τῆς ἐνσάρκου οἰκονομίας τοῦ ἑνὸς τῆς ἁγίας τριάδος, κυρίου ἡμῶν Ἰησοῦ Χριστοῦ, καὶ μίαν ἐνέργειαν δογματίσαντες . . . αἰτοῦμεν τὸ θεόστεπτον ὑμῶν κράτος εἰπεῖν τοῖς τοῦ μέρους τῆς ἁγιωτάτης ἐκκλησίας Κωνσταντινουπόλεως πόθεν ἡ τοιαύτη ἐφεύρηται καινοφωνία.

Macarius, the patriarch of Antioch, undertook the role of defender of the creed of the accused, a creed to which he himself was an ardent adherent. Then Constantine IV, who was presiding over the council, asked for evidence in support of the monothelete theses. Following the formulation of the fifth ecumenical council mentioned above (p. 4), he stated that the evidence would be accepted on condition that it was taken from the ecumenical councils and the ἔκκριτοι fathers.[98]

So the main procedure began with the reading of the acts of the third ecumenical council provided by the patriarchal library. Macarius failed to convince the assembly by appealing to the contents of a letter of Cyril of Alexandria included in these acts.[99]

The second session (10 Nov. 680, CPG 9421) was devoted to the reading of the acts of the fourth ecumenical council, with no benefit whatsoever to Macarius.[100] His hopes to persuade the council participants on the basis of the acts of the previous councils evaporated during the next session (13 Nov. 680, CPG 9422), when the acts of the fifth ecumenical council were found to be falsified in two instances that favored Monotheletism. In the first instance, a letter of Menas of Constantinople to Pope Vigilius was found, upon closer examination of the manuscript, to have been written on three insert quires that had obviously been added later to the first volume of the official copy of the acts. As a result, the letter was not taken into account.[101]

In the second instance, another falsification was discovered in the second volume of the acts containing the seventh session of the fifth ecumenical council. This falsification was detected again by the papal legates in two *libelli* purportedly sent by Vigilius to Justinian and Theodora respectively.[102] The legates demanded an examination of the manuscript. This examination was later carried out during the fourteenth session (5 April 681, CPG 9433), and the two volumes were collated with other copies of the acts. This revealed that the fifteenth quire of the manuscript had been subject to alterations and that an additional quire had been inserted before the sixteenth quire. The perpetrators of these falsifications were anathematized, along with the spurious letters.[103] Consequently, Macrobius, the bishop of Seleukeia, revealed the agent of a considerable number of similar falsifications in

[98] Ibid., 22.24–26: Εἰ βούλεσθε περὶ τούτου παριστᾶν ἡμῖν, οὐκ ἄλλως ὑμᾶς δεχόμεθα ἀποδείξεις προφέροντας, εἰ μή, καθὼς εἴπατε, ἐκ τῶν ἁγίων καὶ οἰκουμενικῶν συνόδων, καὶ τῶν ἁγίων ἐκκρίτων πατέρων.

[99] Ibid., 24.7–33.

[100] Ibid., 32.12–34.13.

[101] Ibid., 40.18–42.7.

[102] Ibid., 42.12–30.

[103] Ibid., vol. II,2, 646.7–648.4; see also the remarks of Riedinger, ibid., XVI–XVII.

the person of a certain monk named George. He had worked, as he confessed, at the instigation of Macarius of Antioch and had falsified every book of the fifth council that fell into the hands of the archbishop of Antioch. As was further unveiled, other persons were also involved in this enterprise.[104]

To return to the third session, once the text of the acts had been proved useless for Macarius and his followers, he was given the choice of supporting his doctrine on the basis of patristic authority. Macarius asked for a period of time (διωρίας . . . διδομένης), apparently in order to collect the χρήσεις that would serve his own purposes. Before the end of the third *actio*, George, the patriarch of Constantinople, asked for the reading of the *Epistula Synodica* of Pope Agathon and of the *Epistula Agathonis et synodi ad Constantinum IV imp.* (*CPG* 9417 and 9418).[105]

The request of George was granted during the fourth session (15 Nov. 680, *CPG* 9423), and the *Epistula Synodica* of Agathon was read out. The principal points of this *epistula* were generally drawn from the acts of the Lateran Council of 649. In the same *epistula* one finds incorporated a florilegium of fourteen dyothelete quotations,[106] all taken directly from the florilegia of the Lateran Council and another one comprising nine heretical χρήσεις[107] presented for the first time at the Lateran Council also.[108]

---

[104] Ibid., 650.1–654.10

[105] Ibid., vol. II,1, 44.19–46.7

[106] Ibid., 84.1–94.30.

[107] Ibid., 102.29–106.20; see also Diekamp, *Doctrina Patrum*, p. LXII.

[108] The relationship of the quotations in Agathon's letter to the florilegia of the Lateran Council calls for a few comments. It is evident that the first five orthodox quotations were simply copied verbatim from the orthodox florilegium of the Lateran Council. The quotations are: (1) Gregorius Naz., *Orat.* 30.12, C(onstantinople III): 84.1–6 = L(ateran 649): 284.23–29 (no. 20); (2) Gregorius Nyss., *Refutatio confess. Eunomii*, C: 84.8–11 = L: 286.1–5 (no. 22); (3) Gregorius Nyss., *Antirrheticus adv. Apollinarium*, C: 84.13–23 = L: 286.28–288.5 (no. 26); (4) Iohannes Chrys., *De consubstantiali*, C: 84.25–86.6 = L: 288.7–19 (no. 27); and (5) Cyrillus Alex., *Thesaur.* c. 24, C: 86.8–14 = L: 292.31–294.3 (no. 36). Quotation no. 6 in Agathon's letter (C: 88.19–25) is the Greek translation of a Latin passage from the *De trinitate* 9,5 of Hilary of Poitiers. This translation is different from the one found in L (298.4–14). The same holds true for the next fragment (C: 88.27–30, no. 7: Hilarius Pict., *De trinitate* 9,11), but it comes from the *florilegium dyotheleticum* and not from the Lateran acts proper (L: 426, no. 12). The problems start with quotation no. 8 of the letter (Athanasius Alex., *Orat. contra Arianos III* 35): Agathon gives two more lines from the same text (C: 90.22–29 = L: 304.28–35, no. 14). The same situation occurs in quotation no. 11 (Leo papa, *Epist.* 28.4 *ad Flav.*). Agathon again provides two lines more than the Lateran text. Finally, the heretical anthology in the letter of Agathon concludes with four fragments from the *Tomus ad Theodoram aug.* of Theodosius Alex., while in the Lateran Council there exists only the first fragment (C: 104.24–27, no. 6 = L: 326.16–20, no. 16) and part of the second (C: 106.1–5, no. 7 = L: 326.22–25, no. 17). Now, since the letter of Agathon was originally written in Latin and translated into Greek after its arrival at Constantinople, the question is: where did the Greek translators find the Greek passages of the florilegium? The acts of the Lateran Council offer one possible source, but this does not explain the presence of

Later, when it came to the question of the orthodoxy of this *epistula*, Patriarch George declared that after a detailed examination he could assure the emperor of the conformity with the orthodox faith not only of the letter but also of the quotations of the first florilegium. These quotations, in addition, were in accordance with the actual text of the works of the ἔκκριτοι fathers, as a collation with the books of the patriarchal library proved.[109]

One month later (fifth session, 7 Dec. 680, *CPG* 9424), Macarius offered two books (κωδίκια) with *testimonia* taken from the works of the holy fathers that favored the single will and operation of Christ. They were read out loud,[110] and more than two months later (12 Feb. 681, *CPG* 9425), during the sixth session, a third κωδίκιον with χρήσεις presented by Macarius was also read out and then sealed.[111] Thereupon, the legates of the pope objected that the quotations offered by Macarius and his followers were mutilated and asked for them to be collated with the original texts from the books of the patriarchal library. They also offered a κωδίκιον of their own with orthodox and heretical *testimonia* to be read.[112]

In the seventh session (13 Feb. 681, *CPG* 9426), the Roman florilegium of orthodox and heretical extracts was cited and the papal legates inquired if the participants agreed with the letter of Agathon and that of his synod. George of Constantinople and Macarius of Antioch requested the collation of the quotations with the original text of each work. Accordingly, all the κωδίκια were sealed to ensure that nothing would be altered after their official submission.[113]

In the next session, the eighth (7 March 681, *CPG* 9427), after the declaration of Patriarch George that he accepted as orthodox the letters and *testimonia* sent by Agathon and his synod, the bishops who were present at the council, one by one, stated their agreement with the dogmatic content of the letter of Agathon. Macarius alone and his followers stood in opposition in their refusal to accept two wills or two operations in Christ, and they continued to defend Monotheletism. The *confessio fidei* of Macarius was also recited.[114]

---

the two, more extended, quotations of Constantinople together with the two heretical fragments of Theodosius of Alexandria that do not occur in L. A second solution could be the hypothesis that the actual books from which the fragments had been extracted were available along with the text of the Lateran acts. For more on the subject, however, see below, p. 27, and Chapter IV.

[109] *ACO Ser. II*, vol. II,1, 196.18–24.
[110] Ibid., 168.8–14.
[111] Ibid., 176.14–178.5.
[112] Ibid., 187.10–28.
[113] Ibid., 186.6–188.23.
[114] Ibid., 212.5–232.13.

The time came for the collation of the quotations included in the κωδίκια of Macarius with the original text of the works from the books of the patriarchal library in Constantinople. The first five quotations of the florilegium of Macarius were found to be drastically abridged, and the patriarchal secretaries read out the suppressed parts of the original text.[115] Macarius was accused of using heretical methods.[116]

The reading of the florilegium of Macarius was continued in the ninth session (8 March 681, *CPG* 9428). The seventh quotation (Ps.-Athanasius, *De incarn. contra Arianos*), after a brief discussion, was judged to be prodyothelete, while the last one (Cyrillus Alex., *Comm. in Matt.*) was again found to be abridged.[117] At that moment Macarius found himself deprived of any patristic argument in support of his views. The verdict of the assembly held that the extracts presented by him not only did not favor his monothelete belief, but also, on the contrary, lent support to the orthodox dyothelete views, when placed in their context. Consequently Macarius was deposed, and any further discussion on the remaining quotations he had submitted was denied.[118]

It then came time for the collation of the Roman florilegium with the original texts. In the tenth meeting of the council (18 March 681, *CPG* 9429), the sealed κωδίκιον was presented before the assembly and unsealed. The recitation of the orthodox quotations began, and each extract was compared with the corresponding passage from the books of the patriarchal library or those that the papal legates had brought with them. All of the quotations, according to the secretaries of the patriarchate, agreed with the passages of the original text. The orthodox extracts were followed by another florilegium of twenty heretical quotations from the same Roman codex.[119]

---

[115] Ibid., 234.1–260.16. The quotations were extracted from the following works:

1–2. Ps.-Athanasius, *De incarn. contra Apoll.* (*CPG* 2231) (2 fragments)
3–4. Ambrosius, *De fide* (*CPL* 150) (2 fragments)
   5. Ps.-Dionysius Areopagita, *De divinis nominibus* (*CPG* 6602)
   6. Iohannes Chrys., *In illud: pater, si possibile est, transeat* (*CPG* 4369).

Also, at some point during the examination of this florilegium, Theophanes, abbot of the monastery of Baion, presented two short dyothelete quotations (one from Ps.-Athanasius, *De incarn. contra Apoll.*, and the second by Augustinus, *Contra Iulian. Pelag.* [*CPL* 326]). Ibid.15–248.2.

[116] Ibid., 242.3–6: Ἡ ἁγία σύνοδος εἶπεν· ἰδοὺ καὶ ταύτην τὴν χρῆσιν τοῦ ἁγίου πατρὸς περιεῖλες· οὐχ ἁρμόζει ὀρθοδόξοις οὕτως περικεκομμένας τὰς τῶν ἁγίων πατέρων φωνὰς παρεκβάλλειν, αἱρετικῶν δὲ μᾶλλον ἴδιον τοῦτο καθέστηκεν.

[117] Ibid., 268.15–272.2.

[118] Ibid., 274.10–19, 276.20–22.

[119] Ibid., 288.4–368.10 (orthodox florilegium); 370.6–390.4 (heretical). For a list of authors, see *CPG* 9429.1 and 2. Sansterre has also provided a similar list and some of the heretical works, as well as a few remarks on the relationship of these florilegia to those of the Lateran

The orthodox florilegium drew basically on that of the Lateran Council of 649. A closer look, however, reveals some significant differences.[120] It included forty-eight orthodox quotations taken from twenty-nine works of fourteen authors,[121] but they were not divided into sections as the extracts of the Lateran florilegium had been. Of the forty-eight quotations, eighteen appear for the first time in the acts of the sixth ecumenical council. Among those eighteen there are three extracts from the works of Emperor Justinian: one from the *Adversus Nestorianos et Acephalos* and two from his *Epistula dogmatica ad Zoilum* (*CPG* 6879).[122]

There are also two other fragments[123] in the orthodox florilegium which, although they were not included in the four florilegia of the Lateran Council, were found in the dyothelete florilegium of codex Vaticanus graecus 1455 (a. 1299). The Vatican florilegium contained a considerable number of *testimonia* that did not appear in the Lateran Council. They were, however, closely related in content to those of the Lateran Council.

A comparison of the remaining thirty extracts common to both the Lateran Council and the sixth ecumenical council (hereafter L and C respectively, even for page references) uncovers a wide spectrum of differences and similarities between the two lines of transmission of these fragments.

Council (*Les moines grecs*, 120, nn. 63–64). Another list is provided by K. Manaphes, Αἱ ἐν Κωνσταντινουπόλει βιβλιοθῆκαι αὐτοκρατορικαὶ καὶ πατριαρχικὴ καὶ περὶ τῶν ἐν αὐταῖς χειρο-γράφων μέχρι τῆς ἁλώσεως *(1453)*, Μελέτη φιλολογικὴ (Athens, 1972), 76–81.

[120] On the subject, in addition to the notes of Sansterre (above, n. 119), see also the remarks of Riedinger, in *ACO Ser. II*, vol. II,2, p. XIII.

[121] Ps.-Athanasius of Alexandria, Ambrose of Milan, Anastasius of Antioch, Augustine of Hippo, Cyril of Alexandria, Epiphanius of Salamis, Ephraem of Antioch, Gregory of Nazianzus, Gregory of Nyssa, Justinian, Justin Martyr, John Chrysostom, John of Scythopolis, and Pope Leo I. Basil of Caesarea is the only major author not included here.

[122] *ACO Ser. II*, vol. II,1, 350.5–356.16. The remaining fifteen are the following:

1. Iohannes Chrys., *Hom. de consubstantiali* (*CPG* 4320), 292.1–21
2–3. Idem, *In Matthaeum Homiliae* 1–90 (*CPG* 4424), two extracts; (a) 296.9–298.2; (b) 310.1–312.2
4. Idem, *In illud: pater, si possibile est, transeat* (*CPG* 4369), 306.13–312.2
5. Gregorius Nyss., *De opificio hom.* (*CPG* 3154), 304.21–306.3
6. Idem, *Contra Eunomium libri* c. 35 (*CPG* 3135), 306.5–9
7–8. Cyrillus Alex., *Contra Iulianum imp.* (*CPG* 5233h), two extracts: (a) 316.12–21; (b) 318.1–8
9–10. Idem, *Commentarii in Iohannem* (*CPG* 5208), two extracts: (a) 324.10–326.4; (b) 326.11–20
11. Ps.-Athanasius Alex., *De incarnatione contra Apollin.* (*CPG* 2231) 336.1–8
12. Augustinus, *Fragmenta contra Iulianum* (*CPL* 326), 336.12–15
13. Leo papa, *Epist.* 11 *ad Flav.* (*CPL* 1656), 336.20–338.3
14–15. Ephraem Antioch., *Apologia concilii Chalced.* (*CPG* 6902), two extracts; (a) 356.18–358.17; (b) 360.1–362.2.

[123] These are: Gregorius Nyss., *Contra Eunomium* (*CPG* 3135), *ACO Ser. II*, vol. I, 428 (quot. 24) = vol. II,1 340.20–342.15; and Cyrillus Alex., *Oratio ad Theodosium imp. de recta fide* (*CPG* 5218), *ACO Ser. II*, vol. I, 432 (quot. 55) = vol. II,1, 348.1–11.

Starting with the text proper of the fragments, it is noticeable that C always begins with a more accurate lemma and usually gives the incipit of the work. But then again, in most cases there is an almost verbatim correspondence between L and C or a few variants, or omissions of particles or even words on both sides. Even the excerpt from the Greek translation of Pope Leo's *Epistula* 165,8 *ad Leonem* (*CPL* 1656) is almost identical in both C (288.4–13) and L (302.1–9). The differences are all the more serious between the two fragments from the *De fide* (*CPL* 150) of Ambrose of Milan in L (274.16–19 and 276.10–19) and a more extensive fragment in C (288.17–290.14) that includes both. In this case, however, it is evident that we are dealing with two different Greek translations of the same Latin original.

Another, more noteworthy, point of difference between L and C is the length of their common quotations. In general, C provides much more extensive fragments than L, although on two occasions L does so,[124] and in another three both L and C give the same lines.[125] Furthermore, L and C display partly overlapping fragments[126] or passages from the same work that supplement each other.[127]

---

[124] (1) Ambrosius Mediol., *De fide* L 276.21–77, C 288.19–23; and (2) Leo papa, *Ep.* 165,6 *ad Leonem imp.* L 298.34–300.19, C 338.7–14.

[125] (1) Ps.-Iustinus, *Expos. rectae fidei* (*CPG* 6218) L 304.10–15, C 340.10–15; (2) Ps.-Iohannes Chrys., *Sermo in s. Thomam* (*CPG* 4574) L 312.5–9, C 340.11–16; and (3) Cyrillus Alex., *Thesaurus* c. 32 (*CPG* 5215) L 268.19–23 and 268.1–4 (also in *flor. dyoth.* L 431 [quot. 43]), C 348.17–350.2. The case of quotation 15 of C (Cyrillus Alex., *Thesaurus* [*CPG* 5215] c. 24, C 314.22–316.9) is a little odd: in the florilegia of L (quot. 31), there is a small part of the C fragment (L 312.21–24 = C 314.21–316.2); however, the entire C passage already exists in L embedded in the long speech of Bishop Deusdedit (L 354.35–356.10).

[126] For example, the excerpts from *Ep.* 165,6 *ad Leonem imp.* of Leo I (*CPL* 1656): in C 338.7–16 (= quot. 32) the fragment corresponds to the first five lines of the L quotation (L 298.36–300.2: [Τοιγαροῦν: add. C] εἰ καὶ τὰ μάλιστα . . . τῆς θεότητος ἐπικλίνεται). Then L continues for another twelve lines (L 300.2–14), while in C there is no corresponding text. Finally, in C 338.16–26 (= quot. 33) we have an extract that covers the last five lines of the quotation in L (300.14–19: καὶ τὸ δὴ πέρας . . . πιστεύει καὶ λόγον) but goes six more lines beyond the point where L stops and concludes with the words ἐκ τῆς τῶν ἔργων ποιότητος αἰσθανόμεθα. The same or slightly modified picture is also provided by the following excerpts (with corresponding quotation numbers): (1) Epiphanius Const., *Panarion* (*CPG* 3745) C 328.1–20 (= quot. 25), L 290.11–21 (31), 290.23–26 (32), and 290.28–35 (33); (2) Gregorius Naz., *Oratio* 30.12 (*CPG* 3010) C 330.1–16 (26), L 270.20–14 (2), 284.23–29 (20), and 284.31–35 (21).

[127] Compare the fragments from Gregorius Nyss., *Ep.* 189,6 *ad Eustathium* (*CPG* 2900/3137):

C 344.19–346.11 (= quot. 38)	= *PG* 32, 692c5–693a8
L 262.31–33 (15)	= *PG* 32, 693a8–12
L 262.37–38 (16)	= *PG* 32, 693c12–15
C 346.15–20 (39)	= *PG* 32, 696a9–b4
L 264.3–4 (17)	= *PG* 32, 696a13–15.

As far as the heretical florilegium of the same Roman κωδίκιον in C is concerned, matters stand rather differently. Among the nineteen quotations the Romans included in it,[128] only three were shared with the florilegium of the Lateran Council.[129]

It seems, *prima facie,* that the Roman legates were not satisfied with the florilegia of the Lateran Council and, before their departure for Constantinople, compiled a new florilegium of dyothelete quotations. In most cases the florilegia of the Lateran Council served as a guide, but the search went on for new authors and works, an effort which is more apparent in the heretical florilegium of C.[130] However, comparison of the common extracts in L and C suggests that, despite the textual differences, the florilegia of the Lateran Council of 649 and the κωδίκιον submitted by the Roman legates to the assembly in 681 were based on the same sources. This distinct possibility implies the presence in Rome of major collections of anti-monothelete works,[131] and not only florilegia. An additional argument in support of this assumption is that at least seven of the books used for the collation of the orthodox and heretical fragments were brought from Rome. The rest were taken from the patriarchal library in Constantinople. Many of them were described in detail in the proceedings.[132]

After the anathematization of Macarius and his followers, the council continued its work. The reading of the written documents, many of which had not been examined by the Lateran Council, occupied most of the last

---

[128] The last quotation (no. 20, Apollinaris Laodic., *Contra Diodorum ad Heracl.*, CPG 3356) was not originally included in this florilegium, but was read out from a book of the patriarchal library at the request of the Roman legates (C 388.11-390.4). This is rather peculiar because part of this extract was originally part of the L florilegium (L 320.38-39).

[129] (1) Themistius diac. Alex., *Antirrheticus contra tomum Theodosii* c. 41 (*CPG* 7285) C 370.8-14, L 326.31-34; (2) idem, *Antirrheticus* c. 34, C 374.7-10, L 328.9-12 (the lemma here reads: *Ep. ad Salamitanos, CPG* 7190); (3) Theodosius Alex., *Tomus ad Theodoram aug.* (*CPG* 7133) C 380.7-11, L 326.16-20.

[130] The monothelete florilegium of the Lateran Council contained forty-two fragments from thirty-two works of thirteen authors, while in that of Constantinople there appeared nineteen (twenty) fragments from nine (ten) works of six (seven) authors. However, C presented sixteen new fragments and three new authors (Paulus Antioch., Anthimus Trap., and Theodorus Bostr.). Even Severus of Antioch, whose name features in both florilegia, is represented in C by six fragments totally different from those of L.

[131] For a detailed list of the sources and works related to the monothelete controversy, see F. Winkelmann, "Die Quellen zur Erforschung des monenergetisch-monotheletischen Streites," *Klio* 69 (1987) 515–59. From this article Riedinger has listed the works that appeared in the acts of the sixth ecumenical council, in *ACO Ser. II,* vol. II,2, 961–62.

[132] See, for example, the description of the books used in the collation of the texts of the orthodox florilegium in *ACO Ser. II,* vol. II,1,1 286.20-21, 290.15, 296.3, 298.3, 298.19-20, 304.19, etc.

meetings. The citation of the orthodox *Epistula* of Sophronius of Jerusalem in the eleventh session[133] was followed by and contrasted with the writings of Macarius.[134]

In the twelfth session (22 March 681, *CPG* 9431), other monothelete works were read from χαρτία and κωδίκια that Macarius had submitted to the emperor in 680. They contained material already examined during the previous sessions as well as two letters of Sergius of Constantinople and the reply of Honorius to the second letter of Sergius.[135] Because many other letters were included among the papers of Macarius, the synod asked for the collation of the letters with the texts in the official registers of the patriarchate. The remainder of the session was spent on this task.[136]

During the thirteenth session (28 March 681, *CPG* 9432),[137] writings of Cyrus of Alexandria, Sergius, Pyrrhus, Paul, Peter of Constantinople, Theodore of Pharan, and Honorius of Rome were read from the registers of the patriarchal library. All of these authors were condemned and anathematized on the basis of their works.[138] The most interesting part of this session was the recitation of a small florilegium of eleven quotations from two works of Theodore of Pharan.[139] The very same fragments were already present in the acts of the Lateran Council, and it seems that this poor collection had hoarded the only existing specimens of Theodore's work from the time of the Lateran Council.[140] Therefore, the use of the word βιβλίον as the form in which this collection was presented is rather questionable here.[141]

The final sessions of the council, apart from the fourteenth that has already been mentioned[142] and the eighteenth which was the last session (16

---

[133] *ACO Ser. II*, vol. II,1, 410.12–494.9.

[134] Ibid., 500.9–512.15; list of works in *CPG* 9430.

[135] Ibid., 524–58.8.

[136] Ibid., 558.10–564.16.

[137] Ibid., 576.19–626.21.

[138] A list of the works that were read is found in *CPG* 9432.

[139] Theodorus Pharan., (1) *Ad Sergium* (*CPG* 7601/9400.1); (2) *De interpretationibus* (*CPG* 7602/9400.2). For the critical edition of these fragments, see above, n. 69. Maximus the Confessor, in his *Epistula ad Marinum Cypri presbyterum*, written in Carthage and dating from 645–646, says that he happened to find a book of Theodore of Pharan (ἐνέτυχον σχέδει Θεοδώρου τοῦ τῆς Φαράν, *PG* 91, 136c). Should we trace the origin of the present florilegium back to that context?

[140] Riedinger, *Übersetzungen*, 13.

[141] *ACO Ser. II*, vol. II,2, 602.1–3: Ἔτι λαβὼν ὁ αὐτός . . . Ἀντίοχος ⟨ἀναγνώστης καὶ νοτάριος⟩ βιβλίον Θεοδώρου ἐπισκόπου γενομένου τῆς Φαρὰν ἀνέγνω λόγον.

[142] In addition to the whole procedure of manuscript examination during this session, I should add here the offering of an extensive excerpt from the *Homilia in illud: nunc anima mea turbata est* of Athanasius of Alex. (*CPG* 2161) by three Cypriot bishops (ibid., 656.3–662.17). According to their account, they had brought a florilegium of their own from Cyprus and had

Sept. 681, *CPG* 9437)[143] (in the course of which the *horos* was issued), present no particular interest for this study.

In conclusion, the sixth ecumenical council had little to do with the substance of the monothelete controversy, on which much had already been said (or rather, written) during the Lateran Council. There were no dogmatic arguments,[144] and the main concern was the authenticity and textual correctness of the patristic extracts that supported the monothelete or the dyothelete views. In brief, the greatest part of the council revolved around the question of what exactly had been written and by whom. Inevitably, florilegia and other documents occupied a preponderant position in the minutes of the acts.

Simplistic as it may seem, Macarius emerged as the villain in this confrontation not only because he adopted heretical attitudes, but also because (from the philological point of view) he supported them with poor texts. In this council we witness, besides the enormous significance of the florilegia for the entire procedure, the imposition of higher standards of textual accuracy for the quotations they included. This accuracy became the decisive point for their validity as sources of orthodox doctrine.

7. The Iconoclastic Florilegia of the Synods of Hiereia (754) and St. Sophia (815)

If any of the Iconoclastic literature survives today, it is only to the extent that Iconoclastic fragments were inserted into Iconophile works for the purposes of refutation. It is unfortunate that we do not have a complete edition of the existing Iconoclastic works and fragments. Excerpts of these texts have been treated or sometimes edited in studies that have dealt primarily with their interpretation.[145]

---

finally been able to collate this χρῆσις with the text of an old manuscript in Constantinople before its presentation. But, as Riedinger has pointed out ("Griechische Häretikertexte," 12 n. 5), two fragments from this passage were already to be found in the acts of the Lateran Council.

[143] *ACO Ser.* II, vol. II,2, 752 ff.

[144] With one exception: the verbal exchanges between Theophanes, abbot of the monastery of Baion, Macarius, and others during the eighth session (*ACO Ser. II*, vol. II,1, 242.14–246.12).

[145] There are three basic surviving Iconoclastic texts.

(1) the Πεύσεις of Constantine V, which are prior to the Council of Hiereia. The Iconophile patriarch Nicephorus preserved fragments in his first and second *Antirrhetici, PG* 100, 206–373, and parts of the florilegium appended to them in his *Contra Eusebium* (ed. J. B. Pitra, *Spicilegium Solesmense*, I [Paris, 1852], 371–503) and *Adversus Epiphanidem* (idem, *Spicilegium Solesmense*, IV [Paris, 1858]], 292–380). Modern edition: G. Ostrogorsky, *Studien zur Geschichte des byzantinischen Bilderstreites* (Breslau, 1929) and also H. Hennephof, *Textus byzantinos ad icono-*

From the Synod of Hiereia we have first a florilegium that was inserted into its *horos*. It was a small collection of apparently iconophobic texts.[146] The list included in the first place some citations from the Old and New Testaments,[147] followed by extracts from the following works:

1. Epiphanius Constantiensis, with no title (= *CPG* 3751, *Testamentum ad cives* [fragmenta]; most recent edition: Thümmel, *Frühgeschichte*, 302), Mansi XIII 292D–E

2. Gregorius Naz. (*CPG* 3035.2), *Carmina moralia* 31, 39 ff. (*PG* 37, 913), Mansi XIII 297A

3. Iohannes Chrys., with no title (= *CPG* 4415, *In Psalmum* 145, *PG* 55, 521B), Mansi XIII 300A

4. Basilius Caes., extract with no title (= *CPG* 2900, *Epistula I ad Gregorium Naz.*), ed. Y. Courtonne, *S. Basile, Lettres*, I (Paris, 1957), 8, Mansi XIII 300B

5. Athanasius Alex., with no title (= *CPG* 2090, *Oratio contra Gentes*, *PG* 25, 29A; the last phrase comes from *CPG* 2098, *Epistula ad Adelphium*, *PG* 26, 1081C), Mansi XIII 300E

6. Amphilochius Iconiensis, with no title (= *CPG* 3252, *Encomium s. Basilii magni* [*BHG* 260z], extant only in Syriac),[148] Mansi XIII 301D

7. Theodotus Ancyranus, with no title (= *CPG* 6133, *Fragmentum contra imagines*), Mansi XIII 310E–312A

---

machiam pertinentes (Leiden, 1969). For further discussion of the Πεύσεις and their florilegium, see Gero, *Constantine V*, 37–52.

(2) The *Horos* of the Council of Hiereia, found in the acts of the seventh ecumenical council, where it is refuted (sixth *actio*, Mansi XIII 208–364). The *Horos* without its refutation is in Hennephof, *Textus*, 61–78. For English translation and commentary, see Gero, *Constantine V*, 53–110.

(3) The *Horos* of the Synod of St. Sophia (815) and its florilegium, preserved by Nicephorus again in his as yet unpublished *Refutatio et eversio* (transmitted by Paris. gr. 1250 saec. XIII [XIV?], fols. 173–332 and Paris. Coislin. 93 saec. XV [XII?], fols. 1–159. Modern edition: P. Alexander, "The Iconoclastic Council of St. Sophia (815) and Its Definition," *DOP* 7 (1953), 58–66, which improves the previous editions by D. Serruys, "Les actes du concile iconoclaste de l'an 815," École Française de Rome, *Mélanges d'archéologie et d'histoire* 23 (1903), 345–51, and Ostrogorsky, *Studien*, 48–51. See also P. Alexander, *Nicephorus*, 137–40 and passim, and Gero, *Constantine V*, passim.

[146] Mansi XIII, 280D: Πρὸς τούτῳ οὖν τῷ διεξεταστικῷ καὶ διεσκεμμένῳ ἡμῶν δόγματι, παρέξομεν καὶ ἐκ τῆς θεοπνεύστου γραφῆς καὶ τῶν ἐγκρίτων ἡμῶν πατέρων ἐναργεῖς τὰς μαρτυρίας συμπνεούσας ἡμῖν καὶ ἐπικυρούσας τὸν τοιοῦτον ἡμῶν εὐσεβῆ σκοπόν· A treatment of the nature of some of these extracts is attempted by Sr. Charles Murray, "Art and the Early Church," *JTS* 28 (1977), 322 ff. For the letter to Constantia by Eusebius, see S. Gero, "The True Image of Christ: Eusebius' Letter to Constantia Reconsidered," *JTS* 32 (1981), 460–70.

[147] Joh. 4:24, 1:18, 5:37, 20:29, found in Mansi XIII 280E; Exod. 20:4, Deut. 5:8, 4:12, in Mansi XIII 284C; Rom. 1:23, 25; 2 Cor. 5:16, 7; Rom. 10:17, in Mansi XIII 285B–C.

[148] See Gero, *Constantine V*, 83 n. 106; also Thümmel, *Frühgeschichte*, 288–89.

8. Eusebius Caesar., *CPG* 3503, *Epistula ad Constantiam Augustam* (Thümmel, *Frühgeschichte*, 282–83), Mansi XIII 313A–D.

The main characteristics of this florilegium are the paucity of the citations and the slipshod appearance of the extracts in the *horos*. Only two of the eight quotations bear a title, but this does not necessarily imply that the lemmata were missing from the original florilegium; they may have been omitted by the person who drafted the refutation of the *horos*.[149] However, the authenticity of quotations 1 and 7 was denied in the refutation, and the orthodoxy of Eusebius was questioned. Finally, the genuineness of other extracts was rejected for various reasons.

On the other hand, according to the testimony of Gregory of Neocaesarea, Theodosius of Amorium, and Theodore of Myra, who had participated in the Synod of Hiereia and were finally accepted as penitents by the council of 787, another florilegium had circulated in the form of loose sheets (πιττάκια) during the synodal proceedings at Hiereia. We know only that on one of those πιττάκια there was a letter of St. Nilus to Olympiodorus (*CPG* 6043, *PG* 79, 580–81), which in some parts—possibly falsified—favored Iconoclasm.[150] A second passage was also presented in the same form, taken from the *Apocrypha Acta Iohannis*.[151]

The florilegium of the Πεύσεις has not survived in its entirety in the works of Nicephorus; therefore, it is impossible to ascertain the degree to which Hiereia depends on it. To be sure, two items at least are common to both florilegia: (1) the *Epistula ad Constantiam Aug.* of Eusebius,[152] and (2) the letter of St. Nilus to Olympiodorus. In addition, we know nearly all the names of the authors represented in the florilegium of the Πεύσεις: Basil of Caesarea, Gregory of Nazianzus, Gregory of Nyssa, Athanasius of Alexandria, Cyril of Alexandria (*Comm. in Isaiam*), John Chrysostom,[153] Eusebius, Nilus, etc. Still, this information provides little help. Paul Alexander, citing Ostrogorsky (*Studien*, 13 ff), states: "It is noteworthy that the . . . Council of Hiereia (754) asserted its independence from the Emperor omitting from its

---

[149] According to the *Scriptor incertus de Leone Armeno* (*PG* 108, 1025B = F. Iadevaia, *Scriptor Incertus* [Messina, 1987], 60.278–80), however, the incipits of the works were given; see Mango, "Availability," 35.

[150] Mansi XIII 37A–D. For this letter of St. Nilus, see H. Thümmel, "Neilos von Ankyra über die Bilder," *BZ* 71 (1978), 10–21. Thümmel (p. 21) suggests that the Iconoclastic version was the original one.

[151] Mansi XIII 173E, text ibid., 168D–169B. It is the story of the icon of John the Apostle, set up by Lykomedes.

[152] See Gero, *Constantine V,* 48. The most recent edition of the letter is in Thümmel, *Frühgeschichte*, 282–84, with all previous editions listed on p. 282.

[153] Nicephorus, *Contra Eusebium*, ed. Pitra, 378.33–379.4.

own *florilegium* some of the patristic passages compiled under the Emperor's supervision and by adding new quotations."[154] Thus the Synod of Hiereia did not deviate from the pattern established by the previous councils as far as the use of florilegia was concerned, apart from one detail to which I will return after discussing the synod of 815.

In the same manner, and in similar circumstances, were the Iconoclastic florilegia of the Synod of St. Sophia (815) compiled. The story is very well attested by the *Scriptor Incertus de Leone Armeno:* in the year 814 Emperor Leo V appointed a committee of six[155] to compile an Iconoclastic florilegium. The committee, led by John the Grammarian, was given quarters in the imperial palace, where they met:

> John asked authority to examine books everywhere. . . . And so they brought together a great multitude of books and searched through them, but they found nothing . . . until they laid their hands on the *synodicon* of Constantine the Isaurian . . . and, taking from it the *incipits* (τὰς ἀρχάς), they began finding the passages in the books, and these they stupidly brought forward, making marks in the places they had found.[156]

As is the case for the Synod of Hiereia, two florilegia are attested to have been recited in the course of this synod. There is no information available in the sources for the florilegium presented in the first session,[157] but it should not be different from that presented in the second and found in the *horos* ("definition") issued by the synod. Perhaps this florilegium "represents . . . with some additions or omissions, the labours of the committee appointed by Leo V in 814."[158] Its dependence on the florilegium of Hiereia is evident: five of the eight excerpts of the *horos* of Hiereia were repeated in 815, either verbatim or in slightly improved form.[159] However, the 815 florilegium introduced the following excerpts:[160]

[154] Alexander, *Nicephorus*, 127–28. See also ibid., 128 n. 1, another related piece of information from Nicephorus' *Refutatio et eversio:* "Constantine V wanted to delete some quotations from the *florilegium* compiled by the Council but was dissuaded from doing so by the most prominent number of the clergy."

[155] For the members of this committee and the preponderance of the Armenian element among them, see Alexander, *Nicephorus*, 126–27.

[156] *Scriptor incertus*, PG 108, 1025A–B = Iadevaia ed., 59.270–60.283, trans. Mango, "Availability," 35.

[157] See Alexander, *Nicephorus*, 127, 137–38.

[158] Ibid., 128. See also idem, "Church Councils and Patristic Authority: The Iconoclastic Councils of Hiereia (754) and St. Sophia (815)," *HSCPh* 63 (1958), 502.

[159] Both the *horoi* of 754 and 815 shared quotations 1, 2, 3, 6, and 7 in the list above, p. 32. To these we may add a sixth fragment taken from the letter of St. Nilus to Olympiodorus, which in Hiereia appeared, as noted, in the form of a πιττάκιον.

[160] For the text, see Alexander, "Iconoclastic Council," 60–66.

1. A fragment supposedly from the *Constitutiones apostolorum,* which is not contained in F. X. Funk, *Didascalia et Constitutiones apostolorum* (Paderborn, 1905)[161]
2. Asterius Amasenus, *Homilia de divite et Lazaro* (= *CPG* 3260, *Homiliae* i–xvi), *PG* 40, 168B (Thümmel, *Frühgeschichte,* 308–9)
3. A fragment attributed to "a certain Leontius," with no further indication of provenance[162]
4. Another fragment by Basilius Seleuciensis; no lemma[163]
5. Basilius Caes., *De creatione hominis* (= *CPG* 3215, *Homilia I de creatione hominis,* among the *spuria* of Gregorius Nyss.), *PG* 44, 273A–B
6. Gregorius Nyss., *CPG* 3175, *De tridui inter mortem et resurrectionem domini nostri . . . spatio* (vulgo: *In Christi resurrectionem i*), ed. E. Gebhardt, *Gregorii Nysseni Opera,* IX.1 *Sermones* (Leiden, 1967), 304
7. Iohannes Chrys., *CPG* 4510 (*BHG* 1602), *In Sanctum Romanum homilia 2, PG* 50, 616
8. Idem, Λόγος εἰς τὸν Ἀβραάμ, not among the published works of this author[164]
9. Epiphanius Constantiensis, *CPG* 3749, *Tractatus contra eos qui imagines faciunt*[165]
10. Idem, *CPG* 3750, *Epistula ad Theodosium imp.* (fragmenta)[166]
11. Idem, *CPG* 3754, *Epistula ad Iohannem Hierosolymitanum.*[167]

As in 754, the florilegium of 815 is also riddled with fragments of dubious attribution and genuineness in addition to some others from minor authors. The quotations were probably presented in a more accurate fashion in the acts of the synod than they are in the works of Nicephorus. If we believe the *Scriptor Incertus,* books with the relevant passages marked were used, at least by the committee. Whether these books were brought forward during the sessions of the synod is uncertain.

The significance of the florilegia for the Iconoclasts becomes evident by

[161] Alexander, *Nicephorus,* 256 n. 1; text: idem, "Iconoclastic Council," 60.

[162] Text: Alexander, "Iconoclastic Council," 60.

[163] Text: ibid., 61.

[164] Ibid., 62.

[165] There are three different editions of these fragments based on the two manuscripts of the *Refutatio et eversio* of Nicephorus. Because in many instances it is difficult to draw the line between the quotation proper and Nicephorus' comments on it, the editions disagree as to the number of the actual extracts from this work. Ostrogorsky, *Studien,* 68–71, has recognized nineteen fragments, whereas Alexander, "Iconoclastic Council," 63–64, accepts only ten. K. Holl, *Die Schriften des Epiphanius gegen die Bilderverehrung,* in *Gesammelte Aufsätze zur Kirchengeschichte* II,2 (Tübingen, 1928), 356–59, also gives a different number of extracts.

[166] Ostrogorsky, *Studien,* 71–73, gives nine excerpts (Holl, *Schriften,* 360–62, eleven). However, Alexander ("Iconoclastic Council," 64–65) cites only two fragments (Ostrogorsky, ibid., frag. 23 and 27) as derived from the 815 florilegium, the rest being introduced by Nicephorus himself who had the whole *Epistula* at his disposal.

[167] Ostrogorsky, *Studien,* 73–75; Alexander, "Iconoclastic Council," 65.

the extraordinary care invested in their preparation by both of the emperors who most actively campaigned for Iconoclasm. The preparatory committee of Leo V was given authority to look for manuscripts in all possible places and was housed in the Great Palace. The interest of Constantine V and Leo V in this matter is comparable only to that of Justinian I in the preparation of the Three Chapters dossier. One may assume that the discussions at Hiereia and St. Sophia were conducted in the same manner as at the previous councils and that florilegia played the same role there. Finally, according to Alexander, it is in the Iconoclastic florilegium of 815 that one can find any original contribution of the Second Iconoclasm to the advancement of Iconoclast theology.[168]

To conclude this discussion of the florilegia of the Iconoclastic synods, I should add a few words about the way these florilegia were presented. As we have seen, in every council examined up to now, the orthodox florilegia were always (with the exception of the Council of Chalcedon) followed by a heretical one. Applying the same pattern to the Hiereia and St. Sophia synods, one would expect to find a heretical florilegium in the preserved parts of their acts. This would lead to the following surprise: supposing that the orthodox doctrine was represented by the Iconoclastic florilegia, the place of the heretical florilegia was inevitably reserved for those that comprised openly Iconophile quotations, for example, the fragment from the *De Sancto Meletio Antiocheno* of John Chrysostom (*PG* 50, 515A–B), and many others that were read during the seventh ecumenical council. If the Iconoclasts were to be consistent, one should expect the anathematization, at least, of the Iconophile extracts and (by implication) works of many eminent church fathers. However, to my knowledge, there is not a single allusion to such an incident.[169] If this argument has any value, we have one more pos-

---

[168] Alexander, ibid., 39 ff. For a refutation of this thesis, see M. Anastos, "The Ethical Theory of Images Formulated by the Iconoclasts in 754 and 815," *DOP* 8 (1954), 153–60. Alexander eventually responded to Anastos' criticism in his "Church Councils and Patristic Authority," (above, n. 158). In this article, Alexander seems to have accepted Anastos' objections; after a thorough examination of the sources concerning the patristic documentation of the 815 synod, Alexander shifted his focus: what the Iconoclastic committee did was to "find many patristic quotations that had not appeared in the Decree of Hiereia, to improve on the identification of some passages quoted in the earlier document [= *Horos* of Hiereia] and in some instances to supply further fuller excerpts than the Decree of Hiereia had done" (ibid., 502).

[169] Only John of Damascus, George of Cyprus, and Patriarch Germanus were anathematized at Hiereia. But this does not imply the anathematization of the authors that John of Damascus, for example, included in his Iconophile florilegia, because, according to the *horos* of Hiereia, it was the way John interpreted the quotations that made him a heretic. Cf. the anathemas: Τῷ εἰκονολάτρῃ καὶ φαλσογράφῳ Μανσούρ, ἀνάθεμα. . . . Τῷ τῆς ἀσεβείας διδασκάλῳ καὶ παρερμηνευτῇ τῆς θείας γραφῆς Μανσούρ, ἀνάθεμα. Mansi XIII 356C–D.

sible reason why it was always a difficult case to defend the Iconoclastic posi-
tions on the basic level of patristic argumentation.

8. The Florilegia of the Roman Synods of 731 and 769

For the Roman Synod of 731 we possess some scanty information found
mainly in the letter of Pope Hadrian I addressed to Charlemagne probably
in the year 793,[170] commonly known as the *Hadrianum* (JE 2483).[171]

In this letter Hadrian defends the second Nicaean council of 787 and
the orthodoxy of the veneration of images against the criticism of the theologians of Charlemagne, as expressed in his *Capitulare adversus Synodum pro
sacrarum imaginum erectione*.[172] To each objection expressed in the heading
of each chapter of the *Capitulare,* Hadrian opposed a small florilegium of
scriptural, conciliar, or patristic extracts.

Because in many cases Charlemagne's criticism targeted, among other
issues, the particular use of some of the Iconophile quotations occurring in
the acts of Nicaea II, Hadrian had to answer him with new and, at the same
time, different quotations in order to convince him of the rightness of the
extracts already used or the dogmatic correctness of the opinions that he
criticized. This meant that Hadrian had at his disposal a number of second-

---

[170] See A. Freeman, "Carolingian Orthodoxy and the Fate of the Libri Carolini," *Viator* 16
(1985), 90, 105.

[171] For the text see above, p. 3 n. 7 and the list of abbreviations. For the Council of 731,
see W. Hartmann, *Die Synoden der Karolingerzeit im Frankreich und in Italien*, Konziliengeschichte,
ed. W. Brandmüller, Reihe A: Darstellungen 6 (Paderborn, 1989), 40–41. For the Council of
769, see ibid., 84–86. The *Hadrianum* refers repeatedly to the acts of those two councils, but
the following passage is the most telling: *Hadrianum*, 15.27–16.3:

> Nam et predecessores nostros, videlicet beatissimos pontifices Gregorium et Gregorium,
> Zachariam et Stephanum, Paulum et iterum Stephanum, repperimus eos pro sacris ima-
> ginibus erectione in Spiritu sancto ferventes, recte fidei zelum habere. Pro quo domnus
> Gregorius papa secundus iunior, una cum LXXVIIII sanctissimis episcopis ante confessi-
> onem beati Petri apostolorum principis praesedentem, multorum sanctorum patrum tes-
> timonia roborantes, venerari et adorari sacras imagines in eorum concilio censuerunt.
> Porro et praedecessor noster, sanctae recordationis quondam dominus Stephanus papa
> similiter cum episcopis partibus Francie atque Italie praesedente in basilica salvatoris do-
> mini nostri Iesu Christi, quondam Constantiniana, praedecessoris sui venerabilem conci-
> lium confirmans atque amplectens, magis magisque et ipse una cum omnibus episcopis
> praesidentibus sanctorum patrum testimonia adherentes, adorari atque venerari sacras
> imagines statuerunt.

[172] This *Capitulare* is now lost, but the *Hadrianum* preserves the titles of its chapters. For
its relationship to the *Libri Carolini*, see S. Gero, "The Libri Carolini and the Image Controversy," *GOTR* 18 (1973), 7–8 n. 8; also the more detailed and thorough study by Freeman,
"Carolingian Orthodoxy," 71–75, 105, and passim. The recent study by A. Melloni, "L'Opus
Caroli Regis contra Synodum' o 'Libri Carolini,'" *Studi medievali,* ser. 3, 29.2 (1988), 873–86,
does not seem to go beyond the point reached by Freeman.

class Iconophile quotations, because most of the "first-rate" Iconophile extracts had already been used by Nicaea II in 787 and were, consequently, disputed by Charlemagne.

The result was that 185 quotations were finally included in the *Hadrianum*. Forty-eight of them were derived from works of Greek fathers, five from the acts of the sixth ecumenical council (Constantinople III), one from the Council in Trullo, one from the Constantinopolitan synod of 536, and additional ones from Nicaea II. Of all the Greek patristic fragments, only fifteen deal directly with the veneration of images. The remainder are related to other issues, for example, the procession of the Holy Spirit (Capitula 1 and 3) and the falsification or destruction of patristic books (Cap. 66–67). Most of the fragments from Latin fathers were taken from the works of St. Augustine (fifty-four) and Pope Gregory the Great (twenty-four).

Hadrian, in some cases, refers directly to the acts of the Roman Councils of 731 and 769, and either gives an extract from them or quotes an Iconophile *testimonium* from their florilegia. Accordingly, we can be sure of the provenance of some Iconophile quotations. One other possible source for some Iconophile extracts in the *Hadrianum* may have been the *Synodica rectae fidei* of the three Oriental patriarchs that arrived in Rome about the year 764/65. There are three references to it in the *Hadrianum* which provide the information that this *Synodica* was included (after being translated into Latin) in the acts of the 769 council[173] and that it contained an extensive florilegium of Iconophile quotations.[174] As for the quotations from the Latin fathers in the *Hadrianum,* there should have been another source; if not their actual books, then, possibly, a Latin florilegium.

Although the exact function of florilegia in these two councils cannot be investigated, it does not seem to have been different from that described above in the sections concerning the fifth and sixth ecumenical councils. However, it seems necessary to try to restore some bits and pieces from their contents because they will prove useful to the study of the Iconophile florilegium of codex Parisinus graecus 1115.

---

[173] *Hadrianum,* 11.12–28. The surviving parts from the acts of this council have been edited by A. Werminghoff, *MGH, Conc. II, Karolini Aevi* 1.1 (Hannover-Leipzig, 1904–8), 74–92. Two more fragments from the 769 acts have been recently edited by L. Böhringer, "Zwei Fragmente der römischen Synode von 769 im Codex London, British Library, Add. 16413," in *Aus Archiven und Bibliotheken, Festschrift für Raymund Kottje zum 65. Geburtstag,* ed. H. Mordek (Frankfurt, 1992), 93–105 (text, pp. 102–5).

[174] *Hadrianum,* 23.19–22: "Item de synodica trium patriarcharum, videlicet Cosme Alexandrie, Theodori Antiochie et Theodori Hierosolime, quam in predicto concilio (= 769) relecta, ab omnibus fideliter honorata et venerabiliter suscepta est, ubi post multa sanctorum patrum testimonia Theodorus patriarcha Hierosolimorum inquid."

What should also be stressed is that only the Roman Council of 731 was directly involved in the image worship problem, while the Lateran Council of 769 spent time on this issue (actually its fourth session) simply in reconfirming the acts, decisions, and canons of the 731 council. It also endorsed the *Synodica rectae fidei* of the Oriental patriarchs.[175] Hence, whenever I mention a florilegium, I mean a florilegium already existing in the year 731 and augmented by a number of quotations offered in the 769 council (see the list below).

One of the quotations that occurs in the *Hadrianum* and that was derived from the florilegium of the Council of 731 (*Hadrianum*, 47.10–17)[176] can also be found in a small florilegium incorporated into the synodal letter of Pope Hadrian I (Mansi XII 1067A), addressed in the year 785 to Constantine VI and his mother Irene (= *Synodica* of Hadrian I, JE 2448). Therefore, it is more than possible that the thirteen fragments which constitute the florilegium of the synodal letter of the year 785 were lifted from the acts of the 731 and 769 councils.[177]

Taking all these into account, one can draw up the following list of quotations belonging to the florilegium of the 731 and 769 councils:

1. *Exodus* 25.1–22 (*Hadrianum*, 19.20–23)
2. *Regum* III, 6.23/6.32 (ibid., 19.24–29)
3. Gregorius I Papa, *Epistula ad Secundinum* (ibid., 20.2–13) = *Registrum epistularum* 9.147, 41 (*CPL* 1714)
4. Ambrosius Mediol., *Epistula supposititia II* (ibid., 20.20–26) (*CPL* 160)
5. *Numeri*, 21.8–9 (ibid., 27.32–34)
6. Ps.-Athanasius, *Quaestiones ad Antiochum ducem* (ibid., 31.29–32.1), *PG* 28, 621A (*CPG* 2257)[178]
7. Ps.-Dionysius Areopag., *Epistula X ad Iohannem theologum* (ibid., 32.26–29), *Corpus Dionysiacum II*, 208.6–10 (*CPG* 6613)
8. Idem, *De coelesti hierarchia* (ibid., 32.30–33.4), *Corpus Dionysiacum II*, 8.15–9.2 (*CPG* 6600)

---

[175] See the remarks of Werminghoff, in *MGH, Conc. II*, 88.

[176] It is a fragment attributed to John Chrysostom but originally belonging to the *Homilia de lotione pedum* of Severian of Gabala (*CPG* 4216). See below, Chapter III, sec. 5, no. 10.

[177] On the provenance of the image worship *testimonia* of the synodal letter of Hadrian, see Wallach, *Diplomatic Studies*. The second chapter of this book, "The *Testimonia* of Image Worship in Hadrian I's *Synodica* of 785 (*JE 2448*)," concludes with the theory that these quotations, or at least some of them, were taken either from the collections of *testimonia* of John of Damascus or "from chains of testimonia contained in the no-longer-extant *gesta* of the Lateran Council of 769" (ibid., 42, 88–89, 98–99, 104–5, 130–31).

[178] The full text of this quotation as it appeared in the acts is provided by Böhringer, "Zwei Fragmente," 102–3.

9. Cyrillus Alex., *Thesaurus de sancta et consubstantiali Trinitate* (ibid., 33.12–14), *PG* 75, 184D–185A (*CPG* 5215)

10. Gregorius Naz., *Oratio 45 in Sanctum Pascha* (ibid., 36.31–36), *PG* 36, 637A (*CPG* 3010.45)

11. Gennadius Massiliensis, *Liber sive diffinitio ecclesiasticorum dogmatum cap.* 73 (ibid., 41.33–36) (*CPL* 958)

12. *Preces clericorum et monachorum ad Iohannem CPolitanum et synodum* (ibid., 41.37–42.5), *ACO* III, 60.35–61.3 (*CPG* 9329.6)

13. Ps.-Iohannes Chrys., *Sermo in quinta feria paschae* = Severianus Gabalensis, *Homilia de lotione pedum* (ibid., 47.1–6; also Mansi XII 1067A), *REB* 25 (1967), 226.8 (*CPG* 4216)

14. Augustinus, untraced quotation,[179] Mansi XII 1066A–B (Greek), 1065C (Latin)

15. Gregorius Nyss., *De deitate Filii et Spiritus Sancti* (Mansi XII 1066B Gr., 1065C–D Lat.), *PG* 46, 572C (*CPG* 3192)

16. Idem, *In Canticum canticorum hom. XV* (Mansi XII 1066B–C Gr., 1065D Lat.), *PG* 44, 776A (*CPG* 3158)

17. Basilius Caes., *Epistula* 360 (Mansi XII 1066C–D, 1065D), *PG* 32, 1100 (other version), (*CPG* 2900)

18. Idem, *Sermo in XL martyres Sebastenses* (Mansi XII 1066D–E, 1068A–B), *PG* 31, 508D–509A (*CPG* 2863)

19. Ps.-Iohannes Chrys., *De parabola seminis* = Severianus Gabalensis, *De sigillis sermo* (Mansi XII 1066E–1067A, 1068B–C), *PG* 63, 544.7–15 (*CPG* 4209)

20. Cyrillus Alex., *Commentarii in Matthaeum* (Mansi XII 1067B, 1068D), *CPG* 5206

21. Athanasius Alex., *Oratio de incarnatione Verbi* (Mansi XII 1067C, 1068 D–E), *PG* 25, 96 and 120C (*CPG* 2091)

22. Ambrosius Mediol., *De incarnationis dominicae sacramento* (*Hadrianum* 52.35–39; Mansi XII 1067C–D, 1068E–1069A), *PL* 16, 873B (*CPL* 152)

23. Epiphanius Constantiensis, *Panarion* (*Adversus haereses*) (Mansi XII 1067D, 1069A), *GCS* 37, 12.10 (*CPG* 3745)

24. Stephanus Bostrensis, *Contra Iudaeos fragmenta* (Mansi XII 1067 D–1070D, 1069A–1072B), (*CPG* 7790)

25. Hieronymus Hierosolymitanus, *Dialogus de cruce* (Mansi XII 1070E, 1072B), *PG* 40, 865C–D (*CPG* 7817).

Quotations 3 and 4 were presented for the first time at the Lateran Council of 769[180] and cannot be included in the original florilegium of the 731 council. The investigation of the Iconophile florilegium of codex Parisinus graecus 1115, combined with that of Mosquensis Hist. Mus. 265 and Venetus Marcianus gr. 573 in Chapter III below, may shed further light on

---

[179] See Wallach, *Diplomatic Studies*, 31.
[180] See *Hadrianum*, 20.2–3 and 20.23–26.

this florilegium, as well as on the problem of the contribution of the florilegium of the *Synodica* of 764 to it.

9. Conclusions

First, concerning an apparent disagreement between the received opinion on the meaning of the phrase "recorded proceedings of conciliar acts" and the reality disclosed by the preceding survey: the modern reader usually expects to find in the acts of a council the minutes of spontaneous reactions and interactions of the participants and, recalling Riedinger, of their "freien Discussionen." As we have seen, however, this was not always the case, and the extent of spontaneous and improvised actions ranges from zero (as in the Lateran Council, which is merely a theological treatise with dogmas expounded and explained in the form of a dialogue) to the limited interventions of the participants, usually in the form of acclamations or, sometimes, brief exchanges of arguments that took place in the course of the fourth and sixth ecumenical councils. We have also seen that, on some occasions, actions that appear to be spontaneous were actually premeditated (see above, pp. 11, 12, 15–16, 19–20). Hence, in the conciliar acts, it is the written material that forms the basis on which everything else moves.[181] And since the basic stages through which the conciliar procedure evolved were always standard,[182] the written material had to be carefully prepared in advance. Its presentation in turn

[181] Unfortunately, statistics about the percentage of the written against that of the spoken word are available only for the Lateran Council of 649, which, however, cannot be used in order to infer what happened with the other councils. Riedinger ("Die Lateransynode und Maximos," 115) reckons that "Der Text der Lateranakten besteht etwa zu 44% aus Reden der Konzilsteilnehmer, zu 44% aus Übersetzungen griechischer Briefe und Florilegien und zu etwa 12% aus original lateinischen Briefen." Furthermore, the part covered by speeches (44 percent) is distributed among Martin I (26 percent) and five other bishops (18 percent). The percentage taken up by the speeches and dialogues is considerably lower in the other councils, because speeches such as that of Pope Martin (*ACO Ser. II,* vol. I, 336–42) followed by those of Maximos bishop of Aquileia (ibid., 344–352.9) and Deusdedit of Calaris (ibid., 352.15–358.17)—all of them embroidered with excerpts from holy scripture and patristic quotations—are missing from the acts of the other councils. The reason is very simple: assuming that they had been delivered orally, their length was enormous and the verbatim citation of patristic extracts would have required exceptional memory or the use of written notes. These speeches were made so long because the acts of the Lateran Council were from the very beginning a written text.

[182] Here I give a rough outline of these stages: (1) reading of the imperial letter(s) which officially announced the convocation of the council; (2) reading of synodal letters of the pope or the patriarchs that stated the problems; (3) reading of written accusations of specific heresy against named individuals; (4) presentation of the heretical dogma through the citation of heretical writings and florilegia; (5) refutation of the heretical dogma with the presentation of orthodox writings and florilegia; and (6) condemnation of the heresy and its supporters and official closing of the council with the promulgation of an *horos* or of some canons. Note that this framework has its exceptions, for example, the fourth ecumenical council, but some basic parts of the procedure always remained the same (e.g., n. 1 above).

should follow an already well-trodden path with which the *primicerii notari-orum* were in principle well acquainted. Inevitably this left little room for spontaneous interventions which, in addition, were usually triggered by the contents of the texts that were read.

Second, concerning the florilegia proper: in a conciliar context perceived as a series of prearranged events based on written material, the florilegia are not an exception. As we have seen, their dependence on previous collections implies that some preparatory work had preceded the official opening of any council.[183] As has also been shown, even details of their presentation to the assembly had been carefully planned some time ahead, and on some occasions what we read in the minutes does not correspond to the actual course of events.

One can also observe that their significance increases from council to council along with their length. From the twenty fragments of the sixth session of Ephesus (431) we come to the 123 of the Lateran Council. From the virtual non-existence of florilegia in the acts of Chalcedon (451) we witness the tedious scrutinization of monothelete and dyothelete anthologies in the most significant sessions of Constantinople III (680/81). Finally, another interesting aspect of the use of florilegia is that at the sixth ecumenical council at least, and, possibly, at the Iconoclastic Synod of St. Sophia (815), "back-up" copies of the anthologized books appear along with the florilegia.

The following chapters will deal with the question of how much the reality described in this chapter applies to the seventh ecumenical council and with the relationship between the Iconophile florilegium of codex Parisinus Graecus 1115, other dated Iconophile florilegia (that of the 731 and 769 Roman councils above included), and the acts of the 787 council.

---

[183] I cite one exception here: Macarius of Antioch was given some time after the third session of the sixth ecumenical council in order to prepare his monothelete florilegia. It took him three months to compile the anthologies he finally submitted (above, pp. 24–25).

ILLUSTRATIONS

1 Paris. gr. 1115, fol. 1. Written by a fourteenth-century scribe on an additional sheet of paper; the older numberings are present on the upper margin. (photo: courtesy Bibliothèque Nationale, Paris)

2 Paris. gr. 1115, fol. 2. Written by the same scribe who wrote fol. 1. (photo: courtesy Bibliothèque Nationale, Paris)

3 Paris. gr. 1115, fol. 8ᵛ. The upper nine lines are written by scribe X1 (see p. 53) and the remainder by Leo Cinnamus. (photo: courtesy Bibliothèque Nationale, Paris)

4 Paris. gr. 1115, fol. 208. Note the Greek *Filioque* on lines 21 and 22. (photo: courtesy Bibliothèque Nationale, Paris)

5–6 Paris. gr. 1115, fols. 224ᵛ–225. The opening lines of the *Chronographiae* of Julius Sextus Africanus start at line 35 (see pp. 86–87). (photo: courtesy Bibliothèque Nationale, Paris)

p. 10. λογος

7 Paris. gr. 1115, fol. 235ᵛ. The beginning of the frontispiece of the Iconophile florilegium (*Adversus Iconoclastas*). (photo: courtesy Bibliothèque Nationale, Paris)

8 Paris. gr. 1115, fol. 283ᵛ. The end of the Iconophile florilegium with the anathemas against the Iconoclast bishops of Hiereia. (photo: courtesy Bibliothèque Nationale, Paris)

9 Paris. gr. 1115, fol. 306ᵛ. The colophon of the manuscript; a note by a later hand is on the lower part of the page. (photo: courtesy Bibliothèque Nationale, Paris)

10 Codex Venetus Marc. gr. 573, fols. 3ᵛ–4. (photo: courtesy the Biblioteca Marciana, Venice)

† ΤΟΥ ΑΥΤΟΥ ΓΡΗΓΟΡΙΟΥ ΠΑΠΑ ΠΡΟΣ ΛΕΩΝΤΑ ΤΟ[Ν]
ΒΑΣΙΛΕΑ ΕΠΙΣΤΟΛΗ ΔΕΥΤΕΡΑ ⁘

11 Codex Mosquensis Hist. Musei 265, fol. 209. (photo: courtesy the Historical Museum, Moscow)

CHAPTER II

Codex Parisinus Graecus 1115

1. Introduction

A considerable number of the quotations listed in the previous chapter among those contained, for example, in the florilegia of the Lateran Council can be found in Parisinus graecus 1115 (= P) along with many other texts and extracts related to the ecumenical councils. Although in general terms P is classified as a manuscript of *miscellanea theologica*,[1] the texts that have appeared in the acts of the councils examined up to now—mostly epistles and parts of florilegia—occupy roughly half of this manuscript.[2]

Forty years ago R. Devreesse promised to give "une analyse complète de cet important manuscrit,"[3] but he died in 1978 without having published anything on the subject. Such an analysis is attempted in this chapter, which focuses on the particular characteristics that will provide a better understanding of the nature of this manuscript and the history of its archetype.

A detailed list of the contents of the manuscript will be found below in Appendix I, where each passage is given a number. Passages belonging to the Iconophile florilegium of fols. 235^v–283^v are listed in Appendix II; therefore the text numbering of Appendix I does not take into account the number of the texts listed in Appendix II buts runs continuously, ignoring the lacuna of fols. 235^v–283^v.[4]

2. Bibliographic Survey

Manuscript P has already been described in great detail and from every aspect—codicological, palaeographical, and historical—by J. Munitiz.[5] A

---

[1] See, for example, the introduction to the edition of the *Hodegos* of Anastasius the Sinaite by K-H. Uthemann, *Anastasii Sinaitae, Viae Dux, CCSG* 8 (Louvain, 1981), p. xxxiii.

[2] Relevant to this is the remark of Combefis cited above, p. 1.

[3] R. Devreesse, *Introduction à l'étude des manuscrits grecs* (Paris, 1954), 187 n. 7.

[4] Reference to the quotations in Appendix II will be made by the relevant number accompanied by an asterisk (e.g., 14*). If a fragment is unedited, I give my own edition; if it is edited, I give the starting and concluding words.

[5] Munitiz, "Parisinus," 51–67. Also H. Omont, *Inventaire sommaire des manuscrits grecs de la Bibliothèque Nationale et des autres bibliothèques de Paris et des départements*, vol. I (Paris, 1886), 223; idem, *Fac-similes des manuscrits grecs datés de la Bibliothèque Nationale du IXe au XIVe siècle* (Paris, 1891), pl. lxii (fol. 221^v); Munitiz has also written a shorter version of his article in Ch. Astruc

technical description may be summarized as follows: codex Parisinus graecus 1115 (former 15; 83 DCCCCXXXVI; 9; 1026; Regius 2951), 14 March
1276, Constantinople, paper with parchment covers, 240 × 170 mm, 38
lines per page (average): collection of theological works (extracts from the
third to seventh ecumenical councils, Anastasius the Sinaite *Hodegos*, *Doctrina Patrum*, etc.).

The part of the original manuscript that is preserved today (fols. 8–306)
consists of thirty-eight quires of Oriental paper of good quality. Two smaller
quires of Western paper of the fourteenth century have been added, one
at the beginning (fols. 1–7) and the other at the end (fols. 307–314). The
numeration of the folia in the upper right-hand corner was written in Arabic
numbers in the seventeenth century.[6]

The only scribe of the original part of the manuscript, the majority of
the marginalia included, who has subscribed his work on fol. 306[v] was Leo
Cinnamus (*PLP* 11723). He is otherwise unknown, but the quality of his
handwriting suggests a professional scribe. On the other hand, the quality
of his work has been severely criticized by many scholars, and the faults
must be attributed in most cases to his negligence and low level of philological training. He often commits grammatical mistakes, misreads or misspells
words of his exemplar, and, above all, omits particles, words, and phrases
from his exemplar.[7] What the present study also reveals is that, in the case
of some long texts, Cinnamus mutilated or drastically abridged them. The
overall impression is that the copyist did not care much about the correctness of his transcription and in many cases displayed signs of hasty and
uncritical work.

Finally, recent research has proved that his archetype was written in
majuscule.[8] Nevertheless, there is a possibility, as will be shown in the next
chapter, that the largest part of the Iconophile florilegium that was included
in the archetype of this manuscript was already written in minuscule.[9]

---

et al., *Les manuscrits grecs datés des XIIIe et XIVe siècles conservés dans les bibliothèques publiques de
France*, vol. I (XIIIe s.) (Paris, 1989), 46–48.

    [6] Munitiz, "Parisinus," 52–53.

    [7] Ibid., 54–55. On Cinnamus see also E. Gamillscheg and D. Harlfinger, *Repertorium der
griechischen Kopisten 800–1600*, Veröffentlichungen der Kommission für Byzantinistik, Band III,
2. Teil, Handschriften aus Bibliotheken Frankreichs (Vienna, 1989), Part A, 130; Part B,
123–24; Part C, pl. 330.

    [8] See R. Riedinger, "Der Tomus des Papstes Damasus (CPL 1633) im Codex Paris. gr.
1115," *Byzantion* 54 (1984), 635 n. 6, and R. Riedinger and H. Thurn, "Die Didascalia
CCCXVIII Patrum Nicaenorum und das Syntagma ad Monachos im Codex Parisinus Graecus
1115 (a. 1276)," *JÖB* 35 (1985), 83 n. 21.

    [9] See also Munitiz, "Parisinus," 55.

There has been an attempt to associate the script of Cinnamus with the one that occurs in the manuscripts of the so-called group of Karahissar (Leningrad Bibl. Publ. 105, Chicago Univ. Libr. 965 [= Codex 2400, the Rockfeller-McCormick New Testament], Athous Lavra B 26, etc.).[10] Although some characteristics of the script of this group can also be traced in Cinnamus' handwriting, the only concession that can be granted to this suggestion is that Cinnamus was simply influenced by this script.[11] Besides, the latest dating proposed for this group (1153–1210)[12] is incompatible with the dating of Parisinus graecus 1115.

A handwriting similar to that of Cinnamus is that of scribe L of codex Oxford Bodl. Libr., Roe 22 (dating from 1286), who wrote fols. 550 lines 24–33 and 553^v of this manuscript.[13] Furthermore, the script of Cinnamus is close to that of some manuscripts deriving from the imperial chancery.[14] This indicates that Cinnamus might have been an official scribe of this service and not necessarily of an imperial scriptorium, but this suggestion is highly hypothetical.

Finally, the script of the two additional quires belongs, according to Munitiz,[15] to the hand that wrote the marginalia on fols. 125^v, 129^{r-v}, 134^v, 211^v–213, and 294–297,[16] while E. Schwartz sees two different handwritings, one for fols. 2–7^v, 8^v lines 1–8, and 307^{r-v}, and a second for the rest (fols. 1 and 308–314^v).[17]

The colophon of the manuscript has been the source of almost all the problems that have made this codex the subject of so many remarks and discussions beginning in the year 1708, when Montfaucon published it for the first time.[18] The colophon reads as follows:

[10] Uthemann, "Ein Beitrag," 42–49.

[11] Ibid., 57.

[12] See P. Canart in *La paléographie grecque et byzantine,* Colloques Internationaux du CNRS 559 (Paris, 1977), 310–11.

[13] See A. Turyn, *Dated Greek Manuscripts of the Thirteenth and Fourteenth Centuries in the Libraries of Great Britain,* DOS 17 (Washington, D.C., 1980), 53, pl. 39.

[14] See, for example, the script in the chrysobull of November 1347 addressed by John VI Cantacuzenus to the Monastery of Dionysiou on Mount Athos. *Actes de Dionysiou,* ed. N. Oikonomides, *Archives de l'Athos,* IV, Album (Paris, 1968), pl. II.

[15] Munitiz, "Parisinus," 55.

[16] For this copyist who worked in the second half of the fifteenth century in North Italy, see S. Kotzabassi, "Der Kopist des Geschichtswerkes von Dukas," in *Symbolae Berolinenses für Dieter Harlfinger,* ed. F. Berger, Ch. Brockmann, et al. (Amsterdam, 1993), 307–23 and esp. 313.

[17] *ACO* I,1,7, pp. VIII–X.

[18] B. de Montfaucon, *Palaeographia graeca* (Paris 1708), 41, 65–66. The same colophon is also published, among others, by J. Munitiz with French translation ("Parisinus," 55–56) and by K.-H. Uthemann with German translation of some parts ("Ein Beitrag," 27–29). Mango ("Availability," 33) also gives the English translation of some lines.

+ τὸ παρὸν βιβλίον ἐγρά(φ)η διὰ χειρὸς ἐμοῦ λέοντος τ(οῦ) [2] κινάμου·
τελειωθὲν σὺν θ(ε)ῷ μηνὶ μαρτ(ίω) ιδ´ (ἰνδικτιῶνος) δ´· [3] ἡμέρα ἑβδόμη·
ἔτους ͵ϛψπδ´, ἐπὶ τῆς βασιλεί(ας) [4] τῶν εὐσεβεστάτ(ων) καὶ πιστοτάτων
καὶ ἐκ θ(εο)ῦ ἐστεμ(μ)ένων [5] μεγάλων βασιλέων ἡμῶν, τοῦ τε κυρ(οῦ)
μιχ(αὴλ) δούκα [6] ἀγγέλου κομνηνοῦ τοῦ παλαιολόγου καὶ νέου κωνσταν-
τ(ί)ν(ου) [7] καὶ θεοδ(ώ)ρ(ας), τῆς εὐσεβεστάτ(ης) αὐγούστ(ης), καὶ τοῦ
κυρ(οῦ) ἀνδρον(ίκ)ου [8] κομνηνοῦ, τοῦ παλαιολόγ(ου) καὶ ἄννης, τῆς
εὐσεβεστάτης [9] αὐγούστης· καὶ ἐναπετέθη ἐν τῇ βασιλικῇ βιβλιοθήκῃ·
[10] μετεγράφη δὲ ἀπὸ βιβλίου εὑρεθέντος ἐν τῇ παλαιᾷ [11] βιβλιοθήκῃ
τῆς ἁγίας ἐκκλ(ησίας) τῆς πρεσβυτέρας ῥώμης· [12] ὅπερ βιβλίον ἐγράφη
καὶ αὐτὸ ἐν ἔτει ͵ϛσξζ´ ὡς ἀριθ [13] μεῖσθαι τοὺς χρόνους τοῦ τοιούτου
βιβλίου ἄχρι τοῦ παρόντος [14] ιζ´ πρὸς τοῖς πεντακοσίοις+ [15] ἔχει δὲ τὸ
παρὸν βιβλίον τετράδ(ια) γεγραμμένα μη´ καὶ φύλλα [16] τπα´ καὶ τετράδια
ἄγραφα β´.

The present book/codex was written by the hand of Leo Cinnamus; it
was finished with (the help of) God on the fourteenth of March of the
fourth indiction, on the seventh day (= Saturday) of the year 6784, in
the reign of the most pious and faithful and crowned by God great
emperors of ours, sire Michael Doucas Angelus Comnenus [the] Palaeologus and new Constantine, and Theodora the most pious augusta, and
sire Andronicus Comnenus [the] Palaeologus, and Anna, the most pious
augusta; and it was deposited in the imperial library. It was copied from
a book that had been found in the old library of the Holy Church of
Old Rome, which had been written (καὶ αὐτὸ) in the year 6267, so that
the age of that book may be reckoned as 517 years up to the present.
The present book consists of 48 written (γεγραμμένα: see Munitiz, "Parisinus," 56, 62) quaternions and 381 folios and 2 unwritten (ἄγραφα)
quaternions.

The problems posed by the last sentence of this colophon have been
resolved by J. Munitiz in a satisfactory way. His conclusion is that the original
manuscript counted 392 folia instead of the 299 that are extant.[19] It follows
that what remains today from this manuscript is probably the part including
fols. 94–392 of the original product of Cinnamus. In any case, it is certain
that a number of folia were torn from the beginning of this manuscript, no
fewer than 82 (381 [τπα´] minus 299) and no more than 101.[20] (Chapter V
below suggests a possible reason for this.)

Another serious problem has been pointed out by Uthemann and has

---

[19] Munitiz, "Parisinus," 61–62.

[20] This is the number resulting from the subtraction of 299 from 400 which is the total
number of folios of 50 quires (48 γεγραμμένα + 2 ἄγραφα). Munitiz ("Parisinus," 61–62) made
some more complicated calculations that yielded a total of 392 folios for the 50 quires.

to do with the fact that both dates in the above colophon show signs of correction.[21] An inspection of fol. 306^v of the manuscript under ultraviolet light yielded the following results. The paper of this page is rather worn out by excessive use. Many letters have been effaced, and some of them have been rewritten in ink that is darker than that used for the original text. This is clearly visible in the words βασιλέων ἡμῶν in line 5, or the two lambdas and possibly the πα and ογ in the word παλαιολόγου in line 6 and elsewhere. The first date (σψπδ in line 3) has also been partially rewritten over some erased letters or characters. More specifically, under the two first letters (σψ) there is nothing visible, and they seem to have been written on plain paper. However, the two last letters (πδ), especially δ, have been written over some characters that look like N followed by something like ευ. I discuss this situation further in Chapter VI. For now, it must be stressed that the indiction that is also given for that date (= δ, line 2) is the original one and the year σψπδ corresponds to the fourth indiction. Concerning the second date (line 12: ςοξζ), it is clear that we have the original letters by the hand of Cinnamus.

The most serious problem of the codex, however, comes from the chronological indications themselves: although there is no particular objection to taking at face value the completion date of this manuscript, that is, 14 March 6784 or A.D. 1276 according to the Byzantine era (= fourth indiction), it is difficult to accept the date of its archetype which, according to the same era, would have gone back to the year 6267 = A.D. 759. The reason for this is that P includes some texts that give clear chronological indications pointing to a date later than 759.

Already in 1708, Montfaucon noticed the existence of a *Synodicon* of John of Jerusalem among the texts of the Iconophile florilegium on fols. 235^v–283^v of P. In this *Synodicon* there was an allusion to the execution of the Iconoclast Patriarch Constantine II in 766 (fol. 244^v).[22] Montfaucon therefore emended the figure ,ςοξζ' (6267) to ,ςτξζ' (6367 = 859), attributing the original figure to a scribal error (confusion between σ and τ). Since then, many other scholars either accepted the credibility of the colophon[23] or ad-

---

[21] Uthemann, "Ein Beitrag," 31.

[22] Montfaucon, *Palaeographia graeca*, 65–66. The Greek text in P (fol. 244^v) reads as follows: . . . λοιπὸν ποία σύνοδος πατριάρχην μὴ ἔχουσα (= Synod of Hiereia in 754)· ἀλλὰ καὶ ὃν ἐποίησε ἀπέκτεινε· τίς οὐ μὴ καταγελάσῃ τὴν σύνοδον ταύτην τὴν ἀκέφαλον, κεφαλὴν μὴ ἔχουσα ἐποίησεν ἑαυτὴν (leg.: ἑαυτῇ) κεφαλὴν καὶ στραφεῖσα ἔρριψεν αὐτὴν μᾶλλον δὲ ἀπέτεμεν αὐτήν . . .

[23] This is the case of Th. Schermann, "Die Geschichte der dogmatischen Florilegien vom V.-VIII. Jahrhundert," *TU* 28.1 (1904), 6–10; F. Cavallera, "Les fragments de Saint Amphiloque dans l'Hodegos et le tome dogmatique d'Anastase le Sinaite," *RHE* 8 (1907) 476–77; E.

hered to Montfaucon's solution,[24] regarding the second date of the colophon as a scribal error or, at times, as a falsification.

Diekamp, trying to reconcile the discrepancy between the second date
of the colophon and that of the contents of the archetype of P, proposed the
theory that parts of P were copied from more than one manuscript, one of
which dated from 759.[25] In a similar vein, E. Zettl thought that a "wandering" colophon of a single earlier manuscript bearing the year 759 was incorporated by a later compiler into the archetype of P.[26]

A more ingenious attempt in this direction was made by Melioranskij
who, taking into account the chronological evidence provided by some texts
of the Iconophile florilegium of P, observed that the use of the Alexandrian
era, which was current during the eighth century, for the calculation of the
date of the archetype yields the year 774/5, a date that saves the credibility
of the colophon.[27]

The most recent contribution on the subject is due to Uthemann. For
the date of the archetype of P he is inclined to accept the hypothesis of a
"wandering" colophon, which was deliberately used by the Byzantines in
favor of their dogmatic theses in the thirteenth-century *Filioque* controversy.[28] He bases that assumption on the existence of the following texts in P:

Schwartz, *ACO* I,1,7 (Berlin, 1924), pp. VIII–IX; B. Granić, "Der Inhalt der Subscriptionen in
den datierten griechischen Handschriften des 11., 12., und 13. Jahrhunderts," *Byzantion* 1
(1924), 267; R. Browning, "Recentiores non Deteriores," *Bulletin of the Institute of Classical Studies
of the University of London* 7 (1960), 12 n. 9 (repr. in *Griechische Kodikologie und Textüberlieferung*,
ed. D. Harlfinger [Darmstadt, 1980] 261 n. 9); E. Chrysos, "Νεώτεραι ἔρευναι περὶ Ἀναστασίων
Σιναϊτῶν," *ΚΛΗΡΟΝΟΜΙΑ* 1 (1969), 134–35; J. Straub, *ACO*, IV,1, pp. XXIV–XXV.

[24] The list includes M. Le Quien, *Oriens Christianus in quatuor patriarchatus digestus*, vol. I
(Paris, 1740), cols. 590–91; *PG* 109, 501–2; P. Batiffol, "Librairies byzantines à Rome," in *Mé-
langes d'archéologie et d'histoire* 8 (1888), 297–98; Vogel-Gardthausen, *Griechische Paläographie*, vol.
II (Leipzig, 1913), 439; Devreesse, *Introduction*, 182; Gouillard, "Origines," 244 n. 8; Gero, *Leo
III*, 64 n. 16; Munitiz, "Parisinus," 63–64. Most recently, P. Chrestou also has implicitly placed
the creation of the Iconophile florilegium of P in the period of the Second Iconoclasm; see his
"Testimonia Neglected by the Seventh Ecumenical Council," *AHC* 20 (1988), 251.

[25] Diekamp, *Doctrina Patrum*, pp. XX–XXI and XLV.

[26] E. Zettl, "Die Bestätigung des V. Ökumenischen Konzils durch Papst Vigilius. Untersuchungen über die Echtheit der Briefe *Scandala* und *Aetius* (JK. 936. 937)," *Antiquitas, Reihe* 1:
Abhandlungen zur Alten Geschichte 20 (Bonn, 1974), 37 n. 4.

[27] B. M. Melioranskij, *Georgij*, 83. This theory was later rediscovered by C. Mango, "La
culture grecque," 710–12 and idem, "Availability," 33–34; H. Belting and G. Cavallo not only
accept this thesis but also use it as an example of a case similar to that of the original of codex
Taurinensis gr. B.I.2. The original of the Taurinensis provides in its colophon some chronological data which can make sense only with the use of the Alexandrian era: H. Belting and G.
Cavallo, *Die Bibel des Niketas (Ein Werk der höfischen Buchkunst in Byzanz und sein antikes Vorbild)*
(Wiesbaden, 1979), 12–15, esp. 13–14 for P. See also Sansterre, *Les moines grecs*, 179–80.

[28] Uthemann, "Ein Beitrag," 31: "Insbesondere das Datum 759 ist mit grösstem Vorbehalt
zu betrachten. Es könnte sich um eine bewußte Frühdatierung mit polemischer Tendenz zu-

1. A canon περὶ τοῦ μὴ δεῖν τὸν ἱερέα β΄ λειτουργίας ποιεῖν (fol. 235ʳ⁻ᵛ), the full version of which is attributed by other manuscripts to Photius.[29]

2. Some fragments from works of St. Basil, Cyril of Alexandria, and others which constitute an anti-Latin florilegium on the subject of the procession of the Holy Spirit (*Filioque*). This florilegium in his opinion can possibly be dated in the thirteenth century and, in any case, not before Photius (fols. 180ᵛ–215ᵛ, 221ᵛ–224ᵛ).[30]

3. The Iconophile florilegium on fols. 235ᵛ–283ᵛ, in which are included the following dated texts:

(a) The Διάλογος στηλιτευτικὸς γενάμενος περὶ πιστῶν καὶ ὀρθοδόξων καὶ πόθον καὶ ζῆλον Θεοῦ ἐχόντων πρὸς ἔλεγχον τῶν ἐναντίων τῆς πίστεως καὶ διδασκαλίας τῶν ἁγίων καὶ ὀρθοδόξων πατέρων, commonly known as *Adversus Iconoclastas*.[31] This text in P is anonymous, however it is generally attributed to John of Jerusalem,[32] a delegate of the Oriental patriarchs to the second Nicaean council of 787 and a very active participant in it. The *Adversus Iconoclastas* offers an explicit, though complicated, statement of its date, which is the year 770.[33]

(b) A recension of the treatise *De sacris imaginibus contra Constantinum Caballinum* (or otherwise *Adversus Constantinum Caballinum*),[34] for which the *termini post* and *ante quem* are the years 754 and 775 respectively.[35] It is considered a work of John, patriarch of Jerusalem, but in this case there is manuscript evidence, for example, P (fol. 239): Συνοδικὸν Ἰωάννου ἀρχιεπισκόπου Ἱεροσολύμων.

(c) The *Narratio* of John of Jerusalem,[36] an account of the beginning of Iconoclasm in Syria which, according to Melioranskij, had been composed

---

gunsten des patristischen Arguments der Byzantiner im Filioque-Streit des 13. Jahrhunderts handeln."

[29] Ibid., 34. For this canon, see the end of the present chapter.

[30] Ibid., 37–42.

[31] Parisinus gr. 1115, fol. 235ᵛ–239, *PG* 96, 1348–61; *CPG* 8121.

[32] See Beck, *KThL*, 488.

[33] Uthemann, "Ein Beitrag," 34–35. The text reads as follows: Paris. gr. 1115, fol. 238ᵛ: ὑμεῖς δὲ οἱ νεοκήρυκες καὶ καινοὶ θεολόγοι . . . ἀπὸ τοῦ Κυριακοῦ πάθους καὶ τῆς σωτηρίου ἀναστάσεως μέχρι τῆς παρούσης ἰνδικτιῶνος ὀγδόης ἔτη ἑπτακόσια με΄ λέγουσιν εἶναι . . . ἕως ὅτου γὰρ τὴν ἔρευναν ταύτην ἤρξασθε ποιῆσαι, εἰσὶ ἔτη πλεῖον ἢ ἔλασσον με΄· ἀπὸ γὰρ ἐννάτης ἐπινεμήσεως ἤρξασθε τῇ ἀληθείᾳ ἀντιπίπτειν . . . The author of the *Adversus Iconoclastas* uses a primitive chiliastic era in which the Incarnation of Christ falls in the year 5500, his passion in 5533, and the date of the composition of the *Adv. Icon.* in 5533 + 745 = 6278, which according to the Byzantine era gives the year 770. Beck also accepts the same date in *KThL*, 488.

[34] It is the *Synodicon* mentioned above, p. 47; Paris. gr. 1115, fols. 239–245, with different incipit from that of the recension in *PG* 95, 309–44 (*CPG* 8114).

[35] Uthemann, "Ein Beitrag," 35–36.

[36] Parisinus gr. 1115, fols. 280ᵛ–281ᵛ, Mansi XIII 197A–200B, *PG* 109, 517–20.

for the synod of the three Oriental patriarchs in 764[37] that condemned the
Iconoclast bishop Cosmas of Epiphania. However, according to Uthemann,
this διήγησις was written in order to be cited at Nicaea II because: "Der Text
des Parisinus zeigt im Vergleich mit jenem der Akten der Synode von Nikaia
keinen auffälligen Unterschied; er beginnt mit derselben Anrede an eine
Synode; er bezeichnet die Ikonoklasten mit einem für die Synode von Nikaia typischen Neologismus als χριστιανοκατήγοροι."[38]

(d) Furthermore, he claims that the Iconophile florilegium of P was
based on the acts of Nicaea II because it includes almost all the Iconophile
testimonia cited during the fourth session of the council, apart from those
found in Mansi XIII 32C–33C, 36A–D, 57D–60B, the three letters of Patriarch
Germanus I (100B–128A), and the small extract from the treatise *De Spiritu
Sancto* of St. Basil. P also includes all the orthodox quotations on the issue
of image worship that appear in the fifth session of the same council "und
zwar weitgehend in der gleichen Textfolge wie die Gesta."[39]

Finally, J. Munitiz, arguing from the identification of the anti-Latin florilegium among the texts of P, came to question the validity of the other
information of the colophon. His points, which may be taken as the logical
implications of the work of K.-H. Uthemann, are presented in the following
passage which is quoted here in full as the best possible account of the results
and suggestions put forward by many of the scholars who have touched
upon the problems of P.

> Pour évaluer la valeur historique de chaque élément de la souscription
> il ne suffit pas de croire à la bonne foi de Kinnamos. Il faudra voir son
> oeuvre dans le contexte post-conciliaire de Lyon (1274), à un moment
> où le camp anti-unioniste, qui comptait trois des personnages impéri-
> aux mentionnés dans la souscription, cherchait des matériaux qui serv-
> iraient d'armes contre la campagne violente menée par Michel VIII.
> Un livre qui contenait des textes anti-latins (à propos du *Filioque*), qui
> avait le prestige d'être la copie d'un manuscrit d'origine romaine du
> VIIIᵉ s., et qui avait été déposé dans la Bibliothèque impériale, serait
> d'une valeur polémique considérable. Mais une fois qu'on a démontré
> que le modèle ne pouvait être antérieur au IXᵉ s. (post-photien), on se
> demande s'il était vraiment d'origine romaine, si l'Empereur Michel
> VIII aurait accepté (juste en 1276!) un tel livre dans sa bibliothèque,
> et, par conséquent, si l'année 1276, écrite comme on a remarqué en
> surcharge, ne serait pas aussi une "exagération pieuse." Les éléments

---

[37] Melioranskij, *Georgij,* 98.
[38] Uthemann, "Ein Beitrag," 36.
[39] Ibid., 36–37.

certains sont les suivants: le modèle du *Paris. gr.* 1115, au moins pour la première partie (Florilèges conciliaires), devait être très ancien (vraisemblablement du IXᵉ s.); le modèle en question, s'il n'y a eut qu'un, n'était pas antérieur au IXᵉ s.; Kinnamos travaillait au XIIIᵉ s., et pas au XIVᵉ s., la preuve en est dans le papier qu'il a utilisé et dans sa manière d'écrire. Pour le reste, il semble qu'on n'a pas trouvé encore de textes dans la partie originelle du *Paris. gr.* 1115 qui soient certainement postérieurs au IXᵉ s., et il n'est pas impossible que Kinnamos ait travaillé en 1276, bien qu'une date postérieure à la mort de Michel VIII (11.12.1282) soit plus vraisemblable. L'origine romaine du modèle est très suspecte.[40]

At first sight, the theory of Uthemann and Munitiz seems to have given some very satisfactory answers to the problems of P, although some points still remained undecided, for example, the exact date of the archetype of P or even the date of P itself.

However, another scholar appeared unwilling to accept these conclusions. R. Riedinger indirectly criticized the position of Munitiz by opposing the results of his own work on some texts that P includes. The main points of Riedinger's theses can be summarized as follows:

1. On fol. 39 lines 16–31 of P there is an extract from the letter of Victor of Carthage addressed to Pope Theodore in 646. This epistle was originally written in Latin and then translated into Greek. Both versions can be found in the acts of the Lateran Council of 649. The implications of this fact are obvious: by being a piece of correspondence between Rome and one of its suffragan bishops, this letter gives some additional support to the Roman origin of the archetype of P.[41]

2. The version of the *Epistula Synodica* of Sophronius of Jerusalem (*CPG* 7635) that P offers (fols. 73ᵛ–86ᵛ) is a text whose peculiarities suggest a transmission that derives from a version that could have existed only in Rome.[42]

3. The Greek translation of the *Tomus Damasi* (*CPL* 1633) found in P (fols. 196 line 6 from bottom to 197ᵛ line 10) displays clear signs that it was made within the period between the fifth and eighth centuries by Byzantine monks attached to the papal curia.[43]

4. There is a series of selected extracts from the *Epistula Synodica* in P,

---

[40] Munitiz, "Parisinus," 64.

[41] Riedinger and Thurn, "Die Didascalia," 80.

[42] R. Riedinger, "Die *Epistula Synodica* des Sophronios von Jerusalem im Codex Parisinus BN Graecus 1115," *BYZANTIAKA* 2 (1982), 153.

[43] R. Riedinger, "Der Tomus des Papstes Damasus (CPL 1633) im *Codex Paris. gr.* 1115," *Byzantion* 54 (1984), 634–37.

fols. 201–203 (see above, no. 2), the redaction of which has to be placed in Rome during the first quarter of the eighth century.[44]

5. Finally, the textual condition of the *Didascalia CCCXVIII patrum Nicaenorum* in P (fols. 221ᵛ–224ᵛ) suggests that it was copied from an exemplar belonging to an early (mid-8th cent.) and very good textual tradition.[45]

Such is the *état des recherches* concerning the problems of P. This and the following chapters add a few more *tesserae* missing from the puzzle of this highly important manuscript. The anti-Latin florilegium identified by Uthemann and the chronological implications that it entails are examined in the present chapter, while Chapter III is devoted to the Iconophile florilegium and a detailed discussion of Uthemann's points.

First, a list of the contents of P is given below, with chapterlike divisions corresponding to the manuscript's major clusters of texts:

1.	(fol. 1)	John of Damascus, *De unione*
2.	(fols. 2–4)	Barlaam, Δόγμα Λατίνων
3.	(fols. 4ᵛ–87ᵛ)	Conciliar texts (letters from the third to sixth councils, plus one from the Lateran Council of 649, fol. 39)
3A.	(fols. 39–40)	Gregory Naz., extracts from *Orat.* 43, 21, 37, a canon from the *Constitutiones apostolorum,* and an extract from Philo the historiographer
3B.	(fols. 40–60ᵛ)	Ps.-Leontius, *Liber de sectis*
4.	(fols. 87ᵛ–108)	Anastasius the Sinaite, *Viae dux* (first part)
5.	(fols. 108–116ᵛ)	Ps.-Athanasius of Alex., *Testimonia e scriptura*
6.	(fols. 116ᵛ–121)	Ps.-Cyril of Alex., *De dogmatum solutione*
7.	(fols. 121–129ᵛ)	*Doctrina Patrum*
8.	(fols. 129ᵛ–173ᵛ)	Anastasius the Sinaite, *Viae dux* (second part)
9.	(fols. 173ᵛ–180ᵛ)	*Doctrina Patrum*
10.	(fols. 180ᵛ–219ᵛ)	Florilegium on the Holy Spirit
10A.	(fols. 188–190ᵛ)	Synoptic account of the five ecumenical councils
10B.	(fols. 197ᵛ–198)	*Libellus satisfactionis Petri episcopi Nicomediae* (= sixth ecumenical council)
11.	(fols. 219ᵛ–235ᵛ)	Miscellaneous (dogmatic and historical)
12.	(fols. 235ᵛ–283ᵛ)	Iconophile florilegium
13.	(fols. 283ᵛ–306ᵛ)	Miscellaneous (canonical)

---

[44] R. Riedinger, "Die Nachkommen der *Epistula Synodica* des Sophronios von Jerusalem (a. 634; CPG 7635)," *Römische historische Mitteilungen* 26 (1984), 106.

[45] Riedinger and Thurn, "Die Didascalia," 82. Note that this article concludes with some more indications found in P which point strongly to the Roman origin of its archetype, ibid., 82–83.

14.   (fol. 307^{r-v})   Sequel of no. 3 above (two letters of Cyril of
                                   Alex. from the acts of the third ecumenical
                                   council)
15.   (fols. 308–314^v)   Matthew Blastares, *Contra Latinos*

Leaving aside items 1, 2 (fols. 1–4), and 15 (fols. 308–314^v) which are fourteenth-century additions, I proceed to the investigation of the remainder, paying particular attention to those that are of crucial significance for the dating and origin of P and its archetype, as well as for the final decision as to the exact nature of Parisinus graecus 1115.

3. The Additional Part of Codex P (fols. 4^v–7^v, 307^{r-v}; Appendix I, quotations 3A–11A, 1, 12A–13A) and the Epistles Related to the Council of Ephesus (fols. 8–14, quot. 2–7)

Starting from the contents of the additional quires at the beginning and end of the manuscript (quot. 1A–11A, fols. 1–7^v; quot. 12A–14A, fols. 307–314^v), I may repeat what Schwartz had already noted in his introduction to the edition of the acts of the Council of Ephesus.

The first piece (Appendix I, quot. 1A, fol. 1: John of Damascus, *De unione*) seems to be the latest of all the additions that were made to the mutilated manuscript. According to Munitiz, the addition of the second text (2A, fols. 2–4) dates from 1335–41.[46] The script of these folia is different, according to Schwartz, from that of fols. 4^v–7^v and 307^{r-v}. This last script is attributed to a scribe that Schwartz has designated X1.[47]

Quotations 3A–13A, which were copied by scribe X1, are closely related to the material existing in the first folia of the original part of the manuscript, especially to quotation no. 1. The surviving part of the original codex begins with a small fragment from the *Commentarii in Iohannem* of Cyril of Alexandria (= quot. 1). After that begins a collection of letters from the third ecumenical council (*Collectio Minor HX*, provided also by codex Arundelianus 529; see Schwartz, *ACO* 1,1,7, p. VIIII). The bottom lines of fol. 8 and the upper part of fol. 8^v had been left blank by Cinnamus, probably because of damage in his exemplar. These missing lines were supplemented by scribe X1, who used a codex containing the whole series of these letters. Apart from that, X1 took from the same exemplar quotations 3A–11A and with them completed the additional first part. The same scribe went on to add another quire at the end, where he copied two more texts (12A–13A)

---

[46] Munitiz, "Parisinus," 65.
[47] *ACO* I,1,7, p. VIII. For this scribe see now Kotzabassi, "Der Kopist," esp. 313 for his work on P.

from the same collection. Finally, the refutation of the pro-Latin florilegium by Blastares (14A) at the end of the second additional quire was written by the scribe of quotations 1A and 2A.[48]

It is also worth noting that scribe X1 retained, though not strictly, the order in which the texts were included in his exemplar. If one looks at the texts' numbers in *CPG*, one observes that 3A–7A and 9A come from the *Ante Ephesum* part, while 8A and 10A–11A come from the *Gesta Ephesina*. Then the original part of P begins with texts from the *Post Ephesum* (quot. 2–7).

Another point is that when scribe X1 worked on P, the actual extent of the manuscript was the same as today. The proof for this is a note of X1 on fol. 4ᵛ that reads as follows: Ἐν τῷ παρόντι τετραδίῳ τετάρτῳ εὑρήσεις κεφάλαια τῆς πέμπτης συνόδου. ἀνάγνωθι οὖν κεφάλαιον ιγ΄ καὶ ἐπιστολὴν Βιγιλίου πάπα. Indeed, the letter of Vigilius is included in the fourth quire. This also implies that the codex was already mutilated fifty years after its completion.

Here I might take a first step toward considering the reasons for the mutilation of the first part of the manuscript. This step can be facilitated by examining the very first extract of the surviving part of P (quot. 1, fol. 8: Cyril of Alex., *Commentarii in Iohannem*). Schwartz gives a transcription of the entire extract in his introduction and concludes "locum in Cyrilli qui servati sunt libris frustra quaesivi." But the existence of this extract was a clear indication to Schwartz that a whole florilegium concerning the Holy Spirit preceded the collection of the Ephesian letters.[49] This florilegium was possibly as long as the missing part of P.

The passage in question comes from the ninth book of the *Commentarii in Iohannem* of Cyril of Alex. (*PG* 74, 257c). But the more interesting thing is that it can be found in the Greek version of the acts of the Council of Ferrara-Florence (1438–39), and was adduced by the pro-Latin bishop of Rhodes in support of the *Filioque*.[50] Of course the two versions (P and Ferrara) differ in some minor details, and the Ferrara one is slightly shorter than that of P, since some phrases have been omitted. However, even if in fact P was not the actual source for the quotation in Ferrara, it is enough for the time being to connect it with the debate about the *Filioque*.

Thus, from the outset of this study, the suggestion of Uthemann and Munitiz that this manuscript has to be associated with the *Filioque* dispute is proved to have some basis. We may keep in mind the information provided

[48] *ACO* I,1,7, pp. viiii–x.

[49] Ibid., p. viiii. Besides, almost all of quot. 3A–10A are small excerpts from the whole works and their content deals with the Holy Spirit.

[50] See *Concilium Florentinum, Series B*, ed. J. Gill, *Quae supersunt auctorum graecorum Concilii Florentini*, pars I, vol. V, fasc. 1–2 (Rome, 1953), 99.7–19.

by this passage until we come, later on, to examine the florilegium that Uthemann identified as anti-Latin.

4. The *Collectio Epistularum* from the Fourth, Fifth, and Sixth Ecumenical Councils (fols. 14–39, 60ᵛ–87ᵛ; quot. 8–36, 43–46)[51]

Fourth Ecumenical Council (fols. 14–31ᵛ, quot. 8–29)

The letters taken from the acts of the fourth ecumenical council (8–29, fols. 14–31ᵛ) begin after a note of historical nature on fol. 14: Κυρίλλου τελευτή-σαντος τοῦ Ἀλεξανδρείας καὶ Ἰωάννου τοῦ Ἀντιοχείας, τούτων τοὺς θρόνους διεδέξαντο, ἐν μὲν τῇ Ἀλεξανδρείᾳ Διόσκορος, ἐν δὲ τῇ Ἀντιοχείᾳ Δόμνος.

This collection, just like the previous and the following ones, is a minor and abridged selection from the vast corpus of letters exchanged in the period before the Council of Chalcedon (448–451).[52] In fact, almost half of them (nos. 10–15, 17, 18, and 29) are related to the Council of Ephesus of 449,[53] one coming from the Synod of Constantinople of 448 (no. 9), the rest being all from the preparatory correspondence of the Council of Chalcedon. Epistles 24–28, which follow the heading Ἀρχὴ συνόδῳ (sic) τῇ ἐν Χαλκηδόνι, had never been cited at the ceremonial opening of the council and were issued as official documents aiming at a convocation of the council.[54] The last piece connected with the 451 council stops at fol. 31ᵛ, and is the famous Tome of Pope Leo I (quot. 29). On the margin of this letter there is an excerpt from the *Pratum spirituale* of John Moschos, written by the hand of Cinnamus.[55]

Fifth Ecumenical Council (fols. 31ᵛ–40, quot. 30–41)

Codices P and Arundelianus 529 (= Ar) are the main sources for the existing Greek fragmentary material from the acts of the fifth ecumenical council of

---

[51] For the whole collection of conciliar letters, see also E. Zettl, "Die Bestätigung," 36–45, where he examines this anthology along with another similar one that exists in codex Arundelianus 529 (British Mus. Add. 10445). A more detailed study of the relationship between the two manuscripts also exists in the edition of the *Hodegos* of Anastasius the Sinaite by Uthemann, *Anastasii Sinaitae*, pp. XCI–XCVII.

[52] Schwarz has called it *Epistularum Collectio H, ACO* II,1,1, p. VIIII.

[53] See *CPG* [8910] ff. Synodus Ephesina (a. 449), ("latrocinium"), I. Epistulae ad synodum spectantes ante gesta scriptae.

[54] See Schwartz, *ACO* II,1,1, p. VIII.

[55] It is the narration of the wondrous correction of the *Tomus Leonis* by the Apostle Peter who appeared in a vision, *PG* 87,3, 3012A–B. It seems that Cinnamus retained the same arrangement of the texts as that of the archetype of P, while another apograph of the very same original of P, namely, the already mentioned codex Arundelianus 529, has transferred this passage in the main text, and put it out of sequence among some fragments from the *Doctrina Patrum*. See Uthemann, *Anastasii Sinaitae*, p. XCII.

553.[56] Although Ar offers more passages than P,[57] the witness of P is equally valuable. The part surviving in P (30–35, fols. 31ᵛ–39) comes under the heading Ἐκ τῶν ὑπομνημάτων τῆς ἁγίας οἰκουμενικῆς ε΄ συνόδου. On fol. 38ᵛ there is also the indication Τέλος βιβλίου η΄ τῆς ἁγίας συνόδου τῆς ἐν Κωνσταν-τινουπόλει συναχθείσης. Χριστὲ ὁ Θεός, δόξα σοι.

The last two quotations (34, 35) from the fifth council seem to belong to another selection of the codex which was written under the *rubrica:* Ὅτι οὐ δεῖ σιωπεῖν (sic) καὶ ὑποστέλλεσθαι τοῖς ἀντιλέγουσι τῇ ἀληθείᾳ περὶ τῆς εὐσεβείας, κἂν οἰουδήποτε βαθμοῦ τύχιεν (sic) εἶναι τοὺς ἀντιλέγοντας, εἰ καὶ λίαν εἰσὶ τῶν εὐτελῶν καὶ ἀπόρων· πιστοὶ δὲ οἱ ἀντεχόμενοι τῆς ὀρθοδόξου πίστεως.

Under the same heading, after the last two quotations from the acts of the fifth council, follows a small piece extracted from the Greek version of the acts of the Lateran Council of 649 (quot. 36). The implications of this presence for the provenance of the archetype of P have already been discussed.[58] The five quotations, however, that come after the *epistula Victoris* (quot. 37–41) are a little difficult to be classified within their context. According to Zettl: "Der Sammler scheint den Zweck verfolgt zu haben, eine Apologie vorzubereiten gegen diejenigen, die das V. Konzil wegen der Verurteilung der Drei Kapitel bekämpften." He also assigns to this small florilegium a date after the year 646.[59] As for the last quotation (41, fols. 39ᵛ–40), it is a fragment from the lost *Historia ecclesiastica* of Philo the Historiographer cited by Anastasius the Sinaite.[60] The fragment tells the story of a presbyter who, after having been excommunicated by his bishop, died in martyrdom. However, owing to the excommunication, he could not see the face of Christ, even though he was a martyr. The story appears to illustrate the consequences of the *post mortem* anathematization of Origen and Theodore of Mopsuestia by the fifth ecumenical council, otherwise there seems to be no reason for its insertion in this place. It also seems possible that quotations 36–41 might have been marginal notes in the archetype of P along with the *rubrica,* just like the extract from the *Pratum spirituale* on fol. 31ᵛ.

P concludes quotation 41 with the following sentence: Τοὺς δὲ ὑπὸ τοῦ βασιλέως χειροτονημένους ἄρχοντας, κἂν λήσταρχοί εἰσι, κἂν κλέπται, κἂν λησταί, κἂν ἄδικοι, κἂν ὅτι οὖν (lege: ὁτιοῦν) εἰσιν ἕτερον, δεδοικέναι χρή, οὐ

---

[56] Straub, *ACO* IV,1, pp. XXIV–XXV.
[57] See Zettl, "Die Bestätigung," 39–42.
[58] See above, p. 51.
[59] Zettl, "Die Bestätigung," 42–43.
[60] See G. Mercati, "Un preteso scritto di san Pietro vescovo d'Alessandria e martire sulla bestemmia e Filone l'istoriografo," in *Opere minori,* II, *ST* 77 (1937) 436–38.

διὰ τὴν πονηρίαν καταφρονοῦντες αὐτῶν, ἀλλὰ διὰ τὴν ἀξίαν τοῦ χειροτονήσαν-τος δυσωπούμενοι. Perhaps this was also a marginal note in the archetype of P transposed by Cinnamus into the main text. What is more, it seems to continue the meaning of the above *rubrica* (ὅτι οὐ δεῖ σιωπεῖν, etc.), and this offers an additional argument toward the assumption that the aforementioned passages were originally marginalia.

The digression from the conciliar texts continues for another twenty folia, and we have in this part of P the whole text of the *Liber de sectis* (*CPG* 6823) of Ps.-Leontius Byzantius (quot. 42, fols. 40–60ᵛ). We are interested in only two things as far as this text is concerned: (a) P along with codex Arundelianus 529 are the most reliable witnesses to this treatise;[61] and (b) the *De sectis* was written no earlier than the year 579.[62]

Sixth Ecumenical Council (fols. 60ᵛ–87ᵛ, quot. 43–46)

The sixth ecumenical council is represented in this manuscript by three letters and one excerpt from the acts. Among these letters we can find the long *Epistula Synodica* of Sophronius of Jerusalem (quot. 45, fols. 73ᵛ–86ᵛ; see above, p. 51). There is also another extract from the tenth *actio* of the same council among the texts of the *Filioque* florilegium, seemingly out of place (quot. 167, fols. 197ᵛ–198, = *Libellus satisfactionis Petri episc. Nicomediae, CPG* 9429.3).[63]

5. Dogmatic Texts in the Form of Ἐρωταποκρίσεις: *Hodegos* (parts I and II), *Testimonia e scriptura*, and *De dogmatum solutione* (fols. 87ᵛ–121, 130–173ᵛ; quot. 47–49 and 111)

The collection of conciliar texts is followed by part of the *Hodegos* (*Viae dux*) (*CPG* 7745) of Anastasius the Sinaite (quot. 47, fols. 87ᵛ–108); one ψευδεπί-γραφον, the *Testimonia e scriptura* of Ps.-Athanasius (*CPG* 2240), for which P gives a version longer than the one published in *PG*;[64] and the *De dogmatum solutione* of Cyril of Alexandria (*CPG* 5231) (quot. 48 and 49, fols. 108–116ᵛ and 116ᵛ–121). The second part of the *Hodegos* comes after an interruption of nine folia occupied by a part of the *Doctrina Patrum* (121–129ᵛ).

Even if the *Testimonia e scriptura* is not exactly a text comprising ἐρωταπο-

---

[61] M. Waegeman, "The Text Tradition of the Treatise *De Sectis* (Ps. Leontius Byzantinus)," in *L'antiquité classique* 45 (1976), 191.

[62] S. Rees, "The *De Sectis:* A Treatise Attributed to Leontius of Byzantium," *JTS* 40 (1939), 358–60.

[63] For further discussion on P and the sixth ecumenical council, see *ACO Ser.* II, vol. II,1, p. VIII and n. 4.

[64] See *CPG* 2240 nota.

κρίσεις, it can nevertheless be classified under the same structural category with the other two because it is a collection of citations from scripture assembled, according to their content, under a particular title. It resembles, from this point of view, the *Sacra Parallela* of St. John Damascene. The dating of the two minor texts is not of particular significance. The *Hodegos*, however, according to Uthemann, who edited this text, should possibly be dated 686–689.[65]

6. The Parts from the *Doctrina Patrum* (fols. 121–129ᵛ and 173ᵛ–180ᵛ; quot. 50–110, 112–30)

Apart from the two clusters of quotations belonging to the *Doctrina Patrum* (*CPG* 7781) on fols. 121–129ᵛ and 173ᵛ–180ᵛ, there exist a few other quotations from the same anthology that are to be found among the texts of the Iconophile florilegium on fols. 246–247ᵛ and 248–251. Five more quotations derived from or connected with the last chapter of the *Doctrina Patrum* are interspersed among the extracts of the same florilegium and will be examined in the next chapter.

   F. Diekamp dates the final form of the *Doctrina Patrum* to the years 685–726,[66] and there is no apparent reason to deny, for the time being, the correctness of this dating which, besides, is so broad. In his edition the total of the quotations amounts to the enormous figure of 977. The greatest part of them, namely 901, are transmitted by Bodleianus Misc. gr. 184 (12th cent.) and Parisinus gr. 1144 (15th cent.). Nevertheless, the earliest sources for the text of the *Doctrina Patrum* are codex Vaticanus gr. 2200 (Columnensis 39, 8th–9th cent.) and, of course, the archetype of P.

   Compared to Vaticanus gr. 2200, P is a much poorer source. On the folia of P that the *Doctrina Patrum* occupies, we count 117 extracts, the ones belonging to the Iconophile florilegium not included, while Vaticanus gr. 2200 offers a good 644. A quick look through the quotations of P is enough to prove that what we find here is a random extraction of quotations from the original of the *Doctrina*, which, nevertheless, was partly done in accordance with the sequence of the chapters as they are arranged in the printed edition.[67]

---

[65] Uthemann, *Anastasii Sinaitae*, p. CCXVIII. See also ibid., pp. LXXXVI–XCVII for the relation between P and codices Arundelianus 529, Mosquensis Bibl. Synod. gr. 443 (Vlad. 232), and Vaticanus gr. 1702. Of interest is also his conclusion that "Zumindest *quoad nos* ist die Vorlage von X1 und X2 [*viz.* the original of P] als *eine* Handschrift zu betrachten."

[66] *Doctrina Patrum*, p. LXXX.

[67] In the edition the extracts are cited according to the sequence established by Vat. gr. 2200, Bodleianus Misc. 184, Paris. gr. 1144, and partly by Athous Vatopedinus 507. See *Doctrina Patrum*, p. XXXIII.

The group of quotations on fols. 121–129ᵛ of P starts with the first part of the heading of the second chapter as it reads on p. 11 of the *Doctrina*.[68] Therefore, we have in P the following sequence of chapters of the printed edition:

(A) P, fols. 121–129ᵛ:
chap. B: 3 extracts (plus 1 not included in Diekamp's edition = quot. 50–53),
chap. Γ: 1 extract (54),
chap. Δ: 1 extract (55),
chap. E: 3 extracts (56–58),
chap. ΣΤ: 3 extracts (59–61),
chap. Z: 5 extracts (62–66),
chap. H: 8 extracts (67–74).

Quotations 75–78 do not appear in the edition, and the extraction goes on to:
chap. ΙΔ: 2 extracts (79–80),
chap. ΙΕ: 13 extracts (81–93),
chap. ΙΣΤ: 5 extracts (94–98),
chap. ΙΗ: 7 extracts (99–105),
chap. K: 5 extracts (106–110).

(B) P, fols. 173ᵛ–180ᵛ:
chap. ΚΑ: 2 extracts (112–113),
chap. ΚΓ: 3 extracts (114–116).

From this point on the order is disturbed, and the quotations are arranged at random. Therefore, it seems more convenient to prefix the numbers of the quotations as found in Appendix I (page numbers refer to Diekamp's edition).
117: chap. Z (page 48 IV)
118–119: not in the edition
120: chap. ΛΖ (284 II)
121–123: chap. Z (53–54, XX–XXII)
124–125: not in the edition
126: chap. A (4 XI)
127–130: chap. B (15, 13, 11, XVI–XVII, X, I)

(C) P, fols. 246–247ᵛ (the numbers refer to Appendix II; see also note 4 of this chapter):
4*: not in the edition
5*–6*: chap. B (76 XVI, XVIII)

---

[68] P, fol. 121: Ὅτι ἐκ δύο φύσεων τὸν Χριστόν, καὶ ἐν δύο φύσεσιν, ὀρθοδόξως οἱ θεόπνευστοι πατέρες ἐκήρυξαν καὶ ὅτι τὸ μίαν λέγειν φύσιν τοῦ λόγου σεσαρκωμένην εὐσεβῶς ταὐτόν ἐστι τῷ εἰπεῖν δύο φύσεις.

7*: chap. IZ (116 IV)
8*: chap. H (56 VII)
9*–11*: not in the edition
12*, 14*: chap. Z (48 V, 54 XXI)
[16*: chap. ME (329 XIII)]

(D), fols., 248–251:
24*: chap. ME (326 III)
25*: chap. A (4. XI)
26*, 27*, 29*: not in the edition
28*, 30*–32*, 34*, 35*: chap. B (74 II, V; 73 I; 74 VI; 75 XIII; 76 XV)
33*: chap. IZ (115 III)
36*: chap. A (3 X)
37*: chap. IZ (115 I)
38*: chap. B (11 I)
39*–40*: chap. Z (52 X, 47–48 I–III)
41*–42*: chap. B (16–17 XIX–XXI)
43*: chap. ME (328 X).[69]

From these data it is clear that P contains sixteen extracts that do not appear in Diekamp's edition.[70] There are also eight quotations that are repeated one more time in the anthology under the same lemma:

62 and 117 (= chap. Z, page 48 IV)
64 and 121 (= chap. Z, 53 XX)
51 and 42* of Appendix II (= chap. B, 17 XXI)
52 and 13* of App. II (= chap. B, 19 XXVIII)
67 and 8* of App. II (= chap. H, 56 VII)
122 and 14* of App. II (= chap. Z, 53 XXI)
126 and 25* of App. II (= chap. A, 4 XI)
130 and 38* of App. II (= chap. B, 11 I).

A second point apparent from the above list is the following: from quotation 50 up to quotation 116 (fols. 121–129^v and 173^v–174^v), the sequence of chapters (B–KΓ) seems to be almost uninterrupted with the major exception of the lacuna between quotations 74 and 79. There, in place of some extracts that should belong to Chapters Θ–IΓ, we encounter four fragments that Diekamp excluded from his edition.

On the other hand, in one single instance we can observe a continuous

---

[69] Quotations 60*, 68*, 70*, 75*, and 91* of the Iconophile florilegium can also be found in chapter ME of the *Doctrina Patrum* (330 XVI, 327 VII, VIII, VI, and 330 XVIII). See below, Chapter III, sec. 4.

[70] I.e., quotations 53, 75–78, 118, 119, 124, 125 of Appendix I and 9*–11*, 26*, 27*, and 29* of Appendix II.

correspondence between the quotations in P and those of the *Doctrina,* and it is quotations 67–74 that find their counterparts in quotations VII–XVI of chapter H of the *Doctrina.* The usual practice of the copyist, be it the one who produced the archetype of P or Cinnamus, was to choose two or more, but never the whole number of extracts belonging to a particular chapter, sometimes skipping more than one chapter.

Apart from the heading of the second chapter mentioned above, there does exist in P a small part of the heading of chapter Z of the *Doctrina* (fol. 175) and three scholia that will be examined below. Diekamp has rejected the quotations of P[71] that I have listed above, considering them as extracts belonging to an earlier period or perhaps an earlier florilegium. He claims that: "Zur Unterscheidung spätere Zusätze von dem ursprünglichen Bestande läßt sich ein ziemlich sicheres Kriterium aus dem Umstande herleiten, daß die Doctrina in den Überschriften der einzelnen Zitate die Autoren nicht mit den in anderen Florilegien so gebräuchlichen Beiwörtern ἅγιος, μακάριος u. ä. auszuzeichnen pflegt."[72]

Of course there are some exceptions to this rule, but they are very few. And indeed five of the fifteen suppressed quotations of P display in their lemma adjectives such as ἅγιος, etc.[73] It is then very strange how it could be possible to discover five examples of the adjective ἅγιος among just sixteen quotations of P, when only ten such words exist in the first thirty chapters of the *Doctrina.*

The first objection that can be raised on behalf of P is that all the quotations from the *Doctrina* were copied at random and with no particular purpose on the part of the scribe apart from that of a hasty transcription of what he had in front of him. In such a case, where only chance has permitted the survival of those particular texts of the *Doctrina* through P, why have these sixteen fragments appeared among the extracts from the *Doctrina*?

There are two possible explanations for this: either Cinnamus copied, at the same time, from another codex, or the original of the *Doctrina* counted, possibly, more than 977 quotations.

At this point, it seems that the examination of the content of the texts in question, in connection with their context, may provide a better answer.

---

[71] At least the ones on fols. 121–129, 173ᵛ–180ᵛ, because he did not collate fols. 246–251 of P; see *Doctrina Patrum* 326.

[72] Diekamp, *Doctrina Patrum,* pp. XXXIV–XXXV.

[73] Quotations 53: Τοῦ ἁγίου Σιλβέστρου ἐπισκόπου Ῥώμης . . . ; 76: Τοῦ ἁγίου Ἰσιδώρου πρεσβυτέρου Πηλουσιώτου . . . ; 77: Τοῦ ἁγίου Φωστηρίου πρεσβυτέρου καὶ ἀρχιμανδρίτου . . . ; 78: Τοῦ ἁγίου Ἐπιφανίου ἀρχιεπισκόπου Κωνσταντίας . . . ; 124: Τοῦ μακαρίου Ἐφραὶμ εἰς τό . . .

The first quotation that Diekamp omitted is the one that bears the lemma Τοῦ ἁγίου Σιλβέστρου ἐπισκόπου Ῥώμης ἐκ τῆς ἀντιλογίας τῆς πρὸς Ἰουδαίους (quot. 53). In the manuscript it comes after three quotations from the second chapter of the *Doctrina* and just before another one from the third chapter.

We know next to nothing about the literary activities of Pope Silvester, if any,[74] and the nature of this fragment suggests a dating later than the fourth century. Since it is a *Disputatio contra Iudaeos*, the most appropriate period for its composition seems the seventh century,[75] although the simplicity of the theological argumentation might point to an earlier period, possibly connected with Theopaschitism (second quarter of the 5th cent.). The following is the whole text as it appears in P (the original is a fragment from the Greek *Vita Silvestri*, part of a letter of Constantine I to his mother Helen).[76]

(P, fol. 121ᵛ)

    Τοῦ ἁγίου Σιλβέστρου ἐπισκόπου Ῥώμης ἐκ τῆς ἀντιλογίας
                τῆς πρὸς Ἰουδαίους.

    Ἰουβὰλ λέγει· ἀδύνατόν ἐστι πεῖσαί με ἀνθρώπινον λογισμὸν ἐν ἑνὶ δύο εἶναί τινα καί, ἅμα μὲν κατέχεσθαι, ἅμα δὲ σταυροῦσθαι καὶ τὸ
5 ἐν τούτων ὑπομένειν τὴν ὕβριν. Σίλβεστρος ἔφη· εἰ οὖν τοῦτο (cod. τούτω), οἱῳδήποτε ἀνθρωπίνῳ ὑποδείγματι δυνηθῶ ἀποδεῖξαι, ὁμολογεῖς ἐπὶ τῶν παρόντων ἀρχόντων ἡττεῖσθαι; (sic) Κωνσταντῖνος αὔγουστος εἶπε· καὶ ἄκων καὶ μὴ βουλόμενος καταδικασθήσεται συναινέσαι (cod. συνενέσαι), ἀποδεικνύντος σου δύο φύσεις ἡνωμένας
10 κατ᾽ αὐτὸν (cod. καταυτόν), τὴν μὲν μίαν πάσχειν, τὴν δὲ ἑτέραν ἐλευθέραν τοῦ πάθους εἶναι. Σίλβεστρος ἔφη· ἵνα τῇ παρούσῃ βασιλικῇ πορφυρίδι ἐν τῷ ὑποδείγματι χρήσωμαι (cod. χρώσωμαι), ἔριον ἦν· τούτῳ (cod. τοῦτο) μιγὲν (cod. μηγὲν) τῆς κογχύλης τὸ αἷμα, χροιὰν πορφυραίαν αὐτῷ παρέσχεν· ὅτε οὖν ἐνήθετο τοῖς δακτύλοις καὶ
15 ἐκλώθετο γενόμενον στήμων, ποῖον ἆρα τὴν στρέψιν (cod. στέρψιν) ὑπέμεινε, τῆς βασιλικῆς ἀξίας ἡ βαφή, ἢ τὸ πρὸ τοῦ γενέσθαι αὐτὸ (cod. αὐτῶ) πορφυρίδα, ἔριον μόνον ὑπάρχον; οὐ γὰρ ὁ τῆς βασιλικῆς ἀξίας κόσμος, ἀλλὰ τοῦτο, ὅπερ καὶ ἐν τῷ τίκτεσθαι αὐτὸ (cod. αὐτῶ)

---

[74] See *BHG* 1634f.

[75] See V. Déroche, "L'authenticité de l'Apologie contre les Juifs' de Léontios de Néapolis," *BCH* 110 (1986), 660–64.

[76] To my knowledge, this *Vita* has been edited only once by Combefis in 1659, and it was included one year later in his *Illustrium Christianorum martyrum lecti triumphi* (Paris, 1660), 258–336. The passage given here can be found ibid., 317.14–320.23, but with numerous variants. For a more thorough study of the *Actus Silvestri*, and its dating see F. J. Dölger, *Konstantin der Grosse und seine Zeit* (Freiburg, 1913), 377–447. Dölger locates that text in Rome ca. 450. For further bibliography see A. Kazhdan, "'Constantin Imaginaire' Byzantine Legends of the Ninth Century about Constantine the Great," *Byzantion* 57 (1987), 209 n. 81.

εὐτελὲς ἔριον ὑπῆρχεν· ἀναγκαῖόν ἐστιν ὁμοιῶσαι τῷ ἐρίῳ τὸν
20 ἄνθρωπον καὶ τῇ πορφυραίᾳ χροιᾷ τὸν θεὸν λόγον· ὡς ἥνωτο ἐν τῷ
πάθει, ἥνωτο ἐν τῷ σταυρῷ, ἀλλὰ τῷ πάθει παντελῶς οὐχ ὑπέπεσε.
Τοῦ βασιλέως τοίνυν Κωνσταντίνου καὶ πάντων ὁμοῦ κραζόντων καὶ
λεγόντων τῇ ἀληθείᾳ συμβαίνειν τὸ ὑπόδειγμα, Θαρᾶ Φαρισαῖος
λέγει· οὐκ ἀρκεῖ μοι τὸ ὑπόδειγμα τοῦτο, ἐπειδὴ ἅμα καὶ τέμνεται, ἅμα
25 καὶ νήθεται ἐρίῳ. Ἀντιλεγόντων δὲ αὐτῷ σχεδὸν πάντων καὶ λεγόντων
ἅμα μὲν εἶναι, τὸ δὲ ἔριον μόνον τῷ πάθει ὑποπίπτειν δύνασθαι, οὐ
τὴν χροιάν, ὁ Σίλβεστρος ἔφη· δέομαι ὑμῶν, τέκνα μου ποθεινότατα,
παράσχετέ μοι σιωπήν (cod. σιωπεῖν)· ἐναργέστερον δὲ ὑπόδειγμα
ἐρῶ, ὃ μὴ δυνήσεται ὁ Ἰουδαῖος ὑπερβῆναι (fol. 122) καὶ προσθεὶς
30 εἶπεν· ἄκουε Θαρᾶ· δυνατόν ἐστι τὸ δένδρον ἔχον ἐν ἑαυτῷ τὴν ἀκ-
τῖνα τοῦ ἡλίου τμηθῆναι; Θαρᾶ λέγει· δυνατόν ἐστι. Σίλβεστρος ἔφη·
ἐν τῷ οὖν τέμνεσθαι αὐτὸν (cod. αὐτῷ) οὐ θεωρεῖς ὅτι τὴν πληγὴν τοῦ
τέμνοντος σιδήρου ἡ ἀκτὶς πρώτη ὑποδέχεται πρὶν ἢ (cod. πρινὴ) τὸ
ξύλον ὑποδέξασθαι; ἀλλ᾽ ἡ λαμπηδών, καίτοι ἐκεῖ οὖσα, οὔτε τμηθῆ-
35 ναι οὔτε διακοπῆναι δύναται· οὕτως τοίνυν καὶ ἡ θεότης οὔτε χωρι-
σθῆναι ἠδύνατο, οὔτε τμηθῆναι, τοῦτο δὲ ὑπέπεσε τῷ πάθει, ὅ,
καθάπερ ξύλον, καὶ δεθῆναι ἠδύνατο καὶ κρατηθῆναι· καὶ ταῦτα μὲν
τὰ ὑποδείγματα εἶπον (cod. εἰπών), ὦ Ἰουδαῖε, οἷα θνητὸς ἄνθρωπος
καὶ φθαρτὸς ὑπάρχων· εὐτελῆ γὰρ παρὰ εὐτελοῦς ἐλέχθη (cod. ἠλέγ-
40 χθη), ἀμυδράν τινα ἔννοιαν τῆς φρικτῆς οἰκονομίας τοῖς πιστοῖς πα-
ραστῆσαι ὀφείλοντα· οὐ γὰρ ὡς τοῦ παντὸς ἐφικνούμενος ταῦτα εἶπον·
οὔτε γὰρ δύναται κτιστὴ φύσις καταλαμβάνειν τὴν ἄκτιστον καὶ ἀκατάληπτον οὐσίαν ἐκείνου (cod. -ην)· τούτου γὰρ ἕνεκε<ν> κατηξίω-
σεν ἀναλαβεῖν σάρκα ἐκ τοῦ ἡμετέρου φυράματος, ἵνα ἡμᾶς θείας
45 κοινωνοὺς ἀπεργάσηται φύσεως καὶ ἑνῶσαι ἑαυτῷ τὴν ἡμετέραν
φύσιν· ἕνωσιν δέ φημι ἀσύγχυτον καὶ ἄτρεπτον καὶ ἀναλλοίωτον καὶ
ἣν ἐπίσταται μόνος αὐτός.

This passage records a debate over the problem of the two natures of
Christ in one hypostasis. On the other hand, the heading of the second
chapter of the *Doctrina* reads as follows: Ὅτι ἐκ δύο φύσεων τὸν Χριστὸν καὶ
ἐν δύο φύσεσιν οἱ θεόπνευστοι πατέρες ἐκήρυξαν καὶ ὅτι τὸ λέγειν μίαν φύσιν
τοῦ λόγου σεσαρκωμένην εὐσεβῶς, ταὐτόν ἐστι τῷ εἰπεῖν δύο φύσεις ἐν τῷ
Χριστῷ . . . (*Doctrina*, 11).

The three lines at the end of the fragment (lines 49–51) offer a statement that also appears in the heading of the fifth chapter of the *Doctrina* (p.
33: Ὅτι ἄτρεπτοι μεμενήκασιν αἱ πρὸς ἑνότητα συνελθοῦσαι φύσεις καὶ ἀσύγ-
χυτοι).[77]

---

[77] Besides that, the heading of the fourth chapter (p. 29) seems equally relevant to the
formulation of the question by the Jew: Ὅτι διπλοῦς ὁ Χριστὸς ὑπὸ τῶν πατέρων ὠνόμασται διὰ
τὸ διττὸν τῶν φύσεων καὶ πάλιν οὐ διπλοῦς διὰ τὸ τῆς ὑποστάσεως μοναδικόν, ἤγουν τοῦ προσώπου.

In conclusion, as far as the extract in question is concerned, it does not seem irrelevant to the context within which it is found in P. Even if it belonged to a different florilegium, we should not forget that the *Doctrina* itself is a compilation based on earlier florilegia,[78] and this remark is also valid for the fragments that will be examined next.

After the fragment by Silvester, we come across another four fragments (quot. 75–78) that were rejected by Diekamp on the same ground: fragments 76–78 display the adjective ἅγιος in their lemma. These quotations occur in a position where extracts taken from chapters Θ–ΙΓ were to be expected. However, the four extracts fill in this lacuna. One of them belongs to an author who, to my knowledge, is otherwise unknown (quot. 77): Τοῦ ἁγίου Φωστηρίου. Apart from the extract of St. Epiphanius (quot. 78), the other three are very short and read as follows:

75 (P, fol. 124ᵛ):
Παύλου ἐπισκόπου Ἐμέζης, ἐκ τοῦ λόγου τοῦ λεχθέντος ἐν Ἀλεξανδρείᾳ παρόντος τοῦ ἁγίου Κυρίλλου.

Ταῦτα πάντα εἰργάσατο ἵνα γνῷς ὅτι συνῆν τῷ πάσχοντι καὶ τὰ μὲν πάθη οἰκειοῦτο (sic), αὐτὸς δὲ ἀπαθὴς ἅπαντα εἰργάζετο.

76 (P, fol. 124ᵛ):
Τοῦ ἁγίου Ἰσιδώρου πρεσβυτέρου Πηλουσιώτου ἐπιστολὴ Δωροθέῳ κώμητι (sic) <ρκδ′>.

Χριστοῦ πάθος λέγεται Χριστοῦ τὸ πάθος· γέγονε γὰρ σαρκωθέντος καὶ τῇ προσλήψει τῆς σαρκὸς τὸ πάθος ὑπομείναντος· θεότης γὰρ γυμνὴ οὐ μόνον πάσχειν οὐ δύναται, ἀλλ᾽ οὔτε κρατεῖσθαι οὐδ᾽ ὁρᾶσθαι, εἰ μὴ τῇ φύσει τῶν ἀνθρώπων ἡνώθη φιλανθρώπως.

For quotation 77 (P, fol. 124ᵛ), see Appendix I, p. 275.

As for the passage of St. Epiphanius (quot. 78, P, fols. 124ᵛ–125), it is a somewhat more extensive excerpt from the *Panarion* and expresses in a more elaborate way the same ideas as those found in quotation 77.[79] As is evident, the main idea expressed by those four passages is that of the two natures of Christ and the πάθος of the human one during the crucifixion. Is it possible for these four passages to find a place under a chapter heading

[78] For these florilegia see *Doctrina Patrum*, pp. LIII–LXVI.
[79] E.g., *Panarion* (ed. K. Holl, GCS 37, 517.18–22): Ὁ ὑπὲρ ἡμῶν τὸ πάθος ὑπομείνας ἐν ἀληθείᾳ ἐν τῇ σαρκὶ καὶ ἐν τῇ τελείᾳ ἐνανθρωπήσει, παθὼν ἐν ἀληθείᾳ ἐπὶ τοῦ σταυροῦ, συνούσης αὐτῷ τῆς θεότητος, ἀλλ᾽ οὐ τραπείσης εἰς τὸ πάσχειν, οὔσης δὲ ἀπαθοῦς καὶ ἀτρέπτου, τῶν δύο ἀκολουθιῶν σαφῶς κατανοουμένων, "Χριστοῦ πάσχοντος ὑπὲρ ἡμῶν σαρκί", ἀπαθοῦς δὲ μένοντος ἐν θεότητι . . . etc. (= P, fol. 124ᵛ, line 6 from bottom to line 1 from bottom).

of the *Doctrina*? The most suitable one seems to be the heading of the chapter to which also belong the preceding quotations (67–74). This heading reads as follows: Ὅτι ἡ "ἐν" πρόθεσις ἔγνωσται τοῖς πατράσι προτασσομένη τῶν Χριστοῦ φύσεων, καὶ ὅτι οὐ δεῖ λέγειν, ὡς ἡ θεότης ἔπαθε σαρκί ἢ Θεὸς διὰ σαρκὸς ἔπαθεν (*Doctrina*, 55). In addition, I cite another quotation taken at random from the same chapter. It is quotation 72 (= *Doctrina*, 57 XIV):

Ἀμφιλοχίου ἐκ τῆς πρὸς Σέλευκον ἐπιστολῆς·
Πάσχει τοίνυν ὁ Χριστός, ὁ Υἱὸς τοῦ Θεοῦ οὐ θεότητι ἀλλ᾽ ἀνθρωπότητι· τουτέστι ὁ Θεὸς ἔπαθε σαρκί, ἀλλ᾽ οὐχ ἡ θεότης σαρκὶ ἔπαθεν· ἄπαγε τὸ δυσμενὲς καὶ βλάσφημον, δείλαιε. Ἡ ληφθεῖσα πάσχει φύσις, ἡ δὲ λαβοῦσα ἀπαθὴς μένει. Οἰκειοῦται δὲ ὁ Θεὸς Λόγος ἀπαθῶς τὰ τοῦ ἰδίου ναοῦ ἀνθρώπινα πάθη, σταυρόν φημι καὶ θάνατον καὶ τὰ ἄλλα, ὅσα περὶ αὐτὸν οἰκονομικῶς θεωρεῖται, οἰκειοῦται, αὐτὸς πάσχων οὐδέν.

The similarities between quotations 75–78 and the last one (72) are clear, and therefore the possibility of the former ones belonging to the original of the *Doctrina* gains further ground. It is also worth noting that these four quotations come right after the extract which is the last that is included in chapter H of the printed edition (P, quot. 74, *Doctrina*, 58 XVI).

In the second portion of the excerpts from the *Doctrina* there do occur another four texts not included in the edition: two from works of John Chrysostom (quot. 118, 125, fols. 174ᵛ, 179ᵛ), one by Ephraim (quot. 124, fols. 176–179ᵛ), and the fourth seemingly a verse passage by an anonymous author (quot. 119, fols. 174ᵛ–175).[80]

Quotations 118 and 119 fall under the heading of chapters Z and B respectively. Compare:

(A) *Doctrina*, 49:
Ὅτι Θεὸς ἅμα καὶ ἄνθρωπος ὁ Χριστὸς καὶ εἷς ὁ Χριστὸς καὶ περὶ τοῦ τρόπου τῆς οἰκονομίας . . .
(A1) 118, P, fol. 174ᵛ, lines 28–29:
Εἶπεν ὅτι ἡ μορφὴ τοῦ δούλου ἀληθής, καὶ οὐδὲν ἐλάττων· οὐκοῦν καὶ ἡ μορφὴ τοῦ Θεοῦ τελεία καὶ οὐκ ἐλάττων . . .

(B) *Doctrina*, 11:
Ὅτι ἐκ δύο φύσεων τὸν Χριστὸν καὶ ἐν δύο φύσεσιν ὀρθοδόξως οἱ θεόπνευστοι πατέρες ἐκήρυξαν καὶ ὅτι τὸ μίαν λέγειν φύσιν τοῦ λόγου σεσαρκωμένην εὐσεβῶς ταὐτόν ἐστι τῷ εἰπεῖν δύο φύσεις.

---

[80] For the text see Appendix I, pp. 280–81.

(B1) 119, P, fol. 174ᵛ:

Γραφὴ καὶ μαρτυρίαι . . . περὶ τῶν δύο φύσεων τοῦ ἑνὸς τῆς ἁγίας τριάδος . . .
τὸν ἐκ Θεοῦ πατρὸς υἱὸν μονογενῆ Θεὸν Λόγον καὶ ἄνθρωπον γεγονότα ἐν πνεύματι καὶ ἀληθείᾳ προσκυνήσωμεν, θατέραν αὐτοῦ φύσιν μηδαμῶς ἀπαρνούμε-
νοι, εἴτε τὴν θείαν λέγω, εἴτε τὴν ἀνθρωπίνην . . .

Again, the rejection of these two extracts is not so easily justifiable because they seem to satisfy the requirements of the heading of the second
and seventh chapters of the *Doctrina*. What is more, quotation 119 is also
included in Arundelianus 529 (fols. 74–75),[81] under the lemma Συμβουλία
τῶν ἁγίων πατέρων, preceded by what in P is the heading of chapter B and
followed by quotation 52 (= *Doctrina*, chap. B, 19 XXVIII).

Quotation 124 is the text of the entire *Sermo in transfigurationem Domini
et Dei Salvatoris* (*CPG* 3939) attributed to Ephraim the Syrian. The whole
work revolves around the topic of the two natures of Christ, the divine and
the human. Starting from the interpretation of the Transfiguration as a
proof Christ offered to the three Apostles in order to testify to his divine
nature, Ephraim continues with the logical implications of the two natures.
Extracts such as the one cited next (and many more from the same work)
could have found a place in the anthology of the *Doctrina*:

Καὶ αὐτῷ ἔκραξεν ὁ πατήρ· "οὗτός ἐστιν ὁ υἱός μου ὁ ἀγαπητός", οὐ κε-
χωρισμένη (cod. -ος) ἡ δόξα τῆς θεότητος αὐτοῦ ἐκ τῆς ἀνθρωπότητος αὐτοῦ, ἀλλ᾽ εἰς ἕνα ἔκραξε τὸν φαινόμενον ἐν σώματι εὐτελεῖ καὶ ἐν δόξῃ
φοβερᾷ· καὶ ἡ Μαρία αὐτὸν υἱὸν ἔκραζεν οὐ κεχωρισμένον τῷ σώματι αὐτοῦ τῷ ἀνθρωπίνῳ ἐκ τῆς δόξης αὐτοῦ τῆς θεϊκῆς· εἷς ἐστι γὰρ ὁ ἐν τῷ
σώματι καὶ τῇ δόξῃ φανεὶς τῷ κόσμῳ καὶ ἡ δόξα αὐτοῦ ἐμήνυσε τὴν φύσιν
αὐτοῦ τὴν θεϊκήν, τὴν ἐκ τοῦ πατρός· καὶ τὸ σῶμα αὐτοῦ ἐμήνυσε τὴν φύσιν
αὐτοῦ τὴν ἀνθρωπίνην, τὴν ἐκ Μαρίας . . .[82]

Ephraim continues with a series of clauses of the following structure: Εἰ
οὐκ ἦν σάρξ, Μαρία ἐν τῷ μέσῳ τί παρήχθη; Καὶ εἰ μὴ ἦν Θεός, Γαβριὴλ Κύριον
τίνα ἐκάλει; If he were not God, why did this happen, and if he were not
man, why did that happen, and so on until the end. So this work could, as
well, fit in one of the first nine chapters of the *Doctrina*, but especially in
chapters B, Γ, or H.

Next to Ephraim's text we have a fragment (quot. 125) from the *De fide*
of Severian of Gabala (*CPG* 4206), which, however, is attributed by P to John
Chrysostom. Its content allows for its classification among the extracts from
the first chapter of the *Doctrina*. The text is given in this place:

---

[81] Uthemann, *Anastasii Sinaitae*, p. XCII.
[82] P, fol. 178, line 3 from bottom to 178ᵛ, line 8.

(P, fol. 179ᵛ)

Ἰωάννου ἐπισκόπου Κωνσταντινουπόλεως ἐκ τοῦ
περὶ πίστεως λόγου.

Πρῶτον οὖν ἐστιν ἁπάντων πίστις, ἡ εἰς τὸν Θεόν, πρᾶγμα ἀψηλάφητον, ἀκατάληπτον, ἀθεώρητον, ἀπολυπραγμόνητον, ἀκαταζήτητον,
5 ἀκατηγόρητον, σιωπῇ τιμώμενον καὶ νῷ προσκυνούμενον· πίστις ἀπὸ
Πατρὸς μὲν ἄρχεται, ἐπὶ Υἱὸν δὲ ἔρχεται, εἰς δὲ τὸ Πνεῦμα πληροῦ-
ται· πίστις ἕδρα ψυχῆς, θεμέλιος ζωῆς, ἀθάνατος ρίζα, πίστεως δὲ ρίζα
ζῶσα ὁ Πατήρ, κλάδος ἀμάραντος ὁ Υἱός, καρπὸς ἀθάνατος τὸ Πνεῦμα
τὸ ἅγιον, τριὰς ἁπλῆ, ἀσύνθετος, ἀσυνείκαστος, ἀνέκφραστος, ἀδιή-
10 γητος, ἀδιαίρετος κατὰ συμφωνίαν, κατὰ δύναμιν, κατὰ ἐνέργειαν,
κατὰ θειότητα, κατὰ μέγεθος, ἐν ὑποστάσεσι καὶ ὀνόμασι μόνον (cod.
-ην) διῃρημένη, ἐν δὲ πράγμασι καὶ δυνάμεσι ἡνωμένη· τριὰς πρὸ
αἰώνων ὑπάρχουσα, οὐκ ἀπὸ χρόνου ἀρξαμένη τὸ εἶναι, ἀλλ᾽ ἄναρχος,
ἄχρονος, ἀγήρατος, ἀκήρατος, ἀθάνατος, ἀτελεύτητος, οὐκ αὔξουσα,
15 οὐ λήγουσα, οὐ γηράσκουσα, ἀλλὰ ἀεὶ κατ<ὰ τ>αὐτὰ καὶ ὡσαύτως
ἔχουσα καὶ δοξαζομένη εἰς τοὺς αἰῶνας τῶν αἰώνων· ἀμήν.

Right before the two texts mentioned above, P gives three quotations
(121–123, fols. 175–176) under the heading Περὶ τῆς ἐν Ἅδῃ τοῦ Θεοῦ λόγου
μετὰ τῆς ἡνωμένης αὐτῷ νοερᾶς ψυχῆς καθόδου, ὅπως οἱ θεόσοφοι ἡμῶν πατέρες
ἐδίδαξαν. This heading is a different version of part of the heading of chapter Z of the *Doctrina*,[83] and the three quotations are the three last ones to be
found in the same chapter of the *Doctrina*. Diekamp suggested that "Doctrina und P zwei getrennte Zweige der Überlieferung dieses kurzen Florile-
giums darstellen." The reasons he presented were (a) the different readings
provided by P, and (b) the fact that quotation 123 was longer in P than in
the *Doctrina*.[84]

Examining the variants of P in relation to the *Doctrina*, we have the
following list for quotation 121:

συνεκλάσθησαν *DP*	συνεπριάσθησαν P
ὁ υἱὸς *DP*	καὶ ὁ υἱὸς P
ἐχωρήθη *DP*	ἐχωρίσθη P
γυμνῇ τῇ θεότητι *DP*	γυμνῇ θεότητι P

These do not seem to be very significant. On the other hand, the part of
quotation 123 that in P does not overlap with that of the *Doctrina* reads
as follows:

---

[83] Cf. *Doctrina Patrum*, 47: Ὅτι Θεὸς ἅμα καὶ ἄνθρωπος ὁ Χριστός . . . καὶ περὶ τοῦ πάθους
καὶ τῆς ἐν τῷ ἅδῃ καθόδου, ὅπως οἱ πατέρες παρέδωκαν.

[84] *Doctrina Patrum*, p. LIV.

(P, fol. 175ᵛ)

Πολλῶν δὲ ὄντων τῶν πανσόφως ὑπὸ τῶν θεοφόρων ἡμῶν πατέρων εἰρημένων πρὸς δήλωσιν τῆς εὐσεβοῦς πίστεως καὶ τῆς εἰς ἕνα Θεόν,
τὸν ἐν τρισὶν ὑποστάσεσι δοξαζόμενον καὶ προσκυνούμενον, ὁμολογίας, ἔτι γε μὴν καὶ περὶ τῆς ἐνσάρκου οἰκονομίας τοῦ σωτῆρος ἡμῶν
5 Χριστοῦ, τοῦ ἑνὸς τῆς ἁγίας τριάδος, ἀρκεῖν ἡγοῦμαι τὰ παρατεθέντα
τοῖς εὐπειθῶς καὶ φιλοθέως τούτων ἀκροωμένοις· ἱκανὰ γὰρ ταῦτα
σαφῶς τοῖς ἀφιλερίστως καὶ μετὰ φόβου Θεοῦ (fol. 176) ἐντυγχάνουσι
καὶ εὐσεβῶς καὶ φιλομαθῶς ζητοῦσι τῆς τε πανσέπτου τριάδος τὸ
ὁμοούσιον καὶ τῆς τοῦ σωτῆρος ἡμῶν Χριστοῦ, τοῦ ἑνὸς τῆς ἁγίας τρι-
10 άδος, φιλανθρώπου σαρκώσεως τὴν ἀληθῆ δόξαν· καὶ ὡς οὐ κατὰ συνουσίωσιν ἢ φυρμὸν ἢ σύγχυσιν ἢ ἔκστασιν ἢ τῶν δύο φύσεων (θεότητος λέγω καὶ ἀνθρωπότητος) καθ' ὑπόστασιν γέγονεν ἕνωσις, ἀλλ' ὅτι
καὶ ἐν τῇ ἑνώσει καὶ μετὰ τὴν ἕνωσιν μένουσι τὰ ἑνωθέντα τὴν φυσικὴν σώζοντα ἰδιότητα ἄτρεπτον, ἀναλλοίωτον, ἀδιάσπαστον, ἀδι-
15 αίρετον, ἀμέριστον. Ἀλλ' ἵνα μὴ εἰς μῆκος τὸν λόγον ἐκτείνωμεν, ἐνταῦθα πέρα⟨ς⟩ τοῖς λεγομένοις ἐπιθῶσωμεν, σὺ δέ, ὦ τέκνον, φιλοπόνῳ
σπουδῇ καὶ πόθῳ θεογνωσίας, ἐπιμελῶς καὶ ἐπαγρύπνως τῇ ἀναγνώσει
πρόσεχε, τὸν φωτισμὸν ἄνωθεν ἐξαιτούμενος, ὃ⟨ς⟩ ἐκ τοῦ πατρὸς τῶν
φώτων, ἐξ οὗ πᾶσα δόσις ἀγαθὴ καὶ πᾶν δώρημα τέλειόν ἐστι καταβαῖ-
20 νον καὶ τοσοῦτον καταυγάζον τῶν φιλοθέων τὰς καρδίας, ὅσον ἡ πίστις
χωρεῖ καὶ τὸ ἡμέτερον ἔχει τῆς προθέσεως, ἤγουν τῆς εἰλικρινοῦς τῶν
θείων λογίων ἐπιθυμίας.

Here we have a scholium that appears to have concluded what in the
Doctrina is the whole sequence of chapters A–Z. Was it actually included in
the original of the *Doctrina*? Or was it the concluding scholium of a separate florilegium?

One should always bear in mind that the *Doctrina* itself was a kind of
florilegium florilegiorum. Therefore, it is by no means impossible for P to have
borrowed parts from a florilegium on which the *Doctrina* had been based
for the first seven chapters at least. Another hypothesis could be that P (or
better: the archetype of P) was a direct apograph of the original of the *Doctrina* whose extent has not, unfortunately, been preserved by any of the main
manuscripts that were used by Diekamp for the edition.

Diekamp himself recognized that the original of P was a direct apograph of the *Doctrina* and the readings that P gives point to a stage of the
textual transmission earlier than that from which the main manuscripts
used in his edition had drawn.[85] I will return to this after examining the

---

[85] Ibid., p. XLV: "Die fraglichen Exzerpte in P. müssen also aus x [= the archetype of the
Doctrina] oder wahrscheinlicher aus einer mit x wesentlich identischen Handschrift geflossen
sein."

third fragmented part from the *Doctrina,* which is on fols. 246–247ᵛ and 248–251 of P.

Among the thirty-five quotations from the *Doctrina* that are included in this part of the Iconophile florilegium of P (4*–16* and 24*–43*), Diekamp has not published quotations 4*, 9*–11*, 26*, 27*, and 29*. It is not necessary to repeat the same process here, comparing the content of those quotations to the chapter headings. I will simply suggest a possible chapter to which each extract could be assigned if we accept that P reflects a true image of the original *Doctrina* throughout the whole extent of its relevant folia. The list is as follows:

4*: Gregorius Thaumaturgus, *De deitate et tribus personis, CPG* 1781 = *Doctrina,* chapter A

9*: Irenaeus Lugdunensis, *Fragmenta varia graeca,* frag. 8 (= Hippolytus, *Commentarii in Reges*), *CPG* 1315.3, *PG* 7, 1233ᴀ = *Doctrina,* chapters B–Z[86]

10*: Amphilochius Iconiensis, *Frag. xv ex epistula ad Seleucum* (spurium; see *CCSG* 3, pp. 263–64), *CPG* 3245.15 = *Doctrina,* chapter Z

11*: Proclus CPolitanus, *Homilia III de incarnatione Domini, CPG* 5802, *PG* 65, 705ᴅ–706ᴀ = *Doctrina,* chapter Δ

26*: Ignatius Antiochenus, *Epistulae suppositiciae, CPG* 1026, *PG* 5, 921ʙ–924ᴀ = *Doctrina,* chapter A

27*: Gregorius Naz., *Oratio XL in sanctum baptisma, CPG* 3010.40, *PG* 36, 417ᴀ–ᴄ = *Doctrina,* chapter A

29*: Cyrillus Alex., *Thesaurus, CPG* 5215, *PG* 75, 557A = *Doctrina,* chapter IB

Quotation 27* concludes with a small scholium that exists only in P (fol. 249). It reads as follows:

Ὅτι ὧν ἡ ἐνέργεια μία τούτων καὶ ἡ οὐσία μία καὶ ἡ βούλησις μία. Καὶ ὧν αἱ φύσεις διάφοροι, τούτων καὶ αἱ ἐνέργειαι διάφοροι. Ἐξ ὧν συνάγεται τὸ μίαν εἶναι τῆς παναγίας τριάδος τὴν οὐσίαν πρὸς ἀνατροπὴν τῆς Ἀρείου καὶ Εὐνομίου κακοδοξίας, οἵτινες τὸ ὁμοούσιον ἀρνούμενοι τὸ ἀνόμοιον ἐπὶ τῶν τριῶν πρεσβεύουσι ὑποστάσεων.

This scholium helps us to classify quotations 26* and 27* under chapter A. Part of quotation 27* does occur in the *Doctrina* incorporated into another text.[87]

---

[86] The same extract occurs twice in the *Hodegos* (Uthemann, *Anastasii Sinaitae,* X.1,2, 185–90 and X.2,7, 142–45). In both cases it is inserted into particular florilegia comprising extracts that deal with the two natures of Christ. In the first instance, many of the other extracts occur also in the *Doctrina,* half of them listed in the seventh chapter (X.1,2, 93–94, 104–8, 176–78), and the situation is similar in the second instance (X.2,7).

[87] See *Doctrina Patrum,* 189.13–16.

The last item P can offer to supplement the edition of Diekamp is another scholium that comes after quotation 39* and, obviously, is not related to it.

(P, fol. 250)

Ἀπώχρει (sic) ταῦτα πρὸς τὸ δεῖξαι σαφῶς ὅτι, ὥσπερ μία τῆς ἁγίας τριάδος ἡ οὐσία, οὕτω καὶ μία δύναμις καὶ μία ἐνέργεια καὶ μία βούλησις· οὐ γὰρ σκοπὸς ἡμῖν πρὸς μῆκος τὸν λόγον ἐκτεῖναι, ἀλλὰ διὰ βραχέων τοὺς ἐντυγχάνοντας πρὸς τὴν τῶν ἱερῶν τῆς ἐκκλησίας διδασκάλων εὐσεβῆ παράδοσιν. (lacuna) Εἰρήσεται δὲ λοιπὸν καὶ περὶ τῆς θείας ἐνανθρωπήσεως, ἤγουν τῆς κατὰ σάρκα τοῦ Θεοῦ λόγου οἰκονομίας καὶ ὅπως δεῖ περὶ τῆς ἑνώσεως δοξάζειν καὶ ὅτι ἐκ δύο φύσεων καὶ ἐν δύο φύσεσιν ὁ κύριος ἡμῶν Ἰησοῦς Χριστὸς ὑπὸ τῶν θεοπνεύστων τῆς ἀποστολικῆς ἐκκλησίας διδασκάλων κηρύττεται ἀδιαιρέτως καὶ ἀδιασπάστως, ἀτρέπτως τε καὶ ἀσυγχύτως.

The natural place for this scholium would be after the end of the first chapter as a link between it and the second chapter.[88]

In conclusion, we cannot be completely certain that the extracts of P that Diekamp rejected were among the quotations included in the original *Doctrina*. The following arguments may lead one to opt for them belonging to the original anthology, but all of them are no more solid than those on which Diekamp based his rejection of them. In any case, I recapitulate them.

(A) At first sight it is clear that either Cinnamus or the copyist of the archetype of P transcribed at random and in a very hasty manner some parts from the *Doctrina*. He initially followed the sequence of the chapters as dictated by the original, but after quotation 116 he started skipping pages forward or backward before deciding what to copy. Under these circumstances, it is strange that the sixteen additional quotations of P appeared among those belonging to the main corpus. The most reasonable solution is that they were actually part of the original florilegium.

The postulation by Diekamp of another florilegium that the scribe of P or of its archetype used in combination with the *Doctrina* makes things more complicated. What is more, even the fullest manuscripts, as we have seen, do not give the entire number of quotations that the original florilegium comprised, the chapter headings are not everywhere the same, and the scholia as well.[89] In addition, all manuscripts give fewer than forty-five chapters, which is the number of chapters in Diekamp's edition.

On the same line of argument, one cannot but observe that the last three chapters of the *Doctrina* are attested by only two manuscripts, and

---

[88] Cf. ibid., 1: Περὶ τῆς ἐν τριάδι καὶ μονάδι θεολογίας.
[89] Ibid., pp. XL–XLII.

chapter ME only by Bodleianus Misc. gr. 184. Why should one accept as part of the original that chapter (which, in addition, advances the terminus ante quem up to a later date), and not the quotations of P that seemingly belong to less problematic chapters?

(B) The second argument in support of the derivation of these sixteen quotations from the original *Doctrina* is the close relation of their content with other quotations included in the first chapters of the work.

(C) In the end, I may come back to the assertion by Diekamp of the chronological priority of the archetype of P over that of Vaticanus gr. 2200, which is the earliest witness to the textual tradition of (part of) the *Doctrina*. It is not easily understandable why, while he recognized the direct connection of P with the archetype of the *Doctrina,* he refused to exploit this advantage. R. Riedinger, who has compared the two manuscripts in relation to a collection of extracts from the *Epistula Synodica* of Sophronius of Jerusalem common to both of them, has stressed the "Ursprünglichkeit" of P in comparison to the Vatican manuscript. In addition, he thinks that, while the provenance of P is, in all probability, Roman, that of Vaticanus gr. 2200 is perhaps Palestinian,[90] something that brings P closer to the most likely milieu that produced the *Doctrina,* namely, Rome.[91]

Thus, if it is accepted that the witness of P has to be taken into account, then we have the following sixteen quotations that should be added to the edition of Diekamp:

Chapter A: 125, 4*, 26*, 27*, plus two scholia
Chapter B: 53, 119, 124, 9*
Chapter Δ: 11*
Chapter Z: 118, 10* plus a scholium
Chapter H: 75–78
Chapter IB: 29*.

7. The Florilegium on the Procession of the Holy Spirit (fols. 181–219ᵛ; quot. 131–235)

This particular anthology had first attracted the attention of R. Devreesse, who thought it was one of the first attempts of Greek theology to support its theses on the procession of the Holy Spirit.[92] Uthemann in his turn came

---

[90] Riedinger, "Die Nachkommen der *Epistula Synodica*," 98, 106. For more about the Eastern (Syro-Palestinian) provenance of codex Vaticanus gr. 2200 see also L. Perria, "Il *Vat. gr.* 2200. Note codicologiche e paleografiche," *Rivista di studi bizantini e neoellenici,* N.S. 20–21 (1983–84), 25–68 and esp. 67. Cf. also B. L. Fonkič and F. B. Poljakov, "Paläographische Grundlagen der Datierung des Kölner Mani-Kodex," *BZ* 83 (1990), 22–30 esp. 24.

[91] Riedinger, "Griechische Konzilsakten," 257 n. 14.

[92] Devreesse, *Introduction,* 188.

to examine many passages of the same florilegium and their use by some pro- and anti-Latin authors and compilers of the thirteenth century, who were involved in the dispute over the *Filioque* issue.[93] Consequently he concluded that: "Es (= P) liefert patristische Argumente gegen das filioque der Lateiner."[94] This identification served as one of his main arguments in order to discredit the credibility of almost every piece of information in the colophon of P, as has already been noted,[95] for if the anti-*Filioque* florilegium is not a work of the thirteenth century, then it should have been compiled during or after the period of Photius.

Here a short historical digression on the doctrine of the procession of the Holy Spirit is in order. What is known about the first appearance of the idea that the Holy Spirit proceeds from the Son as well as from the Father, an idea that led to the insertion of the word *Filioque* (or its equivalent, e.g., *et Filio*) into the Nicene-Constantinopolitan creed?

The temporal and geographical origins of the introduction of the Holy Spirit's procession from the Son appear somewhat muddled in the works of modern theologians and church historians. J. M. Hussey, for example, gives credit to Pope Martin I (649–655) for the official introduction of the double procession into (one of?) his synodal letter(s?). The monotheletes of Constantinople accused him of that, and it was "the earliest instance of this accusation being brought against the West."[96]

For J. Pelikan it was a local synod held in Fréjus in 796 under the presidency of Paulinus of Aquileia "that set down what appears to be the earliest documentation for the Western recension of the Nicene Creed."[97]

The issue, however, being a delicate point of conflict between Eastern and Western Christianity, has always been the subject of numerous studies by theologians of the nineteenth and earlier centuries. Among them, H. B. Swete in his book[98] has shown in a very comprehensive way the whole procedure of the expansion of the use of the augmented version of the creed, basing his comments exclusively on written sources of the relevant periods. Recent research has also contributed much to our understanding of the

---

[93] I.e., John Beccus *Epigraphae*, Const. Meliteniotes *De processione*, Andronicus Camaterus *Testimonia*, Nicephorus Blemmydes *Sermones*, Georg. Metochites *Antirrhesis, Historia Dogmatica*, etc. Uthemann, "Ein Beitrag," 40–41.

[94] Ibid., 42.

[95] See above, p. 48–49, 54.

[96] Hussey, *The Orthodox Church*, 20.

[97] Pelikan, *Eastern Christendom*, II, 184.

[98] H. B. Swete, *On the History of the Doctrine of the Procession of the Holy Spirit from the Apostolic Age to the Death of Charlemagne* (Cambridge, 1876).

whole problem and its Spanish parameters. It seems helpful for the present study to retain the frame established by Swete and supplement it with the findings of modern scholarship.

The view that the Holy Spirit proceeds not only from the Father but also from the Son initially found its theoretical bedrock in the teachings of St. Augustine of Hippo (d. 430).[99] After his death, "Western Europe appears to have generally adopted the Augustinian view of the Procession, almost without being conscious of the change thus made in its theology."[100]

A line of Western bishops and other ecclesiastical figures, starting from a period between the years 430 and 450, are reported to have either written or preached that the Holy Spirit proceeds from the Father *and* the Son. The list includes the names of St. Eucherius, bishop of Lyons (d. 450), Faustus, bishop of Riez (d. ca. 485), Gennadius, a priest of Marseilles (d. ca. 495), and Julianus Pomerius, a priest of Arles (d. ca. 500).[101]

The pro-*Filioque* authors and preachers from the West are multiplied in the sixth century, and the names of Avitus, archbishop of Vienne (d. 518) and St. Fulgentius, [102] bishop of Ruspe (d. 532) are to be listed along with those of the fifth century.

While the Gallic provinces openly supported the *Filioque,* at Rome during this period "S. Augustine's view appears to have received occasional sanction even from Popes,"[103] and Pope Leo the Great as well as Pope Hor-

[99] See Pelikan, *Eastern Christendom,* II, 188–89. On the procession of the Holy Spirit in some earlier Latin fathers, see (in addition to the first chapters of Swete's book), M. Simonetti, "La processione dello Spirito Santo nei Padri Latini," *Maia* 7 (1955), 308–24, where he basically treats Tertullian, Hilary of Poitiers (d. 367), Ambrose of Milan, Marius Victorinus, et al. For these fathers see also J.N.D. Kelly, *The Athanasian Creed* (New York-Evanston, Ill., 1964), 87–90. For the procession of the Holy Spirit in the early Greek fathers (Origen, Athanasius of Alexandria, Basil of Caesarea, Didymus the Blind, and Cyril of Alexandria), see Simonetti, "La processione dello Spirito Santo secondo i Padri Greci," *Aevum* 26 (1952), 33–41, a rather unconvincing article, however, because the author adheres to the Latin way of understanding the Greek words that denote procession of the Holy Spirit *through* the Son. See also Pelikan, *Eastern Christendom,* II, 188–90, and the excellent article by D. Ramos-Lissón, "Die Synodalen Ursprünge des 'Filioque' im römisch-westgotischen Hispanien," *AHC* 16 (1984), 287–89.

[100] Swete, *History,* 153.

[101] Ibid., 154. The relevant passages are printed in the following series: Eucherius episcopus Lugdunensis, *CPL* 489, *Instructionum ad Salonium l. ii, PL* 50, 774, *CSEL* 31 (1894), 67.10; Faustus episcopus Reiensis, *CPL* 962, *De Spiritu Sancto l. ii* (Ps.-Paschasius), *PL* 62, 9, *CSEL* 21 (1891), 116.1; Gennadius presbyter Massiliensis, *CPL* 958a, *Libri ecclesiasticorum dogmatum, PL* 58, 980; Iulianus Pomerius presbyter Arelatensis, *CPL* 998, *De vita contemplativa, PL* 59, 433.

[102] The ἅγιος Φωστήριος of quotation 77 of P? Texts: Alcimus Avitus episcopus Viennensis, *CPL* 990, *Dialogi cum Gundobado rege vel librorum contra Arrianos relliquiae, PL* 59, 385–86, *MGH, Auctores Antiquissimi,* VI, 6.14–19; Fulgentius episcopus Ruspensis, *CPL* 826, *De fide ad Petrum, PL* 65, 696, *CCSL* 91A (1968), 747.1055–60.

[103] Swete, *History,* 156.

misdas seem to have ranged from hesitating acceptance[104] to purportedly open admission.[105] To these we may add the names of Boethius and Cassiodorus.[106]

The *Filioque*, however, had officially been introduced into the creed much earlier in Spain.[107] Victricius of Rouen already in 396 had spoken in his creed of: "Sanctus Spiritus vero de Patre et Filio."[108] Next we have the first Council of Toledo (A.D. 400) in the *Regula fidei* of which the creed is included *without* the *Filioque*.[109] However, the same creed was later in 447 expanded by Pastor of Palencia in his *Libellus*, and the words *Filioque* appear in it.[110]

The same formulation is repeated much later in the sixth century, when Reccared, the king of the Visigoths of Spain, renounced Arianism and he and his people embraced the Catholic dogma. On the occasion of his conversion a council was convened at Toledo in 589 (Toledo III), and Reccared publicly confessed his faith in the Holy Spirit which "predicandus est a Patre et a Filio procedere."[111] However, it is not yet certain that the words *a Patre et Filio procedere* did actually appear in the Constantinopolitan Creed recited by Reccared, since the manuscript tradition of the acts of this council is not uniform on this point.[112] One is on safe ground when it comes to the anathe-

---

[104] Pope Leo, *CPL* 1657 *Sermo LXXVI*, *PL* 54, 402, 404, *CCSL* 138, (1973), 467.56. Also in his letter to Turibius of Astorga (*Epist. XV, PL* 54, 681) he speaks of the Holy Spirit as "Alius qui de utroque processit."

[105] Pope Hormisdas (d. 523), Letter to Emperor Justin, *Epist. LXXIX, PL* 63, 514, although the relevant passage seems corrupt. For a better edition of the letter see *Collectio Avellana* (= ep. 236), *CSEL* 35.2, 714.17–18. In the apparatus criticus it is rather clear that the words "et Filio" were a later addition.

[106] Swete, *History,* 158–60. The double procession of the Holy Spirit is stated in: Boethius, *CPL* 890.1, *Quomodo Trinitas unus Deus ac non tres dii, PL* 64, 1254; Cassiodorus *CPL* 900, *Commenta psalterii, PL* 70, 23; *CCSL* 97 (1958), 23.20–23.

[107] For details, causes, and particular developments on the adoption of the interpolated creed in Spain, see Ramos-Lissón, "Die Synodalen Ursprünge," 286–99.

[108] Reproduced in his *De laude sanctorum* IV, *PL* 20, 446 (*CPL* 481).

[109] See J. Orlandis and D. Ramos-Lissón, *Die Synoden auf der Iberischen Halbinsel bis zum Einbruch des Islam (711), Konziliengeschichte,* ed. W. Brandmüller, Reihe A: Darstellungen (Paderborn, 1981), 48.

[110] J. A. De Aldama, *El Simbolo Toledano I,* Analecta Gregoriana 7 (Rome, 1934), 66. The text reads as follows: ibid., 30–31: "Spiritum quoque Paraclitum esse, qui nec Pater sit ipse nec Filius; sed a Patre Filioque procedens. Est ergo ingenitus Pater, genitus Filius, non genitus Paraclitus, sed a Patre Filioque procedens." The theory that this creed was also adopted by a council summoned the same year in Toledo by Turibius of Astorga (Swete, *History,* 164–67; De Aldama, ibid., 66) is now rejected (see Ramos-Lissón, "Die Synodalen Ursprünge," 294 n. 57).

[111] For the text see J. Vives, *Concilios visigóticos e hispano-romanos,* España Cristiana, Textos 1 (Barcelona-Madrid, 1963), 109–10.

[112] On the subject see J.N.D. Kelly, *Early Christian Creeds* (London, 1960), 361–62, where he rather pleads for the existence of the addition. The negative option is followed by G. Dos-

mas pronounced by this council. The third anathema reads as follows: "Qui-
cumque Spiritum Sanctum non credet aut non crediderit a Patre et Filio
procedere . . . anathema sit."[113]

After the Council of Toledo the words *Filioque* and expressions that im-
plied the double procession of the Holy Spirit[114] were to be heard in most of
the churches of Spain, not only as interpolated into the Constantinopolitan
Creed, but in other instances also during the liturgy. The interpolated form
of the creed had also been solemnly recited at Toledo in the years 633 (Toledo IV),[115] 638 (Toledo VI),[116] 653 (Toledo VIII),[117] 681 (Toledo XII), 693
(Toledo XVI),[118] and at Braga (Braga III) in 675.[119] So "before the year 700
there was at least one part of Western Christendom where the *Filioque* had
taken such firm root that its excision from the Creed would have seemed
nothing less than an abandonment of the Faith."[120]

As it has become evident from this brief survey, the period between
the fifth and the seventh century witnessed a wider movement toward the
adoption of the *Filioque* by many Western Christians. It implies that the
ground was prepared for a possible theological debate on, and even documentation of, the subject. Since, in addition, the popes were usually reluc-
tant to "tamper with the authorized text" of the creed,[121] it seems that Rome
was the most fertile part of this ground for any kind of confrontation, be it
with the Eastern church, which strictly rejected the interpolation, or with
the ardent supporters of the *Filioque* in the Spanish, French, and German
provinces.

What was the reaction of the East to this gradually evolved departure by the
West from the traditional form of the dogma?

Hussey is right in asserting that the accusation brought against the

---

setti, *Il Simbolo di Nicea e di Constantinopoli* (Rome, 1967), 176–78 n. 2, and K. Schäferdiek, *Die
Kirche in den Reichen der Westgoten und Sueven bis zur Errichtung der westgotischen katholischen Staatskirche,* Arbeiten zur Kirchengeschichte 39 (Berlin, 1967), 211–12 n. 226.

[113] Orlandis and Ramos-Lissón, *Die Synoden,* 108 n. 50; Vives, *Concilios,* 118.

[114] For the various formulations by which the double procession of the Holy Spirit is expressed in the creeds of this period, see De Aldama, *El Simbolo,* 124–31.

[115] Orlandis and Ramos-Lissón, *Die Synoden,* 149; text: Vives, *Concilios,* 187.

[116] Orlandis and Ramos-Lissón, *Die Synoden,* 181.

[117] Ibid., 204; text: Vives, *Concilios,* 267–68.

[118] Orlandis and Ramos-Lissón, ibid., 252 and 304 respectively.

[119] Ibid., 241.

[120] Swete, *History,* 174–76.

[121] Kelly, *Early Creeds,* 366. And that despite the examples stated above by Swete. For more
on the cautious/reserved or even anti-*Filioque* stance of Rome, see Kelly, ibid., 360–67.

pope was the first clash between East and West on the subject.[122] It emerged at a time when the patriarchal throne of Constantinople was occupied by a monothelete patriarch, and we learn this from a fragment of a letter of St. Maximus the Confessor addressed to a certain Marinus, a priest on the island of Cyprus.[123] This letter, according to P. Sherwood, was written in the year 645/6.[124] The pope therefore who, in all probability, had inserted the *Filioque* in his synodal letter was Theodore I (642–649) and not Martin I, as Hussey and Swete[125] believe.

There had been a problem concerning the interpretation of a small passage from this letter at Florence in 1439, but its genuineness had not been challenged.[126] Combefis in his notes to the edition presented some reservations on the issue.[127] The letter, nevertheless, seems to be genuine and to its authenticity concurs the testimony of Anastasius Bibliothecarius, who in the ninth century translated part of it.[128] Stylistic and other internal evidence exclude the possibility of a ninth-century fabrication.[129]

At any rate, the relevant passage of the letter reads as follows:

Ἀμέλει τοι γοῦν τῶν τοῦ νῦν ἁγιωτάτου Πάπα συνοδικῶν οὐκ ἐν τοσούτοις, ὅσοις γεγράφατε, κεφαλαίοις οἱ τῆς βασιλίδος τῶν πόλεων ἐπελάβοντο· δυσὶ δὲ μόνοις, ὧν, τὸ μὲν ὑπάρχει περὶ θεολογίας, ὅτι τε, φασίν, εἶπεν "ἐκπορεύεσθαι κἀκ τοῦ Υἱοῦ τὸ Πνεῦμα τὸ ἅγιον . . ." Καὶ τὸ μὲν πρῶτον συμφώνους παρήγαγον χρήσεις τῶν Ῥωμαίων πατέρων· ἔτι γε μὴν καὶ Κυρίλλου Ἀλεξανδρείας, ἐκ τῆς πονηθείσης αὐτῷ εἰς τὸν εὐαγγελιστὴν ἅγιον Ἰωάννην ἱερᾶς πραγματείας· ἐξ ὧν οὐκ αἰτίαν τὸν Υἱὸν ποιοῦντας τοῦ Πνεύματος σφᾶς αὐτοὺς ἀπέδειξαν· μίαν γὰρ ἴσασιν Υἱοῦ καὶ πνεύματος, τὸν Πατέρα, αἰτίαν, τοῦ μὲν κατὰ τὴν γέννησιν τοῦ δὲ κατὰ τὴν ἐκπόρευσιν, ἀλλ᾽ ἵνα τὸ δι᾽ αὐτοῦ προϊέναι δηλώσωσι καὶ ταύτῃ τὸ συναφὲς τῆς οὐσίας καὶ ἀπαράλλακτον παραστήσωσι.[130]

It is more than clear that Maximus here accepts the fact of the interpolation and defends the pope, although he was not quite happy about it. He

---

[122] See above, p. 72. For a second possibly similar incident during the reign of Constantine V between the Iconoclast delegates of Constantinople and the Iconophile bishops of Rome during the Council of Gentilly (767), see Kelly, *Early Creeds*, 363.

[123] *CPG* 7697.10 Maximus Confessor, *Exemplum epistulae ad Marinum Cypri presbyterum*, *PG* 91, 133–37.

[124] P. Sherwood, *An Annotated Date-List of the Works of Maximus the Confessor*, Studia Anselmiana 30 (Rome, 1952), 53–55.

[125] Swete, *History*, 183.

[126] Gill, *Quae supersunt*, 132.

[127] See *PG* 91, 139–40, *monitum*.

[128] *PL* 129, 577 ff.

[129] See Sherwood, *Date-List*, 54.

[130] *PG* 91, 133D8–136B2.

says in the sequel that he had asked the Latins for a more precise explanation of their dogma but the difference of language did not permit a better elucidation of the situation.[131]

What he says, in addition, is that the Romans on the other hand produced a florilegium of quotations (χρήσεις) of Latin fathers and also an extract (or extracts?) from the commentaries of Cyril of Alexandria on the Gospel of John in order to prove the following points: (a) they did not introduce two principles of the Holy Spirit, (b) the *Filioque* was inserted so as to declare that the Holy Spirit proceeds *through* the Son, and (c) by this addition they meant to represent the fact that the essence of all three members of the Holy Trinity is united/connected and in no way differing (τὸ συναφὲς τῆς οὐσίας καὶ ἀπαράλλακτον παραστήσωσι).

Going back to P, the first thing worth noting is that the letter of St. Maximus to Marinus is to be found among the texts of the *Filioque* florilegium (fols. 185ᵛ–187, quot. 152). What is more, the quotation of Cyril of Alexandria mentioned in this letter is, in all probability, quotation no. 1 on fol. 8 of the original part of P[132] or quot. 163. Recall here that, according to Schwartz, this fragment is the last remnant of a florilegium on the Holy Spirit that existed in the missing part of the manuscript.[133]

The assumption that the two florilegia—the missing one and the one under examination here—were connected may be supported by a marginal note written by the hand of Cinnamus on fol. 193. This scholium is written in the margin of another letter of Cyril, *Epistula* 17, and reads as follows: Σχόλιον· Τοῦ ἁγίου Μαξίμου ἐκ τῶν ἐπιστολῶν διὰ τὸ συναφὲς τῆς οὐσίας τῶν ὑποστάσεών φησι ὁ ἅγιος Κύριλλος ὁμοίως καὶ ἐν τῇ ἑρμηνείᾳ τοῦ κατὰ Ἰωάννην εὐαγγελίου. Possibly this scholium on fol. 193 refers to quotation no. 1, although quotation 163 may equally well be the case or even all three of them, which may be the better option as will be shown below.

What should be taken for certain is that, when Maximus spoke of Latin

---

[131] Ibid., 136c1-9. Μεθερμηνεύειν δὲ τὰ οἰκεῖα, τοῦ τὰς ὑποκλοπὰς χάριν διαφυγεῖν τῶν ὑποπιπτόντων κατὰ τὴν ὑμετέραν κέλευσιν, παρεκάλεσα τοὺς Ῥωμαίους· πλὴν ἔθους κεκρατηκότος οὕτω ποιεῖν καὶ στέλλειν, οὐκ οἶδα τυχὸν εἰ π(ε)ισθεῖεν, ἄλλως τε καὶ τὸ μὴ οὕτως δύνασθαι διακριβοῦν ἐν ἄλλῃ λέξει τε καὶ φωνῇ τὸν ἑαυτῶν νοῦν ὥσπερ ἐν τῇ ἰδίᾳ καὶ θρεψαμένῃ, καθάπερ οὖν καὶ ἡμᾶς ἐν τῇ καθ' ἡμᾶς τὸν ἡμέτερον. Γενήσεται δὲ πάντως αὐτοῖς, πείρᾳ τὴν ἐπήρειαν μαθοῦσι, καὶ ἡ περὶ τούτου φροντίς.

[132] See above, p. 54.

[133] A closer look at the contents of the first additional quire of the manuscript can prove that quotations 4A–7A and 9Ai are small extracts dealing with the procession of the Holy Spirit as well. Besides that, quotation 4A is absolutely the same as quotation 156 of the *Filioque* florilegium.

fathers quoted in that florilegium of the mid-seventh century, he apparently did not mean to exclude the Greeks. His detailed mention of the extract of Cyril of Alexandria probably entails that it was not the only one to be included in the anthology. But to this we may return below. For the time being we can concentrate on the external characteristics of the florilegium on the procession of the Holy Spirit.

The point where this florilegium starts is easily discernible since its first quotation (131, fol. 180ᵛ) follows one small extract that definitely belongs to the *Doctrina Patrum*. It probably breaks off at fol. 219ᵛ, where quotation 235 ends. No particular title or lemma is assigned to this florilegium as, for example, in the case of the second chapter of the *Doctrina Patrum*, as has been shown above.

The florilegium runs to an approximate number of 167 fragments, the length of which varies from three lines of a manuscript's page to several folios. Almost seventy different works of no fewer than sixteen authors were used for the compilation of this anthology, some of whom I have not been able to identify (e.g., quot. 173, 230). Some other excerpts have been impossible to trace within the work of the particular author that their lemma indicates (e.g., quot. 132, 204, 212).[134]

Much of the space is occupied by fragments from the *Adversus Eunomium* II–V of Basil (fols. 183ʳ⁻ᵛ, 208, 210–213, 214–215ᵛ), who is one of the most favorite authors of the compiler of this florilegium. The main bulk of the quotations comes from the ἔγκριτοι fathers who usually appear in most florilegia on any dogmatic subject, namely, Basil (5 works plus one unidentified), Cyril of Alexandria (8 works plus 2 unidentified), Gregory of Nazianzus (10 plus 1), Gregory of Nyssa (6), John Chrysostom (4 plus 2), Maximus the Confessor (6 plus 1). The rest have been excerpted from works of Amphilochius of Iconium, Ps.-Dionysius, Epiphanius, Methodius Olympius, Sophronius of Jerusalem, Ephraim, conciliar acts, and so on.

Finally, quotation 158 (fols. 188–190ᵛ), which is an unpublished treatise on the *Confessiones fidei* of the first five ecumenical councils, seemingly interrupts the florilegium as it appears out of context. In Chapter V below it will be shown that this is not the case.

It has already been stressed that, according to the letter of St. Maximus to Marinus, the quotations of the florilegium that the Romans compiled in

---

[134] For the identification and location of many of the quotations in P, I have used the *Ibycus* and *Pandora* programs of the *Thesaurus Linguae Graecae*. The texts that, despite the attribution to a certain author in their lemma, were not to be found within the particular work are pointed out in Appendix I by the words "Not in *TLG*."

defense of their views on the procession of the Holy Spirit supported the points that the addition of the *Filioque* did not imply two principles of the Holy Spirit, explained the procession *through* the Son, and declared the *homoousion* of the three persons of the Holy Trinity.

What is the content of the extracts of the florilegium of P? Do they satisfy the requirements set out in the letter of St. Maximus? The obstacle posed by the information of St. Maximus that the florilegium comprised mainly excerpts from Latin authors while here it is an anthology of Greek authors can be set aside for the time being, for what is of interest now is the nature of the florilegium and not its dating. Therefore, we can proceed to the examination of the content of the quotations of P, taking into account the information provided by the letter of St. Maximus.

The following quotations taken at random seem to tally with the framework set above:

(A) Paris. gr. 1115, fol. 8 (quot. no. 1):
Τοῦ ἁγίου Κυρίλλου ἑρμηνεία εἰς τὸ ῥητὸν τοῦ κατὰ Ἰωάννην εὐαγγελίου . . .

. . . Ὅτε τοίνυν τὸ ἓν καὶ τὸ αὐτὸ πνεῦμα τοῦ τε Θεοῦ καὶ πατρός ἐστι καὶ τοῦ υἱοῦ, πῶς οὐχὶ πάντως μίαν ἕξουσι καὶ τὴν οὐσίαν; Ἐπεὶ οὖν ὁμοούσιον ὁ πατὴρ καὶ ὁ υἱός, λεκτέον ὅτι ὁ πατὴρ διδοὺς τὸ πνεῦμα χορηγεῖ αὐτὸ δι' υἱοῦ καὶ ὁ υἱὸς διδοὺς δηλοῖ ὅτι ὁ πατὴρ δίδωσιν, ἐξ οὗ τὰ πάντα.

(B) Paris. gr. 1115, fol. 181ᵛ (quot. 133)
Τοῦ ἁγίου Ἐπιφανίου ἐκ τοῦ ἀγκυρωτοῦ . . .

. . . τὸ δὲ ἅγιον πνεῦμα Θεοῦ, ἀεὶ ὂν ἀπὸ πατρὸς ἐκπορευόμενον, καὶ τοῦ υἱοῦ λαμβανόμενον· ἀλλ' ὁ μὲν υἱὸς μονογενὴς ἀκατάληπτος, τὸ δὲ πνεῦμα παρὰ πατρὸς ἐκπορευόμενον καὶ ἐκ τοῦ υἱοῦ λαμβανόμενον. καὶ μετὰ βραχέα· αὐτὸς γὰρ ὁ μονογενὴς λέγει τὸ πνεῦμα τοῦ πατρὸς καὶ τὸ ἐκ τοῦ πατρὸς ἐκπορευόμενον καὶ τοῦ ἐμοῦ λήψεται, ἵνα μὴ ἀλλότριον νομισθῇ πατρὸς καὶ υἱοῦ, ἀλλὰ τῆς αὐτῆς οὐσίας, τῆς αὐτῆς θεότητος.

(C) Paris. gr. 1115, fol. 187ᵛ (quot. 156 = 4A)
Κυρίλλου ἐκ τοῦ λόγου τοῦ πρὸς τὰς βασιλίδας·

Πιστεύομεν δὲ ὁμοίως καὶ εἰς τὸ πνεῦμα τὸ ἅγιον, οὐκ ἀλλότριον αὐτοῦ τῆς θείας φύσεως καταλογιζόμενοι· καὶ γάρ ἐστι τὸ ἐκ πατρὸς ἐκπορευόμενον, φυσικῶς προχεόμενον δι' υἱοῦ τῇ κτίσει· νοεῖται γὰρ οὕτως μία τε καὶ ὁμοούσιος καὶ ἐν ταυτότητι δόξης ἡ ἁγία καὶ προσκυνουμένη τριάς.

(D) Paris. gr. 1115, fol. 195ᵛ (quot. 165)
Τοῦ ἁγίου Γρηγορίου Νύσης ἐκ τοῦ βίου τοῦ ἁγίου Γρηγορίου τοῦ Θαυματουργοῦ.

Ἐν πνεῦμα ἅγιον, ἐκ Θεοῦ τὴν ὕπαρξιν ἔχον, καὶ διὰ τοῦ υἱοῦ πεφηνὸς δηλαδὴ τοῖς ἀνθρώποις.

There are many more quotations of this sort in the florilegium of P, and, what is more, the constant repetition of the formula *through* the Son and its equivalents (διὰ τοῦ υἱοῦ, παρὰ τοῦ υἱοῦ λαμβανόμενον, ἐν υἱῷ ἀναπαυόμενον, etc.) occurs throughout.[135] But this is reasonable, as the formula "who proceeds from the Father through the Son" had mainly served the cause of the *Filioque* because, in the words of J. Pelikan: "The supporters of the West contended that if the Eastern tradition contained—and therefore authorized—the phrase, 'through the Son,' it was obvious that 'there is no difference between saying "from the Son" and saying "from the Father through the Son,"' for the two phrases were 'identical in force.'"[136]

There are, however, many instances where P provides the original formulation—καὶ εἰς τὸ Πνεῦμα τὸ ἅγιον . . . τὸ ἐκ τοῦ πατρὸς ἐκπορευόμενον, τὸ σὺν πατρὶ καὶ υἱῷ συνπροσκυνούμενον[137]—but even so, the following passages are of crucial importance for establishing the identity of the florilegium:

1. Paris. gr. 1115, fol. 181ᵛ lines 11–13 (Epiphanius of Salamis, *Ancoratus*):
. . . οὐδὲ τὸ πνεῦμα τίς (sic) οἶδεν εἰ μὴ ὁ πατὴρ καὶ ὁ υἱός, παροῦ (sic) ἐκπορεύεται καὶ παρ' οὗ λαμβάνει. (quot. 133)
Repeated slightly altered on lines 18–20 of the same folio and lines 9–11 of fol. 182:
. . . οὕτω τολμῶ λέγειν οὐδὲ τὸ πνεῦμα, εἰ μὴ ὁ πατὴρ καὶ ὁ υἱός, ἐξ οὗ λαμβάνει καὶ παρ' οὗ ἐκπορεύεται. (quot. 134, 138)
Compare with:
1a. Council of Florence (Gill, *Quae Supersunt*) 127.17-19:
. . . οὕτω τολμῶ λέγειν οὐδὲ τὸ πνεῦμα, εἰ μὴ ὁ Πατὴρ καὶ ὁ Υἱὸς παρ' οὗ ἐκπορεύεται καὶ παρ' οὗ λαμβάνει.
1b. *PG* 42, 439A14-B1:
. . . οὕτω τολμῶ λέγειν οὐδὲ τὸ πνεῦμα, εἰ μὴ ὁ Υἱός, ἐξ οὗ λαμβάνει, καὶ ὁ Πατήρ, παρ' οὗ ἐκπορεύεται.[138]

---

[135] E.g., Paris. gr. 1115, fol. 181, line 10; fol. 181ᵛ, lines 5, 7, 23; fol. 182, line 4 from bottom; fol. 184, line 1 from bottom; fol. 187, lines 14–15, 18; fol. 194, lines 8 and 11 from bottom; fol. 199, line 5 from bottom; fol. 199ᵛ, line 13; fol. 200ᵛ, lines 20–21; fol. 207, lines 10–11 from bottom; fol. 207ᵛ, line 10 from bottom; fol. 219, lines 10–11 from bottom, etc.

[136] Pelikan, *Eastern Christendom, II*, 277.

[137] E.g., Paris. gr. 1115, fol. 191ᵛ, lines 12–13.

[138] The *PG* version is repeated in the edition of the *Ancoratus* by K. Holl in *GCS* 25 (Leipzig, 1915), 91.21-22. In the apparatus criticus, though, the Florence version is cited as given by Laurentianus VI 12 and Jenensis mscr. Bose 1.

2. Paris. gr. 1115, fol. 188 lines 7–9 (Cyril of Alexandria, *Oratio ad Theod. imp. de recta fide.* = quot. 157):

. . . τὸ δὲ πνεῦμα ζωὴ διὰ δικαιοσύνης· ἄρα οὖν ὅτι καὶ ἴδιόν ἐστι τοῦ πατρὸς ἐξ οὗ ἐκπορεύεται· ὡσαύτως καὶ τοῦ υἱοῦ. καὶ οὔτι που μόνον ἢ λόγος ἐστὶν ἐκ πατρός, . . .

Compare with *PG* 76, 1189A:

. . . τὸ δὲ πνεῦμα ζωὴ διὰ δικαιοσύνης (τὸ δὲ πνεῦμα ζῶν διὰ δικαιο-σύνην *ACO* I,1,1, 67.14). Ἄραρεν οὖν, ὅτι καὶ ἴδιόν ἐστι τὸ πνεῦμα τοῦ Υἱοῦ, καὶ οὔτι που μόνον ἢ Λόγος ἐστὶ πεφηνὼς ἐκ Πατρός, . . .

3. Paris. gr. 1115, fol. 208 lines 19–22 (Basil, *Adversus Eunomium II,* = quot. 209):

. . . ὑμεῖς δὲ οὐ τὸ πνεῦμα τοῦ κόσμου ἐλάβετε, ἀλλὰ τὸ πνεῦμα τὸ ἐκ τοῦ Θεοῦ· τοῦτο δὲ τοῦ Κυρίου πνεῦμα τῆς ἀληθείας λέγοντος ἐπειδὴ αὐτὸς ἡ ἀλήθεια καὶ παρὰ τοῦ πατρὸς καὶ υἱοῦ ἐκπορεύεται.

Compare with *PG* 29, 652B12–C1:

. . . Ὑμεῖς δὲ οὐ τὸ πνεῦμα τοῦ κόσμου ἐλάβετε, ἀλλὰ τὸ πνεῦμα τὸ ἐκ τοῦ Θεοῦ· τοῦτο δὲ τοῦ Κυρίου τὸ πνεῦμα τῆς ἀληθείας λέγοντος, ἐπειδὴ αὐτὸς ἡ ἀλήθεια, καὶ παρὰ τοῦ Πατρὸς ἐκπορεύεται.

These examples are rather striking in their pro-*Filioque* bearing.

Apart from that, I may examine the florilegium from another aspect trying to answer the following question: which party has used quotations included in this florilegium? Here the situation is somewhat delicate, as the same quotations were used in many cases by both the pro- and the anti-Latin authors. And this has to do with a particular trait of the *Filioque* debate: in Greek patristic literature there has never been, to the best of my knowledge, a direct allusion to the procession of the Holy Spirit from the Son in the concise form of ἐκ τοῦ Πατρὸς καὶ τοῦ Υἱοῦ ἐκπορευόμενον. Support of the *Filioque* was attempted on the basis of interpretation of the various passages in the Greek fathers, a strategy that left the same texts open to counterinter-pretation.[139] So it is not surprising that some of the quotations of P also feature, for example, in the anti-Latin florilegium of Mark of Ephesus, the leading opponent of the unionist Council of Ferrara-Florence (1438–39).[140]

[139] A good illustration of this fact is offered by the debate between John of Montenero and Mark of Ephesus over the meaning of the passage from the *Ancoratus* of Epiphanius cited above, p. 80, during the Council of Florence (Gill, *Quae supersunt,* 256–59). The interpretation of the passage even included analysis of the syntax of the sentence ἀφ' οὗ λαμβάνει καὶ ἀφ' οὗ ἐκπορεύεται (ibid., 257.23–26).

[140] Quotations 151, 157, 162, 165, 181, 182, 183, 185, 186, 187, 191, and 201 of P corre-spond either partially or word for word to quotations 36, 74, 22, 120, 52, 56, 57, 54, 55, 61–63 (= 187), 67–68 (= 191), and 50 of the anti-Latin florilegium of Mark of Ephesus (*Concilium Florentinum, Documenta et Scriptores, Series A,* Vol. X, Fasc. II, *Marci Eugenici Metropolitae Ephesi: Opera anti-Unionistica,* ed. L. Petit [Rome, 1977], 34–59: *Testimonia a Marco Ephesio collecta*).

There are, however, a great many quotations in P that were adduced by the Latins during the debates at Ferrara-Florence,[141] and only by them. Some examples will make this point clearer:

1. The aforementioned passage from the *Ancoratus* of Epiphanius (quot. 133) is invoked during the council of 1439 nine times,[142] always by the papal envoys.

2. Only the legates of the pope produced extracts from works of Maximus the Confessor, starting with the already mentioned *Epistula ad Marinum* (quot. 152)[143] and another extract from the *Quaestiones ad Thalassium* (quot. 214).[144] It is also remarkable that an extract from the *Epistula Romae scripta* of Maximus (quot. 153)[145] presented by the Latins was not in support of the *Filioque* but of another issue connected with the *Filioque*, that of the primacy of the Roman church.

3. The same holds good for some other extracts such as quotations 161 (Cyril of Alex., *Epistula* 17),[146] 164 (Gregory of Nyssa, *De Orat. Domin.*),[147] 165 (Gregory of Nyssa, *Vita Gregorii Thaumat.*),[148] 188 (Gregory of Naz., *Epist.* CII),[149] not to mention the extracts from the *De Spiritu Sancto* and the *Adversus Eunomium II–V* of Basil.

Taking all this into consideration, it becomes apparent that the florilegium on the procession of the Holy Spirit is a pro-Latin one and not an anti-Latin collection as Devreesse and Uthemann assumed. But if so, when should it be dated?

It has already been explained that, according to the information provided by the *Epistula ad Marinum* of Maximus the Confessor, a florilegium on the subject had been compiled around 645. The only problem is that

---

[141] In contrast to the long theological discussions of the Ferrara-Florence Council in 1438–39, the first council on the subject, namely that of Lyons (1274), is characterized by complete lack of any exchange of arguments. At this council the Byzantines, upon reaching Lyons on 24 June, simply expressed their obedience to the Holy See and declared that there was no difference between the Greek and the Roman beliefs. See A. Franchi, *Il Concilio II di Lione (1274) secondo la Ordinario Concilii generalis Lugdunensis* (Rome, 1965), 85–92; also B. Roberg, *Die Union zwischen der griechischen und der lateinischen Kirche auf dem II. Konzil von Lyon (1274)* (Bonn, 1964), 137–50, with further details and bibliography. Of the dogmatic discussions before the 1274 council, there is an entirely new aspect in Chapter V below.

[142] *Concilium Florentinum*, Gill, *Quae supersunt*, 127, 256, 259, 260, 265, 266, 271–72, 337, 397.

[143] Ibid., 132, 392, 411.

[144] Ibid., 126, 402.25–28.

[145] Ibid., 390.8–10.

[146] Ibid., 347, 398, 419.

[147] Ibid., 125.28–30.

[148] Ibid., 367.

[149] Ibid., 93.25–94.2.

it comprised (mainly?) excerpts from works of Latin fathers although the presence of at least one passage from Cyril of Alexandria is attested by the same letter. We should not be wrong in assuming that it was not the only one but that there should have existed at least a core of the Greek quotations found in P by that period. Besides, one very significant characteristic of the *Filioque* florilegium of P is that it includes some quotations in which mention is simply made of the Holy Spirit, without any theological bearing on the procession. I would suggest that this is a strong indication that the primary concern of the compiler was to make an anthology on the Holy Spirit and not specifically on the *Filioque*. Consequently, it is more likely that here we have a compilation that was created at a very early stage of the history of the *Filioque*.[150]

If this is so, then at least a part of this florilegium might originate from a period around the year 645. However, there still exists another witness to this florilegium which is not much later than the year 774/5, namely, the *Hadrianum* of the year 793.[151]

It is clearly indicative of the ambiguity of any quotation concerning the procession of the Holy Spirit that, while Hadrian I uses, in all probability, quotations that existed in the archetype of P, he does so in order to defend the non-*Filioque* version of the creed. In the first *capitulum* of the *Capitulare adversus Synodum*, Charlemagne reprehends Patriarch Tarasius "qui Spiritum sancto non ex Patri et Filio secundum Niceni symboli fidem . . . profitetur."[152] Hadrian, taking up the defense, cites twenty-one quotations in support of the *per Filium* formulation. In this small florilegium are almost equally represented the Latin and the Greek fathers: eleven quotations from the former and ten from the latter.[153] Almost one-third of them (6) can possibly claim as a source the archetype of P or a parallel source.[154]

---

[150] The fragments, for instance, of Amphilochius of Iconium (quot. 197, 198) or the excerpts from the *Convivium X Virginum* of Methodius Olympius (quot. 141–143) have never been connected with the *Filioque*.

[151] See above, Chapter I, pp. 37–38.

[152] *Hadrianum*, 7.23–25.

[153] The list includes the following: Latins: Hilary (1 quotation), Ambrose (1), Augustine (4), Leo the Pope (2), and Gregory the Pope (3); Greeks: Athanasius (2), Eusebius (= Gregory of Nyssa) (1), Basil (1), Gregory Nazianz. (1), Cyril of Alex. (4), and Sophronius of Jerus. (1).

[154] (1) *Hadrianum*, 8.14–21: Gregorii martyris et episcopi Neocessarie fides = P, quot. 165; (2) *Hadrianum*, 9.7–14: Gregorii theologi de secundis Epiphanii = P, quot. 181; (3) *Hadrianum*, 9.39–10.2: . . . de sentencia sancti Cyrilli . . . = P, quot. 9A; (4) *Hadrianum*, 10.3–10: Cyrilli ad Iohannem Antiochenum = P, quot. 178; (5–6) two small extracts from the *Tomus Leonis* (*Hadrianum*, 10.18–20) of Pope Leo, and the *Epistula Synodica* of Sophronius of Jerusalem (*Hadrianum*, 11.5–6). In this case P includes both the works in their entirety (quot. 29 and 45, 192 respectively).

In one instance at least the text of the *Hadrianum* is a verbatim translation of the extract in P.[155] In another instance—the case of the Creed of Gregory of Neocaesarea, quot. 165—the Latin text of the *Hadrianum* is inferior to that of P and appears under a different lemma than that of P (Eusebius of Caesarea, *Historia ecclesiastica*). However, Hadrian does seem to be aware of all the information included in the lemma of P (fol. 195ᵛ).[156]

A third quotation that P has in common with the *Hadrianum* is an extract from *Oratio* 39 of Gregory of Nazianzus (quot. 181). P preserves three fragments from this speech that correspond to *PG* 36, 345C9–15, 348A9–12, B6–C4, while the *Hadrianum* gives a translation of lines 348A9–B4 of the Migne edition.[157]

So the *Hadrianum* can be taken as a terminus ante quem (= 793) for this florilegium, although it is a little later than the date provided by the colophon of P.

In conclusion, the *Filioque* florilegium should be considered a pro-Latin one. The fact that it also includes some quotations that are irrelevant to the procession of the Holy Spirit and simply praise its divinity, but ignore completely the *Filioque* issue, could justify a dating as early as the seventh century.[158] The ideal period for the compilation of at least a considerable part

---

[155] *Hadrianum*, 10.3–10 (. . . sancti Cyrilli ad Iohannem Antiochenum) = P, fol. 190 (Τοῦ ἁγίου Κυρίλλου ἐκ τῆς πρὸς Ἰωάννην πατριάρχην Ἀλεξανδρείας (sic), quot. 178).

[156] *Hadrianum*, 8.21–24: ". . . Et non solum istoriografus iste haec memorat sancti Gregorii fides, sed et maximus predicator sanctus Gregorius Nysenus in sermone Greco . . . ea explanavit, qualiter a quibus eidem sancto Gregorio disposita atque ostensa et visa est."

[157] Assuming that the original of P was the actual source for the appearance of this quotation in the *Hadrianum*, then here is another example that may strengthen the suspicion that Cinnamus has mutilated or abridged many extracts that belonged to his original. But on this there is more in the following chapters.

[158] Father Munitiz of Campion Hall, Oxford, had the kind generosity to let me have a copy of a letter sent to him on 11/10/1974 by Father J. Paramelle. In this letter the French savant discussed some problems of P. Among other things he wrote the following words about this particular florilegium (I have emphasized the crucial parts): "Or, le recueil christologique [= fols. 8–235ᵛ of P] (je l'appelle ainsi pour le charactériser en gros par opposition au second [= fols. 235ᵛ–306]), même si, dans les *ff. 196–215*, il y a bien des textes qui parlent de la *Théologie notamment du Saint-Esprit: mais sans aucune espèce d'allusion, ceci est à noter, aux controverses post-Photiennes, bien qu'un lecteur postérieur ait ajouté en marge* "Κατὰ Λατίνων" *cf. les textes des fᵒs additionnels du début et de la fin du codex, 1–7 et 307–314 plusque de l'Économie.*" I wish to thank Father Paramelle for granting me permission to cite from this letter and from an article of his, which is unpublished at the moment these lines are written: J. Paramelle, "Morceau égaré du *Corpus Dionysiacum* ou Pseudo-pseudo-Denys? Fragment grec d'une *Lettre à Tite* inconnue," in Ysabel de Andia (ed.), *Denys l'Areopagite et sa posterité en Orient et en Occident*, Actes du Colloque, Paris, 21–24 septembre 1994 (Paris, 1996), 237–266. In this article he examines quotation 150 (Ps.-Dionysius Areopagite, *Letter to Titus*) along with a number of quotations that precede and follow it in P (148, 149, 151–158). One of his most significant suggestions is that the procession of the

(if not all) of this florilegium would be a date after 645/6, after the arrival in Rome of Maximus the Confessor and his followers,[159] who carried a wealth of books in their luggage.[160]

8. The Collection of *Miscellanea:* (a) *Historica et canonica* (fols. 219ᵛ–235ᵛ, quot. 236–245), (b) *Canonica et dogmatica* (fols. 283ᵛ–306, quot. 246–254)

Between the *Filioque* florilegium and the Iconophile one are inserted ten rather extensive works (quot. 236–245), most of which comprise historical (quot. 236, 238, 241–244) and canonical material (quot. 237, 245), plus two excerpts from theological works (quot. 239, 240). The space next to the Iconophile florilegium (P, fols. 283ᵛ–306) is held by a second collection of canonical and dogmatical texts (quot. 246–254), which seems to be similar in nature to the first one. As far as the second group of miscellaneous texts is concerned, it is worth noting that, although quotations 247 and 248 can usually be found at the beginning of collections of formal disavowals of heresies in which later texts are also included, both are no later than the second half of the fifth century.[161] Works of Basil, Gregory of Nyssa, and Ps.-Athanasius and fragments from the Old Testament complete this short collection. When exactly these texts were first put together is impossible to determine.

However, a closer examination of some of the items included in the first collection is needed because some fragments are problematic in their actual dating, namely, quotations 236, 238, and 241–45.

(1) Quotation 236 (P, fols. 219ᵛ–221ᵛ): A *Tractatus de sex Synodis* opens this section of the manuscript and its attribution in P to Cyril of Jerusalem is at least strange, since Cyril died in 386 just after the second ecumenical council. According to Munitiz: "This fanciful attribution weakens still further the credibility of the final colophon of Leon Kinnamos (fol. 306ᵛ)."[162] Despite this attribution, which is impossible to explain, the date of the composition of this text does not endanger the date of the colophon of P. The P

Holy Spirit was first debated well before the Council of Lyons (1274) or Photius (9th century) by a number of people who were in contact "—peut-être simplement par correspondance, communication de livres—avec Maxime le Confesseur ou avec certains de ses disciples, restés ou revenus à Rome après son transfert à Constantinople, son procès et sa mort." (ibid., 262–3).

[159] See P. Sherwood, *St. Maximus the Confessor (the Ascetic Life, the Four Centuries on Charity)* (London, 1955), 23.

[160] See the references to the articles of R. Riedinger in the previous chapter.

[161] See G. Ficker, "Eine Sammlung von Abschwörungsformeln," *ZKG* 27 (1906), 445, 448.

[162] J. Munitiz, "Synoptic Greek Accounts of the Seventh Council," *REB* 32 (1974), 151 n. 17.

version itself is very similar to the well-known anonymous *Tractatus de Synodis*.[163] The differences between P and the anonymous *Tractatus* are limited to omissions of words or short phrases on both parts (although P omits less), changes in the word order, and different readings. P concludes with a scholium that does not exist in the Munitiz version and which reads as follows (P, fol. 221ᵛ): Ἰδοὺ πρός γνῶσιν μείζονα τῶν φιλοπόνων ἐγράφησαν αἱ ἅγιαι ἓξ σύνοδοι, πότε καὶ διατὶ καὶ ἐν ποίοις τόποις συνηθροίσθησαν καὶ τίνας ἀνεθεμάτισαν καὶ ποῖα δόγματα ὀρθόδοξα ἐβεβαίωσαν. Obviously this text cannot be much later, from the sixth ecumenical council, and since in the same work Justinian II is mentioned, the date cannot be later than that of his death (711).[164]

(2) Skipping quotation 237 (for which see above, p. 52 n. 45), we go to a small fragment under the lemma Ἀφρικανοῦ ἱστορίας (quot. 238, P, fols. 224ᵛ–225). The full name of the author is Julius (Sextus) Africanus (d. post-240), but in the Middle Ages he was usually known as Ἀφρικανός.[165] I give here a full transcription of the text in P:

> Paris. gr. 1115, fols. 224ᵛ–225:
> Ἀφρικανοῦ ἱστορίας. Ἐν ἀρχῇ ἐποίησεν ὁ Θεὸς τὸν οὐρανὸν καὶ τὴν γῆν τουτέστι τὸ πᾶν κατ᾽ εἰδέαν ἢ ἀπὸ μέρους τῶν ἄκρων, εἴτι ἕτερον διὰ τούτων σημαίνεται. α΄ Πρώτη μὲν ἡμέρα τὸ φῶς, ὃ ἐκάλεσεν ἡμέραν. β΄ Δευτέρα δὲ (fol. 225) στερέωμα πρὸς διάκρισιν ὕδατος,
> 5 οὐρανὸν ἐπονομάσας. γ΄ Τρίτη δὲ ἦν γῆς φανέρωσις, καὶ θαλάσσης σύνοδοι. δ΄ Τετάρτη φωστῆρες. ε΄ Πέμπτη ἐξ ὑδάτων ψυχαὶ νηκτῶν (cod. ψυκτῶν) τε καὶ ἀερίων. ϛ΄ Ἕκτη τε ἐκ τῆς γῆς ζῶα, ἄνθρωπος κατ᾽ εἰκόνα Θεοῦ, τὸ χοϊκὸν ἀπὸ γῆς πλασθείς, καθ᾽ ὁμοίωσιν δὲ ἐμψυχωμένος, ἢ ὅτι τὸ μὲν κατ᾽ εἰκόνα προσδοὺς (cod. προσδεὺς) τὸ δὲ
> 10 καθ᾽ ὁμοίωσιν προσδοκᾶται.

Most of the works of Africanus have come down to us in the form of fragments embedded in later texts, and this is especially true for his main historical work, the *Chronographiae* (CPG 1690). A number of these fragments are preserved by George Syncellus in his *Chronicle*, which starts with the same biblical sentence as that cited above (Ἐν ἀρχῇ ἐποίησεν ὁ Θεὸς τὸν οὐρανὸν καὶ τὴν γῆν). In the sequel, Syncellus, speaking of the first day of

---

[163] Ed. J. Munitiz, "The Manuscript of Justel's *Anonymi Tractatus de Synodis*," *Byzantion* 47 (1977), 239–57, text: 253–57. In this article Munitiz has used only one manuscript on which the 1615 edition of Ch. Justel was based: the Bruxellensis 11376. For other manuscripts of the same version see Munitiz, "Synoptic Greek Accounts," 154.

[164] Munitiz proposed (a) the first period of Justinian's reign (685–695); (b) a date in the 730s, ibid., 248–49.

[165] See the entry by E. Amman, in *DTC* 8 (1925), col. 1921.

the Creation, refers to Julius Sextus and stresses that Τὴν πρώτην ἡμέραν ὁ Ἀφρικανὸς νοητὴν λέγει διὰ τὸ ἀδιοργάνιστον εἶναι τέως τὸ πρωτόκτιστον φῶς καὶ κεχυμένον.[166] Certainly, this passage does not resemble the one presented above at all, however it is commonly accepted that in the work of Syncellus "it is often difficult to distinguish between what comes from him and what comes from his sources when the latter are no longer at our disposal."[167] If this is the case here, then the word νοητὴ of Syncellus must be his own condensed rendering of the Ἐν ἀρχῇ ἐποίησεν ὁ θεὸς τὸν οὐρανὸν καὶ τὴν γῆν, τουτέστιν τὸ πᾶν κατ' εἰδέαν of Africanus.

On the other hand, Photius in his *Bibliotheca* gives the information that Julius Sextus starts his work with the Mosaic hexaemeron (ἀπὸ τῆς Μωυσαϊκῆς κοσμογενείας) exactly like the fragment above. Apart from that, the text complies stylistically with another observation of Photius, that Africanus Ἔστι ... σύντομος μέν, ἀλλὰ μηδὲν τῶν ἀναγκαίων ἱστορηθῆναι παραλιμπάνων.[168] In brief, it is highly possible that quotation 238 of P represents the opening lines of the now lost *Chronographiae* of Julius Sextus Africanus, and, to my knowledge, P is the unique witness to this particular fragment.

(3A) Quotation 241: Ἱππολύτου Θηβαίου ἐκ τοῦ χρονικοῦ αὐτοῦ συντάγματος (P, fols. 226ᵛ–228).

(B) Quotation 242: Περὶ τῶν γ΄ ἡμερῶν τῆς ἀναστάσεως τοῦ Χριστοῦ (P, fols. 228ʳ⁻ᵛ).

P transmits only the fragment from the first "edition" of the *Syntagma* of Hippolytus, the composition of which is placed by its last editor between 650 and 750, with more possibilities for the first half of this period.[169]

The next quotation (242) lays out a systematic treatment on the computation of the three days and nights after the crucifixion of Christ (for text, see Appendix I). I have been unable to identify it, and any attempt to date it is prone to major errors. It seems to be a fragment from a chronography, but this is the most I can say.

(4A) Quotation 243: Τοῦ ἁγίου Ἐπιφανίου ἐπισκόπου Κύπρου περὶ τῶν προφητῶν, πῶς ἐκοιμήθησαν καὶ ποῦ κεῖνται (*CPG* 3777, *De prophetarum vita et obitu, recensio prior*), P, fols. 228ᵛ–233.

---

[166] A. Mosshammer, ed., *Georgii Synkelli Ecloga Chronographica* (Leipzig, 1984), 3.1–2. The fragments of Africanus have been collected by M. J. Routh, *Reliquiae sacrae*, II (Oxford, 1846), 238–308. The fragment from Syncellus is on p. 238.

[167] I. Ševčenko, "The Search for the Past in Byzantium around the Year 800," *DOP* 46 (1992), 281.

[168] *Photius, Bibliothèque*, I, ed. R. Henry (Paris, 1959), 19. See also W. Adler, *Time Immemorial*, DOS 26 (Washington, D.C., 1989), 45–46.

[169] F. Diekamp, *Hippolytos von Theben, Texte und Untersuchungen* (Münster, 1898), 157.

(B) Quotation 244: Τοῦ αὐτοῦ περὶ τῶν ἁγίων ἀποστόλων ποῦ ἕκαστος ἐκήρυξε καὶ πότε καὶ ποῦ ἐτελεύτησαν καὶ τὰ ἅγια αὐτῶν σώματα ποῦ κεῖνται καὶ ἐν ποίοις τόποις. (*CPG* 3780, *Index apostolorum*), P, fols. 233ᵛ–234ᵛ.

(C) Quotation 244a (= *CPG* 3781, *Index discipulorum*), P, fols. 234ᵛ–235.

(D) Quotation 244b: Εἰσὶ τὰ ὀνόματα τῶν γονέων τῶν ιβ΄ ἀποστόλων καὶ τοῦ Μελχισεδέκ. P, fol. 235.

This group of four Epiphanian or Pseudo-Epiphanian texts has been edited by Th. Schermann in his *Prophetarum vitae fabulosae indices apostolorum discipulorumque domini, Dorotheo, Epiphanio, Hippolyto, aliisque vindicata* (Leipzig, 1907). Parallel to the edition, Schermann published a study of the textual tradition of all these and other related texts.[170] Therein he traced the origins of the transmission and the historical value of these texts. Unfortunately, in constructing his framework Schermann placed much emphasis on the Oriental (mainly Syriac and Hebrew) lines of the tradition of these texts and somehow neglected their Latin translations.[171]

P is the unique source for quotation 243. This text has been described by the monophysite Jacob of Edessa (640–708) as one of the works that have been "falsely ascribed to Epiphanius."[172] Consequently this text conforms to the chronological data of the colophon of P.

However, for the next two texts (244 and 244a), Schermann vaguely proposes a date no later than the mid-eighth century.[173] But when Schermann published his edition he was not aware that a rather simple version of these two lists included in Vaticanus graecus 1506, fols. 78ʳ⁻ᵛ also existed translated into Latin. What is more, the Latin translation is transmitted by a manuscript of the late sixth century that belongs to the Chapter Library of Verona (ms LI, fols. 156ᵛ–157ᵛ). These lists were appended to an early translation of the Apostolic Constitutions.[174] So it is reasonable to assume that they were as early as the Apostolic Constitutions.[175] Even if the P version

---

[170] T. Schermann, *Propheten- und Apostellegenden nebst Jungerkatalogen*, TU 31.3 (Leipzig, 1907).

[171] See the review by H. Delehaye in *AB* 27 (1908), 205.

[172] Information found in a letter of Jacob preserved in the 9th-century Syriac manuscript London British Museum Add. 12172; see W. Wright, *Catalogue of Syriac Manuscripts in the British Museum*, II (London, 1871), 601. Also Schermann, *Prophetarum vitae*, XIII–XIV; *Propheten-*, 4. See also the stemma on 132, where he places this text in the 6th century.

[173] Schermann, *Propheten-*, 351.

[174] See C. H. Turner, "A Primitive Edition of the Apostolic Constitutions and Canons: An Early List of Apostles and Disciples," *JTS* 15 (1913–14), 53–65. For a more detailed description of the Verona manuscript, see idem, "An Arian Sermon from a MS in the Chapter Library of Verona," *JTS* 13 (1912), 19–28, and A. Spagnolo and C. H. Turner, "A Fragment of an Unknown Latin Version of the Apostolic Constitutions," ibid., 492–514.

[175] Turner, "Primitive Edition," 62.

of these lists seems to be a later, rather augmented one, it still cannot be far removed from the fourth century.

A final point concerning quotations 244 and 244a is that in P part of the *Index apostolorum* along with the first third of the *Index discipulorum* are missing. Schermann supplemented these parts from Vindobonensis Theol. gr. 77 (13th cent.). Quite recently a Latin translation of the whole text including the parts missing from P has been published, and it is finally possible to restore the original list of the seventy disciples,[176] in a more accurate fashion than Schermann did (*Propheten-*, 315–17). For the full text of quotation 244b, see Appendix I.

(5) Dating problems are also presented by quotation 245 (P, fol. 235[r-v]), which is a canon περὶ τοῦ μὴ δεῖν τὸν ἱερέα β´ λειτουργίας ποιεῖν.[177] Uthemann gets the credit of having reminded us that this canon appears under the name of Photius in many manuscripts, and it has been edited by J. Hergenröther in *Monumenta Graeca ad Photium pertinentia* (Regensburg, 1869), 11.[178]

This text can possibly be of the ninth century, although we cannot exclude an earlier date of composition and its subsequent adoption by Photius. In any case, it occurs in numerous manuscripts, and its attribution to a particular author is not uniform in them. Grumel also attributes it to Photius,[179] but he is aware of the complexities concerning its authorship. First, Hergenröther (ibid., 11) had noticed that some manuscripts transmit this canon anonymously, and then Beneševič gave an extensive list of manuscripts along with the varying lemmata they provide.[180] The text itself does not differ significantly from manuscript to manuscript,[181] but much more interesting are the lemmata in their various transmissions. The following lists all

---

[176] See F. Dolbeau, "Une liste ancienne d'Apôtres et de Disciples, traduite du Grec par Moïse de Bergame," *AB* 104 (1986), 299–314.

[177] The whole text reads as follows: Paris. gr. 1115, fol. 235: Περὶ τοῦ μὴ δεῖν τὸν ἱερέα β´ λειτουργίας ποιεῖν· ⟨Ὁ⟩ ὀρθὸς λόγος καὶ ἡ ἀκριβὴς τῶν πραγμάτων κατανόησις τὸν ἱερέα ἅπαξ τῆς ἡμέρας ἐπιτρέπει τὴν ἀναίμακτον θυσίαν ἐπιτελεῖν, ἀλλ᾽ οὐ πολλάκις· εἰ γὰρ εἰς τὸ ἓν θυσιαστήριον οὐ συγχωρεῖται δευτέραν (fol. 235ᵛ) θυσίαν ποιεῖν, πολλῷ μᾶλλον τὸν ἱερέα τῆς ἡμέρας οὐ θέμις δὶς ἱερᾶσθαι, ἐπεὶ καὶ Χριστός, ὁ ἀληθινὸς ἀρχιερεύς, . . .

[178] Uthemann, "Ein Beitrag," 34 n. 32.

[179] V. Grumel, *Regestes*, vol. I, fasc. II–III, 163 (= N. 587 [588]).

[180] V. N. Beneševič, "Monumenta Vaticana ad ius canonicum pertinentia," *Studi Byzantini* 2 (1927), 159–60.

[181] Hergenröther based his edition on the following mss: (1) Vat. gr. 1150, fol. 127; (2) Vat. gr. 1119, fol. 7ᵛ; (3) Vat. gr. 430, fol. 221ᵛ; (4) Monacensis gr. 380, fol. 151. I have also been able to collate the same text in mss (5) Vat. gr. 828, fol. 281 and (6) Sinaiticus gr. 1117 (482), fol. 355.

the available lemmata divided into five groups and the manuscripts that transmit them:

I

(1) Περὶ τοῦ μὴ δεῖν τὸν ἱερέα β´ λειτουργίας ποιεῖν.

Paris. gr. 1115 (a. 1276), fol. 235

(2) Περὶ τοῦ μὴ ποιεῖν ἱερέα λειτουργίας δύο.

Vindob. hist. gr. 7 (ca. 1200), fol. 14. The canon appears as a "quasi appendix" to the thirty *capitula* of the *Constitutiones Apost.*[182]

(3) Περὶ τοῦ μὴ ποιεῖν ἱερεὺς λειτουργίας δύο.

Sinait. gr. 1121 (14th–15 cent.), fol. 283ᵛ. Here the canon occupies chapter 85 of a collection under the title Ἐκλογὴ τοῦ παρὰ Θεοῦ δοθέντος νόμου τοῖς Ἰσραηλίταις.

Neapolitanus II C 7 (a. 1140), fol. 88 and Mediolanensis di Brera AF. IX. 31 (16th cent.), fol. 10 were inaccessible to me, and I could not verify the lemma, but the fragment is included in them as canon 15 of Peter and Paul.[183]

II

(1) Τόμος συνοδικὸς περὶ τοῦ ἄπαξ τῆς ἡμέρας ὀφείλειν γίνεσθαι τὴν ἀναίμακτον θυσίαν.

Vat. gr. 430 (16th cent.), fol. 220ᵛ

(2) Περὶ τοῦ ἄπαξ ὀφείλειν λειτουργεῖν τὸν ἱερέα.

Monacensis gr. 380 (14th cent.), fol. 151. Here follows the nomokanon in fourteen chapters ascribed to Photius.

(3) With no lemma, but—as in II(2)—after a work of Photius.

Vat. gr. 828 (13th–14 cent.), fol. 281

III

(1) Φωτίου τοῦ ἁγιωτάτου πατριάρχου περὶ τῆς θείας λειτουργίας.

Vat. gr. 1119 (13th cent.), fol. 7ᵛ

Vat. gr. 1150 (16th cent.), fol. 127

Mosqu. Synod. 398 (= Vladimir 315), (12th cent.), fol. 176ᵛ

IV

(1) Τοῦ ἁγιωτάτου καὶ οἰκουμενικοῦ πατριάρχου κυροῦ Νικολάου τοῦ Νέου (= Nicholas II Chrysoberges [979–991] or Nicholas III Grammatikos [1084–1111]?), περὶ τοῦ μὴ λειτουργεῖν τὸν ἱερέα δὶς τῆς ἡμέρας.

Sinait. gr. 1117 (482), (14th cent.), fol. 355

(2) Νικολάου πατριάρχου τοῦ νέου περὶ τοῦ μὴ δεῖν τὸν ἱερέα δὶς τῆς ἡμέρας λειτουργεῖν.

Vat. gr. 640 (14th cent.), fol. 195ʳ⁻ᵛ

---

[182] See F. X. Funk, ed., *Didascalia et Constitutiones Apostolorum*, vol. II (Paderborn, 1905), 143.

[183] Beneševič, "Monumenta Vaticana," 159.

V

(1) Τοῦ ἁγίου Νικηφόρου, πατριάρχου Κωνσταντινουπόλεως, περὶ ⟨τοῦ⟩ οὐ χρὴ τὸν ἱερέα ἱερουργεῖν καθεκάστην.
Sinait. gr. 1109 (321), (a. 1424), fol. 253ᵛ.

The manuscript tradition of this fragment is obviously very complicated, and no doubt there are many other manuscripts that transmit it. Almost all the manuscripts that attribute the canon to a particular patriarch
are later than the thirteenth century (exception: Photius in Mosqu. Synod.
398), whereas the two earliest manuscripts (Vindob. hist. gr. 7 and Neapol.
II C 7) ascribe it to the pseudo-Apostolic tradition. P also places the canon
in virtually the same context next to the *Index apostolorum* of Ps.-Epiphanius
(incidentally, a setting very similar to that of the early Latin translations in
the Verona manuscript mentioned above, p. 88). A critical edition of this
small text could possibly solve the problems, but for the time being it is
enough to have demonstrated the many lines of its transmission. The line
that links it with Photius is by no means the most reliable, while that of
P includes, at least, the earlier manuscripts. The fact also of the multiple
attribution in itself is a good reason for questioning any claim of paternity
on behalf of Photius or any other patriarch.

CHAPTER III

The Iconophile Florilegium of Parisinus Graecus 1115

1. Introduction

A very extensive anthology on the subject of image veneration covers fols. 235ᵛ–283ᵛ of the codex. It contains 133 extracts, but some of them seem irrelevant to the subject of the florilegium. As has been shown above, twenty-eight of them derive from the *Doctrina Patrum* (quot. 4*–14*, 26*– 42*; fols 246–247ᵛ, 248ᵛ–251).[1] Therefore, the Iconophile florilegium includes 105 quotations in defense of image worship.

There has been a tendency on the part of the compiler of this florilegium to follow certain rules in the way he assembled it. One clearly discernible principle is that he cited the works according to the importance of the names of their authors. Putting aside quotations 1* and 2*, which both serve as an introduction to the florilegium itself, it can be demonstrated that the first Iconophile quotations are taken from the main ἔγκριτοι fathers in the following sequence: (a) Basil (quot. 15*–19*, 25*); (b) Gregory of Nazianzus (21*–24*); (c) Gregory of Nyssa (43*–48*, 51*, 52*); (d) Gregory of Neocaesarea (49*, 50*); (e) John Chrysostom (53*–59*); (f) Cyril of Alexandria (61*–67*); and (g) Athanasius of Alexandria (68*–71*). These authors are also arranged in alphabetical order, except for Athanasius of Alexandria. Moreover, it is worth noting that the quotations from Basil and John Chrysostom conclude with a fragment from their *vitae* (quot. 20* and 60* respectively). The compilation continued with extracts from authors that the compiler considered somehow minor compared to the previous ones (e.g.,

---

[1] See above, pp. 69–70. However, the fact that these quotations deal mainly with christological problems may give them a *raison d'être* among the texts of an Iconophile florilegium: it was mainly christological issues that constituted the basis of Iconoclasm. See Pelikan, *Eastern Christendom*, II, 125–33; also J. Meyendorff, *Christ in Eastern Christian Thought* (Washington, D.C., 1969), 135–48; Ch. von Schönborn, *L'icône du Christ*, 3rd ed. (Paris, 1986), 54 ff, 179–238; L. Ouspensky, *Theology of the Icon*, trans. A. Gythiel and E. Meyendorff (Crestwood, N.Y., 1992), vol. I, 119–50.

Hypatius of Ephesus, 74*; Dionysius the Areopagite, 75*–80*;[2] Anastasius of Antioch 81*–82*; Cyril of Jerusalem 91*).

A considerable section toward the end of the anthology was devoted to hagiographic material,[3] and the florilegium closed with some biblical extracts[4] and the letter of Pope Gregory II to Patriarch Germanus that ends with the (interpolated?) anathemas against the leaders of the Iconoclastic Council of Hiereia.[5]

There are, in addition, some instances where the compiler tried to gather together in small clusters texts of similar nature such as Dionysius the Areopagite and Hypatius of Ephesus, the three quotations on fols. 265ᵛ–269ᵛ that belong to the literary genre of the *sermones* or *disputationes contra Iudaeos* or *paganos* (quot. 101*–103*),[6] and a little further on the two fragments from the historians Sozomen and Evagrius.[7] In general, the main sources of this florilegium were patristic, hagiographic, and historical works. To these one may add the conciliar acts, which are represented by three extracts.[8]

This chapter examines the relationship of the florilegium of P with all the other existing anthologies (earlier and, some, later than the seventh ecumenical council, Nicaea II in 787) that are related to image veneration. This examination establishes a date for the entire florilegium and perhaps solves the chronological problems already mentioned.

2. The *Adversus Iconoclastas* (*CPG* 8121), (quot. 1*, fols. 235ᵛ–239)

The chronological evidence provided by the introductory piece of this florilegium, the Διάλογος στηλιτευτικὸς (*Adversus Iconoclastas*), allows for a dating

---

[2] The placing of Hypatius of Ephesus right before Dionysius is noteworthy in the sense that both are similar from one evident point of view: Hypatius uses the same language and *seemingly* the same ideas as Dionysius. See E. Kitzinger, "The Cult of Images in the Age before Iconoclasm," *DOP* 8 (1954), 138. Rather well-founded objections on the relationship Hypatius-Dionysius have been expressed by S. Gero, "Hypatius of Ephesus on the Cult of Images," in *Christianity, Judaism and Other Greco-Roman Cults: Studies for Morton Smith at Sixty*, ed. J. Neusner, Part II (Leiden, 1975), 211–13. Still, the compiler of P seems to have put Dionysius next to Hypatius based on superficial considerations such as their common vocabulary.

[3] Quot. 107*–124*, fols. 270ᵛ–277ᵛ; also quot. 72*, fol. 254ᵛ and quot. 87*–88*, fols. 261ᵛ–262.

[4] Quot. 127*–130*, 132*, fols. 280ʳ⁻ᵛ, 281ᵛ.

[5] Quot. 133*, fols. 281ᵛ–283ᵛ.

[6] Fols. 265ᵛ–269ᵛ. To the same genre also belongs quot. 95*, fols. 263ᵛ–264 (Stephen of Bostra, *Contra Iudaeos fragmenta*).

[7] Quot. 105*, 106*, fol. 270ʳ⁻ᵛ.

[8] Quot. 94*, 104*, and 125*, fols. 263ᵛ, 269ᵛ–270, and 278 respectively.

as early as A.D. 770.[9] A second chronological indication found in the same text consolidates this dating. It reads as follows: ἐξ ὅτου γὰρ τὴν ἔρευναν ταύτην ἤρξασθε ποιῆσαι εἰσὶν ἔτη πλεῖον ἢ ἔλασσον με΄· ἀπὸ γὰρ ἐννάτης ἐπινεμήσεως ἤρξασθε τῇ ἀληθείᾳ ἀντιπίπτειν . . . (P, fol. 238ᵛ). If we take into account that the "official" Iconoclasm (= τῇ ἀληθείᾳ ἀντιπίπτειν) began in the year 726, which corresponds to the ninth indiction, then, by adding more or less forty-five years, we obtain the year 770/1, which partly corresponds to the eighth indiction (= 769/70).[10] This is the indiction in which the author of the *Adversus Iconoclastas* places himself in time.

Having settled, therefore, a definite date for this work, we can proceed to its analysis. The text appears twice in Migne, once under the name of John of Damascus or of a certain John, patriarch of Jerusalem (*Opusculum adversus Iconoclastas*, PG 96, 1348C–1361C), and for a second time anonymously in *PG* 109, 501A–516C. In both cases it is the same text that was first published as an appendix to the edition of Theophanes' *Chronographia* by Combefis (Paris, 1685, pp. 303–11) from the unique manuscript that preserves it, that is, P. In P the work is anonymous.

An extremely detailed study of the text by P. Speck has recently been published,[11] but unfortunately has very little to offer toward a better understanding of it. Since Speck has examined the work as it is in the Migne edition,[12] and therefore taken out of its original context, the Iconophile florilegium of P, his conclusions are rather complicated and misleading. As it is impossible to give here a detailed summary of his remarks on the text, I simply present an outline of his final conclusions.

Speck believes that the *Adversus Iconoclastas* was a text that had gradually developed in different periods. According to him, what we possess today is a fragmentary form of the original text which had been lost through a damaged exemplar.[13] In any case, the text of P, as it is today, stands in three parts.

> Die Mitte (die Kapitel δ΄ [= *PG* 109, 505C] –ιγ΄ genau bis in 513A) bietet ein Glaubensbekenntnis, das sicher vorikonoklastisch ist und hier einfach übernommen wurde. Sein Text zeigt keine Korruptellen.

[9] See above, Chapter II, p. 49 n. 33.

[10] See V. Grumel, *La chronologie* (Paris, 1958), 248–49.

[11] P. Speck, *Ich bin's nicht, Kaiser Konstantin ist es gewesen*, ΠΟΙΚΙΛΑ ΒΥΖΑΝΤΙΝΑ 10 (Bonn, 1990) (hereafter *Kaiser Konstantin*), 579–635.

[12] He used the text in *PG* 109, 501A–516C. For reasons of convenience I will also refer to the same text, at the same time taking into account the text of the manuscript. Also, when the manuscript provides readings different from those of *PG*, preference will be given to the manuscript.

[13] Speck, *Kaiser Konstantin*, 584, 587, 588, and elsewhere.

Daran schließen sich (kapitel ιγ´ [der Rest] – ιε´ 513B–C) mehr schlecht als recht verbundene Auszüge aus einer katechismusartigen Schrift an, die Hinweise gibt, welches Gebet von welchem Bild gesprochen werden soll. Auch diese Kapitel haben nichts mit der eigentlichen Invectiva zu tun, sondern sind bei einer späteren Redaktion hinzugefügt worden.

Die Reste des eigentlich alten und jetzt nochmals zu datierenden Textes sind also ziemlich kurz; sie umfassen die Kapitel α´–γ´ und ις´ . . . (*PG* 109, 501A–505C, 513C–516C).[14]

Moreover, he claims that one of the chronological indications (ἀπὸ τοῦ κυριακοῦ πάθους . . . μέχρι τῆς παρούσης ἰνδικτιῶνος ὀγδόης, ἔτη ἑπτακόσια με´ λέγουσιν εἶναι) was originally a marginal note to the work transposed later into the main text.[15]

Speck may be right in that the text presents some problems, especially in its syntax,[16] but this does not necessarily imply that it is a clumsy patchwork of fragments introduced or removed from the main body of the original work at different times. He may also be right in that the word διάλογος in its title does not depict the true genre of the text, yet I cannot agree with his inference that it is a λόγος, in the sense that it was written to be recited before an audience.[17]

It must be said from the beginning that the *Adversus Iconoclastas*, despite its problematic syntax which, in all probability, was the result of omissions by Cinnamus himself, and of the poor knowledge of the Greek tongue on the part of the author (note that he did not even know the correct name of the palace where the 754 Iconoclastic council took place: P, fol. 236, Ἔρια), is a rather homogeneous text that deals chiefly with a single problem. The problem addressed by the *Adversus Iconoclastas* is present in its title: it is a Διάλογος (or whatever) . . . πρὸς ἔλεγχον τῶν ἐναντίων τῆς πίστεως καὶ τῆς διδασκαλίας τῶν ἁγίων καὶ ὀρθοδόξων ἡμῶν πατέρων.

The anonymous author, referring explicitly to the participants at the Council of Hiereia, accuses them of introducing a δόξα κενὴ (to be more

---

[14] Ibid., 628.

[15] Ibid., 616–17.

[16] E.g., clauses with infinitive in the place of a verb: Πιστεύομεν τοιγαροῦν εἰς μίαν ἁγίαν καθολικὴν καὶ ἀποστολικὴν τοῦ Θεοῦ ἐκκλησίαν, ἐν ᾗ μαθητευθῆναι ἐν τῇ κατηχήσει (P, fol. 238). Clauses with no apparent connection to the context: . . . ἀλλ᾽ ὅμως καὶ ταῦτα πράττοντες, καθ᾽ ὑμῶν αὐτῶν ἀκονᾶτε τὸ ξίφος τῆς δικαιοκρισίας τοῦ Θεοῦ, καὶ πολλῆς μακροθυμίας καὶ ἀγαθότητος· διὸ παρακαλῶ ὑμᾶς ἀπορρίψαι . . . (P, fol. 239), etc.

[17] Speck, *Kaiser Konstantin*, 582–84. Professor E. Chrysos has suggested to me that Διάλογος is an acceptable possibility, supposing that the author perceives his monologue as a "conversation" with the Iconoclasts.

specific, a heresy: *PG* 109, 501A; P, fol. 235ᵛ). But this is not the main point of the author's charge. His concern focuses on the fact that the Iconoclasts did so by distorting (στρεβλοῦν, παραχαράττειν) quotations/fragments (φωναί) taken from the orthodox fathers, not only on the subject of image worship but also on the dogma of the incarnation of God the Logos. The following cites all the relevant passages from the *Adversus Iconoclastas*.

(A) *PG* 109, 501A4–10; P, fol. 235ᵛ

οὗτοι δέ, . . . ἐπίσκοποι καὶ ποιμένες τῶν λογικῶν τοῦ Χριστοῦ λαχόντες εἶναι προβάτων, διὰ δόξαν κενὴν καὶ μόνον τῶν πατέρων τὰς φωνὰς παρωσάμενοι, κατὰ τῆς πίστεως ἑαυτοὺς ὁπλίσαντες, τὰ ὀρθῶς ὑπ' αὐτῶν ῥηθέντα στρεβλοῦσι, κατὰ τὸν ἀδόκιμον αὐτῶν καὶ τεθολωμένον νοῦν, διδάσκοντες, . . .

(B) *PG* 109, 504B2–6; P, fol. 235ᵛ

. . . καταφλυαροῦσι τοίνυν τινὲς τῶν τῆς ἀληθείας πατέρων καὶ διδασκάλων, καὶ δὴ καὶ σκαιότητος διαβολικῆς τὸν οἰκεῖον ἐμπλήσαντες νοῦν, παραχαράττειν ἐπείγονται τὸ τῆς ἀληθείας μυστήριον καὶ τῆς μετὰ σαρκὸς οἰκονομίας τοῦ μονογενοῦς. . .

(C) *PG* 109, 504B12–D2; P, 1115, fol. 236

. . . ὥσπερ γὰρ ἀληθῶς αὐτοὶ ἠρνήσαντο τὸν υἱὸν τοῦ Θεοῦ σαρκὶ ἐληλυθότα, οὕτως καὶ νῦν νεοκήρυκες μὴ θέλοντες προσκυνεῖν καὶ σεβάζεσθαι τῆς ἐνσάρκου τοῦ Χριστοῦ παρουσίας καὶ τῆς κατὰ σάρκα αὐτοῦ ἀχράντου μητρὸς καὶ κατὰ ἀλήθειαν Θεοτόκου . . . Μαρίας καὶ πάντων τῶν ἁγίων αὐτοῦ τάς . . . ἁγίας εἰκόνας, ἀλλὰ νέαν κενοτομοῦντες (sic) ἐτεκτονήσαντο πίστιν παρὰ τὴν ἀρχῆθεν ἐκ τῶν ἁγίων ἡμῶν πατέρων καὶ μαθητῶν καὶ διαδόχων τῶν ἁγίων ἀποστόλων ὑπαρχόντων, ὡς γὰρ αὐτοῖς ἔδοξεν, νῦν λέγοντες πλέον τῶν ἁγίων πατέρων, ὧν οἱ λόγοι καὶ αἱ ἀρεταὶ στήριγμα καὶ στήλη τῆς . . . ἐκκλησίας ὑπάρχουσιν οὗτοι τὴν πίστιν φυλάττειν διαβεβαιοῦντες· τὰς γὰρ αὐτῶν τῶν πατέρων φωνάς, ἃς αὐτοὶ τρανῶς ἐκήρυξαν περὶ τῶν σεβασμίων καὶ προσκυνητῶν εἰκόνων, οὗτοι οἱ νεόσοφοι λαβόντες . . . κατὰ τὰς ἰδίας ἐπιθυμίας πρὸς τὸν ἴδιον νοῦν στρεβλοῦσιν . . .

Then the author proceeds to accuse them of having used what the fathers have said against the idols in order to support Iconoclasm. Here the anonymous author seems to echo what has already been said by St. John of Damascus. Compare:

PG 109, 504D2–6; P, 1115, fol. 236

Ὡς γὰρ αὐτοὶ (= the fathers) περὶ τῶν εἰδωλικῶν ξοάνων καὶ δαιμονικῶν στηλῶν φράσαντες εἴρηκαν, οὗτοι (= the Iconoclasts) εἰς τὰς ἁγίας εἰκόνας μετέστρεψαν τοὺς ἁγίους πατέρας καὶ διδασκάλους τῆς . . . πίστεως, παρωσάμενοι τὰς αὐτῶν φωνὰς καὶ μαρτυρίας.

John of Damascus, *Contra imaginum calumniatores oratio* (ed. Kotter, *Schriften III*, I 24, II 17.1–5)

Ἃς μέντοι χρήσεις (sc. by the fathers) παράγεις, οὐ τῶν παρ᾽ ἡμῖν εἰκόνων βδελύσσονται τήν προσκύνησιν, ἀλλὰ τῶν ταύτας θεοποιούντων Ἑλλήνων.[18]

Therefore, since the Iconoclasts rejected the testimony of the fathers who taught the veneration of images, the author makes clear his intention first to deliver an admonition (or speech? διάλεκτος) to the Iconoclasts and then to complete his duty by citing some Iconodule quotations from the works of the fathers which obviously will prove the error and the malignity of the Iconoclasts.[19]

The διάλεκτος begins with the author asking, in a rhetorical manner, the participants at the Council of Hiereia:[20]

PG 109, 505A1–8; P, 1115, fol. 236

Λεγέτωσαν ἡμῖν (= the Iconoclasts of Hiereia) . . . ποίῳ τρόπῳ καὶ σκοπῷ τὰς τῶν πατέρων παρακρουόμενοι φωνὰς κατὰ τὰς ἰδίας ἐπιθυμίας ἑαυτοὺς ἐξαπατῶντες, ἐξελκόμενοι καὶ δελεαζόμενοι στρεβλεῖτε; (sic).

Next we come across a short passage that may offer an additional argument toward the assumption that the author already had in front of him the florilegium that follows. Compare:

PG 109, 505A8–11; P, fol. 236

. . . ποῖον ἐπὶ τῆς γῆς προσκυνητὸν καὶ σεβάσμιον καὶ λατρευτὸν ἐστιν ἀχειροποίητον . . .

P, fol. 263ᵛ (Stephen of Bostra, *Adv. Iudaeos*)

. . . ⟨ποῖον⟩ ἐπὶ ⟨τῆς⟩ γῆς οὐκ ἔστι χειροποιητόν . . . [21] (and continues with the citation of some objects of veneration that were χειροποίητα, such as the Ark of the Covenant, the Lantern, and the Tabernacle).

[18] Despite the received opinion on the date of the three Iconophile homilies of St. John Damascene in ca. 730, this passage may serve as an indication for the dating of the two first homilies after 753. On this see more below in section 4.

[19] Paris. gr. 1115, fol. 236: . . . παρωσάμενοι τὰς αὐτῶν φωνὰς καὶ μαρτυρίας περὶ ⟨τάς⟩ . . . ἀγίας εἰκόνας, ἄσπερ ἡμῖν τρανῶς σέβειν καὶ προσκυνεῖν ἐδίδαξαν· διὸ καὶ μετ᾽ ὀλίγην διάλεκτον πρὸς τοὺς νεοκήρυκας ποιησάμενοι, Θεοῦ διδόντος ἡμῖν καὶ τὸ ἀναπνεῖν, ὀλίγα ἐκ πολλῶν παραθήσομεν . . . Note that the emphasized words constitute a standard expression that usually occurs in a text right before the introduction of a florilegium (cf. *ACO* II,1,3, 114.1–3; *ACO Ser. II,* vol. II,1, 81.27–29).

[20] Ἔρια in the text of P and not ᾽Ονέρια as printed in the edition of Combefis.

[21] This is not the only instance where the author incorporates material from the florilegium in the *Adv. Iconoclastas*. See below, pp. 189–90, which demonstrate a clear example of dependence of the *Adv. Icon.* on phrases of the anonymous *Disputatio Iudaei et Christiani* (quot. 102*).

The greatest part of the remainder of the work is a very elaborate expansion on the creed (*PG* 109, 505c-512d9; P, fols. 236ᵛ-238), which in itself does not offer anything in particular to the cause of image worship. It is, however, the essential context on which the author bases his claim that, in addition to the creed and the Bible, the holy fathers who investigated all these matters in faith and in the right manner have taught us the way to venerate and worship the symbols of the faith, such as the cross, the Gospels, and the icons of the Mother of God, of the apostles, the martyrs, and the saints. And he repeats his intention to compile a florilegium that will include the corpus of this tradition:

> *PG* 109, 513c10–13; P, fol. 238ᵛ
> Ταῦτα οὕτως παρελάβομεν ἐκ τῶν ἁγίων πατέρων, ὧν καὶ τὰ ὀνόματα καὶ τοὺς λόγους ἐν τῷ τεύχει παρασημειωσόμεθα, Θεοῦ βουλήσει καὶ προνοίᾳ.

According to B. Atsalos, the word τεῦχος basically means codex, but one of its particular senses, namely, that of a "volume contenant un ouvrage d'un auteur,"[22] seems to suit perfectly the case of the *Adversus Iconoclastas* complete with its florilegium that follows.

After the chronological information in *PG* 109, 513d5-516a1, which has already been discussed, the author censures the Iconoclasts for the last time ('Ηπίστητε τοῖς πατράσι καὶ τῷ βαπτίσματι ὃ παρ' αὐτῶν εἰλήφατε καὶ δέξασθε αὐτῶν τὴν πίστιν καὶ τοὺς λόγους. *PG* 109, 516a5-7; P, fol. 238ᵛ) and finally admonishes them to adhere to the teachings of the fathers (as expounded in the quotations) and join the Orthodox in the veneration of icons (καὶ τὰς ἁγίας φωνὰς τῶν πατέρων σὺν ἡμῖν ὑποδέξασθε καὶ σὺν αὐτοῖς τε καὶ ἡμῖν ταῖς ἁγίαις εἰκόσι τὸ σέβας ἀναπέμψατε. *PG* 109, 516c8-10; P, fol. 239).

The preceding analysis must have made clear that the *Adversus Iconoclastas* was written with a specific purpose. Its author, though unknown to us,[23] was

---

[22] See B. Atsalos, *La terminologie du livre-manuscrit à l'époque byzantine (Première partie)* (Thessalonike, 1971), 119.

[23] We can, however, be almost certain about his origin: since the Iconophile florilegium includes, as will be shown below, items that could be found only in Rome, it is evident that the author of the *Adversus Iconoclastas* had worked in Rome as well. One more argument supporting the non-Constantinopolitan origin of the author could possibly offer the name of the place where the 754 synod took place: Ἔρια is very unlikely to have been written by a Constantinopolitan author to whom Ἱέρεια was a familiar place. Of course, there is always the possibility of a scribal error introduced by Cinnamus or by the copyist that produced the exemplar of P. A different opinion is held by Speck (*Kaiser Konstantin*, 635), who believes that the *Adversus Iconoclastas* was written in Palestine.

also the compiler of the Iconophile florilegium of P. He wrote the *Adversus Iconoclastas* with the intention of endowing the whole florilegium with an introductory piece in which he would give a summary description of the nature of the contents of the florilegium and their agreement with the orthodox tradition as well as their open support of the icon veneration that was part of this tradition. But his overriding concern was to defend the λόγοι of the orthodox fathers which had suffered various falsifications at the hands of Iconoclasts and, through them, the veneration of icons. In other words, the author of the *Adversus Iconoclastas* tried to refute the florilegium of the *horos* of Hiereia, not in a direct and detailed way as Nicephorus did in the second part of his *Refutatio et eversio*,[24] but by opposing to the poor Iconoclastic florilegium the impressive bulk of his own Iconophile anthology.

Since the *Adversus Iconoclastas* was not meant by definition to be recited before an audience, the words διάλογος of the title or α´ λόγος or even δ´ λόγος, according to the suggestion of Speck,[25] do not seem to be the correct ones in this case. A possibly acceptable emendation could be πρόλογος, but it is very rarely attested in the sense of "introduction" (cf. *PG* 28, 1201B).

The fact that the author borrowed and elaborated phrases from quotations included in the florilegium is sound evidence that the latter was already in existence in the year 770. The allusion, also, that the Iconoclasts παραχαράττειν ἐπείγονται τὸ τῆς ἀληθείας μυστήριον τῆς μετὰ σαρκὸς οἰκονομίας τοῦ Μονογενοῦς (*PG* 109, 504B5–6; P, fol. 235ᵛ) may allow for the conclusion that even the twenty-eight quotations from the *Doctrina Patrum* were originally included in the Iconophile florilegium, since almost all of them deal with christological problems (e.g., the two natures of Christ).

These conclusions lead to some new questions. What were the sources that the compiler of the year 770 had at his disposal? Does P preserve the whole of the original of the florilegium of 770? Does the florilegium in all of its extent date from 770, or do we have to accept as later interpolations some quotations, such as the *Narratio* of John of Jerusalem (quot. 131*) and the anathemas of Theodosius of Ephesus, Sissinius Pastillas, and other Iconoclasts (end of quot. 133*) that seem to have been derived from the acts of the Nicaea II in 787?[26] I begin with the second question.

---

[24] See Alexander, *Nicephorus*, 255–62.

[25] *Kaiser Konstantin*, 582.

[26] See C. J. Stallman, *The Life of St. Pancratius of Taormina* (Oxford University, D.Phil. thesis, 1986), vol. II, 77.

3. Restoring the Initial Extent of the Iconophile Florilegium of 770: P and
the Iconophile Florilegia of M and V

Codex Mosquensis Hist. Mus. 265 (= M)[27] is well known as the only source
of one of the earliest Iconophile works, the Νουθεσία γέροντος περὶ τῶν ἁγίων
εἰκόνων. It is written in a very early minuscule dating sometime between the
ninth and eleventh centuries. The prevailing opinion favors the earlier
date.[28]

Apart from the Νουθεσία (fols. 142–171ᵛ), M presents a collection of
Iconophile *testimonia* similar to that of P. Fifty-five Iconophile texts, the
length of which varies from a few lines to nine folia, are to be found on fols.
171ᵛ-241 of M.[29] After the elimination of quotation 39M, which is simply a
repeat of quot. 25M, there remain fifty-four quotations that belong to the
Iconophile florilegium of M.

More than half of them (twenty-eight) are common to both M and P.[30]
However, although in many cases an extract in P is absolutely the same as
in M,[31] there are many instances where P provides a more extended fragment than M[32] and vice versa.[33]

An excellent example of the relationship of the two manuscripts with a
possibly common archetype are the extracts from the *Vita* of St. Silvester
(P = quot. 124*, fol. 277ᵛ; M = quot. 36M, fols. 234–235). If we suppose
that the part of the *Vita* transmitted by both manuscripts consists of four

[27] About this manuscript see Vladimir (Archimandrite), *Sistematičeskoe opisanie rykopisej
Moskovskoj sinodalnoj (patriaršej) biblioteki,* vol. I (Moscow, 1894), 226–30; Uthemann, *Anastasii
Sinaitae,* XXXII, LXX ff. See also the lengthy review of the book of Melioranskij by E. Kurz, in
BZ 11 (1902), 538–42. Finally, see now B. L. Fonkič and F. B. Poljakov, *Grečeskie rykopisi sinodalnoj biblioteki* (Moscow, 1993), 73–74.
[28] Vladimir, *Opisanie,* 226: 9th century; Gouillard, "Origines," 255: 10th century; Kotter,
Schriften III, 36: 9th century; Fonkič-Poljakov, *Grečeskie,* 73: 9th/10th.
[29] For these quotations see Appendix III. Reference to the quotations of M will be made
as in the following example: 19M.
[30] Here is an exhaustive list of these quotations:

1M includes 66*, 97*, 132*	24M = 55*	46M = 104*
2M = 103*	26M = 53*	48M = 123*
7M = 2*	34M = 52*	49M = 94*
10M = 71*	36M = 124*	50M = 63*
12M = 3*	37M = 73*	51M = 52*
14M = 17*	38M = 92*	52M = 69*
16M = 96*	40M = 56*	53M = 16*
19M = 100*	41M = 54*	54M = 46*
22M = 121*	42M = 44*	55M = 47*

[31] E.g., quot. 12M and 3*, 22M and 121*, 24M and 55*, 41M and 54*, 49M and 94*, 50M
and 63*.
[32] Quot. 53* and 26M, 55* and 24M, 92* and 38M, etc.
[33] Quot. 7M and 2*, 10M and 71*, 14M and 17*, 19M and 100*, 52M and 69*, 55M and 47*.

paragraphs (a, b, c, and d), then P preserves a, c, and d, while M has included b and c. Moreover, the textual differences between the two manuscripts are not particularly significant and in many cases point to an archetype written in minuscule (οὕτως P: ὄντος M; ἀφορίσαντες P: ἀφανίσαντες M; συνλειτουργεῖ P: σοι λειτουργεῖ M; σχηματίζεσθαι P: ὀνομάζεσθαι M).

Another example concerns the 82nd canon of the Quinisext Council (Mansi XI 977ε-980β; P = quot. 94*, fol. 263ᵛ; M = quot. 49ᴹ, fol. 239). The acts of Nicaea II (787) display the same canon four times (Mansi XII 1079 A-C, 1123ε-1126A, XIII 40ε-41A, 220C-E), while in one case it was read from the very sheet of papyrus of the acts of the Quinisext that bore the signatures of the bishops (Mansi XIII 40ε-41A). In all these instances the opening phrase of the canon runs as follows: Ἔν τισι τῶν σεπτῶν εἰκόνων γραφαῖς, ἀμνὸς δακτύλῳ τοῦ Προδρόμου δεικνύμενος ἐγχαράττεται . . . On the other hand, P and M give the following incipit: Ἔν τισι τῶν σεπτῶν εἰκόνων γραφαῖς, ἀμνὸς τῷ δακτύλῳ τοῦ Προδρόμου . . . The same formula appears also in the Νουθεσία γέροντος,³⁴ whose author used the Iconophile florilegium (or part of it).

A third trait that possibly points toward the dependence of P and M on a common archetype is the following: M is one of the few manuscripts that transmits the second *Oratio contra imaginum calumniatores* of John of Damascus. However, the work is scattered over various parts of this manuscript, broken into five fragments (paragraphs refer to Kotter ed., *Schriften III*):

M, fols. 182ᵛ-191ᵛ = para. II 1–10; 14–23 (quot. 4ᴹ)
M, fol. 192 = para. II 69.1-10 (quot. 5ᴹ)
M, fol. 192 = para. II 11.1-24 (quot. 6ᴹ)
M, fols. 230–233 = para. II 10.8-14.14 (quot. 32aᴹ)
M, fols. 240ʳ⁻ᵛ = para. II 45–47 (quot. 54ᴹ-55ᴹ).

This phenomenon is usually explained in terms of palaeography by the assumption that M is the apograph of a manuscript in which the order of the folios had been disturbed. And this accounts also for the fact that quot. 32aᴹ (= para. II 10.8-14.14, Kotter ed.) is interpolated into another irrelevant fragment from a letter of Ignatius of Antioch.³⁵ Now in P, as will be seen further on, parts of paragraphs 16 and 14 of John of Damascus' second *Oratio* are inserted into the text of the *Adversus Constantinum Caballinum* (P, fol. 242ᵛ lines 16–30 and fols. 243ᵛ line 33–244 line 18). If P (or its exemplar)

---

³⁴ Melioranskij, *Georgij*, xxxv.
³⁵ See J. Darrouzès, "Deux textes inédits du Patriarche Germain," *REB* 45 (1987), 6: "Cela signifie que le modèle utilisé par le copiste avait des folios déplacés de telle manière que les lacunes n'étaient pas trop choquantes."

has also copied a manuscript with the folios that contain the same second speech of John of Damascus out of sequence, the coincidence is too striking.

Finally, one further example will make the dependence of P and M on the same archetype more apparent and, at the same time, will help to set the cornerstone for a possible solution of some problems that P presents in certain instances in comparison with the text of the Acts of Nicaea II. Compare (the spelling of M is given as in the manuscript):

Paris. gr. 1115 (fol. 247ᵛ)

Τοῦ αὐτοῦ ἐκ τῆς ἐπιστολῆς τῆς πρὸς Ἰουλιανὸν τὸν βασιλέα καὶ παραβάτην.
Κατὰ τὴν θεόθεν ἐπικεκληρω-μένην ἡμῖν ἀμώμητον τῶν χριστι-ανῶν πίστιν· καὶ μεθ' ἕτερα·

            δέχομαι δὲ καὶ τοὺς ἁγίους ἀποστόλους, προ-φήτας τε καὶ μάρτυρας καί εἰς τὴν πρὸς Θεὸν ἱκεσίαν τούτους ἐπικα-λοῦμαι, τοῦ δι' αὐτῶν, ἤγουν τῆς μεσιτείας αὐτῶν, ἵλεών μοι γενέσθαι τὸν φιλάνθρωπον Θεὸν καὶ λύτρον μοι τῶν πται-σμάτων δωρήσασθαι· ὅθεν καὶ τοὺς χαρακτῆρας τῶν εἰκόνων αὐτῶν τιμῶ καὶ προσκυνῶ καὶ κατ' ἐξαίρετον τοῦτο παραδεδομένον, ἐκ τῶν ἁγίων ἀποστόλων καὶ οὐκ ἀπηγο-ρευμένον, ἀλλ' ἐν πάσαις ταῖς ἐκ-κλησίαις ἡμῶν τούτων ἀνιστορου-μένων.

Mosqu. Hist. Mus. 265 (fol. 233ʳ⁻ᵛ).

Ἐπιστολὴ τοῦ ὁσίου πατρὸς ἡμῶν Βασιλείου πρὸς Ἰουλιανὸν τὸν παραβάτην.
Κατὰ τὴν θεόθεν ἐπικεκληρο-μένην ἡμῶν ἀμώμητον χριστιανοῖς πίστιν, ὁμολογῶ καὶ συντίθημι· πιστεύω εἰς ἕνα Θεὸν πατέρα παν-τοκράτορα, Θεὸν τὸν πατέρα, Θεὸν τὸν υἱόν, Θεὸν τὸ πνεῦμα τὸ ἅγιον· ἕνα Θεὸν τὰ τρία προσ-κυνῶ καὶ δοξάζω· ὁμολογῶ δὲ καὶ τὴν τοῦ υἱοῦ ἔνσαρκον οἰκο-νομίαν καὶ θεοτόκον τὴν κατὰ σάρκα τεκοῦσαν αὐτὸν ἁγίαν Μαρίαν· δέχομε δὲ καὶ τοὺς (fol. 223ᵛ) ἁγίους ἀποστόλους προ-φήτας καὶ μάρτυρας καὶ εἰς τὴν πρὸς Θεὸν ἱκεσίαν

ἤγουν τῆς μεσητίας αὐτῶν, ἤλεον μοι γενέσθε τὸν φιλάνθρωπον Θεὸν καὶ λύτρον μοι τῶν πτε-σμάτων χαρήσασθαι· ὅθεν καὶ τοὺς χαρακτῆρας τῶν εἰκόνων αὐτῶν τιμῶ καὶ προσκυνῶ κατεξ-αίρετον τοῦτο παραδεδομένον, ἔκ τε τῶν ἁγίων ἀποστόλων καὶ οὐκ ἀπηγορευμένον, ἀλλ' ἐν ἁπάσαις ταῖς ἐκκλησίαις ἡμῶν τούτων ἀν-ιστορουμένων.

Neither P nor M gives the whole text, as P omits the entire creed, re-placing it with the formula καὶ μεθ' ἕτερα, while M has dropped one line from the main text. The variants are not of particular importance (ἡμῖν P:

ἡμῶν M; χριστιανῶν P: χριστιανοῖς M; πάσαις P: ἀπάσαις M), but the word δωρήσασθαι in P which becomes χαρήσασθαι (with η) in M is a possible indication that the original of both P and M was written in minuscule: the complex δωρη– is more easily misread as χαρη– when the archetype is in minuscule than in majuscule (ΔΩΡΗ–, ΧΑΡΗ–). The most significant observation, however, has to do with the omission of the creed in P: in all likelihood, the missing creed should have existed in the archetype but Cinnamus chose to omit it and put the formula καὶ μεθ᾽ ἕτερα in its place. This is something that Cinnamus has repeated many times, as we will see.

Apart from these arguments, there is also another piece of evidence that can be brought forward at this point, a small florilegium compiled by Nicetas of Medicion, who died in April 824.[36] He was one of the leading post-Nicaean Iconophile personalities who flourished during the second period of Iconoclasm.[37] The sole witness to this florilegium is codex Vaticanus gr. 511[38] (fols. 66ᵛ-69ᵛ). In the epilogue of this florilegium Nicetas explains that he compiled a collection of a small number of quotations written in an abridged form because it was impossible to mention all the fathers and their works in detail.[39] What is of major importance is that in this small florilegium (twenty-seven extracts) we can find quotations that are common to (a) P and the florilegium of Nicetas (= N); (b) M and N; and (c) all three: P, M, and N. Here I give some examples of each case. Compare (the spelling of P, M, and N is given as in the manuscripts):

(A) Quotations common to P and N
    I. Paris. gr. 1115, fol. 254ᵛ (quot. 72*)
    Ἐκ τοῦ βίου τοῦ ἁγίου ἱερομάρτυρος Παγκρατίου· Καὶ φησὶν ὁ μακάριος Πέτρος ὁ ἀπόστολος· τέκνον Ἰωσήφ, ἐξένεγκε τὴν εἰκόνα τοῦ Κυρίου ἡμῶν Ἰησοῦ Χριστοῦ καὶ ἐντύπωσον αὐτὴν ἐν τῷ πυργίσκῳ, ἵνα ἴδωσιν οἱ λαοὶ ποίαν μορφὴν ἀνέλαβεν ὁ υἱὸς τοῦ Θεοῦ καὶ ἰδόντες, ἐπὶ πλέον πιστεύσωσι καὶ ἐπὶ πλέον λαμβάνωσι τὴν γνῶσιν τῶν παρ᾽ ἡμῶν εἰς αὐτοὺς κηρυχθέντων.

---

[36] See Beck, *KThL*, 496.

[37] See also the *Vita Nicetae Mediciensis* by Theosterictus (*BHG* 1341) in *AASS, Aprilis* I, Appendix, XXII-XXXIII, esp. XXIX ff.

[38] See R. Devreesse, *Codices Vaticani Graeci*, vol. II (Rome, 1937), 365.

[39] Vat. gr. 511, fol. 69ᵛ: Ταῦτα μὲν πνευματικοὶ ἡμῶν ἀδελφοὶ ἐκ πολλῶν ὀλίγα συλλέξαντες ἐκ περικοπῆς, ἐγράψαμεν ὑμῖν ἐν συντόμῳ· οὐδὲ γὰρ ἦν δυνατὸν οὔτε πάντας τοὺς θείους πατέρας μνημονεῦσαι, οὔτε (sic) τὰς βίβλους αὐτῶν καὶ τὰς μαρτυρίας καὶ τὰς χρήσεις πλατυτέρως γράψαι, ἀλλ᾽ ὅσον μόνον τὸν νοῦν ὑμῶν διεγείραι εἰς τὴν τοῦ Κυρίου ἀγάπην καὶ ἔχητε ἀπολογίαν πρὸς τοὺς ἐπερωτῶντας ὑμᾶς περὶ τῆς ἐν ἡμῖν ἐλπίδος. The last phrase of this conclusion may serve as an indication that this summary of a florilegium was compiled during the second period of Iconoclasm.

Ia. Vat. gr. 511, fol. 66ᵛ

Ἐν τῇ ἱστορίᾳ τοῦ μαρτυρίου τοῦ ἁγίου Παγκρατίου ἔστιν οὕτως· τέκνον Ἰωσήφ, ἐξένεγκε τὴν εἰκόνα τοῦ Κυρίου ἡμῶν Ἰησοῦ Χριστοῦ καὶ ἐν-τύπωσον αὐτὴν ἐν τῷ πυργίσκῳ, ἵνα ἰδόντες ἐπὶ πλέον (fol. 67) πιστεύσωσιν, ὁρῶντες τὸν τύπον τῆς μορφῆς αὐτοῦ καὶ ὑπόμνησιν λαμβάνωσι τῶν παρ᾽ ἡμῖν εἰς αὐτοὺς κηρυχθέντων.

II. Paris. gr. 1115, fol. 261ᵛ (quot. 86*)

Τοῦ ἁγίου Ἐπιφανίου· Μὴ γὰρ βασιλεὺς ἔχων εἰκόνα δύο βασιλεῖς εἰσίν, ἀλλ᾽ ὁ βασιλεὺς εἷς ἐστι καὶ μετά τῆς εἰκόνος.

IIa. Vat. gr. 511, fol. 68

Τοῦ ἁγίου Ἐπιφανίου· Μὴ γὰρ ὁ βασιλέως ἔχων εἰκόνα, δύο ἔχει βασιλεῖς; ἀλλ᾽ ὁ βασιλεὺς εἷς ἐστι καὶ μετὰ τῆς εἰκόνος.⁴⁰

(B) Quotations common to M and N

I. Mosqu. Hist. Mus. 265, fol. 238 (quot 47ᴹ)

Ἐκ τοῦ μαρτυρίου τοῦ ἁγίου Γρηγορίου Ἀρμενίας· . . . καὶ ἀντὶ τῶν ξύλων ἔπιξεν (sic) τὸν σταυρὸν ἐν μέσω τῆς οἰκουμένης, ἵνα οἱ ἐθισθέντες προσκυνεῖν τὰ ξύλα διὰ τοιαύτης συνηθείας πιστεύσωσιν προσκυνεῖν τὸν σταυρὸν αὐτοῦ καὶ τὴν ἐπάνω ἀνθρωπόμορφον εἰκόνα.

Ia. Vat. gr. 511, fol. 67ᵛ

Τοῦ ἁγίου Γρηγορίου τῆς Μεγάλης Ἀρμενίας· καὶ ἀντὶ τῶν ξύλων ἔπηξε τὸν σταυρὸν ἐν μέσω τῆς οἰκουμένης, ἵνα οἱ ἐθισθέντες προσκυνεῖν τὰ ξύλα διὰ τῆς τοιαύτης συνηθείας πιστεύσωσι προσκυνεῖν τὸν σταυρὸν καὶ τὴν ἐπάνω ἀνθρωπόμορφον εἰκόνα.⁴¹

II. Mosqu. Hist. Mus. 265, fol. 228ᵛ (quot. 25ᴹ)

Τοῦ αὐτοῦ (= ἁγ. Ἰωάννου τοῦ Χρυσοστόμου) ἐκ τῆς ἑρμηνίας τῆς παραβολῆς τοῦ σπόρου· ἔνδυμα βασιλεικὸν ἐὰν ὑβρίσῃς, οὐ τὸν ἐνδεδυμένον ὑβρίζεις; οὐκ οἶδας ὅτι ἐὰν εἰκόνα βασιλέως ὑβρίσῃς εἰς τὸν προτότυπον (sic) τῆς ἀξίας φέρῃς τὴν ὕβριν; οὐκ οἶδας ὅτι ἐὰν τὴν εἰκόνα τὴν ἀπὸ ξύλου ἢ ἀπὸ ἀνδριάντος χαλκοῦ κατασύρῃς, οὐχ ὡς εἰς ἄψυχον ὕλην τολμήσας κρίνεσαι, ἀλλ᾽ ὡς κατὰ βασιλέως κεχρημένος; εἰκόνα ὅλως βασιλέως φέρουσα τὴν ἑαυτῆς ὕβριν ὡς εἰς τὸν βασιλέα ἄγει.

---

⁴⁰ For a detailed analysis of this passage see below, pp. 177–78. Despite the textual differences between P and N, this particular version is attested only by P. A comparison of N with the other versions of this extract (below, p. 177) can easily prove that the text transmitted by the original of P stands behind the N version.

⁴¹ This is a fragment from the Greek translation of the Armenian *Vita* of St. Gregory the Illuminator by Agathangelos. The translation was possibly made in the 6th century (see Gero, *Constantine V,* 98 n. 147; also A. Kazhdan and H. Maguire, "Byzantine Hagiographical Texts as Sources on Art," *DOP* 45 [1991], 11 n. 94). It is extremely interesting that part of this quotation as it appears in M (but not the extract cited here) is also found in a much earlier Iconophile treatise of the 7th century written in Armenian by a certain Vrthanes (see Sirarpie Der Nersessian, "Une apologie des images du septième siècle," *Byzantion* 17 [1944–45], 61).

IIa. Vat. gr. 511, fol. 67ᵛ

Τοῦ αὐτοῦ· ἔνδυμα γὰρ βασιλικὸν ἐὰν ὑβρίσῃς τὸν τοῦτο ἐνδυόμενον ὑβρίζεις. Οὐκ οἶδας ὅτι ἐὰν εἰκόνα βασιλικὴν ὑβρίσῃς εἰς τὸ πρωτότυπον (fol. 68) τῆς ἀξίας ἀναφέρρεις τὴν ὕβριν; οὐκ οἶδας ὅτι ἐὰν εἰς εἰκόνα τὶς τὴν ἀπὸ ξύλου, οὐχ ὡς εἰς ἄψυχον ὕλην τολμήσας κρίνεται, ἀλλ᾽ ὡς κατὰ βασιλέως· εἰκὼν δὲ ὅλως φέρουσα τὴν ἑαυτῆς ὕβριν εἰς τὸν βασιλέα ἀνάγει. Πάντως καὶ ἡ εἰκὼν τοῦ Χριστοῦ ὑβριζομένη εἰς τὸν Χριστὸν ἀναφέρει τὴν ὕβριν.

(C) Quotations common to P, M, and N

I. Paris. gr. 1115, fol. 252 (quot. 56*)

Τοῦ αὐτοῦ (Ἰωάννου Χρυσοστ.), εἰς τὴν τεσσαρακοστὴν καὶ περὶ μετανοίας· πολλὰς πολλάκις εἶδον εἰκόνας καὶ γραφέας ἐθεασάμην χρώμασι τὴν ἀλήθειαν μιμουμένους καὶ χειρὶ καὶ τέχνῃ διασύροντας ἅπερ ἡ φύσις ἤγαγε, τουτέστιν ἡ ἀλήθεια.

Ia. Mosqu. Hist. Mus. 265, fol. 235ᵛ (quot. 40ᴹ)

Τοῦ αὐτοῦ ἐκ τοῦ λόγου τῆς τεσσαρακοστῆς· πολλὰς πολλάκης ἰδὼν εἰκόνας καὶ γραφαῖς ἐθεασάμην χρώμασιν τὴν ἀλήθειαν μιμουμένους καὶ χειρὶ καὶ τέχνῃ διασύρωντας ἅπερ ἡ φύσις εἰσήγαγεν τοῦ τέστιν ἡ ἀλήθεια.

Ib. Vat. gr. 511, fol. 68

Τοῦ αὐτοῦ· πολλὰς πολλάκις εἶδον εἰκόνας καὶ γραφέας ἐθεασάμην χρώμασι τὴν ἀλήθειαν μιμουμένους.

II. Paris. gr. 1115, fol. 253 (quot. 63*)

Τοῦ αὐτοῦ (= Κυρίλλου Ἀλεξ.), ἐκ τοῦ λόγου τοῦ εἰς μάρτυρας· πάλιν μαρτυρικῆς ἀνδραγαθείας τὰ γνωρίσματα λάμπουσιν· εἶδον κατὰ τοῖχον γραφῆς ἐναθλοῦσαν τοῖς σκάμμασι κόρην καὶ οὐκ ἀδακρυτὶ τὴν θέαν κατώπτευσα. Ταῦτα δέ μοι προὐξένησεν ἡ ἐντοιχογραφὴ διὰ χρωματουργίας τὴν ἀνδρίαν ὑφηγουμένη τῆς μάρτυρος.

IIa. Mosqu. Hist. Mus. 265, fol. 239ᵛ (quot. 50ᴹ)

Κυρίλλου ἀρχιεπισκόπου Ἀλεξανδρείας εἰς τὴν ὁσίαν μάρτυρα· πάλιν μαρτυρικῆς ἀνδραγαθίας τὰ γνωρίσματα λάμπουσιν· ἴδων ἐγὼ κατὰ τύχον γραφῆς ἐναθλοῦσαν τοῖς σκάμμασιν κόρην καὶ οὐκ ἀδακρυτὶ τὴν θέαν κατόπτευσα. καὶ μετ᾽ ὀλίγα· ταῦτα γὰρ προεξένισεν ἡ ἐντυχωγραφὴ διὰ χρωματουργίας τὴν ἀνδρίαν ὑφηγουμένη τῆς μάρτυρος.

IIb. Vat. gr. 511, fol. 68

Τοῦ αὐτοῦ· εἶδον ἐγὼ κατὰ τοίχου γραφὴν κόρην ἐναθλοῦσαν τοῖς σκάμμασι καὶ οὐκ ἀδακρυτὶ τὴν θέαν κατόπτευσα. καὶ αὖθις· ταῦτα γάρ μοι προεξένισεν ἡ ἐν τοίχῳ γραφὴ διὰ χρωματουργίας τὴν ἀνδρείαν ὑφηγουμένη τῆς μάρτυρος.

The divergences that in some examples mark the text of N can possibly be explained by the hypothesis that Nicetas had in his hands a copy of the original of P and M, which was the result of successive transcriptions. Apart from those common fragments, N also contains a small passage under the vague title Λεοντίου (fol. 68). It so happens that Nicetas has copied here a scholium from the first and second Iconophile florilegia of John of Damascus. As the scholium was inserted in a work of Leontius of Neapolis, the confusion is understandable.[42] Of enormous significance, however, is the fact that the source of N included also the two first florilegia of John of Damascus. (For more on this, see below in this chapter, especially section 4.)

Last but not least in this argument is a fourth florilegium which is more reliable than N. It is the Iconophile florilegium of Venetus Marcianus gr. 573 (9th cent., hereafter: V), which contains no less than fifty-three Iconophile quotations.[43] J. Pinard, in a study of some fragments of Dionysius the Areopagite common to both P and V (P 75*–77*, fols. 255ᵛ–256; V 20, fols. 6ᵛ–8), has proved beyond doubt that P and V draw independently of each other on the same archetype.[44]

Despite the presence of three very small pieces in V that may be a later interpolation[45] (a four-verse epigram of Germanus, a two-verse epigram by Tarasius, and a third one of four verses by Nicephorus: V 17–19, fol. 6ʳ⁻ᵛ),

---

[42] The text in the ms reads: N, fol. 68: Λεοντίου. Εἰ οὖν τοῦ σταυροῦ τὸν τύπον προσκυνοῦμεν, εἰκόνα σταυροῦ ποιοῦντες ἐξ οἱασοῦν ὕλης, τοῦ σταυρωθέντος τὴν εἰκόνα πῶς μὴ προσκυνήσωμεν. This is scholium I 55, II 51 of John of Damascus (see Kotter, *Schriften III*, 156). See also V. Déroche, "*L'Apologie contre les Juifs* de Léontios de Néapolis," *TM* 12 (1994), 49–50 n. 31.

[43] See E. Mioni, *Bibliothecae Divi Marci Venetiarum Codices Graeci Manuscripti*, vol. II (Rome, 1981), 476–78.

[44] To my knowledge, this study is still unpublished (cf. Munitiz, "Parisinus," p. 55). I would like to express my grateful thanks to Father Munitiz for his kind offices in gaining access to a copy of this study. Apart from the arguments produced by J. Pinard that were based on his textual study, I may add here some information that will further consolidate the overall dependence of V on the original of P and M: in addition to the eleven quotations examined by Pinard we can count another sixteen excerpts that offer a text identical with that of P word for word. (Quot. in App. IV 2 = 64*; 3 = 65*; 6 = 50*; 11 = 51*; 12 = 52*; 13 = 82*; 14 = 83*; 16 = 84*; 22 = 49*; 23 = 16*; 25 = 20*; 26 = 24*; 27 = 23*; 28 = 67*; 31 = 56*; 37 = 100*). On the other hand, for the relationship between V and M, the following piece of information is essential: the last work that is included in the florilegium of V (fols. 23ᵛ–26) is a treatise Περὶ ἀχειροποιήτων εἰκόνων, in which the anonymous author gives a brief description of nine icons. The passage concerning the third one reads as follows: (V, fol. 24): Ἡ ἐν Καμουλιανοῖς τῆς Καισαρείας ἀχειροποίητος τοῦ δεσπότου εἰκών, ἣν ἐξηγεῖται ὁ Νύσης Γρηγόριος ὑπάρχειν ἐν κιδάρει καθαρᾷ. The author had in mind the text offered only by Mosquensis Hist. Mus. 265, fols. 177ᵛ–182ᵛ (see App. III, 3ᴹ: Τοῦ ἁγίου Γρηγορίου ἐπισκόπου Νύσσης εἰς τὴν εὕρεσιν τῆς ἁγίας ἀχράντου ἀχειροποιήτου Καμουλιανῶν . . .).

[45] As suggested by a short scholium that introduces these epigrams and reads as follows: Venetus Marcianus gr. 573, fol. 6: Προσπαρέκουσαν οὖν βεβαίωσιν αὐτῶν τῶν ἁγίων εἰκόνων καὶ ἐπισφράγησιν τῶν ἐμαυτοῦ λόγων, καὶ ἑτέρων πατέρων ἰάμβια <u>εὑρημένα ἐν ἐκκλησίαις</u> ἐνθήσομαι.

the majority of the quotations can also be found in P.[46] Some of these quotations are common to P, M, and V.[47] From an approximate number of twelve fragments that do not occur in P, I can list the following two that are common to V and M:

1. Iohannes Chrys., *De parabola seminis,* V 44 (fol. 17ᵛ) = M 25ᴹ.

2. Sophronius, *Pratum Spirituale,* V 51 fols. 21–22 = M 23ᴹ.

Finally, the following piece appears only in V and the first Iconophile florilegium of John of Damascus (= Dam.):

1. Basilius Caesar., *Homilia dicta in Lacizis,* V 42, fol. 17ʳ⁻ᵛ = Dam. I 48 (transmitted solely by codex Athous Dionys. 175).[48]

And one more piece is common to V and the *Doctrina Patrum* alone:

2. Gregorius Nyss., *Encomium in s. Stephanum protomartyrem i,* V 47, fol. 18ʳ⁻ᵛ = *Doctrina,* ΜΕ' XI (= *PG* 46, 720c9–15).

On the evidence assembled above, it is reasonable to conclude that P, V, and M have drawn from the same (or from copies of the same) original, and that the extent of its Iconophile florilegium was larger than that preserved by each one of P, M, and V, and, perhaps, even larger than what the combination of P, V, M, chapter 45 of the *Doctrina Patrum,* and at least the first two florilegia of John of Damascus can offer.[49] Of course, this conclusion does not rule out the possibility of some of the items found in P, V, or M being later independent additions from other sources. Still, this might possibly

---

[46] As can be seen in Appendix V, quot. 1–16, 20–38, and 50 of Marcianus 573 fall into this category.

[47] These are the following nine quotations:

P 63* = M 50ᴹ = V 1 (fol. 2)

P 73* = M 37ᴹ = V 5 (fol. 3)

P 53* = M 26ᴹ = V 10 (fol. 4ʳ⁻ᵛ)

P 69* = M 52ᴹ = V 21 (fol. 8ᵛ)

P 55* = M 24ᴹ = V 30 (fol. 11ʳ⁻ᵛ)

P 56* = M 40ᴹ = V 31 (fol. 11ᵛ)

P 92* = M 38ᴹ = V 34 (fol. 12ʳ⁻ᵛ)

P 94* = M 49ᴹ = V 38 (fols. 15ᵛ–16)

P 96* = M 16ᴹ = V 50 (fol. 21)

[48] See Kotter, *Schriften III,* 153.

[49] Here we encounter yet another problem that M poses: quot. 29ᴹ–33ᴹ (32aᴹ excluded) deal in general with a different subject, that of the obligation of the orthodox Christian to avoid any contact with the heretics. A small collection appended to the florilegium of Nicetas of Medicion (Vat. gr. 511, fols. 68ᵛ–69ᵛ) comprises eleven quotations under the title Περὶ τοῦ μὴ συνοικεῖν τοῖς αἱρετικοῖς ἐκ τῶν διατάξεων τῶν ἁγίων ἀποστόλων. No quotation in M corresponds to any one in N, but Ignatius of Antioch and the *Constitutiones Apostolorum* are common to both. The question remains open whether the original of P, V, and M included a section with extracts on this particular issue or not.

apply to very few items preserved by P or V. In any case, it is permissible to speak of a common archetype (= F) of the Iconophile florilegia of P, M, and V that was composed in 770.

The most significant conclusion of this part of the study has to do, however, with the colophon of P. Since the *Adversus Iconoclastas* and F date from 770, it implies that the chronological indication provided by the colophon of P is correct on condition that one uses the Alexandrian era for the calculation of the year of P's original. And P's original, according to the colophon, dates to ͵ϛοξϛ´, which corresponds to the year 774/5. So PV (and possibly M) have not directly copied the τεῦχος of 770 but a slightly later apograph of it. Here it should be stressed that whenever I mention the original of P, V, and M (= F) I mean in fact the original (the τεῦχος as the author of *Adv. Iconoclastas* calls it) of 770 and not the actual exemplar of PV, which dates from 774/5.[50] This has been adopted for reasons of convenience and only for the third and fourth chapters.

The Two Letters of Pope Gregory II to Leo III

The assumption that P, V, and M copied partly overlapping parts of the same florilegium introduces an additional problem: M is one of the basic sources of the two letters of Pope Gregory II (715–731) to Emperor Leo III (JE 2180 and JE 2182, quot. 8[M] and 9[M], fols. 199[v]–208[v], 209–212[v]). J. Gouillard, the modern editor of these letters, has argued against their authenticity[51] and, with much skepticism, placed their composition in Constantinople "entre la fin du VIIIe siècle, . . . et la première moitié du IXe siècle," by an author who should have been "sans doute un moine ayant des lectures."[52] If Gouillard is right, then the only solution to that problem would be the hypothesis that these two letters were a later interpolation.

Gouillard, however, was a single case among a great number of scholars that have pronounced opinions for and against the authenticity of these two letters (plus a third one by the same pope addressed to Germanus [P, fols. 281[v]-283[v], quot. 133*]). In recent years serious research carried out by H. Grotz and H. Michels has placed the understanding of these letters on a better basis. First, Grotz, an advocate of the authenticity of these letters, presented significant arguments on behalf of their genuineness and, above all, made clear that the letters were originally written in Greek, possibly by

---

[50] For the exemplar of M the situation is a little more difficult because it certainly is different from the exemplar of PV.

[51] Gouillard, "Origines," 259–66.

[52] Ibid., 275–76.

Pope Gregory II himself.[53] Also, according to Grotz, their date has to be placed some time between 726 and 729.

On the other hand, Michels, who tried to refute some of the arguments of Grotz, places the fabrication of these letters in Constantinople. Even if in some cases his criticism of Grotz is plausible, the specific termini post quem he has been able to come up with do not go beyond the year 754,[54] while his vague connection of these two letters with the "anscheinend um 800 im Osten zirkulierenden Briefen" does not stand on firm ground. Therefore, even if the dating to the second half of the eighth century (and more specifically after 754)[55] of Michels is accepted, it still leaves much time before

---

[53] See H. Grotz, "Beobachtungen zu den zwei Briefen Papst Gregors II. an Kaiser Leo III.," *Archivum Historiae Pontificiae* 18 (1980), 9–40. The original language and the authorship of the letters is discussed on pp. 14–20, after a brief recapitulation of the existing bibliography on the subject (ibid., 9–14). Grotz further argued that (a) the word Σεπτέτον, which has been one of the main supports of the inauthenticity of the first letter, can be dismissed as a scribal error (ibid., 20–22); (b) two passages, the first of which displays wrong chronological indications and the second of which alludes to later events (capture of Ravenna in 751), are obviously later interpolations by an unknown "Glossator" (ibid., 22–27); (c) for the existence of correspondence between Gregory II and Leo III we have the witness of the *Epistula Synodica* (Mansi XII 1060 ff) and of the *Hadrianum* (*MGH, Epp.* 5, 55–57) of Pope Hadrian I (ibid., 27–30); and (d) the image of Edessa mentioned in the first *epistula* which, according to Gouillard ("Origines," 263 ff), came to the knowledge of the Romans after 767, was actually known at Rome much earlier (Grotz, op. cit., 37–38). See also idem, "Weitere Beobachtungen zu den zwei Briefen Papst Gregors II. an Kaiser Leo III.," *Archivum Historiae Pontificiae* 24 (1986), 365–75, and "Die früheste römische Stellungnahme gegen den Bildersturm (Eine These, die es zu beweisen gilt)," *AHC* 20 (1988), 150–61, where Grotz elaborates further on some arguments he first presented in his 1980 article and especially on the meaning of the words Σεπτέτον and συλλαβή. For an exhaustive study and recapitulation of the problems concerning the letters of Pope Gregory and for further bibliography, see P. Conte, *Regesto delle lettere dei Papi del secolo VIII, Saggi* (Milan, 1984), 46–79.

[54] H. Michels, "Zur Echtheit der Briefe Papst Gregors II. an Kaiser Leon III." *ZKG* 99, (1988), 390.

[55] Ibid., 391 and 390. The latest terminus post quem proposed by Michels is based on some lines in both letters, in which the Pope speaks of his plans to visit the "inner West." Michels associates this information with the visit of Pope Stephen II to the Franks that took place in 754. The connection is a little thin on the ground, because Pope Gregory II could also have planned a visit to Northern Europe in the context of his intensive proselytizing activities directed through Boniface to Bavaria and other neighboring Frankish areas (see J. N. D. Kelly, *The Oxford Dictionary of Popes* [Oxford, 1986], 87). As far as the capture of Ravenna is concerned, it is worth noting that neither Michels nor Grotz mention an earlier fall of this city to the Lombards which, however, did not last long. I see no reason why this should not be the event alluded to in the letter. The only problem is that the details are rather confusing in the sources and earlier historians had placed this incident in 729, but recent research shifted it a decade later to the papacy of Gregory III. (737 to 740 with 738 as the best estimate; see T. F. X. Noble, *The Republic of St. Peter, The Birth of the Papal State 680–825* [Philadelphia, 1984], 41–42 and n. 131 for further bibliography and primary sources). I wish to thank Professor W. Treadgold for bringing this historical incident to my attention.

the year 770 which I have postulated as the date of the compilation of F. (I will return to these letters below in section 4.)

The *Adversus Constantinum Caballinum* and the Νουθεσία γέροντος περὶ τῶν ἁγίων εἰκόνων

Starting from the assumption that P, V, and M contain parts of the same florilegium, I should attempt to give an answer to a different problem: what is the relationship of the *Adversus Constantinum Caballinum* (= *CC, BHG* 1387f) with the Νουθεσία. Of course a complete answer can be given only on the basis of a critical edition of *CC* which does not exist. Here I set out some basic considerations on the problem and only up to the point that P and M are involved, in the hope of undertaking a critical edition of *CC* in the near future.

We may recall that the Νουθεσία, written by a certain monk(?) called Theosebes, occurs only in M,[56] while *CC*, which is often attributed to John of Damascus, exists in a number of manuscripts in several recensions.[57] What appears in *PG* 95, 309A–344B is the longer recension of *CC* composed, possibly, after the death of Constantine V and before the seventh ecumenical council of Nicaea (780–787).[58] This version (= *BHG* 1387e) is not of particular relevance, since it is included in various manuscripts[59] with no connection whatsoever to any Iconophile florilegium.

The first to present a thorough study on the relationship of the *CC* with the Νουθεσία was B. M. Melioranskij, but, regrettably, he lacked any means of access to P. All he had at his disposal was the longer recension in Migne, which led him to very complicated conclusions, culminating in the postulation of three (or four) different versions of the same text.[60]

On the other hand, he noticed that the Νουθεσία was divided into three parts which he dated to different periods: 765–775 for the first and 750–754

---

[56] Text in M, fols. 142–171ᵛ. In addition to the edition of Melioranskij, *Georgij*, V–XXXIX, there is a new, rather improved, one by A. Misides, Ἡ παρουσία τῆς Ἐκκλησίας Κύπρου εἰς τὸν ἀγῶνα ὑπὲρ τῶν εἰκόνων (Leukosia, 1989), 153–92. For a further discussion of the dating and other problems of the Νουθεσία, see Gero, *Constantine V*, 25–36.

[57] See, for example, Gero, *Leo III*, 63 n. 12. For other manuscripts see *BHG* 1378f–g and *BHG Nuov. Auct.* 1378f–g. Also J. Noret, "Le palimpseste 'Parisinus gr. 443'," *AB* 88 (1970), 149.

[58] See Melioranskij, *Georgij*, 31.

[59] Bodleianus 274 (= Bodl. Roe 28), Caesareus 144 (= Vindob. Theol. gr. 10), and Regius 1829 (= Paris. gr. 767), according to Combefis, the first editor. See his introduction to the edition in *Auctar. Biblioth. PP Gr.*, vol. II, reprinted in *PG* 95, 305–8. The text in the *PG* edition is divided into twenty-four paragraphs of unequal length. For a complete but not so clear analysis of this version, see Speck, *Kaiser Konstantin*, 321–440.

[60] See Melioranskij, *Georgij*, 77–84 and esp. the stemma on p. 87.

for the other two.[61] It is to his credit, also, that he gave a complete list of passages common to *CC* and the Νουθεσία. He actually discovered twelve passages with literal similarities and ten with looser ones, all occurring in the second and third parts of the Νουθεσία.[62]

The conclusions of Melioranskij can be summarized as follows. The *Urtext* has to be traced in parts II and III of the Νουθεσία, which were probably written before 754, since no allusion to the Council of Hiereia exists therein. The text of the Νουθεσία, as it is transmitted by M, is a later version (ca. 770) of the pre-754 text with the addition of the introductory part I, which was possibly written in 765–775.

As far as *CC* is concerned, Melioranskij suggested that the recension found in M—the very codex of the Νουθεσία—was a reworked version of the Νουθεσία. The text of *CC* as it is in P was a rehash of M made in 774, subsequently reordered and updated in the form of the extended version of *PG* in 780–786. Unfortunately, very few of the suggestions of Melioranskij are of any value today, and the whole work has to be repeated from the beginning.

To start with, putting aside the *ex silentio* argument for the early dating of parts II and III of the Νουθεσία, the parallel passages cannot prove in themselves the priority of the Νουθεσία over the P version of *CC*. Some of the passages in *CC* seem to be an elaboration of their counterparts in the Νουθεσία. Compare, for example:

Νουθεσία (M, fol. 149^v)

κατανόησον τοὺς ἐπὶ γῆς βασιλεύοντας· τοὺς ἀτιμάζοντας αὐτῶν τὰς εἰκόνας οὐχὶ κεφαλικῆς αὐτοὺς ἀξιοῖ τιμωρίας;

CC (*PG* 95, 317в)

πολλάκις ἄφρων ἄνθρωπος, ἐὰν εὑρεθῇ ἐμπτύων τὴν εἰκόνα τοῦ ἐπιγείου βασιλέως, τί πανθάνει (sic); οὐ κεφαλικῆς τιμωρίας ἀξιοῦται;

CC (P, fol. 241)

ἐὰν εὑρεθῇ ἄνθρωπος ἐμπτύων τὴν εἰκόνα τοῦ ἐπιγείου βασιλέως οὐχὶ κεφαλικὴν τιμωρίαν ὑποκείσεται.

Some other passages, however, seem to abridge what the Νουθεσία presents. Compare:

Νουθεσία (M, fol. 146^v)

φανεροῖ τοῦτον τοῦ ἁγίου Πνεύματος ἡ φάσις, ἡ διὰ Δαβὶδ τοῦ προφήτου λέγουσα· τὰ εἴδωλα τῶν ἐθνῶν ἀργύριον καὶ χρυσίον ἔργα χειρῶν

---

[61] Ibid., 33.
[62] Ibid., 4–14.

ἀνθρώπων· στόμα ἔχουσιν καὶ οὐ λαλήσουσιν· ὀφθαλμοὺς ἔχουσιν καὶ οὐκ ὄψονται . . .

CC (PG 95, 324в = P, fol. 243ᵛ)

Θέλεις εἰπεῖν κατὰ τὸν προφήτην Δαβίδ· τὰ εἴδωλα τῶν ἐθνῶν ἀργύ-ριον καὶ χρυσίον, ἔργα χειρῶν ἀνθρώπων· στόμα ἔχουσι καὶ οὐ λαλήσουσι καὶ τὰ ἑξῆς . . .

For more examples one can always go back to the detailed list of parallel passages drawn up by Melioranskij.[63] One caveat, however: P is on many occasions different from what the *PG*-Melioranskij text provides. Therefore, the only thing that these correspondences can prove is the interdependence of the two works and nothing else.

A comparison of the P and M versions of *CC* reveals the following: In both P and M are missing paragraphs 1, 8, 10, 12, and 18–24 of the *PG* version; hence, at first sight, P and M offer the same version. The text itself appears to support this observation. On fols. 239–240 line 9 of P and fols. 192ᵛ–193ᵛ of M, the differences are not of great importance; P omits words that appear in M and vice versa. Then, M omits the text that is included in fols. 240 line 10–241 line 11 of P, a loss that ought to be attributed to the disappearance of a page from M.

From fol. 195 of M the divergences between P and M are more weighty. M seems to adopt expressions and words of a lower style than that of P. Compare:

(A) P, fol. 243

Πάλιν ὡς οἶμαι ἀντερεῖς μοι ὅτι οἱ πατέρες τῆς ἕκτης συνόδου οἱ συμ-παραγενάμενοι, ἑτέρας βλασφημίας καὶ αἱρέσεις ἀναφυούσας, καταλῦσαι καὶ ἀφανίσαι ἔσπευδον, καὶ περὶ τούτων οὐκ ηὐκαίρεισαν·

M, fol. 195ᵛ

Θέλεις εἰπεῖν ὅτι οἱ πατέρες τῶν ἐξ συνόδων ἄλλας βλασφημίας καὶ αἱρέσεις ἐπολεμοῦσαν καταλῦσαι καὶ περὶ τούτου οὐκευκέρισαν· (sic).

(B) P, fol. 243

μὴ οἱ πατέρες οὐ προσεκύνουν αὐτάς·

M, fol. 196

Ἀλλ᾽ ἐρ⟨ε⟩ῖς μοι ὅτι οἱ πατέρες οὐδὲ προσεκυνοῦσαν (sic) αὐτά, οὐδὲ εἶχαν αὐτὰ εἰς ψῆφον.

(C) P, fol. 244ᵛ

κελεύεις θανάτῳ ὑποπίπτειν καὶ τὸν προσκυνήσαντα καὶ τὸν προσ-κυνηθέντα;

---

[63] Ibid.

M, fol. 197
κελεύεις ἀποθνίσκει (sic) καὶ ὁ προσκυνηθεὶς καὶ ὁ προσκυνήσας;

Strangely enough, M comes again much closer to P after fol. 197ᵛ line 6 (ἄρτι εἰπέ μοι . . .), and the differences become smoother, like the ones occurring in the first folia of the work in both manuscripts.

Another very important difference between P and M is that on fols. 241ᵛ line 7–242ᵛ line 6 from the bottom P gives a very extended (interpolated) passage that is missing, not only from M, but also from the longer version of Migne. What is more, this extended passage of P concludes with a short paragraph from the second *Oratio contra imaginum calumniatores* of John of Damascus.[64] But this is not the only fragment of John of Damascus that is interpolated in the P version of *CC*. A little further on in fol. 243ᵛ, line 8 from the bottom, the P version of *CC* introduces an extensive answer to the Iconoclast refusal to venerate handmade objects (ἐγὼ χειροποιητὰ οὐ προσκυνῶ). The first seven lines sound almost like fragments from paragraph 15 of the first *Oratio* of John of Damascus, but the following twenty lines (P, fol. 243ᵛ line 2 from the bottom: ἐγὼ δὲ οὐ προσκυνῶ τῇ ὕλῃ . . . to fol. 244, line 18: καὶ τῶν φίλων Χριστοῦ) are lifted word for word from paragraph 14 of the second *Oratio* of John of Damascus.[65] M, on the other hand, devotes to the subject just four lines which roughly correspond to the two concluding lines of this paragraph in P. The Migne version of *CC* is also different (*PG* 95, 325A–C).

Finally, the P version of *CC* may also have been the introductory piece to an earlier version of the Iconophile florilegium, and there are some arguments in favor of this. First, *CC*, apart from the fragment of John of Damascus, presents six Iconophile *testimonia* that exist in the Iconophile florilegium;[66] second, there are some indirect allusions to the works of the church fathers,[67] and the work closes with a straightforward admonition to the Christians to investigate the holy scripture and the traditions of the fathers,[68] a topic that had been further elaborated by the author of the *Adversus Iconoclastas*, as has already been demonstrated.

The fact that the author of the P version of *CC* had already at his dis-

[64] It is paragraph II 16 as found in Kotter, *Schriften III*, 111.1–6, 112.33–113.63 (Paris. gr. 1115, fol. 242ᵛ, lines 16–30: Οὐ μόνον δὲ γράμμασι . . . τί περὶ τὰς εἰκόνας σμικρολογεῖτε;).

[65] Kotter, *Schriften III*, 104–5, par. II 14.12–34.

[66] These are extracts from quot. 16*, 25*, 52*, 54*, 55*, and 94* of P.

[67] Cf. P, fol. 244ᵛ: Ἄρτι εἰπέ μοι τίνι ἐξακολουθήσωμεν, τῶν θεοφόρων ⟨πατέρων⟩ ἢ τῶν σαλσικαρίων; εἰπέ μοι τίνος ἐπακούσωμεν, τὸν ἅγιον Βασίλειον . . . ἢ τὸν Παστιλλᾶ, . . . τὸν ἅγιον Ἰωάννην τὸν Χρυσόστομον . . . etc.

[68] Cf. P, fol. 245: Ἐγὼ παρακαλῶ ὑμᾶς ἵνα ἀνανήψωμεν . . . καὶ ἐρευνῶμεν τὰς θείας γραφὰς καὶ τὰς παραδόσεις τῶν πατέρων . . .

posal a florilegium in which the second *Sermo contra imaginum calumniatores* of John of Damascus was included has some very significant implications. First, it offers one further argument in support of the theory that P and M copied partly overlapping pieces of the same original[69] since the second *Sermo* is included only in M (quot. 4^M–7^M, fols. 182^v–192 and 32a^M, fols. 230–233).[70] Furthermore, the second homily of John of Damascus, at least, along with its florilegium was known at Rome before 770, since P is a Roman product, as has already been said and will further be proved below.

From the comparisons made above, we may conclude that there are only two basic versions of *CC:* the shorter one that is represented by P and M and which dates from 766 to 770[71] and the longer one (*PG* 95, 309A–344B) which is a little later (780–787).

It has already been explained that the only certain aspect, as far as the relationship between the Νουθεσία and *CC* is concerned, lies in their interdependence. What, in addition, becomes apparent from the investigation of M and P is that not only *CC*, but also the Νουθεσία presuppose the existence of a florilegium from which they draw quotations and either incorporate parts of or elaborate on some phrases extracted from them. In the Νουθεσία this dependence is more evident simply because there are more quotations embedded in it[72] than in *CC*. If the theory of Melioranskij is accepted, then we should also accept that a great part of the Iconophile florilegium was already compiled before 754, which is not impossible.

The other possibility that has to be checked by the future editor of *CC*

---

[69] The fact that there are textual differences between P and M can easily be explained if one accepts that M belongs to a different line of transmission of a common original, something that I have already suggested for the florilegium of Nicetas of Medicion.

[70] Quot. 32a^M offers a part of the second *Sermo* which corresponds to paragraphs II 10.8–14.14 (ἐν μὲν γὰρ—δι' ἐμὲ γενάμενον) of Kotter's edition. This passage has escaped the attention of the editor and should be added to the general description of the manuscripts, Kotter, *Schriften III*, 36. See also Darrouzès, "Deux textes inédits," 6.

[71] This version provides paragraphs (or part of paragraphs) 2–7, 9, 11, 13–17, and 25 of the *PG* recension. For a third version of *CC* with different desinit see *BHG* 1387g.

[72] In the Νουθεσία there occur the following quotations: 17* = 14^M, 52* = 51^M, 54* = 41^M, 63* = 50^M, 94* = 49^M, 104* = 46^M, 66*, 132*, 18^M, and 97*. The last quotation offers a very clear indication that the texts of the Iconophile florilegium, as they appear in P, do not reflect in some cases the extent of the quotation in its original form. To be exact, quot. 97* is common to P, the Νουθεσία, and the acts of the seventh ecumenical council (= Mansi XIII 160D–161E). It is the *Epistula ad Iustinum imp.* of Symeon, the younger Stylite (*CPG* 7366). Mansi preserves the text of the entire letter, P gives what corresponds to Mansi XIII 161A.9–B.5, while in the Νουθεσία is included another fragment corresponding to Mansi XIII 161C.1–9. Evidently the original of 770 included the whole of the letter. On the other hand, the presence of this extract along with quot. 66* and 132* in the Νουθεσία is a further proof that the original Iconophile florilegium of 770 included at least all the extracts in P and M, since these three quotations do occur in P but not in M.

is that of the priority of *CC* over the Νουθεσία. In such a case, the original version of *CC* accompanied by a massive florilegium—which certainly included, among other texts, the second *Sermo contra imaginum calumniatores* of St. John of Damascus and a considerable portion of its florilegium—was in existence some time after 766 and before 770. It then implies that all three parts of the Νουθεσία were written after 770 (or, at least, after 766), something that is established only for its first part.[73]

Finally, it has been shown that an earlier version of the Iconophile florilegium of the original of 770 included a number of quotations and *CC,* perhaps as an introductory piece. This corpus of quotations was extant after 766. Then, in 770, it was probably enlarged and completed at Rome by the author of the *Adversus Iconoclastas,* who added his work as a general preface to the whole florilegium.

Since the Νουθεσία—if we are to believe its closing paragraph[74]—seems to have been written in Syria, the following theory might be taken into consideration. After 770 and before 775 a copy of the τεῦχος created by the author of the *Adversus Iconoclastas* traveled to Palestine. There the author of the Νουθεσία (a certain Θεοσεβής), after having completed the selection of pieces from that copy, added the Νουθεσία at the beginning of this abridged edition of the τεῦχος, as an introduction to the, so to speak, Oriental version of the τεῦχος of 770, which in fact is the florilegium of M. The problem, of course, with this theory is that it cannot definitely exclude the original possibility of the priority of the Νουθεσία over the P version of *CC.* The reason is that the theory of the priority of the Νουθεσία has the advantage of conforming to the usual pattern of the transmission of texts: from the East (Jerusalem, Damascus, and so on) to the West (Rome).[75] But, still, we have no indication whatsoever that the Νουθεσία was known at Rome. So the question remains open for the editor of these two works, but, for the time being, the most plausible suggestion that can be offered is the following. Assuming that in 766–770 there was an Iconophile florilegium that included the P version of *CC* as its introductory piece, the Νουθεσία looks like a cut-and-paste work of somebody who used this florilegium *and CC.* The opposite is impossible because, while M transmits the Νουθεσία *and CC,* P preserves *only*

---

[73] P. Speck, also, thinks that the Νουθεσία cannot be the original of *CC* (Speck, *Kaiser Konstantin,* 342), and postulates an earlier version of *CC* as the original of both. However, he has gone as far as to suggest that the *Urtext* of *CC* and of the Νουθεσία was an Iconoclastic work, converted later to an Iconophile one (ibid., 347).

[74] See Melioranskij, *Georgij,* xxxix.

[75] See Sansterre, *Les moines grecs,* 177–79 and passim.

CC and there is no reason to assume that the Roman original of PV included the Νουθεσία.

4. The Original of P, M, and V (= F) and Other Florilegia

The Florilegium of the Roman Councils of 731 and 769

Chapter I, section 8 of this study presented a list of the quotations included in the acts of the Iconophile councils at Rome in 731 and 769.[76] This list contains twenty-five quotations, three from the Bible (nos. 1, 2, 5), five from Latin fathers (nos. 3, 4, 11, 14, and 22), and seventeen from Greek fathers (nos. 6–10, 12, 13, 15–25).[77]

The Greek version of these seventeen extracts is also included in PV and M. Extracts 13 and 15–25 on the list are examined in detail below in section 5 of this chapter. Here I will concentrate only on extracts 6–10 and 12.

6. Ps.-Athanasius, *Quaestiones ad Antiochum ducem* (*CPG* 2257), *PG* 28, 621A–D

This fragment is included in a snippet of the acts of the Roman Synod of 769 that has been recently edited by L. Böhringer.[78] This edition added the missing parts of that fragment, which appears to be much more extensive than the seven lines provided by the *Hadrianum*.[79] P (fols. 253ᵛ–254, quot. 70*) and the *Doctrina Patrum* (*Doctrina*, 327.11–328.22) offer the Greek original on which the Latin translation was based, while John of Damascus (*Schriften III*, 169, III 59) transmits almost half of the same Greek fragment. There is no doubt that the *Doctrina*-P Greek version is behind the Latin translation of this fragment. Of course, there are some textual differences, most of which can be traced in the first lines of the fragment. Compare:

(1) P, fol. 253ᵛ
Τοῦ αὐτοῦ ἐκ τῆς πρὸς ἀντίοχον δοῦκα διαλέξεως καὶ ἐρωτήσεως κεφάλαιον (?) ρλζ´.

Doctrina, 327.11–12
Ἐκ τῶν γραφέντων ρ´ κεφαλαίων πρὸς Ἀντίοχον τὸν ἄρχοντα κατὰ πεῦσιν καὶ ἀπόκρισιν κεφάλαιον λη´. (= same as John of Damascus *Schriften III*, III 59.1–2)

---

[76] See above, pp. 39–40. References will be made to this list.
[77] See their concordance with quotations of other florilegia in Appendix V.
[78] See above, Chapter I, p. 38 n. 173 and p. 39 n. 178.
[79] *Hadrianum*, 31.29–32.1; for the text of the new edition, see L. Böhringer, "Zwei Fragmente," 102–3.

Böhringer ed., 102
Interrogacio Antiochi ad sanctum Athanasium propter imaginem.

(2) P, fol. 253ᵛ-*Doctrina*, 327.13–15
(Ἐρώτησις add. *Doctr.*) Τοῦ θεοῦ διὰ τῶν προφητῶν ἐπιτρέποντος μὴ προσκυνεῖν χειροποίητα, διατί προσκυνοῦμεν τὰς εἰκόνας καὶ τὸν σταυρὸν ἔργα τεκτόνων ὑπάρχοντα, καθὼς καὶ τὰ εἴδωλα τυγχάνουσιν; (–οντα *Doctr.*)

Böhringer ed., 102
Quomodo lex et prophete dicentes "Statuas et similitudines non adoretis," quomodo vos facitis imaginem et adoratis eam?

For the rest of the text there is an almost word-for-word correspondence between the *Doctrina*-P Greek versions and the Latin translation. Even some words that are missing from the Migne edition[80] of the Greek text are provided by P, the *Doctrina*, or even John of Damascus. If Böhringer had taken into account these versions, her edition would have been more complete, and it would have saved her the following error. Compare:

P, fol. 253ᵛ-*Doctrina*, 328.7–8
πῶς βέλος (βέλος om. P) δεξαμένη ἁγίου ἄψυχος στήλη (εἰκὼν P), ὡς ἔνσωμος (ἔμψυχος: P) φύσις αἷμα παραδόξως ἐξήγαγε.

London, British Library Add. 16413, fol. 4ᵛ
Quomodo autem framea suscipiens sanctis sine anima imago sicut corporalis natura sanguinem glorificae produxit.

PG 28, 621ʙ
πῶς βέλος δεξαμένη ἄψυχος στήλη, ὡς ἐνσώματος φύσις αἷμα παραδόξως ἐξήγαγεν;

Böhringer ed., 103
Quomodo autem frameam [Böhr.: framea *L*] suscipiens [Böhr.: *folgt sinnloses* sanctis] sine anima . . . etc.

This fragment yields some interesting conclusions. The first is that we can safely assume that the *Hadrianum* as a source for the acts of the 731 and 769 Roman synods is a rather poor one and what is found in there should usually be the minimum one could expect. The second conclusion gives us the terminus ante quem for the *Doctrina*-P version of the Greek fragment, which is the year 731. The fact also that John of Damascus (III 59) provides less than this fragment is an indication that either the critical edition of Kot-

[80] Böhringer, "Zwei Fragmente," 102: "filios nostros" and "dilectionem animae nostrae demonstremus."

ter needs further improvements or that John of Damascus already copied other florilegia and not actual books.

7. Dionysius Areopagita, *Epistula ad Iohannem theologum* (*CPG* 6613), *Corpus Dionysiacum II*, 208.6–10

This particular fragment does not occur in P, and the *Hadrianum* transmits a somewhat more extensive excerpt than the single line provided by John of Damascus (*Schriften III*, 144, III 43) and the *Doctrina* (326.26–29). Although this passage is missing from PVM, it is interesting to note that P and V share a group of eleven excerpts from the *De ecclesiastica hierarchia* and the *De coelesti hierarchia* (P, fols. 255ᵛ–256, quot. 75*–77*; V, fols. 6ᵛ–8ᵛ, quot. 20). P in addition provides three much more extensive portions from the *De coelesti hierarchia* (P, fols. 256–258ᵛ, quot. 78*–80*) which include a considerable number of the previous eleven short excerpts. This is a peculiarity of P which possibly implies that the compiler (of 770 or of 731?) had, side by side, the florilegium and the complete books of Ps.-Dionysius. Now, since the *Hadrianum* quotation is more extensive than the *Doctrina*-John of Damascus one, it is permissible to hypothesize that the 731 synod used the books of Dionysius that also served as a source for the Dionysian collection of P.

8. Dionysius Areopagita, *De coelesti hierarchia* (*CPG* 6600), *Corpus Dionysiacum II*, 8.15–9.2

The *Hadrianum* gives a very poor translation of the passage indicated above (καὶ τὰς εἰρημένας . . . τῆς νοητῆς διαδόσεως). On the other hand, M (fol. 225ᵛ, quot. 18ᴹ) is the only apograph of F that has preserved the same passage but not exactly the same lines. The passage in M corresponds to *Corpus Dionysiacum II*, 8.14–21 (Διὸ τὴν ὁσιωτάτην . . . χειραγωγία χρήσοιτο). It is obvious that both the 731 synod and M utilized a more extensive part of the same passage.

9. Cyrillus Alexandrinus, *Thesaurus de sancta et consubstantiali Trinitate* (*CPG* 5215), *PG* 75, 184ᴅ

For this fragment "de sermone sancti Cyrilli Alexandrini episcopi," K. Hampe, the editor of the *Hadrianum*, notes that "hunc locum in Cyrilli operibus non inveni." Compare, however, the Latin text with the first part of quot. 67*, which is also provided by V, fol. 10ᵛ (quot. 28):

Hadrianum, 33.12–14
Quemadmodum imaginem quis designata iucunda respexit, mirabitur quidem regis figura, et quae illo apparet: haec et ejus noscens conscriptionem pariter cernens delectabitur, ut ipsum regem aspiciat etc.

Paris. gr. 1115, fol. 253

Τοῦ αὐτοῦ ἐκ τῶν θησαυρῶν ιβ΄ κεφαλαίου· ῞Ωσπερ ἄν τις εἰς εἰκόνα διαγεγραμμένην ἄριστα βλέποι καὶ ἀποθαυμάζοι μὲν τὸ τοῦ βασιλέως σχῆμα
καὶ ὅσαπερ ἐν ἐκείνῳ φαίνεται, ταῦτα καὶ ἐν τῇ γραφῇ δυνάμενός τε καὶ
ἔχων ὁρᾶν εἰς ἐπιθυμίαν ἔλθοι τοῦ καὶ αὐτὸν ἰδεῖν τὸν βασιλέα.

The lemma in P is more precise than in the *Hadrianum* and helps to
locate the extract in *PG* 75, 184D6 ff. Although the Latin fragment is a
clumsy translation of the Greek text, there should be no doubt that its actual
source was the original of PV and M. Thus we can be sure that this quotation, like no. 6 above, belongs to a part of the florilegium that was certainly
earlier than the year 731.

10. Gregorius Nazianzenus, *Oratio* 45 *in Sanctum Pascha* (*CPG* 3010.45),
PG 36, 637A

This is the only patristic *testimonium* from the 731 and 769 synods for
which I have not been able to find the Greek original among the quotations
of any Iconophile florilegium. This could be an indication that the florilegium of 731 was already very extensive.

12. *Preces clericorum et monachorum ad Iohannem CPolitanum et synodum*
(*CPG* 9329.6), *ACO* III, 60.35–61.3

P (fols. 269ᵛ–270, quot. 104*) and M (fols. 237ᵛ–238, quot. 46ᴹ) preserve
the same passage from the acts of the Constantinopolitan Synod of 536.

These fragments are a good testimony to the existence, already before 731,
of a florilegium of Greek Iconophile quotations, many (if not all) of which
had been translated into Latin for the needs of the 731 synod. Unfortunately it is impossible to decide about the extent of this florilegium and
whether the compiler of 770 added new fragments to or removed already
existing ones from this early anthology in order to complete his τεῦχος. A
very important conclusion that follows is that the production of Iconophile
florilegia started in the first moments of the Iconoclastic controversy, possibly throughout the Christian world, but certainly in Rome and Palestine.
As for Rome, I have already given a precedent for this practice: the case of
the florilegium on the procession of the Holy Spirit (above, pp. 76–77 and
esp. pp. 84–85).

It is fitting in this context to examine some aspects of the two letters of Pope
Gregory II to Emperor Leo III (above, pp. 108–10) and of his letter to
Patriarch Germanus I.

On condition that their genuineness is accepted, the two letters to Leo

III present some good evidence for the fact that the bibliographic preparation of the Iconophiles had started as early as 726–729. More specifically, the first initiative for and the initial undertakings of such an enterprise can be traced in the following passage of the first letter:

Gouillard, "Origines," 279.30–40

Καὶ ἔγραψας (sc. Leo III) ὅτι οὐ δεῖ προσκυνεῖν χειροποίητα καὶ πᾶν εἶδος καθ᾽ ὁμοίωμα καθὼς εἶπεν ὁ Θεός, μήτε ἐν οὐρανῷ μήτε ἐπὶ τῆς γῆς, καὶ ὅτι πληροφόρησόν με τίς ἡμῖν παρέδωκε σέβεσθαι καὶ προσκυνεῖν τοῦ Θεοῦ νομοθετοῦντος μὴ προσκυνεῖν χειροποίητα; . . . (line 36) Ὅμως σὺ ἀπώσω καὶ ἠρνήσω καὶ ἐξέβαλες ἔξω τοὺς ἁγίους ἡμῶν πατέρας καὶ διδασκάλους οὓς ἰδιοχείρως καὶ ἐγγράφως ὡμολόγησας πείθεσθαι καὶ ἀκολουθεῖν. Ἡ γραφὴ ἡμῶν καὶ τὸ φῶς καὶ ἡ σωτηρία ἡμῶν οἱ ἅγιοι καὶ θεοφόροι πατέρες καὶ διδάσκαλοι ἡμῶν τυγχάνουσι, καὶ αἱ ἐν Χριστῷ ἓξ σύνοδοι παρέδωκαν ἡμῖν, καὶ οὐ παραδέχῃ αὐτῶν τὰς μαρτυρίας.

It is clear in the above passage that Leo III in one of his letters to Gregory II, among other things, expressed the belief that Christians should not worship handmade objects. The answer of the pope implies that he had already consulted the scriptures, patristic literature, and the acts of the six ecumenical councils on the subject (the relevant words are underscored above) and had found that there was no such prohibition in them. The compilation of an Iconophile florilegium is the most likely event that lies behind these words, since this is the only way the pope could respond to the demand of Leo III: καὶ ὅτι πληροφόρησόν με τίς ἡμῖν παρέδωκε σέβεσθαι καὶ προσκυνεῖν τοῦ Θεοῦ νομοθετοῦτος μὴ προσκυνεῖν χειροποίητα; . . .

In the second letter, Gregory cites the names of some of the ecclesiastical authorities whose works openly support the veneration of images (Gouillard, "Origines," 299.289–292):

ἆρα φρονιμώτεροί εἰσι Γρηγορίου τοῦ θαυματουργοῦ ἢ Γρηγορίου τοῦ Νυσσαέως καὶ Γρηγορίου τοῦ θεολόγου καὶ Βασιλείου Καππαδοκίας ἢ Ἰωάννου τοῦ Χρυσοστόμου, ἵνα μὴ γράψω τῶν μυρίων μυριάδων τῶν ὁμοίων ἐκείνων ἁγίων καὶ θεοφόρων πατέρων ἡμῶν καὶ διδασκάλων.

It is really striking that Gregory II begins the list of Iconophile fathers with the name of Gregory of Neocaesarea (Θαυματουργός). Gregory of Neocaesarea contributed to the whole Iconophile literature just two spurious quotations (P, fol. 251ᵛ, quot. 49*–50*; also V, quot. 22 and 6), which, in addition, were never officially used by the seventh ecumenical council. There is no doubt, therefore, that these two quotations were known in Rome even before the Synod of 731. Moreover, Gouillard has correctly indicated that on some occasions, and especially in the first letter, there are some references to Iconophile fragments that were included in F.[81]

More rich in quotations, however, is the third letter of Gregory II to Patriarch Germanus I (JE 2181).[82] This letter has also been studied by Gouillard ("Origines," 246–51 and esp. 246–47), who has almost exhausted the subject of the patristic extracts that are cited in it. So here I repeat only the list of *testimonia* that are embedded in this letter:

1. Basilius Caesar., *De Spiritu Sancto* = P 25*, V 8
2. Severianus Gabalensis, *Homilia de legislatore* = P 55*, M 24^M, V 30
3. The story of the statue of Paneas found in the ecclesiastical histories of Eusebius and Sozomen = P 105*
4. Part of the 82nd canon of the Quinisext Council = P 94*, M 49^M, V 38
5. Leontius Neapol., *Contra Iudaeos orat. v*, = P 103*, M 2^M
6. Stephanus Bostrensis, *Contra Iudaeos fragmenta* = P 95*, V 35.

That Pope Gregory was capable of writing these letters in Greek and having that wealth of patristic literature included in them is beyond any doubt. The following passage from his *Vita* is highly illustrative of that (Duchesne, *Liber Pontificalis*, I, 396.4–14):

Hic (sc. Gregory II) a parva aetate in patriarchio nutritus, sub sanctae memoriae domno Sergio papa subdiaconus atque sacellarius factus, *bibliothicae illi est cura commissa;* deinde ad diaconatus ordinem provectus est et cum viro sancto Constantino pontificae regiam profectus est ur-

---

[81] I give here just one example. Compare:
Gouillard, "Origines," 289.164–291.165:
    Τίς ὁρῶν τὴν ἱστορίαν τοῦ Ἀβραάμ, ἐπικειμένην τὴν μάχαιραν εἰς τὸν τράχηλον τοῦ παιδίου, οὐ κατανύσσεται καὶ δακρύει;
P, fol. 251, quot. 43*; John of Damascus, *Schriften III*, 154–55; I 52; II 48; III 50:
    Εἶδον πολλάκις ἐπὶ γραφῆς εἰκόνα τοῦ πάθους καὶ οὐκ ἀδακρυτὶ τὴν θέαν παρῆλθον . . . Πρόκειται ὁ Ἰσαὰκ παρ᾽ αὐτῷ τῷ θυσιαστηρίῳ . . . ὁ δὲ ἐπιβεβηκώς . . . καὶ τὴν δεξιὰν καθωπλισμένος τῷ ξίφει πρὸς τὴν σφαγὴν κατευθύνει. Καὶ ἅπτεται ἤδη τοῦ σώματος ἡ τοῦ ξίφους αἰχμή.
Note that part of this passage is also found in the acts of the 731 and 769 synods (quot. 15 on the list of pp. 39–40 above).

[82] Gouillard claims that this letter is a product of Germanus' pen on account of its many similarities to the letter of Germanus to Thomas of Claudiopolis (Mansi XIII 108A–128A). D. Stein, *Der Beginn der byzantinischen Bilderstreites und seine Entwicklung bis in die 40er Jahre des 8. Jahrhunderts* (Munich, 1980), 156, 269, attributes it to Pope Zacharias and dates it to the year 743, and P. Speck, *Artabasdos. Der rechtgläubige Vorkämpfer der göttlichen Lehre*, ΠΟΙΚΙΛΑ ΒΥΖΑΝΤΙΝΑ 2 (Bonn, 1981), 155–78 claims that the author was Gregory II but the middle part of the text is a 9th-century interpolation. Grumel, *Regestes*, vol. I, fasc. 2–3, 3–4 (N 327) places the letter in as early a period as 723–725, although he doubts its authenticity. On this subject, see also G. Ostrogorsky, "Les débuts de la querelle des images," in *Mélanges Ch. Diehl*, I (Paris, 1930), 243 ff; E. Caspar, "Papst Gregor II. und der Bilderstreit," *ZKG* 52 (1933), 32–42.

bem; atque a Iustiniano principe *inquisitus de quibusdam capitulis optimam responsionem unamquamque solvit quaestionem.* Erat enim vir castus, divinae Scripturae eruditus, facundus loquela . . . ecclesiasticarum rerum defensor et contrariis fortissimus impugnator. (For an English translation of the passage see R. Davis, *The Lives of the Eighth-Century Popes* (*Liber Pontificalis*) [Liverpool, 1992], 3).

One more minor point: it is rather strange that the whole Iconophile florilegium of P (which, as I have suggested, is the only one that may have retained the original arrangement of the fragments as they were in F) closes with this very letter of Gregory II (P, fols. 281ᵛ–283ᵛ, quot. 133*). I could advance two hypotheses for this situation. (a) If F had simply reproduced, with not the slightest change in order and content, an older corpus of citations, then this letter as a concluding piece could possibly stand as a kind of "authorizing seal" to that corpus put there by Pope Gregory himself. (b) If we assume that the compiler of the year 770 was responsible for this arrangement, this could be interpreted as a symbolic gesture on his part by which he meant to pay tribute to the spiritual father and possible original compiler of the pre-731 florilegium. Certainly both suggestions are highly hypothetical, though not impossible.

What of the possibility that the letters are later fabrications? As I have shown, the scholars who oppose their authenticity have not been able to produce a terminus post quem that goes beyond the year 754 for the letters to Leo III (above, p. 108–10) and 743 for the third letter to Germanus I. So, even the possibility of the letters being fake allows for a date much earlier than 770 as a terminus ante quem for the existence of an Iconophile florilegium that was used by the author(s?) of the letters. However, since these letters and the Roman Synod of 731 share at least two quotations (P 43* and 95*), one could see an additional reason for accepting that the year 731 could also be the terminus ante quem for their production.

In conclusion: it seems to be certain that part of (if not the whole of, or more than) what is preserved by F was already collected before the year 731.[83] On the other hand, the acceptance of the authenticity of the three letters of Gregory II simply helps to determine more accurately the circumstances and the period in which this compilation took place (723/725–729).[84]

---

[83] This part of the present study, as well as section 8 of Chapter I, provide an answer to the question raised by Sansterre, *Les moines grecs*, 182: "on peut se demander si un florilège du même genre que celui réuni par Jean († vers 750) ne circulait pas à Rome dès 731."

[84] By inverting the argument, one might claim that the letters are genuine for the additional reason that they fit perfectly within the framework of the prerequisites, in matters of written documentation, for the synod of 731.

One can only dispute whether some of the quotations found in these letters and F were included in the pre-731 collection or not.

The *Doctrina Patrum*

Apart from the twenty-eight quotations of the *Doctrina Patrum* that are included in the Iconophile florilegium of P, but have no direct bearing on image worship, F included another nine (eight in PMV and one more only in V) that also occur in the final chapter (ΜΕ′) of Diekamp's edition of the *Doctrina*.

Diekamp has postulated the year 726 as terminus ante quem for this chapter, thus assigning to it the place of the first Iconophile collection. It is, however, strange that we should find the scholium III 57 of John of Damascus in ΜΕ′ XII of the *Doctrina*. If all the scholia came from his pen, then the date of chapter 45 has to be placed a little later, after 730 at least,[85] or even possibly after 753.[86]

This chapter consists of eighteen quotations, but unfortunately we are unable to decide on its exact extent. This is because it is provided by only one manuscript (Bodleianus Misc. gr. 184) whose last page (fol. 191ᵛ) does not seem to coincide with the actual end of this collection: it stops abruptly in the middle of an extract from the second *Catechesis ad illuminandos* of Cyril of Jerusalem (*CPG* 3585.2; *PG* 33, 421).[87]

---

[85] See Kotter, *Schriften III*, 5–7.

[86] See Beck, *KThL*, 477.

[87] The problem of the critical edition of the *Doctrina* is enormously complicated, and the way it was solved by Diekamp cannot be the definitive one. It seems that the *Doctrina* continued being expanded beyond the year 726 which was considered by Diekamp the, so to speak, "year of death" of the *Doctrina*'s growth. To my knowledge, codex Athonensis Vatopedinus gr. 594 (see S. Eustratiades and Arcadios Vatop., *Catalogue of the Greek Manuscripts in the Library of Vatopedi on Mount Athos*, Harvard Theological Studies 11 [Cambridge, Mass., 1924], 116–17, which is the Athous Vatopedinus 507 of Diekamp; see *Doctrina*, pp. xiv–xv), of the 11th–early 12th century, preserves on fols. 21 ff a different version of the *Doctrina*. Diekamp took it into account for his edition as long as it conformed with the order established by his main manuscripts (see above, Chapter II, n. 67), but ignored the last part of Vatopedinus because it was much different from his plan. (For a list of contents of this part of the ms, see D. Serruys, "Anastasiana," in *Mélanges d'archéologie et d'histoire* 22 [1902], 168–70.) In the Vatopedi version of the *Doctrina*, Chap. Μ′ (fols. 151–159) bears the title: Περὶ τῆς ἀθέου τῶν εἰκονομάχων δεινοτάτης αἱρέσεως. This chapter consists of twenty-four Iconophile quotations, but its most interesting feature is that it has excerpted the following sources: (a) F (Vatop. gr. shares *only* with P and V quotation 84*/V 16 = Vatop. gr. 594, fol. 155ᵛ), (b) the florilegia of John of Damascus (Vatop. 594 provides at least five quotations from the first and second florilegia along with the scholia that John of Damascus had attached to them; see Vatop. gr. 594, fols. 151, 153, 156), and (c) the *Refutatio et eversio* of Patriarch Nicephorus I. From this work the compiler of the Vatopedi manuscript has excerpted a number of quotations along with the introductory remarks of the patriarch (see, for example, the passage in Vatop. gr. 594, fols. 152ʳ⁻ᵛ, which is included in Paris.

Two of the eighteen quotations of chapter 45 of the *Doctrina* do not appear in any other florilegium.[88] Three are common to P and the *Doctrina* only.[89] One more is included only in Marcianus gr. 573, which implies that it was also included in the original of P and M.[90] Another four reappear in the third florilegium of John of Damascus.[91] A further seven are common to the *Doctrina*, P, and the three florilegia of John of Damascus.[92] Finally, there is also a quotation common to the *Doctrina*, the acts of the 731 and 769 councils, and Dam.[93]

What possibly happened in the case of the six quotations common to P, the *Doctrina*, and Dam. is that they may have ended up in P by way of the florilegia of John of Damascus, as did, for example, quotation 60* (Georgii Alexandrini *Vita S. Johannis Chrysostomi*, CPG 7979). The *Doctrina* (ME′ XVI) gives one more sentence from the incipit of a text which otherwise is almost identical in all its three versions. In one instance, however, P presents an extract that is more extended, while the *Doctrina* gives even less than John of Damascus. Compare:

P 24* (fol. 248)
　　τοῦ αὐτοῦ (= Τοῦ ἁγίου Γρηγορίου τοῦ Θεολόγου)· ἐκ τοῦ δευτέρου λόγου τοῦ περὶ υἱοῦ. οἱ τὰς μορφὰς γράφοντες καὶ τὰ γράμματα διὰ τὸ μὴ

Coislinianus gr. 93, fols. 87ᵛ–88: συνφθεγγέσθω τούτοις καὶ ὁ θεῖος Βασίλειος . . . ἔχει δὲ ἡ λέξις οὕτως· τοῦ ἁγίου Βασιλείου ἐκ τοῦ εἰς τὸν ἅγιον Βαρλαάμ . . . etc.). This particular version of the *Doctrina* is, therefore, later than the 830s, and is enough to prove that this enormous dossier was still expanded in the 9th century. As is stated by Professor P. Chrestou ("Testimonia Neglected by the Seventh Ecumenical Council," *AHC* 20 [1988], 252), Professor B. Phanourgakis is currently working on the edition of this version of the *Doctrina*.

[88] *Doctrina*, chap. ME′: (1) V, 327.1-2: Τοῦ ἁγίου Διονυσίου περὶ μύρου· τοὺς δὲ ἱεροὺς ἄγουσιν ἐπὶ τὰς θείας εἰκόνας καὶ ἐποψίας αὐτῶν κοινωνίας. (2) IX, 328.23-26: Τοῦ ἁγίου Γρηγορίου τοῦ Θεολόγου ἐκ τοῦ εἰς τὰ ἅγια γενέθλια λόγου· καὶ τὴν φάτνην προσκύνησον, δι᾽ ἧς ἄλογος ὢν ἐτράφης ὑπὸ τοῦ λόγου. For this, however, cf. Mansi XIII 309D.

[89] P 68* = *Doctrina*, chap. ME′ VII; P 75* = *D.* ME′ VI; P 91* = *D.* ME′ XVIII.

[90] *Doctrina*, chap. ME′, XI: Τοῦ ἁγίου Γρηγορίου ἐκ τοῦ εἰς τὸν ἅγιον Στέφανον ἐκ τοῦ μείζονος λόγου· οὕτως γὰρ ἂν ὁ τῆς εἰκόνος—ἐν τῇ εἰκόνι χαρακτηρίζεται. = Ven. Marc. 573, fol. 18ʳ⁻ᵛ (quot. 47).

[91] These are:
(1) *Doctrina*, chap. ME′ I = John Dam. III 61
(2) *Doctrina*, ME′ II = Dam. III 62
(3) *Doctrina*, ME′ XII = Dam. III 56, 57
(4) *Doctrina*, ME′ XV = Dam. III 58.

[92] (1) P 16* = *Doctrina*, chap. ME′, XIII = Dam. I 44, 46/ II 40, 42/ III 47, 106
(2) P 24* = *Doctrina*, ME′, III = Dam. III 64
(3) P 25* = *Doctrina*, ME′, XIV = Dam. I 35/ II 31/ III 48
(4) P 43* = *Doctrina*, ME′, X = Dam. I 52/ II 48/ III 50
(5, 6) P 60* = *Doctrina*, ME′, XVI, XVII = Dam. I 61/ II 57/ III 54
(7) P 70* = *Doctrina*, ME′, VIII = Dam. III 59.

[93] *Doctrina*, chap. ME′ IV = *Acta* 7 = Dam. III 43.

εἶναι τῆς ἀληθείας ἄλλως ἐπιτυχεῖν, εἰ μὴ πρὸς τὸ ἀρχέτυπον βλέποντας κἀκεῖθεν χειραγωγουμένους. [(εἰκόνος φύσις μίμημα τοῦ ἀρχετύπου) καὶ οὗ λέγεται].

The sentence in parentheses corresponds to the extract in *Doctrina*, ME′ III, and the brackets indicate what John of Damascus (III 64) offers. Here two choices are in order: either P draws from a florilegium that was also the source of Dam. and of the *Doctrina*, or the compiler of 770 used the extract of the *Doctrina* (or of John of Damascus) in order to locate within the actual work the longer fragment that he finally gave.

As for the remaining three quotations of the *Doctrina*, they may have been the source of P. It seems possible for quotations 68* (= *Doctrina*, ME′ VII) and 91* (= *Doctrina*, ME′ XVIII) at least.[94] Quotation 75* (Dionysius the Areopagite, *De ecclesiastica hierarchia*, PG 3, 473B–C, *Doctrina*, ME′ VI), however, is more likely to have been derived from a book containing the works of Dionysius or from a particular florilegium of his writings, as it is followed by many other extracts from works of the same author (quot. 76*– 80*) that do not exist in the *Doctrina*.

Thus it may be concluded that the *Doctrina* could be indirectly connected with F in four cases (quot. 16*, 43*, 60*, 70*), directly in two (quot. 68*, 91*), and may have supplied the indications for the location of an extract within the whole work in another two instances (quot. 24* and 75*). Nevertheless, the most serious possibility is that the *Doctrina* and the original of P, V, and M (= F) have copied partly overlapping segments of a common archetype.

The Florilegia of John of Damascus[95]

Despite the attempts of Kotter (*Schriften III*, 5–7), the dating of the three homilies of John of Damascus still cannot be ascertained. Since even the date of his death has not yet been fixed,[96] we may be content with the assumption that a terminus ante quem for them and their florilegia could be the end of the second (if not the beginning of the third) quarter of the eighth century.[97]

It has already been proved that the original of PV and M included the whole of the second *Oratio contra imaginum calumniatores* of John of Damascus (nos. 39–41 and 45 on the list below). In addition, PV and M offer another

---

[94] See below, Chapter III, sec. 5, the examination of quot. 14 and 22 respectively.

[95] Text in Kotter, *Schriften III*, 144–200.

[96] See Beck, *KThL*, 477; also Gero, *Constantine V*, 109 n. 183.

[97] Stein, *Bilderstreit*, 204, dates the two first sermons before 741; Speck, *Artabasdos*, 207–9, suggests a period after 752–754 for the first *sermo* and a date just before 754 for the second (ibid., 223).

forty-one quotations that can also be found in the three florilegia of John of Damascus. The list includes the following extracts:

1.	P 15*	= V 24		= Dam. I 34	II 30	III 46
2.	P 16*	= V 23	= M 53^M	= Dam. I 44, 46	II 40, 42	III 47, 106
3.	P 19*			= Dam. I 48	II 44 *Schol.*	
4.	P 20*	= V 25		= Dam. I 60	II 56	III 53
5.	P 21*	= V 9		= Dam.		III 109
6.	P 24*	= V 26		= Dam.		III 64
7.	P 25*	= V 8		= Dam. I 35	II 31	III 48
8.	P 43*			= Dam. I 52	II 48	III 50
9.	P 46*		= M 54^M	= Dam. I 49	II 45	
10.	P 47*		⟨ M 55^M	= Dam. I 50, 51	II 46, 47	
11.	P 53*	= V 10	= M 26^M	= Dam.	II 62	
12.	P 54*		= M 41^M	= Dam.		III 122
13.	P 55*	= V 30	= M 24^M	= Dam.	II 60	III 105
14.	P 59*			= Dam. I 53	II 49	III 51
15.	P 60*	= V 32		= Dam. I 61	II 57	III 54
16.	P 69*	= V 21	= M 52^M	= Dam.		III 114
17.	P 70*			= Dam.		III 59
18.	P 76*	= V 20		= Dam. I 11.5–10		III 21.7–13
19.	P 77*	= V 20		= Dam. I 32	II 28	III 44
20.	P 80*			= Dam. I 32	II 28	III 44.2–4
21.	P 82*	= V 13		= Dam.	II 66	III 127
22.	P 85*			= Dam.		III 116
23.	P 89*			= Dam.		III 138
24.	P 90*			= Dam. I 58	II 54	III 52
25.	P 92*	= V 34	= M 38^M	= Dam.	II 65	III 131
26.	P 94*	= V 38	= M 49^M	= Dam.		III 137
27.	P 95*	= V 35		= Dam.		III 73, 72
28.	P 96*	= V 50	= M 16^M	= Dam.		III 125
29.	P 100*	= V 37	= M 19^M	= Dam.		III 130
30.	P 103*		= M 2^M	= Dam. I 54, 56		III 84, 86–89
31.	P 108*			= Dam.		III 132
32.	P 112*			= Dam.		III 55
33.	P 114*			= Dam.		III 92
34.	P 116*			= Dam.		III 135
35.	P 123*		= M 48^M	= Dam. I 64	II 67	III 13
36.	P 130*			= Dam.	II 22.29–39	
37.		V 42		= Dam. I 48 *Schol.*		III 56
38.		V 44	= M 25^M	= Dam.	II 61	
39.			M 4^M	= Dam.	II 1–10, 14–23	
40.			M 5^M	= Dam. I 66	II 69	

41.	M 6^M = Dam.	II 11	
42.	M 15^M = Dam.		III 69
43.	M 17^M = Dam.		III 134
44.	M 20^M = Dam.		III 136
45.	M 32a^M = Dam.	II 10–14	

It becomes evident from the above list that the compiler of the Iconophile florilegium (F) had certainly had at his disposal all the three florilegia of John of Damascus and not only the second one as might have been expected. Moreover, if we examine the above list reversing the correspondence and starting from the florilegia of John of Damascus, it will become apparent that the original of PVM included almost all the quotations found in the first and second florilegia of John of Damascus and almost half of the quotations of the third one.

It should be noted that the first florilegium of John of Damascus is repeated in its entirety in the second florilegium. Actually, the second florilegium has added only another seven quotations at the end of the first one and, although both florilegia appear to be very extensive, the quotations they display are relatively few, since almost every quotation is followed by a scholium penned by John of Damascus himself. Therefore, the first florilegium numbers twenty-three quotations taken from seventeen works of eleven authors, and the second exceeds the first by another seven fragments from John Chrysostom (4), Ambrose of Milan (1), Anastasius of Antioch (1), and Anastasius Apocrisiarius (1). The third florilegium is much more extensive, including almost eighty quotations apart from the ones that are shared with the other two florilegia.[98]

Another striking trait of the first florilegium is that it follows in the arrangement of the quotations a pattern similar to that adopted by the compiler of F. John of Damascus cites the fragments in the following sequence: major fathers: Dionysius the Areopagite (I 28, 30, 32), St. Basil (I 34, 35, 37, 39, 40, 42, 44, 46), Gregory of Nyssa (I 49, 50, 52), and John Chrysostom (I 53); minor fathers: Leontius of Neapolis (I 54, 56), Severian of Gabala (I 58); hagiography (I 60–63) and an extract from the *Pratum spirituale* (I 64).

Here I shall treat quotations 4, 9, 10, 14, 18–20, 23, 24, 29, 37, and 42–44 on the above list, as nos. 6, 15, and 17 have already been examined (section 4 above), and the remainder is investigated below (section 5).

(I) Vita Basilii Caesariensis (= 4)
P 20* (fol. 248), V 25 (fol 9^v), Dam. I 60; II 56; III 53

---

[98] For quotations in the three florilegia of Dam. that are missing from P, V, and M, see Appendix V.

This small excerpt from the life of St. Basil in P seems to have been taken from the florilegia of St. John of Damascus. The fragment in Dam. starts with a brief introduction of two lines which the compiler of 770 reduced to a simpler lemma. Compare:

Dam.: Ὅτι δὲ οὐ καινὸν ἐφεύρημα τὸ τῶν εἰκόνων, ἀλλὰ ἀρχαῖον καὶ τοῖς ἁγίοις καὶ ἐκκρίτοις πατράσιν ἐγνωσμένον τε καὶ εἰθισμένον, ἄκουε· Γέγραπται ἐν τῷ βίῳ Βασιλείου τοῦ μάκαρος τῷ δι᾽ Ἑλλαδίου, τοῦ αὐτοῦ μαθητοῦ καὶ διαδόχου τῆς αὐτοῦ ἱεραρχίας, ὡς παρειστήκει . . .

PV: Ἑλλαδίου τοῦ μαθητοῦ αὐτοῦ καὶ διαδόχου τῆς ἱεραρχίας αὐτοῦ ἐκ τοῦ βίου αὐτοῦ (= St. Basil)· Παρειστήκει . . .

The striving of the compiler to turn the introduction into a typical lemma is evident in the triple repetition of the word αὐτοῦ. Any other textual differences between P and Dam., especially omissions and mistakes, should rather be attributed to the negligence of Cinnamus, although one omission is also present in manuscript A (Scorialensis Ψ. III. 8) of Dam. (Μερκουρίου τοῦ ἀοιδίμου [om. PVA] μάρτυρος).

(II) Gregorius Nyssenus, *De opificio hominis* (*CPG* 3154; *PG* 44, 136C5–15: Ὥσπερ κατὰ τὴν ἀνθρωπίνην—καὶ τοῦ ὀνόματος) (= 9)

P 46* (fol. 251ᵛ), M 54ᴹ (fol. 240ʳ⁻ᵛ), Dam. I 49; II 45

P gives only lines 4–8 of the fragment as it is in Dam., while M offers a text identical with that of John of Damascus, excepting the noun ἐπισκόπου and the indication κεφαλαίου τετάρτου that are missing from the lemma, plus one καὶ omitted from the main text.

The intervention of Cinnamus is clearly visible in the P version of the fragment. Since it starts with the word ὥσπερ, which usually entails the introduction of a second sentence starting with οὕτω, Cinnamus, not having the intention to copy the whole fragment whose second clause (the one introduced with οὕτω) was irrelevant to image worship, deleted the word ὥσπερ. On the other hand, on two occasions where P diverges from the printed text, the variants are also transmitted by manuscript A of Dam.: συμπαραγράφουσι Kotter: συμπεριγράφουσι PA; καὶ εἰκὼν καὶ βασιλεὺς Kotter: καὶ ἡ εἰκὼν βασιλεὺς PA.

(III) Idem, *De opificio hominis* (*PG* 44, 137A3–10) (= 10)

P 47* (fol. 251ᵛ), M 55ᴹ (fol. 240ᵛ), Dam. I 50, 51; II 46, 47

P, again, is a drastically fragmented part of the quotation in Dam., offering only lines 5–9 of the text in the edition by Kotter. On the other hand, M not only presents a quotation absolutely identical with that in Dam., but

also includes the subsequent scholium by John of Damascus (Kotter ed., I
51, II 47).

The lemma, however, of P is much closer to Dam. than that of M.
Compare:

Dam.: Τοῦ αὐτοῦ ἐκ τοῦ πέμπτου κεφαλαίου τῆς αὐτῆς πραγματείας.
(= ἐκ τοῦ ἀναπληρωματικοῦ, τουτέστι τοῦ περὶ κατασκευῆς ἀνθρώπου).
P: Τοῦ αὐτοῦ ἐκ τοῦ ε΄ κεφαλαίου, τοῦ ἀναπληρωματικοῦ.
M: Τοῦ αὐτοῦ.

(IV) Iohannes Chrysostomus, Ἐκ τῆς ἑρμηνείας τῆς πρὸς Ἑβραίους ἐπιστολῆς. Locus non inventus[99] (= 14)

P 59* (fol. 252^{r-v}), Dam. I 53; II 49; III 51

P and Dam. present exactly the same text, and the few variants of P are
also transmitted by codex D of Dam. (= Neapolitanus 54 [II B 16]).[100]

(V) Dionysius Areopagita, De coelesti hierarchia (CPA 6600, Corpus Dionysiacum II, 11.11–15) (= 18)

P 76* (fol. 255^v), V 20 (fol. 7), Dam. I 11.5–10; II 21.7–13

(VI) Idem, De ecclesiastica hierarchia (CPG 6601, Corpus Dionysiacum II,
65.14–15) (= 19)

P 77* (fol. 256), V 20 (fol. 8), Dam. I 32; II 28; III 44.7–8

(VII) Idem, ibid., (Corpus Dionysiacum II, 65.8–10) (= 20)

P 80* (fol. 261), Dam. I 32; II 28; III 44.2–4

All these quotations constitute a small part of the Dionysian fragments
that PV have in stock. The case of these fragments is very strange in that P
offers on fols. 255^v-256 (quot. 76*, 77*) eleven tiny fragments that are followed by the complete chapters of the works of Dionysius from which they
have been extracted (P, fols. 256–261, quot. 78*–80*) (see also above, p. 118,
no. 7). It is obvious, therefore, that the compiler of 770 had at his disposal
a florilegium comprising perhaps only fragments from the works of Dionysius the Areopagite, so he did not have to turn to Dam. for fragments V–VII.

(VIII) Methodius Patarensis, De resurrectione (CPG 1812; PG 18, 289A–
B = GCS 27, 379.9–16) (= 23)

P 89* (fol. 262), Dam. III 138

[99] See Kotter, Schriften III, p. 155.
[100] E.g., Kotter, I 53, line 8: χρώμασι Kotter: σώμασι PD.

Unexpected as this is, we have here the first instance where P offers a text better and fuller than that found in Dam. Compare:

P: Τοῦ ἁγίου Μεθοδίου, ἐπισκόπου Πατάρων καὶ μάρτυρος ἐκ τοῦ βʹ ἀντιρρητικοῦ λόγου περὶ ἀναστάσεως, οὗ ἡ ἀρχή· Ἴδωμεν δὴ οὖν, ἃ τὸ πρῶτον εἰς τὸν ἀπόστολον προήχθημεν εἰπεῖν. αὐτίκα γοῦν τῶν . . .

Dam. Τοῦ ἁγίου Μεθοδίου, ἐπισκόπου Πατάρων, περὶ ἀναστάσεως, λόγου δευτέρου· Αὐτίκα οὖν τῶν . . .

Moreover, Dam. omits words on ten occasions, resulting in some cases in a poor text.[101] Compare:

P: καὶ ὁ δυσφημήσας εἰς ὁποτέραν οὔτε ὡς πηλὸν ἀτιμάσας ἀφίεται . . .
Dam.: καὶ ὁ δυσφημήσας εἰς ὁποτέραν οὔτε ὡς εἰς πηλὸν ἀφίεται . . .

On the other hand, P omits the last sentence of the Dam. version, which reads as follows:

Τὰς μὲν ἀπὸ χρυσοῦ κατεσκευασμένας εἰκόνας τῶν αὐτοῦ ἀγγέλων, τὰς ἀρχὰς καὶ τὰς ἐξουσίας, εἰς τιμὴν καὶ δόξαν αὐτοῦ ποιοῦμεν.

This sentence, however, does not relate directly to what precedes it. The whole passage deals with the punishment of anyone who calumniates the images of emperors as an offender of the emperor himself. The concluding sentence, by focusing on the icons of angels, appears out of context. Thus it is not impossible that it was omitted by Cinnamus.

Under these circumstances one is entitled to question the originality of the florilegia of John of Damascus. It has been proved that in the previous cases Dam. was more likely to be the source of many quotations of P and also of chapter 45 of the *Doctrina Patrum*. However, there are some other instances—such as the present one and extract no. 6 (above, pp. 116–18)— where the question emerges: did John of Damascus compile his three florilegia himself and if not, did he use a preexisting florilegium? If the answer to the last question is positive, then to what extent does PVM represent this archetypal florilegium? I return to this question at the end of this chapter.

(IX) Severianus Gabalensis, *Oratio in dedicationem . . . crucis* (*CPG* 4270; *PG* 56, 499) (= 24)

P 90* (fol. 262ʳ⁻ᵛ), Dam. I 58; II 54; III 52

P displays a text almost identical to that of John of Damascus, but omits the incipit: Πῶς ἡ εἰκὼν τοῦ ἐπικαταράτου ζωὴν ἤνεγκε τοῖς ἡμετέροις προγό-

---

[101] A glance at the apparatus criticus of the critical edition (Kotter, *Schriften III*, 200) shows that in three cases the editor felt obliged to supplement the missing words from the edition of the works of Methodius, ed. N. Bonwetsch, *Methodius, GCS* 27 (Leipzig, 1917), 379.9–18.

νοις. The very few mistakes ought to be attributed to Cinnamus. In one instance, his effort to repair an omission caused by a homoioteleuton is apparent. Compare:

Dam.: Ἀλλ᾽ ἐκεῖνα, φησίν, ἐνομοθέτησα, ἵνα ἐκκόψω τὰς ὕλας τῆς ἀσεβείας καὶ τὸν λαὸν ἀπαγάγω πάσης ἀποστασίας καὶ εἰδωλολατρείας· νυνὶ δὲ χωνεύω τὸν ὄφιν χρησίμως . . .

P: ἀλλ᾽ ἐκεῖνα φησὶν ἐνομοθέτησα, ἵν᾽ ἐκκόψω τὰς ὕλας τῆς ἀσεβείας· νυνὶ δὲ χωνεύω τὸν ὄφιν, καὶ τὸν λαὸν ἀπάγω πάσης ἀποστασίας καὶ εἰδωλολατρείας· νῦν χωνεύω τὸν ὄφιν χρησίμως . . .

The least that can be postulated here is a common source for both F and Dam.

(X) Theodorus Anagnostes, *Historia ecclesiastica* (*CPG* 7503; *PG* 86, 220D–221A = *GCS* 54, 107.11–108.3) (= 29)

P 100* (fol. 265ᵛ), V 37 (fol. 15), M 19ᴹ (fols. 225ᵛ-226), Dam. III 130

It seems that Dam. and P have copied different versions of the same text. The lemma in Dam. is more complete than that of PV and M.[102] On the other hand, the divergences between P and Dam. are more significant, and P offers five more lines beyond the point where Dam. stops. In brief, everything leads to the exclusion of Dam. as a possible source for F. Neither the original of PV and M could have served as such to Dam., since the latter's incipit is different from that of PV and M. In addition, both versions seem equally corrupt and do not allow for a safe detection of a possible common source.

(XI) Basilius Caesar., *Homilia dicta in Lacisis* (*CPG* 2912; *PG* 31, 1456C–D) (= 37)

V 42 (fol. 17ʳ⁻ᵛ), Dam. I 48; II 44 Scholium; III 56

A very small part from the beginning of this fragment appears in Dam., while V continues for a few more lines. Dam., however, gives the incipit of the work and one line before the point where V starts. In the lines common to both V and Dam., V presents a slightly better text (V: ὥσπερ εἴ τις ἄνθρωπος ὀργισθεὶς πρὸς βασιλέα τὴν εἰκόνα λιθάζει Dam.: ὥσπερ εἴ τις ἄνθρωπος ὀργισθεὶς τὴν εἰκόνα λιθάζει).

---

[102] Dam. III 130: Θεοδώρου ἱστοριογράφου Κωνσταντινουπόλεως ἐκ τῆς ἐκκλησιαστικῆς ἱστορίας περὶ Γενναδίου, ἀρχιεπισκόπου Κωνσταντινουπόλεως.
P: Θεοδώρου ἀναγνώστου Κωνσταντινουπόλεως περὶ τῆς ἐκκλησιαστικῆς ἱστορίας.
M, V: Ἐκ τῆς ἐκκλησιαστικῆς ἱστορίας Θεοδώρου ἀναγνώστου Κωνσταντινουπόλεως.
The preposition περὶ in the lemma of P, which makes no sense, offers some ground for the assumption that Cinnamus may have abridged a title similar to that of Dam.

(XII) Eusebius Caesar., *Historia ecclesiastica* (*CPG* 3495; ed. E. Schwartz and Th. Mommsen, *GCS* 9.2, 670.10–674.6 (M), 672.3–24 (Dam.))

M 15^M (fols. 223^v–225), Dam. III 69

M presents a more extended text, the middle part of which corresponds to the quotation in Dam. The divergences between M and Dam. are such as to exclude the possibility of their interdependence or, at least, their reference to a common source. Compare some of the differences between M and Dam. from the text printed in *GCS* (= A):

(a) εἰς μνήμην ἐλήλυθα A: ἐμνήσθημεν Dam., εἰς μνήμην ἐλθὼν M
(b) ἀπαλλαγὴν εὕρασθαι μεμαθήκαμεν A: ἀπαλλαγὴν εὑρέσθαι μεμ. Dam., ἀπηλλαγμένην μεμαθήκαμεν M
(c) ἐπὶ τὸ πρόσθεν A, M: ἐπὶ τοὔμπροσθεν Dam.
(d) τούτου δὲ ἄντικρυς A, M: οὗ ἀντικρὺ Dam.
(e) ἀλεξιφάρμακόν τι παντοίων νοσημάτων A, M: ἀλεξιφάρμακον τῶν πάντων νοσημάτων Dam.

Examples (a) and (c)–(e) make clear the closer proximity of M to A in comparison to the Dam. version. The next example, however, will make still clearer the textual inferiority of Dam. Compare:

A: καὶ αὐτοῦ δὴ τοῦ Χριστοῦ διὰ χρωμάτων ἐν γραφαῖς σῳζομένας ἱστορήσαμεν, ὡς εἰκός, τῶν παλαιῶν ἀπαραφυλάκτως, οἷα σωτῆρας ἐθνικῇ συνηθείᾳ παρ᾽ ἑαυτοῖς, τοῦτον τιμᾶν εἰωθότων.

M: καὶ αὐτοῦ τοῦ Χριστοῦ διὰ χρωμάτων ἐν γραφαῖς σῳζομένας ἱστορήσαμεν· εἰκὸς τῶν παλαιῶν ἀπαραφυλάκτως, ὃς ἂν (sic) σωτηρίας ἐθνικῇ συνηθείᾳ παρ᾽ ἑαυτοῖς τοῦτον τιμᾶν ἰοθώτων (sic).

Dam.: καὶ αὐτοῦ τοῦ σωτῆρος διαχρωματιζομένας ἱστορήσαμεν, ὡς εἰκός, τῶν παλαιῶν ἀπαραφυλάκτως, οἷα ἐθνικῆς συνηθείας οὔσης παρ᾽ αὐτοῖς, τοῦτον τιμᾶν εἰωθότων τὸν τρόπον.

One thing is certain: even if M in many cases differs considerably from A, in some crucial instances it is much closer to the original than Dam.

(XIII) *Vita Danielis*, ed. M. L. Clugnet, *ROC* 5 (1900), 258 (= 43)

M 17^M (fol. 225^r–v), Dam. III 134

M gives not only a longer fragment, but a slightly fuller text. Only the lemma in Dam. is partially more precise, but still M cannot be excluded as a source for the tiny (three lines) fragment in Dam. Compare:

M, fol. 225: Τοῦ ἁγίου Σωφρονίου, ἐπισκόπου Ἱεροσολύμων· περὶ τοῦ βίου τοῦ λατόμου· . . . τότε ὀλιγορίσας (sic) ἀπῆλθον καὶ ἔρρηψα (sic) ἑαυτὸν ἔμπροσθεν τῆς (fol. 225^v) εἰκόνος τῆς ἁγίας Θεοτόκου μετὰ κλαυθμοῦ λέγων οὕτως· Κύριε λῦσον (sic) τὴν ἐγγύην τοῦ ἀνθρώπου τούτου (sic) ἀπ᾽ ἐμοῦ . . .

Dam. Ἐκ τοῦ βίου τοῦ ἀββᾶ Δανιὴλ περὶ Εὐλογίου τοῦ λατόμου· Τότε ὀλι-γωρήσας ἀπῆλθε καὶ ρίψας ἑαυτὸν ἔμπροσθεν τῆς εἰκόνος τῆς θεοτόκου μετὰ κλαυθμοῦ ἔλεγε· "Κύριε λῦσον τὴν ἐγγύην τοῦ ἀνθρώπου τούτου ἀπ᾽ ἐμοῦ."

The text in M is much closer to the edition (which is far from being a critical one) of the work than Dam. Compare:

ROC 5 (1900), 258.30–32
Περὶ τοῦ λοτόμου (sic) Εὐλογίου . . . Τότε ὀλιγωρήσας ἀπῆλθον καὶ ἔρριψα ἐμαυτὸν ἔμπροσθεν τῆς <u>πύλης</u> τῆς θεοτόκου μετὰ κλαυθμοῦ καὶ λέγω· Κύ-ριε λῦσον (sic) τὴν ἐγγύην τοῦ ἀνθρώπου τούτου ἀπ᾽ ἐμοῦ.

Compared with the edition, the M version shows signs of deliberate alterations followed by Dam. which, in its turn, has further altered the syntax. M has added the name of an author in the lemma (Sophronius) and has substituted the word τῆς πύλης for the words τῆς εἰκόνος τῆς ἁγίας. Of course, M again is more extended than Dam., which allows the supposition that M may reflect the source of Dam.

(XIV) *Vita Eupraxiae,* (*BHG* 631) *AASS* Martii II (1668), 729c
M 20ᴹ (fol. 226ʳ⁻ᵛ), Dam. III 136
Both M and Dam. are textually very close to the edited text, although Dam. appears to have censored a small phrase (ἀπελθοῦσα δὲ ἡ παῖς κατεφί-λει τὸν χαρακτῆρα). M offers a longer incipit, but Dam. has extracted one more fragment from the same *vita*. It would not be impossible to claim a common source for both transmissions.

The comparative analysis of the interrelationship between the *Doctrina Patrum,* the florilegia of John of Damascus, and the acts of the Roman Councils of 731 and 769 with the original of P, M, and V may lead to some interesting remarks, and some still not definitive conclusions, but nevertheless useful ones.

The collation of the *testimonia* that were common to these florilegia was made on the basis of the received chronological succession of the florilegia in question. Assuming that chapter 45 of the *Doctrina* was prior to the acts of the 731 Roman council and the florilegia of John of Damascus, an attempt was made to establish a clear link between them and the possible original of P, M, and V.

In the course of this study, however, some new elements emerged, which, in some cases, contradicted each other. How is it possible, for example, to find in the *Doctrina Patrum* the scholium III 57 of John of Damascus and, at the same time, a quotation that cannot be detected among the *testimonia* of other florilegia (*Doctrina*, ΜΕ′ IX: Gregory Naz. καὶ τὴν φάτνην προσκύνησον, δι᾽ ἧς ἄλογος ὢν ἐτράφης ὑπὸ τοῦ λόγου)?[103] If we suppose that Dam. was the source of the *Doctrina*, why is the aforementioned fragment of Gregory of Nazianzus missing from all three florilegia of John of Damascus?

Furthermore, if Dam. was the actual source of a number of quotations incorporated into the original of P, M, and V, how can we explain the fact that in some cases PV or even M—despite the deficiencies of its copyist that are evident in all the passages quoted above—offer more extended fragments (see above, V, VI, VII, XII, XIII) or a better text (above, VIII, XII, XIII)? One may, however, observe that the texts of Dam. that are inferior to their counterparts in the original of P exist only in his third florilegium. Even so, this fact provides a terminus ante quem for the supposed original (or part of it) as early as the death of John of Damascus.

In addition, the case of quotations where Dam. offers less than the original of P, M, and V corroborates the aforementioned terminus ante quem, if we base our conjectures on the rule that a fragment of a certain number of words (A) is prior to another one of fewer words (A′), on condition that they are confined to a single (and not contaminated) line of transmission. What we have here is the succession: P or V or M ⟩ Dam. which may be decoded as: ⟨original of⟩ PVM prior to Dam. To this assumption contributes also the fact that in many cases P, M, and V reflect an abridged form of what their original included, while the texts in Dam. and in the *Doctrina* are apparently preserved in the form in which John of Damascus or the compiler of chapter 45 of the *Doctrina* had decided to incorporate them into their florilegia.

Conclusions

To sum up, P, M, and V have, in all probability, copied parts of an immense florilegium which was the work of an anonymous compiler in the year 770. As we have seen, however, many events had taken place in the period ca. 731–770. Two major collections were compiled in this period. The first is the Greek florilegium that dates between 725 and 729 and was compiled in Rome. Its Latin translation was used by the 731 Iconophile synod. This pre-731 florilegium (which was the basis of F) contained only the Greek portion

---

[103] It is noteworthy, though, that the author of the refutation of the *horos* of the Iconoclastic Council of Hiereia was aware of this passage. See Mansi XIII 309D6–8.

of what seems to have been available at Rome before 731. However, it bears no witness to the Iconophile fragments from Latin fathers which were also part of the Iconophile arsenal, as the *Hadrianum* allows one to assume by its numerous Latin Iconophile quotations.

The second collection is represented by the three florilegia of John of Damascus. It is not possible to decide with certainty whether the saint excerpted real books or used a collection similar to (if not identical with) the pre-731 anthology as the basis for the formation of at least his first and second (and possibly third) florilegium. The Iconophile fragments, as they are preserved in P, M, and V, give in some instances a better and more extended text, while in other cases this relation is reversed with Dam. giving the better and more extended text. So this situation possibly implies that behind F and Dam. there is already a common source and that even John of Damascus reproduced a florilegium.

Now, for what happened to this pre-731 corpus and to the florilegia of John of Damascus only hypotheses can be advanced. It is certain that some time in this period the second speech of John of Damascus traveled to Rome with his florilegia. Should one connect the arrival of the Damascenian works in Rome with the sending of the *Synodica rectae fidei* of the three Oriental patriarchs in 764/5? It is a possibility. What is more, this *Synodica* also included an Iconophile florilegium.[104] Was this different from those of Damascene? What other quotations did this florilegium offer to the compiler of F? An answer is impossible.

Nevertheless, the existence, for example, of an initially separate florilegium composed exclusively of quasi-Iconophile fragments from Dionysius the Areopagite should not be excluded. P, M, V, Dam., and the *Doctrina Patrum* constitute strong evidence of that, since they all provide fragments that are common to some or all of them but, in some instances, occur only in one of them.

Above all, extremely essential to this study is the fact that the great majority of the quotations that are to be found in P, M, or V were well known in Iconophile circles from the early stages of Iconoclasm. Quotation 104*, for instance, which occupies a place toward the end of the Iconophile florilegium of P (fols. 269ᵛ–270), was utilized by the Roman Council of 731. Thus what the compiler of 770 possibly did was to put in a relative order a mass of *testimonia* that had already been deposited in the papal *Scrinium* on various occasions. It also seems possible that a number of quotations were to be found twice in this florilegium of 770: the first time as part of the core of

[104] Cf. *Hadrianum*, 11.12–23.

the anthology that dated back to ca. 731, and in the second place incorporated into one of the florilegia of John of Damascus. This is perhaps the
reason why the excerpt from the *De parabola seminis* of Ps.-Chrysostom occurs twice in M (quot. 25[M] and 39[M])

So, even if one cannot finally decide who copied whom (John of Damascus the pre-731 kernel [or corpus?] of the original of P, M, and V, or the
opposite), it is enough to conclude that almost all the Iconophile quotations
were already known and collected before the death of St. John of Damascus.
What happened next was a process of sporadic additions to (or possibly
even subtractions from) an existing, rather very extensive corpus that dated
before 731. The year 770, just one year after the second Iconophile synod
at Rome, was a perfect date for someone to gather a body of material that
had obviously served the proceedings of a local synod at Rome the preceding year.

These considerations may also help to make clear that the question
whether the original of P has copied the *acta* of the seventh ecumenical
council (Nicaea II) or not is actually a pseudo-dilemma. The existence of
this dilemma is the responsibility of modern scholarship, which focused exclusively on the question: which copied what? P—and only P, since M and
V have been ignored up to now—the acts of 787, or the opposite? As has
been shown, the original of PVM has copied fragments that did already
exist in the acts of the 731 council, the florilegia of John of Damascus, and
other very early anthologies. For that very reason, the acts of Nicaea II cannot be considered a source for the original of PVM. The preceding analysis
must have made clear that almost every (if not every) *testimonium* had already
been collected in Rome (by Gregory II?) and in Jerusalem (by John of Damascus) no later than the first appearance of Iconoclastic ideas.[105] And this
is in accordance with the historical reality that has been described in the
first chapter. Florilegia were not compiled exclusively for the needs of an
impending council but as soon as a theological question arose. The work of
any council in the field of patristic documentation was that of selecting extracts from already existing collections and not that of fresh compilations.

Nevertheless, it is far from sure that among the quotations of the original Iconophile florilegium there are no later interpolations to be discovered.
I have already pointed out that three quotations in V were obviously not

---

[105] It is too tempting to suggest that collections of Iconophile extracts had already existed
much earlier, namely, in the 7th century. In the Armenian Iconophile treatise translated by
Sirarpie Der Nersessian ("Une apologie des images du septième siècle," *Byzantion* 17 [1944–45],
61), we find some Iconophile quotations, and among these part of quot. 47[M] of M and part of
quot. III 123 of John Damascene (*Schriften III*, 194, III 123, lines 10–14).

included in F (App. IV, quot. 17, 18, and 19). Also it is not certain whether the seventh ecumenical council made use of a florilegium or of actual books. The collation of the texts of P, M, and V with the acts of the seventh ecumenical council may offer some new answers.

5. F and the Acts of Nicaea II (787)

Introduction

The close relationship of the Iconophile florilegium of Paris. gr. 1115[106] to many of the texts that appear in the acts of Nicaea II[107] has already been stressed by scholars.[108] The consensus of opinion (which up to now has been based only on the examination of P but not of V and M) is that the texts of the Paris manuscript have been copied from the acts of the council of 787. At first sight that seems to be true since on fols. 251–283^v of P almost all of the texts that had been used during the fourth and fifth sessions of the council are included, sometimes in the same order.[109] Furthermore, it can be noted that the extracts provided by the acts give, in some cases, a more extended text than those of Parisinus.

This section provides a thorough textual study of the two florilegia: that of P, M, and V on the one hand, and that of the *acta* on the other, but before offering a collation, some considerations should be set down.

First, one should keep in mind that the original part of Paris. gr. 1115[110] is the result of the work of Leo Cinnamus. In spite of the high quality of his script, Cinnamus was no more than a simple copyist depending always on the condition of the text he had before him. Therefore, improvements of the original text by Cinnamus himself are not to be expected, although in some cases the text of Marcianus gr. 573 combined with P will help to establish a better text. For Mosquensis Hist. Mus. 265, the situation is much worse, as has already been made obvious by the texts transcribed for the needs of the present study. Under these circumstances the texts provided by the acts may possibly be more correct than the ones of Parisinus. It is self-evident that at least the misreadings of Vat. gr. 1181 and Vat. gr. 836 (the ones used for the edition of the acts) have been corrected by the editors

---

[106] Paris. gr. 1115, fols. 235^v–283^v.

[107] J. D. Mansi, *Sacrorum Conciliorum Nova et Amplissima Collectio* (Florence, 1759 ff; repr. Graz, 1960), XII 951–1154, XIII 1–496bis.

[108] On the subject see, among others, Gero, *Leo III*, 63 n. 16; Mango, "Availability," 28–35; Uthemann, "Ein Beitrag," 36.

[109] See Uthemann, "Ein Beitrag," 36.

[110] Fols. 8–306. Fols. 1–7^v and 307–314^v are a later addition of the 14th or 15th century. See Munitiz, "Parisinus," 52, 54, 59–60, etc.

of the acts, whereas Cinnamus has obviously added to the misreadings of his archetype and, in addition, abridged in many cases the text of his archetype, as has already been demonstrated and will be further illustrated by more examples. It is not, therefore, easy to judge at first sight which collection is prior to the other on the basis of which text is more corrupt.

The second and more serious problem is that there still does not exist a critical edition of the acts of the second Nicaean council. The existing edition of J. D. Mansi (= A) is the only one available. Based on the *Editio Conciliorum Romana,* which is very often referred to as the collection of Pope Paul V and relies essentially on two manuscripts, that is, Vat. gr. 1181 (15th cent.) and Vat. gr. 836 (13th cent.),[111] its accuracy is not assured. However, this was the edition that later reappeared in the major series of the seventeenth and eighteenth centuries.

For that reason, any other sources for the acts are indispensable. So it is very helpful that the Latin translation of Anastasius Bibliothecarius, which replaced the poor text of the no-longer-extant first Latin translation of the year 788, is included in Mansi's edition. This translation is, in some cases, closer to the original Nicaean text than the Greek text itself. The reason for this fidelity is that Anastasius' translation goes back to 873 and is based on a Byzantine manuscript of the Greek acts of Nicaea II originating at some time between 858 and 871.[112] Hence it is obvious that it will be taken into account whenever necessary.

However, since the translation of Anastasius has not been so successfully edited,[113] other sources are also enormously useful. In this category belong the Latin versions of some *testimonia* [114] included in P and in the acts which are also incorporated into the *Libellus Synodalis* (= *LS*)[115] of the Paris Council of 825, into the *Libri Carolini* (= *LC*),[116] and into Hadrian's refutation of the lost *Capitulare adversus Synodum,* the *Hadrianum* of ca. 793. *LS, LC,* and the *Hadrianum* are based for their *testimonia* on the first Latin translation of the second Nicaean council, which goes back to the year 788.[117] The *Hadrianum,* in addition, transmits many fragments that had been translated into

---

[111] See P. van den Ven, "Patristique," 339, 360 n. 2. It has to be noted also that the manuscripts that preserve the acts of 787 are all later than the 13th century.

[112] See Wallach, *Diplomatic Studies,* 14–15.

[113] See *Acta Iohannis,* ed. E. Junod and J. D. Kaestli, *CCSA* 1 (Brepols-Turnhout, 1983), 355–56.

[114] I.e., the *testimonia* included in the synodal letter of Pope Hadrian I addressed to Empress Irene and Constantine VI. Mansi XII 1065C–1071A (= *Synodica* of A.D. 785).

[115] Ed. A. Werminghoff, *MGH, Concilia* 2.2, *Aevi Karolini* 1, 2 (Hannover-Leipzig, 1908), 480–532.

[116] Ed. H. Bastgen, *Libri Carolini sive Caroli Magni Capitulare de Imaginibus, MGH, Legum Sectio III, Concilia 2, Supplementum* (Hannover-Leipzig, 1912–24).

[117] See Wallach, *Diplomatic Studies,* 13–14.

Latin much before 787 for the Roman synods of 731 and 769. The significance of these texts is evident.

Concerning the Greek text of the acts, there has been an attempt by E. Junod and J. D. Kaestli to identify the manuscripts that transmit the acts of Nicaea II and distribute them among a number of families.[118] Their efforts led to the discovery of another nine manuscripts containing the acts of the 787 council in addition to the ones of the *editio Romana,* all of which are no earlier than the thirteenth century. I may simply give here a short notice of each one:

1. Vat. gr. 836 (13th cent.) = Va
2. Taurinensis Bibl. Nation. 110 (B II 9) (13th cent.) = T
3. Breslau, gr. 437 (14th–15th cent.)
4. Venetus Marcianus gr. 166 (15th cent.) = Ma
5. Mediolan. Bibl. Nat. Brerae, AF. X. 47 (15th cent.) = B
6. Vat. gr. 660 (16th cent.) = Na
7. Vat. gr. 834 (16th cent.) = X
8. Vat. gr. 835 (16th cent.)
9. Vat. gr. 1181 (16th cent.) = Y
10. Vat. Ottobonianus gr. 27 (16th cent.) = O
11. Vindob. hist. gr. 29 (16th cent.) = W
12. Scorial. gr. 449 (Ψ. II. 14) (16th cent.) = S.

Junod and Kaestli collated only three quotations from the *Acta Iohannis* that were included in the acts and, on the basis of this collation, they concluded that all these manuscripts, with the exception of Va, can be divided into two groups: the first comprising codices MaO and the second codices BNaSTWXY. According to Junod and Kaestli, as far as the *Acta Iohannis* are concerned, the *editio Romana* offers a text "de bonne qualité."[119]

Since the collation of the text of the acts in all these manuscripts with the text of P belongs to a major project, that of the critical edition of the seventh ecumenical council, I chose to compare one text common to P and the acts of 787, namely, the *Narratio* of John of Jerusalem (quot. 131*), whose textual condition may illustrate better than any other text the transmission of the acts. One additional reason was that part of this text is preserved translated into Latin in the *Libellus Synodalis* of the Paris Council of 825, which was based on the original text of the acts of 787. A detailed comparison of the P version of this text can be found below (pp. 208–9, no. 49).

For the time being, what we are interested in is the transmission of this

---

[118] See Junod and Kaestli, *Acta Iohannis,* 344–51. For a reevaluation and confirmation of their findings, see now V. Déroche, "L'*Apologie contre les Juifs* de Léontios de Neapolis," *TM* 12 (1994), 52–57.

[119] Ibid., 351.

text by the manuscripts of the 787 council in comparison with the edition of Mansi (= Va and Y on the above list). I have collated this text as it is found in the oldest manuscript of the family MaO, namely, in Venetus Marcianus gr. 166 (Ma), and in one specimen of the family BNaSTWXY, the Taurinensis Bibl. Nation. 110 (B II 9) (T). The following lists the most significant variants:

Va and Y (= Mansi)	Ma, fols. 367–368	T, fol. 98ᵛ
διηγήσασθαι	ἀποδεῖξαι	διηγήσασθαι
ἁγίας ὑμῶν καὶ ἱερᾶς	καὶ ἁγίας	ἁγίας ὑμῶν καὶ ὁσίας
εἰκονοκλαστῶν	εἰκονοκαυστῶν	εἰκονοκλαστῶν
ἐξήγησιν	διήγησιν	ἐξήγησιν
μηδέν με	μηδέν μοι	μηδέν με
Σελεμὰν ἦν	Σουλιμὰν δὲ ἦν	Σελεμὰν δὲ ἦν
Τεσσαρακοντάπηχυς	Σαραντάπηχυς	Τεσσαρακοντάπηχος
διακείμενος	διακαιόμενος	διακείμενος
κατέχριον	κατέχεον	κατέχριον

There are some other variants as well, but the picture does not change. At any rate, it becomes evident that the edition of Mansi and T are almost identical, and this is reasonable simply because Mansi drew on Va and Y, of which the latter belongs to the same family as T. Family MaO does not seem to produce anything better than what the BNaSTWXY family does.

Here we come to P, which has some further variants to offer. Most of them are discussed below. This is, however, the place to concentrate on a very significant one. The name of the Jewish soothsayer who converted Leo III to Iconoclasm is transmitted in various forms: Mansi (Va and Y): Τεσσαρακοντάπηχυς; Ma: Σαραντάπηχυς; T: Τεσσαρακοντάπηχος. Only P gives the reading Σεραντάπηχος, which was certainly the name that John of Jerusalem mentioned during the fifth session of the 787 council.[120] This conclusion is corroborated by the Latin fragment of this *Narratio* in the *Libellus Synodalis*, where the same name reads *Serantapicus*.[121] Although the transmission of the name is a very small piece of evidence, one may not be wrong in assuming that a critical edition of the acts of the seventh ecumenical council will not give a dramatically improved text if it is to be based on the two families of manuscripts described above. Therefore, the Mansi edition possibly provides a text that can adequately serve our purposes.

Finally, there is one further complication because the question "which text is posterior, the original of PVM or the original of the acts of the 787

---

[120] See also Gero, *Leo III*, 195–98.
[121] *MGH, Concilia* 2, 2, 520.1.

council?" implies the collation of texts that do not actually exist in their original form. This question can be illustrated by the following stemma, where F is the archetype of fols. 235ᵛ–283ᵛ of Paris. gr. 1115, fols. 2–26 of Venetus Marcianus gr. 573, and fols. 142–241 of Mosqu. Hist. Mus. 265:

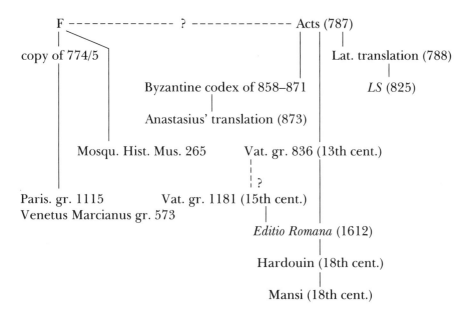

PVM and the Quotations of Nicaea II

Within the framework of all the above limitations, I may endeavor to restore the relationship between F and the acts by collating the texts of P, V, and M with those of the Mansi edition (= A).

The collation of the texts that P, M, and V and the acts have in common will follow the order in which they occur in the Paris manuscript. After the name of the author and the title (for which I have adopted the *CPG* standards) are given the Greek lemma along with the position the text occupies in P (and in M or V if it also occurs in them) and in the acts. There follow the incipits and the desinits in two separate sections, (A) and (B), if they are different. The same holds for the Greek lemmata.

1. Basilii Caesariensis Cappadociae (*Sermo*) *in Barlaam martyrem* (*PG* 31, 489A–B); *CPG* 2861 (Spurium); *BHG* 223

(A) P, fol. 247ᵛ (P 15*); V, fol. 9ʳ⁻ᵛ (V 24)

(Dam. I 34; II 30; III 46)

Τοῦ ἁγίου Βασιλείου ἐπισκόπου Καισαρείας Καππαδοκείας (sic) μαρτυρίαι περὶ τῶν ἐν τοῖς ἁγίοις οἴκοις εἰκόνων. P

Τοῦ αὐτοῦ ἐκ τοῦ εἰς Βαρλαὰμ τὸν μάρτυρα. V

Inc. Πρότερον μὲν τῶν ἁγίων οἱ θάνατοι· καὶ μετὰ βραχέα· (πρότερον—βραχέα om. V) ἀνάστητέ μοι νῦν (om. V) οἱ (ὦ V) λαμπροί . . .

Des. . . . καὶ ὁ τῶν παλαισμάτων ἀγωνοθέτης Χριστός.

(B) Mansi XIII, 80B–D

Τοῦ ἁγίου Βασιλείου ἐκ τοῦ εἰς τὸν μακάριον Βαρλαὰμ τὸν μάρτυρα· οὗ ἡ ἀρχή·

Inc. Πρότερον μὲν τῶν ἁγίων οἱ θάνατοι· καὶ μεθ᾽ ἕτερα. ἀνάστητέ μοι νῦν, ὦ λαμπροί, . . .

Des. . . . καὶ ὁ τῶν παλαισμάτων ἀγωνοθέτης Χριστός· ᾧ ἡ δόξα εἰς τοὺς αἰῶνας, ἀμήν.

Parisinus gives this quotation under the general title: . . . Βασιλείου . . . μαρτυρίαι περὶ τῶν ἐν ἁγίοις οἴκοις εἰκόνων, since the four extracts that follow belong to the same author. The full title of the work is given by the acts, and it is worth noting that it is almost the same as the title appearing in John of Damascus' *Orationes I–III pro sacris imaginibus* (Dam., I 34; II 30; III 46).[122] V also offers a somewhat shorter lemma.

In the acts the quotation was cited from a book produced by Theodosius, bishop of Catane. Comparing the extract in the acts with that in P, it is evident that the differences between them are minor. Parisinus omits the final sentence: ᾧ ἡ δόξα εἰς τοὺς αἰῶνας. Some other omissions and mistakes can be attributed to Cinnamus, but especially this one:

τοῖς τῆς ὑμετέρας σοφίας περιλάμψατε χρώμασιν: A, Dam., V

τοῖς τοῖς ὑμετέροις περιλάμψατε χρώμασιν: P

On the other hand, there are two points where P is in accordance with Dam. against A. First, the final sentence which P and V omit does not exist in some manuscripts of Dam.[123] Then there is this small part of a sentence:

ζωγράφοι, καὶ (om. V) τὴν τοῦ στρατιώτου κολοβωθεῖσαν εἰκόνα: A, V

ζωγράφοι, τὴν τοῦ στρατηγοῦ κολοβωθεῖσαν εἰκόνα: Dam., P

The Latin translation of the acts (Mansi XIII 79C) reads as follows: *militis abbreviatam imaginem*. There is no doubt, therefore, that this extract in P is taken directly from Damascene's florilegium and not from the acts. Never-

---

[122] Τοῦ ἁγίου Βασιλείου ἐκ τοῦ εἰς τὸν μακάριον Βαρλαὰμ τὸν μάρτυρα A λόγου add. Dam. (Kotter, *Schriften III*, 146).

[123] Ibid., 146. The mss are D = Neapol. 54 (II B 16), and F = Athous Dionys. 175 (3709); see ibid., 36–37 and 34.

theless, a closer look at the text of the acts reveals some cases where A draws also on Dam. Compare the examples:

Dam.: Τοῦ ἁγίου Βασιλείου ἐκ τοῦ εἰς τὸν μακάριον Βαρλαάμ, τὸν μάρτυρα λόγου, οὗ ἡ ἀρχή.

A: Τοῦ ἁγίου Βασιλείου ἐκ τοῦ εἰς τὸν μακάριον Βαρλαάμ, τὸν μάρτυρα, οὗ ἡ ἀρχή.

Dam.	P	A
ὦ λαμπροὶ (= V)	οἱ λαμπροὶ	ὦ λαμπροὶ
τῇ γραφῇ (= V)	τὴν γραφὴν	τῇ γραφῇ

The intervention of V helps us to restore the text of the original of the year 770 (or better its copy of the year 774/5) in a form almost identical with that transmitted by Dam. and gives a measure of the negligence of Cinnamus. In any case, the text of the original of P is closer to the Dam. version than to that of the acts. Therefore, since it has already been proved that almost all the quotations of the first two florilegia of Dam. were included in the original of P, M, and V (= F), and a considerable part of the third, we may assume that there is a possibility of Dam. being, through F, the source of the appearance of this quotation in the acts.

2. Basilii Caesar. (*Sermo*) *in XL martyres Sebastenses* (*PG* 31, 508D–509A); *CPG* 2863; *BHG* 1205

(A) P, fol. 247ᵛ (16*); V, fol. 9 (V 23); M, fol. 240 (53ᴹ)
(Dam. I 44, 46; II 40, 42; III 47, 106)
Τοῦ ἁγίου Βασιλείου, (τοῦ αὐτοῦ P) ἐκ τοῦ λόγου τοῦ εἰς τοὺς τεσσαράκοντα μάρτυρας.
Inc. Δεῦρο οὖν εἰς μέσον αὐτοὺς ἀγαγόντες διὰ τῆς ὑπομνήσεως, . . .
Des. . . . ταῦτα γραφικῇ σιωπῇ (σιωπὼς M) διὰ τῆς (om. M) μιμήσεως δείκνυσιν.

(B) Mansi XIII 277B–C and XIII 300C, inserted in both cases in the *refutatio* of the *horos* of Hiereia. This extract also occurs in XII 1066D–E. It is one of the thirteen extracts that constitute a small florilegium included in Pope Hadrian's synodal letter or *Synodica* of 785. The first part of this extract is also cited in XII 1014E.
Βασίλειος ἐν τῷ ἐγκωμίῳ τῶν ἁγίων τεσσαράκοντα μαρτύρων λόγῳ αὐτοῦ οὕτως φησί·
Inc. Δεῦρο δὴ οὖν εἰς μέσον αὐτοὺς ἀγαγόντες διὰ τῆς ὑπομνήσεως . . .
Des. . . . ταῦτα γραφῇ σιωπῶσα διὰ μιμήσεως δείκνυσιν.

The Dam. version of this quotation (I 44; II 40 and I 46; II 42) reads as follows:

Δεῦρο δὴ οὖν εἰς μέσον αὐτοὺς ἀγαγόντες διὰ τῆς ὑπομνήσεως κοινὴν τὴν ἀπ᾽ αὐτῶν ὠφέλειαν τοῖς παροῦσι καταστησώμεθα, προδείξαντες πᾶσιν ὥσπερ ἐν γραφῇ τὰς τῶν ἀνδρῶν ἀριστείας. Ἐπεὶ καὶ πολέμων ἀνδραγαθήματα καὶ λογογράφοι πολλάκις καὶ ζωγράφοι διασημαίνου-
5 σιν, οἱ μὲν τῷ λόγῳ κοσμοῦντες, οἱ δὲ τοῖς πίναξιν ἐγχαράττοντες, καὶ πολλοὺς ἐπήγειραν εἰς ἀνδρείαν ἑκάτεροι. Ἃ γὰρ ὁ λόγος τῆς ἱστορ-ίας διὰ τῆς ἀκοῆς παρίστησι, ταῦτα γραφικὴ σιωπῶσα διὰ μιμήσεως δείκνυσι.

Sigla:
A = Mansi XII 1014ᴇ ‖ B = Mansi XII 1066ᴅ-ᴇ ‖ C = Mansi XIII 277ʙ-ᴄ ‖ D = Mansi 300ᴄ ‖ P = Paris. gr. 1115 ‖ M = Mosqu. 265 (3 Ἐπεὶ—8 δείκνυσιν) ‖ V = Marc. gr. 573
Apparatus criticus
1 Δεῦρο—3 ἀριστείας om. AB 1 Δεῦρο—6 ἑκάτεροι om. D δὴ om. PV 2 ἀπ᾽: παρ᾽ C 3 post ἀνδρῶν add. τούτων PV post ἀριστείας add. ἐοικώς PV 3 Ἐπεὶ καὶ om. PV post πολέμων add. γὰρ PV 4 ἀνδραγαθήματα: τρόπαια καὶ νίκας B 4 διασημαίνουσιν: κατασημ- PV 6 ἐπήγειραν: διήγειραν ACM, ἐξήγ- P, πρὸς ἀνδραγαθίαν διήγ. B εἰς: πρὸς PV εἰς—6 ἱστορίας om. M 7 ἅ—7 δείκνυσι om. A τῆς ἱστορίας om. D ταῖς ἱστορίαις C: τοῖς λογογράφοις PV διὰ τῆς ἀκοῆς om. B τῆς om. C 7 παρίστησι: ὑπέγραψε B γραφικὴ: γραφὴ BCD σιωπῶσα: σιωπῇ PV, σιωπὼς M post διὰ add. τῆς PV.

The most complete version of this quotation is the one provided by C,[124] which corresponds to the P extract. The words διήγειραν and γραφὴ instead of ἐπήγειραν and γραφικὴ, in lines 6 and 7 respectively, occur in one of the manuscripts of Dam. and appear in the apparatus criticus of Kotter's edition.[125] The mistakes of PV are more serious in this fragment, and it is difficult to establish a clear link between PV and either Dam. or A. Nevertheless, most of the major errors in P can be attributed to Cinnamus again or to the copyist of 774/5. The word τούτων in line 3 seems to have been arbitrarily added. The word ἐοικὼς in the same line that occurs in both PV is an obvious misspelling of ἐπεὶ καὶ at the beginning of the next sentence. This misspelling left the sentence pending with no introductory conjunction, a deficiency that the copyist of 774/5 tried to restore by inserting a γὰρ after πολέμων in line 3. As for the words ὁ λόγος τοῖς λογογράφοις instead of ὁ λόγος τῆς ἱστορίας and σιωπῇ instead of σιωπῶσα in lines 6 and 7, they are

---

[124] The B version, which is the retranslation of the Latin version of Basil's *Sermo*, although in most cases adhering to the Greek original, is not so accurate because the Byzantine translator tried to compromise between the original text he had recognized and the Latin quotation. See Wallach, *Diplomatic Studies*, 32–33.
[125] Kotter, *Schriften III*, 151.

common examples of psychological errors.[126] Finally, for the word κατασημαίνουσι which PV give in the place of διασημαίνουσι in line 4, a misspelling of δια– as κατα– is possible, especially if the exemplar of PV was written in minuscule.

This attempt to restore the original of the PVM extract gives finally a text very close to both Dam. and A. It again seems possible that Dam. was the common source of both F and A, unless Dam. also drew on an ultimate common source.

3. Basilii Caesar. *Epistula ad Iulianum transgressorem* (*PG* 32, 1100, after the acts;[127] also Y. Courtonne, *Saint Basile, Lettres,* III [Paris, 1966], 220), *CPG* 2900 = *Epistula* 360 (Spuria)

(A) P, fol. 247ᵛ (17*); M, fols. 165ᵛ–166, 223ʳ⁻ᵛ (14ᴹ)
Τοῦ αὐτοῦ ἐκ τῆς ἐπιστολῆς τῆς πρὸς Ἰουλιανὸν τὸν βασιλέα καὶ παραβάτην. P
Ἐπιστολὴ τοῦ ὁσίου πατρὸς ἡμῶν Βασιλείου πρὸς Ἰουλιανὸν τὸν παραβάτην. M, fol. 223
ἄκουσον τί καὶ ὁ μέγας θεοφόρος πατὴρ ἡμῶν Βασίλειος ἐν τοῖς ἀντιθέτοις τοῦ Ἰουλιανοῦ δόγμασιν φησίν. M, fol. 163ᵛ
Inc. Κατὰ τὴν θεόθεν ἐπικεκληρωμένην ἡμῖν (ἡμῶν M) ἀμώμητον . . .
Des. . . . ἐν πάσαις (ἀπάσαις M) ταῖς ἐκκλησίαις ἡμῶν τούτων ἀνιστορουμένων.

(B) 1. Mansi XIII 72ᴇ–73ᴀ
Τοῦ ἐν ἁγίοις πατρὸς ἡμῶν Βασιλείου ἐκ τῆς ἐπιστολῆς αὐτοῦ πρὸς Ἰουλιανὸν τὸν παραβάτην.
Inc. Κατὰ τὴν θεόθεν ἐπικεκληρωμένην ἡμῖν ἀμώμητον πίστιν τῶν Χριστιανῶν, . . .
Des. . . . ἐν πάσαις ταῖς ἐκκλησίαις ἡμῶν τούτων ἀνιστορουμένων.
2. Mansi XII 1066ᴄ–ᴅ Greek text; *MGH, Conc.* 2. 2 (= *LS*) 511.3–12
Latin text
. . . ἐν τῇ ἐπιστολῇ τοῦ ἁγίου Βασιλείου τῇ πρὸς Ἰουλιανὸν τὸν παραβάτην ἐμφέρεται·
Inc. καθὼς ἐκληρονομήσαμεν ἐκ τοῦ Θεοῦ τὴν ἡμετέραν ἄμεμπτον πίστιν τῶν Χριστιανῶν . . .
Latin: Secundum id quod divinitus datam, haereditariam nobis immaculatam Christianorum fidem . . .

---

[126] See M. L. West, *Textual Criticism and Editorial Technique* (Stuttgart, 1973), 23: "There are several ways in which an individual word may be miswritten without having been misread. By far the commonest is partial assimilation to some other word nearby."
[127] See Van den Ven, "Patristique," 348–49.

Des. . . . ἐν πάσαις ταῖς ἐκκλησίαις ἡμῶν τὴν αὐτῶν ἀναστηλοῦμεν ἱστορίαν.
Latin: . . . sed in omnibus ecclesiis nostris eorum designantes historiam.

Apart from the acts, this extract appears in the third part of the Νουθεσία[128] (M, fols. 164ᵛ–165) and is also included in the Iconophile florilegium that follows the Νουθεσία in the same manuscript (M, fol. 223ʳ⁻ᵛ). On
both occasions the fragment contains almost the same mistakes and omissions.

I have already cited above the P and M versions of this fragment[129] as
a typical example of the dependence of P and M on a common original.

In the acts this quotation was read out from a book that was offered by
the legates of Pope Hadrian. It is strange that the formula ἧς ἡ ἀρχὴ is absent
here, an omission that arouses the suspicion that this extract was the only
extant piece of the letter.

This quotation in M (fols. 165ᵛ–166) reads as follows:
. . . Βασίλειος ἐν τοῖς ἀντιθέτοις τοῦ Ἰουλιανοῦ δόγμασίν φησιν· κατὰ
τὴν θεόθεν ἡμῶν ἐπικεκληρωμένην ἀμώμητον πίστιν τοῖς χριστιανοῖς
ὁμολογῶ καὶ συντίθημι· πιστεύω εἰς ἕνα Θεὸν πατέρα παντοκράτορα,
Θεὸν τὸν πατέρα, Θεὸν τὸν υἱόν, Θεὸν τὸ πνεῦμα τὸ ἅγιον, ἕνα Θεὸν
5   τὰ τρία (fol. 166) προσκυνῶ καὶ δοξάζω· ὁμολογῶ δὲ καὶ τὴν τοῦ υἱοῦ
ἔνσαρκον οἰκονομίαν, καὶ θεοτόκον τὴν κατὰ σάρκα τεκοῦσαν αὐτὸν
ἁγίαν Μαρίαν· δέχομαι δὲ καὶ τοὺς ἁγίους ἀποστόλους, προφήτας καὶ
μάρτυρας καὶ εἰς τὴν πρὸς Θεὸν ἱκεσίαν τοῦ δι᾿ αὐτῶν ἤγουν τῆς μεσιτείας αὐτῶν ἵλεών μοι γενέσθαι τὸν φιλάνθρωπον Θεὸν καὶ λύτρον
10   μοι τῶν πταισμάτων χαρίσασθαι. ὅθεν καὶ τοὺς χαρακτῆρας τῶν ἁγίων
εἰκόνων αὐτῶν τιμῶ καὶ προσκυνῶ, κατ᾿ ἐξαίρετον τοῦτο παραδεδομένον ἔκ τε τῶν ἁγίων ἀποστόλων καὶ οὐκ ἀπηγορευμένον, ἀλλ᾿ ἐν
ἁπάσαις ταῖς ἐκκλησίαις ἡμῶν τούτων ἀνιστορουμένων.

Although, as I have argued above, the Νουθεσία made use of a copy of
the τεῦχος of 770 (F), this fragment differs in some cases from the quotation
in F. The most significant difference is the following:

P: καὶ εἰς τὴν πρὸς Θεὸν ἱκεσίαν τούτους ἐπικαλοῦμαι, τοῦ δι᾿ αὐτῶν,
ἤγουν τῆς μεσιτείας αὐτῶν, ἵλεών μοι γενέσθαι . . .
M: καὶ εἰς τὴν πρὸς Θεὸν ἱκεσίαν
ἤγουν τῆς μεσητίας αὐτῶν, ἤλεον μοι γενέσθαι . . .

---

[128] Melioranskij, Georgij, p. XXXIII.
[129] See above, pp. 102–3.

Νουθ.: καὶ εἰς τὴν πρὸς Θεὸν ἱκεσίαν   τοῦ δι᾽ αὐτῶν,
ἤγουν etc.

This omission, which is more extensive in the florilegium of Mosquensis, is once more clear evidence of the negligence of the copyist of M. In any case, the variants that P, M, A and the *LS* offer are the following:

Sigla
P = Paris. gr. 1115, fol. 247ᵛ ‖ M = Mosqu. Hist. Mus. 265, fols. 223ʳ⁻ᵛ ‖ A = Mansi XIII 72ᴇ–73ᴀ ‖ L = *Libellus Synodalis* of 825 (*MHG, Conc.* 2.2, p. 511.4–12), which gives a better version of the *Synodica's* text.
Apparatus criticus
1 Βασίλειος—φησιν: τοῦ αὐτοῦ ἐκ τῆς ἐπιστολῆς τῆς πρὸς Ἰουλιανὸν τὸν βασιλέα καὶ παραβάτην P, Ἐπιστολὴ τοῦ ὁσίου πατρὸς ἡμῶν Βασιλείου πρὸς Ἰουλιανὸν τὸν παραβάτην M, . . . ἐκ τῆς ἐπιστολῆς αὐτοῦ πρὸς Ἰουλιανὸν τὸν παραβάτην A, . . . Sancti Basilii in epistulam ad Julianum imperatorem missa L 2 ἡμῶν om PMA post ἐπικεκληρωμένην add. ἡμῖν PA, ἡμῶν M πίστιν—χριστιανοῖς: τῶν χριστιανῶν πίστιν P, χριστιανοῖς πίστιν M, πίστιν τῶν Χριστιανῶν A 3 ὁμολογῶ—7 Μαρίαν om. P inserens καὶ μεθ᾽ ἕτερα. πιστεύω: πιστεύειν A, credo L 7 post προφήτας add. τε P 8 post ἱκεσίαν add. τούτους ἐπικαλοῦμαι PA τοῦ—αὐτῶν om. M 9 φιλάνθρωπον: misericordissimum L 10 χαρίσασθαι: δωρήσασθαι P, γενέσθαι καὶ δοθῆναι A ἁγίων om. PMAL 11 post προσκυνῶ add. καὶ P 12 τε om. PA 13 ἁπάσαις: πάσαις PA

It is possible that the papal translator had a partially corrupt original in front of him, such as the quotation in the Νουθεσία. The correspondence between L on the one hand and P combined with Mosqu. 265, fol. 223ᵛ, where the same passage occurs, on the other is interesting. Compare:

MP: κατὰ τὴν θεόθεν ἐπικεκληρωμένην ἡμῖν ἀμώμητον ⟨τοῖς⟩ Χριστιανοῖς (τῶν Χριστιανῶν P) πίστιν
L: Secundum id, quod divinitus datam, haereditariam nobis, immaculatam Christianorum fidem.

The following extract from L, is obviously a translation of a mutilated part of the extract like the one appearing in the Νουθεσία or in M.

Νουθεσία: δέχομαι δὲ καὶ τοὺς ἁγίους ἀποστόλους . . . καὶ εἰς τὴν πρὸς Θεὸν ἱκεσίαν, τοῦ δι᾽ αὐτῶν, ἤγουν τῆς μεσιτείας αὐτῶν ἵλεών μοι γενέσθαι.
Libellus Synodalis: Suscipio vero et sanctos apostolos . . . et ad Deum deprecationem quae per eos—scilicet illis mediantibus—propitiatorem mihi efficit.

Here the redactor found himself in an awkward position because the text he was translating had omitted the words τούτους ἐπικαλοῦμαι after ἱκεσίαν. It is difficult to explain this relation between the Νουθεσία-M version and the Latin translation of this extract. P in this case gives the most complete text, but is not the one that served as the basis for the Latin translation.

On the other hand, the omission of almost five lines by P has been discussed elsewhere, and it is fairly certain that they were included in the original (F) since they are transmitted through M. Moreover, P agrees four times with A against the Νουθεσία, whereas it comes closer to the Νουθεσία only once, in line 10 (χαρίσασθαι Νουθεσία: δωρήσασθαι P: condonari L: γενέσθαι καὶ δοθῆναι M).

In conclusion, the two versions that appear in the acts can be connected in the following way with the existing transmissions of this fragment.

(A) The extract in the chain of *testimonia* incorporated into the *Synodica* of 785 (Mansi XII 1066c-d or, for a better text, *LS*, 511.4–12) seems to have relied in its Latin form on a slightly corrupt passage like that of the Νουθεσία. Since this quotation was originally included in the acts of the 731 council in Rome, it is possible that the defective Greek fragment was already available in Rome before 731. If this hypothesis is correct, then the compiler of 770 or the copyist of 774/5 are the only persons who can have improved the text.

(B) The quotation that was read out during the fourth session of the council (Mansi XIII 72e-73a) appears to have drawn on F because the combination of the P and M versions seems to correspond to the text of the acts. Compare:

A: Τοῦ ἐν ἁγίοις πατρὸς ἡμῶν Βασιλείου ἐκ τῆς ἐπιστολῆς αὐτοῦ πρὸς Ἰουλιανὸν τὸν παραβάτην.
M: Ἐπιστολὴ τοῦ ὁσίου πατρὸς ἡμῶν Βασιλείου πρὸς Ἰουλιανὸν τὸν παραβάτην.
P: Τοῦ αὐτοῦ ἐκ τῆς ἐπιστολῆς πρὸς Ἰουλιανόν, τὸν βασιλέα καὶ παραβάτην.

A: Κατὰ τὴν θεόθεν ἐπικεκληρωμένην ἡμῖν ἀμώμητον πίστιν τῶν Χριστιανῶν ὁμολογῶ καὶ συντίθημι πιστεύειν . . .
M: Κατὰ τὴν θεόθεν ἐπικεκληρωμένην ἡμῶν ἀμώμητον χριστιανοῖς πίστιν ὁμολογῶ καὶ συντίθημι· πιστεύω . . .
P: Κατὰ τὴν θεόθεν ἐπικεκληρωμένην ἡμῖν ἀμώμητον τῶν Χριστιανῶν πί-στιν[. . . . . . .]
L: Secundum id, quod divinitus datam haereditariam nobis, immaculatam Christianorum fidem confiteor et promitto. credo . . .

In this example we can observe an almost word-for-word correspondence between P and L from Κατὰ . . . until πίστιν and between M and L for the rest of the sentence. Apparently no copy of F has preserved a perfect text.

4. Basilii Caesar. *Sermo contra Sabellianos et Arium et Anomaeos* (*PG* 31, 605ᴅ–608ᴀ); *CPG* 2869

P, fol. 248 (19*); (Dam. I 48; II 44)
Mansi XIII 72ᴀ–ʙ and XIII 273ᴇ (only the incipit)
Τοῦ ἁγίου Βασιλείου (τοῦ αὐτοῦ P) ἐκ τοῦ λόγου τοῦ κατὰ Σαβελλιανῶν καὶ Ἀρείου καὶ τῶν Ἀνομοίων, ⟨οὗ ἡ ἀρχή·⟩ A
Inc. Μάχεται Ἰουδαϊσμὸς Ἑλληνισμῷ καὶ ἀμφότεροι Χριστιανισμῷ· καὶ μεθ' ἕτερα: ἀλλ' ὁ τῆς ἀληθείας λόγος ἑκατέρωθεν τὰ ἐναντιώματα διαπέφευγεν . . .
Des. . . . τὴν τιμὴν ἐβεβαίωσε διὰ τῆς τούτου ὁμολογίας.

The earlier attestation of this quotation comes from one of the manuscripts that preserve the first and second *Orationes pro sacris imaginibus* of John of Damascus, namely, from Athous Dionys. 175, appended to a scholium that bears the number I 48, II 44 in the printed edition.

The differences among the three versions (P, A, and Dam.) are minor:

1. καὶ Ἀρειανῶν καὶ Ἀνομ. Dam.: καὶ Ἀρείου καὶ τῶν Ἀνομ. PA
2. καὶ ἀμφότεροι Χριστιανισμῷ PA om. Dam.
3. ὁ τῆς Dam. A: ὅτι τῆς P
4. οὐ Dam.: οὐδὲ PA
5. δείξας Dam., P: δεικνὺς A
6. τὸ πρωτότυπον Dam.: τὸν πρωτότυπον PA
7. εἰ γὰρ ἡ εἰκὼν βασιλεύς, πολλῷ δήπου εἰκὸς βασιλέα εἶναι τὸν τῇ εἰκόνι παρασχόμενον τὴν αἰτίαν Dam.: om. PA.

As we can see, A agrees with P against Dam. in five instances (1, 2, 4, 6, 7), A agrees with Dam. against P in one case, but it is crystal clear that this is a misspelling introduced by Cinnamus (3, ὁ τῆς Dam. A: ὅτι τῆς P), and Dam. agrees with P against A just once (5, δείξας Dam. P: δεικνὺς A), which, however, is sufficient for the establishment of a direct link between Dam. and P. On the basis of these agreements, it can be claimed that F was the source of A.

5. Gregorii Naz. *Carmina moralia, De Virtute* (*PG* 37, 737–38); *CPG* 3035

(A) P, fol. 248 (21*); V, fols. 3ᵛ–4 (V 9); (Dam. III 109)
Τοῦ ἁγίου Γρηγορίου τοῦ θεολόγου ἐκ τῶν ἐπῶν περὶ ἀρετῆς λόγου καὶ εἰς Πολέμωνα. P

Γρηγορίου τοῦ θεολόγου ἐκ τοῦ περὶ ἀρετῆς καὶ εἰς Πολέμωνα λόγου. V

Inc. Θεὸν τὸν πάντων αἴτιον πρῶτον καλῶ, (om. V)

Οὐδ᾿ ὁ Πολέμων ἐμοὶ (ἐμοίγε V) σιγηθήσεται.

Des. Καὶ τοῦτο πολλοῖς οἶδα τῶν λαλουμένων.

(B) Mansi XIII 13B–C

Τοῦ ἁγίου Γρηγορίου τοῦ Θεολόγου ἐκ τῶν ἐπῶν ἐκ τοῦ περὶ ἀρετῆς
λόγου, οὗ ἡ ἀρχή·

Inc. Θεὸν τὸν πάντων αἴτιον πρῶτον καλῶ. Καὶ μεθ᾿ ἕτερα·

Οὐδ᾿ ὁ Πολέμων ἔμοιγε σιγηθήσεται . . . .

Des. . . . ὡς ζῶντ᾿ ἐπαισχυνθεῖσα τὸν γεγραμμένον.

On this quotation P. Van den Ven remarks: "L'incipit de la pièce complète donné par les Actes après la formule οὗ ἡ ἀρχή: Θεὸν τὸν πάντων αἴτιον
πρῶτον καλῶ, *PG* 37, 693, l. 13 (vers 184), ne correspond pas à celui de
l'édition: Πολλῶν ἀκούω καὶ λέγοιμι μὴ μάτην, *PG* 37, 680 (vers 1), ce qui
semble indiquer que le concile avait en main un manuscrit incomplet."[130]

Although, compared with the acts, P is full of mistakes, it is more than
possible that the manuscript that Van den Ven had in mind was the archetype of PVM. The reason for this is that PV provide at the end one more
verse: Καὶ τοῦτο πολλοῖς οἶδα τῶν λαλουμένων, which comes after the
whole excerpt in the edition of Migne. The quotation is also included in
Dam. III 109, though the desinit there is the same as the one in the acts
and the incipit does not include the supposedly initial verse (Θεὸν τῶν
πάντων . . .).

A list of the variants common to P and A in comparison with the text in
PG and Dam. might be of some help.

Dam.	P	A
—(= V)	Θεὸν τὸν πάντων αἴτιον πρῶτον καλῶ	P
Οὐδὲ	Οὐδ᾿ ὁ (= V)	P
ἔμοιγε (= V)	ἐμοὶ	Dam.
γ᾿ αἰσχρὸς	γὲ αἰσχρῶν (= V)	Dam.
δ᾿ ἔρωτι (= V)	δὲ ἔρωτι	Dam.
τιν᾿	τὶ (τινὰ: V)	Dam.
εἴθ᾿ ἑαυτὸν	εἴτε αὐτὸν (= V)	Dam.
ὥσθ᾿ ἕν τι	ὥστ᾿ ἕν τι (= V)	Dam.
ὑπερκύπτων (= V)	ὑποκύπτων	Dam.
ταύτην (= V)	ταύτ᾿	Dam.
ζῶντ᾿ ἐπαισχυνθεῖσα	ζῶντα αἰσχυνθεῖσα (= V)	Dam.

[130] Van den Ven, "Patristique," 352.

Compare also:

PG: Έταίραν εἰσεκάλει τις ἀκρατὴς νέος

Dam.: Έταίραν εἰσκαλεῖ τις ἀκρατὴς νέος·

PV: ἑταιρίδα εἰσκαλεῖταί τις ἀκρατὴς νέος·

A: ἑταιρίδ' εἰσκαλεῖταί τις ἀκρατὴς νέος·

PG, Dam., and A give a metrically correct verse, while P in all the cases where it differs from Dam. results in metrical errors. This leads to the following conclusions: Cinnamus is to be held responsible for some of the errors, something that can be verified by the witness of V in five cases; his exemplar also was corrupt, which is possible in another five instances.

What the above analysis may point out is that the text which finally appeared in the acts was a version that drew equally on Dam. and F aiming at the best possible metrical result. One simple question is in order here. It has already been proved that F included almost all the *testimonia* of the first and second Iconophile florilegia of John of Damascus and at least part of the third. Did these florilegia arrive in Constantinople as one τεῦχος, as I have suggested for the florilegium that was compiled in 770? Or did they come to Constantinople as separate codices? It is difficult to answer, but if the answer to the first question is positive, then F should have included some quotations more than once. We have already seen the case of quotation 25ᴹ, which is the same as 39ᴹ; here we possibly have a second instance of the same phenomenon with the P and Dam. versions of the present fragment. As is normal under the circumstances described above, the two quotations are not textually identical.

At any rate, it seems likely that the persons in charge of the preparation of the conciliar procedure had access to both F and Dam.[131] Whether they were to be found in a single volume or in different books is a matter of little significance, although the first option seems more probable.

The most significant point that can be made about this fragment is related to the wrong incipit given by both P and A. Two sources quoting the same wrong verse as the opening line of the poem is an extraordinary coincidence. One has to accept that one of these sources has provided the fragment to the other. So the possible solutions are two: either this excerpt is a post-787 interpolation to the original of PV, or Nicaea II made use of florilegia.

6. Basilii Caesar. *De Spiritu Sancto*, ed. B. Pruche, *Basile de Césarée. Sur le Saint-Esprit*, 2nd ed., *SC* 17bis (Paris, 1968), 45.15–46.9 (*PG* 32, 149.33–39); *CPG* 2839

---

[131] See also below, the study of quot. 46.

(A) P, fol. 248ʳ⁻ᵛ (25*); V, fol. 3ᵛ (V 8)

(Dam. I 35; II 31; III 48)

Inc. mutile propter lacunam, sine nomine auctoris . . . λέγεται καὶ ἡ τοῦ βασιλέως εἰκών· P

Τοῦ αὐτοῦ ἐκ τοῦ πρὸς Ἀμφιλόχιον περὶ ἁγίου Πνεύματος κεφαλαίου ΙΗ΄. βασιλεὺς λέγεται καὶ ἡ τοῦ βασιλέως εἰκὼν V

Des. . . . τοῦ δὲ τρόπου τῆς ὑπάρξεως ἀρρήτου φυλαττομένου P

ἐν τῇ κοινωνίᾳ τῆς θεότητος ἔστιν ἡ ἕνωσις V

(B) Mansi XIII 69D

Τοῦ ἁγίου Βασιλείου ἐκ τῶν πρὸς Ἀμφιλόχιον τριάκοντα κεφαλαίων περὶ τοῦ ἁγίου πνεύματος, ἀπὸ κεφαλαίου ιζ΄.

Inc. Ὅτι βασιλεὺς λέγεται καὶ ἡ τοῦ βασιλέως εἰκών, . . .

Des. . . . διότι ἡ τῆς εἰκόνος τιμὴ ἐπὶ τὸ πρωτότυπον διαβαίνει.

The passage was very well known to the participants of the council owing to the citation διότι ἡ τῆς εἰκόνος τιμὴ ἐπὶ τὸ πρωτότυπον διαβαίνει, which is included in it. The *Doctrina Patrum* is perhaps its earliest source.[132] Although it is provided by the last chapter of the *Doctrina*, P relies on the first chapter of the work (4, XI) and gives the most extended version of the quotation. The P version is almost identical with the modern edition of the text.

In the acts only a small part of the quotation is cited, probably from Dam. I 35; II 31; III 48. The lemma is exactly the same in both Dam. and A, and there is only one difference in the text: διαμερίζεται Dam. (= *Doctrina*, P, V, edition): μερίζεται A.

The relation of the four quotations can be depicted in the following stemma:

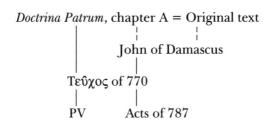

Doctrina Patrum, chapter A = Original text

John of Damascus

Τεῦχος of 770

PV　　　Acts of 787

7. Gregorii Nysseni (*Sermo*) *de deitate Filii et Spiritus Sancti* (*PG* 46, 572c); *CPG* 3192; *BHG* 2354

---

[132] *Doctrina Patrum*, chap. Α΄ 4, XI and chap. ΜΕ΄ 329, XIV.

(A) P, fol. 251 (43*); (Dam. I 52; II 48; III 50)

Τοῦ ἁγίου Γρηγορίου ἐπισκόπου Νύσης ἐκ τοῦ περὶ θεότητος λόγου καὶ εἰς τὸν Ἀβραάμ.

Inc. . . . Οἷόν τι πάσχουσι πρὸς τοὺς πολυανθεῖς τῶν λειμόνων (sic) καὶ μεθ' ἕτερα· εἶδον πολλάκις ἐπὶ γραφῆς εἰκόνα. . .

Des. . . . καὶ περιηγμένας ἔχων εἰς τοὐπίσω τὰς χεῖρας.

(B) Mansi XIII 9c–d. The work is also mentioned in XIII 117a. In XII 1066b a very small extract is given inserted in the *Synodica* of 785:

Ἐκ τοῦ λόγου τοῦ ἁγίου Γρηγορίου Νύσσης λεχθέντος ἐν Κωνσταντινουπόλει. περὶ θεότητος υἱοῦ καὶ πνεύματος καὶ εἰς τὸν Ἀβραάμ, οὗ ἡ ἀρχή

Inc. Οἷόν τι πάσχουσι πρὸς τοὺς πολυανθεῖς τῶν λειμώνων· καὶ μεθ' ἕτερα: εἶδον πολλάκις ἐπὶ γραφεῖς (sic) εἰκόνα . . .

Des. . . . καὶ τότε αὐτῷ γίνεται θεόθεν φωνὴ τὸ ἔργον κωλύουσα.

The main part of the quotation, Εἶδον πολλάκις ἐπὶ γραφῆς εἰκόνα τοῦ πάθους καὶ οὐκ ἀδακρυτὶ τὴν θέαν παρῆλθον, ἐναργῶς τῆς τέχνης ὑπ' ὄψιν ἀγούσης τὴν ἱστορίαν, appears in the *Doctrina* (328 X), but it is Dam. (I 52; II 48; III 50) that gives a longer incipit and desinit. In the acts, the quotation is cited after Dam. with almost the same title:

Dam.: Τοῦ ἁγίου Γρηγορίου τοῦ Νύσης ἀπὸ λόγου ῥηθέντος ἐν Κωνσταντινουπόλει περὶ θεότητος υἱοῦ καὶ πνεύματος καὶ εἰς τὸν Ἀβραάμ, λόγου μδ΄, οὗ ἡ ἀρχή· Οἷόν τι πάσχουσι πρὸς τοὺς εὐανθεῖς . . .

A: Ἐκ τοῦ λόγου τοῦ ἁγίου Γρηγορίου Νύσσης λεχθέντος ἐν Κωνσταντινουπόλει, περὶ θεότητος υἱοῦ καὶ πνεύματος, καὶ εἰς τὸν Ἀβραάμ· οὗ ἡ ἀρχή· Οἷόν τι πάσχουσι πρὸς τοὺς πολυανθεῖς. . . .

The different readings are very few, and A omits two lines from the incipit that are given by Dam.

The first part of the quotation (Εἶδον—ἱστορίαν) in P is identical with Dam. and A, although the lemma is considerably shorter (Τοῦ ἁγίου Γρηγορίου Νύσης ἐκ τοῦ περὶ θεότητος λόγου καὶ εἰς τὸν Ἀβραάμ). The reading τοὺς πολυανθεῖς, which is given by P and A, is εὐανθεῖς in Dam.

The second part of the quotation, which is an *ekphrasis* of an image of the sacrifice of Abraham, poses a considerable problem: P omits the last seven lines of the passage, as it appears in the acts. The initial question emerges again: who is responsible for that, the compiler of the florilegium himself or Cinnamus? If we take into account the quotations examined so far, the intervention of Cinnamus seems more than possible. A more reliable answer to the problem may be given after the examination of the next quotation.

8. Gregorii Nyss. *In Canticum canticorum, hom. XV,* ed. H. Langerbeck, *Gregorii Nysseni Opera VI* (Leiden, 1960), 28.7–17 *(PG* 44, 776A); *CPG* 3158

(A) P, fol. 251 (44*); M, fol. 236 (42ᴹ)

Τοῦ αὐτοῦ ἐκ τῆς ἑρμηνείας τοῦ ἄσματος τῶν ἀσμάτων P
Τοῦ ἁγίου Ἰωάννου τοῦ Χρυσοστόμου ἐκ τῆς ἑρμηνίας τοῦ ἄσματος τῶν ἀσμάτων M

Inc. Κατὰ τὴν ζωγραφικὴν ἐπιστήμην ὕλη πάντως ἐστὶ ἐν διαφόροις βαφέσι (sic) συμπληροῦσα . . . P
Ὥσπερ δὲ κατὰ τὴν γραφικὴν ἐπιστήμην . . . M

Des. . . . ὃ διὰ τῶν χρωμάτων ὁ τεχνίτης ἀνέδειξεν. P and M

(B) Mansi XII 1066B–C, Latin = XII 1065D–E

ἐκ τῆς ἑρμηνείας αὐτοῦ τῆς εἰς τὰ ἄσματα τῶν ἀσμάτων, καθὼς ἡ γεγραμμένη διδαχὴ λέγει.
Latin: . . . de interpretatione ejus in cantica canticorum, sicut conscripta doctrina dicit.

Inc. ὕλη τίς ἐστι παντελῶς ἐν διαφόροις βαφαῖς ἀναπληροῦσα . . .
Lat. Materia quaedam est omnino in diversis tincturis, quae complet . . .
Des. . . . ἀλλὰ πρὸς τὴν θεωρίαν τοῦ πρωτοτύπου ἀνάγεται.
Lat. . . . quam per colores magister demonstravit.

The various transmissions of the passage are the following:

(A) *Gregorii Nysseni Commentarius in Canticum Canticorum,* ed. H. Langerbeck (Leiden, 1960), 28.7–17 *(PG* 44, 776A)
ὥσπερ δὲ κατὰ τὴν γραφικὴν ἐπιστήμην ὕλη μέν τις πάντως ἐστὶν ἐν διαφόροις βαφαῖς ἡ συμπληροῦσα τοῦ ζῴου τὴν μίμησιν, ὁ δὲ πρὸς τὴν εἰκόνα βλέπων τὴν ἐκ τῆς τέχνης διὰ τῶν χρωμάτων συμπληρωθεῖσαν οὐ ταῖς ἐπιχρωσθείσαις τῷ πίνακι βαφαῖς ἐμφιλοχωρεῖ τῷ θεάματι, ἀλλὰ πρὸς τὸ εἶδος βλέπει μόνον, ὃ διὰ τῶν χρωμάτων ὁ τεχνίτης ἀνέδειξεν.

(B) P, fol. 251: . . . ἐκ τῆς ἑρμηνείας τοῦ ἄσματος τῶν ἀσμάτων·
Κατὰ τὴν ζωγραφικὴν ἐπιστήμην ὕλη πάντως ἔστι ἐν διαφόροις βαφέσι συμπληροῦσα τοῦ ζῴου τὴν μίμησιν, πρὸς τὴν εἰκόνα δέ τις βλέπων τὴν ἐκ τῆς τέχνης διὰ τῶν χρωμάτων συμπληρωθεῖσαν τοῦ πινακίου ταῖς βαφαῖς, φιλοχωρεῖ τῷ θεάματι, ἀλλὰ πρὸς τὸ εἶδος βλέπει μόνον, ὃ διὰ τῶν χρωμάτων ὁ τεχνίτης ἀνέδειξεν.

(C) M, fol. 236: Τοῦ ἁγίου Ἰωάννου τοῦ Χρυσοστόμου (sic !) ἐκ τῆς ἑρμηνίας τοῦ ἄσματος τῶν ἀσμάτων·
Ὥσπερ δὲ κατὰ τὴν γραφικὴν ἐπιστήμην ὕλη μέν τίς ἐστιν παντὸς ἐν διαφόροις βαφαῖς ἡ συμπληρούμενη (–σα supra lineam) τοῦ ζῴου τὴν μίμησιν· ὁ δὲ πρὸς τὴν εἰκόνα βλέπων τὴν ἐκ τέχνης διὰ τῶν χρωμάτων συμπληρωθῆ-

σαν (sic) τῶ πήνακι (sic), οὐ ταῖς βαφαῖς ἐμφιλοχωρεῖ τῶ θεάματι, ἀλλὰ πρὸς τὸ εἶδος βλέπει μόνον, ὃ διὰ τῶν χρωμάτων ὁ τεχνήτης (sic) ἀνέδειξεν.

(D) Latin translation of the quotation in the *Synodica* of 785 cited in *LS*, 513.25–29.[133]

Item ipse in interpretationem in cantica canticorum: Sicut vero conscripta doctrina materia quaedam est, ita omnino in diversis tincturis, quae complent animantis imitationem. Qui vero imaginem conspicit ex eadem arte per colores completam tabulam, non tincturis praefert contemplationem, sed visionem depictam conspicit tantummodo, quam per colores magister demonstravit.

The Greek quotation in B differs from the edited text in A, and some emendations are necessary. The reading βαφέσι (sic!) is an evident misreading of βαφαῖς ἡ, and the reading τοῦ πινακίου stands for the original τῷ πίνακι, οὐ. Some other omissions or alterations (ὥσπερ δέ, μέν τις, etc.) are, in all probability, part of the contribution of Cinnamus. It is a happy incident, however, that M preserves a much better text than that of P.

As L. Wallach claims: "The Latin translation of Gregory's original text in *JE 2448* (= *Synodica*), as cited in the *Libellus Synodalis* of 825, is by and large a literal one."[134] Indeed, the Latin translator follows almost verbatim the Greek original but for one case. Compare the sentences:

A: ὁ δὲ πρὸς τὴν εἰκόνα βλέπων τὴν ἐκ τῆς τέχνης διὰ τῶν χρωμάτων συμπληρωθεῖσαν οὐ ταῖς ἐπιχρωσθείσαις τῷ πίνακι βαφαῖς ἐμφιλοχωρεῖ τῷ θεάματι (Langerbeck)

B: πρὸς τὴν εἰκόνα δέ τις βλέπων τὴν ἐκ τῆς τέχνης διὰ τῶν χρωμάτων συμπληρωθεῖσαν τοῦ πινακίου (=τῷ πίνακι, οὐ) ταῖς βαφαῖς φιλοχωρεῖ τῷ θεάματι P

C: ὁ δὲ πρὸς τὴν εἰκόνα βλέπων τὴν ἐκ τέχνης διὰ τῶν χρωμάτων συμπληρωθῆσαν τῷ πίνακι, οὐ ταῖς βαφαῖς ἐμφιλοχωρεῖ τῷ θεάματι M

D: Qui vero imaginem conspicit ex eadem arte per colores completam tabulam, non tincturis praefert contemplationem (*LS*)

There is no doubt that the papal redactor translated the archetype of the quotation in the original of M and P (F), because D is much closer to B (= P) and especially to C (= M) than to A (= Langerbeck ed.).

Now we may return to quotation no. 7. The two fragments (7 and 8) are both included, one next to the other, in Hadrian I's *Synodica* of 785,

---

[133] See Wallach, *Diplomatic Studies*, 86–87. The study of the Greek text in Mansi XII 1066B–C is useless because it is a retranslation of the Latin translation of the Greek original, ibid., 88.

[134] Ibid., 88.

which implies that they were lifted from the acts of the 731 and 769 Roman synods. Quotation no. 7 has also been preserved in the *Libellus Synodalis* of 825 and reads as follows: Vidi . . . multoties imaginem passionis . . . deducens historiam, et cetera. The underlined words could well stand for the fragment of the *ekphrasis* that P gives, and which in the translator's opinion was not worth translating, an opinion that some centuries later Cinnamus obviously shared.

Thus this quotation, along with the previous one, must have been part of the florilegium compiled in 770 since their Latin versions were included in the acts of the 731 and 769 councils, as I have suggested in Chapter I.

9. Iohannis Chrysostomi *De s. Meletio Antiocheno* (*PG* 50, 515A–B); *CPG* 4345; *BHG* 1244

(A) P, fols. 251ᵛ–252 (53*); V, fol. 4ʳ⁻ᵛ (V 10); M, fols. 228ᵛ–229 (26ᴹ); (Dam. II 62)

Τοῦ ἁγίου Ἰωάννου τοῦ Χρυσοστόμου ἐκ τοῦ λόγου εἰς Μελέτιον ἐπίσκοπον Ἀντιοχείας καὶ εἰς τὴν σπουδὴν τῶν συνελθόντων. P

Τοῦ ἐν ἁγίοις πατρὸς ἡμῶν Ἰωάννου τοῦ Χρυσοστόμου ἐκ τοῦ λόγου τοῦ πρὸς Μελέτιον ἐπίσκοπον Ἀντιοχείας καὶ μάρτυρα, ἐν ᾧ καὶ εἰς τὴν σπουδὴν τῶν συνελθόντων. V

Τοῦ αὐτοῦ· ἐκ τῆς ἐπιστολῆς τῆς πρὸς Μελέτιον ἐπίσκοπον M

Inc. Πανταχοῦ τῆς ἱερᾶς ταύτης ἀγέλης περιφέρω τοὺς ὀφθαλμούς· καὶ μετὰ βραχέα· καὶ ἦν εὐσεβείας διδασκαλία τὸ γινόμενον . . . P

Ὅπερ οὖν ἐπ᾽ ὀνόματι αὐτοῦ ἐποιήσατε . . . V

Καὶ ἦν εὐλαβείας διδασκαλία τὸ γινόμενον . . . M

Des. . . . καὶ διπλήν (sic) τινα τῆς ἀποδημίας ἔχειν τὴν (om. VM) παραμυθίαν.

(B) Mansi XIII 8C–D

Τοῦ ἁγίου πατρὸς ἡμῶν Ἰωάννου τοῦ Χρυσοστόμου ἐκ τοῦ εἰς Μελέτιον ἐγκωμίου, οὗ ἡ ἀρχή·

Inc. Πανταχοῦ τῆς ἱερᾶς ταύτης ἀγέλης περιφέρων τοὺς ὀφθαλμοὺς καὶ τὴν πόλιν ἅπασαν ἐνταῦθα παροῦσαν βλέπων, οὐκ ἔχω τίνα μακαρίσω· καὶ μεθ᾽ ἕτερα· καὶ ἦν εὐλαβείας (Lat.: reverentiae) διδασκαλία τὸ γινόμενον.

Des. . . . καὶ διπλῆν τινα τῆς ἀποδημίας ἔχειν παραμυθίαν.

Dam. (II 62, *Schriften III*, 163) seems to be the primary source of this passage. Compare the titles:

Dam.: Τοῦ αὐτοῦ Ἰωάννου τοῦ Χρυσοστόμου ἐκ τοῦ εἰς Μελέτιον, ἐπίσκοπον Ἀντιοχείας καὶ μάρτυρα λόγου καὶ εἰς τὴν σπουδὴν τῶν συνελθόντων, . . .

P: Τοῦ ἁγίου Ἰωάννου τοῦ Χρυσοστόμου ἐκ τοῦ λόγου εἰς Μελέτιον ἐπίσκοπον Ἀντιοχείας (καὶ μάρτυρα add. V) καὶ εἰς τὴν σπουδὴν τῶν συνελθόντων·

A: Τοῦ ἁγίου πατρὸς ἡμῶν Ἰωάννου τοῦ Χρυσοστόμου ἐκ τοῦ εἰς Μελέτιον ἐγκωμίου, . . .

Apart from the title, P and Dam. cite the same incipit, whereas A gives two more lines. There is only one instance where P agrees with A against Dam. (ἐχάραξαν Dam.: διεχάραξαν PVMA), but the definite conclusion is that the original of P drew on Dam. It is not necessary, however, to deduce that P was the intermediate link between Dam. and A. The organizing committee of the council probably used as a model the quotation in Dam. (or in F), but they were able to provide another manuscript with the works of Chrysostom during the debate in the fourth session. That is probably the reason why A adds two more lines after the pattern οὗ ἡ ἀρχὴ and provides a text that in some cases is closer to the *PG* edition than the Dam. and PMV versions.

10. Iohannis Chrys. *Sermo in lavationem quintae feriae* (Λόγος εἰς τὸν νιπτῆρα) = Severiani Gabalensis *Homilia de lotione pedum*, ed. A. Wenger, "Une homélie inédite de Sévérien de Gabala sur le lavement des pieds," *REB* 25 (1967), 226, 8; *CPG* 4216

P, fol. 252 (54*); M, fol. 235ᵛ (41ᴹ); (Dam. III 122)
Mansi XIII 68ᴅ–ᴇ; also XII 1067ᴀ
Τοῦ ἁγίου πατρὸς ἡμῶν Ἰωάννου τοῦ Χρυσοστόμου (=τοῦ αὐτοῦ PMDam.) ἐκ τοῦ λόγου τοῦ (ἐκ—τοῦ om. ADam.) εἰς τὸν νιπτῆρα.
Inc. Πάντα (οὖν add. M) ἐγένοντο διὰ δόξαν Θεοῦ, χρῆσιν δὲ ἡμετέραν·
Des. . . . οὐ τὸ γήινον σχῆμα (τιμᾷ add. AM) ἀλλὰ (αὐτὸν add. M) τὸν οὐράνιον χαρακτῆρα αἰδεῖται.

The quotation is taken from a very popular *Sermo* as can be judged from the abundance of the manuscripts that preserve it.[135] The attribution of the work to John Chrysostom in these manuscripts is unanimous, but recent research has given the authorship to Severian of Gabala.[136]

L. Wallach[137] has examined this quotation by comparing the Greek text, as it appears in five manuscripts of the Vatican Library and in Mansi, to the Latin versions of it included in the *Hadrianum* (47.11–17) and in the *Synodica*

---

[135] Wenger, "Une homélie . . ." 221, lists twenty-five manuscripts, a figure that is not exhaustive.
[136] Ibid., 223.
[137] *Diplomatic Studies*, 94–102.

of 785 as it is cited in the *Libellus Synodalis* (*LS*, 510.25–31) and the *Libri Carolini* (*LC*, II.19, 78.19–26). The same comparison, with the addition of the versions provided by PM and the edition by Wenger (based on Paris. gr. 582, 10th cent.), is attempted in the following.

I. Original Greek text of the quotation as restored on the basis of the following manuscripts:

    Vat. Ottobon. gr. 85, fol. 197ʳ (9th cent.)
    Oa: Vat. Ottobon. gr. 14, fol. 178ʳ (10th cent.)
    Ba: Vat. gr. 1255, fol. 99 (10th cent.)
    C: Vat. gr. 2013, fol. 91 (10th cent.)
    D: Vat. Pii II gr. 23, fol. 50ᵛ (11th cent.)
    Fa: Paris. gr. 582, fol. 340 (10th cent.)
    P: Paris. gr. 1115, fol. 252 (13th cent.)
    M: Mosqu. Hist. Mus. 265, fol. 235ᵛ (9th cent.)
    A: Mansi XIII 67D–E

a. εἰς τὸν νιπτῆρα in Vat. Ottobon. gr. 85, Inc. Ἔλεον θεοῦ καὶ φιλανθρωπίαν

b. Τὰ πάντα γὰρ ἐγένετο διὰ δόξαν μὲν αὐτοῦ, χρῆσιν δὲ ἡμετέραν·

b1. ἥλιος, ἵνα ἀνθρώπους μὲν καταλάμπῃ

c. νεφέλαι εἰς τὴν τῶν ὄμβρων διακονίαν,

d. γῆ εἰς τὴν τῶν καρπῶν εὐθηνίαν

e. καὶ θάλαττα εἰς τὴν τῶν ἐμπόρων ἀφθονίαν·

f. πάντα λειτουργεῖ τῷ ἀνθρώπῳ, μᾶλλον δὲ τῇ εἰκόνι τοῦ δεσπότου.

g. Οὐδὲ γὰρ ὅταν βασιλικοὶ χαρακτῆρες καὶ εἰκόνες εἰς πόλιν εἰσφέρονται καὶ ὑπαντῶσιν ἄρχοντες καὶ δῆμοι μετ᾽ εὐφημίας καὶ φόβου, οὐ σανίδα τιμῶντες, οὐ τὴν κηρόχυτον γραφὴν ἀλλὰ τὸν χαρακτῆρα τοῦ βασιλέως τιμῶντες,

h. οὕτω καὶ ἡ κτίσις οὐ τὸ γήινον σχῆμα τιμᾷ, ἀλλὰ τὸν οὐράνιον χαρακτῆρα αἰδεῖται.

Apparatus criticus

a. λόγος εἰς τὸν νιπτῆρα τῇ ἁγίᾳ καὶ μεγάλῃ Εʹ Fa: ἐκ τοῦ λόγου τοῦ εἰς τὸν νιπτῆρα. PM

b. Τὰ, γὰρ om. PA; γὰρ: οὖν M; ἐγένετο: ἐγένοντο PMA; μὲν αὐτοῦ: Θεοῦ PMA

b1. om. PMA

c. νεφέλαι: νεφέλη PMA

e. καὶ om. BaDPMA; θάλαττα: θάλασσαι M θάλατται A

f. λειτουργεῖ: σοὶ λειτουργεῖ OaP, συλλειτουργεῖ Fa, συνλειτουργεῖ M; ἀνθρώπῳ: Θεῷ P

g. οὐδὲ γὰρ: ὥσπερ γὰρ A; ὅταν: ὅτε POa εἰσφέρονται: ἐμφέρονται P; καὶ om. P; post ὑπαντῶσιν add. αὐταῖς A; μετ᾽: μετὰ DP; καὶ φόβου om.

PMA; τιμῶντες: τιμῶσιν A; οὐ τὴν: οὐδὲ τὴν PA ἢ τὴν OaBaFa; post γραφὴν add. τοῦτο ποιοῦσιν OaFa; τιμῶντες om. OaBaCDFaPMA

h. τιμᾶ om. P; post ἀλλὰ add. αὐτὸν M

II. *Hadrianum* II, chap. 13, 47.11–17

   a. Nam in praedecessoribus nostris sanctis pontificibus conciliis sancti Iohannis Chrysostomi ita fertur sententiam inter cetera:

b–e. (desunt)

   f. Omnia tibi ministrant homini, magis autem imagini (Dei);

   g. quia nec quando imperiales vultus et imagines in civitatem introibunt et obviant iudices et senatus, cum laude et honore, non tabulam honorantes, neque effuse cere scripturam, sed vultum imperatoris,

   h. sic et mundus hominum non terrenam speciem honorantes, sed caelestem vultum venerentur etc.

III. *Synodica* of 785 cited in *LS*, 510.25–31; *LC*, II 19, 78.19–26

a. *LS:* Item Iohannis archiepiscopi Constantinopolitani, qui et Chrysostomi. Iohannis Chrysostomi in sermone coenae Domini: *LC:* Et iterum idem de eodem patre, sermone in quinta feria Pasche:

b. *LS* and *LC:* Omnia facta sunt propter gloriam Dei, usui autem (vero *LC*) nostro:

c. nubes ad imbrium ministerium,

d. terra (–m *LC*) ad frumenti (fructuum *LC*) abundantiam,

e. mare ad negotiandum copiose (mare navigantium *LC*),

f. absque invidia omnia famulantur homini, magis autem imagini Domini (Dei *LC*).

g. Neque enim quando imperiales (imperialis *LC*) vultus et imagines in civitates introducuntur et obviant iudices et plebes cum laudibus, non tabulam honorantes neque effusas ex aere figuras (effusae cerae scripturas *LC*), sed figuram imperatoris,

h. sic et creatura (–m *LC*) non terrenam speciem honorat, sed eandem (eadem *LC*) ipsam caelestem figuram reveretur.

IV. Anastasius' version of I (above), Mansi XIII, 67D–E

a. Sancti patris nostri Joannis Chrysostomi sermo in lavationem quintae feriae.

b. Omnia facta sunt propter gloriam Dei et usum nostrum.

c. Nubes ad imbrium ministerium,

d. terra ad fructuum abundantiam,

e. mare ad mercatorum copiam.

f. Omnia tibi ministrant, imo autem imagini Dei.

g. Nam quando imperiales characteres et imagines in civitatem introducuntur, obviam veniunt principes et vulgus cum laudatione, non

tabulam honorantes, neque perfusam cera picturam, sed chara-
cterem imperatoris:
h. sic creatura non terrenum habitum, sed caelestem figuram ven-
eratur.

V. Anastasius' version of *Synodica* of 785, Mansi XII 1068c–d

    a. Et iterum de sermone ejusdem patris habito in quinta feria
       Pasche:
b, c, d. identical with IV (above), b, c, d.
    e. mare navigantibus absque invidia est;
    f. omnia famulantur homini, magis autem imagini Dei;
    g. neque enim quando imperiales vultus et imagines in civitates
       introducuntur, et obviant judices et plebes cum laudibus, tabu-
       lam honorant, vel supereffusam cera scripturam, sed figuram
       imperatoris.
    h. Sic et creatura non terrenam speciem honorat, sed caelestem
       ipsam figuram reveretur.

According to Wallach again: "The comparison of I with the Latin versions II, III, and IV, proves that I is their ultimate, not immediate source.
The omission of Ib1 in the three Latin versions and the substitution in IIIb
and IVb of *Dei* for αὐτοῦ in Ib indicate that the Latin versions depend on a
common, second-hand Greek transmission and its Latin rendering which
was present in some collection of χρήσεις or testimonia advocating image-
worship."[138]

We can leave this argument for a while and concentrate on P. At first
sight the fact that P follows A against I in at least ten cases is impressive,
although in some instances M agrees with I. P furthermore gives the reading
Θεῷ instead of ἀνθρώπῳ in (f) and ἐμφέρονται, which is an obvious misspelling of εἰσφέρονται, and omits two words (καί, αὐταῖς) in (g) and one (τιμᾷ)
in (h).

The key sentence in the whole passage is (g). Compare the various
transmissions of it:

I: L. Wallach and A. Wenger:

g. Οὐδὲ γὰρ ὅταν βασιλικοὶ χαρακτῆρες καὶ εἰκόνες εἰς πόλιν εἰσφέρονται
   καὶ ὑπαντῶσιν ἄρχοντες καὶ δῆμοι μετ' εὐφημίας καὶ φόβου, οὐ σανίδα
   τιμῶντες, οὐ τὴν κηρόχυτον γραφὴν ⟨τοῦτο ποιοῦσι⟩, ἀλλὰ τὸν χαρακτῆρα τοῦ βασιλέως τιμῶντες,
h. οὕτω . . .

---

[138] Ibid., 98.

PM:

g. Οὐδὲ γὰρ ὅτε (ὅταν M) βασιλικοὶ χαρακτῆρες καὶ εἰκόνες εἰς πόλιν ἐμφέρονται (εἰσφέρονται καὶ M) ὑπαντῶσιν ἄρχοντες καὶ δῆμοι μετὰ (μετ᾽ M) εὐφημίας οὐ σανίδα τιμῶντες, οὐδὲ (οὐ M) τὴν κηρόχυτον γραφήν, ἀλλὰ τὸν χαρακτῆρα τοῦ βασιλέως (τιμῶντες om. PM)

h. οὕτω . . .

II (= *Hadrianum*):

g. quia nec quando imperiales vultus et imagines in civitatem introibunt et obviant iudices et senatus, cum laude et honore, non tabulam honorantes, neque effuse cere scripturam, sed vultum imperatoris,

h. sic . . .

III (= *Synodica* of 785 in *LS* and *LC*):

g. Neque enim quando imperiales (imperialis *LC*) vultus et imagines in civitates introducuntur et obviant iudices et plebes cum laudibus, non tabulam honorantes neque effusas ex aere figuras (effusae cerae scripturas *LC*), sed figuram imperatoris,

h. sic . . .

V (= Anastasius' version of the *Synodica* in Mansi XII 1068D):

g. neque enim quando imperiales vultus et imagines in civitates introducuntur, et obviant judices et plebes cum laudibus, tabulam honorant, vel supereffusam cera scripturam, sed figuram imperatoris.

h. Sic . . .

John of Damascus: Dam. III 122: . . . εἰς τὸν νιπτῆρα·

Ὥσπερ γάρ, ὅταν βασιλικοὶ χαρακτῆρες καὶ εἰκόνες εἰς πόλιν καταπέμπωνται καὶ εἰσφέρωνται, ὑπαντῶσιν ἄρχοντες καὶ δῆμοι μετ᾽ εὐφημίας καὶ φόβου, οὐ σανίδα τιμῶντες, οὐ τὴν κηρόχυτον γραφήν, ἀλλὰ τὸν χαρακτῆρα τοῦ βασιλέως, οὕτως καὶ ἡ κτίσις.

A (= Mansi XIII 67D–E):

g. ὥσπερ γὰρ ὅτε βασιλικοὶ χαρακτῆρες καὶ εἰκόνες εἰς πόλιν εἰσφέρονται καὶ ὑπαντῶσιν αὐταῖς ἄρχοντες καὶ δῆμοι μετ᾽ εὐφημίας, οὐ σανίδα τιμῶσιν, οὐδὲ τὴν κηρόχυτον γραφήν, ἀλλὰ τὸν χαρακτῆρα τοῦ βασιλέως.

h. οὕτω . . .

IV (= Anastasius' version, Mansi XIII 68D–E):

g. Nam quando imperiales characteres et imagines in civitatem introducuntur, obviam veniunt principes et vulgus cum laudatione, non

tabulam honorantes, neque perfusam cera picturam, sed charac-
terem imperatoris;
   h. sic . . .

Despite the assertion by both Wallach and Wenger, the reading Οὐδὲ
γὰρ I, P (Lat: quia nec II, Neque enim III, V) cannot be the original one.
Two lines after that οὐδὲ we have a second negation (οὐ σανίδα τιμῶντες
οὐ(δὲ add. P) τὴν I, P, Lat. non tabulam honorantes, II, III). Of course, the
second negation is so distant from the first that it could be regarded as a
reinforcing repetition. However, if one abides by the basic rules, we have
instead of a desirable negation, a strong affirmation. On the other hand, the
participle τιμῶντες I, P (Lat. honorantes II, III) stands in the position of a
verb, leaving the whole section with two dependent clauses and no main
clause on which to depend. In addition, the next sentence (h) is introduced
by the demonstrative pronominal adverb οὕτω (I, P, Dam., A, Lat.: sic II,
III, IV, V), which is not the appropriate *apodosis* to the preceding Οὐδὲ of
the main clause.

Things look much smoother with the text of John of Damascus and of
the acts. The main clause is introduced by ὥσπερ γὰρ and the verb in Dam.
is ὑπαντῶσιν, while in A it is τιμῶσιν, which both make perfect sense.

It is interesting to note that Anastasius first observed the unevenness of
the syntax and gave a translation that solved the problems by omitting in
IV the introductory *Neque* and the second negation in V, where he also
changed the participle *honorantes* into the indicative mood of the same
verb (*honorant*).

The final conclusions could be the following. (a) The original version
of this quotation must be closer to the one given by John of Damascus and
not to that restored by Wallach or Wenger. (b) The quotation in the acts
(Mansi XIII 68D–E) belongs to a transmission that takes into account the
version of Dam. combined, perhaps, with the P and M (= F) version, while
the text of Parisinus and Mosquensis is related to the Latin extract in Mansi
XII 1068C–D), and it can be placed before the Latin translations of the extract and after the original proposed by Wallach and Wenger (see above,
pp. 158 and 160). (c) The quotation in P seems to come from a text available
in Rome before and after Nicaea II. Anastasius in IV is translating almost
verbatim the quotation in P and M. In this case he must have had both the
Paris and the Nicaean versions available, and he might have been confused
by the differences of the two manuscripts in (f) (πάντα σοι λειτουργεῖ τῷ
ἀνθρώπῳ A: τῷ Θεῷ P) and in (g) (ὥσπερ M: οὐδὲ P), so he decided not to
translate them.

11. Iohannis Chrys. *Sermo quod veteris et novi Testamenti unus sit legislator et in vestem sacerdotis* = Severiani Gabalensis *Homilia de legislatore* (*PG* 56, 407D); *CPG* 4192

P, fol. 252 (55*); V, fol. 11ʳ⁻ᵛ (V 30); M, fol. 228ᵛ (24ᴹ)
(Dam. II 60; III 105)
Mansi XIII 9A; also XIII 93C and XIII 300C–D, 324C

Τοῦ αὐτοῦ (Τοῦ ἁγίου Ἰωάννου τοῦ Χρυσοστόμου M) ἐκ τοῦ λόγου (τοῦ add. V) ὅτι παλαιᾶς καὶ καινῆς διαθήκης εἷς ὁ νομοθέτης· (ἐστὶ add. M) καὶ εἰς τὸ ἔνδυμα τοῦ ἱερέως· PVM

Τοῦ ἐν ἁγίοις πατρὸς ἡμῶν Ἰωάννου τοῦ Χρυσοστόμου λόγος· ὅτι παλαιᾶς καὶ καινῆς διαθήκης εἷς ὁ νομοθέτης· καὶ εἰς τὸ ἔνδυμα τοῦ ἱερέως, οὗ ἡ ἀρχή A.

Τῆς Χριστοῦ βασιλείας τὸ εὐαγγέλιον προκηρύττουσι μὲν (οἱ add. P) προφῆται· καὶ μεθ᾽ ἕτερα· (Τῆς—ἕτερα om. VM) Ἐγὼ καὶ τὴν κηρόχυτον ἠγάπησα γραφὴν εὐσεβείας πεπληρωμένην· εἶδον γὰρ ἄγγελον ἐν εἰκόνι ἐλαύνοντα βαρβάρων στίφη (στίφη PV, Mansi XIII 300; νέφη Mansi XIII 9A, M; cuneos Mansi XIII 10A). εἶδον πατούμενα βαρβάρων φῦλα (φῦλον V), καὶ τὸν Δαυὶδ ἀληθεύοντα· κύριε ἐν τῇ πόλει σου τὴν εἰκόνα αὐτῶν ἐξουδενώσεις.

The text is preserved in the Paris manuscript in perfect condition. In the acts it is cited by various speakers with almost no difference from the text in P, the citation in the refutation of the *horos* (Mansi XIII 300C–D) of the Hiereian council being absolutely identical with it. The earliest work that cites this quotation is the letter of Gregory II sent to Germanus of Constantinople, which is inserted in the acts (Mansi XIII 93C). However, the divergences are more than negligible, thus pointing to a separate line of transmission, but still testifying to the existence of this fragment at Rome before 731.

John of Damascus includes this extract in the florilegia of the second and third homilies on the Images (II 60; III 105). Apart from the omission of the initial line of the work (Τῆς Χριστοῦ . . . προφῆται) and of the word διαθήκης in the lemma, the rest of the text in II 60 is identical with P and A XIII 300C–D.

In Mansi XIII 9A the quotation is taken from a book offered by Theodosius, abbot of the monastery of St. Andrew τοῦ Νησίου. It is difficult to decide whether this book had been used for the quotation in XIII 300C–D and 324C, since it gives, along with M, the reading νέφη instead of στίφη, or Parisinus was the model for this quotation. According to Wallach, "John of Damascus' version of the excerpt from *De legislatore,* and not the treatise itself, was the actual source for the quotation's appearance in the *Acta* of II

Nicaea."[139] Comparing Dam. with P, it becomes evident that the quotation in Parisinus is more apt to meet the requirements of a source for the excerpt in the acts, since in addition to the parts missing from Dam., it provides the same text, letter by letter.

Then, what about the text offered to the assembly by Theodosius? The possible options are two: either Theodosius indeed gave a real codex, which is not improbable, or the seemingly spontaneous intervention of various clerics and monks and the offer of books during the proceedings of the council had been prearranged by the organizing committee.[140]

12. Cyrilli Alexandrini *Commentarii in Matthaeum*,[141] *CPG* 5206

(A) P, fol. 252ᵛ (61*)

Τοῦ ἁγίου Κυρίλλου Ἀλεξανδρείας· ἐκ τοῦ εἰς τὸν Ματθαῖον ἁγίου εὐαγγελίου.

Ζωγραφεῖ γὰρ ἡ πίστις τὸν ἐν μορφῇ θεοῦ ὑπάρχοντα λόγον, ὃς τῆς ζωῆς ἡμῶν λύτρωσις προσηνέχθη τῷ Θεῷ τὴν καθ᾽ ἡμᾶς ὁμοίωσιν ὑποδὺς καὶ γενόμενος ἄνθρωπος· καὶ μετ᾽ ὀλίγα· εἰκόνων ἡμῖν ἀποπληροῦσι χρείαν αἱ παραβολαί, τὴν δύναμιν τῶν σημαινομένων οἰονείπως καὶ ὀφθαλμῶν παρενθέσεις καὶ ἀφὴ⟨ν⟩ χειρὸς ὑποβάλουσαι καὶ τὰ ἐν ἰσχναῖς ἐννοίαις ἀφανῶς ἔχοντα τὴν θεωρίαν.

(B) Mansi XII 1067ʙ

. . . τοῦ μακαρίου Κυρίλλου ἐκ τῆς εἰς τὸ κατὰ Ματθαῖον ἅγιον εὐαγγέλιον ἑρμηνείας . . .

ζωγραφεῖ γὰρ ἡ πίστις τὸν ἐν μορφῇ τοῦ Θεοῦ ὑπάρχοντα λόγον, ὡς καὶ ἡ τῆς ζωῆς ἡμῶν λύτρωσις προσηνέχθη τῷ Θεῷ, τὴν καθ᾽ ἡμᾶς ὁμοίωσιν ὑποδὺς καὶ γενόμενος ἄνθρωπος· καὶ πάλιν ὁ αὐτὸς μετὰ μικρόν. εἰκόνων ἡμῖν ἀποπληροῦσι χρείαν αἱ παραβολαί, τῶν σημαινομένων τὴν δύναμιν οἰονείπως καὶ ὀφθαλμῶν παραθέσει, καὶ ἀφῇ χειρὸς ὑποβάλλουσαι καὶ τὰ ἐν ἰσχναῖς ἐννοίαις ἀφανῶς ἔχοντα τὴν θεωρίαν.

(B1) Mansi XII 1068ᴅ. . . . beati Cyrilli ex interpretatione sancti evangelii secundum Mattheum . . . (= Anastasius' version)
Depingit enim fides quod in forma Dei existit verbum, sicut et nostrae vitae redemptio oblata est Deo, secundum nos carne indutus et factus homo. Et idem ipse post pauca: Imaginum nobis explent opus parabolae, significantes virtutem, ac si oculorum adhibitione et palpatu manus

---

[139] Ibid., 118.

[140] See Mango, "Availability," 32–33, and Chapter IV below.

[141] According to Wallach, *Diplomatic Studies*, 106, this passage "has not been traced as yet. . . . The two testimonia in JE 2448 are to be added to the fragments of Cyril's lost *Commentary on Matthew*, collected by Joseph Reuss" (*Matthäus-Kommentare aus der griechischen Kirche*, TU 62, V. Reihe, Bd. 6 [Berlin, 1957], 153–69).

suggerant etiam ea quae inexilibus cogitationibus invisibiliter habent contemplationem.

(B2) *Synodica* of 785 cited in *LS*, 511.25-30, *LC*, II.20, 79.22-23/26-28:
Item beati Cyrilli Alexandrini episcopi in sermone (expositione *LC*) Matthei evangelistae
Depingitur enim fides, quod in forma Dei existit (exsistit *LC*) verbum, sicut et nostrae vitae redemptione oblatus est Deo secundum nostram (nos *LC*) similitudinem indutus (om. LC) et factus homo. Et idem ipse post pauca: Imaginum nobis explent opus parabolae significantium virtutem, cuidam (cui *LC*), quomodo et oculorum adhiberi et palpatu manus afferri, in vestigiis mentibus inapparabiliter habens visionem.

The meaning of these two excerpts is more or less obscure in all of the four versions. Parisinus gives the impression that it stands closer to the original since it is the only manuscript that gives the reading ὃς instead of ὡς in the first extract. If we accept that the original one was the pronoun ὃς and not the particle ὡς, then the following participles acquire the subject that was missing.

In the second extract, the readings παρενθέσεις, ἀφή⟨ν⟩, of P make better sense than παρενθέσει or παραθέσει, ἀφῆ. The Latin translations also demonstrate the difficulties the redactor had to overcome, failing in some cases to understand the real meaning of the corrupt passage he was translating, for example, *vestigiis mentibus* in (c). The essential thing about this quotation is that it comes from the acts of the 731 and 769 Roman synods since it is only included in the *Synodica* of 785.

Here is a tentative depiction of the relationship of the four versions:

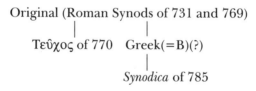

Original (Roman Synods of 731 and 769)

Τεῦχος of 770   Greek(=B)(?)

Synodica of 785

13. Cyrilli Alex. *Epistula ad Acacium Scythopoleos episcopum* (*ep*. 41), *ACO* 1,1,4, 40.1/47.21-24/30–48.22 (*PG* 77, 217, 220A–D); *CPG* 5341

P, fol. 252ᵛ–253 (62*)
Mansi XIII 12ʙ–13ᴀ
Τοῦ ἁγίου Κυρίλλου ἐπισκόπου Ἀλεξανδρείας (τοῦ αὐτοῦ P) ἐκ τῆς ἐπιστολῆς τῆς πρὸς Ἀκάκιον ἐπίσκοπον Σκυθοπόλεως, περὶ τοῦ ἀποπομπαίου· (ἧς ἡ ἀρχὴ add. A)

Inc. Τοῖς παρὰ τῆς σῆς ὁσιότητος ἀρτίως ἐπεσταλμένοις, (ἀπεστ. P)
ἐντυχὼν ἠγάσθην ἄγαν· καὶ μεθ' ἕτερα· Φαμὲν οὖν ὅτι σκιά . . .
Des. . . . ἤγουν τῶν ἐνδεχομένων, ἐν ἑνὶ κατιδεῖν αὐτὸν πάντα δρῶντα
τὰ εἰρημένα.

There is no easy way to decide whether this piece was interpolated in
the original of P or whether the Council of 787 used F for this citation.
Unfortunately, since this excerpt is not included in any of the existing florilegia of St. John of Damascus or anywhere else, any inference can be based
only on P and A. Parisinus gives a text considerably inferior to that of the
acts. First, it omits some clauses that appear in the acts, whereas two or three
words missing from the text of the acts do exist in the Latin translation of
Anastasius. Second, in Parisinus there are some characteristic misreadings
of the exemplar. Compare: πόσον P: πῶς ἂν A; ἐμφανίζοντα P: ἐφιζήσαντα A;
ἑνικῶς P: ἦν εἰκὸς A; in all three cases the correct readings are provided
by A.

This is the first quotation, so far, that may have been a later interpolation in F. But in the context of the other extracts examined up to now this
possibility should be viewed with skepticism. If Cyril's fragment was part of
the 770 collection, the intervention of Cinnamus must have been considerable. It is noteworthy, however, that the clauses Cinnamus omits all belong
to biblical quotations inserted into the text of the *epistula*.

In conclusion, the quotation itself, as it appears in P, though inferior to
the text in the acts, might have been the source of the acts, on condition that
Cinnamus was held responsible for the alteration of an original otherwise
identical with the one the organizing committee of the council had at their
disposal.

14. Athanasii Alex. *Oratio de incarnatione Verbi,* ed. Ch. Kannengiesser,
Sur l'incarnation du Verbe, SC 199 (Paris, 1973), 256.1–2 and 314.1–4 (*PG* 25,
96 and 120c); *CPG* 2091

(a) P fol. 253ᵛ (68*)
Τοῦ ἁγίου Ἀθανασίου περὶ τῆς ἐνανθρωπήσεως τοῦ κυρίου·

Ἱκανῶς μὲν ἐκ πολλῶν ὀλίγα λαβόντες ἐγράψαμεν· ἔπειτα· καὶ
ταῦτα τὰ ἐν ξύλοις γραφόμενα,
μορφῆς παρελθούσης δίχα ῥύπου
καὶ πάλιν

(b) Mansi XII 1067c
τοῦ ἁγίου Ἀθανασίου ἐπισκόπου
Ἀλεξανδρείας περὶ τῆς ἐνανθρωπήσεως τοῦ Κυρίου· οὗ ἡ
ἀρχή·

Ἱκανῶς μὲν ἐκ πολλῶν ὀλίγα λαβόντες ἐγράψαμεν· ἔπειτα· καὶ
αὐτὰ τὰ ἐν ξύλοις γραφόμενα,
μορφῆς παρελθούσης ἐκ τοῦ ἔξω
ῥύπου, πάλιν ἀναγκαῖον τὸν αὐ-

οὗ τινος ἐστὶν ἡ μορφὴ τοῦ ἀνα-
καινίσαι δυνηθῆναι εἰκόνα ἐν τῇ
αὐτῇ ὕλῃ καὶ στοιχείῳ· διὰ γὰρ
τὴν αὐτὴν μορφὴν καὶ ὕλην ὅπου
    γράφεται οὐ καταβάλλεται,
ἀλλ᾽ ἐν αὐτῇ συνιστορεῖται.

τὸν ἀναλαβέσθαι καὶ ἑνῶσαι (in
marg: ἴσ. ἀνανεῶσαι).
οὗ τινός ἐστιν ἡ μορφή, τοῦ ἀνα-
καινίσαι δυνηθῆναι εἰκόνα ἐν τῇ
αὐτῇ ὕλῃ καὶ στοιχείῳ. διὰ γὰρ
τὴν αὐτοῦ μορφὴν καὶ ἡ ὕλη, ὅπου
καὶ γράφεται, οὐ καταβάλλεται,
ἀλλ᾽ ἐν αὐτῇ συνιστορεῖται.

(c) Mansi XII 1068D–E: sancti Athanasii episcopi Alexandrie de humanatione Domini, cujus initium est:
Sufficienter quidem de multis pauca sumentes, intimavimus; et post; Et
ipsa quae scribuntur in lignis, abolita forma per exteriores sordes, iterum idipsum necesse est in omnibus resumere et unire, cujus est
forma, renovari possit imago in eadem materia et elemento. Per (in
marg: Gr. propter) eamdem enim formam et materia (sic), ubi et conscribitur, non dejicitur, sed in ea ipsa configuratur; et cetera (= Anastasius' version)

(d) Hadrian I's *Synodica,* cited in *LS,* 513.14 f
Item sancti Athanasii episcopi Alexandrini de humanatione Domini, cuius initium: Sufficienter quidem de his multis pauca sumentes intimavimus.
Et post: (*LC,* II.14, 74.3–6; *LS,* 513.15–18)
Sicut ea quae scribitur in lignis, forma abolita exterioribus sordibus,
iterum necesse est in (est in om. *LS*) idipsum (id ipsum *LS*) recuperari
atque uniri his (ei *LS*), cuius est forma, ut innovari possit imago in
eadem materia atque elemento. Per eius enim formam et ipsa materia,
ubi et conscribitur, non deicitur, sed in ea ipsa configuratur.

(e) Athanasius, *De incarnatione verbi Dei* (after the edition mentioned
above)
Αὐτάρκως ἐν τοῖς πρὸ τούτων ἐκ πολλῶν ὀλίγα διαλαβόντες. Ὡς γὰρ τῆς
γραφείσης ἐν ξύλῳ μορφῆς παραφανισθείσης ἐκ τῶν ἔξωθεν ῥύπων, πάλιν
χρεία τοῦτον παραγενέσθαι, οὗ καὶ ἔστιν ἡ μορφή, ἵνα ἀνακαινισθῆναι ἡ
εἰκὼν δυνηθῇ ἐν τῇ αὐτῇ ὕλῃ· διὰ γὰρ τὴν ἐκείνου γραφὴν (μορφὴν Mt.
Athos, MS Dochiariou 78) καὶ αὐτὴ ἡ ὕλη ἐν ᾗ καὶ γέγραπται, οὐκ ἐκβάλ-
λεται, ἀλλ᾽ ἐν αὐτῇ ἀνατυποῦται

This text has also been thoroughly examined by Wallach[142] because it
is one of the excerpts in the catena of *testimonia* inserted in the *Synodica* of
785. The quotation, in its version of the Greek translation of the *Synodica,*
differs considerably from the edited text (e) and also from the quotation

---

[142] *Diplomatic Studies,* 102–4.

preserved in the *Doctrina Patrum* (ME, 327 VII). As far as concerns the Greek Nicaean version, Wallach assumes that: "The Byzantine translator does not insert the Greek original e in his translation of [the *Synodica*], but his own translation of d. We therefore read . . . Ἱκανῶς instead of Αὐτάρκως (*sufficienter*), and . . . we do not read with e Ὡς γὰρ but Καὶ αὐτά."

Wallach seems to be right, but the date of the retranslation of the text into Greek must be left open at present, since there is a possibility that it might have first taken place before 785. This possibility comes with the fact that both the Greek and the Latin versions are introduced by the formula οὗ ἡ ἀρχή/*cuius initium est,* which can be taken as evidence that Hadrian took this quotation from a preexisting florilegium.

The quotation in P (a) is evidently much inferior to the (b) version and it is equally evident that it belongs along with (b) to the same line of transmission. Its overall condition, if considered out of the general context, pleads for its dependence on (b), but this is one out of very few such cases. Besides, the presence of the Greek original fragment in the *Doctrina* and its retranslation from Latin into Greek in the *Synodica* of 785 implies that it was known before 731 at Rome. If this retranslation took place after 787, then this fragment is a later addition to F.

15. Athanasii Alex. *Oratio contra Arianos iii* (PG 26, 332A–B); *CPG* 2093

(A) P, fol. 253ᵛ (69*); V, fol. 8ᵛ (V 21); M, fols. 239ᵛ–240 (52ᴹ); (Dam. III 114)

τοῦ αὐτοῦ· ἐκ τοῦ κατὰ Ἀρειανῶν. P

Ἀθανασίου τοῦ ἁγιωτάτου ἀρχιεπισκόπου Ἀλεξανδρείας ἐκ τοῦ λόγου τοῦ κατὰ Ἀρειανῶν· V

Τοῦ ἁγίου Ἀθανασίου ἀρχιεπισκόπου Ἀλεξανδρείας ἐκ τοῦ τετάρτου λόγου κατὰ Ἀριανῶν· M

Inc. Ὁ γὰρ οὕτως ⟨lac.⟩ ὅτι ἕν εἰσιν ὁ υἱός. . . M

Ἐν τῇ εἰκόνι τοῦ βασιλέως τὸ εἶδος καὶ ἡ μορφή ἐστι . . . PV

Des. . . . ἡ γὰρ ἐκείνου μορφὴ καὶ τὸ εἶδός ἐστιν ἡ εἰκών. MP

. . . ὁ ἐν τῇ εἰκόνι γεγραμμένος. V

(B) Mansi XIII 69B–C, XIII 273A

Τοῦ ἁγίου Ἀθανασίου ἐκ τοῦ κατὰ Ἀρειανῶν λόγου τετάρτου, οὗ ἡ ἀρχή·

Inc. Οἱ Ἀρειομανῖται, ὡς ἔοικε, κρίναντες ἅπαξ ἀποστάται γενέσθαι· καὶ μεθ᾽ ἕτερα. τοῦτο καὶ ἀπὸ τοῦ παραδείγματος τῆς εἰκόνος τοῦ βασιλέως προσεχέστερόν τις κατανοεῖν δυνήσεται. ἐν γὰρ τῇ εἰκόνι . . .

Des. . . . ἡ γὰρ ἐκείνου μορφὴ καὶ τὸ εἶδός ἐστιν ἡ εἰκών.

The florilegium of the third speech of St. John of Damascus is, possibly, the first witness to this extract (III 114.14–24). The quotation, however, in PV is much closer to the one in A. On the other hand, A gives a more extended version than P does. First of all, A starts with the incipit of the work and then gives two more lines before the point from which Parisinus starts. Any divergence between PV and A leads to the classification of PV within the corrupt line of the transmission. One example will suffice:

καὶ ἐν τῷ βασιλεῖ δὲ τὸ ἐν τῇ εἰκόνι εἶδός ἐστιν. ἀπαράλλακτος δέ ἐστιν . . . A

καὶ ἐν τῷ βασιλεῖ καὶ ἐν τῇ εἰκόνι καὶ ἀπαράλλακτός ἐστιν . . . PV

Here again it is almost impossible to find which is the original and which the apograph. If the copyist of Parisinus were to take the blame for the omissions and mistakes, then the quotation in P could definitely be the source for the acts, but the same reading is transmitted by V as well, something that entails the presence of the corrupt passage in the exemplar of P and V. In spite of its textual inferiority in general, Mosquensis comes to offer substantial help with the restoration of the 770 archetype.

In the first place, it should be stressed that Dam. is the only source that gives the right reference to the work from which this fragment was taken, whereas M offers the wrong indication in its lemma which finally appeared in the acts. Compare:

Dam.: Τοῦ ἁγίου Ἀθανασίου Ἀλεξανδρείας κατὰ Ἀρειανῶν βιβλίου τρίτου.

M: Τοῦ ἁγίου Ἀθανασίου, ἀρχιεπισκόπου Ἀλεξανδρείας, ἐκ τοῦ τετάρτου λόγου κατὰ Ἀρειανῶν·

A: Τοῦ ἁγίου Ἀθανασίου ἐκ τοῦ κατὰ Ἀρειανῶν λόγου τετάρτου, οὗ ἡ ἀρχή.

Then the M version is more extended than A, corresponding to Dam. III 114.8–23, while A corresponds to Dam. III 114.12–23. Moreover, the passage that is corrupt in P and V appears in M in a much better shape, although, again, three words are missing. In any case, the complete passage can finally be restored by the intervention of all three: P, V, and M. Compare:

A: ἐν γὰρ τῇ εἰκόνι τοῦ βασιλέως τὸ εἶδος καὶ ἡ μορφή ἐστι· καὶ ἐν τῷ βασιλεῖ δὲ τὸ ἐν τῇ εἰκόνι εἶδός ἐστιν, ἀπαράλλακτος δέ ἐστιν ἡ ἐν τῇ εἰκόνι τοῦ βασιλέως ὁμοιότης . . .

M: ἐν γὰρ τῇ εἰκόνι τοῦ βασιλέως τὸ εἶδος καὶ ἡ μορφή ἐστιν καὶ ἐν τῷ βασιλεῖ δὲ τῷ (sic) ἐν τῇ εἰκόνι εἶδός ἐστιν,
    ἡ ἐν τῇ εἰκόνι τοῦ βασιλέως ὁμοιώτης (sic) . . .

PV: ἐν   τῇ εἰκόνι τοῦ βασιλέως τὸ εἶδος καὶ ἡ μορφή ἐστιν καὶ ἐν τῷ
βασιλεῖ καὶ   ἐν τῇ εἰκόνι   καὶ ἀπαράλλακτός ἐστιν ἡ ἐν
τῇ εἰκόνι τοῦ βασιλέως ὁμοιότης . . .

The only thing missing from M is the incipit of the *oratio* (Οἱ Ἀρειομανῖται—γενέσθαι), but this happens with all the extracts in M, with the exception, of course, of the works that are included in M in their entirety. Two
minor variants of M are given in the correct form by P or V (ἐπορῶντα M:
ἐνορῶντα PVA; ἀλλάττειν M: διαλλάττειν PA).

This situation allows for some interesting remarks. It has already been
claimed that P and V represent one line in the transmission of the florilegium of 770 and M a second line independent of PV. This fragment is strong
evidence of that. Furthermore, P and V copied parts of an original that was
already corrupt. It means that the exemplar of PV was already a direct(?)
apograph of the τεῦχος of the year 770. In fact, another piece of information
leads to this conclusion, namely, the date of the colophon of P. We may recall
that, according to this colophon, the archetype of P was written in the year
774/5 (,ϛοξζ' according to the Alexandrian era) and not in 770. So it seems
that the exemplar of P and V was a copy of the florilegium of 770 produced
in the year 774/5, while M, in all probability, draws from another copy of
the τεῦχος of 770, if not of the τεῦχος itself.

16. *Narratio de cruce seu imagine Berytensi*, falsely attributed to St. Athanasius (*PG* 28, 805–812); *CPG* 2262; *BHG* 780–788b

(A) P, fol. 254ʳ⁻ᵛ (71*); M, fols. 213–217 (10ᴹ)
τοῦ αὐτοῦ· P
Λόγος τοῦ ἐν ἁγίοις πατρὸς ἡμῶν Ἀθανασίου ἀρχιεπισκόπου Ἀλεξανδρείας περὶ τῆς εἰκόνος τοῦ κυρίου ἡμῶν Ἰησοῦ Χριστοῦ τοῦ γεναμένου
θαύματος ἐν Βηρυτῷ τῇ πόλει. M:
Inc. Δεῦρο (om. M) ἄρατε τοὺς ὀφθαλμοὺς τῆς διανοίας ὑμῶν καὶ ἴδετε τὸ
καινὸν θέαμα τοῦτο· . . .
Des. . . . τὸ θαῦμα τοῦτο ἐν Βηρυτῷ τῇ πόλει γέγονεν. P
      . . . καὶ δοξάσωμεν τὴν αὐτοῦ ἀγαθότητα τοῦ ἀληθεινοῦ (sic) υἱοῦ
τοῦ Θεοῦ τοῦ ζῶντος· αὐτῷ γὰρ πρέπει δόξα . . . etc. M

(B) Mansi XIII 24ε–32ᴀ
Λόγος τοῦ ἐν ἁγίοις πατρὸς ἡμῶν Ἀθανασίου περὶ τῆς εἰκόνος τοῦ κυρίου ἡμῶν Ἰησοῦ Χριστοῦ τοῦ ἀληθινοῦ Θεοῦ ἡμῶν, γενομένου θαύματος
ἐν Βηρυτῷ τῇ πόλει.
Inc. Ἄρατε τοὺς ὀφθαλμοὺς τῆς διανοίας ὑμῶν καὶ ἴδετε τὸ καινὸν θέαμα
τοῦτο, ὅπερ γέγονε νῦν . . .
Des. . . . ὅτι τῆς αὐτοῦ πίστεως ἡμᾶς κατηξίωσε καὶ τῆς αὐτοῦ ἐπιγνώσεως,

μεθ᾿ οὗ τῷ πατρὶ ἅμα τῷ ἁγίῳ πνεύματι δόξα νῦν καὶ ἀεὶ καὶ εἰς τοὺς αἰῶνας τῶν αἰώνων, ἀμήν.

The whole narration was cited during the fourth session of the council (Mansi XIII 24E–32A) from a book offered by Peter, bishop of Nicomedia, and it is the same as the one included in *PG*.

The version appearing in P is a dramatically abridged one and leaves no place for detailed commentary. Some brief remarks, are, however, necessary.

The fact that the work in P occupies almost one folium, as against four columns in the acts, is highly indicative of the size of the abridgement performed probably by the copyist of Parisinus gr. 1115. In other words, Parisinus gives in the first fourteen lines a summary of the initial part of the work, as in cols. 24D–28A of the Mansi edition. The rest of the quotation in P corresponds almost verbatim to the parts included in col. 28 lines 11–19 and 22–40 of the same edition. At the end, P closes abruptly with the sentence: Τὸ θαῦμα τοῦτο ἐν Βηρυτῷ τῇ πόλει γέγονεν, a sentence that does not exist in any of the editions of the text. On the other hand, Mansi continues for another one and a half columns (Mansi XIII 28D–32A).

It might be useful, nevertheless, to observe that the parts omitted by P are not directly connected with image worship. The beginning of the *Narratio* in A is a rhetorical introduction and a detailed exposition of how an icon was found by the Jews. Then, in the rest of the part missing from P, the narrative shifts to the miracles that the blood from the icon performed among the Jews and their consequent conversion to the Christian faith.

Again, M provides an integral version of the work and, although the variants are too many, its dependence on a source common with that of the second Nicaean council seems possible. The lemma is almost identical in both M and A:

A: Λόγος τοῦ ἐν ἁγίοις πατρὸς ἡμῶν Ἀθανασίου περὶ τῆς εἰκόνος τοῦ κυρίου ἡμῶν Ἰησοῦ Χριστοῦ τοῦ ἀληθινοῦ Θεοῦ ἡμῶν, γενομένου θαύματος ἐν Βηρυτῷ τῇ πόλει.

M: Λόγος τοῦ ἐν ἁγίοις πατρὸς ἡμῶν Ἀθανασίου, ἀρχιεπισκόπου Ἀλεξανδρείας, περὶ τῆς εἰκόνος τοῦ κυρίου ἡμῶν Ἰησοῦ Χριστοῦ τοῦ γεναμένου θαύματος ἐν Βηρυτῷ τῇ πόλει.

Both versions give also an equally mediocre text, with M omitting phrases or words in some instances, while in other cases A fails to provide the whole text. However, we must assume that this text was included in the florilegium of 770 in its entirety. The textual condition in which this work occurs in M suggests that Mosquensis and the florilegium of 770 are separated by more than one manuscript older than M.

Finally, the major discrepancy between the two versions is located in the desinit, but in the case of M the text appears as a faithful reproduction of the closing paragraph of a *sermo* delivered before an audience. This possibly means that M stands closer to the original of the discourse than A. Compare:

A: δότε οὖν αὐτῷ δόξαν μετ' εὐφροσύνης ἐν κατανύξει καὶ θρήνῳ, χαίροντες καὶ εὐχαριστοῦντες, ὅτι τῆς αὐτοῦ πίστεως ἡμᾶς κατηξίωσε, καὶ τῆς αὐτοῦ ἐπιγνώσεως· μεθ' οὗ τῷ πατρὶ ἅμα τῷ ἁγίῳ πνεύματι δόξα νῦν καὶ ἀεὶ καὶ εἰς τοὺς αἰῶνας τῶν αἰώνων. ἀμήν.

M: . . . καὶ ἵνα δῶμεν αὐτῷ δόξαν μετ' εὐφροσύνης καὶ εὐχαριστεῖαν (sic) ἐπὶ τῇ αὐτοῦ μεγαλιώτητι (sic), ὅτι τῆς αὐτοῦ πίστεως ἡμᾶς ἠξίωσεν καὶ τῆς αὐτοῦ γνώσεως. Ναὶ τέκνα, γνῶμεν καὶ ἐπὶ τοῦ παρόντος τοῦ Κυρίου ἡμῶν Ἰησοῦ Χριστοῦ τὴν δύναμιν καὶ δοξάσωμεν τὴν αὐτοῦ ἀγαθότητα (sic) τοῦ ἀληθεινοῦ υἱοῦ τοῦ Θεοῦ τοῦ ζῶντος. Αὐτῷ γὰρ πρέπει δόξα τιμὴ καὶ προσκύνησις καὶ εὐχαριστεῖα (sic), ἅμα τῷ εὐλογημένῳ καὶ ἀθανάτῳ καὶ ὑπερενδόξῳ πατρὶ σὺν τῷ ἁγίῳ πνεύματι, εἰς τοὺς αἰῶνας τῶν αἰώνων ἀμήν.

17. An extract that does not actually appear in written form in the acts, but is cited by Gregory, bishop of Pesinus, during the first session of the council; ed. F. X. Funk, *Didascalia et Constitutiones Apostolorum II* (Paderborn, 1906), 144–46.

(A) P, fol. 254ᵛ (73*); V, fol. 3 (V 5); M, fol. 235 (37ᴹ)
Παμφίλου ἱερομάρτυρος· ἐκ τῆς ἐν Ἀντιοχείᾳ τῶν Ἀποστόλων γενομένης (–αμένης VM) συνόδου, ⟨ὑπὸ τῶν ἀποστόλων⟩ M, τουτέστιν ἐκ τῶν συνοδικῶν (τουτέστιν—συνοδ. om. M) κεφαλαίων τοῦ τετάρτου (κεφάλαιον τέταρτον M). Πρὸς τὸ (τοῦ M) μηκέτι ἀποπλανᾶσθαι (πλανᾶσθαι M) εἰς (τὰ add. M) εἴδωλα τοὺς σωζομένους ἀντεικονίζομεν (ἀλλ' ἀντεικονίζειν M) τὴν θεανδρικὴν ⟨ἄχραντον, χειροποίητον⟩M στήλην (στολὴν M) του ἀληθινοῦ Θεοῦ καὶ σωτῆρος ἡμῶν Ἰησοῦ Χριστοῦ καὶ τῶν αὐτοῦ θεραπόντων τὰς μορφὰς (om. M) ⟨ἀντικρυς τῶν εἰδώλων (om. M) καὶ (om. M) Ἰουδαίων⟩ VM καὶ (om. V) μηκέτι ἀποπλανᾶσθαι (πλανᾶσθαι M) εἰς εἴδωλα μηδὲ ὁμοιοῦσθαι Ἰουδαίοις καὶ Ἕλλησιν (ἔθνεσιν: V, om. M).

(B) Mansi XII 1018ᴄ–ᴅ
Γρηγόριος ἐπίσκοπος Πισινοῦντος εἶπεν· ἐν τῇ κατὰ Ἀντιόχειαν συνόδῳ τῶν ἁγίων ἀποστόλων εἴρηται: τοῦ μηκέτι πλανᾶσθαι εἰς τὰ εἴδωλα τοὺς σωζομένους, ἀλλ' ἀντεικονίζειν τὴν θεανδρικὴν ἄχραντον στήλην τοῦ κυρίου ἡμῶν Ἰησοῦ Χριστοῦ.

There is no point in discussing this extract, since in the acts it is mentioned from memory and not from a written document. It is, however, significant because it indicates that the participants were aware of a great number of Iconophile quotations that were not officially included in the agenda.

18. Anastasii Antiocheni *Epistula ad scholasticum* (frag.) (*PG* 89, 1408A); *CPG* 6954

> P, fol. 261 (81*)
> Mansi XIII 56A–B
> Τοῦ ἁγίου Ἀναστασίου ἐπισκόπου Θεουπόλεως· ἐπιστολὴ πρός τινα σχολαστικὸν (τινας σχολαστικοὺς P), δι᾽ ἧς ἀπεκρίνατο πρὸς αὐτὸν πρὸς τὴν ἐνεχθεῖσαν ⟨αὐτῷ⟩ A παρ᾽ αὐτοῦ ἀπορίαν· (ἧς ἡ ἀρχή add. A).
> Inc.: Εἰ τῷ μόνον ἐπερωτήσαντι σοφίαν σοφία λογισθήσεται· καὶ μεθ᾽ ἕτερα· καὶ μηδεὶς προσκοπτέτω . . .
> Des.: . . . μήπω τῆς ἔνδον ἀναγνώσεως πεῖραν εἰληφώς.

The passage was read out from a book offered to the assembly by John, the representative of the Oriental patriarchs. Both versions, apart from the differences that occur in the title, are absolutely identical.

There is only one case where P and A disagree. Compare:

προσκυνοῦμεν γὰρ καὶ ἀνθρώπους καὶ ἀγγέλους καὶ ἁγίους P
προσκυνοῦμεν γὰρ καὶ ἀνθρώπους καὶ ἀγγέλους ἁγίους A

Version A is confirmed by the Latin translation of Anastasius: *Adoramus enim homines et angelos sanctos.* Parisinus' reading is rather better because ἄγγελοι are not usually referred to as ἅγιοι.

Therefore, if the omission of αὐτῷ and the change of the singular accusative τινα σχολαστικὸν into τινας σχολαστικοὺς in P can be attributed to the copyist (misreading of an abbreviation), it becomes evident that P's archetype had given a better text and it is almost sure that it was the source for the quotation in A.

19. Anastasii Antiocheni *Ad Symeonem Bostrensem* (frag.) (*PG* 89, 1405A, B); *CPG* 6955

> (A) P, fol. 261 (82*); V, fols. 4ᵛ–5 (V 13)
> (Dam. II 66; III 127)
> Τοῦ αὐτοῦ· ἐκ τῆς πρὸς Συμεών, ἐπίσκοπον Βοστρῶν περιέχουσα περὶ Σαββάτου. P
> Ἀναστασίου τοῦ ἁγιωτάτου ἐπισκόπου Θεουπόλεως, ἐπιστολὴ πρὸς Συμεών, ἐπίσκοπον Βόστρης, περιέχουσα περὶ Σαββάτου: V

Inc. Ὥσπερ ἀπόντος βασιλέως ἡ εἰκὼν αὐτοῦ ἀντ᾽ αὐτοῦ προσκυνεῖται . . .
Des. . . . εἰς αὐτὸν ἐκεῖνον, οὗ ὁ (om. V) τύπος, ἀναφέρει τὴν ὕβριν.

(B) Mansi XIII 56ε–57α, also XIII 273α
Τοῦ ὁσίου πατρὸς ἡμῶν Ἀναστασίου πρὸς Συμεὼν ἐπίσκοπον Βόστρης
λόγος περὶ Σαββάτου, οὗ ἡ ἀρχή·
Inc. Εἰ πατέρας δεῖ κατὰ τὸ λόγιον, καὶ ὡς σὺ φῇς, ἐπερωτᾶν, ἔτιγε μὴν
καὶ πρεσβυτέρους. καὶ μετ᾽ ὀλίγα· ὥσπερ γὰρ ἀπόντος μὲν βασιλέως,
ἡ εἰκὼν αὐτοῦ ἀντ᾽ αὐτοῦ προσκυνεῖται. . .
Des. . . . εἰς αὐτὸν ἐκεῖνον, οὗ ὁ τύπος ἐστί, ἀναφέρει τὴν ὕβριν.

This text, like the previous extract of Anastasius of Antioch, is derived
from a book produced by another member of the assembly, the bishop of
Constantia in Cyprus.

It was first included in two of the florilegia appended to John of Damascus' *orationes* (II 66 and III 127), and the extract in II 66 must have been
the model for the later anthologies.

The version appearing in the acts is a little more extended than the one
in P and also in Dam. (II 66): A starts with the real incipit of the lost work:
Εἰ πατέρας δεῖ κατὰ τὸ λόγιον, καὶ ὡς σὺ φῇς, ἐπερωτᾶν, ἔτιγε μὴν καὶ πρεσβυτέρους. The three versions (Dam. II 66, PV, and A) present some minor
differences in twelve cases. In seven cases, A agrees with Dam. against P,
in two A agrees with P against Dam., in another two the text of A is a combination of Dam. and PV, but the general impression is that all three of the
versions are almost identical, as the following examples illuminate:

Ὥσπερ γὰρ ἀπόντος μὲν βασιλέως Dam.A γὰρ, μὲν om. PV; ἐπεὶ Dam.A:
ἐπειδὴ PV; καὶ μετ᾽ ὀλίγα Dam.A: γὰρ PV; τιμωρίαν ὑφίσταται Dam.: τιμωρίαν δικαίαν ἐπίσταται PV: τιμωρίαν δικαίαν ὑφίσταται A; and so on.

Their major difference, though, lies in the titles. Compare:

A: Τοῦ ἁγιωτάτου καὶ μακαριωτάτου ἀρχιεπισκόπου Θεουπόλεως καὶ πα-
τριάρχου Ἀναστασίου περὶ σαββάτου, καὶ πρὸς Συμεὼν ἐπίσκοπον Βόστρης
(= Dam. II 66)
B: Τοῦ ἁγίου Ἀναστασίου ἐπισκόπου Θεουπόλεως ἐκ τῆς (ἐπιστολή V)
πρὸς Συμεὼν ἐπίσκοπον Βοστρῶν (Βόστρης V) περιέχουσα περὶ σαββάτου.
(= PV)
B1: Ἀναστασίου, ἀρχιεπισκόπου Ἀντιοχείας, πρὸς Συμεών, ἐπίσκοπον
Βόστρων, περὶ τοῦ σαββάτου. (= Dam. III 126)
C: Τοῦ ὁσίου πατρὸς ἡμῶν Ἀναστασίου πρὸς Συμεὼν ἐπίσκοπον Βόστρης
λόγος περὶ σαββάτου, οὗ ἡ ἀρχή· (= A)

It looks as though B is trying to compromise between A and B1, and C appears as a final reshaping of B and B1. Moreover, in some cases A seems to be aware of Dam. Compare:

Dam.	PV	A
τὸν πρωτότυπον	τὸ πρωτότυπον	PV
ἐπεὶ	ἐπειδὴ	Dam.
—	ἐν	Dam.
τιμωρίαν ὑφίσταται	τ. δικαίαν ἐπίσταται	τ. δικαὶαν ὑφίσταται
καίτοι	καίτοιγε	Dam.
κεκραμένα	ἀνακεκραμμένα	Dam.
τύπος (=V)	ὁ τύπος	P
ἐστίν	—	Dam.

Therefore, the possibility that A combined Dam. and the original of PV should not be excluded, although the more extensive incipit of A might suggest that the council had at its disposal a collection of the letters of the patriarch.

20. Ambrosii Mediolanensis *De incarnationis dominicae sacramento*, ed. O. Faller, *CSEL* (Vienna, 1964), 79, chap. 7. 75.125–27 (*PL* 16, 873B); *CPL* 152

(a) Paris. gr. 1115, fol. 261ᵛ (85*)
Τοῦ ἁγίου Ἀμβροσίου ἀρχιεπισκόπου Μεδιολάνων πρὸς Γρατιανὸν τὸν βασιλέα, ἐκ τοῦ τρίτου βιβλίου κεφάλαιον θ´.
Τί γὰρ μήποτε καὶ τὴν θεότητα
καὶ τὴν σάρκα αὐτοῦ προσκυνοῦντες μερίζωμεν τὸν Χριστὸν ἢ ὅτε
ἐν αὐτῷ τὴν θείαν εἰκόνα καὶ τὸν
σταυρὸν προσκυνοῦμεν μερίζομεν αὐτόν; μὴ γένοιτο.

(b) Mansi XII 1067D
. . . τοῦ μακαρίου Ἀμβροσίου
πρὸς Γρατιανὸν τὸν βασιλέα, ἐκ
τοῦ τρίτου βιβλίου, κεφαλαίου ἐν-
νάτου.
Τί γάρ; μή ποτε καὶ τὴν θεότητα
καὶ τὴν σάρκα αὐτοῦ προσκυνοῦντες, μερίζομεν τὸν Χριστὸν ἢ ὅτε
ἐν αὐτῷ τὴν θείαν εἰκόνα καὶ τὸν
σταυρὸν προσκυνοῦμεν μερίζομεν αὐτόν; μὴ γένοιτο.

(c) Mansi XII 1068E–9A: Item beati Ambrosii (Mediolanensis episcopi add. *LS*) ad Gratianum imperatorem ex libro tertio capitulo (capite *LS*) nono. Numquidne (–nam Lat. A) quando et deitatem et carnem eius (om. Lat. A) adoramus, dividimus Christum? aut quando in ipso et Dei imaginem et crucem adoramus, dividimus eum? Absit.

(d) *PL* 16, 873B; *CSEL* 79, 7.75.125–27
Sed verendum est, inquis (–t: *CSEL*), ne si duos principales sensus aut geminam sapientiam Christo tribuimus, Christum dividamus? Numquid cum et divinitatem eius adoramus et carnem, Christum dividimus?

Numquid, cum in eo imaginem Dei, crucemque veneramur, dividimus eum? . . .

(e) Dam. III 116

Ἀμβροσίου, ἐπισκόπου Μεδιολάνων, πρὸς Γρατιανὸν τὸν βασιλέα περὶ τῆς ἐνσάρκου οἰκονομίας τοῦ Θεοῦ λόγου· Θεὸς πρὸ τῆς σαρκὸς καὶ Θεὸς ἐν σαρκί. Ἀλλὰ φόβος, φησί, μὴ δύο ἡγεμονικὰ ἢ σοφίαν διττὴν ἀπονέμοντες Χριστῷ μερίζειν δόξωμεν Χριστόν. Ἆρα οὖν μή, ὁπότε καὶ τὴν θεότητα αὐτοῦ καὶ τὴν σάρκα προσκυνοῦμεν, μερίζομεν τὸν Χριστὸν ἤ, ὅτε ἐν τῷ αὐτῷ καὶ τὴν τοῦ Θεοῦ εἰκόνα καὶ τὸν σταυρὸν προσκυνοῦμεν, διαιροῦμεν αὐτόν; Μὴ γένοιτο.

Much of the textual study of this small excerpt has already been carried out by Wallach. His main point is that the Latin quotation above (c), which is supposed to be the basis for the Greek translation (a, b), was actually the retranslation into Latin of a Greek redaction of the text, apparently the one listed by John of Damascus in III 116 (e).[143] Then he claims that the aforementioned Latin version of the Greek redaction in Dam. III 116 "was inserted in a collection of patristic testimonia of image-worship that belonged to the *Acta* of the Lateran Council [sc. the Roman Council of 769]. This Greek-Latin Ambrose testimonium was subsequently inserted, together with other testimonia of the same synodal source . . . in Hadrian I's *Synodica* of 785."[144]

The quotation that is incorporated into P is the same as the one in A and contains, in addition, the title ἀρχιεπισκόπου Μεδιολάνων, which is missing from A but not from the Latin version preserved in *LS*. The case is much more complicated in comparison with the other quotations of the *Synodica* of 785, but it seems possible that (e), (a), (c) were all available at Rome before 770. On the basis of the relationship between the Greek and Latin versions of the *testimonia* in the *Synodica* of 785, I may introduce the following hypothesis. The (e) version of the extract was possibly included in the corpus of patristic quotations translated into Latin for the 731 Roman council (= version (c)). Some time after 731 it was retranslated into Greek in order, perhaps, to be included in the correspondence conducted between Rome and the East.[145] Dam. III 116 draws, in all probability, on the Greek corpus of

---

[143] Ibid., 127.

[144] Ibid., 131.

[145] It is impossible to suppose that the compiler of 770 made the translation, since, as is shown below in quotation 21, he was unable to realize that the two small fragments from the *Panarion* of Epiphanius were identical in the sense that the second was the basis for the Latin translation and the first was the Greek retranslation of the Latin version. However, this does not exclude the possibility of the Ambrose Greek version [(a) and (b)] being the result of the translations made after 785 for the needs of the seventh ecumenical council. If this is the case then the fragment is a post-774/5 addition.

pre-731, as is evident in some other cases (see above, pp. 120–23, etc.), and it is likely that the participants in the Roman Councils of 731 and 769 were unaware of the original excerpt (d) from the work of Ambrose. This is why in the *Synodica* of 785 there appears the corrupt version (c).[146]

21. Epiphanii Constantiensis *Panarion* (= *Adversus haereses*), ed. K. Holl, *Epiphanius*, Bände 1–3: *Ancoratus und Panarion, GCS* 37 (Leipzig, 1922); *CPG* 3745 (P 86*)

(A) P, fol. 261ᵛ: Τοῦ ἁγίου Ἐπιφανίου· Μὴ γὰρ βασιλεὺς ἔχων εἰκόνα δύο βασιλεῖς εἰσίν, ἀλλ' ὁ βασιλεὺς εἷς ἐστι καὶ μετὰ τῆς εἰκόνος.

(A1) P, ibid.: τοῦ αὐτοῦ· καὶ γὰρ καὶ οἱ βασιλεῖς διὰ τὸ ἔχειν εἰκόνας, οὐ δύο εἰσὶ βασιλεῖς, ἀλλὰ βασιλεὺς εἷς σὺν τῇ εἰκόνι.

(A2) *Panarion, Haer.*, GCS 37, 12.10–11: Καὶ γὰρ καὶ οἱ βασιλεῖς οὐ διὰ τὸ ἔχειν εἰκόνα δύο εἰσὶ βασιλεῖς, ἀλλὰ βασιλεὺς εἷς σὺν τῇ εἰκόνι.

(A3) Mansi XII 1067ᴅ: πάλιν τοῦ ἁγίου Ἐπιφανίου Κωνσταντίας τῆς Κύπρου· μὴ γὰρ εἰ βασιλεὺς ἔχει εἰκόνα, δύο εἰσὶ βασιλεῖς; οὔμενουν· ὁ βασιλεὺς εἷς ἐστι καὶ μετὰ τῆς εἰκόνος.

(B) Mansi XII 1069ᴀ: Item sancti Epiphanii Constantiae Cypri: Numquid enim et imperator pro eo quod habet imaginem, duo sunt imperatores? non sane; sed imperator unus est etiam cum imagine.

(B1) The original text of this quotation in the *Synodica* as is preserved in *Libellus Synodalis* of the Paris Synod of 825, 511.34–35:
Item sancti Epyphanii episcopi Constantiae Cypri: Etenim imperatores pro eo quod habent imagines, non duo sunt imperatores, sed imperator unus cum imagine.

It appears that Parisinus gives not only the original version of the extract (A1), but also the Greek retranslation (A) of the Latin redaction (B1). Another interesting point is that the Latin translation B1 is not a literal translation of the original in A2, as Wallach claims,[147] but renders verbatim version A1 of P.

Since the original quotation in A2 cannot have been supplied by Cinnamus himself, the Parisinus version is once more prior to the acts. The Greek version in A presents also a reading different from the quotation in A3 (βασι-

[146] For the Latin version of the florilegium in the *Synodica* of 785, it has already been said that it was based on the lost acts of the Roman Synod of 731 which were repeated in the Lateran Council of 769. See also W. von den Steinen, "Entstehungsgeschichte der *Libri Carolini*," *Quellen und Forschungen aus Italienischen Archiven und Bibliotheken* 21 (1929–30), 28, 50. See also the *scholium* by A. Werminghoff in *MGH, Concilia 2, 1., Aevi Karolini* 1.2 (Hannover-Leipzig, 1904), 88.
[147] *Diplomatic Studies*, 34.

λεὺς ἔχων P: εἰ βασιλεὺς ἔχει A), which might indicate that even the Greek retranslation in P is prior to the one in A3. The fact that P provides the Greek retranslation along with the original version of the text allows the supposition that among the collections the compiler of the τεῦχος of 770 had access to should have been one that included the Greek original text of some quotations, possibly their Latin translation, and also—for reasons that I am unable to explain—their retranslation into Greek.

22. Cyrilli Hierosolymitani *Catechesis ad illuminandos ii,* ed. W. K. Reischl, *Cyrilli Hierosolymorum Archiepiscopi opera quae supersunt omnia* (Munich, 1848), 60 (*PG* 33, 421); *CPG* 3585.2

> P, fol. 262ᵛ (91*)
> Mansi XIII 160ᴀ–ʙ
> Τοῦ ἁγίου Κυρίλλου ἀρχιεπισκόπου Ἱεροσολύμων ἐκ τοῦ τῆς β΄ κατηχήσεως P
> Τοῦ ἁγίου Κυρίλλου ἀρχιεπισκόπου Ἱεροσολύμων κατήχησις δευτέρα, ἧς ἡ ἀρχή· A
> Inc. Δεινὸν ἡ ἁμαρτία καὶ νόσος (νόσῳ P) χαλεπωτάτη ψυχῆς ἡ παρανομία· καὶ μεθ᾽ ἕτερα· τίνα γὰρ ὑπόνοιαν ἔχεις (ἔχει P) περὶ Ναβουχοδονόσορ;
> Des. ... τὰ ἐπὶ τὸ ἱλαστήριον τῆς κιβωτοῦ, ὧν ἀναμέσον (ἀνὰ μέσον P) ἐλάλει (ὁ add. A) κύριος.

The quotation is one of the eighteen extracts included in chapter 45 of the *Doctrina* (330.13–15). In all probability, the original of P drew from the same source as the *Doctrina,* omitting one or two clauses and adding the incipit of the work. The version of the acts, apart from the slightly different title, is identical with the text provided by P, while the same passage in the edition of Reischl is considerably different. Therefore, the line of the transmission of the text could be the following:

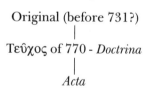

Original (before 731?)
|
Τεῦχος of 770 - *Doctrina*
|
Acta

23. Anastasii Apocrisiarii *Acta in primo exsilio seu dialogus Maximi cum Theodosio ep. Caesareae in Bith.* (*PG* 90, 156ᴀ-ʙ, 164.9–15); *CPG* 7735; *BHG* 1233[148]

---

[148] For this fragment see also R. Bracke, *Ad Sancti Maximi Vitam* (Louvain, 1980), 107–10. Unfortunately, he has ignored in his analysis codex Marcianus gr. 573, which is of particular significance here, and also Mosquensis Hist. Mus. 265.

P, fol. 262ᵛ (92*); V, fol. 12ʳ⁻ᵛ (V 34); M, fol. 235 (38ᴹ)
(Dam. II 65; III 131)
Mansi XIII 37ε–40β
Ἐκ τῶν κινηθέντων δογμάτων μεταξὺ τοῦ ἐν ἁγίοις Μαξίμου καὶ Θεοδοσίου ἐπισκόπου Καισαρείας τῆς Βιθυνίας καὶ τῶν σὺν αὐτῷ (ὑπάτων· ὧν
ἡ ἀρχή· add. A) PA
     Ἐκ τοῦ τόμου τῶν κινηθέντων δογμάτων μεταξὺ τοῦ ἐν ἁγίοις Μαξίμου
καὶ Θεοδοσίου ἐπισκόπου Καισαρείας τῆς Βιθυνίας. V
     Μαξίμου φιλοσόφου καὶ ὁμολογητοῦ ἐκ τῶν περὶ αὐτὸν πεπραγμένων
μεταξὺ αὐτοῦ τε καὶ Θεοδωσίου (sic) ἐπισκόπου. M
Inc. Τὰ κεκηρυγμένα (κεκινημένα A) περὶ τῆς ἀμωμήτου ἡμῶν τῶν Χριστιανῶν πίστεως (πίστεως τῶν Χριστιανῶν A)· καὶ μεθ᾽ ἕτερα· Μάξιμος
εἶπε· Δεσπόται . . . PA,
     Καὶ ἐπὶ τούτοις ἀνέστησαν πάντες . . . M,
     Ἀνέστησαν οὖν μετὰ φόβου καὶ δακρύων . . . V.
Des. . . . καὶ τῆς αὐτὸν τεκούσης παναγίας ἀειπαρθένου Μαρίας (μητρὸς
     A), PA,
     . . . ἐπὶ βεβαιώσει τῶν λαληθέντων M,
     . . . τῷ βασιλεῖ τὴν αἰτίαν παρέπεμψεν V.

The almost absolute likeness of the two quotations becomes apparent
at first sight. A smaller part of this extract appears in John of Damascus'
florilegia (II 65; III 131).

Here is a list of the divergences among the three versions:

Dam.	PM	A
—(= M)	Τὰ κεκηρυγμένα (om. M)	Τὰ κεκινημένα
—(= M)	πίστεως τῶν Χριστ. (om. M)	τῶν Χριστ. πίστεως
ταῦτα	τοῦτο (om. M)	τοῦτο
γένοιτο	γένηται (om. M)	γένοιτο
καὶ μετὰ δα-κρύων	μετὰ χαρᾶς καὶ δακρύων	μετὰ χαρᾶς καὶ δ.
τεθεικότες	τεθεικότες (–ικώτες M)	τεθηκότες
χεῖρας	ἰδίας ⟨αὐτῶν⟩M, χεῖρας	ἰδίας χεῖρας
—(= M)	καὶ μετὰ βραχέα (om. M)	καὶ μετὰ βραχὺ
—(= M)	πάντως (om. M)	πάντες
—(= M)	Μαρίας (om. M)	μητρὸς

In Dam. III 131, the following title precedes the quotation:
Τοῦ ἀββᾶ Μαξίμου καὶ Θεοδοσίου ἐπισκόπου καὶ τῶν ἀρχόντων τῶν ἀποσταλέντων παρὰ τοῦ βασιλέως.

From the evidence furnished by the three versions, it can be inferred that A takes into account both Dam. and the original of P. This conclusion becomes more evident if we take a look at the title in Dam. III 131: the word ὑπάτων that A adds to the end of the title provided by P seems to stand for the καὶ τῶν ἀρχόντων τῶν ἀποσταλέντων παρὰ τοῦ βασιλέως in Dam. III 131.

What is more, the contribution of V helps to restore an original which was longer than that extant in the A (and PM) version. Two examples will make this point clear. After the words ἐπὶ βεβαιώσει τῶν λαληθέντων, A and P introduce the formula καὶ μεθ᾽ ἕτερα, while V reads as follows: καὶ οὕτως ἠσφαλίσαντο ἀλλήλους· τοῦ δὲ ἐπισκόπου Θεοδοσίου τὸν ὅρκον πειρωμένου καταλύειν . . .

Compare also the passages:

V, fol. 12ᵛ	A XIII, 40A10–B3
. . . εἶπεν πρὸς αὐτὸν ὁ ἅγιος Μάξιμος μετὰ δακρύων·	στραφεὶς τοίνυν ὁ ἀββᾶς Μάξιμος πρὸς τὸν ἐπίσκοπον, μετὰ δακρύων εἶπεν αὐτῷ·
κύρι ὁ μέγας, ἡμέραν κρίσεως ἐκδεχόμεθα · οἶδας τὰ τυπωθέντα καὶ δόξαντα ἡνίκα τὰς χεῖρας τεθείκαμεν ἐπὶ τῶν ἁγίων εὐαγγελίων καὶ τοῦ ζωοποιοῦ σταυροῦ καὶ τῆς ἁγίας εἰκόνος τοῦ Κυρίου καὶ σωτῆρος ἡμῶν καὶ ἐπὶ τῆς ἁγίας εἰκόνος τῆς παναγίας παρθένου Μαρίας· καὶ βαλὼν κάτω τὸ πρόσωπον Θεοδόσιος ἐπὶ τῷ βασιλεῖ τὴν αἰτίαν παρέπεμψεν.	κύρι ὁ μέγας, ἡμέραν κρίσεως ἐκδεχόμεθα πάντες· οἶδας τὰ τυπωθέντα καὶ δόξαντα ἐπὶ τῶν ἁγίων εὐαγγελίων καὶ τοῦ ζωοποιοῦ σταυροῦ καὶ τῆς εἰκόνος τοῦ Θεοῦ καὶ σωτῆρος ἡμῶν καὶ τῆς αὐτὸν τεκούσης παναγίας ἀειπαρθένου Μαρίας.

On the basis of the passages presented above, it is not difficult to conclude that the original of P, M, and V (F) comprised two versions: the one of the florilegia of John of Damascus P and M, and a second which included a more extended version of the same passage, since the additional lines provided by V briefly summarize the missing parts of the text (*PG* 90, 156B–164A). Dam. and the version preserved by P were taken into account in the acts, but not V.

24. Constantini diaconi et chartophylacis sanctissimae Dei magnae ecclesiae Constantinopoleos *Laudatio omnium martyrum* (*PG* 88, 408A, 496D–497D, 500A–B); *CPG* 7403; *BHG* 1191

(A) P, fols. 262ᵛ–263ᵛ (93*)

Κωνσταντίνου διακόνου καὶ χαρτοφύλακος τῆς ἁγιωτάτης ἐκκλησίας Κωνσταντινουπόλεως, ἐκ τοῦ ἐγκωμίου τοῦ εἰς πάντας τοὺς ἁγίους τοὺς κατὰ τὴν οἰκουμένην μάρτυρας.

Inc. Εἶτα οἴεσθαι (sic) ᾧ οὗτοι ἔφησαν οἱ δικάζοντες . . .

Des. . . . καὶ οὐ καθ' ὑμᾶς ποικιλίας παράγοντες καὶ σχήματα κατὰ τὸ δοκοῦν διαγλύφοντες.

(B) Mansi XIII 185A–188A

Κωνσταντίνου διακόνου καὶ χαρτοφύλακος τῆς ἁγιωτάτης τοῦ Θεοῦ μεγάλης ἐκκλησίας Κωνσταντινουπόλεως εἰς πάντας τοὺς ἁγίους μάρτυρας, οὗ ἡ ἀρχή.

Inc. Αἱ μὲν Χριστοῦ πανηγύρεις· καὶ μεθ' ἕτερα· εἶτα οἴεσθε, ὦ οὗτοι, ἔφησαν οἱ δικάζοντες . . .

Des. . . . καὶ οὐ καθ' ὑμᾶς ποικίλας ἰδέας παράγοντες, καὶ σχήματα κατὰ τὸ δοκοῦν διαγλύφοντες.

There seem to be no striking differences between A and P. A closer examination of the two texts, however, will reveal some interesting hints as to the relationship of these two versions.

Parisinus omits the incipit of the work. Its readings are in some cases better than those of the acts, but sometimes inferior. In any case, the following readings are evident misreadings that must be attributed to Cinnamus: αἰδεῖτο P: ἐδεῖτο A; ἀναστήσαντος P: ἀναστήσοντος A; οὐδὲν αὐτὴν P: οὐδὲ νῦν τὴν A; προσώποις P: τρόποις A; ποικιλίας P: ποικίλας ἰδέας A.

On the other hand, P is closer to the original reading in the following cases: ἐγχαράττετε A: ἐγχαράττεται P (exaratur Lat. A); περὶ τοῦτο A: περὶ τούτων P (ab horum Lat. A); ἐξ ἀρχῆς A: ἐξ αὐτῆς P (scrib. αὐτῆς sive ἑαυτῆς) (ex se Lat. A). Still, P omits four words, while A omits one.

Compare also the sentences:

    I. P: οὐ γὰρ οἷά τε ἦν ἐξ αὐτῆς κάτω κειμένην τὴν ἧτταν ἀναπαλαῖσαί τε καὶ ἀνακαλέσασθαι, . . .

    Acts: οὐ γὰρ οἴατε ἦν ἐξ ἀρχῆς κάτω κειμένη, ἢ τὴν ἧτταν ἀναπαλαῖσαί τε καὶ ἀνακαλέσασθαι, . . .

The original should read as follows:

οὐ γὰρ οἷόν τε (οἷα τε PG) ἦν ἐξ αὐτῆς (ἑαυτῆς PG) κάτω κειμένην (–μένη PG) τὴν ἧτταν ἀναπαλαῖσαί τε καὶ ἀνακαλέσασθαι, . . .

    II. P: οὔτε μὴν τοὺς δι' οὓς ὁ ἀγὼν λυσιτελής τε καὶ ὠφέλιμος ὁ ἡμέτερος πρόμαχος, . . .

    Acts: οὔτε μὴν (μὲν PG) τοῖς δι' οὓς ὁ ἀγών, λυσιτελεῖς τε καὶ ὠφελίμους ὁ ἡμέτερος πρόμαχος, . . . (= PG)

The original probably had the following:

οὔτε μὴν τοὺς δύο, οἷς ὁ ἀγὼν λυσιτελής τε καὶ ὠφέλιμος ὁ ἡμέτερος πρόμαχος ⟨γενήσεται⟩, . . .

Parisinus is closer to the original, which, in both cases, was too difficult for any copyist to decipher.

III. P: ὅσα καὶ ἐξ ὧνπερ ὁ ἄνθρωπος καὶ μήτε (= μὴ τῇ?) δοκήσει τὸ σὰρξ φανῆναι σχηματισάμενος. (= PG)

Acta: ὅσα καὶ ἐξ ὧν περ ὁ ἄνθρωπος, καὶ μὴ τῇ δοκήσει τό σῶμα σχηματισάμενος.

Acta1: (A, in marg.): ὅσα καὶ ἐξ ὧν περ ὁ ἄνθρωπος, καὶ μὴ τῇ δοκήσει τὸ σὰρξ παγῆναι σχηματισάμενος/ καὶ μὴ τὸ σὰρξ φανῆναι σχηματισάμενος.

It is certain that both P and A draw from the same original, which provided a text that was not in perfect condition. Both copyists were compelled to commit errors. The final inference is that the quotation from F should be the source for the extract provided in the acts. The incipit that exists in A but not in P can be explained in two ways: either by the supposition that Cinnamus himself omitted the sentence (or sentences) for reasons known only to him, or by the theory (which may apply to some other quotations as well) that the organizing committee in some cases was able to provide the actual work according to the indications (incipit and desinit) established by a florilegium and then, after tracing the extracts within the work, have them recited in public.

25. *Canon sextae synodi octuagesimus secundus* (= *Quinisextum canon* 82, Mansi XI 977ε–980β); *CPG* 9444

> P, fol. 263ᵛ (94*); V, fols. 15ᵛ–16 (V 38); M, fol. 239 (49ᴹ)
> (Dam. III 137)
> Ἐκ τῶν κανόνων τῶν συνελθόντων πατέρων ἐν τῇ ἕκτη συνόδω, κανὼν πγ´ (sic) P
> Ἐκ (om. V) τῆς ἁγίας καὶ (om. M) οἰκουμενικῆς ἕκτης συνόδου. VM
> Mansi XIII 40ε–41α; also XIII 220c–ε
> Κανὼν τῆς ἁγίας καὶ οἰκουμενικῆς ς´ συνόδου, (octuagesimus secundus Mansi XIII 39ε)
> Inc. Ἔν τισι τῶν σεπτῶν εἰκόνων γραφαῖς, ἀμνὸς ⟨τῷ⟩PM δακτύλω τοῦ Προδρόμου . . .
> Des. . . . καὶ τῆς ἐντεῦθεν γε(ι M)νομένης τῷ κόσμω (γεναμένης τοῦ κόσμου V) ἀπολυτρώσεως.

Concerning the provenance of this canon of the Quinisext council there is no doubt: it was cited from a χάρτης which was, as the subsequent debate revealed, the original copy of the canons of that council bearing the signatures of the fathers.

Since it is the only canon up to this period dealing directly with the icons, it is included in almost every Iconophile work and florilegium composed before and after the council of 787. In the acts the whole canon is read out four times. The opening phrase reads in all four cases as follows: Ἔν τισι τῶν σεπτῶν εἰκόνων γραφαῖς, ἀμνὸς δακτύλω τοῦ Προδρόμου δεικνύμενος ἐγχαράττεται. The omission of the article τῷ before the noun δακτύλῳ gives a sense of unevenness, but still this is how the text reads in the acts. On the other hand, the text in the Νουθεσία and in M gives the complex τῷ δακτύλω which is also present in P.

26. Stephani Bostrensis *Contra Iudaeos* (frag.), ed. G. Mercati, "Stephani Bostreni nova de sacris imaginibus fragmenta e libro deperdito Κατὰ Ἰου-δαίων," *ST* 76 (1937), 202–6; *CPG* 7790

(A) P, fol. 263ᵛ–264 (95*); V, fols. 12ᵛ–14 (V 35); also in cod. Ambrosianus gr. A 84 sup. (12th or 13th cent.)
(Dam. III 72, 73)
Στεφάνου τοῦ ἁγιωτάτου ἐπισκόπου Βοστρῶν περὶ ἁγίων εἰκόνων· (περὶ εἰκόνων τῶν ἁγίων V) PV
Inc. Περὶ δὲ τῶν εἰκόνων τῶν ἁγίων θαρροῦμεν . . .
Des. . . . ἄξιον γάρ ἐστι μνημονεύειν τῶν ἡγουμένων ἡμῶν καὶ εὐχαριστίας προσφέρειν τῷ Θεῷ. P,
. . . οἱ ἅγιοι ὑπὲρ ἡμῶν τὸ θεῖον ἐξιλεοῦνται. V.

(B) Mansi XII 1067ᴅ–1070ᴅ (Latin: XII 1069ᴀ–1072ᴀ = *LS* 511.36–512.30)
. . . τοῦ ἁγίου Στεφάνου ἐπισκόπου Βόστρων·
. . . sancti episcopi Stephani Bostron de imagine sanctorum. (Lat. A)
Item sancti Stephani episcopi Bostron ad quosdam de imaginibus sanctorum (*LS*, 511.36)
Inc. οἵ τινες δὴ περὶ τῶν εἰκόνων τῶν ἁγίων ὁμολογοῦμεν, ὅτι πᾶν ἔργον τὸ γινόμενον ἐν ὀνόματι τοῦ Θεοῦ . . .
De imaginibus vero (om. *LS*) sanctorum confitemur (confidimus *LS*), quoniam omne opus, quod fit in Dei nomine . . .
Des. . . . ἄξιον δέ ἐστιν μνημονεύειν τῶν ἡγουμένων ἡμῶν καὶ εὐχαριστίας προσφέρειν τῷ Θεῷ.
. . . Dignum enim est commemorari praepositorum (doctorum *LS*) nostrorum et gratias referre Deo.

One of the sources of this extract is the florilegium appended to the third *Sermo de imaginibus* of John of Damascus (III 72, 73). The text, as it is included in PV and A, differs considerably from that of Dam.: it is more extended, and the vocabulary is different. Mercati published the same text from Ambrosianus gr. A 84 (12th or 13th cent.). When he published his version, he was aware neither of the Greek translation of the text in the *Synodica* nor of the existence of the fragment in PV. For more on this, see my article, "Stephen of Bostra: *Fragmenta contra Iudaeos* (CPG 7790): A New Edition," *JÖB* 43 (1993), 45–60.

Here I give a brief summary of my conclusions. A Greek version of

Stephen's text which was somewhat different from the version provided by Dam. III 72, 73 was translated into Latin for the Roman Synod of 731. Then it was retranslated into Greek before 770. PV preserve part of the original Greek version interpolated with the final part of the Greek retranslation. The Ambrosianus version seems to rely more on Dam. and the Greek retranslation, while A is an almost word-by-word retranslation of the Latin translation. The stemmatic depiction of the relationship among the various versions (but not that of the manuscripts) might be as follows:

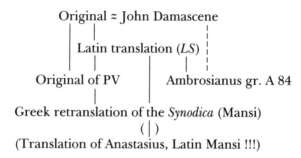

Original ≂ John Damascene

Latin translation (*LS*)

Original of PV   Ambrosianus gr. A 84

Greek retranslation of the *Synodica* (Mansi)
(|)
(Translation of Anastasius, Latin Mansi !!!)

27. Hieronymi Hierosolymitani *De effectu baptismati* (*Dialogus de cruce?*) (*PG*, 40, 865c-d); *CPG* 7817

(a) Paris. gr. 1115, fol. 264 (96*)
Τοῦ ἁγίου Ἱερωνύμου πρεσβυτέρου Ἱεροσολύμων·

Καὶ γὰρ ὡς συνεχώρησεν ὁ Θεὸς
προσκυνεῖν πᾶν ἔθνος   χειροποιητά, Ἰουδαίους   τὰς πλάκας
ἐκείνας,   ἃς ἠλατόμησε
Μωυσῆς καὶ τὰ δύο χερουβὶμ
τὰ χρυσά, οὕτως καὶ ἡμῖν τοῖς
χριστιανοῖς ἐδωρήσατο τὸν
σταυρὸν καὶ τῶν ἀγαθῶν ἔργων
τὰς εἰκόνας γράφειν καὶ προσκυνεῖν καὶ δεῖξαι τὸ ἔργον ἡμῶν.

(b) Mansi XII 1070ε
Ἐκ τοῦ λόγου τοῦ μακαρίου
Ἱερωνύμου πρεσβυτέρου Ἱεροσο-
λύμων·

Καὶ γὰρ ὡς συνεχώρησεν ὁ Θεὸς
προσκυνεῖν πᾶν ἔθνος τὰ χειροποίητα, Ἰουδαίοις δὲ τὰς πλάκας
ἐκείνας εὐδόκησεν, ἃς ἐλατόμησεν ὁ Μωυσῆς καὶ τὰ δύο χερουβὶμ τὰ χρυσᾶ· οὕτω καὶ ἡμῖν τοῖς
Χριστιανοῖς ἐδωρήσατο τὸν
σταυρὸν καὶ τῶν ἀγαθῶν ἔργων
τὰς εἰκόνας γράφειν καὶ προσκυνεῖν, καὶ δεῖξαι τὸ ἔργον ἡμῶν.

Latin text: Mansi XII 1072β
De sermone beati Hieronymi presbyteri Hierosolymitani: Etenim sicut permisit Deus adorare omnem gentem manufacta, Judaeos autem tabulas quas dolavit Moyses, et duos cherubim aureos, sic et nobis Christianis donavit crucem et bonarum operationum imagines pingere et adorare, venerari, et demonstrare opus nostrum.

V and M give a slightly different version of the same passage which reads as follows: V, fol. 21 (V 50); M, fol. 225 (16ᴹ)

Τοῦ ἁγίου Ἰερωνύμου ἐπισκόπου (πρεσβυτέρου Μ) Ἱεροσολύμων· Χάριν τούτου συνεχώρησεν ὁ Θεὸς παντὶ ἔθνει προσκυνεῖν (τι add. Μ) χειροποίητον· Ἰουδαίοις (–ους Μ) μὲν τὰς πλάκας, ἃς ἐλάξευσεν Μωυσῆς καὶ τὰ δύο Χερουβὶμ τὰ χρυσᾶ· οὕτως καὶ ἡμᾶς (ἡμῖν Μ) τοὺς (τοῖς Μ) χριστιανοὺς (–οῖς Μ) ἐχαρίσατο τὸν σταυρὸν καὶ τὰ τῶν ἁγίων ἀνδραγαθήματα ἐν εἰκόσιν διαγράφειν (καὶ ταῦτα ἀσπάζεσθαι add. Μ) καὶ προσκυνεῖν καὶ δεικνύειν τὴν διάθεσιν ἡμῶν τὴν πρὸς αὐτὸν (αὐτοὺς Μ).

John of Damascus (III 125) represents, possibly, the ultimate source of this quotation, but the text provided by him is much different from the quotation in the Greek translation of the *Synodica*. It is certain that the P and A versions represent a retranslation of the Latin redaction which in its turn had, in all possibility, been based on the VM version.

The text in both A and P is almost identical, apart from the abridged title in P and some differences at the beginning. Compare also:

I. De sermone beati Hieronymi presbyteri Hierosolymitani (Mansi XII 1072ʙ)
Etenim sicut permisit Deus adorare omnem gentem manufacta, Judaeos autem tabulas, quas dolavit Moyses . . .

II. Mansi XII 1070ᴇ: Ἐκ τοῦ λόγου τοῦ μακαρίου Ἰερωνύμου πρεσβυτέρου Ἱεροσολύμων· Καὶ γὰρ ὡς συνεχώρησεν ὁ Θεὸς προσκυνεῖν πᾶν ἔθνος τὰ χειροποίητα, Ἰουδαίοις δὲ τὰς πλάκας ἐκείνας εὐδόκησεν, ἃς ἐλατόμησεν ὁ Μωυσῆς, . . .

III. P
Τοῦ ἁγίου Ἰερωνύμου πρεσβυτέρου Ἱεροσολύμων· Καὶ γὰρ ὡς συνεχώρησεν ὁ Θεὸς προσκυνεῖν πᾶν ἔθνος χειροποιητά, Ἰουδαίους δὲ τὰς πλάκας ἐκείνας, ἃς ἠλατόμησεν ὁ Μωυσῆς, . . .

P is closer to the Latin text than A, so Anastasius might have used the text preserved in P for this translation. Apart from that, P gives the reading Ἰουδαίους, which is better than the Ἰουδαίοις provided by A. Finally, F included the Greek archetype of the same piece as witnessed by V and M and not only the Greek retranslation of P, a situation similar to the one we have already seen above in no. 21.

28. Symeonis Stylitae Iunioris *Epistula ad Iustinum Iuniorem* (*PG* 86, 2, 3216); *CPG* 7366

(A) P, fol. 264^{r-v} (97*); V, fol. 12 (V. 33)

Τοῦ ἁγίου Συμεῶνος τοῦ εἰς τὸ θαυμαστὸν ὄρος· ἐκ τῆς ἐπιστολῆς τῆς πεμφθείσης πρὸς τὸν βασιλέα Ἰουστιανόν· (sic) P

Συμεὼν τοῦ Στυλίτου τοῦ ἐν τῷ Θαυμαστῷ ὄρει ἐκ τῆς ἐπιστολῆς τῆς πεμφθείσης πρὸς τὸν βασιλέα Ἰουστῖνον· V

Inc. Οἱ πανευσεβεῖς καὶ καλλίνικοι (τῶν καλλινίκων V) ὑμῶν νόμοι παρα-κελεύονται, . . .

Des. . . . τοιαῦτα τετολμηκότες, μηδεμία εἰς αὐτοὺς γένηται φιλανθρωπία.

(B) Mansi XIII 160ᴅ–161ᴇ

Τοῦ ἁγίου Συμεὼν τοῦ Στυλίτου, τοῦ εἰς τὸ Θαυμαστὸν ὄρος ἐπιστολὴ πέμπτη πρὸς τὸν βασιλέα Ἰουστῖνον τὸν νέον.

Inc. Τίς δώσει, ἀεισεβέστατε καὶ ἀγαθὲ δέσποτα, τοῖς ὀφθαλμοῖς μου πηγὰς δακρύων . . .

Des. . . . ἡ φιλόχριστος ὑμῶν βασιλεία ὑπὲρ πάσας τὰς ἔμπροσθεν βασι-λείας· ὅτι αὐτῷ ἡ δόξα εἰς τοὺς αἰῶνας . . . etc.

It is impressive how small a part of the original letter is included in P and V. The text, however, is almost the same in the part where PV overlap A. There are only two words missing from PV, and the different setting of the words of the first sentence in PV seems to be a deliberate arrangement so that the extract becomes autonomous out of its context. Compare:

A: ἀναφέρομεν . . . ὅτι εἰ οἱ πανευσεβεῖς τῶν καλλινίκων ὑμῶν νόμοι παρα-κελεύονται . . . τολμῶντας, πόσης ἄρα ἄξιοί εἰσι καταδίκης . . .
P: Οἱ πανευσεβεῖς καὶ καλλίνικοι ὑμῶν νόμοι παρακελεύονται . . . τολμῶν-τας. πόσης ἄρα . . .

Cinnamus fell, of course, into a major error by transforming the καλλί-νικος emperor to καλλινίκους νόμους, but this is of no great importance, since V gives the correct reading. It should also be noted that the last clause in PV gives better sense than the corresponding one in A. Compare:

PV: πόσης ἄρα ἄξιοί εἰσι καταδίκης (εἰς ἀπώλειαν add. V) οἱ . . . τοιαῦτα τετολμηκότες· μηδεμία εἰς αὐτοὺς γένηται φιλανθρωπία.
A: πόσης ἄρα ἄξιοί εἰσι καταδίκης εἰς ἀπώλειαν οἱ . . . τοιαῦτα τετολμηκό-τες· μηδεμιᾶς εἰς αὐτοὺς γενομένης φιλανθρωπίας:

The extract in P is too short compared to the whole letter that was read out during the fifth session of the council, and it is dangerous to claim that the original of P was the source for A. A closer look, however, at the text of the letter offers a basis for the justification of the omission of more than 85 percent of the text: apart from the quotation included in P, the rest of the letter has nothing to do with image worship. It contains complaints of St. Symeon the Stylite against some Samaritans living near the town of Porphy-reon and some admonitions for the handling of their case addressed to Emperor Justin II. Therefore, it may be possible that the whole letter was included in F but the copyist of the year 774/5 decided to cut it short for obvious reasons. On the other hand, even if V contains exactly the same fragment as P, it does not necessarily imply that the whole letter was missing from their common original (F): I have already demonstrated (above, p. 114 n. 72) that the Νουθεσία included a different part from this *epistula*.

Finally, it is worth noting that whereas in the text provided by A the lemma is *Epistula ad Iustinum imp.*, the original text of the acts, as can be inferred by the first Latin translation and the *Capitulare adversus Synodum*,[149] had repeated a different lemma that was partially (Ἰουστιανὸν) given by P: *Epistula ad Iustinianum imperatorem*, although the witness of V (Ἰουστῖνον) leaves open the question about the name of the addressee in F.

29. Antipatri Bostrensis *Homilia in mulierem quae fluxum sanguinis passa est* (frag.) (*PG* 85, 1793c–d); *CPG* 6683

P, fol. 264ᵛ (98*)
Mansi XIII 13d-e
Ἀντιπάτρου ἐπισκόπου Βόστρων· ἐκ τοῦ λόγου τοῦ εἰς τὴν αἱμόρρουν· (οὗ ἡ ἀρχή· add. A)
Ὅτι μὲν πρώτη Ἰουδαίων κλῆσις, ἐδίδαξεν ἡ γραφή· καὶ μεθ' ἕτερα· ταῦτα τοῦ σωτηρίου κρασπέδου λαβομένη ἔλεγεν ἡ αἱμόρρους, ὡς βασιλέα τῆς φύσεως κρατοῦσα τὸν Κύριον καὶ τοῦ πάθους τὴν τυραννίδα διδάσκουσα· καὶ τυχοῦσα (τυχοῦσι P) τῆς δωρεᾶς, ἀνδριάντα ἤγειρε τῷ Χριστῷ, τὸν μὲν πλοῦτον ἰατροῖς ἀναλώσασα, τοῦ δὲ πλούτου τὰ λειπόμενα προσενέγκασα τῷ Χριστῷ.

The text in A is the same, letter by letter, with the one in P, and it is possible that the original of Parisinus is the actual source for the appearance of this quotation in the acts.

30. Asterii episcopi Amasiae *Relatio in Euphemiam martyrem*, ed. C. Datema, *Asterius of Amasea, Homilies I–XIV* (Leiden, 1970), 153–55 (*PG* 40, 333–37); *CPG* 3260.1 *homiliae i–xiv* (= *xi*); *BHG* 623–23a

P, fols. 264ᵛ–265ᵛ (99*)
Mansi XIII 16a–17d and XIII 308a–309b
Τοῦ μακαρίου Ἀστερίου ἐπισκόπου Ἀμασείας ἔκφρασις εἰς Εὐφημίαν τὴν μάρτυρα·
Inc. Πρώην, ὦ ἄνδρες, Δημοσθένην εἶχον ἐν χερσὶ τὸν δεινόν, . . .
Des. . . . ἵνα κατίδῃς ἀκριβῶς εἰ μὴ πολὺ κατόπιν τῆς ἐξηγήσεως ἤλθομεν.

---

[149] See *Hadrianum*, 21–22.

The whole work was cited at the fourth session from a book presented by a certain Thomas, a monk from the monastery τοῦ Χηνολάκκου. It is also inserted into the refutation of the *horos* of Hiereia (Mansi XIII 308A–309B).

There are no significant differences between P and A, and most of them are the outcome of misreadings on the part of Cinnamus. A few examples will suffice:

τὴν αἰσχύνην P: τὸν Αἰσχίνην A; εἶδεν ἡ θέα εὖ φὰν ὁρῶσαν εἰ παῖς (sic!) P: εἷλεν ἡ θέα Εὐφράνορος ἂν εἶπες; θεριστήριον P: τέρετρον A.[150]

Cinnamus, in some cases, also mistakes the letter Λ for the letter Δ, the diphthong ΕΙ for the letter Η and vice versa (εἶδος P: ἦθος A; δῆλον P: δειλὸν A; εἴδει P corrig.: ἤδη). This is an indication that might point to the possibility of the original of the *ekphrasis* being written in uncial.

Here again the text of the archetype of P may have been the source for the citation in the acts. I cannot be sure about the spontaneity of the offering of the book by the monk Thomas, or even about whether Thomas did indeed offer a real book and not a copy of the τεῦχος of 770. In any case, one should not forget that the very same text was inserted into the refutation of the *horos* of Hiereia, a text that should have taken much time to compose and which, presumably, was ready before the opening of the council.

31. Iohannis Thessalonicensis *Fragmentum de imaginibus* (*Sermo? Contra paganos et Iudaeos*),[151] ed. A. Gallandius, *Bibliotheca veterum Patrum anticorumque scriptorum ecclesiasticorum*, vol. 13 (1779), 196–97, after the acts; *CPG* 7923

P, fols. 265ᵛ–266 (101*)
Mansi XIII 164C–165C
Ἰωάννου ἐπισκόπου Θεσσαλονίκης ἐκ τοῦ λόγου· (οὗ ἡ ἀρχὴ add. A)
Inc. Μέχρι τότε πειράζων τὸν κύριον ἡμῶν καὶ Θεὸν Ἰησοῦν τὸν Χριστὸν προσεκαρτέρησεν ὁ ἐχθρὸς εἰς τὴν ἔρημον· καὶ μετ᾽ ὀλίγα· Ἕλλην εἶπεν· . . . P
Μέχρι τότε πειράζων τὸν κύριον ἡμῶν καὶ Θεὸν Ἰησοῦν Χριστόν· καὶ μετ᾽ ὀλίγα· Ὁ Ἕλλην εἶπε· . . . A
Usque nunc Dominum nostrum et Jesum Christum tentans perseverat inimicus in eremo; et post pauca; Gentilis dixit . . . Mansi XIII 163C.
Des. . . . τοῖς (τοὺς P) ἐφ᾽ οὓς ἀπεστάλησαν ὑπὸ τοῦ μόνου Θεοῦ γεγένηνται.

---

[150] In his edition Datema decided to exclude P because "the text which this codex gives is too poor to attach much importance to it" (Datema, *Asterius of Amasea*, 150).

[151] See Alexander, *Nicephorus*, 31 n. 2.

The incipit in P corresponds to the incipit preserved by the translation of Anastasius. Cinnamus is responsible for some minor omissions and misreadings, but the general point is that we are dealing with two almost identical versions. In addition to the extended incipit, P gives readings closer to the translation of Anastasius in the following instances:

P: προσκυνεῖτε αὐτὰς; A: προσκυνεῖτε αὐτοὺς; Lat.: adoratis illas.
P: ἀσώματοι; A: ἀόρατοι; Lat.: incorporei.
Compare finally:
P: εἰ δέ που εὕροις ἀσωμάτους καλουμένους τοὺς ἀγγέλους . . . , οὕτως αὐτοὺς προσαγόρευσον (προσηγόρευσαν A). P is evidently better.

The original of P may again have been the source of the citation in the acts. As the quotation was derived from a book offered by Nicholas, bishop of Cyzicus, the inference that the intervention of the bishop was not spontaneous is unavoidable. The problem of the use of books or florilegia by the council also remains open.

32. Anonymi *Disputatio Iudaei et Christiani* (unidentified)

P, fol. 266^{r–v} (102*)
Mansi XIII 165E–168C
Ἐκ τῆς διαλέξεως Ἰουδαίου (τε add. P) καὶ Χριστιανοῦ.
Inc. Ὁ Ἰουδαῖος λέγει· ἐπείσθην εἰς πάντα (–ας P) καὶ πιστεύω τῷ ἐσταυρωμένῳ . . .
Des. . . . ὁρᾷς πῶς ὁ παραγγέλλων Μωυσῆς ὁμοίωμα μὴ ποιῆσαι ὁμοίωμα ἐποίησεν;

The text in P is almost flawless, and Cinnamus must be responsible for only three misspellings and one or two possible omissions. A, on the other hand, omits two or possibly four words and gives in some instances an inferior text. It is not, however, necessary to proceed to a further comparison between the two versions, since there is more significant evidence to be presented.

The *Adversus Iconoclastas* is a work written no doubt in 770 by the compiler of this florilegium.[152] Compare the following passages:

I. *Disputatio Iudaei et Christiani* (P, fol. 266^v)
Τὴν δὲ τοῦ σωτῆρος εἰκόνα θεωροῦντες καὶ προσκυνοῦντες πνευματικοῖς ὄμμασι καρδίας, ὡς τὸν τῶν ὅλων Θεὸν καὶ δεσπότην εὐχαριστοῦμεν, τὸν καταδεξάμενον ἐν μορφῇ δούλου τὸν ἄνθρωπον λαβεῖν καὶ σῶσαι τὸν κόσμον καὶ ὁμοιωθῆναι ἡμῖν χωρὶς πάσης ἁμαρτίας κατὰ πάντα.

[152] See above, pp. 93 ff.

Adversus Iconoclastas (P, fol. 238ʳ⁻ᵛ)

Καὶ λοιπὸν τὸ αἰσθητὸν ὄμμα πρὸς τὴν εἰκόνα (= τοῦ Χριστοῦ) ἀτενῶς βλέπον, τὸ νοητὸν τῆς καρδίας ὄμμα σὺν τῷ νῷ εἰς τὸ μυστήριον τῆς ἐνσάρκου οἰκονομίας ἀκοντίζω καὶ περὶ τῶν ἀσυγγνώστων καὶ πολλῶν μου ἁμαρτημάτων δέομαι τὴν ἀγαθότητα καὶ εὐσπλαγχνίαν αὐτοῦ λέγων: δόξα σοι ὁ Θεός, ὁ σωτήρ μου, ἐλέησόν με τὸν ἁμαρτωλὸν καὶ συγχώρησον τὰς πολλάς μου ἁμαρτίας, ὁ δι᾿ ἐμὲ τὸ κατ᾿ ἐμὲ φορέσας δίχα μόνης τῆς ἁμαρτίας.

II. *Disputatio* (ibid.)

εἰκόνας . . . προσκυνοῦντες, τὸν τῶν ἁγίων ἐπικαλοῦνται Θεόν, λέγοντες· εὐλογητὸς εἶ ὁ Θεὸς τοῦδε τοῦ ἁγίου καὶ πάντων τῶν ἁγίων, ὁ δοὺς αὐτοῖς ὑπομονὴν καὶ ἀξιῶν τῆς σῆς βασιλείας.

Adversus Iconoclastas (P, fol. 238ᵛ)

. . . ὅταν δὲ ἴδω εἰκόνα ἀποστόλου ἢ μάρτυρος ἤ τινος τῶν ἁγίων ἱστορίαν τῶν παθημάτων αὐτῶν, ὧν διὰ Χριστὸν ὑπέμειναν γενναίως λέγω· δόξα σοι ὁ Θεὸς τοῦδε τοῦ ἀποστόλου ἢ τοῦδε τοῦ μάρτυρος ἢ τοῦδε τοῦ ἁγίου καὶ ταῦτα οὕτως λέγων, εἰς Θεὸν τὴν δόξαν ἀναπέμπω.

It can easily be seen that the author of the *Adversus Iconoclastas* elaborates on the extracts from the *Disputatio Iudaei et Christiani*. The first extract of *Adv. Icon.* helps also to resolve the following disagreement between P and A. Compare:

A: . . . προσκυνοῦντες, πνευματικοῖς ὀφθαλμοῖς καὶ <u>καρδίας ὄμμασι</u> Θεῷ τῷ τὸν ὅλων δεσπότῃ εὐχαριστοῦμεν, . . .

P: . . . προσκυνοῦντες πνευματικοῖς ὄμμασι καρδίας, ὡς τὸν τῶν ὅλων Θεὸν καὶ δεσπότην εὐχαριστοῦμεν, . . .

Adv. Icon.: . . . τὸ αἰσθητὸν ὄμμα πρὸς τὴν εἰκόνα ἀτενῶς βλέπον, τὸ <u>νοητὸν τῆς καρδίας ὄμμα</u> σὺν τῷ νῷ . . . ἀκοντίζω.

It is beyond doubt that P is closer to the original than A. A minor point gives further support to the priority of P: the allocution ὦ Ἰουδαῖε in P has been substituted for ὦ ἀδελφὲ in A in an attempt by the organizing committee to bring the whole passage (Διάλεξις Ἰουδαίου! καὶ Χριστιανοῦ) into the historical context of the circumstances (on this see next quotation).

33. Leontii Neapolitani *Contra Iudaeos orationes v* (frag.), ed. V. Déroche, "L'*Apologie contre les Juifs* de Léontios de Neapolis," *TM* 12 (1994), 66–72 (*PG* 93, 1597–1608), *sermo 3*; *CPG* 7885.1

P, fols. 266ᵛ–269ᵛ (103*); M, fols. 171ᵛ–177 (2ᴹ)
(Dam. I 54, 56; II 50, 52; III 84, 86, 87–89)
Mansi XIII 44A–53C

Λεοντίου ἐπισκόπου Νεαπόλεως τῆς Κύπρου (Κυπρίων νήσου P) ἐκ τοῦ πέμπτου λόγου ὑπὲρ τῆς Χριστιανῶν ἀπολογίας (καὶ add. P) κατὰ Ἰουδαίων καὶ περὶ εἰκόνων τῶν ἁγίων (τῶν ἁγίων εἰκ. P).

Inc. Φέρε δὴ λοιπὸν περὶ τῶν σεπτογράφων εἰκόνων ἀπολογίαν ποιήσωμεν . . .

Des. . . . καὶ τὸν τύπον τοῦ σταυροῦ αὐτοῦ καὶ τοὺς χαρακτῆρας τῶν ἁγίων αὐτοῦ· ὅτι αὐτῷ πρέπει δόξα, σὺν τῷ πατρὶ etc.

This is a very extensive text and it was read out from a βίβλος brought forward by Peter and Peter, the vicars of Pope Hadrian, during the fourth session of the council.

P, M, and A are in about the same condition. There are instances where P omits words, even lines, which are supplemented by M, but the same holds in other cases for A and M, so it can be inferred that the three versions, being almost equally corrupt, draw from the same archetype.

Furthermore, P differs from A in a decisive detail. At fol. 267ᵛ of P we read the address ὦ Ἰουδαῖε, which in A has become ὦ ἀδελφέ, and, a few lines further down, the clause εἰ δὲ ἐγκαλεῖς μοι πάλιν, ὦ Ἰουδαῖε, λέγων . . . has vanished in A. As in the previously examined text of the *Disputatio*, it is a clear indication that these alterations are the result of the change of the historical context. In the words of V. Déroche: "l'omission des attaques spécifiquement destinées aux Juifs, . . . indique une époque où l'ennemi n'est plus le Juif, mais le chrétien iconoclaste, et une occasion où le texte devait être cité comme pièce d'un dossier."[153] It is, nevertheless, noteworthy that the organizing committee did not persist in the adaptation of the whole text of Leontius to the circumstances, and the mention of Jews passes uncensored on other occasions later on in the text.

One can find more details in the very recent edition of this fragment by Déroche. According to him, the text as transmitted by PM belongs to the same line of transmission that gave us two manuscripts of the acts of 787, Venetus Marcianus gr. 166 (Ma) and Vaticanus Ottobonianus gr. 27 (O). However, PM compared to MaO give a text "dans un état bien supérieur."[154] Moreover, Déroche's summary of his comparison of all the existing versions is as follows:

. . . le *passus* de Nicée II provient d'un travail d'abréviation de l'*Apologie* fait en vue du Concile de Nicée II, qui a cherché à sélectionner les éléments directement adaptables à la problématique iconodule du

[153] V. Déroche, "L'authenticité de l'Apologie contre les Juifs' de Léontios de Néapolis," *BCH* 110 (1986), 667.
[154] Déroche, "L'Apologie," 54.

concile. . . . Jean Damascène et les *excerptores* anonymes [i.e., P and M] ont au contraire découpé des passages dans le texte original, d'une façon plus habituelle qui nous donne selon toute vraisemblance une image plus fidèle de ce dernier.[155]

It seems likely once more that the βίβλος that was produced by the two Peters was a copy drawn from F. It is also interesting that they "spontaneously" presented a book that offered a text which had been slightly "modified" in order to meet the circumstances of that time.

34. *Preces clericorum et monachorum ad Iohannem Constantinopolitanum et Synodum, ACO* III, 60.35–61.3; *CPG* 9329.6 (9202 nota)

    (A) P, fols. 269ᵛ–270 (104*); M, fols. 237ᵛ–238 (46ᴹ)

    Ἐκ τῆς δεήσεως τῶν μοναχῶν καὶ κληρικῶν Ἀντιοχείας κατὰ Σεβήρου πρὸς τὴν ε′ σύνοδον.

    Inc. Οὐ μὴν οὐδὲ αὐτῶν ἐφείσατο τῶν ἁγίων θυσιαστηρίων . . .

    Des. . . . ὅτι οὐ χρὴ ἐν εἴδει περιστερᾶς σχηματίζεσθαι (ὀνομάζεσθε Μ) τὸ ἅγιον πνεῦμα.

    (B) Mansi XIII 181ε–184α

    Ἐκ τῆς δεήσεως τῆς ἐπιδοθείσης τῇ ἁγίᾳ συνόδῳ, τῇ συνελθούσῃ ἐν ταύτῃ τῇ βασιλίδι πόλει κατὰ Σεβήρου τοῦ αἱρετικοῦ καὶ Ἀκεφάλου, παρὰ τῶν κληρικῶν καὶ μοναχῶν τῆς Ἀντιοχέων μεγαλοπόλεως ἁγίας τοῦ Θεοῦ ἐκκλησίας, ἧς ἡ ἀρχή.

    Inc. Νῦν εἴπέρ ποτε (sic) καιρός, ὦ μακαριώτατοι, καὶ μετ᾽ ὀλίγα· οἷα καὶ ὁσιώτατοι καὶ ἃ περὶ τὰς ἐν Δάφνῃ . . .

    Des. . . . οὐ χρῆναι ἐν εἴδει περιστερᾶς ὀνομάζεσθαι τὸ ἅγιον πνεῦμα.

The quotation in the acts is a few lines longer in the incipit than the P version, cited obviously from the actual manuscript of the acts of the Constantinopolitan Council of 536, which the organizing committee must have had at its disposal. P offers a text identical to that in A, with the exception of one word: ὀνομάζεσθαι AM: σχηματίζεσθαι P. The source of P must have been another copy of the acts of this council, deposited perhaps in Rome or in Jerusalem.

35. Evagrii *Historia ecclesiastica*, ed. J. Bidez and L. Parmentier, *The Ecclesiastical History of Evagrius* (London, 1898), 174.15–175.17; (*PG* 86, 2748ᴀ–49ᴀ); *CPG* 7500

    P, fol. 270ʳ⁻ᵛ (106*)

    Mansi XIII 189ε–192ᴄ

    Ἐκ τῆς ἐκκλησιαστικῆς ἱστορίας Εὐαγρίου, ἐκ τοῦ δ′ λόγου·

---

[155] Ibid., 58.

Inc. Μετὰ γὰρ τὸ προσβαλεῖν τῇ πόλει τὸν Χοσρόην, . . .
Des. . . . ἀπανθρακωθέντα (ἀπ' ἀνθρ. P) τοῖς ὑπερτέροις μετεδίδοσαν, ἄπαντα τοῦ πυρὸς ἀμφινεμομένου.

The omission of words and letters by Cinnamus is frequent in this passage. He is responsible for the disappearance of letters and words in eleven instances at least. Moreover in one case, being unable to decipher a Latin term, he simply transcribed letter by letter what he saw. The result is peculiar: ὅπερ ἄγες· τὰ πρὸς Ῥωμαίων κέκληται (= ὅπερ ἀγέστα πρὸς Ῥωμαίων καλεῖται). On the other hand, he succeeds in another case in preserving the erudite style of Euagrius: ὡς ἂν τῇ φλογὶ τὰ ξύλα φθειρόμενα τὸν χοῦν καταγά- γοι, while in the acts the same clause is simplified like this: ὡς ἂν τῇ φλογὶ τὰ ξύλα φθειρόμενα τὸν χοῦν εἰς γῆν καταγάγωσι, but P omits the words εἰς γῆν after τὸν χοῦν (see also ed. cit., 175.2-3). P also agrees with the edited text against A in the following cases:

Edition	P	A
ἐπεποίητο	= Ed.	ἐποιεῖτο
ἐπήγγελεν	= Ed.	ἐπήγγειλεν/praecipiebat, Lat.A
καταγάγοι	= Ed.	καταγάγωσι
τὴν ὕλην	= Ed.	τῆς ὕλης
ἀφεῖσαν	ἀφίησαν	ἀφῆκαν
ἐσεδέξαντο	εἰσεδέξαντο	εἰσεδέξατο,

while P and A agree against the edition in the following instances:

Edition	P	A
ἐπετετέλεστο	ἐτέλεστο	ἐτετέλεστο
πυρὰν	πυρᾶς	= P
προσάψαντες	προσανάψαντες	= P

Evidently P is some steps closer to the original than A, while both move on the same line of transmission.

In the acts this quotation was read out after a comment of the assembly on the fate of some Iconophile books under the Iconoclastic regime. A certain deacon Cosmas informed the assembly that he had found in the patriarchal *skeuophylakion* a βίβλος containing various *martyria* and the story of the Camuliana image, with the folios containing the story of the image torn out. After a brief discussion of the issue, another monk named Stephen showed a second book having ἐν δυσὶ καταβατοῖς ἀπαλειφάς. Then Gregory, the abbot of the monastery τοῦ Ὑακίνθου, produced another book with the same text, and the passage was finally read out. If the book offered by the aforementioned abbot is again a copy from F, then it becomes evident that the whole process of the spontaneous interventions had been carefully prearranged.

36. Sophronii Hierosolymitani (I) *Laudes in ss. Cyrum et Iohannem* (*PG* 87, 3, 3388A); *CPG* 7645; *BHG* 476. (II) *Miracula C. et I.* (*PG* 87, 3, 3557D–3560D); *CPG* 7646; *BHG* 478

    P, fols. 270ᵛ–271 (107*, 108*); V, fol. 5ʳ⁻ᵛ (V 15, only the *Laudes*); (Dam. III 132)

    Mansi XIII 57B–60B

    (I) Τοῦ ὁσίου πατρὸς ἡμῶν Σωφρονίου ἐπισκόπου (ἀρχιεπισκόπου Α) Ἱεροσολύμων ἐκ τοῦ ἐγκωμίου (ἐγκώμιον Α) τοῦ (om. Α) εἰς τοὺς ἁγίους Κῦρον καὶ Ἰωάννην. ΡΑ

    Σωφρονίου τοῦ ἁγιωτάτου ἐπισκόπου Ἱεροσολύμων ἐκ τοῦ ἐγκωμίου τοῦ εἰς Κῦρον καὶ Ἰωάννην τοὺς μάρτυρας. V

Inc. Ἄλλοι μὲν ἄλλως τοὺς ἁγίους τιμάτωσαν πολυμερῶς . . .

Des. . . . τοὺς ἐραστὰς ἀμείβεσθαι τοῖς δώροις εἰώθασιν· ΡΑ

    . . . τῶν μαρτύρων τιμὴν ἁμιλλάσθωσαν (sic). V.

    (II) καὶ μεθ' ἕτερα· ἀπὸ θαύματος· P

    Ἐκ τῆς αὐτῆς συγγραφῆς τοῦ αὐτοῦ πατρός, τῶν αὐτῶν ἁγίων θαῦμα (in marg.: tricesimo sexto), οὗ ἡ ἀρχή· Α

Inc. Ἀλεξάνδρειαν Αἰγύπτου καὶ Λιβύων ἀκούω μητρόπολιν· καὶ μεθ' ἕτερα· ἐλθόντες οὖν εἰς νεών τινα . . .

Des. . . . καὶ παραχρῆμα τὴν νόσον ἀπέθετο καὶ τὴν ῥῶσιν ἀνέλαβε (ἀπέλαβεν P).

There are no significant differences. The mistakes of Cinnamus are few and indicate an original written in minuscule (he mistakes α for ο and vice versa, μ and υ for ν, and so on). The title in P is also more precise than in A.

It is probably another quotation drawn from the original of 770, and its citation might have been staged, as it was read out from a book presented by Gregory, the abbot of the monastery of Hormisdas.

John of Damascus in his third homily (III 132) includes the miracle under a more detailed lemma (Τοῦ ἁγίου Σωφρονίου ἐκ τῶν θαυμάτων τῶν ἁγίων μαρτύρων Κύρου καὶ Ἰωάννου εἰς Θεόδωρον τὸν ὑποδιάκονον ποδαγριοῦντα·) and different incipit and desinit. Interesting enough is the fact that Dam. includes a part that both P and A have skipped and in its place have introduced the formula καὶ μεθ' ἕτερα. Finally, V includes a somewhat shorter part of quotation 107*, with no noteworthy variants.

37. *Miracula Sanctorum Cosmae et Damiani*, ed. L. Deubner, *Kosmas und Damian* (Leipzig-Berlin, 1907): (I) 173–74 [= 30th], (II) 132–34 [13th], (III) 137–38 [15th]); *BHG* 387, 389

    I. P, fol. 271ʳ⁻ᵛ (109*)

    Mansi XIII 64B–D

Ἐκ τῶν θαυμάτων τῶν ἁγίων Κοσμᾶ καὶ Δαμιανοῦ (τῶν Ἀναργύρων add. P).

Inc. Ἕτερός τις ἀνὴρ ἐπιεικὴς σφόδρα, σύριγγα ἐσχηκώς . . .

Des. . . . καὶ λέγουσαν αὐτοῖς· ἴδε οὗτός ἐστι βοηθήσατε αὐτῷ διὰ τάχους.

II. P, fols. 271ᵛ–272 (110*)
Mansi XIII 64ᴇ–65ᴅ
Ἐκ τῶν αὐτῶν θαυμάτων· περὶ τῆς γυναικὸς Κωνσταντίνου τοῦ ἐν Λαοδικείᾳ.

Inc. Συνέβη τινὰ ἄνδρα ἐν στρατείᾳ ἐξεταζόμενον, ὀνόματι Κωνσταντῖνον . . .

Des. . . . ὅτι ὄντως (οὕτως P) σὺν αὐτοῖς ἐκεῖσε διῆγον (διήγουν P) οἱ ἅγιοι κατὰ τὴν αὐτῶν φωνήν· (καὶ εὐθέως ἀπηλλάγη ἡ γυνὴ τοῦ νοσήματος add. A).
Latin: . . . quod vere secum ibidem degerent sancti secundum vocem ipsorum. in marg: Gr. add.: ac statim liberata est femina morbo. Lat. Mansi (XIII 66ᴅ).

III. P, fol. 272 (111*)
Mansi 68ᴀ–ᴅ
Ἐκ τῶν αὐτῶν (θαυμάτων add. A). περὶ τῆς γυναικὸς τῆς ἐχούσης τοὺς στρόφους (τὸν στρόφον P).

Inc. Καλῶς ὁ σοφώτατος Παῦλος, ὁ στύλος καὶ διδάσκαλος τῆς ἐκκλησίας βοᾷ ὅτι . . .

Des. . . . τὴν διὰ τῶν ἁγίων προσγενομένην αὐτῇ ἐν τῷ τοιούτῳ σχήματι θεραπείαν.

The case of these quotations is similar to that of no. 36, but this time the text provided by P is in better condition compared to the one in A. That P and A also belong to the same line of transmission is corroborated by their numerous agreements against the edition of Deubner. Compare:

37 I

Deubner (p. 174)	PA
τῶν τε ἰατρῶν ἀπειρηκότων	τ. τε ἰ. εἰρηκότων
ὅθεν θαρσήσας	θαρσήσας τοίνυν
τὸν πάνσεπτον καὶ ἔνδοξον . . . οἶκον	τὸν ἔνδοξον οἶκον
ἐξελθὼν ἐν τῷ ὑπαίθρῳ	ἐξελθὼν ἐν τῷ ὑπερθύρῳ
κατὰ τὴν δεξιὰν	κατὰ τὸ δεξιὸν
οὗτός ἐστιν ὁ νοσῶν· βοηθήσατε	οὗτός ἐστι· βοηθήσατε

37 II

Deubner (132–33)	PA
τῆς τῶν ἁγίων προσεδρίας	τῇ (τῆς A) τῶν ἐνδόξων ἁγίων Κοσμᾶ καὶ Δαμιανοῦ προσεδρείᾳ (−ας A),

ἐν εἰκόνι　　　　　　　　　　　ἐν εἰκονιδίω
ἐπωνόμασται　　　　　　　　　ἐπωνομάσθη
πράγματος　　　　　　　　　　προστάγματος
τούτους ἐν γραφῇ ἐπεφέρετο　τούτους ἐπεφέρετο
ἀσθενοῦντας　　　　　　　　　ἀσθενεῖς

37 III

κaὶ μηδεὶς ἐπιλάβοιτο τούτου πιστοί, ἀκατηγόρητον γὰρ ἐπ' ὠφελείᾳ ψυχῆς πανταχοῦ τὸ ἄπληστον κρίνεται (Deubner 137, *Mir.*, 13.12–13),

κaὶ μηδεὶς ὑπολάβοι τοῦτο πιστοί· ἀκατηγόρητον γὰρ ἐπ' ὠφελείᾳ ψυχῆς πανταχοῦ τὸ πιστὸν κρίνεται P,

κaὶ μηδεὶς ὑπολάβοι τοῦτο ἄπιστον· οὐδὲ γὰρ ἀκατηγόρητον ἐπ' ὠφελείᾳ ψυχῆς πανταχοῦ τὸ ἄπιστον κρίνεται A,

et nemo suspicetur hoc o fideles: sine accusatione quippe super utilitate animae ubique quod non creditur, judicatur. Lat. A

κυλιομένη τε ἐν τῷ κραββάτῳ ἄπαυστον εἶχεν τὴν ὀδύνην (Deubner)
κυλιομένην τε ἐν τῷ κραββάτῳ ἄπαυστον ἔχειν τὴν ὀδ. PA.

Furthermore, the Latin translation of Anastasius agrees with P against A in ten instances. Highly illustrative of that is the different desinit in 37 II. According to Tarasius, the book containing those extracts had been offered by the clerics of the Church of Cosmas and Damian at Constantinople.

38. Theodoreti Ep. Cyri *Historia religiosa,* ed. P. Canivet and A. Leroy-Molinghen, *Théodoret de Cyr. L'histoire des moines de Syrie,* vol. 2 (Paris, 1977), 158, par. 1.1/ 182, par. 11.19–22 (*PG* 82, 1473A); *CPG* 6221; *BHG* 1439–40

P, fol. 272ᵛ (112*); (Dam. III 55)
Mansi XIII 73ʙ
Θεοδωρήτου ἐπισκόπου Κύπρου (sic)· ἐκ τῆς φιλοθέου ἱστορίας ἐκ τοῦ βιβλίου Συμεῶνος τοῦ Στυλίτου. P.
Θεοδωρήτου ἐπισκόπου Κύρου, ἐκ τοῦ βίου Συμεὼν τοῦ Στυλίτου, οὗ ἡ ἀρχή. A
Ἐκ τῆς Φιλοθέου ἱστορίας Θεοδωρήτου, ἐπισκόπου Κύρου, εἰς τὸν βίον τοῦ ἁγίου Συμεῶνος τοῦ Κιονίτου· Dam.
Συμεώνην τὸν πάνυ, τὸ μέγα θαῦμα τῆς οἰκουμένης. (καὶ μεθ' ἕτερα add. A) (Συμεώνην—ἕτερα om. Dam.) (Περὶ γὰρ Ἰταλίας περιττόν ἐστι κaὶ λέγειν add. Dam.) Φασὶ γὰρ οὕτως ἐν Ῥώμῃ τῇ μεγίστῃ πολυθρύλλητον γενέσθαι τὸν ἄνδρα, ὡς ἐν ἅπασι τοῖς τῶν ἐργαστηρίων προπυλαίοις εἰκόνας αὐτῷ βραχείας ἀναστῆσαι φυλακήν τινα (ἑαυτοῖς add. A/ σφίσιν αὐτοῖς add. Dam.) κaὶ ἀσφάλειαν ἐντεῦθεν πορίζοντα (–ας Dam.) (ποριζομένους A).

The quotation makes its first appearance in the third *Oratio* in defense of the images of John of Damascus (III 55). The text is almost the same in all three (Dam., P, and A), but the title of the P version is closer to the Dam. version than to that in A. P has obviously added the incipit, which does not exist in Dam. The A version is the only one that gives ποριζομένους instead of πορίζοντα P, (–ας) Dam., acquirentes Lat. A. Although P omits the formula καὶ μεθ᾽ ἕτερα, its original must have been the source for the quotation in A.

39. Arcadii(?) *Vita Symeonis Stylitae Iunioris mirabilis montis, capit.* CXVIII, ed. P. Van den Ven, *La vie ancienne de S. Syméon Stylite le Jeune (521–592),* vol. 1, SubsHag 32 (Brussels, 1962), (I): 96–98, (II): 139–41; *CPG* 7369; *BHG* 1689

    I. P, fols. 272–273 (113*)
    Mansi XIII 73c–76c
    Ἐκ τοῦ βίου (βιβλίου P) τοῦ ἁγίου (ὁσίου P) πατρὸς ἡμῶν Συμεῶνος τοῦ ἐν τῷ Θαυμαστῷ ὄρει κεφάλαιον ριή· Περὶ τῆς γυναικὸς τῆς ἐν Ῥωσοπόλει ἀτέκνου οὔσης (ἀτεκνούσης P) καὶ βιαίῳ κατεχομένης δαίμονι, ἥτις ἰαθεῖσα καὶ παιδοποιήσασα εἰκόνα τοῦ δικαίου (τῷ δικαίῳ P) ἀνέθετο ἐν τῷ οἴκῳ αὐτῆς, ἥτις μεγάλως ἐθαυματούργει.
    Inc. Γυνή τις ἦν ἐν Ῥωσοπόλει τῆς Κιλικίας, Θεοτέκνα λεγομένη . . .
    Des. . . . δοξάζουσα τὸν Θεὸν καὶ ἀπαγγέλλουσα τὸ γεγονὸς εἰς αὐτὴν
        παράδοξον.
    Note that the Latin text stops four lines before the actual end of the Greek text (Mansi XIII 75c).

    II. P, fol. 273 (114*); (Dam. III 92)
    Mansi XIII 76d–77b
    Ἕτερον θαῦμα τοῦ ὁσίου πατρὸς ἡμῶν Συμεών· P
    Ὁ αὐτὸς ἀνέγνω ἕτερον θαῦμα τοῦ ὁσίου πατρὸς ἡμῶν Συμεών. A
    Ἐκ τοῦ βίου τοῦ ἁγίου Συμεῶνος τοῦ θαυματουργοῦ ἐξήγησις Ἀρκαδίου, ἀρχιεπισκόπου Κύπρου, θαῦμα ἑκατοστὸν τριακοστὸν δεύτερον· (Dam.)
    Inc. Συνέβη δὲ ἐν ταῖς ἡμέραις ἐκείναις ἄνδρα τινὰ ἀγοραῖον τῆς πόλεως Ἀντιοχείας . . .
    Des. . . . καὶ προσκυνοῦντες μετὰ προσευχῆς τῇ εἰκόνι ἀνεχώρουν.

Very few mistakes on both sides. Initially, it seems that there is no reason to assert anything else than P's original being the source of A. In 39 I the most significant difference between P and A is the one cited next. Compare:

P: Γυνή τις ἦν ἐν Ῥωσοπόλει . . . οἰκήσασα μετὰ τοῦ ἀνδρὸς αὐτῆς ἔτη εἴκοσιν καὶ τέκνον οὐκ ἔσχε.

A: Γυνή τις ἦν ἐν Ῥωσοπόλει . . . ἥτις οἰκήσασα μετὰ ἀνδρὸς ἔτη εἴκοσιν τέκνον οὐκ ἔσχε.

P gives a fuller meaning and, besides, preserves a syntax in biblical style.[156]

In the case of this quotation, P might represent the earliest version of the text, but it was not taken into account by Van den Ven in his critical edition. Nevertheless, P agrees with that edition against A in the following twelve instances:

Van den Ven-P	A
39 I	
αὐτοῖς (–ης P)	αὐτῇ
χωρίζω	χωρίσω
ὦ βία	ὦ βίας
ἠλαύνετο	ἐλαυ-
ἀλαλάζων	ὀλολύζων
γὰρ	om.
ὁ δύστηνος	ὁ δύστηνος ἐγὼ
τὴν εὐχὴν	εὐχὴν
39 II	
αὐτῶν	αὐτοῖς
τότε	om.
ἐλέγξαντα	ἐξελέγξαντα
τοῦ ποιῆσαι	ποιῆσαι

On the other hand, P and A come together against the edition in the following eight cases:

Van den Ven	PA
39 I	
γλῶτταν	γλῶσσαν
κλαίων	καίων
ὄχλου	λαοῦ
ἐξέρχομαι	om.
αὐτοῦ	αὐτῆς
ἐκαθαιρίζοντο	-αρίζοντο
θαῦμα	om.
39 II	
ὑφ' οὗ	om.

---

[156] Cf. some examples taken at random from Mark: ἦν . . . πειραζόμενος 1,13; ἦν . . . ἐπισυνηγμένη 1,33; ἦν . . . δεδεμένος 15,7.

And the third combination, that of A and the edition against P, gives seventeen cases:

Van den Ven-A	P
39 I	
ἀνθρωπίνη φωνῇ	ἀνθρωπίνην φωνὴν
ἐπιόντι	ἐπιδέοντι
ἠλάλαξε	ὕλαξε (sic)
σὸν	σοὶ
ταῦτα δὲ αὐτοῦ	ταῦτα αὐτοῦ
κύκλῳ τῆς στάσεως	κύκλω στάσεως
ηὐθύνθη	ἠδύνθη
αὐτῆς οἴκῳ	ἑαυτῆς οἴκω
εἶπε γὰρ—σωθήσομαι	om.
39 II	
τῆς πόλεως τόπῳ	τόπω τῆς πόλ.
τοῦτο πεποιηκότα	τούτου πεπ.
διαχειρίσασθαι	διαχειρίζεσθαι
νομίσαντες	νομίζοντες
ὡς οὖν οὐκ	ὡς οὐκ
ἀναγαγεῖν	ἀγαγεῖν
ἑαυτοῖς	αὐτοῖς
μεμηνότες	μεμηνικότες

The only safe conclusion in view of this abundance of variants is that P and A draw independently of one another on a common source.

The second miracle is also included in the third florilegium of John of Damascus (III 92). Dam. gives a more detailed title, but the text is more or less identical with the other two versions. Although Dam. presents virtually no variant compared to the edition of Van den Ven, in the acts the text must have been read out from another anthology because the name of the author that is provided by Dam. is not mentioned by A. So it is not easy to decide on the possibility of the archetype of P being a source for the appearance of the *miraculum* in the acts.

40. Photini presbyteri et defensoris magnae ecclesiae CPoleos *Vita Ioannis Ieiunatoris episcopi Constantinopoleos, CPG* 7971; *BHG* 893

> P, fols. 273–275 (115*)
> Mansi XIII 80ᴅ–85ᴄ
> Φωτεινοῦ τοῦ θεοφιλεστάτου πρεσβυτέρου καὶ ἐκκλησιεκδίκου τῆς ἁγιωτάτης ἐκκλησίας Κωνσταντινουπόλεως.

Ἐκ τοῦ βίου τοῦ ἐν ἁγίοις πατρὸς ἡμῶν Ἰωάννου τοῦ Νηστευτοῦ ἐπισκόπου γενομένου τῆς αὐτῆς πόλεως.

Inc.　Ἔτι μηδὲ τοῦτο διαλάθῃ (λάθοι P) τὸ θαῦμα· μηδὲ συγχωρῶμεν (χωροῦμεν P) τῷ θεσπεσίῳ πατρί . . .

Des.　. . . ὁ τύπος δὲ μᾶλλον τῆς παρθένου μητρὸς ἐξιᾶται· τοῦτο μὲν οὖν τὸ πέρας τῆς ὑποθέσεως.

This text in the Mansi edition is not derived from the manuscripts of the acts. In the margin of the Hardouin edition, reprinted by Mansi (XIII 80), we read a note by a Greek scholiast:

Ἔστιν ἀρχαία βίβλος ἐν τῇ ἀποστολικῇ βιβλιοθήκῃ, ἐν ᾗ πολλαὶ ἄλλαι χρήσεις πατέρων καὶ περικοπαὶ παρὰ τὰς ἐν τῇ συνόδῳ ἀναγνωσθείσας δοκοῦσι παρεμβεβλῆσθαι, ἐκτὸς οὔσας δηλαδὴ τῆς συνεχείας τῶν διαλαλιῶν, κἂν ταῖς λοιπαῖς βίβλοις μὴ ἐφευρεθεῖσαι. Μία γοῦν τῶν παρεμβληθεισῶν δοκεῖ περικοπῶν αὐτὴ ἡ ἐκ τοῦ βίου τοῦ Νηστευτοῦ, ἅτε δὴ μὴ ἐν πάσαις ταῖς βίβλοις τῆς συνόδου ταυτησὶ ἐμφερομένη.

The description fits F perfectly, but unfortunately neither Hardouin nor the *editio Romana* specifies which manuscript had this scholium or what period it dates from. What we have, thus, in the Mansi edition is probably another transcription of the archetype of 770. And indeed at fol. 53 of Vaticanus gr. 836, which is one of the two manuscripts the edition was based on, we read: Κωνσταντῖνος διάκονος καὶ νοτάριος ἀνέγνω ἐκ τοῦ βίου τοῦ ἐν ἁγίοις πατρὸς ἡμῶν Ἰωάννου τοῦ Νηστευτοῦ, and at fol. 54ᵛ the desinit ὁ τύπος δὲ μᾶλλον τῆς παρθένου Μαρίας ἐξιᾶται. The name of the author is missing, and the desinit is shorter. The text in P is, however, inferior to the A text, but from the common readings they both share against the ones of the Latin translation of Anastasius, it can be inferred that P and A stand in the same line of transmission.

41. Sophronii Hierosolymitani *Vita Mariae Aegyptiacae* (*PG* 87, 3, 3713B–16A); *CPG* 7675; *BHG* 1042

P, fol. 275ʳ⁻ᵛ (116*); (Dam. III 135)
Mansi XIII 85D–89A
Ἐκ τοῦ βίου τῆς ὁσίας Μαρίας τῆς Αἰγυπτίας. (οὗ ἡ ἀρχὴ add. A)

Inc.　Μυστήριον βασιλέως κρύπτειν καλόν· καὶ μεθ᾽ ἕτερα· κλαίουσα δὲ ὁρῶ τοῦ τόπου ἐν ᾧ ἱστάμην . . . P
　　　Μυστήριον βασιλέως κρύπτειν καλόν· τὰ δὲ ἔργα τοῦ Θεοῦ ἀνακηρύττειν ἔνδοξον. καὶ μεθ᾽ ἕτερα· τοὺς μὲν ἄλλους ὁ ναὸς εἶχε . . . A.

Des.　. . . ταῦτα εἰποῦσα, ἔξειμι (ἐξίημι P) τῆς αὐλῆς τοῦ ναοῦ καὶ συντόνως ἐβάδιζον.

P differs from A in at least twenty-one instances, but most of them are obvious miscopyings by Cinnamus (e.g.: οὕτως P: ὄντως A; οὐδετίποτε [sic] P: οἱασδήποτε A; ἔστότε [sic] P: ἕως τότε A; ἐξίημι P: ἔξειμι A, etc.). The only serious defect of the P version is that it is seventeen lines shorter than A. The part omitted by P deals with the unsuccessful attempts of the heroine of this *vita* to enter the church where the Holy Cross was kept. The incipit of the P text is almost the same as that of the Dam. version (III 135). The Dam. extract may also have drawn from a common archetype. Compared to the other two versions it is almost the same, apart from the omission (which here is more extensive than in P) of clauses that do not directly refer to icons.

42. *Passio sancti martyris Procopii,* ed. A. Papadopoulos-Kerameus, Ἀνάλεκτα Ἱεροσολυμιτικῆς Σταχυολογίας, vol. 5 (St. Petersburg, 1898), 5–6; *BHG* 1577

> P, fol. 275ᵛ (117*)
> Mansi XIII 89ᴀ–ᴅ
> Ἐκ τοῦ μαρτυρίου τοῦ ἁγίου (μάρτυρος add. A) Προκοπίου· (οὗ ἡ ἀρχὴ add. A).
> Inc. Κατὰ τοὺς καιροὺς ἐκείνους ἐβασίλευσε (–ευε P) Διοκλητιανὸς ὁ τύραννος· καὶ μεθ᾿ ἕτερα·
> (a) Ὁ δὲ νεανίας χαρὰν μεγάλην λαβών . . . A
> (b) καὶ προσκαλεσάμενος κρυφίως πᾶσαν τὴν συντεχνίαν . . . P
> Des. . . . εἴλησεν ἐν πορφύρα, καὶ ἐπορεύθη τὴν ὁδὸν αὐτοῦ χαίρων. P
> . . . χαίρων, δεδωκὼς τῷ τεχνίτῃ Μάρκῳ τιμὰς πλείους· καὶ εἰσῆλθε μετὰ τῶν δύο νουμέρων ἐν τῇ πόλει αὐτοῦ. A

The text in P is six lines and one particle shorter than the extract in A, otherwise the concordance between P and A is absolute. Also, both P and A agree twice, at least, against the Papadopoulos-Kerameus edition (1: γραφαῖς ὀνομάτων δεικνύουσαι τῇ ἐβραΐδι διαλέκτω Pap.: καὶ ἐπεγέγραπτο τῇ ἐβρ. δ. PA 2: τὰς εἰκόνας PA: om. Pap.). The missing lines in P again do not deal with images.

43. Georgii Syceotae *Vita Theodori Syceotae,* ed. A.-J. Festugière, *Vie de Théodore de Sykéon, I Texte grec, II Traduction, commentaire et appendice,* SubsHag 48 (Brussels, 1970), 7, par. 8.1–10, 11, par. 13.1–15; *CPG* 7973; *BHG* 1748

> P, fols. 275ᵛ–276 (118*)
> Mansi XIII 89ᴇ–92ʙ
> Ἐκ τοῦ βίου τοῦ ὁσίου πατρὸς ἡμῶν Θεοδώρου ἀρχιμανδρίτου Σικέων (τῆς μονῆς τῶν Συκέων P) οὗ ἡ ἀρχή.

Inc. Εὐλογητὸς ὁ Θεὸς καὶ πατὴρ τοῦ κυρίου ἡμῶν Ἰησοῦ Χριστοῦ· καὶ μεθ᾽ ἕτερα· (ὄντος δὲ αὐτοῦ ὡς ἐτῶν δώδεκα add. A) ἐγένετο θανατικὸν ἐκ τοῦ βουβῶνος (βομβῶνος P) . . .

Des. . . . ἀπὸ τῆς ὥρας ἐκείνης εὐκόλως καὶ εὐμαθῶς ἀπεστήθισε (ἀπεστήθιζε P) τὸ ψαλτήριον.

Again, there are not significant differences between P and A. Two small clauses are missing at the beginning of the P version, but Cinnamus has preserved the word βομβῶνος which appears in the critical edition by Festugière (= Fe). P, in addition, shares the following variants with P against A:

Fe-P	A
μιμήσασθαι	μιμεῖσθαι
ἑξκαιδεκάτου	ἐκκαιδεκάτου
ἑαυτὸν	αὐτὸν
ἀπεστήθιζε	–σε

The other two possible combinations of these three transmissions give the following results:

Fe-A	P
ἀποστηθίσαι	ἐκστηθίσαι
γοῦν	οὖν

PA	Fe
δυσκόλως δὲ μετὰ	δυσκόλως δὲ καὶ μετὰ
ἠδύνατο	ἐδύνατο
τῷ ὄντι ἐκ τοῦ πλησίον	τῷ ὄντι πλησίον

A, finally, agrees with the Latin translation against P in one case, while P and Latin A come together in three instances. All in all, the situation resembles that of quotations 39 I and 39 II above. In the example below, however, P seems to draw from the actual source (as represented by Fe), and A repeats P with some further alterations. Compare:

Fe: . . . ἤσθετο γλυκύτητα ἡδύτερον μέλιτος ἐγχυθεῖσαν ἐν τῷ στόματι αὐτοῦ.

P: . . . ἤσθετο γλυκύτητα ἡδύτερον μέλιτος ἐνεχθεῖσαν ἐν τῷ στόματι αὐτοῦ.

A: . . . ἤσθετο γλυκύτητος ἡδύτερον μέλιτος ἐνεχθείσης ἐν τῷ στόματι αὐτοῦ.

44. *Vita et martyrium sancti Anastasii Persae*, ed. B. Flusin, *Saint Anastase le Perse et l'histoire de la Palestine au début du VIIe siècle* (Paris, 1992), vol. 1, 51, par. 9.1–10; *BHG* 84

P, fol. 276 (119*)
Mansi XIII 21Α–C
Ἐκ τοῦ μαρτυρίου τοῦ ἁγίου (μάρτυρος add. A) Ἀναστασίου τοῦ Πέρσου, (οὗ ἡ ἀρχή· add. A)
Inc. Ὁ μονογενὴς υἱὸς καὶ λόγος τοῦ Θεοῦ, δι᾽ οὗ τὰ πάντα ἐγένετο· καὶ
μεθ᾽ ἕτερα·
(a) ὡς δὲ ἐπλεόνασεν αὐτῷ ὁ πόθος τοῦ φωτισθῆναι . . . A (= 9.1)
(b) ὅμως σὺν αὐτῷ ἀπίει εἰς τὰς ἐκκλησίας . . . P (= 9.4)
Des. . . . κἀκεῖσε τοῦ ἁγίου ἀξιωθῆναι βαπτίσματος.

The text in P is identical with the A version, apart from the omission of
the five lines that follow the incipit. Cinnamus here, as almost everywhere
else, misspells the form ἀπῄει (ἀπίει P) of the verb ἄπειμι. Both P and A
agree on one occasion against the edition (ἀφορήτους βασάνους τὰς παρὰ τῶν
τυράννων ἐπαχθείσας (ἀπ– P) αὐτοῖς AP: ἀφορήτους βασάνους τὰς ἐπαχθείσας
αὐτοῖς παρὰ τῶν τυράννων ed.), but otherwise all three versions are identical.

45. *Miracula Anastasii Persae,* ed. Flusin, 131–32; *BHG* 89

P, fols. 276–277 (120*)
Mansi XIII 21C–24C
Ἐκ τῶν θαυμάτων τοῦ (αὐτοῦ add. P) ἁγίου μάρτυρος (τοῦ Χριστοῦ
add. P) Ἀναστασίου· (ὧν ἡ ἀρχὴ add. A)
Inc. Θαυμάτων διήγησιν προβαλλέσθαι βούλομαι· καὶ μετ᾽ ὀλίγα· φέρε δὴ
καὶ τὰ ἐν Καισαρείᾳ τῆς Παλαιστίνης γενόμενα . . .
Des. . . . δοξάζουσα τὸν Θεόν καὶ μεγαλαυχοῦσα τὸν μάρτυρα.

There are two sentences missing from P, but no other significant differences. Besides, P agrees in three cases with the Latin translation against A.
Again, both P and A are very close to the edited text, and both belong to
the same line of transmission.[157]

46. Ioannis Moschi *Pratum spirituale; CPG* 7376; *BHG* 1442

I. P, fol. 277 (121*); M, fol. 227 (22^M)
Mansi XIII 193D–E (*PG* 87, 3, 2940A–B)
Ἐκ τοῦ (αὐτοῦ add. A) Λειμωναρίου PA
Ἐκ τοῦ παραδεισίου ἐξήγησις M
Inc. Διηγήσαντο ἡμῖν οἱ αὐτοὶ (ἅγιοι M) πατέρες (καὶ τοῦτο add. AM)
λέγοντες ὅτι ἐν ταύταις ταῖς ἡμέραις γυνή τις . . .

---

[157] For a further collation of P with two mss of the 787 acts (Marcianus gr. 166 [15th cent.],
fols. 297^v–299^v and Taurin. Bibl. Nat. B II 9 [13th cent.], fols. 56^v–57) and the Mansi edition
with the basic mss of the *miracula,* see Flusin, 114–15.

Des.   . . . καὶ ἐπίομεν καὶ ἐδοξάσαμεν τὸν Θεὸν (τῶ Θεῶ P) (ἡμῶν add.
PA) (ἀμὴν add. P)

II. P, fol. 277ʳ⁻ᵛ (122*)
Mansi XIII 193ε–196ᴄ (*PG* 87, 3, 3052ᴀ–ᴅ)
Ἐκ τοῦ αὐτοῦ Λειμωναρίου P
Τοῦ αὐτοῦ A

Inc.: Διηγήσατο ἡμῖν Διονύσιος, ὁ πρεσβύτερος τῆς ἐκκλησίας Ἀσκάλωνος
(–ῶνος P) περὶ τοῦ ἀββᾶ Ἰωάννου . . .

Des.:   . . . οὔτε ἐξ ἐρήμου φοιτῶν εἰς τὸ σπήλαιον.

III. (A) P, fol. 277ᵛ (123*)
Mansi XIII 193ᴀ–ᴄ (*PG* 87, 3, 2900ʙ–ᴅ)
Ἐκ τοῦ (αὐτοῦ add. P) Λειμωναρίου

Inc. Ἔλεγόν τινες τῶν γερόντων, ὅτι ἦν τις ἔγκλειστος (–στὸς P) εἰς τὸ ὄρος
τῶν ἐλαιῶν . . .

Des.   . . . ἢ ἵνα ἀρνήσῃ τὸ προσκυνεῖν τὸν κύριον ἡμῶν καὶ Θεὸν Ἰησοῦν
Χριστὸν μετὰ τῆς ἰδίας αὐτοῦ μητρὸς ἐν τῇ εἰκόνι. P
   . . . τὸν δεσπότην καὶ ποιητὴν ἐπιώρκησα, σοῦ δὲ οὐ μὴ ἀκούσω. A

III. (B) M, fols. 238ᵛ–239 (48ᴹ); (Dam. I 64; II 67)
Mansi XIII 60ᴅ–61ʙ
Ἐξήγησις ἐκ τοῦ Παραδεισίου M
Ἐκ τοῦ Λειμωναρίου τοῦ ἁγίου πατρὸς ἡμῶν Σωφρονίου, ἀρχιεπισκό-
που Ἱεροσολύμων. Dam.
   Τοῦ ἐν ἁγίοις πατρὸς ἡμῶν Σωφρονίου ἐκ τοῦ Λειμωναρίου. A

Inc. Ὁ ἀββᾶς Θεόδωρος ὁ Ἐλιώτης διηγήσατο ἡμῖν λέγων· ὅτι . . . M
   Ἔλεγεν ὁ ἀββᾶς Θεόδωρος ὁ Αἰλιώτης, ὅτι . . . Dam., A

Des.   . . . πλὴν τὸν ἐμὸν δεσπότην καὶ ποιητὴν ἐπιόρκησα (sic), ὃς καὶ
συγχωρήσῃ (sic) μοι, σοῦ δὲ τοῦ λοιποῦ οὐ μὴ ἀκούσω. M
   . . . πλὴν τὸν ἐμὸν δεσπότην καὶ ποιητὴν ἐπιώρκησα· σοῦ δὲ οὐκ
ἀκούω. Dam., A

Quotations 46 I and 46 II of P are almost identical with the extracts in
A. Besides, P reflects a state of the text which is very close to the possible
original of the work, deriving from a period before the division of its textual
tradition into particular groups.[158] Quotation 46 III, however, is one of the
most significant for the present study and for the conclusions it will help
us reach.

The extract in question appears in the acts twice: first in the fourth
session (Mansi XIII 60ᴅ–61ʙ), and then at the end of the fifth session (XIII
193ᴀ–ᴄ). During the fourth session, Stephen, the monk and *bibliophylax*, read
out this *testimonium* from a book that was presented by Eustathius, abbot

---

[158] See Ph. Pattenden, "*Pratum Spirituale,*" *JTS* 26 (1975), 40–42.

of the monastery τῶν Μαξιμίνου. Then, in the following session, Patriarch Tarasius came up with the information that he had tried to find the same book in the patriarchal library only to discover that it had the folios dealing with icons cut out. Consequently, the same Stephen announced the recitation of the extracts from the *Pratum spirituale* with these words (Mansi XIII 192ε):

Στέφανος μοναχὸς καὶ βιβλιοφύλαξ εἶπε· βίβλος ἐπιδοθεῖσα παρὰ τοῦ ἡγουμένου τῶν Μαξιμίνου, περιέχουσα τὸν λόγον τὸν φαλσευθέντα εἰς τὸ ἄλλο βιβλίον τὸ περὶ εἰκόνων· καὶ ἀνέγνω ὁ αὐτὸς Στέφανος· Ἐκ τοῦ λειμωναρίου etc.

The above passage has been the source of some misunderstanding on the part of Wallach, who suggested that the ἄλλο βιβλίον refers to the one that was read during the fourth session.[159] From what follows, however, it is clear that the book which is read again is the one offered by Eustathius of Μαξιμίνου, namely, the very same book that was read in the fourth session. Therefore, the φαλσευθὲν book must have been the one that Tarasius mentioned and had probably presented to the assembly.

What may be expected when the same extract from the same book is read out twice is that the two citations be identical letter by letter, word for word, but this is not the case in the acts. The text in the fourth session (Mansi XIII 60ᴅ–61ʙ = Φ) differs perceptibly from that of the second reading in the fifth session (= Ψ, Mansi XIII 193ᴀ–ᴄ). Compare the differences between Φ and Ψ:

Φ: Mansi XIII 60ᴅ–61ʙ	Ψ: Mansi XIII 193ᴀ–ᴄ
Τοῦ ἐν ἁγίοις πατρὸς ἡμῶν Σωφρονίου ἐκ τοῦ Λειμωναρίου· (1)	Ἐκ τοῦ λειμωναρίου·
Inc. Ἔλεγεν ὁ ἀββᾶς Θεόδωρος ὁ Αἰλιώτης . . . (2)	Inc. Ἔλεγόν τινες τῶν γερόντων . . .
καὶ ἦλθε καὶ διηγήσατο πάντα. (3)	καὶ διηγεῖται αὐτῷ ἅπαντα.
. . . συμφέρει δέ σοι μὴ καταλιπεῖν εἰς τὴν πόλιν ταύτην πορνεῖον, εἰς ὃ μὴ εἰσέλθῃς, ἤ . . . (4)	. . . συμφέρει δέ σοι μὴ ἐᾶσαι ἐν τῇ πόλει ταύτῃ πορνεῖον, εἰς ὃ μὴ εἰσέρχῃ, ἤ . . .
. . . μετὰ τῆς ἰδίας αὐτοῦ μητρὸς ἐν εἰκόνι.	. . . μετὰ τῆς αὐτοῦ μητρός.

---

[159] *Diplomatic Studies*, 81; see also Speyer, *Die literarische Fälschung*, 277 n. 5.

The same piece is included also in Dam. and P. In Dam. this extract alone appears in all three of his florilegia (I 64; II 67; III 13) under the title: Ἐκ τοῦ Λειμωναρίου τοῦ ἁγίου πατρὸς ἡμῶν Σωφρονίου, ἀρχιεπισκόπου Ἱεροσολύμων, while in P all three extracts appear under the shorter title: ἐκ τοῦ λειμωναρίου. Compare the differences between Dam. and P first, and then between Dam. and Φ, and P and Ψ above:

John of Damascus (I 64; II 67)	Paris. gr. 1115, fol. 277ᵛ
Ἐκ τοῦ λειμωναρίου τοῦ ἁγίου πατρὸς ἡμῶν Σωφρονίου, ἀρχιεπισκόπου Ἱεροσολύμων.	ἐκ τοῦ αὐτοῦ λειμωναρίου·
(1)	
Inc. Ἔλεγεν ὁ ἀββᾶς Θεόδωρος ὁ Αἰλιώτης . . .	Inc. Ἔλεγόν τινες τῶν γερόντων . . .
(2)	
καὶ ἦλθε καὶ διηγεῖται πάντα.	καὶ διηγεῖται αὐτῷ ἅπαντα.
(3)	
. . . Συμφέρει δέ σοι μὴ ἐᾶσαι εἰς τὴν πόλιν ταύτην πορνεῖον, εἰς ὃ μὴ εἰσέλθῃς, ἤ . . .	. . . συμφέρει δέ σοι μὴ ἐᾶσαι πορνεῖον ἐν τῇ πόλει ταύτῃ εἰς ὃ μὴ εἰσέρχῃ, ἤ . . .
(4)	
. . . μετὰ τῆς ἰδίας αὐτοῦ μητρὸς	. . . μετὰ τῆς ἰδίας αὐτοῦ μητρὸς ἐν τῇ εἰκόνι.

Obviously it is not a simple coincidence that the Φ version in A has almost the same title as Dam. and shares with it all the divergences from Ψ except one (no. 4). It also cannot be a coincidence that P gives the same readings as the Ψ version of A in three of the four fragments above. Besides, Dam. includes only the piece that we find in the fourth session, while P could have provided the three extracts read out in session five.

The only problem here is that P omits again a considerable part at the end of the extract and two small clauses right after the beginning of it. However, the part of the quotation omitted by P but preserved in the Ψ version of A is still different from the text of the Φ version and from Dam. This implies that this part should have been included in the lost exemplar of P if the priority of F is accepted. Moreover, as has already been shown, Cinnamus systematically omitted parts that did not directly deal with image worship, such as the one here.

One final remark: as can be deduced from the tables above, A in Mansi XIII 60ᴅ–61ʙ gives a version that seems to be taking into account both the Dam. and P versions, at least for clause no. 4: μετὰ τῆς ἰδίας αὐτοῦ μητρὸς Dam.; μετὰ τῆς ἰδίας αὐτοῦ μητρὸς ἐν τῇ εἰκόνι P; μετὰ τῆς ἰδίας αὐτοῦ μητρὸς ἐν εἰκόνι Mansi XIII 61A. The same also holds true for the Ψ version of A; while it seems to be depending entirely on P, the fragment in Ψ 4 is much closer to Dam. 4 than to P 4.[160]

This quotation offers very strong evidence that the council relied on the original of P, V, and M (= F), which, as we have postulated, included also the first two Iconophile florilegia of John of Damascus and part, at least, of the third.

47. *Vita Silvestri papae Romae*
P, fol. 277ᵛ (124*); M, fols. 234–235 (36ᴹ)
Mansi XII 1058c–1059c

P has a different version of the incident of the conversion of Emperor Constantine I to the Christian faith by the "in somnio" intervention of Sts. Peter and Paul. The extract, as it appears in the synodal letter of Pope Hadrian, is totally different from the one given by P and M.

48. *Vetus atque Novum Testamentum*
P, fol. 280ʳ⁻ᵛ
Mansi XIII 4D–5c

These are four extracts from "Exodus," "Numeri," "Ezechiel," and from the "epistula S. Pauli ad Hebraeos," which occur in the same order as in the acts, at the end of the Διάλογος Μόσχου μοναχοῦ καὶ ἐγκλειστοῦ (sic) πρός τινα περὶ εἰκόνων ἁγίων (P, fols. 278–280ᵛ; for this text, see the Addenda).

> (i) Ἐκ τῆς ἐξόδου τῶν υἱῶν Ἰσραήλ· (25:16–21) (127*)
> Inc. Καὶ εἶπε κύριος πρὸς Μωυσῆν· ποιήσεις . . .
> Des. . . . ὅσα ἂν ἐντέλωμαί σοι πρὸς τοὺς υἱοὺς Ἰσραήλ.
> (ii) Ἐκ τῶν Ἀριθμῶν· (7.88–90) (128*)
> Inc. Αὕτη ἡ ἐγκαίνισις τοῦ θυσιαστηρίου . . .
> Des. . . . καὶ ἐλάλει πρὸς αὐτόν.
> (iii) Ἐκ τοῦ προφήτου Ἰεζεκιήλ P: Ἰεζεκιὴλ τοῦ προφήτου A (41.1/16–20), (129*)
> Inc. Καὶ εἰσήγαγέ με εἰς τὸν ναόν . . .
> Des. . . . ἐκ τοῦ ἐδάφους ἕως τοῦ φατνώματος τὰ Χερουβίμ.
> (iv) Ἐκ τῆς πρὸς Ἑβραίους ἐπιστολῆς (τοῦ ἁγίου ἀποστόλου add. A) Παύλου· (9.1–5) (130*)

---

[160] The M version is a very peculiar one since its dependence on any of the existing versions cannot be established. Although it gives an incipit similar to the one of Dam. and A vers. Φ (Ὁ ἀββᾶς Θεόδωρος ὁ Ἐλιώτης διηγήσατο ἡμῖν λέγων), the rest of the text approaches the Ψ version of A but with no absolute consistency. Besides, its desinit is more complete than that of any other version. It is hoped that the answer to this problem may appear in the critical edition of the text.

Inc. Εἶχε μὲν οὖν καὶ ἡ πρώτη σκηνή . . .
Des. . . . Χερουβὶμ δόξης κατασκιάζοντα τὸ ἱλαστήριον.

In the light of all the evidence presented above, F might have been one of the sources for the location of these quotations in the biblical text. The fragment from "Exodus" was also cited during the Roman Council of 731 (see above, p. 39). The most reasonable inference is that they were cited from a Bible and not from F.

49. Iohannis Hierosolymitani *Narratio* (*PG* 109, 517–20)

P, fols. 280ᵛ–281ᵛ (131*)
Mansi XIII 197A–200B
Ἰωάννου τοῦ εὐλαβεστάτου Ἰεροσολυμίτου μοναχοῦ διήγησις· P
Ἰωάννης ὁ εὐλαβέστατος πρεσβύτερος καὶ τοποτηρητὴς τῶν ἀνατο-
λικῶν ἀρχιερέων, ἀπὸ πιττακίου ἀνέγνω· A
Inc. Βούλομαι ἐγὼ ὁ μέτριος καὶ πάντων ἔσχατος ἀποδεῖξαι: (διηγήσα-
σθαι A)
Des. . . . ἄξια τὰ ἐπίχειρα (τἀπίχειρα A) τῆς ψευδομαντείας αὐτοῦ κομισα-
μένῳ (κομισάμενον A).

This text is transmitted by P in a considerably better state than that of A. Briefly, P agrees with the Latin translation of the text against A eight times, and gives better readings in four cases. Compare also:

P: . . . θεοστυγὴς αὕτη τῶν Χριστιανῶν, μᾶλλον δ᾽ εἰπεῖν ἀληθέστερον
κατηγόρων καὶ εἰκονομάχων αἵρεσις . . .
A: . . . θεοστυγὴς τῶν χριστιανοκατηγόρων καὶ εἰκονοκλαστῶν αἵρεσις . . .

P obviously points to an earlier stage of the history of the coinage of the word χριστιανοκατήγορος.

Dealing with the content of the text, it must be said that this *Narratio* is the well-known account of the beginning of Iconoclasm in Syria. The current opinion about it is that the original of the manuscript containing this text, Paris. gr. 1115, "was actually copied from the *Acta* of the Council, and so was written after 787."[161] Many years ago Melioranskij had made the conjecture that the *Narratio* was prepared on the occasion of the Jerusalem Synod of 764.[162]

Up to this point, proofs have been presented for the fact that P did not copy the acts but, quite the opposite, the original of P, V, and M must have been the main source for many quotations appearing during the sittings of

---

[161] Gero, *Leo III*, 64 n. 16.
[162] Melioranskij, *Georgij*, 98.

the seventh ecumenical council. This piece can be one certain exception to this rule so far, since it was evidently written to be cited at a council. The introductory comments of John of Jerusalem are very explicit: Βούλομαι ἐγώ, ὁ μέτριος καὶ πάντων ἔσχατος ἀποδεῖξαι μετὰ πάσης ἀληθείας ἐπὶ τῆς παρούσης . . . συνόδου. Melioranskij's suggestion that it was written for the Synod of Jerusalem in 764 should be dismissed for the following reason: the text gives in two instances clear indication of the place of its composition. In the first, it refers to the recall of Masalmas by the caliph Umar after the failure of the former to besiege Constantinople in 717 with the following words: . . . διεδέξατο τοῦτον Οὔμαρος, ὅς, ἐπιβὰς τῆς ἀρχῆς, εὐθὺς μεταστειλάμενος, ἀπέστρεψε τὸν Μασαλμὰν ἀπὸ τῆς γῆς ταύτης (P, fols. 280ᵛ–281). In the second instance, John of Jerusalem mentions that Iconoclasm began during the reign of Yazid, at a time when the evil (= Iconoclasm) had not reached Byzantine territories (πρὸ τοῦ φθάσαι ἐν τῇ γῇ ταύτῃ τὸ κακόν). No doubt in both instances the words ἀπὸ τῆς γῆς ταύτης/ ἐν τῇ γῇ ταύτῃ point to Constantinople.

The only solution is to accept that this *Narratio* is a later interpolation, added to the original of 774/5 (see below, p. 216) shortly after the arrival of the Greek *Acta* of the seventh ecumenical council at Rome in 788. But even so, P should represent the earliest possible version of the text of the acts, as has been suggested above (pp. 137–38).

50. Gregorii Papae Romani *Epistula ad Germanum Constantinopolit.* (*PG* 98, 148–156ʙ); *CPG* 8006; (JE 2181)

P, fols. 281ᵛ–283ᵛ (133*)
Mansi XIII 92c–100a
Ἐπιστολὴ Γρηγορίου τοῦ ἁγιωτάτου πάπα Ῥώμης πρὸς Γερμανὸν (τὸν ἁγιώτατον add. A) πατριάρχην Κωνσταντινουπόλεως.
Inc. Ποία καὶ τίς θυμηδία τὴν ἐμὴν οὕτως οἶδεν εὐφραίνειν ψυχήν . . .
Des. . . . ἡ διαρκὴς (δι' P) ἡμῶν χαρὰ καὶ κοινὸν ὄφελος καὶ
ἀπόλαυσις, ἁγιώτατε, καὶ πᾶσι τοῖς Χριστιανοῖς ποθητέ (ποτέ. P).

This letter in P closes with the following anathema: Ἀνάθεμα τοῖς αἱρετικοῖς Θεοδοσίῳ τῷ ψευδωνύμῳ ἐπισκόπῳ Ἐφέσου, Σισιννίῳ τῷ ἐπίκλην Παστιλλᾷ, Βασιλείῳ τῷ κακεμφάτῳ Τρικακκάβῳ, Ἰωάννῃ Νικομηδείας καὶ Κωνσταντίνῳ Νακολασίας (sic), which is an abridged exposition of the anathemas closing the *horos* of Nicea II in Mansi XIII 400a–ʙ.

As far as the text of the letter of Pope Gregory II to Patriarch Germanus is concerned, there are no significant differences between P and A. Gouillard considers P a copy of A,[163] but it is rather the opposite that we should accept as true.

I have already discussed elsewhere (above, pp. 121–22) the sources and significance of this letter for the whole procedure of the appearance of the first Iconophile florilegia. Here I may add a few words about the anathemas that follow immediately after this letter in P.

Since the anathematization is directed against Theodosius, the bishop of Ephesus, who presided at the Council of Hieria, and other Iconoclast personalities of that early period, it may be possible that it was issued by the Council of Jerusalem in 764. Moreover, although it may equally well have been derived from the acts of the seventh ecumenical council and interpolated into the original florilegium (F), we have an official recording of such an anathematization which took place at Rome in 769. In the *Liber Pontificalis* we read:

> Haec vero omnia promulgata, continuo et diversa sanctorum Patrum testimonia de sacris imaginibus domini Dei . . . Christi sanctaeque . . . ejus genetricis . . . Mariae . . . et beatorum apostolorum omniumque sanctorum . . . in eodem adlata sunt concilio. Et subtilius cuncta perdagantes, statuerunt magno honoris affectu ab omnibus christianis ipsas sacras venerari imagines . . . ; confundentes atque anathematizantes execrabilem illam synodum quae in Graecie partibus nuper facta est pro deponendis ipsis sacris imaginibus.[164]

Certainly both the synods of Jerusalem (764) and Rome (769) could have anathematized these Iconoclasts, but the wording of the anathemas is almost the same as the one that appears in the acts of 787. So it is most likely that they were later interpolated in the Roman original. It is also possible that they were a marginal note transposed into the main text by Cinnamus.

51. Iohannis Chrysostomi *De parabola seminis* = Severianus Gabalensis, *De sigillis sermo; CPG* 4209; *BHG* 2351 (*PG* 63, 544.7–15)

M, (a) fol. 228ᵛ (25ᴹ), (b) fol. 235ʳ⁻ᵛ (39ᴹ); V, fol. 17ᵛ (V 44)
(P, fol. 252, appended to quot. 58*, no lemma, truncated)
(Dam. II 61)
Mansi XII 1066ᴇ–1067ᴀ; XIII 325ᴅ

Τοῦ Χρυσοστόμου (τοῦ αὐτοῦ V) εἰς τὴν παραβολὴν τοῦ σπόρου· V, Mb
Τοῦ αὐτοῦ ἐκ τῆς ἑρμηνείας τῆς παραβολῆς τοῦ σπόρου Ma, Dam II 61

---

[163] Gouillard, "Origines," 244.

[164] *Liber Pontificalis*, 476–77. *Vita Stephani III Papae* (768–772). For English translation of the passage see R. Davis, *The Lives*, 100.

a. Ἔνδυμα βασιλικὸν ἐὰν ὑβρίσῃς, οὐ τὸν ἐνδεδυμένον ὑβρίζεις;
b. Οὐκ οἶδας ὅτι ἐὰν εἰκόνα βασιλέως ὑβρίσῃς, εἰς τὸ (–ν Ma, b) πρωτότυπον τῆς ἀξίας φέρεις τὴν ὕβριν;
c. Οὐκ οἶδας ὅτι ἐάν τις (τὴν Ma, om. V) εἰκόνα τὴν ἀπὸ ξύλου ἢ (om. Dam.) ἀπὸ (καὶ Dam., om. Mb) ἀνδριάντος χαλκοῦ (om. Mb) κατασύρῃ (–ης Ma, κατασύρει τις V), οὐχ ὡς εἰς ἄψυχον ὕλην τολμήσας κρίνεται (–σαι Ma), ἀλλ᾽ ὡς κατὰ βασιλέως κεχωρισμένην V (κεχρημένος Ma, κεχ . . . Dam.¹⁶⁵ om. Mb)
d. Εἰκόνα δὲ (om. Ma) ὅλως (om. V) βασιλέως (χαρακτῆρα add. Mb in margine manu rec.) φέρουσα τὴν ἑαυτῆς ὕβριν εἰς τὸν (om. Dam) βασιλέα ἀνάγει (ἄγη Ma, ἐνάγη Mb).

The Latin version of the quotation occurs in the *Hadrianum* inserted, in all probability, from the *Acta* of the 731 Roman council. In its original form it is preserved by the *Libellus Synodalis*.

LS, 510.32–37: Item beati Iohannis Chrysostomi de parabola seminis:

a. Indumentum imperiale si iniuriaveris, nonne eum qui induitur iniurias?
b. Nescis quia, si quis imaginem imperatoris iniuriat, ad eum ipsum imperatorem, principaliter dignitati eius adfert iniuriam?
c. Nescis quia, si quis imaginem ex ligno aut ex colore detrahit, non sicut ad elementum sine anima ausus iudicatur, sed sicut adversus imperatorem dissegregatam
d. imaginem totidem imperatoris gestans, eius iniuriam ad imperatorem deducit?

Leaving aside the Greek version of Mansi XII 1066E–1067A, which is a retranslation of the Latin redaction and omits the crucial passage (c) and the abridged version of P, the Greek text in all its versions cited above is more or less the same. Ma, Mb, Dam., and V seem to have offered the basis for the Latin translation. What demonstrates the dependence of all these transmissions on a common original are the disturbed phrases (c) and (d), which in all four (Ma, Mb, Dam., and V) give a very poor text. The original passage from the *De sigillis librorum* of Severian of Gabala reads as follows (*PG* 63, 544):

c. οὐκ οἶδας ὅτι, ἐάν τις εἰκόνα τὴν ἀπὸ ξύλου ἢ ἀνδριάντα χαλκοῦν κατασύρῃ, οὐχ ὡς εἰς ἄψυχον ὕλην τολμήσας οὕτω κρίνεται, ἀλλ᾽ ὡς κατὰ βασιλέως χεῖρας ἐκτείνας ἀφανίζεται;

¹⁶⁵ See the apparatus criticus in Kotter, *Schriften III*, 163: "II 61 9 κεχ)ρημένος τῇ ὕβρει om. sed lac. Dᴵᴵ, supplevi ex edd.; unde tamen hae?"

d. Ὕλη ἄψυχος τοῦ βασιλέως εἰκόνα φέρουσα τὴν ἑαυτῆς ὕβριν εἰς βασιλέα ἀνάγει.

The passage from Severian was later discovered by the redactor of the
Hadrianum of 793, and this is the reason why we can find the same passage
under the right lemma and in a more satisfactory Latin translation: *Hadrianum*, 17.13–19:

> Item sancti Severiani episcopi Gavalensis de homilia in qua demon-
> stravit scripturas per Dominum explanatas et cetera:
>
> c. Nescis, quoniam si quis imago quae a ligno detrahet, non sicut ina-
>   nimata materia audens sic iudicatur, sed sicut qui adversum impera-
>   torem manus extendens fedatur materia, sine anima imperatoris se-
>   gregata ab imperatore?
> d. Imago enim omnino ferente, eius iniuria ad imperatorem adtingit,
>   etc.

After the emendations of Wallach,[166] the meaning of the preceding
Latin fragment was made clearer, but it still did not correspond to the Greek
passage of Severian. This implies that even in 793 the Greek original was
corrupt despite its correct attribution.

However, we are still in 731, and the question to be answered is: which
was the version the Latin scribe based his translation on? No doubt it was
the version included in the original of P, M, and V (= F), as has been proved
elsewhere. The next question is: which version has copied F more faithfully,
P, M, or V? P has already been dismissed. There remain M and V, and the
key to the answer is again the Latin translation of the *Synodica* as cited in
the *Libellus Synodalis*. Compare:

> *LS:* Non sicut ad elementum sine anima ausus iudicatur, sed sicut ad-
>   versus imperatorem dissegregatam imaginem totidem . . .
>
> M: οὐχ ὡς εἰς ἄψυχον ὕλην τολμήσας κρίνεται, ἀλλ᾽ ὡς κατὰ βασιλέως
>   κεχρημένος εἰκόνα ὅλως . . .
>
> V: οὐχ ὡς εἰς ἄψυχον ὕλην τολμήσας κρίνεται, ἀλλ᾽ ὡς κατὰ βασιλέως
>   κεχωρισμένην, εἰκόνα δὲ . . .

The word κεχωρισμένην, which corresponds to the *dissegregatam* of the
LS, is the missing piece of the puzzle. The text was so corrupt that the Latin
translator had no other choice than to translate his exemplar word by word.
The result was meaningless simply because the Greek text made no sense.

The conclusions of this examination can be summarized as follows. The
Greek text as it is transmitted by V is closer to the lost original of the florile-

---

[166] *Diplomatic Studies*, 91–94.

gium (F) and served as the basis for the Latin translation of the fragment in 731 at Rome. What is more interesting, the Dam. version seems to adhere to the same line of the textual tradition as V and M, but cannot be considered its archetype, since it gives less than V and M (κεχρημένος Ma; κεχωρισμένην V, κεχ . . . Dam.). Therefore, this fragment provides another occasion to question the originality of the Iconophile florilegia of John of Damascus. If the florilegia of John of Damascus reproduce F, in the case of the quotations examined in the preceding pages one might claim one more time that F not only did not copy the acts of the seventh ecumenical council (apart from one or two exceptions), but, on the contrary, was actually in existence during the early stages of Iconoclasm.

52. Nili Ancyrani *Epistula* 277 (*PG* 79, 580–81); *CPG* 6043
V, fols. 22–23ᵛ (V 52)
Mansi XIII 32c–33c

Τοῦ ἁγίου Νείλου πρὸς Ἡλιόδωρον Σελεντιάριον ἐπιστολὴ σοζ′ V
Ἐπιστολὴ τοῦ μακαρίου Νείλου πρὸς Ἡλιόδωρον σιλεντιάριον A
Inc. Διὰ τῶν κατὰ τόπον καὶ ἐν (τόπον V) διαφόροις χρόνοις
Des. . . . μνήμης τῶν τρισμακαρίστων (μακαρίστων V) μαρτύρων λαμβάνοντι.

There are no significant differences between the two versions. V omits one word, but whenever V differs from A the translation of Anastasius is in agreement with V (παραμυθήτων A: ἀπαραμυθήτων V, nullius consolationis Lat. A; συνδήσαντες A: δήσαντες V, ligantes Lat. A; τρισμακαρίστων A: μακαρίστων V, beatorum Lat. A).

53. Germani I Constantinopolitani *Epistula ad Iohannem episcopum Synadensem* (*PG* 98, 156–61); *CPG* 8002
M, fols. 219–223 (13ᴹ)
Mansi XIII 100a—105a

Ἐπιστολὴ Γερμανοῦ τοῦ μακαριωτάτου πατριάρχου γενομένου Κωνσταντινουπόλεως πρὸς Ἰωάννην ἐπίσκοπον Συνάδων A
Τοῦ αὐτοῦ ἐπιστολὴ πρὸς τὸν ἐπίσκοπον Συνάδων M
Inc. Ἐπιστολὴν τῆς ὑμετέρας θεοφιλίας ἀποδέδωκεν ἡμῖν Ταράσιος . . .
Des. . . . τὴν ὑπερέχουσαν πάντα νοῦν εἰρήνην (τοῦ Θεοῦ add. A)

A and M, despite the presence of many variants between them, point to a common original. The mediocre scribe who produced M has preserved some words that A omits, although in two cases he skipped two or three lines of his exemplar.

54. Iohannis Gabalensis *Vita Severi Antiocheni* (frag.); *CPG* 7525

(A) M, fol. 237ᵛ (45ᴹ)
Ἰωάννου ἐπισκόπου Γαβαλῶν· ἐκ τοῦ κατὰ Σεβῆρον (sic) λόγου·
Inc. Οὐδὲ γὰρ τὴν τῶν ἀγγέλων τιμὴν ἀλώβητον εἴασε . . .
Des. . . . καὶ ταύτην διαίρειν καὶ ἐπ᾽ ἄλλους κινεῖν.

(B) Mansi XIII 184ʙ–ᴄ
Ἰωάννου ἐπισκόπου Γαβάλων εἰς τὸν βίον καὶ τὴν πολιτείαν Σεβήρου
τοῦ αἱρεσιάρχου· οὗ ἡ ἀρχή·
Inc. Εἰ μὲν ἐβούλετο Σεβῆρος ἢ ζωῆς τῆς αὐτῆς. καὶ μετ᾽ ὀλίγα· καὶ οὐδὲ
τὴν ἀγγέλων τιμὴν ἀλώβητον εἴασε . . .
Des. . . . ἐπ᾽ ἀλλήλους κινεῖν οὕτως ἢ ἑτέρως ἔχοντας τοὺς πολλούς.

The main differences between the two versions are apparent in the incipit and the desinit given above. No other significant disagreement is found. The omission of the incipit by the scribe of M is a constant practice in copying his exemplar. Actually there is not a single instance in M where the beginning of a work from which a fragment had been excerpted can be traced.

Conclusions

During the first five sessions of the seventh ecumenical council, Nicaea II, the indication ἀνέγνω (read out), usually after the name of a patriarchal secretary, occurs explicitly or is meant to occur eighty-nine times at the least. This implies that extracts or extensive quotations from at least seventy-seven works had been read out, while in some cases a work was cited in its entirety. Of all these quotations, roughly fifty-six fragments extracted from forty-eight works (plus another thirteen in the *Synodica* of 785) were concerned with image veneration. Of these fifty-six fragments or works, the combination of P, V, M—which roughly yields 148 Iconophile quotations—does not provide the following works:

(1) Germanus I CPolitanus, *Epistula ad Thomam episcopum Claudiopoleos*, Mansi XIII 108ᴀ–128ᴀ (*CPG* 8004)[167]
(2) Idem, *Epistula ad Constantinum episcopum Nacoliae*, Mansi XIII 105ʙ–108ᴀ (*CPG* 8003)
(3) Nilus Ancyranus, *Epistula ad Olympiodorum eparchum*, Mansi XIII 36ᴀ–ᴅ (*CPG* 6043)
(4) Augustinus Hippon., untraced quotation,[168] Mansi XII 1065ᴄ.

---

[167] Note, however, that M, fol. 229ᵛ (28ᴹ) transmits a small fragment from this letter.
[168] See Wallach, *Diplomatic Studies*, 31.

In other words, the original of P, M, and V (= F) should have included perhaps all the image worship *testimonia* that were quoted during the fourth and the fifth sessions of the council. The final number of the existing extracts common to F and the acts is sixty-four, but in the list of the preceding collation of the texts this number is fifty-four because any different extracts that were taken from one single work have been counted as one item, such as, for example, the three extracts from the *Pratum spirituale* (no. 46 in the above list).

It must have become obvious from the collation of the passages in this part of the study that both F and A belonged to the same line of textual transmission (with some exceptions on the line of F represented by M). So, unless things change dramatically with the forthcoming edition of the acts in the *ACO* series, one has to admit that, in the present textual state of the *testimonia*, one transmission must derive from the other or from a common source. And this brings us to the problem of the use of florilegia by the seventh ecumenical council. In its acts much care is taken to give the impression that actual books were presented, spontaneously offered by the participants, or brought forth by the secretaries. Yet this textual study points to an existing florilegium as a source. I will try to explain this peculiarity in the next chapter. For the time being I present some additional arguments in favor of the florilegia as a source for the quotations in the acts.

It must be stressed that there is no doubt that real books were available to the participants at the council. Still, it seems impossible to understand the appearance in the acts of such works as quotation 31 in the above list (John of Thessalonica, *fragmentum de imaginibus*). In a council that had put so much stress on the employment of real books, how can we have a work—which, by the way, is preserved only by P and the acts—cited under the lemma Ἰωάννου ἐπισκόπου Θεσσαλονίκης ἐκ τοῦ λόγου? Which λόγος? The obligation to provide a fuller citation loomed large over the participants of the council if they wanted to play by the rules they had established, but not over the compiler of a florilegium. In other words, the compiler of 770, for example, is more easily allowed to say "that is all I can afford," but not the council. The same or a similar situation is provided by quotations 3 (St. Basil, *Epistula* 360) and 32 (Ἐκ τῆς διαλέξεως Ἰουδαίου ⟨τε⟩ καὶ Χριστιανοῦ).

The most striking case, however, is that of the three fragments of the *Pratum spirituale* (above, quot. 46). The only book available in the patriarchal library was destroyed, and the citation of only the third passage in the fourth session gives a text close to that of Dam., while the three passages read during the fifth session resemble those of P. The facts speak for themselves.

Uthemann has advanced some more arguments in favor of the priority of the acts over P (alone) and, by implication, against the use of florilegia by the council. The reader may find some rather lengthy answers to them in my article, "Some Remarks on the Colophon of Codex *Parisinus Graecus* 1115."[169] Here I give a brief outline of the discussion.

His first point has to do with the order in which the texts appear in P and A, and claims that some of the quotations can be found "in der gleichen Textfolge."[170] This claim, namely, that the texts in P corresponding to the quotations cited during the fifth session follow the succession established by the acts, cannot be valid, as a juxtaposition of the column numbers of the fifth session of the council to the corresponding folios of Parisinus plainly shows.[171] In addition, it is P of all the florilegia (and John of Damascus in the second place) that displays a coherent arrangement of its contents.[172]

The only case where Uthemann is right is that of the *Narratio* (see no. 49), which we have to accept as a later interpolation. It is worth devoting a few remarks to this problem.

The examination of all the existing florilegia has proved, I hope, the immense extent of the original florilegium of the year 770. Its compiler obviously tried to gather in one volume all the possible *testimonia* in favor of image worship. But it should not escape our attention that P is an apograph of a larger volume produced, according to the colophon, in 774/5 and not of the τεῦχος of 770. The volume of 774/5 constituted, in all probability, a *Panoplia dogmatica* on every disputed issue of the Christian faith. Such a significant witness as the *Narratio* of John of Jerusalem would have been deemed worthy of being included in an official collection which aimed to encompass every quotation on image worship. Therefore, it is more likely that the *Narratio* was an interpolation in the original of 774/5 but was not obviously included among the works of the τεῦχος of 770.

One second cluster of texts that I am hesitating to decide whether or not they are post-787 interpolations are nos. 14, 20, 21, 26, and 27 of the list above. The reason is that their text in P represents the Greek retranslation of their Latin translation. A most convenient time for such a work to have been done is a period after the arrival of the Latin *Synodica* of Hadrian I in Constantinople (post 785). I think, however, that F included both their Greek original and the retranslations, since for no. 21 (Epiphanius of Constant., *Panarion*) P provides not only the retranslation but also the Greek

---

[169] *Revue d'histoire des textes* 22 (1992), 131–43; the dating of the *Narratio* (ibid., 135–36, for which I had followed Melioranskij) is wrong, and should be ignored.

[170] Uthemann, "Ein Beitrag," 36–37. Uthemann believes that P was copied from the acts, and this is one of his arguments in defense of his view. His formulation in fact gives the impression that the majority of the texts in P follow the order established by A.

[171] Alexakis, "The Colophon," 137.

[172] See above, Chapter III, Sec. 1.

original of the Latin translation, and for no. 27 (Hieronymus of Jerusalem, *De effectu baptismati*) the Greek original is transmitted by V and M.

The next argument of Uthemann, namely, that P includes almost all the *testimonia* of A, does not prove anything in itself since we have seen that the combination of P, V, and M gives a much larger figure.[173] And the fact alone that P, V, and M are textually closer to the florilegia of John of Damascus than to A is another argument for the priority of almost all the quotations in F over A. Other arguments of Uthemann have been presented above in Chapter II, section 2 (pp. 48–50) and have been discussed in the course of this study.

One issue, however, that could have offered better support for Uthemann's theory is the omission in P (and sometimes in V and M as well) not only of letters, single words, and clauses, but in some cases of whole parts of an extract that are found in A, for instance in nos. 16 (*Narratio de cruce seu imagine Berytensi*) and 28 (*Epistula ad Iustinum imperatorem*) of St. Symeon the Stylite.[174] As I have shown, however, these omissions seem to have been a deliberate action of Cinnamus in most of the cases and the omitted parts do not deal with image worship.[175] Besides, omitting parts from his exemplar is something that Cinnamus has done throughout the whole florilegium, if not through the total extent of the codex.[176] Apart from that, V and M supplement in many cases the part(s) of the text that are missing in P as, for example, in the case of the *Narratio de cruce* (P 71*, M 10^M).

The reasonable conclusion, therefore, is that almost all the omissions must be attributed to Cinnamus who, nevertheless, selected carefully the passages that he decided not to copy. Besides, if it is accepted that both P and A draw from the same archetype, why should Cinnamus follow his original letter by letter at a time when the image worship issue had been resolved for good? The same holds for the copyists that produced M and V, who, even if they did not mutilate the quotations they copied (to the extent that Cinnamus did), proceeded to select a small number of quotations from the more than 150 that were possibly included in F. Taking this into account, it can be deduced that the τεῦχος of 770 provided in all probability the texts in their original extent, as they are found in the acts.

With reference to the results of the collation of the two florilegia (F and A) carried out in the previous pages, the following conclusions can be drawn.

---

[173] Alexakis, "The Colophon," 136.

[174] In fact, the abridged quotations in P are fifteen (see Alexakis, ibid., 138), and if we add quot. 54 above of M, it comes to sixteen fragments out of fifty-four.

[175] Alexakis, "The Colophon," 137–39.

[176] See below, pp. 242–43.

The total number of quotations can be distributed into three major groups:

I. Texts common to F and Hadrian's *Synodica* of 785. Within this category fall the following quotations:

1. (8) Gregorius Nyss., *Hom. XV, In Canticum canticorum*
2. (12) Cyrillus Alex., *Commentarii in Matthaeum*
3. (14) Athanasius Alex., *Oratio de incarnatione Verbi*
4. (20) Ambrosius Mediolan., *De fide ad Gratianum Augustum*
5. (21) Epiphanius Constantiensis, *Panarion*
6. (26) Stephanus Bostrensis, *Contra Iudaeos* (frag.)
7. (27) Hieronymus Hierosolymitanus, *Dialogus de cruce*
8. (51) Iohannes Chrysostomus, *De parabola seminis.*

These eight extracts can be classified into the following subdivisions: (The numbers in parentheses again indicate the place of the quotation in the list of the collation).

(1) Extracts where the fragment in the original of P, M, and V was the source for the Latin translation of the quotation inserted into the original of the *Synodica,* or at least stands between the Greek original of the quotation and the Latin translation. This is the case for nos. 1 (8), 2 (12), and 8 (51)[177] on the above list.

(2) Extracts where the P quotation is a retranslation of the Latin translation of the Greek original. Here nos. 3 (14), 4 (20), 6 (26), and 7 (27) are included.

(3) The interesting case of the short extract from the *Panarion* of St. Epiphanius of Salamis, 5 (21), where P provides not only the Greek retranslation of the Latin translation, but also the Greek original itself, on which the Latin translation had been based. The same can also be demonstrated in the case of the fragment by Hieronymus of Jerusalem (*Dialogus de cruce*): P preserves the Greek retranslation, while M and V preserve the Greek original.

II. A smaller group of four extracts that occur in all three: F, A, and the *Synodica:*

1. (2) Basilius Caes., *Sermo in XL martyres Sebastenses*
2. (3) Idem, *Epistula* 360

---

[177] In quot. 7- (27) P gives the Greek retranslation of the Latin translation, while V (50), and M (16^M) present the Greek original.

3. (7) Gregorius Nyss., *De deitate Filii et Spiritus Sancti*
4. (10) Iohannes Chrys., *Homilia de lotione pedum.*

The PM version of quotations given in nos. 1, 3, and 4 examined in relation to the *Synodica* gives the impression that their original had served as the basis of the Latin translation. It has also been proved that the source for the Latin translation of no. 2 was the extract inserted in the Νουθεσία and M.

On the other hand, the comparison of these texts to the A versions leads to the following conclusions:

(1) No. 1 is not as close to the A as to the Dam. version. No connection, therefore, between P and A.
(2) No. 2: although the initial part of it is missing in P but not in M, F is in all probability the source of A.
(3–4) Nos. 3 and 4: A is a combination of the Dam. and P versions.

III. Texts of PVM found in the fourth and fifth sessions of the council (Mansi XIII 1–202). This is the largest group of all three, amounting to forty-six quotations. (Nos. 17 and 47 are not included in this enumeration for the reasons cited above.) They can also be divided into the following categories:

A. Extracts that undoubtedly were cited during the proceedings of the council from their actual source, but for which either F or Dam. could possibly have given the guideline. These are:

1. (9) Iohannes Chrys., *De s. Meletio Antiocheno.* Although there is a possibility that Dam. or F were the actual sources for the appearance of this quotation in A, the instances where A follows the *PG* readings are five, something rather exceptional. It is likely, therefore, that the text was cited from a book of John Chrysostom.
2. (25) *Quinisextum Canon LXXXII.* In the course of the debate[178] it is made clear that the passage was read out from the original piece of paper that bore the signatures of the fathers that took part in the *Trullanum.*
3. (34) *Preces clericorum et monachorum ad Iohannem CPolitanum.* This is a letter included in the acts of the Constantinopolitan Council of 536, presumably a text easily accessible to the participants.
4. (48 I–IV) The four extracts from the Bible that constitute, so to speak, an answer to the Second Commandment. It was not difficult to have them cited from a Bible.

---

[178] Mansi XIII 40–41.

B. Quotations that seem to have been cited directly from F. This is the most extensive group including thirty-seven extracts from thirty-two works. It seems preferable to include in this category the texts parts of which P or V and M omit, assuming that the exemplar of Cinnamus or F provided the integral extract, and to add the letters of St. Nilus and Germanus I provided by V and M respectively.

The list of these works is as follows:

1. (1) Basilius Caes., *In Barlaam martyrem*
2. (3) Idem, *Epistula 360*
3. (4) Idem, *Contra Sabellianos et Arium et Anomaeos*
4. (6) Idem, *De Spiritu Sancto*
5. (11) Iohannes Chrys., *Homilia de lotione pedum*
6. (13) Cyrillus Alex., *Ad Acacium Scythopoleos*
7. (15) Athanasius Alex. *Oratio III contra Arianos*
8. (16) Idem, *Narratio de cruce*
9. (18) Anastasius Antiochenus, *Epistula ad scholast.*
10. (22) Cyrillus Hierosolym., *Catecheses ad illuminandos II*
11. (24) Constantinus Diacon., *Laudatio omnium Martyrum*
12. (28) Symeon Stylita Iunior, *Epist. ad Iustinum Iuniorem*
13. (29) Antipater Bostrensis, *Homilia in mulierem . . .*
14. (30) Asterius Amasenus, *Homilia XI*
15. (31) Iohannes Thessalonicensis, *Sermo, (frag. de imag.)*
16. (32) *Disputatio Iudaei et Christiani*
17. (33) Leontius Neapolitanus, *Contra Iud., orat. V*
18. (35) Evagrius, *Historia ecclesiastica*
19. (36 I) Sophronius Hierosolym., *Laudes in ss. Cyrum et Iohannem*
20. (36 II) *Miracula Cyri et Iohannis*
21–23. (37 I–III) *Miracula ss. Cosmae et Damiani*
24. (38) Theodoretus Ep. Cyri, *Historia Religiosa*
25–26. (39 I, II) *Vita s. Symeonis Stylitae Iunioris*
27. (40) *Vita Iohannis Ieiunatoris*
28. (41) *Vita Mariae Aegyptiacae*
29. (42) *Passio s. Procopii*
30. (43) Georgius Syceota, *Vita Theodori Syceotae*
31. (44) *Passio scti. Anastasii Persae*
32. (45) *Anastasii Persae Miracula*
33–34. (46 I, II) Iohannes Moschus, *Pratum spirituale*
35. (50) Gregorius II Papa, *Epistula ad Germanum*
36. (52) Nilus Ancyranus, *Epistula 277*
37. (53) Germanus I CPolitanus, *Epistula ad Iohannem ep. Synad.*
38. (54) Iohannes Gabalensis, *Vita Severi Antiocheni.*

This group assembles the overwhelming majority of the texts of F, and the above list is, in all probability, complete.

C. There is finally another group of six quotations, where A gives a text that in some cases is a combination of those provided by Dam. and F. It includes the following extracts:

1. (5) Gregorius Naz., *Carmina moralia*. Here A repeats the wrong incipit and one or two readings provided by P, but in general depends on Dam.
2. (7) Gregorius Nyss., *De deitate Filii et Spiritus Sancti*. A combines the long title of Dam. and the text of P.
3. (10) Iohannes Chrys., *Homilia de lotione pedum*. As has been shown above (pp. 157–62), the Dam. version is used by A in order to render the meaning of a sentence clearer.
4. (19) Anastasius Antiochenus, *Ad Symeonem Bostrensem*. The title in A is an elaboration of the title of P, and the rest of the text gives readings provided by both P and Dam.
5. (23) Anastasius Apocrisiarius, *Acta (Maximi conf.) in primo exsilio*. P reflects the source of the whole A text, but the lemma appears to merge both the Dam. and the P versions.
6. (46 III) Iohannes Moschus, *Pratum spirituale*. This is the most representative sample of this category. Although A copies the same excerpt, in one case from Dam. and in another from the original of P, the copy that was based on Dam. appears to take into account the P version and vice versa.

There is also a single extract which is difficult to classify, namely, St. Basil's *Sermo in XL Martyres Sebastenses* (2). It seems likely to have been taken directly from Dam. rather than from P or the work itself.

The conclusion is that the organizing committee of Nicaea II relied heavily on the texts provided by F.[179] In addition, F in one or two instances dictated the order of the citation of the texts as shown above. Apart from that, it is certain that the committee had at its disposal the florilegia of John of Damascus, since, as has been shown above, they were included in the τεῦχος of 770.[180] They were, in all probability, used for cross-reference. This becomes evident especially in the case of the *Carmina moralia*, where P is full

[179] There is always the possibility of F having included the two letters of Germanus, the one to Thomas of Claudiopolis and the other to Constantine of Nakolia, and the letter of St. Nilus to Olympiodorus *Eparchus*.

[180] It is worth noting that in almost all the cases where the text of Dam. is (possibly?) the ultimate source of a quotation, the correspondence of the readings provided by P and A points to two particular manuscripts of the Dam. works, namely, Neapol. 54 (II B 16), 13 cent., and Athous Dionys. 175 (3709), 13 cent.

of metrical mistakes that do not appear in the acts, since the text provided
by Dam. was correct. It is also evident in some other cases where the extended title of a work is supplemented by Dam., while the whole work draws
from P who provided a shorter title (e.g., no. 3 in the list above, p. 145).

Summing up, it is beyond any reasonable doubt that the τεῦχος of 770,
or perhaps a copy of it, was in most of the cases the actual source of the
quotations that appear in the printed text of the acts, and a critical edition
of the acts of the seventh ecumenical council has to take into account the
text of this manuscript as transmitted by PVM. Moreover, it has become
clear that the acts followed a prearranged course in the discussions of the
fourth and fifth sessions, and the intervention of the participants would not
have been spontaneous at all, barring very few cases.

After all, the selection of the texts to be used for the proceedings of a
council in a florilegium is not a new phenomenon, as has been shown in
Chapter I. Also, concerning the prearranged interventions, many examples
of similar incidents from the previous councils have been given in that same
chapter. The insistence in 787, however, on the pretense of the authenticity
of the books was obviously because the fathers did not desire the charges of
forgery and falsification inflicted upon the Synod of Hiereia to be brought
against the seventh ecumenical council (see below, Chap. IV).

6. F and Works Later than Nicaea II

One instance of a later florilegium based on F has been presented above
(section 3, p. 103) when treating the relationship between P and M and the
Iconophile florilegium of Nicetas of Medicion (N).[181] We saw that Nicetas
epitomized a small number of quotations from the original florilegium.
What was the situation during the second period of Iconoclasm, apart from
the case of Nicetas?

Theodore the Studite is one of the leading Iconophile figures of the
second period of Iconoclasm. A small number of quotations taken from the
fathers and usually corresponding to the extracts in P, M, or V are dispersed
in the relatively few Iconophile works he produced. Nevertheless, he seems
to ignore the existence of F, and this can easily be deduced from his letter
to a certain monk Nicetas (*PG* 99, 1537A–D). Therein Theodore disputes the
ὀρθοφροσύνη of a passage from Hypatius of Ephesus. The same passage is
also included in P (quot. 74*) but with a small alteration that entirely

---

[181] See also my article, "A Florilegium in the Life of Nicetas of Medicion and a Letter of
Theodore the Studite," *DOP* 48 (1994), 179–97.

changes the meaning of a sentence into an openly Iconophile statement, whereas the intention of Hypatius appears to have been the opposite.[182]

Besides that, the Iconophile quotations that he usually cites in his letters and his other dogmatic works do not go beyond the standard extracts from St. Basil, Gregory of Nyssa, Gregory of Nazianzus, Dionysius, Cyril of Alexandria, a fragment from the *Vita Pancratii,* and certainly canon 82 of the Quinisext,[183] which were probably circulating in the Iconophile milieu of that period or were available at the monastery of Studios.

Patriarch Nicephorus is another leading Iconophile in whose work lengthy references to patristic quotations are embedded, and he appears to have had access to a wide range of Iconophile literature. In his *Antirrhetica contra Eusebium,* he quotes from the Greek version of the history of Agathangelos three passages from the life of St. Gregory the Illuminator of Armenia.[184] The first of these passages is almost identical to the one found in M (47^M), but for a few errors that occur in both M and the work of Nicephorus which point to a common source.

Another example, however, is more telling: Nicephorus cites about thirty Iconophile quotations in his as yet unpublished *Refutatio et eversio.*[185] Apart from the fact that most of them present quite a few variants in comparison with the F version, the following fragment appears among them (*Refutatio et eversio:* Paris. gr. 1250, fol. 259; Coislin. gr. 93, fol. 89):

. . . καὶ εἰς τὸν ἅγιον μάρτυρα . . . Βασιλίσκον τοιάδε λέγων· Τὰ μὲν περὶ τῆς ὑπομονῆς τοῦ ἀνδρός, ὅσα περὶ διηγήσεως, ταῦτα ἴσμεν· ἅτινα εἶδον ἐγὼ πολλάκις ἐν τοίχῳ γραφέντα καὶ φοβοῦντα πρὸ τῆς πείρας τοὺς ἀγνοοῦντας τῇ πείρᾳ τε τῆς βασάνου τὸ ἀφόρητον (lac.)· οἶδεν γὰρ καὶ γραφὴ σιωπῶσα λαλεῖν καὶ τὰ μέγιστα ὠφελεῖν.

This quotation, apart from the last sentence, which is derived from the *De sancto Theodoro* (*CPG* 3183; *PG* 46, 737D), is unattested in any source except F (in all P, M, V).

Compare the various transmissions of this fragment:

[182] See ibid., 195–97 where I try to identify Nicetas *monazon* with Nicetas of Medicion.

[183] See *PG* 99, 357B–D, 364A–365A, = *Antirrheticus II;* 468B–469C = *Refutatio poem. Iconomach.;* and the new edition of his letters in G. Fatouros, *Theodori Studitae Epistulae, CFHB* 31.1–2, letters 57, 71, 221, 380, 393, 408, 416, 528, 532, etc. Note that the letter to Nicetas *monazon* is letter 499 in this edition, ibid., II, 737–38.

[184] *Nicephori Antirrhetica contra Eusebium,* ed. J. Pitra, *Spicilegium Solesmense,* I (Paris, 1852), 501–3.

[185] See Alexander, *Nicephorus,* 180–82, 242–62.

51^M, Mosqu. Hist. Mus. 265, fol. 239^v

Τοῦ ἁγίου Γρηγορίου τοῦ Νύσης· εἰς τὸν ἅγιον μάρτυρα Βασιλίσκον·
Τὰ μὲν περὶ τῆς τοῦ ἀνδρὸς ὑπομονῆς, ὅσα περὶ διηγήσεως ἤσμεν (sic)
ταῦτα· ἅτινα καὶ ἐγὼ ἐν τύχω (sic) πολλάκις ἰδὼν (sic) γραφέντα καὶ
φοβοῦντα πρὸ τῆς πείρας τοὺς ἀγνοοῦντας τῇ πείρᾳ τὰς βασάνους τὸ
ἀφόρητον. καὶ μετ᾽ ὀλίγα· οἶδεν γὰρ καὶ γραφὴ σιωπῶσα τὰ μέγιστα
ὠφελεῖν.

52*, Paris. gr. 1115, fol. 251^v; V 12, Ven. Marc. gr. 573, fol. 4^v

Τοῦ αὐτοῦ ἐκ τῆς αὐτοῦ ἑρμηνείας, (Φάσκει τε αὐτὸς καὶ ἐν ἑτέρω
χωρίω· V) Εἶδον ἐγὼ ἐν τοίχω πολλάκις γραφέντα θαύματα καὶ φοβοῦντα τὸ τῆς πείρας ἀγνοοῦντας τῇ πείρᾳ τε τῆς βασάνου τὸ ἀφόρητον
δεικνῦντα (-ς P)· οἶδεν γὰρ καὶ γραφὴ σιωπῶσα λαλεῖν καὶ τὰ μέγιστα ὠφελεῖν·

It is evident that both the M and PV versions supplement each other in
minor points, but Nicephorus relies entirely on the M one. This passage
offers the opportunity for a further remark: perhaps Nicephorus had at
his disposal a copy of the 770 τεῦχος which belonged to the same line of
transmission as M. This offers further support to the hypothesis produced
above that a direct(?) apograph of the τεῦχος of 770 was possibly brought to
Constantinople, while P and V derive from a different copy of the τεῦχος
made in 774/5.

Finally, a possible reconstruction of the "life" of the Iconophile florilegium
(F) would be the following.

After its compilation in the year 770, F was deposited in the papal *scrinium* among other official documents. It was then incorporated into a major
collection assembled in 774/5 (namely, the exemplar on which the whole of
P and possibly other manuscripts are based). After that, a copy of the 770
florilegium was taken to Constantinople in 785 along with the two synodal
letters of Pope Hadrian I by Peter and Peter, the papal legates.[186] This copy
had possibly been collated by Tarasius himself with other existing manu-

---

[186] Cf. *Liber Pontificalis,* I, 511–12:

Hic elegantissimus praesul atque fortissimus rectae fidei praedicator (= Hadrian I) dire-
xit missos suos, videlicet Petrum venerabilem virum archipresbiterum sanctae Romanae
ecclesiae, et Petrum religiosum abbatem venerabilis monasterii sancti Sabbae . . . , apud
imperatorem Constantinum et matrem eius Herenem, adhortans eos atque fideliter
praedicans per suas apostolicas syllabas pro sacris imaginibus erectione, qualiter per testimonia Scripturarum seu traditionum probabilium Patrum a priscis temporibus usque
actenus orthodoxe venerantur in sanctam catholicam et apostolicam Romanam ecclesiam.
For English translation see Davis, *The Lives,* 168–69.

scripts (as many as he was able to find) before being taken to Nicaea.[187] After the synod it was probably deposited in the patriarchal library where Nicephorus may have had the opportunity to consult or even copy it. Concerning the Roman original again, it is quite possible that Anastasius Bibliothecarius used it in the ninth century. Almost five hundred years later it was brought again to Constantinople in the form of the 774/5 collection or a copy of it, as is shown below in Chapter V.

In conclusion, the existence of F, or of a substantial part of it, at such an early period[188] is weighty evidence that the climax of Iconoclasm has to be placed during its first period culminating in the Council of Hiereia. The extent of the τεῦχος of 770—whose *membra disiecta* still survive in the abridged collections of Parisinus, Marcianus, and Mosquensis—and the florilegia of John of Damascus illustrate the intensity of the reaction caused by the measures of Leo III and especially Constantine V. The combined roles of East and West in this confrontation with Constantinople is apparent in F. It strikes one that the bulk of the hagiographic material included in it, with the sole exception of the fragment from the *Vita Pancratii,* consists of fragments from lives of Oriental saints whose cults were also established in Rome (St. Anastasius the Persian, Sts. Cyrus and John, etc.). It is plausible, perhaps, to suppose that most of this hagiographic material came to Rome along with the *Synodica Orientalium Patriarch.* of 765.

In the second period of Iconoclasm the absence of the massive florilegia of the first period is quite apparent. Nicephorus may have quoted about forty fragments in his works. The extracts in the works of Theodore the Studite are even fewer (no more than twenty-five), and the florilegium of Nicetas of Medicion is strong evidence of the decline of the use of florilegia. Does it also confirm the belief that the second period of Iconoclasm was already spiritually exhausted and its intellectual force did not call for the vigorous confrontation that generated the *Adversus Iconoclastas* and the flori-

---

[187] A passage from the *Vita Tarasii* (ed. I. A. Heikel, *Acta Societatis Scientiarum Fennicae* 17 [1891], 404.11–15) may offer some support for this hypothesis: Ταράσιος δὲ (after the unsuccessful convocation of an Iconophile council in August 786) πρὸς τὸ θεῖον ἱερατεῖον γενόμενος μηδὲν δειλίας σημεῖον ἐπιφερόμενος, τῆς ἀναιμάκτου θυσίας ἀπάρχεται καὶ μετὰ τὴν τελεσιουργὸν κοινωνίαν οἴκαδε ἴεται καὶ τῶν προτέρων πόνων περί τε τὴν θείαν γραφὴν καὶ τῶν πατρικῶν λογίων τὰς ἀποδείξεις ἐσχόλαζε καὶ αὖθις σύνοδον κροτηθῆναι τῶν ἀναγκαίων ἐτίθετο, ὡς μὴ τὴν αἱρετικὴν ἐπὶ τὸ χεῖρον προκόψαι κακόνοιαν. Another point is that Tarasius is probably the author of the *refutatio* of the *horos* of Hiereia (see Beck, *KThL,* 489). In this *refutatio,* which was obviously ready before the summoning of the Council of Nicaea, some Iconophile *testimonia* are included which can also be found in P and, of course, in the *Acta* (e.g., Asterius Amas., *Relatio in Euphemiam martyrem,* Mansi XIII 308A–309B).

[188] See also Déroche, "L'authenticité," 656 n. 7.

legium of 770? Perhaps M. Anastos is right in claiming that the Second Iconoclasm was not worthy of the reappraisal of P. Alexander,[189] because "the
florilegium of the Council of 815 does not advance beyond the iconoclastic
theology of the earlier period . . . The most that can be said is that the iconoclasts of 815 added 12 (or 28) patristic references to the florilegium of 754,
none of which, however, can be regarded as constituing an innovation or
substantial addition to the iconoclastic armory."[190] The parallel lives of the
Iconophile and Iconoclastic florilegia constitute a further proof of that.

---

[189] See Alexander, "The Iconoclastic Council," 37–57.

[190] M. Anastos, "The Ethical Theory of Images Formulated by the Iconoclasts in 754 and
815," *DOP* 8 (1954), 159. See also above Chap. I, note 108.

CHAPTER IV

On the Use of Florilegia by the Seventh Ecumenical Council, Nicaea II, 787

The textual study carried out in the previous chapter has proved, I hope beyond any reasonable doubt, that the text we read in the Mansi edition of the acts of Nicaea II is derived from the same source that provided the florilegia of John of Damascus and F. On numerous occasions, however, books were produced during the conciliar deliberations, and there is no reason to doubt their existence, but why does the Mansi edition provide texts so similar to the ones transmitted by all these earlier florilegia examined in Chapter III? Many hypotheses can be suggested. This chapter discusses several with no claim to a full coverage of their wide spectrum. However, some facts must be set forth before any further step.

The basic event that is of crucial interest for the present study took place during the beginning of the fourth session of Nicaea II. At that time Patriarch Tarasius ordered the presentation of the books of the holy fathers which spoke in favor of the images (Mansi XIII 4в): . . . γενήσεται δὲ τοῦτο πῶς; προσαγέσθωσαν εἰς μέσον ἡμῖν πρὸς ἀκρόασιν τῶν περιδόξων ἁγίων πατέρων αἱ βίβλοι· καὶ ἐξ αὐτῶν ἀρυόμενοι, ποτίσωμεν ἕκαστος ἡμῶν τὸ καθ᾽ ἡμᾶς ποίμνιον· . . . A little later Constantine, bishop of Constantia, was more explicit in repeating the order of Tarasius: (ibid. 4c): Κωνσταντῖνος ὁ ὁσιώτατος ⟨ἐπίσκοπος⟩ Κωνσταντίας Κύπρου εἶπε· κατὰ τὴν διαλαλιὰν Ταρασίου τοῦ ἁγιωτάτου καὶ οἰκουμενικοῦ πατριάρχου ἀγέσθωσαν εἰς μέσον αἱ βίβλοι καὶ αἱ ῥήσεις (Lat.: testimonia) τῶν μακαρίων πατέρων καὶ διαρρήδην τῇ ἁγίᾳ ταύτῃ συνόδῳ ἀναγνωσθήτωσαν.

As the session evolves it is clear that these words are carried out faithfully. The secretaries produce the books and read them, and on many occasions individual participants raise and offer particular books that are also read aloud. The following incident is more telling: in Mansi XIII 56A–80D, eighteen extracts derived from thirteen works are quoted.[1] Fifteen of these came from books offered by various monks and clerics, and only three were

[1] Quot. 18, 19, 36i–ii, 46iii, 37i–iii, 10, 15, 6, 4, 3, 38, 39i–ii, and 15 in Chap. III 5.

produced by the patriarchal secretaries.[2] The interval between the recitations is short: in some cases a monk stands up right after the completion of the citation and offers another book, the patriarchal secretary takes it and reads the extract immediately. So if one thinks of F being used on this occasion, then it must be admitted that the whole procedure was carefully stage-managed and that multiple copies of F and of the florilegia of John of Damascus had been prepared in advance for that purpose or that a single manuscript was simply changing hands. But still in four cases the same text was presented twice, once by the secretaries and again by individual participants, so exclusive utilization of F must be excluded. I will come to this hypothesis later on, but for the time being I will proceed with the discussion of my first hypothesis.

(I) The first hypothesis is that the books used for the acts had nothing to do with florilegia but simply belonged to a line of textual transmission very close to that of F. This, however, does not explain, among other things, the two different versions of the *Pratum spirituale* (see above, p. 204, no. 46 III) read during the fourth and the fifth sessions of the council.

(II) The second hypothesis is that F has copied the acts. This can more easily be excluded for a number of reasons. F was produced in 770; F copies John of Damascus (if not, then John of Damascus must have copied a pre-731 corpus that was later reproduced by F), the Greek original of the acts of the Roman Councils of 731 and 769, and other early florilegia. Finally, F should always agree with the acts against any authorized edition of any particular text, but this does not happen at all, as the collation of the texts shows (see above, pp. 192–202, nos. 35, 37, 39, 43, etc.).

(III) The third hypothesis needs much more discussion, and my approach is only tentative, since it deals with the legal aspect of the conciliar procedure on which I must admit lack of competency. According to my third suggestion, we should accept that only F (which included the florilegia of John of Damascus) was used by the seventh ecumenical council, along with a limited number of books, and the whole procedure of their presentation had been carefully prearranged. After all, the insistence on the pretense of the existence of actual books on the part of Nicaea II was an exceptional precaution. It was taken in response to the abuses of the Iconoclastic Council of Hiereia, which had allowed *testimonia* to be presented on loose sheets

---

[2] Quot. 15, 6, and 38 in Chap. III 5.

of paper, thus supporting their theses by texts of ambiguous authenticity and fragments taken out of context.

The organizing committee tried by this elaborate staging to eliminate any possible claim of forgery or encouragement of practices that they openly condemned, although the use of florilegia was part and parcel of the conciliar procedure (as described in Chapter I). This precaution was even more unnecessary in view of the good textual quality of most of the fragments in F. So even if books had to be presented for the sake of verisimilitude (διὰ τοῦ λόγου τὸ ἀληθές), the use of F would not have done any harm.

The use of florilegia and the prearrangement of the entire procedure are more easily understood if we place the whole conciliar procedure within its actual framework: that of a penal trial. Indeed, an ecumenical council can be defined as the highest ecclesiastical court[3] which was summoned only in exceptional cases in order to pass judgment on crimes of heresy. In this context the acts of a council can also be identified as the minutes of a trial.[4]

There is no need to describe in this context the function of other documents such as the *Epistula ad Synodum de Theodoro Mopsuesteno*, which was read during the first session of the fifth ecumenical council (above, p. 11) or the seven ἀναφοραὶ presented during the second session of the Lateran Council (above, p. 16). Likewise, I shall not try to assign to them a judicial term equivalent to the terms employed by any modern judicial system, be it British or Continental. For the florilegia, however, we can be sure that they had served as the basis of what in the modern British system is called "presentation of the written evidence."[5] With the assembly acting as a collective jury, this evidence was presented first in the form of orthodox florilegia[6] in

---

[3] See also S. Troianos, Ἡ ἐκκλησιαστικὴ δικονομία μέχρι τοῦ θανάτου τοῦ Ἰουστινιανοῦ (Athens, 1964), 30–36.

[4] See on the subject the very significant article of E. Chrysos, "Konzilsakten und Konzilsprotokolle vom 4. bis 7. Jahrhundert," *AHC* 15 (1983) 30–40. Chrysos makes the essential distinction between *Konzilsakten* as protocols of "nichtgerichtlichen Synoden" (ibid., 31) and *Konzilsprotokolle* as "eigentlichen Verhandlungsprotokolle der gerichtlichen Prozesse" (ibid., 32). Chrysos also gives a list of the *CPG* numbers which represent the *Konzilsprotokolle*. Needless to say, all the florilegia examined in Chapter I can be found under *CPG* numbers that represent conciliar sessions which Chrysos has classified as *Konzilsprotokolle*. There is only one exception: the florilegium of the fourth ecumenical council which, as I have stressed (above, pp. 8 ff), was not part of the proceedings proper. Furthermore, if we accept the position of Batiffol and Dvornik that "the ecclesiastical gatherings built up their procedure" on the procedures established by the Roman Senate (F. Dvornik, "Emperors, Popes and General Councils," *DOP* 6 [1951], 3–4 and nn. 1, 3 for further bibliography), the element of prearrangement finds its precedent, for this *modus operandi* was inherent in the gatherings of the Roman Senate (ibid., 4).

[5] On the subject, see some remarks from a purely legalistic point of view in S. Troianos, Ἡ ἐκκλησιαστικὴ διαδικασία μεταξὺ 565 καὶ 1204 (Athens, 1969), 114–16.

[6] In Nicaea II in 787, it was the quotations read out during the fourth and fifth sessions.

order to establish the pure orthodox doctrine, and second, in the form of heretical florilegia[7] in order to denote the opposition of the heretical views to the orthodox doctrine. In this way the participants, that is, the jury, were guided in the shaping of what in the Continental legal system is called "total judicial conviction"[8] (πλήρης δικανικὴ πεποίθηση in Greek) on the fact that the crime of heresy had been committed.

What appears, therefore, to be a theatrical performance is the routine operation of a legal system, and this is why the authority of the Lateran Council or the seventh ecumenical council has never been disputed on the basis of being a prearranged procedure. The requisites for a valid council are all assembled in a definition that was formulated shortly after the fifth ecumenical council in 553:

> Οἰκουμενικαὶ δὲ κατὰ τοῦτο ἐκλήθησαν μόναι αἱ πέντε σύνοδοι διότι ἐκ κελεύσεων βασιλικῶν κατὰ πᾶσαν τὴν τῶν Ῥωμαίων πολιτείαν ἀρχιερεῖς μετεκλήθησαν καὶ ⟨ἢ⟩ δι᾽ ἑαυτῶν παρεγένοντο ἢ τοποτηρητὰς ἀπέστειλαν· καὶ ὅτι ἐν ἑκάστῃ τῶν πέντε αὐτῶν συνόδων περὶ πίστεως ἡ ζήτησις γέγονε, καὶ ψῆφος ἤτοι ὅρος δογματικὸς ἐξενήνεκται . . . αἱ δὲ λοιπαὶ σύνοδοι μερι- καὶ γεγόνασιν, οὐ τῶν κατὰ πᾶσαν τὴν οἰκουμένην ἐπισκόπων με- τακληθέντων, οὐ δογματικόν τι ἐκθέμεναι, ἀλλ᾽ ἢ πρὸς βεβαίωσιν τῶν δογ- ματικῶς ταῖς προλαβούσαις ἁγίαις συνόδοις ὁρισθέντων, ἢ πρὸς καθαίρεσιν τῶν ἀσεβῶς αὐταῖς ἐναντιωθῆναι τολμησάντων, ἢ περὶ κανόνων καὶ ζητημάτων εἰς ἐκκλησιαστικὴν ὁρώντων εὐταξίαν τὰ δόξαντα ἔχειν καλῶς διατυπώσασθαι.[9]

No mention is made of any detailed requirements concerning the way a council should be conducted, yet there is a whole complex of regulations and canons that are followed with persistence by the participants at a council. These regulations can be defined as the corpus of Byzantine procedural canon law, about which we know very little. It may have been what Agathias defines as ἡ τῶν δικαστηρίων κομψεία[10] and was part of the stock-knowledge of the officers of the ἐν τῷ Βυζαντίῳ ἀρχεῖα.[11] Unfortunately there does not exist any manual on the subject, apart from a few dispersed and isolated rules and imperial decrees that pertain to judicial procedure. Nevertheless, the corpus of Byzantine procedural canon law can be restored with the help of the proceedings of the church councils, which are in fact the only extant

---

[7] In 787 it was the case of the *horos* of Hiereia and its Iconoclastic florilegium refuted in the sixth session.

[8] Conviction in the sense of persuading here.

[9] V. N. Beneševič, *Kanoničeskij Sbornik XIV titulov* (St. Petersburg, 1905), 78–79.

[10] The word is not attested in that sense by Lampe, Sophocles, and Liddell-Scott.

[11] *Agathiae Historiarum libri quinque*, ed. R. Keydell, *CFHB* 1 (Berlin, 1967), book 4.1.

detailed records of a Byzantine trial for that early period (4th–9th cent.), except for the sixth-century *P. Mich. XIII* 660–661.

In this corpus, provision was probably made for the use of florilegia, and the fact that the quotations included in the florilegia of the councils were usually of high textual quality and sometimes identical with the original text simply testifies to their significance as a means of the presentation of the evidence. But, still, I do not think that restrictions were imposed as to the form in which these texts should be presented. A florilegium or a book had simply to provide a good text, and this is what F could also have done. Any further investigation, however, belongs to the field of *Rechtsgeschichte*.

(IV) The fourth and last hypothesis is based on what I have written in Chapter I especially for the florilegia of the sixth ecumenical council. Recall that the emperor had asked the pope to send along with his delegates the books that would be used by the council.[12] Pope Agathon replied that he was sending his envoys to whom he had given the following items: . . . οἷστισι διακομισταῖς καὶ χρήσεις τινῶν ἁγίων πατέρων, οὓς ἐδέξατο ταύτῃ ἡ ἀποστολικὴ τοῦ Χριστοῦ ἐκκλησία, μετὰ τῶν βιβλίων αὐτῶν παραδεδώκαμεν . . . [13]

That the χρήσεις and the books were two separate things was proved during the tenth session of the council. In that session the Romans provided examples from the books which they had with them in order to verify the citations found in the dyotheletic florilegium which had also been brought from Rome (above, pp. 26–29).[14]

The following passage is much clearer on the subject. During the fourteenth *Actio* of the council, three bishops from Cyprus appeared and addressed the assembly in the following words:

Ἀναδιδάσκομεν τοὺς ἐνδοξοτάτους ὑμᾶς καὶ τὴν ἁγίαν καὶ οἰκουμενικὴν ὑμῶν σύνοδον, ὡς χρήσεις διαφόρων ἁγίων καὶ ἐκκρίτων πατέρων ἐπιφερόμεθα δηλούσας δύο φυσικὰ θελήματα . . . ἐν αἷς ἔγκειται χρῆσις τοῦ ἁγίου Ἀθανασίου τοῦ γενομένου ἀρχιεπισκόπου Ἀλεξανδρείας ἐκ τοῦ λόγου τοῦ ἐπιγεγραμμένου εἰς τὸ εὐαγγελικὸν ῥητὸν τὸ φάσκον· νῦν ἡ ψυχή μου τετάρακται· ὕπεστι δὲ ἡμῖν κατὰ χώραν καὶ ἡ βίβλος τοῦ αὐτοῦ ἁγίου Ἀθανασίου ἡ ἔχουσα ἐφ᾽ ὁλοκλήρῳ τὸν τοιοῦτον αὐτοῦ λόγον. εἰσελθόντων δὲ

---

[12] *ACO Ser. II*, vol. II,1, 6.11: στεῖλαι (sc. the pope) ἄνδρας . . . ἐπιφερομένους καὶ τὰς βίβλους, ἃς δέον ἐστὶ προαχθῆναι.

[13] Ibid., 56.20-22.

[14] See also Sansterre, *Les moines grecs*, 178: "Agathon précisa qu'il avait remis aux légats 'des citations des saints Pères . . . avec les livres eux-mêmes'. Cette dernière affirmation suggère que les envoyés romains emportèrent les trente-neuf écrits cités dans le florilège et non pas seulement les ouvrages mentionnés plus haut."

ἡμῶν ἀρτίως ἐνταῦθα κατὰ κέλευσιν τοῦ εὐσεβεστάτου . . . ἡμῶν βασιλέως
καὶ ἀναζητησάντων βίβλους ὧν ἐπιφερόμεθα πατρικῶν χρήσεων εἰς τὸ ταύτας προκομίσαι τῇ ἁγίᾳ ὑμῶν συνόδῳ, εὕρομεν χαρτῷον παλαιότατον
βιβλίον ἔχον διαφόρους ὁμιλίας τοῦ αὐτοῦ ἁγίου Ἀθανασίου . . . [15]

The above passage is sufficient evidence for the fact that the word χρήσεις
was a *terminus technicus* that defined a collection of quotations/fragments extracted from an entire work or a number of works and presented in the
form of a florilegium.

In addition to the sixth ecumenical council, the Iconoclastic Synod of
St. Sophia in 815 used copies of the entire books from which they had compiled the Iconoclastic florilegium (above, pp. 34–35). We then come to the
question of whether the same thing happened at the seventh ecumenical
council.

I would suggest that a positive answer may best solve the problems of
Nicaea II, but what testimonies do we have for this? The first is found in
the words of bishop Constantine of Constantia, cited from the Mansi edition
in the beginning of the present chapter. He actually asks for the βίβλοι and
the ῥήσεις to be brought forward, but the emendation of the word ῥήσεις to
χρήσεις is necessary. Χρήσεις is not only supported by the Latin translation
of Anastasius (*testimonia*), but appears in one very basic manuscript that preserves the acts, Vat. gr. 836, fol. 35 line 5. To this I may add the following
passage which may remove any doubt. It was written by the later Patriarch
Nicephorus, who took part in this council, and is taken from his *Apologeticus
minor pro sacris imaginibus* (*PG* 100, 848в): Ὅτι καὶ περὶ τῆς προσκυνήσεως τῶν
ἱερῶν εἰκόνων χρήσεις πολλαὶ προσηνέχθησαν τῷ εὐσεβεῖ ἡμῶν βασιλεῖ, δι' ὧν
ἔδει τὴν πληροφορίαν πᾶσι τοῖς ἐντυγχάνουσιν ἀνενδοιάστως γενέσθαι, ὧν τὰ
ὁλόκληρα βιβλία ἡ σύνοδος εἶχεν, ὡς οἱ τῶν εὑρεθέντων ἐν αὐτῇ περιόντες σὺν
τῇ ἀληθείᾳ μαρτυροῦσιν.

So, despite Van den Ven's claim (see above, p. 2), the witness of a participant at the seventh ecumenical council shows things under a different light:
the seventh ecumenical council had books together with florilegia. This
must be the correct hypothesis since, apart from the Iconophile quotations
in the acts of 787, one can count approximately twenty-five patristic and
synodic *testimonia* that were totally irrelevant to the veneration of icons. Quotations such as the fifty-third Apostolic Canon and the eighth canon of the
first ecumenical council (Mansi XII 1020е–1022в), which deal with the obligation of Christians to accept repenting heretics, are not to be found in any
of the Iconophile florilegia examined thus far. There is no reason, therefore,

[15] *ACO Ser. II,* vol. II,2, 656.3–14.

to deny the use of books on the part of the organizing committee, as far as the non-icon-related *testimonia* (plus a few Iconophile ones, listed above in Chap. III, section 5) are concerned.

For the vast majority of the Iconophile excerpts, there may have been no other source than F for two additional reasons: first, because F included a number of *testimonia* that had already been selected by a person as distinguished as John of Damascus, and, second, because the majority of them (with the exception of the *Narratio* of John of Jerusalem) had been officially approved by the Roman Councils of 731 and 769.

The possibility that the florilegium was the unique source of the acts in most of the cases is stronger, for when Nicephorus speaks about books and χρήσεις, he does so in order to enhance the presence of books and not of the florilegium. His overall persuasion and his position when he wrote that work advocate this.[16] But even if we accept that for every Iconophile passage that appears in the acts, the council had at its disposal the respective books, it seems that the secretaries finally inserted in the protocols the text from F.

Finally, the assumption that χρήσεις and books were two different things opens the door to a possibile explanation of a peculiarity of Parisinus. As we have seen (above, pp. 118 and 129), Parisinus offers eleven short Iconophile quotations extracted from works of Dionysius the Areopagite and, additionally, two very extensive passages from the work to which these quotations belong. Should one see in the two extensive Dionysian passages excerpts from the βίβλοι? Or, in other words, does this entail that F included both the χρήσεις and the βίβλοι? It is possible that the Romans provided not only the Iconophile florilegium but also the books that were used for the compilation of F. This would not be the first time this happened. As we saw in Chapter I, the same situation existed ninety-seven years earlier, during the sixth ecumenical council.

---

[16] The work was written between 813 and 815 while Nicephorus was still patriarch (see Alexander, *Nicephorus,* 182). During that period problems of pro-Iconophile or pro-Iconoclast documentation had begun to be investigated again (appointment of an Iconoclast committee by Leo V in order to compile an Iconoclastic florilegium, etc.).

CHAPTER V

The Archetype of Codex Parisinus Graecus 1115, the *Liber de Fide Trinitatis (Libellus)* of Nicholas of Cotrone, and the Treatise *Contra Errores Graecorum* of Thomas Aquinas

In the preceding chapters I have claimed that the original of codex Parisinus Graecus 1115 was a Roman product because of the presence of the pro-Latin florilegium contained in fols. 181–219ᵛ. Some originally Greek Iconophile *testimonia* that were retranslated into Greek after they had been translated into Latin offered additional support to this thesis, for their presence was possible only in Rome.

This chapter attempts to dispel any doubt that may have lingered regarding the Roman provenance of this original and to shed further light on its history during the thirteenth century. I shall follow an inverted process, starting from the remotest repercussions of the original of P and then focusing, step by step, on their cause.

1. The Treatise *Contra Errores Graecorum* of Thomas Aquinas and the *Libellus* of Nicholas of Cotrone[1]

It is well known that the *Contra errores Graecorum* of Thomas Aquinas constitutes a kind of theological commentary on the contents of a *Libellus* submitted to him by Pope Urban IV (1261–64). In the introduction to this work the author wrote: "Libellum ab excellentia vestra mihi exhibitum, sanctissime pater Urbane papa, diligenter perlegi, in quo inveni plurima ad nostrae fidei assertionem utilia expressa." He then proceeded to examine the conformity of the contents of this *Libellus,* which consisted of a great number of quotations from the Oriental fathers, with the beliefs of the Roman Catholic Church on the *Filioque* issue. The problem of the authenticity of the fragments did not concern him; his work concentrated on the explanation of

[1] *Sancti Thomae de Aquino Opera omnia iussu Leonis XIII P.M. edita,* Tomus XL, *Contra Errores Graecorum,* ed. H. F. Dondaine (Rome, 1969) (hereafter *CEG*).

dubia and the use of the Oriental authorities within a theological framework. One of the main problems he had to overcome was the *de verbo ad verbum* translation which resulted in a very poor Latin text and the liberties which in some cases the translator took, thus altering substantially—in favor of the *Filioque*—what the Greek author had in mind.

At any rate, since the request of Urban IV was limited to a theological judgement, Thomas Aquinas responded obediently to this and examined or cited as many as 205 quotations of Greek fathers. For five of them the modern editor of the work reckons that they belong "à la documentation courante des scolastiques," and the remaining two hundred "trouvent leur répondant exact dans le *Liber* exhumé par Uccelli [= the *Libellus*]."[2]

What was this *Libellus* and who wrote it? All the problems related to this work have been resolved beyond any doubt by H. F. Dondaine, who also edited the *Libellus* as an appendix to the *Contra errores Graecorum*. I may briefly repeat here his main conclusions. The *Liber de fide Trinitatis, ex diversis auctoritatibus sanctorum grecorum confectus contra grecos,* or simply *Libellus,* is a very extensive florilegium of 112 quotations excerpted from works of Greek fathers and, in some instances, from synodal acts. It is preserved in only one Latin manuscript (Vat. lat. 808) and is divided into four unequal parts (*tractatus*), the first of which deals with the procession of the Holy Spirit (chaps. 1–93).[3] In the words of the editor: "C'est le corps principal de l'ouvrage, celui que l'épître finale présente à son destinataire."[4] The other three *tractatus* give the impression of appendices to the first one and are concerned with the following issues: *De primatu Romanae ecclesie* (chaps. 94–104), *De azymis* (chaps. 105–10), and *De purgatorio* (chaps. 111–12).

The *Libellus* closes with a dedicatory letter (chap. 113) that contains valuable historical information. The author addresses himself to a Byzantine emperor and offers his work as an answer to a question submitted to him by the emperor (*Libellus,* chap. 113):

> Ecce luce clarius in presenti volumine iam habet theodocta tui sacri imperii celsitudo, o panphron, (id est) omnimode sapiens, clementissime imperator semper auguste, quod sitibundo corde cupiebas audire: scilicet unde et a quibus auctoritatibus sacrosancta catholica mater ecclesia habuit locum addendi in sacro et divo simbolo divorum et sanctorum patrum filioque procedit.

[2] H. F. Dondaine, *CEG,* A8.
[3] Reference to the quotations is made according not to the page number but to the number assigned to each paragraph (*Capitulum*) by the editor (e.g., chap. 28).
[4] *CEG,* A9.

As this passage does not refer to any subject other than the procession of the Holy Spirit, it is evident that the original part of the *Libellus* has to be confined to the first *tractatus* (chaps. 1–93), the remaining three being a later addition. This passage explains the reason and the occasion on which the *Libellus* had been compiled,[5] but still some information is required: who was the author of this *Libellus*, who was the emperor that received it, and, finally, when did the composition of the work take place? Since it is addressed to a Byzantine emperor, the Greek language is, in all probability, the original one and the text of Vat. lat. 808 is obviously a later translation.

There is a Greek document that answers either directly or indirectly all these above questions. Theodore II Laskaris (30 Oct. 1254–30 Nov. 1258), the emperor of Nicaea, composed a *sermo* under the title: Λόγος ἀπολογητικὸς πρὸς ἐπίσκοπον Κοτρώνης κατὰ Λατίνων περὶ τοῦ Ἁγίου Πνεύματος.[6] In the *exordium* of this *sermo* we read:

> Ἐπειδὴ ἐρώτησιν ὑπέθετο ἡ βασιλεία μου πρὸς σέ, ὦ ἱερώτατε ἐπίσκοπε Κοτρώνης, ἀπολογήσασθαι τῇ βασιλείᾳ μου ὅπως ἡ ἁγιωτάτη τοῦ Θεοῦ μεγάλη ἐκκλησία ἡ πρεσβυτέρα Ῥώμη δογματίζει περὶ τῆς ἐκπορεύσεως τοῦ Ἁγίου Πνεύματος, καὶ ἀπολογίαν ἔθου πρὸς τὴν βασιλείαν μου ὅπως ἡ ἁγιωτάτη τοῦ Θεοῦ μεγάλη ἐκκλησία οὕτως σεβάζεται περὶ τῆς ἐκπορεύσεως τοῦ Ἁγίου Πνεύματος, οὐ μόνον ἐκ τοῦ Πατρὸς ἔχειν τὴν ἐκπόρευσιν, ἀλλὰ καὶ ἐκ τοῦ Υἱοῦ, ἀπολογεῖταί σοι ἡ βασιλεία μου ὅτι ἡ καθ᾽ ἡμᾶς ἁγιωτάτη τοῦ Θεοῦ μεγάλη ἐκκλησία, . . . τὸ Πνεῦμα τὸ Ἅγιον ἐκ τοῦ Πατρὸς καὶ μόνου ἐκπορεύεσθαι δογματίζει.[7]

The author (or better the compiler) of the *Libellus* has been identified as Nicholas (*PLP* 20413), bishop of Cotrone (the ancient and modern Croton).[8] I recapitulate the data of his life since they are of importance for the history of the original of P, as will be discussed below.

[5] For more details, see below, pp. 250–51.

[6] Ed. H. B. Swete, *Theodorus Laskaris Junior: De processione Spiritus Sancti oratio apologetica* (London, 1875).

[7] Ibid., 1.1–2.13.

[8] See A. Dondaine, "Nicolas de Cotrone et les sources du Contra errores Graecorum de Saint Thomas," in *Divus Thomas* 28 (1950), 324–32. Beck, *KThL,* 675 f. For more on Nicholas, based on the scanty information provided by Pachymeres (ed. A. Failler, *Georges Pachymérès, Relations historiques,* CFHB 24.2 [Paris, 1984], 463.13–20), see K. M. Setton, "The Byzantine Background to the Italian Renaissance," *Proceedings of the American Philological Society* 100 (1956), 36; D. J. Geanakoplos, *Emperor Michael Palaeologus and the West (1258–1282)* (Cambridge, Mass., 1959), 176–79, 267 n. 38a; D. M. Nicol, "The Greeks and the Union of the Churches: The Preliminaries to the Second Council of Lyons, 1261–1274," in *Medieval Studies Presented to Aubrey Gwynn, S. J.,* ed. J. A. Watt, J. B. Morrall, and F. X. Martin (Dublin, 1961), 457; R. J. Loenertz, "Notes d'histoire et de chronologie byzantines," *REB* 20 (1962), 173–75. B. Roberg, *Die Union zwischen*

Nicholas of Cotrone was a native Greek of Dyrrachium (Durazzo) in Albania, who entered the service of the papal curia possibly some time during the second quarter of the thirteenth century. The first dated document that refers to him is a letter of Pope Innocent IV addressed to John of Aversa (2 Sept. 1254). Therein the pope asked John of Aversa, a provincial minister of the Fratres Minores in Calabria, to install in the bishopric of Cotrone (Croton) "dilectum filium magistrum Nicolaum de Durachio, camerae nostrae clericum, in latina et graeca lingua peritum."[9] But as the episcopal throne of Croton was by that time occupied by a usurper named Maur, the result was, in all probability, that "Nicolas portera désormais le nom d'un siège épiscopal dont il n'a probablement jamais pris possession."[10]

Mention has already been made of the Λόγος ἀπολογητικὸς πρὸς ἐπίσκοπον Κοτρώνης of Theodore Laskaris. We do not know why Nicholas was chosen by the emperor of Nicaea as the addressee of his theological ἐρώτησις, but the fact that Nicholas was acquainted with both the Latin and Greek tongues must have been decisive. On the other hand, it also implies that he was already known to the Byzantines as one of the very few possible intermediaries between two worlds separated by the gap of language.[11]

We also do not know what his answer to the question of the emperor was, but, if we assume that he made a first draft of the *Libellus,* then it was no doubt written in Greek and not in Latin. A quick glance at chapter 113 will be enough to prove this point. The phrase "Ecce luce clarius in presenti volumine iam habet theodocta tui sacri imperii celsitudo, o *panphron,* (id est) omnimode sapiens" could have existed only if the translation went from Greek to Latin and not vice versa.[12]

Another document that is mainly dedicated to Nicholas of Cotrone is a

---

der griechischen und der lateinischen Kirche auf dem II. Konzil von Lyon, Bonner Historische Forschungen 24 (Bonn, 1964), 45–52; G. Dagron, "Byzance et l'Union," in *1274 Année charnière, mutations et continuités,* Colloques Internationaux du Centre National de la Recherche Scientifique 558 (Paris, 1977), 192; G. Podskalsky, "Orthodoxe und westliche Theologie," *JÖB* 31.2 (1981), 514 n. 6; G. Patacsi, "Le Hieromoine Hierothée, théologien du Saint-Esprit," *KΛHPONOMIA* 13 (1981), 303–5. Also N. Festa, "Ancora la lettera di Michele Paleologo a Clemente IV," *Bessarione* 4–6 (1899–1900), 531 f. Most significant for this study is, however, the article by P. Sambin, "Il Vescovo Cotronese Niccolò da Durazzo e un inventario di suoi codici latini e greci (1276)," in *Note e discussioni erudite a cura di Augusto Campana,* Vol. III (Rome, 1954).

[9] See F. Ughelli–N. Coleti, *Italia Sacra,* vol. IX (Venice, 1721), col. 385.

[10] A. Dondaine, "Nicolas de Cotrone," 324.

[11] On this problem, see Roberg, *Union,* 248 ff.

[12] See more examples of this sort in A. Dondaine, "Nicolas de Cotrone," 318. I may note here that chap. 113 was certainly not addressed to Theodore II but to Michael VIII; see below, p. 248.

letter of Michael VIII Palaeologus to Pope Urban IV written in the spring
of 1263 (or 1264). After the formal address to the pope, and the recognition
of the primacy of the latter within the whole Christian church, the emperor
gives a brief exposition of the problems that the negotiations aimed at the
union of the churches stumbled on, mainly due to the lack of competent
interpreters. Then he proceeds to pay tribute to the contribution of Nicholas of Cotrone to the essential progress of the negotiations. It is worth citing
the entire passage of the letter because it is extremely important for the
information it provides:

> Cumque quarto anno nostri imperii primo praeterito vox laetitiae
> ab Occidente cor nostrum tetegerit et insonuerit auribus nostris, quae
> animi nostri accendit affectum, quod a patria et origine gentis nostrae,
> Romaeorum generationis, divina gratia planta proveniens et de viventi
> viridario transplantata et ad hortum similem inserta sanctae Matris Ro-
> manae Ecclesiae atque litteris sacris et scientia divinae Scripturae et
> dogmatibus utriusque Ecclesiae adornat et inspiratione Sanctissimi
> Spiritus animata et augmentata, ad fructum odoris perveniens, ad Im-
> perium nostrum se transportavit Nicolaus videlicet venerabilis praesul
> Citthroniensis [= Cotroniensis], de quo per multorum relationes viro-
> rum venerabilium, veritatem dicentium, sensimus ipsum esse Dei cul-
> torem diligentem et catholicae fidei discretum et verum praedicatorem
> et omnibus sermonibus suae fidei sine personarum acceptionem zela-
> torem reuniendae communis nostrae Matris Ecclesiae, sine falsitate
> utriusque partis verum dispensatorem divinae Scripturae et quae sunt
> Sanctorum Patrum bene expositorem. Cui tertio anno nostri Imperii
> tranquillitatis animi nostri litteras direximus rogantes eundem, qua-
> tenus amore Dei, patriae et omnium nostrorum, *clandestine* ad maie-
> statis nostrae praesentiam personaliter se conferret, ut ex ore ipsius
> veritatem fidei quam confitetur sancta et catholica Romana Dei Ecclesia
> et doctrinam divinarum Scripturarum quam ad eruditionem proponit
> ipsa Romana Ecclesia et formam vestri divini Sacramenti immediate
> graeco audiremus sermone necnon hauriremus vestram et vestrorum
> fratrum plenariam voluntatem. Ipse autem Dei spiritu motus in hac
> hieme praeterita, in vigiliis Dei Christi Nativitatis, ad Imperium no-
> strum accessit, quo viso laetati fuimus acsi sanctae paternitatis vestrae
> faciem videremus. Qui omnia quae sunt verae fidei per ordinem resera-
> vit, quae recte percepimus et corde et animo illustrati invenimus san-
> ctam Dei Ecclesiam Romanam non alienatam a nobis in divinis suae
> fidei dogmatibus, sed ea fere nobiscum sentientem et concantantem.
> Praedictus namque praesul eiusdem Ecclesiae doctrinam et Sanctorum
> Patrum eius, videlicet sancti Silvestri papae, Damasi, Coelestini, Aga-

thonis, Adriani, Leonis Maioris et Junioris, Gregorii Dialogi, Hylarii Pictaviensis, Ambrosii Mediolanensis, Augustini Hypponensis Africae, Hieronymi, Fulgentii et aliorum expositiones et dogmata rectae fidei reseravit nostro Imperio, sicut ista Sancti exposuerunt praedicti; quae invenimus concordantia sermonibus Sanctorum Patrum eius, videlicet Athanasii Alexandrini, Basilii Caesareae Cappadociae, Gregorii magni theologi, Gregorii Nisseni, Iohannis Chrysostomi cum utroque Cyrillo et similia sapientes omnino, quae cum omni fide purissima percepimus, veneramur, credimus et tenemus . . . [13]

The letter reiterates the acceptance of papal primacy and closes with the request by the emperor for the completion of the union of the churches.[14] To sum up the main points of this passage: Nicholas is described as a faithful defender of the union of the churches, with much experience in the works of the Oriental and Latin fathers and holy scripture. It is made clear that Nicholas arrived in secret in Constantinople on the eve of Christmas Day of 1262[15] after a written invitation sent to him by the emperor. After his arrival he undertook to explain the dogmas of the Catholic church and to give a picture of the agreement between the works of the Greek and Latin fathers, something that seems to have encouraged the emperor to further pursue the completion of the union.

It must be stressed that one of the main reasons for which the emperor seemed to be so satisfied was that he heard the whole *expositio fidei* of the Roman church "immediate graeco sermone." Now, since the passage of the letter where mention of the correspondence of the Latin to the Greek fathers is made is almost identical with a small part of chapter 113 of the *Libellus,*[16] there should be no doubt that Nicholas of Cotrone performed his dogmatic exposition based on the *Greek* original of the *Libellus.* According to A. Dondaine, "Toutefois il est évident que l'exposé verbal fait devant Michel Paléologue s'appuyait sur une documentation écrite. Nicolas de Cotrone aura eu recours à son traité composé au temps de Théodore Laskaris."[17]

[13] See, A. Tăutu, *Acta Urbani IV, Clementis IV, et Gregorii X* (Vatican City, 1953), 39.

[14] Ibid., 40.

[15] Or 1263, according to Tăutu, ibid., 40.

[16] *Libellus,* chap. 113: . . . Quoniam quidem teneris et debes recipere beatum dictum Ylarium catholice fidei doctorem et contemporaneum magno patri Athanasio, sicut et recipis eundem sanctum Athanasium: et sicut recipis magnum Basilium, recipere et eius contemporaneum magnum patrem Ambrosium: et sicut recipis beatum Gregorium Nazanzenum, magnum theologum, recipere et eius consimilem . . . magnum patrem Augustinum . . . etc. On the subject see more in A. Dondaine, "Nicolas de Cotrone," 332–33. For the possible contribution of Nicholas to the composition of the 1264 letter of Michael VIII to the pope, see ibid., 333–34.

[17] Ibid., 333.

2. The *Libellus* and the Archetype of Paris. gr. 1115

Here we come to a crucial question: since in the words of Michael VIII this *exposé* was made in Greek, what was the written document that was utilized for this purpose? The answer to this cannot be other than the original of codex Paris. gr. 1115, which was taken to Constantinople by Nicholas of Cotrone on Christmas Eve of the year 1262 (or 1263 according to Tăutu). This needs to be proved in detail. Compare the following fragments:

(1) Paris. gr. 1115, fol. 195ᵛ (quot. 165)

Τοῦ ἁγίου Γρηγορίου Νύσης ἐκ τοῦ βίου τοῦ ἁγίου Γρηγορίου τοῦ Θαυμα-
τουργοῦ· Ἀκοῦσαι γὰρ λέγεται παρὰ τῆς ἐν γυναικείω φανείσης τῷ σχήματι
παρακαλούσης τὸν εὐαγγελιστὴν Ἰωάννην φανερῶσαι τῷ νέῳ τὸ τῆς ἀ-
ληθείας μυστήριον· ἐκεῖνον δέ . . . οὕτως εἰπόντα τὸν λόγον . . . πάλιν μεταστῆναι τῶν ὄψεων·

Ὡς (εἷς leg.) Θεὸς καὶ πατὴρ λόγου ζῶντος σοφίας ὑφεστώσης καὶ δυνάμεως καὶ χαρακτῆρος ἰδίου . . . Ἓν Πνεῦμα ἅγιον . . . εἰκὼν τοῦ υἱοῦ
τελείου τελεία . . . οὔτε οὖν ἐνέλειπέ ποτε υἱὸς πατρί, οὔτε υἱῷ τὸ Πνεῦμα
. . .

Libellus, chap. 55

(Gregorius Cesariensis). Dictus beatus Gregorius Cesariensis episcopus in expositione Spiritus quam Iohannes Evangelista eidem revelavit: Unus Deus Pater verbi viventis, sapientie existentis et virtutis. et paulo post: Spiritus Sanctus est ymago Filii perfecti. et iterum: non enim aliquando deficit Patri Filius, neque Filio Spiritus. Et hic Gregorius fuit ante Nicenam synodum.

It is evident that Nicholas translated single phrases from the more extended original of P, substituting some sentences for the formula "et paulo post" or "et iterum" and omitting words.

(2) Paris. gr. 1115, fol. 181ᵛ (quot. 134)

Τοῦ αὐτοῦ (= Ἀγ. Ἐπιφανίου) ἐκ τοῦ αὐτοῦ βιβλίου καὶ τοῦ λόγου τοῦ
περὶ τῶν δερματίνων χιτώνων· Περὶ τούτου ὁ Κύριός φησιν· ὅταν ἔλθη ὁ
παράκλητος, τὸ πνεῦμα τῆς ἀληθείας, ὃ παρὰ τοῦ πατρὸς ἐκπορεύεται ἐκεῖνος μαρτυρήσει περὶ ἐμοῦ· καὶ αὖθις μετὰ βραχύ. Εἰ τοίνυν παρὰ τοῦ πατρὸς ἐκπορεύεται καὶ ἐκ τοῦ ἐμοῦ φησιν ὁ Κύριος λήψεται, ὃν τρόπον
οὐδεὶς ἔγνω τὸν πατέρα εἰ μὴ ὁ υἱός, καὶ τὸν υἱὸν εἰ μὴ ὁ πατήρ, οὕτω τολμῶ
λέγειν οὐδὲ τὸ πνεῦμα εἰ μὴ ὁ πατὴρ καὶ ὁ υἱός, ἐξ οὗ λαμβάνει καὶ παρ'
οὗ ἐκπορεύεται.

Libellus, chap. 79

Idem in eodem (= de vestibus pellicinis Ade et Eve contra Origenistas): Cum venerit ille Spiritus veritatis, docebit vos in omnem veritatem, non enim loquetur a semet ipso sed quecumque audiet loquetur et que ventura sunt annuntiabit vobis; ille me clarificabit, quia de meo accipiet et annuntiabit vobis, si igitur a padre procedit, et de meo accipiet dicit Dominus, secundum quem modum nemo novit Patrem nisi Filius, neque Filium novit quis nisi Pater, sic audeo dicere, neque Spiritum novit quis nisi Pater et Filius a quo accipit et a quo procedit; neque Filium et Patrem novit quis nisi Spiritus Sanctus . . . etc.

This example depicts a situation quite different from that of example no. 1: P not only omits a sentence, inserting in its place the formula καὶ αὖθις μετὰ βραχύ, but also gives a passage five or six lines shorter than that of the *Libellus*. Moreover, the *Libellus* displays a more detailed lemma and has included one more passage from the same λόγος. Still, the original of P is the only possible source for the *Libellus*. The disputed clause . . . καὶ ὁ υἱός, ἐξ οὗ λαμβάνει καὶ παρ' οὗ ἐκπορεύεται, which in its syntax favors the *Filioque,* was discussed above (Chap. II, section 7). The Latin translation is obviously based on exactly this particular formulation (. . . et Filius a quo accipit et a quo procedit), so there is no difficulty in this matter. On the other hand, it should be accepted that the part which is missing from P certainly existed in its exemplar and it is Cinnamus again who perpetrated the shortening.

This point will be clarified by the next example.

(3) Fragments from four of the five books of the *Adversus Eunomium* of St. Basil (*CPG* 2837 and 2571 for books IV–V which are not genuine; *PG* 29, 497–772) are included in the *Filioque* florilegium of P, and also appear among the chapters of the *Libellus*. The following is a list of all the quotations in P (= quotations 209, 215–25, 228i–xi) and the *Libellus* with their respective references to the *Patrologia Graeca*.

P	= PG 29	*Libellus* (chap.) =	PG 29
1. fol. 208	649c3–652a6/b7–c1		
2.		56	653b–656a
3.		57	657b–660a
4. fol. 210^{r-v}	680d1–681a14		
5. fol. 210^v	661b7–12		
6.	713c12–716a4		
7.	713b1–13/661b13–8/		
	664a8–11		
8. fols. 210^v–211	668a4–d1		
9.	669c8–14		

P	= PG 29	*Libellus* (chap.) =	PG 29
10. fol. 211ʳ⁻ᵛ	681c10–684a6/c5–9/		
	685a2–8		
11. fol. 211ᵛ	692d1–4/736b2–8/		
	748c1 ff./752b6–8/		
	753a11–b3		
12.	732a4–15	58	732a–c
13. fols. 211ᵛ–212	733c7–736b8		
14. fols. 212–213	768b12–773b14		
15. fols. 213ᵛ–215ᵛ	725a15–b9/725c1–2/		
	728d2–729a6/		
	729a6–15/732a3/		
	732a4–9/732a9–15/		
	732b1–9/ b13–c4/		
	733a11–14/	58	732a–c
	733a14–b3/		
	736a5–b5/b5–7		
	736d1–3/737a1 ff.	59	737a
	744c7–15	62	744b–d
	745a13–b4	61	745a–b
	745b12–748c2/		
	753a11–c1/	63	754a–b
	760d4–761a10	64	769a/772b–d
	772c11–13/d1–4		

It is easy to observe that P and the *Libellus* display partly corresponding parts of a common original. It is not necessary to juxtapose a fragment from P and its translation by Nicholas, as it will not give anything more than what is provided by the first two examples, but it is worth paying much attention to the following piece of information. On fol. 215, P reads: Ὅτι οὐκ ἀπὸ ὁμωνυμίας ταυτότητος, ἀλλὰ φύσεως θείας ἑνότητος γνωρίζεται. This sentence appears in *PG* 29, 748c1–2. In the margin, by the side of this subtitle there is the following *rubrica* by the hand of Cinnamus: καὶ μετὰ γ΄ φύλλα. The excerpt that comes next (Τί δὲ ἐναντιοῦτε (sic)—καὶ πνεῦμα στόματος) corresponds to *PG* 29, 753a11–c1, and is interrupted by another *rubrica* that reads: καὶ μεθ᾽ ἕτερα δ΄ φύλλα. Needless to say, the fragment that comes next is to be found a little further on in *PG* 29, 760d4–761a10 (Σπεῖρα γάρ ἐστιν— εἴη μετὰ πάντων ὑμῶν). Finally, the next *rubrica* reveals another omission by Cinnamus: Καὶ ἀλλαχῇ περὶ τοῦ πνεύματος ὁ αὐτὸς ἐν τῷ τέλει τοῦ λόγου, and the quotation that follows is not from the last book of the *Adversus Eunomium* but from a small treatise *De Spiritu* which seemingly was usually copied during the Middle Ages as an appendix to the collection of the five books of the *Adversus Eunomium*. As it is included in *PG* in the same order, it is, again, some columns further on (772c11–13/ D1–4).

I have claimed on many occasions and, with the help of other manuscripts, proved that Cinnamus deliberately omitted not only words, sentences, and extensive passages from his archetype but, on some occasions, whole works that were originally included in the manuscript brought by Nicholas of Cotrone to Constantinople. These three *rubricae* are additional evidence that confirms my assumption. Cinnamus omitted extensive parts from the fifth book of *Adversus Eunomium*, but he was sincere enough to warn the reader about this abridgement. It is, therefore, highly possible that the original of P included all five books of the *Adversus Eunomium* plus the small treatise *De Spiritu*.

On the other hand, it is also evident that Nicholas of Cotrone included in his *Libellus* the Latin translation of some other parts from the same work which in some cases are also abridged in P.

(4) Another passage that supports the dependence of the *Libellus* on the original of P is the following:

Libellus, chap. 81
Iohannes Chrysostomus. Sanctus Iohannes Crisostomus patriarcha Constantinopolitanus, in sermone de epiphania Domini: Hic est Filius meus, qui una mecum mittit ex se spiritum sanctum.

The editor of the *Libellus* was unable to locate this piece in the works of St. John Chrysostom and simply registered it as a *fons non repertus*.[18] However, this excerpt does occur twice in P, but is not to be found in any of the works of John Chrysostom stored in the data base of the *Thesaurus Linguae Graecae*. Compare the Latin translation with the Greek text of P: Paris. gr. 1115, fol. 182 and fol. 210. (quot. 140 and 212):

Τοῦ αὐτοῦ (fol. 182) Ἰωάννου τοῦ Χρυσοστόμου (fol. 210), ἐκ τοῦ λόγου τοῦ εἰς τὰ ἅγια Φῶτα· Οὗτός ἐστιν ὁ υἱός μου ὁ ἀγαπητός, ὁ σὺν ἐμοὶ πέμψας ὑφ᾽ (ἐφ᾽ fol. 210) ἑαυτὸν τὸ πνεῦμα τὸ ἅγιον.

The only reasonable inference is that the original of P was the source of the Latin excerpt in the *Libellus*.

(5) One equally significant fragment of the *Libellus* is this rather extensive one:

[18] *CEG*, A16.

Libellus, chap. 96

Synodus Calcedonensis. Incipit tomus, id est volumen terminativum, sanctorum sexcentorum et triginta patrum sancti Calcedonensis concilii. Sancta et universalis synodus dixit: "Sufficiat ad plenam orthodoxe fidei notitiam et firmam veritatem preclarum et summe sapiens et salutiferum hoc divum symbolum sacri et divi et infallibilis magni concilii Niceni, in hac sancta universali synodo iam consummatum et terminatum, de plena fide et veritate Patris et Filii et Spiritus Sancti et de aliis dogmatibus eiusdem fidei". Et circa finem tomi, omnibus terminatis, interdicitur ab eadem synodo "ut nulli amodo liceat aliam fidem credere, scribere et predicare". Et tandem laudes extollit sacrosancta synodus beato et universali Pape Leoni. Dicit enim: "Omnes nos cum sanctis trecentis decem et octo patribus apud Niceam congregatis, necnon et cum centum quinquaginta patribus in urbe imperiali congregatis, et etiam cum ducentis patribus apud Ephesum convenientibus, clamamus et dicimus: Sic credimus sicut et ipsi; una est fides omnium patrum, una est voluntas, idem sensus, sicut omnes predicamus; hec est fides omnium orthodoxorum, hec fides salvavit et salvat mundum. Leo sanctissimus, apostolicus et ycumenicos, id est universalis, patriarcha per multos annos vivat. Sancti Deo honorabiles et venerabiles hic Deo congregati sint per multos annos. Hec sacrosancta et preclara synodus per multos annos regnet. Hec est fides Romanorum. Confirmet Deus ton isapostolon, id est equalem apostolis, et magistrum throni apostolorum patriarcham nostrum Leonem.

On this passage H. F. Dondaine comments:
Compilator libere amplificavit fragmenta ex Actis Conc. Chalcedonensis: a) "Sancta . . . fidei" (*Lib.* 96.3–11), cf. Act. 5 (Mansi 7, 111C); b) "interdicitur . . . predicare" (12–14), cf. ibid., (Mansi 7, 115C-D); c) "Omnes . . . mundum" (15–23), cf. Act. 2 (Mansi 6, 955C; 971A) et Act. 6 (Mansi 7, 170B); d) Acclamatio "Leo sanctissimus . . ." deprompta videtur ex inscriptionibus quae leguntur in Act. 3 (Mansi 6, 1005B, 1012B, 1021C et 1029C).[19]

In Chapter II it was stated that quotation 158 of P (fols. 188–190ᵛ) appears to interrupt the continuity of the *Filioque* florilegium of P. Munitiz has included it in his list of the contents of P as an unedited "Traité sur les symboles conciliaires."[20] In the following I cite a part of it:

Paris. gr., fol. 189–190
Τόμος τῆς ἐν Χαλκηδόνι τῶν χλ΄ πατέρων ἁγίας συνόδου. Ἡ ἁγία καὶ οἰκουμενικὴ σύνοδος εἶπεν· ἤρκει μὲν εἰς ἐντελῆ τῆς εὐσεβείας ἐπίγνωσίν

[19] Ibid., same page.
[20] Munitiz, "Parisinus," 59.

τε καὶ βεβαίωσιν τὸ σοφὸν καὶ σωτήριον τοῦτο τῆς θείας χάριτος σύμβολον·
περί τε γὰρ τοῦ πατρὸς καὶ τοῦ υἱοῦ καὶ τοῦ ἁγίου πνεύματος ἐκδιδάσκει
τὸ τέλειον . . . (fol. 190) . . . ὥρισεν ἡ ἁγία καὶ οἰκουμενικὴ σύνοδος, ἑ-
τέραν πίστιν μηδενὶ ἐξιέναι (sic) προφέρειν, ἤγουν συγγράφειν (συγγραφὴν
cod.), ἢ συντιθέναι, ἢ φρονεῖν ἢ διδάσκειν ἑτέρως . . . πάντες σὺν αὐτοῖς
ἐκβοῶμεν λέγοντες· πάντες οὕτως πιστεύομεν, μιᾷ πίστει, μιᾷ γνώμῃ· πάντες τὸ αὐτὸ φρονοῦμεν· πάντες συνελθόντες ἀνακηρύττομεν τὴν ὀρθόδοξον
καὶ πανάμωμον πίστιν τῶν ἁγίων ἀποστόλων· αὕτη ἡ πίστις τῶν ὀρθοδόξων·
αὕτη ἡ πίστις τὴν οἰκουμένην ἔσωσεν. Λέοντος τοῦ ἁγιωτάτου ἀποστολικοῦ
καὶ οἰκουμενικοῦ πατριάρχου, πολλὰ τὰ ἔτη. τῶν θεοτιμήτων καὶ πανευσεβῶν ἱερέων πολλὰ τὰ ἔτη. τῆς ἱερᾶς συγκλήτου πολλὰ τὰ ἔτη. αὔξει ἡ
πίστις τῶν ῥωμαίων. στερεώσει ὁ Θεὸς τὸν ἰσαπόστολον καὶ διάδοχον τοῦ
θρόνου τῶν ἀποστόλων πατριάρχην ἡμῶν . . .

Despite the considerable *amplificationes* carried out by Nicholas of Cotrone, the Latin text leaves no doubt as to its source, which actually is more
extended than the Latin translation.

(6) A different aspect of the *Libellus* and, consequently, of its original is
revealed by a penetrating remark of H. F. Dondaine. In discussing its
sources, the editor of the *Libellus* writes:

> Notre *Liber de fide Trinitatis* présente en effet quelques anomalies peu
> explicables dans l'hypothèse d'une libre fabrication des textes. Le *tracta-
> tus I* contient plusieurs pièces qui défendent la divinité du Saint-Esprit,
> mais qui semblent ignorer complètement la querelle du *Filioque*: pièces
> n. 47 (Cyrillus), n. 50 (Cyrillus) et n. 84 (Chrysostomus).[21] . . . Il y a
> même deux pièces où n'est pas question du Saint-Esprit: pièces n. 90
> (Theodoretus) et n. 46 (Cyrillus).[22]

One of these quotations is also included in P. Compare:

Libellus, chap. 84
Idem in sermone de fide: Primo omnium fides in Deum est causa non
attrectabilis, non scrutabilis, indescrutabilis, invisibilis, non indagabilis,
non predicabilis, honorabilis, ex toto veneranda. Fides a patre incipit,
in Filium venit, in Spiritum Sanctum perficitur. Fides est fundamentum
anime, radix vite, radix immortalis. Fidei autem radix viva Pater est;
ramus immarcessibilis semper virens, Filius; fructus vero immortalis ip-
sius rami Filii est Spiritus Sanctus, deitas semper simplex et incom-
posita.

---

[21] Dondaine here cites n. 83 but it is obvious that he means n. 84, since n. 83 is directly
connected with the *Filioque*.
[22] *CEG*, A13.

Paris. gr. fol. 179ᵛ (quot. 125)

Ἰωάννου ἐπισκόπου Κωνσταντινουπόλεως ἐκ τοῦ περὶ πίστεως λόγου·
Πρῶτον οὖν ἐστὶν ἁπάντων πίστις, ἡ εἰς τὸν Θεόν, πρᾶγμα ἀψηλάφητον,
ἀκατάληπτον, ἀθεώρητον, ἀπολυπραγμόνητον, ἀκαταζήτητον, ἀκατηγόρητον, σιωπῇ τιμώμενον καὶ νῷ προσκυνούμενον· πίστις ἀπὸ Πατρὸς μὲν ἄρχεται, ἐπὶ Υἱὸν δὲ ἔρχεται, εἰς δὲ τὸ Πνεῦμα πληροῦται· πίστις ἕδρα ψυχῆς,
θεμέλιος ζωῆς, ἀθάνατος ῥίζα, πίστεως δὲ ῥίζα ζῶσα ὁ Πατήρ, κλάδος
ἀμάραντος ὁ Υἱός, καρπὸς ἀθάνατος τὸ Πνεῦμα τὸ ἅγιον, Τριὰς ἁπλῆ, ἀ-
σύνθετος, ἀσυνείκαστος, ἀνέκφραστος, ἀδιήγητος, ἀδιαίρετος κατὰ συμφωνίαν . . .

PG 60, 767–768 (Severianus Gabalensis, *De fide, CPG* 4206)

Πρῶτον οὖν ἐστι πίστις ἡ πρὸς Θεὸν πρᾶγμα ἀκατάληπτον, ἀψηλάφητον,
ἀθεώρητον, ἀκατηγόρητον, σιωπῇ τιμώμενον καὶ προσκυνούμενον· πίστις
ἀπὸ Πατρὸς μὲν ἄρχεται, ἐπὶ Υἱὸν δὲ ἔρχεται, εἰς δὲ τὸ Πνεῦμα πληροῦται·
πίστις ἕδρα ψυχῆς, θεμέλιος ζωῆς, ἀθάνατος ῥίζα· πίστεως δὲ ῥίζα ζῶσα ὁ
Πατήρ, κλάδος ἀμάραντος ὁ Υἱός, καρπὸς ἀθάνατος τὸ Πνεῦμα τὸ ἅγιον.
Τριὰς ἁπλῆ, ἀσύνθετος, ἀνέκφραστος . . .

P again is no doubt the source of the Latin translation since the Latin
is much closer to the P than to the *PG* version. What is more interesting in
this quotation is that it does not belong to the *Filioque* florilegium. In Chapter II above I postulated that it should originally have belonged to the first
chapter of the *Doctrina Patrum*.[23] Dondaine is correct when he remarks that
"le compilateur . . . aura sans doute emprunté ses textes par paquets à quelques recueils anciens d'objet seulement approchant, sans prendre la peine
de vérifier."[24] Under the circumstances we must slightly correct this remark:
Nicholas of Cotrone did not borrow from "quelques recueils" but only from
a single manuscript which contained a number of particular collections: the
original of P.

The above examples must have elucidated beyond any doubt the dependence of the *Libellus* on the original of P, and since P usually offers a relatively good text,[25] as has been shown, the assumption of Dondaine that "Plu-
sieurs des glosses ou amplifications qui disqualifient ses textes incombent
certainement aux sources par lui utilisées"[26] cannot be accepted. The strik-

[23] See above, pp. 66–67 and 71.

[24] *CEG*, A13.

[25] For the deliberate alterations of the *Greek* text in favor of the *Filioque*, which, by the
way, are very few and which were, in all probability, perpetrated by Cinnamus, see above,
pp. 80–81.

[26] *CEG*, A13.

ingly pro-Latin alterations in the *Libellus* have certainly been the result of the initiative of Nicholas of Cotrone himself.

Apart from the examples that have been presented in the previous pages, P and the *Libellus* have in common an estimated twenty quotations, and a more thorough scrutinization of both may reveal some more.[27]

Finally, chapter 31 of the *Libellus* offers one more argument in favor of the establishment of the lost part of Paris. gr. 1115 as a florilegium on the *Filioque*. As has been explained (Chap. II above), quotations 4A-9A were copied from the lost first part of the manuscript of 1276 and, along with quotation no. 1, constitute the remnants of another florilegium on the *Filioque* issue similar to that of fols. 180–220. This is corroborated not only by the fact that quotation 4A is identical with quotation 161 of the *Filioque* florilegium of P, but also from the appearance of part of quotation 9A among the pieces of the *Libellus* (= chap. 31, S. Cyrilli Alex. *Explanatio xii capitulorum*). The most plausible conclusion is that the part of P that is missing included another more lengthy florilegium on the subject of the procession of the Holy Spirit.

Here we come to another major problem that the *Libellus* and, to some extent, P pose. In chapter 113 the question "unde et a quibus auctoritatibus sacrosancta catholica mater ecclesia habuit locum addendi in sacro et divo simbolo . . . 'filioque procedit'" is answered by Nicholas of Cotrone in the following manner:

> Habuit equidem duo divina angelis et hominibus veriora testimonia. Habuit et sacrosancta universalia concilia, necnon et orientales totius sacre scripture in greco stilo sanctos et divos expositores supravocatos; quibus per omnia consonos . . . habuit etiam in latino stilo mirabiles expositores . . .

All these authorities that are invoked in defense of the *Filioque* only, and not of the *Purgatorium* or the primacy of the Roman church, fall within four categories: scripture, councils, Greek fathers, and Latin fathers. A little further on in chapter 113 Nicholas cites in more detail the names of the Greek and Latin authors included, in all probability, in the original of the *Libellus*. The names of "Hilarius Pictavensis, Ambrosius Mediolanensis, Augustinus Hipponensis, Hieronymus Presbyter, Gregorius I Papa 'Dyalogus,' and Leo

---

[27] Here I give all the quotations I have been able to match: P 134 = *Lib.* 79; P 136 = *Lib.* 78; P 138 = *Lib.* 76; P 139 = *Lib.* 82; P 140 = *Lib.* 81; P 151 = *Lib.* 65; P 153 = *Lib.* 104; P 158 = *Lib.* 96; P 159 = *Lib.* 40; P 161/7A = *Lib.* 41; P 163 = *Lib.* 42; P 164 = *Lib.* 30; P 165 = *Lib.* 55; P 174 = *Lib.* 67; P 182–184 = *Lib.* 26; P 140/212 = *Lib.* 81; P 214 = *Lib.* 91; P 223 = *Lib.* 58; P 225 = *Lib.* 64; P 228iii–v = *Lib.* 58; P 228x = *Lib.* 61; P 125 = *Lib.* 84; P 9A = *Lib.* 31.

Papa" are arrayed along with those of Athanasius of Alexandria, St. Basil, Gregory of Nyssa, Gregory of Nazianzus, John Chrysostom, Cyril of Alexandria, and Cyril of Jerusalem. The same accuracy in the listing of the names of the Greek and Latin authors is also present in the letter of Michael VIII cited above. I repeat again the relevant passage:

> Praedictus . . . praesul eiusdem Ecclesiae doctrinam et Sanctorum Patrum eius, videlicet sancti Silvestri papae, Damasi, Coelestini, Agathonis, Adriani, Leonis Maioris et Junioris, Gregorii Dialogi, Hylarii Pictaviensis, Ambrosii Mediolanensis, Augustini Hypponensis Africae, Hieronymi, Fulgentii, et aliorum expositiones et dogmata rectae fidei reservavit nostro Imperio . . . quae invenimus concordantia sermonibus Sanctorum Patrum eius, videlicet Athanasii Alexandrini, Basilii Caesareae Cappadociae, Gregori magni theologi, Gregori Nisseni, Iohannis Chrysostomi.

The information assembled above is enough to give an idea of the authorities that Nicholas used in his exposition of faith to Emperor Michael VIII. Were all these authorities included in a single manuscript? The *Libellus* does not offer much help toward solving this problem, since all that is found in the first *tractatus* is limited to the Greek fathers (with the exception of chap. 94; see above, example no. 5). What about Parisinus graecus 1115 then? I have chosen to give a list (not exhaustive) as a better way of illustrating the almost complete correspondence between its contents and the data gathered above (the numbers refer to Appendix I).

(1) Scripture: 48 (fols. 108–116^v), 253 (fols. 294–302), etc.
(2) Councils: 1–36 (fols. 8–39), 43–46 (fols. 60^v–87^v), 158 (fols. 188–190^v), etc.
(3) Greek fathers: All the names cited above are represented by more than ten quotations each.
(4) Latin fathers:

(a)	Silvestrus Papa:	53
(b)	Damasus Papa:	167
(c)	Coelestinus:	—
(d)	Agatho Papa	43, 44
(e)	Adrianus Papa:	—
(f)	Leo I Papa:	11, 13–19, 22, 23, 28, 29, 58, 74
(g)	Leo Junior Papa:	—
(h)	Gregorius I Papa:	—
(i)	Hylarius Pictav.:	—
(j)	Ambrosius Mediol.:	63, 67, 68, 82, 127–129
(k)	Augustinus Hippon.:	—

(l)   Hieronymus: —
(m) Fulgentius: 77? (Φωστήριος)

Quotations from five of the thirteen Latin fathers are included in P. The absence of works or at least fragments from works of St. Augustine and Gregory I is striking, but one should never forget that a minimum of 83 folios are missing from the manuscript that Leo Cinnamus produced. It is almost certain that works of all the Latin fathers mentioned in the letter of Michael VIII must have been included in the lost part of Paris. gr. 1115. And this is the best explanation of why these folios are missing today.

On 14 March 1276 Cinnamus completed the copying of the manuscript brought by Nicholas of Cotrone to Constantinople on 24 December 1262 (or 1263 according to Tăutu). The manuscript was deposited in the imperial library, but six years later Michael VIII died (11 Dec. 1282), and his unionist policy[28] was abandoned by his successor, Andronicus II. As early as the end of December 1282, the anti-unionists banned by Michael were recalled.[29] Under these circumstances, it is not difficult to imagine the fate of a manuscript so markedly pro-Latin in the possession of an anti-Latin court. The missing part of it is an eloquent witness to the reversal of the imperial policy and of its possible contents at the same time.

In view of these revelations, there is no reason to deny the accuracy of Cinnamus so far as the date of the completion of Paris. gr. 1115 is concerned, but one may still question the veracity of the date of the original. Was it a Roman or pro-unionist fabrication or not? There are two arguments in favor of the premise that the year 774/5 can still be accepted as the actual date of the compilation of the original of P.

The first argument is predicated on the fact that, in most of the manu-

---

[28] One other noteworthy aspect of the "life" of the archetype of P needs further investigation: it is known from Pachymeres (ed. Failler, I, 487.24–489.5) that John Beccus, who served finally as the much-needed spokesman for the cause of union, was converted from an anti-unionist while in prison. His conversion was the result of much reading of patristic literature that Michael VIII had sent to him (see D. M. Nicol, "The Byzantine Reaction to the Second Council of Lyons, 1274," in *Councils and Assemblies,* ed. G. J. Cuming and D. Baker [Cambridge, 1971], 121). The interesting point in this whole story of learned "persuasion" is in the possibility of the original of P serving as a source for some of the texts provided to Beccus. Beccus in his pro-Latin florilegium (*Epigraphae, PG* 141, 614–724) has included an enormous number of fragments found in P. Only a small number of authors found in the *Epigraphae,* such as Theodore of Raithou (*PG* 141, 621B–C, 637A, 672D, etc.) and Metrophanes of Smyrna (*PG* 141, 692A–B), are not included in P. Further research is also needed on the relationship between P and the Greek texts presented by the Latins in the Council of Ferrara-Florence (see B. Meunier, "Cyrille d'Alexandrie au Concile de Florence," *AHC* 21 [1989], 147–74 and esp. 165 ff.).

[29] See Hussey, *The Orthodox Church,* 243.

script, the Iconophile florilegium excepted, the mistakes of the transcription carried out by Cinnamus point to an original written in uncial.[30] This implies that the exemplar of P dates to a period prior to the end of the eighth century, although we do not know exactly when the minuscule appeared.[31] There are also a number of works in P whose texts correspond to an early stage of their textual transmission, and, despite the mistakes of Cinnamus, P betrays an archetype close to the original text of the works.

The second argument is relevant to the creation of the *Libellus* itself. If we assume that the original of P was extant in the eighth century, then it is possible it was forgotten after the ninth or tenth century,[32] until Nicholas of Cotrone discovered it among the manuscripts of the papal *camera*[33] and began using it in his contacts with Theodore II Laskaris and Michael VIII. If the course of events was the one described above, then the translation into Latin of portions of this manuscript and the creation of the *Libellus* acquire new meaning. Within the context of the contacts between Nicholas and Michael VIII, there is at least one significant reason for the composition of the *Libellus* and its submission to Thomas Aquinas' dogmatic assessment. We may recall that the whole sequence of these contacts and the dogmatic discussion of 1263 were kept secret from the pope, who learned about them from the letter of Michael cited above. In the light of this circumstance the reason for the creation of the *Libellus* becomes clear: the pope wanted to know what dogmatic limits Nicholas had crossed (which explains why Thomas Aquinas was called in) and up to what point the enthusiasm of Michael's letter was based on realistic grounds.[34] This is also the reason why

---

[30] See above, p. 44 n. 8.

[31] See C. Mango, "L'origine de la minuscule," *Colloques Internationaux du C.N.R.S.*, no. 559, *La paléographie grecque et byzantine* (Paris, 1977), 175–80. His theory that the idea of the Greek minuscule came to life in Rome where the Greek monks had the opportunity to see the Latin minuscule may gain some more support from my analysis of the Iconophile florilegium of P in Chapter III above.

[32] It seems that Anastasius Bibliothecarius made use of it, perhaps for his translation of the acts of the seventh ecumenical council and also for the translation of the *Epistula ad Marinum presbyterum Cypri* of Maximus the Confessor.

[33] For the fact that Nicholas had free and unlimited access to the archives and the library of the pope ("un privilège fort rare pour un Grec!"), see A. Dondaine, "Nicolas de Cotrone," 320–22. The *Libellus* contains a fragment attributed to Pope Gregory I (chap. 110). The unique source for this text is the florilegium of Albinus of Milan preserved in Ottobonianus lat. 3057 (ca. 1185). This manuscript "était conservée aux Archives de la Chambre Apostolique depuis la mort de son auteur . . . et aucun autre exemplaire . . . ne fut mis en circulation" (ibid., 321).

[34] There is much space for interpretative work here in light of these new revelations, but I leave it to the historians proper. It seems, however, that the later banishment of Nicholas by Michael VIII to the town of Herakleia of Pontos must be connected with those translations and manipulations of the Greek texts.

the Latin fathers are missing from the *Libellus,* and probably had never been included in it: Thomas Aquinas was unable to comment on the doctrinal correctness of their Greek translation.

From the last consideration it follows that the Latin *Libellus* must have been written after the return of Nicholas of Cotrone from Constantinople in the spring of 1263 (or 1264 according to Tăutu), since chapter 113 seems to have been the translation of Nicholas' address to Michael VIII and not to Theodore II.[35] Accordingly, this implies that the creation of the *Contra errores Graecorum* can be confined to the period from the spring of 1263 (or 1264) to the death of Pope Urban IV (5 Feb. 1265). So much for the Constantinopolitan part of the life of the original of P. Still, there is more to the history of that famous archetype.

The career of Nicholas did not end with his exile to Pontoherakleia (possibly after the spring of 1267).[36] Sambin assumes that he took part in the Council of Lyon (1274) and that he is the same person to whom the monastery of the "eremitani" in Padua granted an "indulgenza" in June 1275.[37] Things become more certain in the next year (1276) when, on 2 October, Nicholas "infirmus corpore, mente tamen et animo sanus" made his will in Venice and a little later (October or November of the same year) died. Everything can be found in fine order in Sambin's article. Of utmost interest to this study, however, is the fact that in his testament Nicholas donated all his personal belongings to the monastery of San Giorgio Maggiore in Venice. All the items had already been deposited at this monastery, but in the testament and in the document by which the property was officially transferred to the monastery there is a basic description of the willed items. As one might expect, the list includes Greek and Latin manuscripts, of which there are eighteen.[38] I reproduce here the description of the Greek manuscripts:

(1–2) Duo alii libri non contenti in testamento de litera greca et in alipis ligati.

---

[35] One may be led to this conclusion after a swift comparison of chap. 113 of the *Libellus* with the letter of Michael VIII and the Λόγος ἀπολογητικὸς of Theodore II. While chap. 113 shares common passages and ideas with the letter of Michael VIII (see A. Dondaine, "Nicolas de Cotrone," 333–34), the Λόγος of Theodore II has no such connection with chap. 113. Another difference: Theodore II simply asked Nicholas ὅπως ἡ ἁγιωτάτη τοῦ Θεοῦ . . . ἐκκλησία ἡ πρεσβυτέρα Ῥώμη δογματίζει περὶ τῆς ἐκπορεύσεως τοῦ Ἁγίου Πνεύματος while Michael VIII wanted to know "unde et a quibus auctoritatibus sacrosancta Catholica mater ecclesia habuit locum addendi in sacro et divo symbolo . . . 'filioque procedit.'"

[36] See Sambin, "Il Vescovo Cotronese," 12–13.

[37] Ibid., 13.

[38] Ibid., 17.

(3) Item alius liber in cartis pecudis et litera greca et in alipis ligatus . . .
LXII libri Iudicum, octo libri Rut.

(4) In alio volumine XVI prophete.

(5) Psalterium totum.

(6) Damascenus in teologia et in philosophia sua.
Et haec omnia sunt volumina greca.

(7) Sunt etiam quaterni in greco stilo excerpti ab originalibus sanctorum
patrum fere LVIII.

It is regrettable that the description is so elementary and rather untech-
nical that one cannot be sure about the identity of items 1 and 2, and one
hesitates for item 6, but there is much certainty in the case of item 7: these
58 quaternions must be identified with the original of codex Parisinus graecus 1115. If we are dealing here with regular quaternions (i.e., four sheets
of paper or parchment folded in half), it gives 58 × 8 = 464 folios, which is
more than what P preserves.

Certainly this identification raises some problems. The first is simply:
how can Nicholas be in Padua in 1275 and his manuscripts copied in Constantinople one year later, the very same year that he died in Venice? One
possible answer is that the Nicholas of the "eremitani" in Padua in 1275 is
not our Nicholas. A second hypothesis is that Cinnamus worked on a first
copy of the materials that Nicholas had with him. Obviously this copy had
been made before his departure.

The second problem is more serious: the colophon of P defines its original as a βίβλος, while in the will only *quaterni* are mentioned. Still, it is possible for these two different terms to designate the same object. What I have
suggested up to now leaves enough room for that. As we have seen, the
mistakes in most of the parts of P point to an archetype written in uncial,[39]
but the majority of the texts in the Iconophile florilegium display misspellings that could have resulted from an archetype written in minuscule.[40] This
means that what Cinnamus copied was either a corpus of texts written in
two different scripts (some in uncial and some in minuscule) or an archetype
that was already a copy of such a corpus. The second possibility implies the
existence of a manuscript between the *quaterni* of 774/5 and the product of
Cinnamus. That certainly explains the presence of Nicholas in Padua in

---

[39] See R. Riedinger, "Die Epistula Synodica des Sophronios von Jerusalem im Codex Parisinus graecus 1115," *BYZANTIAKA* 2 (1982), 150–51, and also two more references above in
Chapter II, n. 8.

[40] Apart from the examples I have given above in Chapter III, sec. 5, see also Munitiz,
"Parisinus," 55. He refers to the unpublished study of M. J. Pinard in which are treated the
Dionysian fragments of the Iconophile florilegium of P.

1275 and the completion of P one year later. Both possibilities, on the other hand, corroborate my suggestion that the original of the year 774/5 could better be described as a dossier rather than as a book proper. However, that leaves the door open to the "wandering colophon theory" of Zettl (above, p. 48). Nevertheless, this theory is not particularly useful since there are no more than three long texts that date after 774/5.[41] In my most generous calculations, the "wandering colophon" does not apply to 1.7 percent of the whole extent of the original manuscript. Even in the unlikely case that the year 754 is accepted as the date of the original, things do not change. One would have to add the works not covered by this date, which are the *Adversus Iconoclastas* and the *Adversus Constantinum Caballinum* (a total of nine-and-a-half folios in P). In this case, the "wandering colophon" would have covered 96 percent of the whole original. Under the circumstances, the whole hypothesis of a "wandering colophon" that covers 96–98.3 percent of the contents of a manuscript sounds rather absurd. On the other hand, the dossier format makes the possibility of later interpolations into the original of 774/5 practically easier and theoretically even more plausible.

Sad to admit, the quest for the original of P stops here. The fate of the library of Nicholas of Cotrone is unknown thereafter. Even the earliest preserved catalogue of the library of the monastery of San Giorgio Maggiore in Venice is silent about the bequest of Nicholas.[42] It is hoped that, now that we know what these *quaterni* contained, someone may yet unearth them in a still uncatalogued library.

---

[41] For the remaining two apart from the *Narratio*, see below, Chapter VI, sec. 1.

[42] See G. Ravegnani, *Le biblioteche del Monastero di San Giorgio Maggiore* (Florence, 1986), 11–12. For the first catalogue of manuscripts drawn up in 1362, see ibid., 73–76.

Conclusions

1. The Nature of the Archetype of Paris. gr. 1115

At the end of this study of Parisinus graecus 1115, the remark of Combefis that "Videri autem potest praeclarus ille codex quasi ὁπλοθήκη universalis"[1] emerges as the most comprehensive one with regard to its nature. I also hope to have established that P does not reflect the actual size of its archetype, even if its missing folios were to be accounted for, but that it does present a true panorama of early Greek patristic literature.

The fact that that archetype was one of the dogmatic weapons stored in the patristic arsenal of the Roman church should no longer be doubted. As such, the archetype of P was an official document of the papal curia, comprising florilegia on every major disputed issue of the Christian faith along with some very significant works such as the *Hodegos* of Anastasius the Sinaite. Still, it has to be stressed that what remains from the archetype of P (through P, M, and V for the Iconophile florilegium) leaves out the possible contribution of Latin fathers, although P includes a considerable number of works of Latin fathers translated into Greek.

There is no apparent reason to deny the accuracy of Cinnamus in dating his work to 1276. Two years after the Council of Lyons, Michael VIII certainly needed a copy of a book such as the archetype of P, since both the pro- and anti-unionist parties displayed increasing activity in pursuing their aims.[2] In addition, all the members of the imperial family named by the colophon were by that time, willingly or not, among the ranks of the pro-unionist party. The problem that in the manuscript the date (1276) is partly written over some other characters may be dismissed on the grounds that the indiction that corresponds to this date (fourth)[3] is included in the same colophon and there is not the slightest trace of any prior writing underneath it.

The date of that archetype appears also perfectly acceptable according

---

[1] *PG* 109, 501–2 in in the *Prolusio.*
[2] See Hussey, *The Orthodox Church*, 235–38; see also above, Chapter V, p. 249 n. 28.
[3] See Grumel, *La chronologie*, 259.

to the Alexandrian era (774/5). No later works are to be found in it with the exception of the *Narratio* of John of Jerusalem which dates from 787, the three epigrams transmitted by V (V 17–19), the anathemas of the Iconoclasts on fol. 283ᵛ, and (possibly) the canon attributed to Photius on fol. 235 along with quot. 14, 20, 26, and 27 in Chapter III 5. Apart from the *Narratio*, the remaining items are so small that one could assume that they were included in the archetype of 774/5 as (later) marginal notes and that Cinnamus (or the scribe who produced V) transposed them into the main text.

However, it is also possible that the archetype of P included two more later interpolations. Among the Latin fathers whom Michael VIII mentions in his letter of 1263/4, the name of Hadrian I features in fifth place. This makes one suppose that among the works included in the lost part of P were Hadrian's two *Epistulae Synodicae* of 785, the first addressed to Tarasius and the second to the rulers Constantine and Irene.

The interpolation of these three works (*Narratio* and Hadrian's letters) can be explained by the nature of the archetype of P: as an official document, it had to be updated from time to time, as long as it was of some importance in matters of Christian faith. It seems that soon after the death of Hadrian I its updating was abandoned, and, although Paschal I (817–824) made use of its contents,[4] it fell into oblivion after the death of Anastasius Bibliothecarius (see above, p. 225) until it was rediscovered by Nicholas of Cotrone.

Another feature in the arrangement of the material that P included must be related to the process of the updating of its archetype. The list below displays the dates of composition of the various texts in P (the numbers refer to Appendix I).

	Quotation	Date
1.	2–7	A.D. 431
2.	8–29	448–451
3.	30–35	553
4.	36–41	646[5]
5.	42	after 579

[4] Paschal I has included some fragments from the Iconophile treatises of John of Damascus in his letter of 819 to Emperor Leo V the Armenian. Part of the letter is preserved in its Greek translation. For more bibliography, see Sansterre, *Les moines grecs*, 130, 182. The letter has been edited by G. Mercati, "La lettera di Pasquale I a Leone V sul culto delle sacre imagini," in his *Note di letteratura biblica e cristiana antica*, ST 5 (1905), 228–35.

[5] They are possibly marginalia transferred into the main text. See above, pp. 56–57.

Quotation	Date
6. 43–46	681
7. 47 and 111	686–689 (quot. 48, 49 out of sequence)
8. 50–110 and 112–130	685–726
9. 131–234	after 645?[6]
10. 235–245	(*Miscellanea Historica*, out of sequence)[7]
11. 1*–133*	770
12. 246–254	(*Miscellanea Canonica*, out of sequence).

According to this list, P and its archetype seem to have followed a loose but coherent chronological arrangement of their contents. With the exception of quotations 48, 49, 235–245(?), and 246–254, which appear out of sequence—all of them being earlier than the seventh century—the only group that does not conform to the situation is the *Filioque* florilegium. Do we have to accept a dating as early as the one proposed above (Chap. II, section 6)? Do we have to place its final compilation between 685 and 770 on the basis of the position it occupies in P? Should it be considered as an additional chapter of the *Doctrina Patrum* or, at least, be simply related to it since in the manuscript it follows immediately after the *Doctrina*? These questions remain open.

One last point that needs clarification is the information provided again by the colophon of P that its archetype was found in the old library of the Holy Church of Old Rome (ἐν τῇ παλαιᾷ βιβλιοθήκῃ τῆς ἁγίας ἐκκλησίας τῆς πρεσβυτέρας Ῥώμης). Which library was this? Batiffol identified it with the library of the Basilica of St. Peter.[8] In support of this view, he pointed to a note that is found in the margin of fol. 141 of Paris. gr. 1470:

Τοῦ ἁγίου Μεθοδίου ἀρχιεπισκόπου Κωνσταντινουπόλεως, σχόλια ἅπερ ἐποίησεν εἰς τὸ μαρτύριον τῆς ἁγίας Μαρίνης ἐν τῷ μαρτυρολογείῳ ὅπερ ἔγραψεν ἰδιοχείρως καθεζόμενος ἐν Ῥώμῃ εἰς τὸν ἅγιον Πέτρον.[9]

---

[6] This is the *Filioque* florilegium.

[7] I would suggest that this historical collection was put together in the first half of the 8th century. Unfortunately, the only argument to support this idea is the position of this collection in P.

[8] P. Batiffol, "Librairies byzantines à Rome," *Mélanges d'archéologie et d'histoire* 8 (1888), 298.

[9] Ibid., 298 n. 2. See also Sansterre, *Les moines grecs*, 175–77, esp. nn. 9, 10, for additional bibliography. There is also one more piece similar to this note, that is, a subscription which the copyist of Londiniensis Brit. Lib. Add. 36821 reproduced from his exemplar and is found on fol. 196 of the ms: Πρώτιστον τόδε τῆς ξενίης Μεθοδίοιο τευκτο/ ἔργον λιτογραφίης ἐν περικλύτῳ Ῥώμῃ/ πρὸς κορυφίου Πέτρου μεγάρῳ τῷ λυσιμόχθῳ. See P. Canart, "Le patriarche Méthode de Constantinople copiste à Rome," in *Palaeographica, diplomatica e archivistica: Studi in onore di Giulio Battelli,* a cura de la Scuola speciale per archivisti e bibliothecari dell'Università di Roma, vol. I (= *Storia e Letteratura* 139 [Rome, 1979]), 346.

However, this identification cannot be correct because it was the "scrinium et bibliotheca patriarchii Lateranensis" where documents such as papal letters and acts of councils (Latin *and* Greek) were kept.[10] So even that indication in the colophon of P is accurate.[11]

The ultimate conclusion is that all the information included in the colophon has to be taken at face value. There is only one little mistake: the number of years separating the exemplar from its apograph is 501 and not 517 as Cinnamus imagined, assuming obviously that the date of the archetype was written in accordance with the Byzantine era.

2. The Availability of Greek Books in Rome until the Ninth Century

The fact that such a *florilegium florilegiorum* as the archetype of P could have been produced in Rome by the end of the eighth century is not a great surprise. J. M. Sansterre has already exhausted the topic of the knowledge of Greek in Rome, especially during the period between the seventh and ninth centuries.[12] Despite his skepticism about the extent of the knowledge of Greek,[13] one could still find in eighth-century Rome a number of bilingual individuals along with some Greeks who could make use of and, of course, produce Greek books. Since most of them were clerics or monks, the papal *scrinium* could have benefited from their skills and knowledge.

However, concerning the possessions of the papal library during that period, information is extremely poor, a situation that persists until the fourteenth century. The first list of books is the *Recensio Perusina* of the year 1311, which gives the description of 624 Latin and 33 Greek manuscripts.[14] But even this list concerns the library of Pope Boniface VIII (post-1295) and not the Lateran library, which was the original papal library and was located in the Lateran Palace. The *Bibliotheca Lateranensis* ceased to exist some time in the twelfth or thirteenth century,[15] and must be distinguished from the library of the Basilica of St. Peter outside the walls of the city.

The information for the period in consideration is provided by various

[10] See I. B. de Rossi, *De origine historia indicibus scrinii et bibliothecae sedis Apostolicae*, in H. Stevenson, *Codices Palatini Latini Bibliothecae Vaticanae* (Rome, 1886), LXXIX–LXXXI.

[11] Note also the resemblance between the Greek wording in the colophon of P and the words in one Latin source describing the Lateran Library: ἐν τῇ παλαιᾷ βιβλιοθήκη τῆς ἁγίας ἐκκλησίας τῆς πρεσβυτέρας Ῥώμης: P, "perscrutato eiusdem *sanctae ecclesiae Romanae scrinio . . .*"; Beda Venerabilis, *Historia ecclesiastica gentis Anglorum, PL* 95, 22.

[12] See Sansterre, *Les moines grecs*, 65–76, 174–206, 214, et passim.

[13] Ibid., 76.

[14] See F. Ehrle, *Historia Bibliothecae Romanorum Pontificum* (Rome, 1890), 26–100.

[15] See de Rossi, *De origine*, XCV ff.

documents (mainly letters, inscriptions, and the *Liber Pontificalis*). These sources usually allude indirectly to the existence of a scriptorium equipped with records of acts (synodal, etc.) and other codices containing theological texts, collections of papal letters, and so on. However, no detailed catalogue exists for this period.

In one instance, de Rossi thought he could give a detailed list of the contents of the Lateran library and its *scrinium,* at least during the seventh century. He assumed that from the florilegia that were presented during the sessions of the Lateran Council of 649, "elicitur pars valde notabilis indicis librorum bibliothecae sedis apostolicae saeculo septimo."[16] Accordingly, he drew up a list of the works utilized by the Lateran Council of 649.[17] Many modern scholars have been skeptical about this attribution.[18] Besides, R. Riedinger has proved that the nature of the acts of the Lateran Council—a text written before 649 and signed by Pope Martin I and his bishops in October 649—does not allow their association with the Lateran library.[19]

One is on safer ground with the florilegia of the sixth ecumenical council. As we have already seen (above, p. 22), according to the letter of Pope Agathon to Emperor Constantine IV (27 March 680), these florilegia were taken to Constantinople by the papal envoys, along with the books from which the quotations had been extracted. Therefore, the acts of the sixth ecumenical council can give us the titles of some of the holdings of the papal library as early as the year 680.[20]

I prefer not to discuss the sending of a small number of books (*antiphonale et responsale, . . . artem grammaticam Aristo[te]lis Dionysii Areopagitis [libros] . . .* etc.) by Pope Paul I to King Pepin the Short, which took place some time between 758 and 763, is of very limited interest,[21] and for which we have no other evidence apart from letter 24 of *Codex Carolinus.*[22] On the other hand, Sansterre has recorded a number of manuscripts that must have been produced by the papal *scrinium.*[23] However, in his discussion of the archetype of

---

[16] Ibid., p. LXIII.

[17] Ibid., pp. LXVIII–LXXI.

[18] On the subject see Sansterre, *Les moines grecs,* 176–77, and esp. n. 26 for further bibliography.

[19] See Riedinger, "Griechische Konzilsakten," 258–60.

[20] See Sansterre, *Les moines grecs,* 177–78.

[21] On the subject see P. Lemerle, *Le premier humanisme byzantin* (Paris, 1971), 13 n. 13; Sansterre, *Les moines grecs,* 182–83.

[22] *MGH, Epistulae,* vol. III, 529.19–22.

[23] *Les moines grecs,* 174–76. The manuscripts are Vat. gr. 1666 and possibly Ambrosianus E 49–50.

Parisinus, Sansterre, following Mango,[24] considers it a product of the Greek (monastic) community of Rome that ended up in the papal library.[25]

The foregoing analysis has presented a number of arguments that support the assumption that the archetype of P was a product of the papal *scrinium*. I may repeat here that in the year 774/5 a scribe collected/copied in a voluminous dossier a number of ecclesiastical documents and theological works already existing in the papal library.[26] Then the dossier was placed among the holdings of the Lateran library. So eventually P is one of the sources that preserve some parts of the Greek works contained in the Lateran library by the end of the eighth century.[27]

In view of its importance and despite the fact that it was probably forgotten for a certain period, the voluminous dossier of the year 774/5 must have been the archetype for more than one manuscript. It is certain that at least the Iconophile florilegium of V draws on the same archetype of the year 774/5. What about the rest of its contents? Not many things are shared between P and V, but V also provides on fols. 30–47ᵛ a collection described by Mioni as *Testimonia martyrum, confessorum et episcoporum de Christi incarnatione*,[28] which is very similar to the *Doctrina Patrum*. This collection in V has in common with P quotation 9* (= V, fol. 34ʳ⁻ᵛ) which I have placed in chapters B–Z of the *Doctrina Patrum* (above, p. 69). Moreover, a swift collation between the P and V transmissions of the *Epistula I ad Amphilochium* (= P, fols. 283ᵛ–287ᵛ, quot. 246; V, fols. 83ᵛ–94ᵛ) points to a common archetype. Noteworthy also is that all the works included in V are earlier than the eighth, if not seventh, century (barring the three short Iconophile epigrams on fol. 6; see App. IV, quot. 17–19). It is safe, therefore, to conclude that the entire V is

---

[24] Mango places the appearance of the original of P in "the milieu of the Levantine colony of Rome" ("Availability," 34).

[25] *Les moines grecs*, 180: "Du moins, voilà un bon exemple d'un livre grec qui finit par arriver dans la bibliothèque pontificale."

[26] No other library in Rome could possibly have copies (if not the originals) of the collection of letters related to the ecumenical councils and the fragments from their acts and especially the *Epistula Synodica* of Sophronius of Jerusalem (see Riedinger, "Die *Epistula Synodica*," 153).

[27] The fact that the archetype of P was a product of the papal *scrinium* implies, among other things, that when in Parisinus (and Arundelianus 529) appear expressions such as: Ἴσον ἀντιγράφου τῆς ἰδιοχείρου πίστεως Φλαβιανοῦ ἐπισκόπου . . . (P, fol. 14) or Ἀντίγραφον λιβέλλου Εὐσεβείου ἐπισκόπου Δορυλαίου (P, fol. 14), or inscriptions of letters starting with the words ἴσον γράμματος etc., the lemma has to be taken at face value. This means that P and Arundel. are apographs at least twice removed from the authentic original of some letters.

[28] Mioni, *Bibliothecae Divi Marci*, II, 477.

an apograph of the 774/5 archetype. Accordingly, what actually survives to-day from this enormous document of the year 774/5 are some *membra disiecta* preserved in fragmentary form by the following manuscripts and works:

(1) Parisinus gr. 1115
(2) Londiniensis Musei Britannici Arundelianus 529 (fols. 7–184)
(3) Venetus Marcianus gr. 573
(4) *Hadrianum* (Latin versions)
(5) *Libellus* of Nicholas of Cotrone (Latin versions).[29]

The appendixes below constitute a catalogue of a significant part of the possessions of the papal library during the eighth to ninth centuries. Moreover, since very often a fragment found in the *Filioque* or in the Ico-nophile florilegia implies the presence of the entire book in the library, it is evident that the Greek patristic literature available in Rome at the end of the eighth century numbered many more volumes than modern research has been willing to concede. Although one could possibly blame the compil-ers and the scribes who worked at the papal *scrinium* for their uncritical selection of some fragments found in the *Filioque* and in the Iconophile flo-rilegia, their contribution to the preservation of a considerable number of good-quality Greek patristic texts is praiseworthy. After all, it is due to them and to Cinnamus that we are now in the fortunate position of being able to cite the names of the authors and titles of works that were kept in the Lat-eran library by the end of the eighth century.

---

[29] The following mss can also be included in this tentative list—which I drew up after a brief survey of the stemmata found in the critical edition of works included in P (*Hodegos, Acta Conciliorum,* etc)—but further research is needed before any definite classification: (1) Mosquensis Hist. Mus. 265: although it belongs to a different milieu (eastern if not Constantin-opolitan), nevertheless the arrangement of the material and its contents are similar to those of P; (2) part of Vat. gr. 1702 (fols. 63–84ᵛ) (see C. Giannelli, *Codices Vaticani graeci, codices 1684–1744* [Vatican City, 1961], 47–49); (3) Vindob. Hist. gr. 127 (H. Hunger, *Katalog der griechischen Handschriften der Österreichischen Nationalbibliothek,* vol. I [Vienna, 1961], 129–30); (4) a consider-able part of Vindobon. theol. gr. 190 (fols. 1–195; see H. Hunger and O. Kresten, *Katalog,* III. 2 [Vienna, 1984], 394–96). Finally, it seems to me that Vat. gr. 2220 (anni 1304–5, see S. Lilla, *Codices Vaticani graeci, codices 2162–2254* [Vatican City, 1985], 224–57) constitutes a, so to speak, Eastern Orthodox dossier dealing with the same issues as the original of P. Its list of contents and its layout are almost the same as those of P. I would suggest that it was a response to the challenges provided by the archetype of P or rather by P itself. However, one other possibility is that P and Vat. gr. 2220 represent the official format of collections of ecclesiastical texts deposited in the libraries of Rome and Constantinople respectively, but these suggestions are highly hypothetical.

APPENDIX I

List of Contents of Parisinus Graecus 1115
(fols. 235ᵛ–283ᵛ not included)

1. Additional Part of the Manuscript (14th–15th cent., fols. 1–7ᵛ)

fol. 1 **1A** Περὶ ἑνώσεως τοῦ Δαμασκηνοῦ
Inc.: Ἕνωσίς ἐστι διεστώτων πραγμάτων κοινωνικὴ συνδρομή, . . .
desin.: . . . . μετὰ τὴν ἕνωσιν τῆς φυσικῆς ἰδιότητος.
CPG 8087.8 Iohannes Damascenus, *De unione, PG* 95, 232–33.

fol. 1ᵛ alia manu: διαφοραὶ γραικῶν καὶ λατίνων; alia manu: πίναξ· συλλογὴ πε(ρὶ) ὧν λατῖνοι τοῖς γραικοῖς διαφέρονται.

fol. 2 **2A** Δόγμα λατίνων γραφὲν ὑπὸ τῶν πρέσβεων τοῦ πάπα, εἶτα ἀνασκευασθὲν παρὰ Βαρλαάμ, μοναχοῦ.
Inc.: Ὁ πατὴρ καὶ ὁ υἱὸς μία εἰσὶν ἀρχὴ τοῦ ἁγίου πνεύματος . . .
fol. 4 desin. mutile: . . . ἰδιότης, πρὸς μὲν τὸ πνεῦμα, προσω . . .
Cf. Sinkewicz, "The *Solutions* Addressed to George Lapithes," 188.

fol. 4ᵛ **3A** Θεοδωρήτου πρὸς Ἰωάννην Ἀντιοχείας
Inc.: Ὁ πάντα σαφῶς πρυτανεύων Θεός . . .
desin.: . . . εἰς ἠχὴν ἡδεῖαν μεταρρυθμίζοντα.
CPG 6266 Theodoretus Episc. Cyri, *Ad Iohannem Antiochenum. ACO* I,1,7, 163–64; *PG* 85, 1484–85.

Post finem excerpti habetur:

> Ἐν τῷ παρόντι βιβλίῳ τετραδίῳ δῳ εὑρήσεις κεφάλαια τῆς πέμπτης συνόδου. Ἀνά-γνωθι οὖν κεφάλαιον ιγ´ καὶ ἐπιστολὴν Βιγιλλίου πάπα.

4A Κυρίλλου· ἐκ τοῦ προσφωνητικοῦ λόγου πρὸς ταῖς εὐσεβεστάταις δεσποίναις, οὗ ἡ ἀρχή· σεμνολόγημα μὲν οἰκουμενικόν.
Inc.: Πιστεύομεν δὲ ὁμοίως καὶ εἰς τὸ πνεῦμα τὸ ἅγιον . . .
desin.: . . . ἡ ἁγία καὶ προσκυνουμένη τριάς.
CPG 5219 [8650] Cyrillus Alexandrinus, *Oratio ad Arcadiam et Marinam augustas de fide. ACO* I,1,5, 63.13–16; *PG* 76, 1204D9–1205A3. Also quotation **156.**

5A Κυρίλλου ἐκ τοῦ λόγου τοῦ πρὸς τὸν βασιλέα Θεοδόσιον, οὗ ἡ ἀρχή· τοῖς ἐν ἀνθρώ-ποις εὐκλείας τὸ ἀνωτάτω. καὶ μεθ᾽ ἕτερα.
Inc.: Καὶ μὴν ἄνδρα λέγων τὸν ὅσον οὔπω . . .
desin.: . . . ὡς εἰκόνα τὴν θείαν Χριστὸν Ἰησοῦν.
CPG 5218 [8648] Cyrillus Alex., *Oratio ad Theodosium imp. de recta fide. ACO* I,1,1, 66.22–26; *PG* 76, 1188A12–B5.

6A Τοῦ αὐτοῦ· ἐκ τοῦ προσφωνητικοῦ λόγου ταῖς εὐσεβεστάταις βασιλίσσι (sic) περὶ τῆς ὀρθῆς πίστεως· οὗ ἡ ἀρχή· τοῖς τὸ θεῖον καὶ οὐράνιον· καὶ μεθ' ἕτερα·
Inc.: Γέγονεν ἄνθρωπος ὁ μονογενής . . .
fol. 5 desin.: . . . καὶ τὸ πνεῦμα τὸ ζωοποιόν.
CPG 5220 [8649] Cyrillus Alex., *Oratio ad Pulcheriam et Eudociam augustas de fide. ACO* I,1,5, 56.3–9; *PG* 76, 1408A10–B6.

7A Τοῦ αὐτοῦ· ἐκ τῆς πρὸς Νεστόριον ἐπιστολῆς, ἧς ἡ ἀρχή· τοῦ σωτῆρος ἡμῶν λέγοντος ἐναργῶς· ὁ φιλῶν πατέρα ἢ μητέρα. καὶ μεθ' ἕτερα·
Inc.: Εἰ γὰρ καὶ ἔστιν ἐν ὑποστάσει τὸ πνεῦμα . . .
desin.: . . . καθάπερ ἀμέλει καὶ ἐκ τοῦ Θεοῦ καὶ πατρός.
CPG 5317 [8644] Cyrillus Alex., *Epist.* 17 *Ad Nestorium. ACO* I,1,1, 39.20–23; *PG* 77, 117C2–7.

8A Ξύστου πάπα πρὸς Κύριλλον·
Inc.: Ἥσθην ἐπὶ τοῖς δηλωθήσοις (sic) μοι . . .
desin.: . . . τοσαύτης ἀσεβείας κοινωνοὺς καὶ μετόχους.
CPG [8792] Xystus Papa, *Epistula Xysti papae ad Cyrillum Alex. ACO* I,1,7, 143–44. *PL* 50, 588–89.

fol. 5ᵛ **9A (i–iii)** Ἐκ τῶν ιβ΄ κεφαλαίων τοῦ ἁγίου Κυρίλλου γραφέντων κατὰ τοῦ δυσεβοῦς Νεστωρίου καὶ μεμφθέντων παρὰ Θεοδωρίτου κεφάλαιον Θ΄.

(i) Inc.: Εἴ τίς φησι τὸν ἕνα Κύριον Ἰησοῦν Χριστόν . . .
desin.: . . . ὑποκείσονται δικαίως τῇ δυνάμει τοῦ ἀναθεματισμοῦ.
(ii) μέμψις Θεοδωρίτου
Inc.: Ἐνταῦθα σαφῶς, οὐ τοὺς νῦν εὐσεβοῦντας . . .
fol. 6 desin.: . . . ἀλλὰ τὸ πνεῦμα τὸ ἐκ Θεοῦ.
(iii) ἀντίθεσις τοῦ ἁγίου Κυρίλλου·
Inc.: Φθάσας ἔφην ὅτι τοῖς Νεστωρίου βατταρισμοῖς . . .
fol. 7 desin.: . . . καὶ οὐκ ἀσυνέτοις σκάζουσαν λογισμοῖς.

(i) *CPG* 5223 Cyrillus Alex., *Explanatio xii capitulorum. ACO* I,1,5, 23.15–27.
(ii–iii) *CPG* 5222 *Apologia xii anathematismorum contra Theodoretum*
ii = *ACO* I,1,6, 133.4–134.15; **iii** = *ACO* I,1,6, 134.16–135.22.

10A Ξύστου, τοῦ μακαριωτάτου πάπα Ῥώμης διαδόχου Κελεστίνου πρὸς Κύριλλον.
Inc.: Χάριν ὁμολογοῦντες τῇ περὶ ἡμᾶς τοῦ Θεοῦ . . .
fol. 7ᵛ desin.: . . . ἡ ὑπὲρ πασῶν τῶν ἐκκλησιῶν μέριμνα.
CPG 8793 Xystus Papa, *Epistula (ad episcopos Aegyptios). ACO* I,1,7, 144–45.

11A Θεῖον γράμμα πρὸς τὴν ἐν Ἐφέσῳ ἁγίαν σύνοδον ἀπολύων (sic) πάντας τοὺς ἐπισκόπους εἰς τὰ ἴδια καὶ ἀποκαθιστῶν (sic) Κύριλλον καὶ Μένονα (sic), τοὺς ἁγιωτάτους ταῖς ἰδίαις ἐκκλησίαις.
Inc.: Ἡμεῖς τὴν τῶν ἐκκλησιῶν εἰρήνην . . .
desin.: . . . ἀλλὰ τοῦ Θεοῦ τοὺς αἰτίους γινώσκοντος.
CPG 8760 *Sacra qua Synodus dissolvitur, Cyrillo et Memnone restitutis. ACO* I,1,7, 142.

2. Original Part of the Manuscript (by Leo Cinnamus, fols. 8–306ᵛ)

fol. 8 **1** Τοῦ ἁγίου Κυρίλλου ἑρμηνεία εἰς τὸ ῥητὸν τοῦ κατὰ Ἰωάννην εὐαγγελίου τό· ὅταν ἔλθῃ ὁ παράκλητος ὃν ἐγὼ πέμψω ὑμῖν, τὸ πνεῦμα τῆς ἀληθείας, ὃ παρὰ τοῦ πατρὸς ἐκπορεύεται.
Inc.: Ἐπειδὴ ὁ υἱός ἐστιν ἡ ἀλήθεια . . .
desin.: . . . δηλοῖ ὅτι ὁ πατὴρ δίδωσιν, ἐξ οὗ τὰ πάντα.
CPG 5208 Cyrillus Alex., *Commentarii in Iohannem, PG* 74, 257c. *ACO* I,1,7, p. VIIII.

2 Ἐπιστολὴ Ἰωάννου ἀρχιεπισκόπου Ἀντιοχείας πρὸς Κύριλλον ἐπίσκοπον Ἀλεξανδρείας περὶ πίστεως·
Inc.: Τῷ δεσπότῃ μου . . . χαίρειν. Πρώην ἐκ θεσπίσματος τῶν . . .
fol. 9 desin.: . . . ἔχουσί τε καὶ τηροῦσι πίστιν.
CPG 6310 [8851] Iohannes I Antiochenus, *Epist. ad Cyrillum Alex. de pace. ACO* I,1,4, 7.20–9.18; *PG* 77, 169–73.

Post finem excerpti P add.:

τούτοις ἑξῆς ὑπετέθη καὶ ἡ διδασκαλία τοῦ ὁσιωτάτου ἐπισκόπου Παύλου τοῦ τῆς Ἐμέσης μεσιτεύοντος καὶ τὴν εἰρήνην βραβεύοντος, ὃς ἐν Ἀλεξανδρείᾳ γενόμενος, οὐ φιλοτιμίας, ἀλλ᾽ ἀποδείξεως χάριν τοῦ συμφωνῆσαι τοὺς ἀνατολικοὺς τῇ οἰκουμενικῇ συνόδῳ.

3 Ὁμιλία Παύλου ἐπισκόπου Ἐμέσης ἐν Ἀλεξανδρείᾳ περὶ εἰρήνης·
Inc.: Εὐλογητὸς ὁ Θεὸς ὁ τοίνυν (sic) πρῶτον . . .
desin.: . . . τῇ οἰκουμένῃ ἐχαρίσατο· αὐτῷ ἡ δόξα ἅμα τῷ πατρὶ etc.
CPG 6367 [8847] Paulus Emesenus, *Homilia III de pace Alexandriae habita* (25/12/432). *ACO* I,1,7, 173 ff, *PG* 77, 1444c.

4 Τοῦ αὐτοῦ ὁμιλία δευτέρα Χοϊὰκ (cod. ἀχιὰκ) κε´ ἐν τῇ μεγάλῃ ἐκκλησίᾳ εἰς τὴν γένναν τοῦ Χριστοῦ καὶ ὅτι Θεοτόκος ἡ ἁγία Παρθένος Μαρία καὶ ὅτι οὐ δύο υἱοὺς λέγομεν ἀλλ᾽ ἕνα υἱὸν Ἰησοῦν Χριστὸν καὶ εἰς τὸν ἐπίσκοπον Ἀλεξανδρείας ἐγκώμια.
Inc.: Εὔκαιρον σήμερον τὴν ὑμετέραν παρακαλέσαι εὐλάβειαν . . .
fol. 10 desin.: . . . καὶ κιθάρα τοῦ ἁγίου πνεύματος, ᾧ ἡ δόξα . . .
CPG 6365 [8847] Paulus Emes., *Homilia I de nativitate Alexandriae habita* (25/12/432). *ACO* I,1,4, 9–11. *PG* 77, 1433–37.

5 Τοῦ αὐτοῦ ὁμιλία γ´ λεχθεῖσα ἐν τῇ μεγάλῃ ἐκκλησίᾳ Τυβὶ καὶ εἰς τὴν ἐνανθρώπησιν τοῦ Χριστοῦ καὶ εἰς τὸν ἀρχιεπίσκοπον Κύριλλον ἐγκώμια.
Inc.: Πρώην πρὸς τὴν ὑμετέραν ἀγωνιστικώτερον διαλεγόμενοι . . .
fol. 11ᵛ desin.: . . . τὰ στίφη καταβαλλούσης, τῷ Θεῷ τοίνυν δόξαν . . .
CPG 6366 [8847] Paulus Emes., *Homilia II de nativitate Alexandriae habita* (1/1/433). *ACO* I,1,4, 11–14; *PG* 77, 1437–44.

6 Κυρίλλου, ἀρχιεπισκόπου Ἀλεξανδρείας εἰς τὸν προεξηγησάμενον καὶ εἰς τὴν ἐνανθρώπησιν.
Inc.: Ὁ μὲν μακάριος προφήτης Ἡσαΐας . . .
fol. 12 desin.: . . . αὐτῷ δι᾽ ἡμᾶς ἐνανθρωπήσαντι λόγῳ . . .
CPG 5247 [8847] Cyrillus Alex., *Homilia iii. De Paulo Emeseno. ACO* I,1,4, 14–15; *PG* 77, 989–92.

7 Τοῦ αὐτοῦ ἐπιστολὴ γραφεῖσα πρὸς Ἰωάννην ἀρχιεπίσκοπον Ἀντιοχείας περὶ τῆς εἰρήνης.
Inc.: Κυρίῳ μου ἀγαπητῷ . . . Εὐφραινέσθωσαν οἱ οὐρανοί . . .
fol. 14 desin.: . . . ἀπεστείλαμεν τὰ ἴσα (sic) τῇ σῇ ὁσιότητι· ἐρρωμένον . . .
CPG 5339 [8848] Cyrillus Alex., *Epist.* 39, *Ad Iohannem Antiochenum (de pace). ACO* I,1,4, 15–20/ II,1,1, 107–11.

Post finem epistulae P add.:

Κυρίλλου τελευτήσαντος τοῦ Ἀλεξανδρείας καὶ Ἰωάννου τοῦ Ἀντιοχείας, τούτους τοὺς θρόνους διεδέξαντο ἐν μὲν τῇ Ἀλεξανδρείᾳ Διόσκορος ἐν δὲ τῇ Ἀντιοχείᾳ Δόμνος.

8 Ἴσον ἀντιγράφου τῆς ἰδιοχείρου πίστεως Φλαβιανοῦ, ἐπισκόπου Κωνσταντινουπόλεως ἐπιδοθείσης παρ' αὐτοῦ αἰτήσαντι τῷ βασιλεῖ.
Inc.: Φλαβιανός . . . χαίρειν. Οὐδὲν οὕτως πρέπει ἱερεῖ Θεοῦ . . .
fol. 14ᵛ desin.: . . . τὴν ἁπλῆν ἐν Χριστῷ ἀναστροφήν.
CPG 5934 Flavianus CPolitanus, *Epistula ad Theodosium imp. ACO* II,1,1, 35–36; *PG* 65, 889–92.

9 Ἀντίγραφον λιβέλλου Εὐσεβείου (sic) ἐπισκόπου Δορυλαίου.
Inc.: Τῷ ἁγιωτάτῳ . . . Φλαβιανῷ . . . ηὔχομεν (sic) μὴ οὕτως παραπληξίας . . .
fol. 15 desin.: . . . τούσδε μου τοὺς λιβέλλους ὑπέγραψα χειρὶ ἐμῇ.
CPG 5941 [8904.1] Eusebius Dorylaeus, *Libellus ad Flavianum episc. Const. et Synodum* (8/11/448). *ACO* II,1,1, 100–101.

10 Ἐπιστολὴ Φλαβιανοῦ ἐπισκόπου Κωνσταντινουπόλεως πρὸς Λέοντα, ἀρχιεπίσκοπον Ῥώμης.
Inc.: Τῷ θεοφιλεστάτῳ . . . Λέοντι . . . οὐδὲν ἵστησιν ἄρα τὴν τοῦ . . .
fol. 15ᵛ desin.: . . . χαρισθείης ἡμῖν, θεοφιλέστατε πάτερ.
CPG 5933 [8914] Flavianus CPolitanus, *Epistula ad Leonem papam. ACO* II,1,1, 36–37.

11 Τῷ ἀγαπητῷ Φαύστῳ υἱῷ πρεσβύτερος ἡμῶν ἐπίσκοπος Ῥώμης
Inc.: Κεχαρισμένον ἐστὶν ἀεὶ ἐμοὶ τὸ τὴν σὴν ἀγάπην . . .
fol. 16 desin.: . . . ἡδέως ἔχουσι πρὸς τοὺς ταῦτα διακομίζοντας.
CPG [8911] Leo I Papa, *Epistula ad Faustum presbyterum. ACO* II,1,1, 37–38.

12 Ἑτέρα ἐπιστολὴ Φλαβιανοῦ ἐπισκόπου Κωνσταντινουπόλεως γραφεῖσα πρὸς τὸν αὐτὸν ἀρχιεπίσκοπον Λέοντα τὸν πρεσβύτερον Ῥώμης.
Inc.: Τῷ ἁγιωτάτῳ. . . . Εὐσεβείας καὶ τοῦ ὀρθοτομεῖσθαι . . .
fol. 17 desin.: . . . ἡμῖν θεοφιλέστατε καὶ ἀξιώτατε πάτερ.
CPG 5935 [8915] Flavianus CPolitanus, *Epist. ad Leonem papam. ACO* II,1,1, 38–40.

13 Ἐπιστολὴ Λέοντος ἀρχιεπισκόπου Ῥώμης πρὸς Ἰουλιανὸν ἐπίσκοπον Κωνσταντινουπόλεως (sic).
Inc.: Τῷ ἀγαπητῷ . . . Λέων, ἐπίσκοπος. Εἰ καὶ διὰ τῶν ἡμετέρων . . .
fol. 18ᵛ desin.: . . . θεραπευθῆναι ὑγιαίνοντά σε/ ἀδελφὲ τιμιώτατε.
CPG [8929] Leo I Papa, *Epistula ad Iulianum episc. Coi* (13/6/449), *ACO* II,1,1, 40–42.

14 Ἐπιστολὴ Λέοντος ἀρχιεπισκόπου Ῥώμης πρὸς τοὺς ἀρχιμανδρίτας Κωνσταντινουπόλεως.
Inc.: Ἀγαπητοῖς τέκνοις . . . Ἐπειδὴ διὰ τὴν αἰτίαν τῆς πίστεως . . .
desin.: . . . μένειν ἐπιθυμοῦμεν· ὁ Θεὸς ὑμᾶς φυλάττοι τέκνα ἀγαπητά.
CPG [8926] Leo I Papa, Epistula ad Faustum et Martinum presbyteros et reliquos archimandritas (13/6/449). ACO II,1,1, 42–43.

15 Ἴσον ἐπιστολῆς γραφείσης παρὰ Λέοντος ἀρχιεπισκόπου Ῥώμης κατὰ Εὐτυχοῦς πρὸς τὴν ἐν Ἐφέσῳ δευτέραν σύνοδον, ἧστινος ὑποβληθείσης μέν, ἀποκρυβείσης δὲ διὰ τὸ μὴ συγχωρῆσαι δημοσιευθῆναι ταύτην τοῖς ἐπισκόποις Διόσκορον.
Inc.: Λέων . . . Ἡ τοῦ ἡμερωτάτου βασιλέως εὐαγεστάτη πίστις . . .
fol. 19ᵛ desin.: . . . καὶ πᾶσα γλῶσσα ἐξομολογήσεται ὅτι Κύριος Ἰησοῦς Χριστὸς εἰς δόξαν Θεοῦ πατρὸς ἀμήν.
CPG [8927] Leo I Papa, Epistula ad synodum quae apud Ephesum convenit (13/6/449). ACO II,1,1, 43–44.

16 Ἐπιστολὴ Λέοντος, ἀρχιεπισκόπου Ῥώμης πρὸς Θεοδόσιον τὸν βασιλέα μεμφομένη τὴν ἐν Ἐφέσῳ γενομένην σύνοδον κατὰ Φλαβιανοῦ καὶ ἑτέραν ἐξαιτοῦντος γενέσθαι.
Inc.: Τῷ φιλανθρωποτάτῳ . . . Τοῖς γράμμασι τῆς ὑμετέρας φιλανθρωπίας. . . .
fol. 20ᵛ desin.: . . . τῇ δεξιᾷ τοῦ Θεοῦ ἐκδικηθείη τὸ κράτος.
CPG [8948] Leo I Papa, Epistula Leonis et sanctae synodi ad Theodosium augustum (13/10/449). ACO II,1,1, 25–27.

17 Ἐπιστολὴ Λέοντος ἀρχιεπισκόπου Ῥώμης πρὸς Θεοδόσιον, τὸν βασιλέα ἐν Ἐφέσῳ ἀποσταλεῖσα.
Inc.: Τῷ ἐνδοξοτάτῳ . . . ὅσων (sic) τῶν ἀνθρωπίνων πραγμάτων . . .
fol. 21 desin.: . . . τὰ ἀποσταλμένα (sic) γράμματα περιέχει.
CPG [8923] Leo I Papa, Epistula ad Theodosium augustum (13/6/449). ACO II,1,1, 45.

18 Τῇ ἐνδοξοτάτῃ καὶ φιλανθρωποτάτῃ θυγατρὶ Πουλχερίᾳ, αὐγούστᾳ· Λέων ἐπίσκοπος·
Inc.: Πόσην πεποίθησιν περὶ τῆς πίστεως τῆς ὑμετέρας . . .
fol. 22 desin.: . . . καὶ συγγνώμης καὶ φιλοτιμίας ἀξιωθήσεται.
CPG [8924] Leo I Papa, Epistula ad Pulcheriam augustam (13/6/449). ACO II,1,1 45–47.

19 Τῇ ἐνδοξοτάτῃ καὶ φιλανθρωποτάτῃ θυγατρὶ Πουλχερίᾳ ἀειαυγούστᾳ, Λέων ἐπίσκοπος καὶ ἡ ἁγία σύνοδος ἡ ἐν Ῥώμῃ συναχθεῖσα.
Inc.: Αἱ ἐπιστολαὶ αἱ περὶ τῆς πίστεως . . .
fol. 22ᵛ desin.: . . . αὐτοῦ φιλαγάθου διατυπώσεως συνεισφερόμενον.
CPG [8949] Leo I Papa, Epistula Leonis et sanctae synodi ad Pulcheriam augustam (13/10/449). ACO II,1,1 47–48.

20 Τῇ φιλανθρωποτάτῃ καὶ εὐσεβεστάτῃ Πουλχερίᾳ αὐγούστᾳ, Ἱλαρίων διάκονος.
Inc.: Σπουδήν μοι γεγενεῖσθαι (sic) μετὰ τὴν σύνοδον . . .
fol. 23 desin.: . . . ζήλῳ μονίμῳ διανοίᾳ συνταξάτω.
CPG [8950] Hilarius Papa, Epistula Hilarii diaconi (postea papae) ad Pulcheriam augustam. ACO II,1,1, 48–49.

21 Γάλλα Πλακιδία, ἡ εὐσεβεστάτη καὶ ἐπιφανεστάτη ἀειαυγούστα, Αἰλία Πουλχερία τῇ εὐσεβεστάτη ἀειαυγούστα, θυγατρί.
Inc.: Ὅτι τὴν Ῥώμην συνσχέειν (sic) ἐκδρομαῖς ὁμοίως . . .

fol. 23ᵛ desin.: . . . καὶ διοικητέον καὶ φυλακτέον ἐπιτρεψάσῃ.
CPG [8960] *Epistula Gallae Placidiae ad Pulcheriam augustam* (2/450). *ACO* II,1,1, 49–50.

22 Λέων, ἐπίσκοπος καὶ ἡ ἁγία σύνοδος, ἡ ἐν τῇ πόλει Ῥωμαίων συναχθεῖσα, κλήρῳ, ἀξιωματικοῖς καὶ παντὶ τῷ λαῷ, τοῖς οἰκοῦσιν ἐν Κωνσταντινουπόλει ἀγαπητοῖς υἱοῖς ἐν Κυρίῳ χαίρειν.
Inc.: Εἰς γνῶσιν ἡμῖν ἐλθόντων, ἅπερ ἐν τῇ Ἐφέσῳ . . .
fol. 24 desin.: . . . τὸν στέφανον τῆς πίστεως λαμβάνειν δυνηθείητε.
CPG [8954] Leo I Papa, *Epistula ad clerum CPolitanum* (13/10/449). *ACO* II,1,1, 50–51.

fol. 24ᵛ **23** Ἐπιστολὴ Λέοντος ἀρχιεπισκόπου Ῥώμης πρὸς τοὺς ἀρχιμανδρίτας Κωνσταντινουπόλεως.
Inc.: Λέων ἐπίσκοπος . . . εἰ καὶ τὰ μάλιστα ἐκεῖνα . . .
fol. 25 desin.: . . . πίστεως ἀκολουθία δεκτέα εἶναι συγχωρεῖ.
CPG [8955] Leo I Papa, *Epistula ad Faustum, Martinum, Petrum, Emmanuelem presb. et archim.* (13/10/449). *ACO* II,1,1, 51–52.

Post συγχωρεῖ P add.

Ἀρχὴ συνόδ⟨ου⟩ τῆ⟨ς⟩ ἐν Χαλκηδόνι.

24 Ἴσον σάκρας ἀποσταλείσης παρὰ τοῦ εὐσεβεστάτου καὶ φιλοχρίστου βασιλέως Μαρκιανοῦ πρὸς τοὺς ἀπανταχοῦ θεοφιλεστάτους ἐπισκόπους περὶ τοῦ συνελθεῖν πάντας εἰς τὴν Νικαέων.
Inc.: Οἱ νικηταί . . . Τῶν πραγμάτων ἁπάντων δεῖ προτιμᾶσθαι . . .
desin.: . . . Μαρκιανοῦ τοῦ αἰωνίου αὐγούστου καὶ τοῦ δηλωθησομένου.
CPG 8982 *Epistula Marciani imperatoris et Valentiniani iii ad (Leonem episc. Romae et) Anatolium episc. CPolis* (23/5/451). *ACO* II,3,1, 27–28.

25 Ἴσον βασιλικοῦ γράμματος ἀποσταλέντος παρὰ τῆς εὐσεβεστάτης καὶ φιλοχρίστου βασιλίδος καὶ αὐγούστης Πουλχερίας πρὸς τὸν κονσουλάριον Βηθυνίας (sic) Στρατήγιον περὶ τοῦ φροντίσαι τῆς κατὰ τὴν σύνοδον εὐταξίας πρὸ τοῦ διῶξαι (sic) ἀπὸ τῆς Νικαέων εἰς τὴν Χαλκηδονέων μεταστῆναι τὴν σύνοδον.
Inc.: Σκοπὸς τῇ ἡμετέρᾳ γαληνότητι πρὸ τῶν πολεμικῶν πραγμάτων . . .
fol. 25ᵛ desin.: . . . οὐχ ὁ τυχών σε παραστήσεται κίνδυνος.
CPG 8997 *Epistula Pulcheriae augustae ad Strategium consularem Bithyniae.* *ACO* II,1,1, 29.

26 Ὁμοίως ἴσον βασιλικοῦ γράμματος δευτέρου πεμφθέντος τῇ ἁγίᾳ συνόδῳ, τῇ ἐν Νικαίᾳ συνδραμούσῃ περὶ τοῦ δεῖν μετελθεῖν εἰς τὴν Χαλκηδονέων·
Inc.: Οἱ νικηταὶ Οὐαλεντινιανός . . . σπεύδοντας ἡμᾶς εἰς τὴν ἁγίαν . . .
fol. 26 desin.: . . . διαφυλάττοι εἰς πολλοὺς ἐνιαυτοὺς ἁγιώτατοι.
CPG 8998 *Epistula Marciani et Valentiniani ad concilium Nicaeae Chalcedonem transferendum.* *ACO* II,1,1, 28–29.

27 Ὁμοίως ἴσον βασιλικοῦ γράμματος τρίτου καταπεμφθέντος ἐν Νικαίᾳ τῇ ἁγίᾳ συνόδῳ, ἔτι τοῦ εὐσεβεστάτου βασιλέως κατὰ τὴν Θρᾴκην ἐπερχομένου περὶ τοῦ δεῖν ἀνυπερθέτως μετελθεῖν ἐν τῇ Χαλκηδονίων.
Inc.: Αὐτοκράτορες . . . Ἤδη μὲν καὶ δι' ἑτέρων θείων ἡμῶν . . .
fol. 26ᵛ desin.: . . . ἐκστρατείαν ἐπανελθεῖν· ὁ Θεὸς ὑμᾶς φυλάξει . . .
CPG 8999 *Epistula eorundem ad idem concilium.* *ACO* II,1,1, 30.

28 Ἴσον ἐπιστολῆς τοῦ ἁγιωτάτου καὶ μακαριωτάτου ἀρχιεπισκόπου τῆς Ῥωμαίων Λέοντος γραφείσης πρὸς τὴν ἁγίαν καὶ οἰκουμενικὴν σύνοδον, ἥτις κομισθεῖσα διὰ τῶν θεοφιλεστάτων ἐπισκόπων Πασχασίνου καὶ Λουκηνσίου καὶ Βονιφατίου πρεσβυτέρου Ῥώμης ἀνεγνώσθη ἐπὶ τῆς ἁγίας συνόδου.
Inc.: Λέων ἐπίσκοπος . . . Ἐμοὶ μὲν εὐκταῖον, ἀγαπητοί . . .
fol. 27ᵛ desin.: . . . ἔρρωσθε ἐν Κυρίῳ ἀδελφοὶ προσφιλέστατοι. ἐδόθη πρὸ πέντε καλανδῶν Ἰουνίων.
CPG [8993] Leo I Papa, *Epistula ad concilium Chalcedonense (synodum Nicaeae constitutam)* (26/6/451). *ACO* II,1,1, 31–32.

29 Ἐπιστολὴ τοῦ μακαρίου Λέοντος, τοῦ τῆς μεγάλης ἀρχιεπισκοπῆς Ῥώμης πρὸς Φλαβιανόν, ἁγιώτατον ἀρχιεπίσκοπον Κωνσταντινουπόλεως· τῷ ἀγαπητῷ ἀδελφῷ Φλαβιανῷ Λέων in margine: ἡ προσαγορευομένη στήλη.
Inc.: Ἀναγνόντες τὰ γράμματα τῆς ἀγάπης τῆς σῆς . . .
fol. 31ᵛ desin.: . . . ἐρρωμένον σε διαφυλάττοι ἀδελφὲ προσφιλέστατε.
CPG [8922] Leo I Papa, *Epistula ad Flavianum CPolitanum (Tomus)* (13/6/449), (*CPL* 1656). *ACO* II,1,1 10–20.

29a Post finem epistulae P add.:

Μετὰ δὲ τὴν ἀνάγνωσιν τῆς προγεγραμμένης ἐπιστολῆς . . . ταῦτα Διόσκορος ἔκρυψεν.

quod est excerptum de actis Concilii Chalcedonensis. *CPG* 9002 *Actio III. ACO* II,1,2, 81.23–31.

29b In margine: ἐκ τῶν Λειμωναρίων κεφ. σαʹ.
Inc.: Διηγήσατο ἐν τῇ Κωνσταντινουπόλει . . .
desin.: . . . χειρὶ τοῦ ἀποστόλου διορθωθεῖσα.
CPG 7376 Iohannes Moschus, *Pratum spirituale*, PG 87.3, 3012A–B.

30 Ἐκ τῶν ὑπομνημάτων τῆς ἁγίας οἰκουμενικῆς εʹ συνόδου. Εὐτυχίου ἀρχιεπισκόπου Κωνσταντινουπόλεως πρὸς Βιγίλλιον πάπα Ῥώμης.
Inc.: Τῷ τὰ πάντα ἁγιωτάτῳ . . . (fol. 32) Ἰδόντες ὁπόσων ἀγαθῶν αἰτία ἐστίν . . .
fol. 32ᵛ desin.: . . . τούτοις δὲ καὶ ὑπεσημηνάμεθα καὶ ὑπογραφή· ἐρρωμένος ἐν Κυρίῳ . . . ὑπέγραψα.
CPG 6937 Eutychius Constantinopolitanus, *Epistula ad Vigilium. ACO* IV,1, 235.1–236.25 et iterum 237.1–238.5; *PG* 86, 2401–6.

Post finem epistulae P add.:

Ὁ αὐτὸς λίβελλος ἐγένετο—πρὸς τὸν αὐτὸν ὁσιώτατον Βιγίλλιον. (*ACO* IV,1, 236.26–29).

31 Ἀντίγραφον ἐπιστολῆς Βιγιλλίου τοῦ ὁσιωτάτου πάπα πρὸς Εὐτύχιον τὸν ἁγιώτατον ἀρχιεπίσκοπον Κωνσταντινουπόλεως καὶ τὴν ὑπ᾽ αὐτὸν σύνοδον.
Inc.: Τῷ ἀγαπητῷ . . . Ἐπληρώθη χαρᾶς τὸ στόμα ἡμῶν καὶ ἡ γλῶσσα . . .
fol. 34 desin.: . . . ἐν ἅπασι τὸ σέβας φυλάττεται. ὑπογραφή. ὁ Θεός . . . τιμιώτατε. ἐδόθη πρὸ ἑπτὰ εἰδῶν . . . ἔτους δωδεκάτου.
CPG [9350] *Epistula Vigilii ad Eutychium CPolitanum* (6/1/553). *ACO* VI,1, 236–38.

Post finem epistulae P add.:

Τῷ αὐτῷ τύπῳ ἔγραψε καὶ πρός—καὶ τὴν ὑπ᾽ αὐτοὺς σύνοδον. (*ACO* IV,1, 238.33-35)

32 Ἐκ τῆς ὀγδόης πράξεως τῆς ἁγίας οἰκουμενικῆς ε´ συνόδου κατὰ Θεοδώρου ἐπισκόπου γεναμένου Μομψοεστίας.

Inc.: Εἴ τις οὐχ ὁμολογεῖ πατρὸς καὶ υἱοῦ καί . . .

fol. 36ᵛ desin.: . . . ὁμοίως καὶ οἱ λοιποὶ ἐπίσκοποι ὑπέγραψαν.

CPG 9362.2 Concilium Oecumenicum CPolitanum II (553), *Gesta, Actio VIII* (2/6/553). *ACO* IV,1, 240.3-245.8 (also *CPG* 9401.7).

33 Βιγιλλίου ἀρχιεπισκόπου Ῥώμης πρὸς Εὐτύχιον ἀρχιεπίσκοπον Κωνσταντινουπόλεως καὶ πᾶσαν τὴν προκειμένην ἁγίαν σύνοδον.

fol. 37 Inc.: Τῷ ἀγαπητῷ . . . Τὰ σκάνδαλα ἅπερ ὁ τοῦ ἀνθρωπίνου . . .

fol. 38ᵛ desin.: . . . περὶ ὧν ἐν ὑπονοίᾳ γέγονεν. Ὁ Θεός . . . τιμιώτατε. ἐδόθη . . . ἔτους ιβ´.

CPG 9364 *Epistula ii Vigilii ad Eutychium CPolitanum* (8/12/553). *ACO* IV,1, 245.9-247.39.

Post ιβ´ add. P:

Τέλος βιβλίου η´ τῆς ἁγίας συνόδου τῆς ἐν Κωνσταντινουπόλει συναχθείσης. Χριστὲ ὁ Θεὸς δόξα σοι· ἀμήν.

Etiam rubricis lit.:

Ὅτι οὐ δεῖ σιωπεῖν (sic) καὶ ὑποστέλλεσθαι τοῖς ἀντιλέγουσι τῇ ἀληθείᾳ περὶ τῆς εὐσεβείας, κἂν οἱουδήποτε βαθμοῦ τύχειεν (sic) εἶναι τοὺς ἀντιλέγοντας, εἰ καὶ λίαν εἰσὶ τῶν εὐτελῶν καὶ ἀπόρων· πιστοὶ δὲ οἱ ἀντεχόμενοι τῆς ὀρθοδόξου πίστεως.

34 Τῆς ἁγίας καὶ οἰκουμενικῆς ε´ συνόδου ἐκ τῆς η´ πράξεως κατὰ Θεοδώρου ἐπισκόπου γενομένου Μομψοεστίας.

Inc.: Ἡ ἁγία σύνοδος εἶπε· τοῦ μεγάλου Θεοῦ καὶ σωτῆρος . . .

fol. 39 desin.: . . . ἐπισπειρομένων τῆς ἀσεβείας ζιζανίων.

CPG 9362.1 Concilium Oecum. CPolit. II (553), *Gesta, Actio VIII* (2/6/553). *ACO* IV,1, 239.1-14.

35 Ἐκ τῆς ἐπιστολῆς Πρόκλου ἀρχιεπισκόπου Κωνσταντινουπόλεως πρὸς Ἰωάννην ἐπίσκοπον Ἀντιοχείας.

Ἠλεὶ ἐκεῖνος (ὁ κεῖνος cod.) ὁ τῷ χρόνῳ καμὼν καὶ ἐν Σιλὼμ τά τοῦ νόμου ἱερουργῶν, αὐτὸς μὲν οὐκ ἐνήργει ἅπερ οἱ παῖδες ἐτόλμων, συνέπραττε δὲ ἐκείνοις δι᾽ ὧν οὐκ ἐκώλυεν ἁμαρτάνοντας, ἐπείπερ κατὰ τὸν ἀληθῆ λόγον τὸ μὴ κωλύειν τὰ ἄτοπα τῷ (τὸ cod.) δρᾶν συγγενές· καὶ πάλιν οἱ παῖδες ταῖς
5 πράξεσι τὸν βαθμὸν ὑβρίζοντες, ἀναξίους τε δι᾽ ὧν ἐπλημμέλουν τῆς ἱερωσύνης ἑαυτοὺς ἐπιφαίνοντες, οὐ μόνον οἷς ἔδρων ἔπιπτον, ἀλλὰ γὰρ καὶ πρὸς τὸ πταίειν τοὺς ἄλλους ἐξεκαλοῦντο, εἰκόνα πλημμελείας ἑαυτοὺς τοῖς ζηλοῦσιν ἀναθέντες. διὸ ἐπ᾽ ἴσης τὰ τῆς δίκης ἐπεῖκται τοῖς τε δυσσεβήσασι καὶ τῷ μὴ κωλύσαντι. τὸν μὲν γὰρ φύσαντα εἰς ἀρετὴν ἔβλαψε τὸ ῥάθυμον, τοῖς δὲ ἐξ
10 ἐκείνου τὸν ἀφανισμὸν (τῶν ἀφανισμῶν cod.) ἐπήγαγε τὸ ἀδιόρθωτον καὶ ὁ

πρεσβύτης ἐν τῷ τῶν νέων ἐναυάγησε χειμῶνι, ὑπὲρ ὧν τῇ σχέσει οὐκ ἐκυβέρνησεν ἐπιπλήξει.

Ἠλεί, Σιλὼμ cf. I Reg. 1.1–4.18.
CPG 5900 Proclus CPolitanus, (Ep. 3) Ad Iohannem Antiochenum. ACO IV,1, 141.12–22; PG 65, 874B–C (Latin).
Fragmentum Graecum primum editum est supra.

36 Ἐκ τῆς ἐπιστολῆς Βίκτωρος τοῦ Καρθαγενισίων (sic) ἐπισκόπου πρὸς Θεόδωρον πάπα Ῥώμης.
Inc.: Ἡμεῖς γὰρ οἱ ἐλάχιστοι τοῦ Κυρίου διακυβερνοῦντος (sic) . . .
desin.: . . . τῷ φανερῷ τοῦτον ἀντιπίπτειν μολύσματι.
CPG [9396] Epistula Victoris episc. Carthaginensis ad Theodorum papam (a. 646 ineunte). ACO Ser. II, vol. I, 102.11–22.

37 Γρηγορίου ἐπισκόπου Ναζιανζοῦ τοῦ Θεολόγου ἐκ τοῦ εἰς Βασίλειον ἐπιταφίου.
Inc.: Κινεῖται οὖν ἐπ' αὐτὸν τῆς ἐκκλησίας ὅσον ἔγκριτον . . .
fol. 39ᵛ desin.: . . . ῥᾷστον δὲ τοῦτο ἦν ἐκ τριῶν τῶν ἰσχυροτάτων.
CPG 3010.43 Gregorius Nazianzenus, Oratio 43, ed. J. Bernardi, Discours 42–43, 188 par. 28.8–190 par. 28.18; PG 36, 533C10–536A6.

38 Τοῦ αὐτοῦ εἰς Ἀθανάσιον ἐπίσκοπον Ἀλεξανδρείας·
Inc.: Καθ' ὃν κινεῖται μὲν ἀφ' ἡμῶν ὅσον φιλόσοφον . . .
desin.: . . . καὶ οὐδὲ νῦν ἔτι λήγει συνανιπτάμενον.
CPG 3010.21 Gregorius Naz., Oratio 21, ed. J. Mossay, Discours 20–23, 162 par. 25.9–18; PG 35, 1112A1–12.

39 Τοῦ αὐτοῦ ἐκ τοῦ εἰς τὸ ῥητὸν τοῦ εὐαγγελίου· ὅτε ἐτέλεσεν ὁ Ἰησοῦς τοὺς λόγους μετῆρεν ἀπὸ τῆς Γαλιλαίας καὶ ἦλθεν εἰς τὰ ὅρια τῆς Ἰουδαίας πέραν τοῦ Ἰορδάνου καὶ ἠκολούθησαν αὐτῷ ὄχλοι πολλοί.
Inc.: Ταῦτα καὶ λαϊκοῖς νομοθετῶ ταῦτα καί . . .
desin.: . . . θάνατός ἐστι ψυχῆς. μέχρι τούτων ὁ λόγος στήτω.
CPG 3010.37 Gregorius Naz., Oratio 37, ed. C. Moreschini, Discours 32–37, 316 par. 23.1–12; PG 36, 308B6–C5. See also quotation **235**.

40 Ἐκ τῶν διατάξεων Παύλου τοῦ ἁγίου ἀποστόλου· περὶ κανόνων ἐκκλησιαστικῶν.
Ὁ διδάσκων εἰ καὶ λαϊκὸς εἴη ἔμπειρος δὲ τοῦ λόγου καὶ τὸν τρόπον σεμνὸς διδασκέτω, ἔσονται γὰρ πάντες διδακτοὶ Θεοῦ.
CPG 1741 Epitoma libri VIII Constitutionum apostolorum seu Constitutiones per Hippolytum. n. (c), ed. F. X. Funk, Didascalia et Constitutiones apostolorum, II (Paderborn, 1905; repr. Turin, 1962), p. 87.17.7–8.

41 Τοῦ ἐν ἁγίοις πατρὸς ἡμῶν Ἀναστασίου πατριάρχου Ἀντιοχείας ἀπόδειξις ὅτι μέγα τὸ ἀρχιερατικὸν ἀξίωμα καὶ γὰρ ἀδύνατον ἀνακρίνεσθαι ἱερέα ὑπὸ λαϊκοῦ, ἀλλ' ὑπὸ μείζονος ἀρχιερέως.
Inc.: Ἐν τῇ ἐκκλησιαστικῇ ἱστορίᾳ Φίλωνος τοῦ φιλοσόφου . . .
fol. 40 desin.: . . . οὐκέτι ἡ λάρναξ ἐκινήθη ἐκ τοῦ τόπου αὐτῆς.
CPG 7512 Philo historiographus, Historia ecclesiastica (frag.), ed. G. Mercati, "Un preteso scritto di san Pietro vescovo d'Alessandria e martire sulla bestemmia e Filone

l'istoriografo," in G. Mercati, *Opere minori*, II, *ST* 77 (1937), 437–38. Also *CPG* 7728 nota, *De dignitate sacerdotali* (2), *PG* 89, 1288c8–d7.

Post αὐτῆς P add.:

Τοὺς δὲ ὑπὸ τοῦ βασιλέως χειροτονημένους ἄρχοντας, κἂν λήσταρχοί εἰσι, κἂν κλέπται, κἂν λησταί, κἂν ἄδικοι, κἂν ὅτι οὖν εἰσιν ἕτερον, δεδοικέναι χρή, οὐ διὰ τὴν πονηρίαν καταφρονοῦντες αὐτῶν, ἀλλὰ διὰ τὴν ἀξίαν τοῦ χειροτονήσαντος δυσωπούμενοι.

42 Ἀπὸ φωνῆς Θεο(δώρου) τοῦ θεοφιλεστάτου ἀββᾶ καὶ σοφωτάτου φιλοσόφου τήν τε θείαν καὶ ἐξωτικὴν καὶ ὡς χρὴ φιλοσοφήσαντος γραφήν.

Inc.: Ἀναγκαῖόν ἐστι μέλλοντας ἡμᾶς χριστινικῶν (sic) αἱρέσεων . . .

fol. 60ᵛ desin.: . . . ἀνοίξει τοῦ στόματος ἡμῶν, ἐχορήγησε Χριστὸς ὁ Θεός, ᾧ ἡ δόξα . . .

CPG 6823 Leontius Scholasticus (Ps.-Leontius), *Liber de sectis*, *PG* 86, 1193–1628.

43 Ἀναφοραὶ Ἀγάθωνι τῷ ἁγιωτάτῳ καὶ μακαριωτάτῳ πάπᾳ τῆς πρεσβυτέρας Ῥώμης πρὸς τὴν ἕκτην σύνοδον.

Inc.: Τοῖς εὐσεβεστάτοις . . . Κατανοοῦντί μοι τοῦ ἀνθρωπίνου βίου . . .

fol. 69 desin.: . . . καὶ ἀγωνιᾶν ἐκείνης ἐστίν.

CPG 9417 *Epistula Agathonis papae ad Constantinum IV imp.* (27/3/680). *ACO Ser. II*, vol. II,1, 52.15–86.6.

44 Ἡ ἐπιγραφὴ τῆς συνοδικῆς ἀναφορᾶς· τοῖς εὐσεβεστάτοις δεσπόταις . . . τῇ συνόδῳ τοῦ ἀποστολικοῦ θρόνου.

Inc.: Πάντων τῶν ἀγαθῶν ἐλπὶς ὑπάρχειν γνωρίζεται . . .

fol. 73 desin.: . . . ὑπέγραψα. (P add.: ὡσαύτως καὶ οἱ λοιποὶ πάντες ὑπέγραψαν ὁμοίως).

CPG 9418 *Epistula Agathonis et Synodi ad Constantinum IV imp. ACO Ser. II*, vol. II,1, 122.8–140.10.

fol. 73ᵛ **45** Δεσπότῃ τῷ τὰ πάντα ἁγιωτάτῳ μακαριωτάτῳ ἀδελφῷ καὶ συλλειτουργῷ Σεργίῳ ἀρχιεπισκόπῳ καὶ πατριάρχῃ Κωνσταντινουπόλεως Σωφρόνιος ἀχρεῖος δοῦλος τῆς ἁγίας Χριστοῦ τοῦ Θεοῦ ἡμῶν πόλεως.

Inc.: Βαβαὶ βαβαὶ παμμακάριστοι, πῶς μοι φίλον . . .

fol. 86ᵛ desin.: . . . πάντες ἀδελφοὶ προσαγορεύομεν. ἐρρωμένος . . .

CPG 7635 Sophronius Hierosolymitanus, *Epistula synodica ad Sergium CPolitanum. ACO Ser. II*, vol. II,1, 410.13–494.9; *PG* 87.3, 3148–3200.

46 Ἐκ τῆς η΄ πράξεως τῆς στ΄ συνόδου ἀπὸ φωνῆς Θεοφάνους πρεσβυτέρου καὶ ἡγουμένου τῆς μονῆς τῶν Βαΐων.

Inc.: Θεοφάνης ὁ θεοσεβέστατος πρεσβύτερος καὶ ἡγούμενος . . .

fol. 87ᵛ desin.: . . . τοῦ ἀληθινοῦ Θεοῦ ἡμῶν ἀποδείκνυται.

CPG 9427 Concilium Oecum. CPolitanum III, *Actio VIII* (7/3/681). *ACO Ser. II*, vol. II,1, 242.14–248.14.

47 Σὺν Θεῷ προγυμνασία κατ᾽ ἐπιτομὴν ὀμματίζουσα τὸν φιλόπονον περὶ ὧν δεῖ πρὸ πάντων ἐξασκεῖν καὶ τὴν εἴδησιν ἔχειν.

Inc.: Ὅτι δεῖ προηγουμένως βίον σεμνὸν καὶ τὸ πνεῦμα τοῦ . . .

fol. 108 desin.: . . . δαμάζεσθαι ὑπὸ τῆς ἀνθρωπίνης φύσεως.

CPG 7745 Anastasius Sinaita, *Viae Dux* (*Hodegos*), ed. K.-H. Uthemann, *Anastasii Sinaitae Viae Dux, CCSG* 8 (Turnhout-Louvain, 1981), P = I,1,1–II,8,137; XIII,1,1–3 πατέρων;   5.85–9.90; XIV,1,1–43 προσευχῆς; XVI,1–XVIII,66; XXI,4,1–40; XXIII,1,30–3,75. See also quotations **111, 194a–e, 239.**

48 Τοῦ ἁγίου Ἀθανασίου μαρτυρίαι ἐκ τῆς γραφῆς κατὰ τὴν τῆς φύσεως κοινωνίαν ἐκ τοῦ ὁμοίους εἶναι τὸν πατέρα καὶ τὸν υἱὸν καὶ τὸ ἅγιον πνεῦμα πρὸς θεωρίαν δυσέφικτον· περὶ ἐλευθερίας.
Inc.: Περὶ πατρὸς ἀναμφίβολον, περὶ υἱοῦ φωνὴ αὐτοῦ . . .
fol. 116ᵛ desin.: . . . ὁ κολλώμενος τῷ Κυρίῳ ἓν Πνεῦμά ἐστιν.
CPG 2240 Athanasius Alexandrinus, *Testimonia e scriptura* (*De communi essentia patris et filii et spiritus sancti*), *PG* 28, 29c–80c.

49 Ἐπιλύσεις δογματικῶν ζητημάτων Κυρίλλου τοῦ ἁγιωτάτου ἀρχιεπισκόπου Ἀλεξανδρείας, ἐπιζητηθέντων παρὰ Τιβερίου διακόνου καὶ τῆς ἀδελφότητος.
fol. 117 Inc.: Εἰ ὁ ἐπὶ πάντων Θεὸς χεῖρας, πόδας, ὀφθαλμούς . . .
fol. 121 desin.: . . . οἱ υἱοὶ τοῦ Θεοῦ τὰς θυγατέρας τῶν ἀνθρώπων.
CPG 5231 Cyrillus Alex., *De dogmatum solutione* (P = chaps. 1–13, 17, 22: *PG* 76, 1077b–1100b, 1105b–1108b, 1117a–1120c).

Ὅτι ἐκ δύο φύσεων τὸν Χριστὸν καὶ ἐν δύο φύσεσιν ὀρθοδόξως οἱ θεόπνευστοι πατέρες ἐκήρυξαν καὶ ὅτι τὸ μίαν λέγειν φύσιν τοῦ λόγου σεσαρκωμένην εὐσεβῶς ταὐτόν ἐστι τῷ εἰπεῖν δύο φύσεις.

CPG 7781 Anastasiana Incertae Originis, *Doctrina Patrum*, ed. Diekamp, 11.2–5.

50 Ἀμφιλοχίου ἐπισκόπου Ἰκονίου ἐκ τῆς πρὸς Σέλευκον ἐπιστολῆς· καὶ μετ᾽ ὀλίγα.
Inc.: Ἡ ληφθεῖσα πάσχει φύσις . . .
desin.: . . . οἰκειοῦται αὐτὸς πάσχων οὐδέν.
CPG 3245.15 Amphilochius Iconiensis, *Fragmentum xv* (*epistula ad Seleucum*), ed. C. Datema, *Amphilochii Opera*, 264.56–57; *PG* 39, 112b–d.
Doctrina Patrum (chap. B′), p. 12.19–24, IX (20–24).

51 Κυρίλλου ἐκ τῆς β´ πρὸς Σούκενσον ἐπιστολῆς. καὶ μετ᾽ ὀλίγα·
Inc.: Ὀρθότατα δὲ καὶ πάνυ συνετῶς ἡ σὴ τελειότης . . .
desin.: . . . ἡ αὐτοῦ γὰρ πέπονθε σάρξ.
Sequitur scholium (Σημειωτέον δὲ καὶ νῦν—δύο εἶναι φύσεις.).
CPG 5346 Cyrillus Alex., *Epist. 46 ad Successum episc. Diocaesareae. ACO* I,1,6, 161.4–8; *PG* 77, 244b.
Doctrina Patrum (chap. B′), p. 17.1–6, XXI.

fol. 121ᵛ **52** Καὶ πρὸς τῷ τέλει τῆς αὐτῆς ἐπιστολῆς.
Inc.: Τούτων τὰς κενοφωνίας ἐκκλίνοντες ἀγαπητέ . . .
desin.: . . . προσάπτειν ἐπείγονται τὴν οἰκονομίαν ἀρνούμενοι.
CPG 4530 Iohannes Chrysostomus, *Epistula ad Caesarium, PG* 52, 760 (also *PG* 64, 496–97).
Doctrina Patrum (chap. B′), p. 19.9–24, XXVIII.

53 Τοῦ ἁγίου Σιλβέστρου ἐπισκόπου Ῥώμης ἐκ τῆς ἀντιλογίας τῆς πρὸς Ἰουδαίους.
Inc.: Ἰουβὰλ λέγει· ἀδύνατόν ἐστι πεῖσαί με ἀνθρώπινον . . .
fol. 122 desin.: . . . καὶ ἀναλλοίωτον καὶ ἣν ἐπίσταται μόνος αὐτός.

BHG 1634f, *Acta Silvestri, Disputatio cum Iudaeis*, ed. F. Combefis, *Illustrium Christi martyrum lecti triumphi* (Paris, 1660), 317.14–320.23. For text, see above, pp. 62–63.

54 Ἀθανασίου ἐκ τῆς πρὸς σωτηριώδους ἐπιφανείας.
Inc.: Ὁ προϋπάρχων Θεὸς πρὸ τῆς ἐν σαρκὶ ἐπιδημίας . . .
desin.: . . . καὶ ἀπαθῆ νοεῖσθαι ἀληθινῶς.
CPG 2231 Athanasius Alex., *De incarnatione contra Apollinarium libri ii*, *PG* 26, 1133B.
Doctrina Patrum (chap. Γ´), p. 25.20–26.10, I.

55 Γελασίου Καισαρείας ἐν ἐξηγήσει τοῦ μαθήματος.
Inc.: Ἦλθε τοίνυν εἰς ταὐτὸν Θεὸς ἅμα καὶ ἄνθρωπος . . .
desin.: . . . καὶ φιμούσθω πᾶν αἱρετικὸν στόμα.
Doctrina Patrum (chap. Δ´), p. 31.18–32.2, XI. See also quotation **83**.

56 Κυρίλλου ἐκ τῆς α´ πρὸς Σούκενσον ἐπιστολῆς.
Inc.: ⟨Ἴ⟩σον γάρ ἐστιν εἰς ἀτοπίας λόγον τὸ εἰπεῖν . . .
fol. 122ᵛ desin.: . . . οὔτε ἡμεῖς οὕτω διακείμεθα.
CPG 5345 Cyrillus Alex., *Epist.* 45 *ad Successum episc. Diocaesareae*. *ACO* I,1,6, 156.11–18; *PG* 77, 236C11–D9.
Doctrina Patrum (chap. Ε´), p. 34.1–2, III. See also quotation **107**.

57 Τοῦ αὐτοῦ ἐκ τοῦ κατὰ Ἰωάννην ὑπομνήματος.
Inc.: Καλῶς δὲ ποιῶν ὁ θεολόγος εὐθὺς ἐπήνεγκε . . .
desin.: . . . σώματι τῷ ἐκ τῆς ἁγίας παρθένου ναῷ.
CPG 5208 Cyrillus Alex., *Commentarii in Iohannem*, *PG* 73, 161B.
Doctrina Patrum (chaps. Β´ and Ε´), pp. 15.22–23, XVIII/ 34.3–5, IV. See also quotations **1, 91, 98, 102.**

58 Λέοντος ἐκ τῆς (sic) πρὸς Φλαβιανὸν τόμον.
Inc.: Ὅπως ἐν αὐτῷ μεμενηκέναι γνωσθῇ ἡ ἰδιότης . . .
desin.: . . . καὶ τὸν λόγον ὁμολογήσωμεν καὶ τὴν σάρκα.
CPG [8922] *Epistula Leonis ad Flavianum CPolitanum (Tomus)*. *ACO* II,1,1, 17.10–13.
Doctrina Patrum (chap. Ε´ and ΙΕ´), p. 34.17–18, VIII/ 96.1–3, XV. See also quotation **29.**

59 Βασιλείου ἐπισκόπου Καισαρείας Καππαδοκίας ἐκ τῶν πρὸς Τερέντιον.
Inc.: Ὅτι δὲ οὐσία καὶ ὑπόστασις οὐ ταὐτόν ἐστι . . .
desin.: . . . τῶν ὀνομαζομένων ὑποστάσει κηρύττεται.
CPG 2900, Basilius Caesariensis, *Epistula* 214, ed. Y. Courtonne, *Saint Basile, Lettres*, II (Paris, 1961), 205–6; *PG* 32, 789A.
Doctrina Patrum (chap. Στ.´), p. 35.14–15, III.

60 Ἀμφιλοχίου ἐκ τῆς πρὸς Σέλευκον ἐπιστολῆς.
Ἀλλ᾽ ἐπειδὴ εἰς ἓν πρόσωπον συντελοῦσιν αἱ φύσεις ἡ ἀπαθὴς τὰ τῆς παθητῆς οἰκειοῦται.
Doctrina Patrum (chap. Στ´), p. 36.1–3, V. See quotation **50.**

61 Γρηγορίου Νύσσης ἐκ τῶν κατ᾽ Εὐνομίου λόγου δευτέρου.
Inc.: Ἡ μὲν γὰρ τῶν ὑποστάσεων ἰδιότης . . .
desin.: . . . τὰς τῶν ὑποστάσεων γνωριστικὰς ἰδιότητας.

CPG 3135 Gregorius Nyssenus, *Contra Eunomium libri*, ed. W. Jaeger, *Gregorii Nysseni Opera*, II, 317.20–27; *PG* 45, 472c.
Doctrina Patrum (chap. Στ´), p. 36.4–6, VI.

62 Βασιλείου πρὸς Ἰωάννην ἐπίσκοπον Ἀντιοχείας.
fol. 123 Inc.: Λέγοντες δὲ Θεὸν παθητόν, τουτέστι τὸν Χριστόν . . .
desin.: . . . καὶ θεότητα παθητὴν οὐ συκοφαντοῦμεν.
Doctrina Patrum (chap. Ζ´), p. 48.9–14, IV. See quotation **117**.

63 Ἀμβροσίου ἐπισκόπου Μεδιολάνων ἐκ τῆς πίστεως περὶ τῆς θείας ἐνανθρωπήσεως.
Inc.: Ὁμολογοῦμεν τὸν Κύριον ἡμῶν Ἰησοῦν Χριστόν . . .
fol. 123ᵛ desin.: . . . τῷ ναῷ καὶ τοῦτον τῇ οἰκείᾳ ἀνέστησε δυνάμει.
Ps.-Ambrosius Mediolanensis, *Expositio fidei frag.*, ed. G. Bardy, "L'Expositio fidei attribuée à saint Ambroise," *ST* 121 (Rome, 1946), 200.1–202.40; *PL* 16, 847A–D.
Doctrina Patrum (chap. Ζ´), p. 49.18–51.17, VIII.

64 Ἱππολύτου ἐπισκόπου Ῥώμης καὶ μάρτυρος.
Inc.: Διὰ τοῦτο "πυλωροὶ ᾅδου ἰδόντες σε ἔπτηξαν" . . .
desin.: . . . πορευθῇ εἰς τὸν ᾅδην καὶ μὴ γυμνῇ τῇ θεότητι.
CPG 1895 nota (b) Hippolytus Romanus, *Frag. iii De Paschate,* ed. H. Achelis, *Hippolyt's kleinere exegetische und homiletische Schriften* (Leipzig, 1897), *GCS* 1,2, 268.23–269.8; *PG* 10, 701A.
Doctrina Patrum (chap. Ζ´), p. 53.14–54.5, XX. See also quotation **121**.

65 Κυρίλλου ἐκ τῆς πρὸς Νεστόριον α´ ἐπιστολῆς.
Inc.: Οὕτω φαμὲν αὐτὸν καὶ παθεῖν καὶ ἀναστῆναι . . .
desin.: . . . καὶ ἐπὶ τοῦ τεθνάναι νοοῦμεν.
CPG 5304 Cyrillus Alex., *Epist.* 4. *ACO* I,1,1, 27.14–19; *PG* 77, 48A.
Doctrina Patrum (chap. Ζ´), p. 54.10–12, XXIII.

66 Τοῦ αὐτοῦ ἐκ τῆς πρὸς Νεστόριον τρίτης ἐπιστολῆς.
Inc.: Ὁμολογοῦμεν δὲ ὅτι αὐτὸς ὁ ἐκ Θεοῦ πατρός . . .
desin.: . . . ἰδίας σαρκὸς ἀπαθῶς οἰκειούμενος πάθη.
CPG 5317 Cyrillus Alex., *Epist.* 17. *ACO* I,1,1, 37.9–12; *PG* 77, 113A.
Doctrina Patrum (chap. Ζ᷇), p. 54.13–14, XXIV. See also quotations **73, 106**.

67 Ἀμβροσίου ἐκ τοῦ περὶ πίστεως πρὸς Γρατιανὸν τὸν βασιλέα.
Inc.: Ὅθεν ἐκεῖνο τὸ ἀναγνωσθὲν ὡς ὁ Κύριος τῆς δόξης . . .
fol. 124 desin.: . . . καθὼς γέγραπται ὁ ἐκ τοῦ οὐρανοῦ καταβάς.
CPL 150 Ambrosius Mediol., *De fide*, lib. II cap. 7, ed. O. Faller, *Sancti Ambrosii Opera*, *CSEL* 78, 76.43–50. *ACO* II,1,1, 22.10–16; *PL* 16, 571B.
Doctrina Patrum (chap. Η´), p. 56.7–18, VII.

68 Τοῦ αὐτοῦ ἐκ τοῦ τετάρτου λόγου τῆς ἐνανθρωπήσεως.
Inc.: Οὐ διῃρημένος ἀλλ᾽ εἷς . . .
desin.: . . . ἀλλ᾽ ὡς (sic) δὲ ἐκ παρθένου.
CPL 152, Ambrosius Mediol., *De incarnationis dominicae sacramento*, cap. 5, ed. Faller, *CSEL* 79, 241.1–4; *PL* 16, 827c].
Doctrina Patrum (chap. Η´), p. 56.19–23, VIII.

69 Ἀθανασίου πρὸς Ἐπίκτητον (3 extracts).
Inc.: Οὐ γὰρ ὥς τινες ὑπενόησαν—τοῦ Θεοῦ λόγος. Καὶ μεθ᾽ ἕτερα.
Καὶ ἦν παράδοξον—ὁ λόγος ἀπαθὴς ἦν. Καὶ μεθ᾽ ἕτερα. Θεὸς γὰρ καὶ Κύριος . . .
desin.: . . . καθηλουμένῳ καὶ ἀτιμαζομένῳ σώματι.
CPG 2095 Athanasius Alex., *Epistula ad Epictetum, PG* 26, 1060A, C, 1065C.
Doctrina Patrum (chap. Η´), p. 57.1-6, IX–XI.

70 Τοῦ αὐτοῦ ἐν τῷ λόγῳ τῷ εἰς τὰ Θεοφάνια κατὰ Ἀπολλιναρίου.
Inc.: Οὐδαμοῦ δὲ αἷμα Θεοῦ καθ᾽ ὑμᾶς παραδεδώκασιν . . .
desin.: . . . καὶ πάθος καὶ ἀνάστασιν κηρύττουσι σῶμα τοῦ Θεοῦ.
CPG 2231 Athanasius Alex., *De incarnatione contra Apol., lib. ii, PG* 26, 1156B.
Doctrina Patrum (chap. Η´), p. 57.7-8, XII. See also quotation **90**.

71 Τοῦ αὐτοῦ ἐκ τοῦ περὶ τῆς σωτηριώδους ἐπιφανείας τοῦ Χριστοῦ κατὰ Ἀπολλιναρίου λόγου·
Inc.: Εἰ γὰρ μὴ πρωτότοκος ἐγεγόνει ἐν πολλοῖς ἀδελφοῖς . . .
desin.: . . . καὶ οὐχὶ Θεὸς διὰ σαρκὸς ἔπαθεν.
CPG 2231 Athanasius Alex., *De incarnatione contra Apol., lib. ii, PG* 26, 1152A.
Doctrina Patrum (chap. Η´), p. 57.9-11, XIII.

72 Ἀμφιλοχίου ἐκ τῆς πρὸς Σέλευκον ἐπιστολῆς.
Inc.: Πάσχει ὁ Χριστός, οὐ θεότητι . . .
desin.: . . . καὶ βλάσφημον δείλαιε.
CPG 3245.15 Amphilochius Iconiensis, *Fragmentum xv (epistula ad Seleucum)*, ed. C.
Datema, *Amphilochii Opera*, 264.53-57; *PG* 39, 113B-D. See also quotation **50**.
Doctrina Patrum (chap. Η´), p. 57.12-19, XIV (P= 57.12-15).

73 = **66** Κυρίλλου ἐκ τῆς πρὸς Νεστόριον τρίτης ἐπιστολῆς.
Inc.: Ὁμολογοῦμεν δὲ ὅτι αὐτὸς ὁ ἐκ Θεοῦ . . .
fol. 124ᵛ desin.: . . . ἀπαθῶς οἰκειούμενος πάθη.
Doctrina Patrum (chap. Η´), p. 58.1-2, XV.

74 Λέοντος ἀρχιεπισκόπου Ῥώμης ἐκ τοῦ πρὸς Φλαβιανόν.
Inc.: Καὶ πάλιν ὁ υἱὸς τοῦ Θεοῦ σταυρωθείς . . .
desin.: . . . τῆς ἀνθρωπίνης ὑπομεμένηκε φύσεως.
CPG [8922] Leo I Papa, *Epistula Leonis ad Flavianum CPolitanum (Tomus)*, (CPL 1656).
ACO II,1,1, 16.11-13; *PL* 54, 772A.
Doctrina Patrum (chap. Η´), p. 58.3-5, XVI. See also quotations **29, 58**.

75 Παύλου ἐπισκόπου Ἐμέζης (sic) ἐκ τοῦ λόγου τοῦ λεχθέντος ἐν Ἀλεξανδρείᾳ παρόντος τοῦ ἁγίου Κυρίλλου.
Ταῦτα πάντα εἰργάσατο ἵνα γνῷς ὅτι συνῆν τῷ πάσχοντι καὶ τὰ μὲν πάθη οἰκειοῦτο (sic), αὐτὸς δὲ ἀπαθὴς ἅπαντα εἰργάζετο.
CPG 6366 Paulus Emes., *Hom. II de nativitate Alexandriae habita. ACO* I,1,4, 14.11-12; *PG* 77, 1444A12-14. See also quotation **5**.

76 Τοῦ ἁγίου Ἰσιδώρου πρεσβυτέρου Πηλουσιώτου ἐπιστολὴ Δωροθέῳ κώμητι (sic), ρκδ´.
Inc.: Χριστοῦ πάθος λέγεται Χριστοῦ τὸ πάθος . . .
desin.: . . . τῇ φύσει τῶν ἀνθρώπων ἡνώθη φιλανθρώπως.

CPG 5557 Isidorus Pelusiota, *Epistularum lib. I* (Κατὰ Θεοπασχιτῶν καὶ τῶν μίαν ἐπὶ Χριστοῦ φύσιν λεγόντων), *PG* 78, 265в.

77 Τοῦ ἁγίου Φωστηρίου πρεσβυτέρου καὶ ἀρχιμανδρίτου ἐκ τῆς ἑρμηνείας τοῦ συμβόλου.

    Αὐτὸς γὰρ ὁ Κύριος τῆς δόξης ὑπὲρ ἡμῶν ἐσταυρώθη καὶ πάσχει ἀπαθῶς· πάσχει γὰρ οὐ τῇ θεότητι, ἀλλὰ τῇ ἀδιαιρέτως συναφθείσῃ αὐτῷ ἰδίᾳ σαρκὶ ἐμψυχωμένῃ καὶ ἀποθνῄσκει, τῆς ψυχῆς δηλονότι χωρισθείσης τοῦ σώματος· ἡ γὰρ θεότης ἀδιαίρετος καὶ ἀσύγχυτος καὶ τῇ ψυχῇ ἡνωμένη ἦν καὶ τῷ σώματι.
5   Κατῆλθεν οὖν ὁ υἱὸς τοῦ Θεοῦ τῇ ἰδίᾳ ψυχῇ πρὸς τὰς τῶν ἁγίων ψυχὰς καὶ πάλιν ἀνέστη τῆς ψυχῆς ἑνωθείσης τῷ σώματι· ἀνέστη οὖν ὁ αὐτός, ὁ μονογενὴς υἱὸς τοῦ Θεοῦ, τῇ ἰδίᾳ δυνάμει, "ἐξουσίαν γὰρ ἔχω", φησί, "τὴν ψυχήν μου θεῖναι καὶ ἐξουσίαν ἔχω πάλιν λαβεῖν αὐτήν". Καὶ εἴ τι ἂν δοκῶμεν θεολογοῦντες λαλεῖν, πάντως ὡς ἔστιν ἀδύνατον εἰπεῖν. Σὺ οὖν, ὀλίγας τὰς ἀφορμὰς
10   λαβών, ἀφθέγκτως λοιπὸν ἐν τῷ ἁγίῳ συμβόλῳ διὰ τῶν ὀλίγων ῥημάτων τὸ ἀκατάληπτον φρῖξον καὶ προσκύνει.

Fragmentum primum editum est supra.

78 Τοῦ ἁγίου Ἐπιφανίου ἀρχιεπισκόπου Κωνσταντίας τῆς Κύπρου ἐκ τῆς πραγματείας κατὰ αἱρέσεων ὀγδοήκοντα, σύντομος ἀληθὴς λόγος περὶ πίστεως καθολικῆς καὶ ἀποστολικῆς ἐκκλησίας.
Inc.: Ὡς ἐκήρυξε τὴν ἀλήθειαν τὸ εὐαγγέλιον . . .
fol. 125ᵛ desin.: . . . ἐρχόμενον κρῖναι ζῶντας καὶ νεκρούς.
CPG 3745 Epiphanius Constantiensis, *Panarion*, ed. K. Holl, *Epiphanius, I. Ancoratus und Panarion*, GCS 37 (Leipzig, 1933), 517.16–519.11.

79 Βασιλείου ἐκ τοῦ περὶ νηστείας λόγου.
Inc.: Ἀπρόσιτος γὰρ ἦν αὐτῷ διὰ τὸ ὕψος . . .
desin.: . . . τοῦ ἀναστάντος πιστούμενος.
CPG 2845 Basilius Caes., *De ieiunio homilia i*, *PG* 31, 177D.
Doctrina Patrum (chap. ΙΔ´), p. 88.7–8, VI.

80 Τοῦ αὐτοῦ ἐκ τοῦ ἐπιγεγραμμένου λόγου πρὸς τὴν Εὐνομίου δόξαν, ἧς Ἀέτιος ἤρξατο.
Inc.: Οὔτε γὰρ οὐσία κατὰ φύσιν ἐνεργείας ἄνευ . . .
desin.: . . . ὅμως τὴν οὐσίαν πιστούμεθα.
Sequuntur scholia: (α) Ὁρᾷς ὡς ἀλλήλοις ταῦτα . . . αὐτὴν ἐκτὸς φύσεως. (β) Εἰ πᾶσα τοίνυν ἐνέργεια . . . ἀνενέργητον δὲ λέγειν αὐτήν.
Doctrina Patrum (chap. ΙΔ´), pp. 88.19–89.19, IX.

81 Ἰωάννου ἐπισκόπου Κωνσταντινουπόλεως εἰς τὴν χήραν τὴν τὰ β´ λεπτὰ προσενέγκασαν.
Inc.: Κάθηται τοίνυν πρὸ τοῦ γαζοφυλακίου ὁ Χριστός . . .
fol. 126 desin.: . . . ὁ ὄχλος βάλλει χαλκόν, καὶ τὰ ἑξῆς.
Doctrina Patrum (chap. ΙΕ´), pp. 91.19–92.12, I.

82 Ἀμβροσίου ἐπισκόπου Μεδιολάνων ἐκ τοῦ πρὸς Γρατιανὸν β´ λόγου.
Inc.: ⟨Ἴ⟩σος οὖν ἐν τῇ τοῦ Θεοῦ μορφῇ ἔλαττον (sic) ἐν . . .
desin.: . . . ὅπου διάφορος οὐσία ἐστίν.

CPL 150 Ambrosius Mediol., *De fide*, lib. II, cap. 8, *CSEL* 78, 81.91–98; *PL* 16, 574c.
Doctrina Patrum (chap. IΕ΄ and IΒ΄), p. 75.8–15, XI/92.13–15, II.

83 = **55** Γελασίου ἐπισκόπου Καισαρείας ἐν ἐξηγήσει τοῦ μαθήματος.
Inc.: Ἦλθε τοίνυν εἰς ταὐτὸν Θεὸς ἅμα καὶ ἄνθρωπος . . .
desin.: . . . καὶ φιμούσθω πᾶν αἱρετικὸν στόμα.
Doctrina Patrum (chap. IΕ΄), p. 92.16–17, III.

84 Κυρίλλου ἐπισκόπου Ἱεροσολύμων ἐκ τῆς εἰς τὸ εὐαγγέλιον ὁμιλίας, ἔνθα ὁ Κύριος
τὸ ὕδωρ οἶνον ἐποίησεν.
Inc.: Ἐσπούδασε μήτε δι᾽ ὅλου φανερῶσαι τὴν ἑαυτοῦ θεότητα . . .
desin.: . . . διὰ τοῦτο συνεχώρησε τῇ σαρκὶ πάσχειν τὰ ἴδια.
CPG 3590 Cyrillus Hierosolymitanus, *Homilia aquae in vinum conversae* (frag.), *PG*
33, 1181A.
Doctrina Patrum (chap. IΕ΄), pp. 92.18–93.10, IV.

85 Τοῦ αὐτοῦ ἐκ τοῦ αὐτοῦ λόγου.
Ἐγεννήθη, ἐθαυματούργησεν, ἔδειξε τὴν διπλῆν ἐνέργειαν, πάσχων μὲν ὡς ἄνθρω-
πος, ἐνεργῶν δὲ ὡς Θεὸς ὁ αὐτός· οὐ γὰρ ἄλλος καὶ ἄλλος εἰ καὶ ἄλλως καὶ ἄλλως.
CPG 3590 Idem, *PG* 33 1181B.
Doctrina Patrum (chap. IΕ΄), p. 93.11–14, V.

86 Κυρίλλου ἐκ τοῦ πρὸς Θεοδόσιον τὸν βασιλέα προσφωνητικοῦ.
Inc.: Καὶ ἐκτείνας ὁ Ἰησοῦς τὴν χεῖρα, φησίν . . .
desin.: . . . εἰ καὶ γέγονε σὰρξ ὁ λόγος.
CPG 5219 Cyrillus Alex., *Oratio ad Arcadiam et Marinam augustas de fide*. *ACO* I,1,5,
111.32–35; *PG* 76, 1320A.
Doctrina Patrum (chap. IΕ΄), p. 94.7–10, X.

87 Γρηγορίου Νύσης ἐκ τοῦ γ΄ λόγου κατὰ Εὐνομίου.
Inc.: Οὔτε ζωοποιεῖ τὸν Λάζαρον ἡ ἀνθρωπίνη φύσις . . .
fol. 126ᵛ desin.: . . . δούλου τῇ δεσποτικῇ δοξαζομένου τιμῇ.
CPG 3135 Gregorius Nyssenus, *Contra Eunomium libri*, ed. W. Jaeger, *Gregorii Nysseni
Opera*, II, 130.28–131.13; *PG* 45, 705c.
Doctrina Patrum (chap. IΕ΄), p. 97.7–9, XIX. See also quotation **61.**

88 Διονυσίου ἐπισκόπου Ἀθηνῶν ἐκ τῆς πρὸς Γάϊον τετάρτης ἐπιστολῆς.
Inc.: Ἔστι δὲ οὐδὲν ἧττον ὑπερουσιότητος . . .
desin.: . . . πρὸς τὸ ἀδιάχυτον συνιστάμενον.
CPG 6607 Pseudo-Dionysius Areopagita, *Epistula iv ad Gaium monachum*, ed. G. Heil
and A. M. Ritter, *Corpus Dionysiacum*, II, 160.9–161.2; *PG* 3, 1073B.
Doctrina Patrum (chap. IΕ΄), p. 97.10–11, XX.

89 Τοῦ αὐτοῦ ἐκ τῆς αὐτῆς ἐπιστολῆς.
Inc.: Καὶ γὰρ ἵνα συνελόντες εἴπωμεν οὐδὲ ἄνθρωπος ἦν . . .
desin.: . . . ἐνέργειαν ἡμῖν πεπολιτευμένος.
Sequitur scholium Maximi Confessoris (*Ambiguorum Liber*, *PG* 91, 1056c–D):
Inc.: Θεανδρικῶς ἤγουν θεϊκῶς ἅμα καὶ ἀνδρικῶς . . .
desin.: . . . τὴν διττὴν παραδιδοῦντος ἐνέργειαν.
Idem, *Corpus Dionysiacum*, II, 161.2–10; *PG* 3, 1073B–C.
Doctrina Patrum (chap. IΕ΄), p. 97.12–98.7, XXI.

90 Ἀθανασίου ἐκ τοῦ κατὰ Ἀπολλιναρίου λόγου.
Inc.: Οὐδαμοῦ δὲ θεότης πάθος προσίεται . . .
desin.: . . . ἐπιδείξει ὑπάρξεως ἐγίνετο τὰ γινόμενα.
CPG 2231 Athanasius Alex., *De incarnatione contra Apollinarium libri ii, PG* 26, 1153в.
Doctrina Patrum (chap. IE´), p. 98.10–11, XXIII. See also quotation **70.**

91 Κυρίλλου ἐκ τοῦ κατὰ Ἰωάννην ὑπομνήματος.
Inc.: Ἐπειδὴ δὲ οὐ Θεὸς κατὰ φύσιν μόνον . . .
desin.: . . . τὰ ὑπὲρ φύσιν ἴδια διδασκομένη φρονεῖν.
CPG 5208 Cyrillus Alex., *Commentarii in Iohannem*, lib. 7 et 8 frag., *PG* 74, 52D.
Doctrina Patrum (chap. IE´), p. 100.1–14, XXX. See also quotations **1, 57, 98, 102.**

92 Ἀθανασίου ἐκ τοῦ γ´ λόγου κατὰ Ἀρειανῶν.
Inc.: Ταῦτα ἀναγκαίως προεξητήσαμεν (sic) ἵνα . . .
fol. 127 desin.: . . . καὶ οὐδήπου τῆς ἀληθείας ἐκπέσωμεν.
CPG 2093 Athanasius Alex., *Oratio iii contra Arianos, PG* 26, 397в.
Doctrina Patrum (chap. IE´), p. 100.15–17, XXXI. See also quotation **96.**

93 Κυρίλλου ἐκ τῆς ἑρμηνείας τῆς πρὸς Ἑβραίους ἐπιστολῆς.
Inc.: Οὐ γὰρ ἦν ἀνθρώπου ψιλοῦ καὶ τῶν καθ᾽ ἡμᾶς ἑνός, . . .
desin.: . . . ἑτέρου κατὰ φύσιν ὑπάρχοντος λόγου.
Doctrina Patrum (chap. IE´), pp. 100.18–101.7, XXXII.

94 Ἀμφιλοχίου ἐπισκόπου Ἰκονίου ἐκ τοῦ περὶ τῆς ἡμέρας καὶ ὥρας λόγου α´· δύο γὰρ αὐτῷ περὶ τούτου πεποίηνται συντάγματα.
Inc.: Ὅταν δὲ εἴπῃ οὐδὲ ὁ υἱός, εἰ μὴ ὁ πατήρ . . .
desin.: . . . οὐχὶ τὴν ἄγνοιαν κατεψεύσατο.
CPG 3245.6 Amphilochius Icon., *Fragmentum vi,* ed. C. Datema, *Amphilochii Opera,* 232–33, PG 39, 104A–C.
Doctrina Patrum (chap. ΙΣΤ´), pp. 108.5–109.7, VI.

95 Ἐκ τοῦ καὶ Ἰησοῦς προέκοπτε σοφίᾳ καὶ ἡλικίᾳ καὶ χάριτι παρὰ Θεῷ καὶ ἀνθρώποις.
Inc.: Προέκοπτε κατὰ τὴν ἡλικίαν ἀνδρουμένου κατὰ φύσιν . . .
fol. 127ᵛ desin.: . . . ἀπὸ τοῦ χείρονος ἐπὶ τὸ κρεῖττον.
CPG 3245.8 Amphilochius Icon., *Fragmentum viii,* ed. C. Datema, *Amphilochii Opera,* 265, *PG* 39, 105A.
Doctrina Patrum (chap. ΙΣΤ´), p. 109.8–19, VII.

96 Ἀθανασίου· ἐκ τοῦ κατὰ Ἀρειανῶν λόγου.
Inc.: Τίς γάρ ἐστιν ἡ λεγομένη—θεοποίησις καὶ χάρις. Καὶ αὖθις. Οὕτω γὰρ αὖξανον (sic) τό . . .
desin.: . . . καὶ Θεὸς ἦν ἐν τῷ σώματι.
CPG 2093 Athanasius Alex., *Oratio iii contra Arianos, PG* 26, 433в–с.
Doctrina Patrum (chap. ΙΣΤ´), p. 109.20–23, VIII–IX. See also quotation **92.**

97 Κυρίλλου ἐκ τοῦ κζ´ κεφαλαίου τοῦ β´ βιβλίου τοῦ θησαυροῦ.
Inc.: ⟨Τ⟩ὸ ἕν τινι προκόπτον—προέκοπτε σοφίᾳ. Καὶ μεθ᾽ ἕτερα. Ἐπιτήρει δὲ ὅτι οὐκ εἶπεν . . .
desin.: . . . ἀναβαινόντων εἰς τὸν τῆς θεότητος λόγον.

CPG 5215 Cyrillus Alex., *Thesaurus de sancta et consubstantiali Trinitate*, PG 75, 428ʙ, 429ᴄ.
Doctrina Patrum (chap. ΙΣΤ´), p. 110.1–5, X–XI.

98 Κυρίλλου ἐκ τοῦ η´ βιβλίου τοῦ εἰς τὸ κατὰ Ἰωάννην ὑπομνήματος.
Inc.: Νῦν φησιν ἡ ψυχή μου τετάρακται . . .
fol. 128 desin.: . . . τὸν τῆς ἰάσεως διαβῆναι τρόπον.
CPG 5208 Cyrillus Alex., *Commentarii in Iohannem*, lib. 8 frag., PG 74, 88ᴅ.
Doctrina Patrum (chap. ΙΣΤ´), pp. 110.13–111.21, XVI. See also quotations **1, 57, 91, 102.**

99 Ἀθανασίου ἐκ τοῦ περὶ τῆς τοῦ Κυρίου ἐνανθρωπήσεως λόγου α´.
Inc.: Ὅταν λέγῃ πάτερ εἰ δυνατὸν τὸ ποτήριον τοῦτο . . .
desin.: . . . τὸ δὲ θεϊκὸν αὐτοῦ πρόθυμον.
CPG 2806 Marcellus Ancyranus, *De incarnatione et contra Arianos*, PG 26, 1021ʙ.
Doctrina Patrum (chap. ΙΗ´), p. 117.13–15, I.

100 Κυρίλλου ἐκ τοῦ κατὰ Ματθαῖον ὑπομνήματος, κεφαλαίου ια´.
Inc.: ⟨Εἰ⟩ γὰρ καὶ ὅτι μάλιστα τὸ συμβᾶν (sic) . . .
desin.: . . . ἀπ᾽ ἐμοῦ τὸ ποτήριον τοῦτο.
CPG 5206 Cyrillus Alex., *Commentarii in Matthaeum*, PG 72, 456ʙ–ᴄ.
Doctrina Patrum (chap. ΙΗ´), pp. 117.16–118.14, II (P= 117.16–118.7).

101 Τοῦ αὐτοῦ ἐκ τοῦ θησαυροῦ, βιβλίου β´ κεφαλαίου κδ´.
Inc.: Γέγονεν ἄνθρωπος ὁ τοῦ Θεοῦ λόγος . . .
desin.: . . . ἡ δὲ σὰρξ ἀσθενής.
CPG 5215 Cyrillus Alex., *Thesaurus de sancta et consubstantiali trinitate*, PG 75, 396ᴅ.
Doctrina Patrum (chap. ΙΗ´), p. 118.22–23, V.

102 Τοῦ αὐτοῦ ἐκ τοῦ κατὰ Ἰωάννην εὐαγγελίου βιβλίου γ´.
Inc.: Οὐχ ὡς ἐγὼ ⟨θέλω⟩, ἀλλ᾽ ὡς σύ . . .
desin.: . . . λόγου εἰς εὐτολμίαν θεοπρεπῆ.
CPG 5208 Cyrillus Alex., *Commentarii in Iohannem*, lib. 4, frag., PG 73, 532ʙ.
Doctrina Patrum (chap. ΙΗ´), p. 119.1–3, VI. See also quotations **1, 57, 91, 98.**

103 Ἰωάννου ἐπισκόπου Κωνσταντινουπόλεως ἐκ τοῦ λόγου τοῦ πρὸς τοὺς ἀπολειφθέντας τῆς συνάξεως καὶ τὸ ὁμοούσιον εἶναι τὸν υἱὸν τῷ πατρὶ ἀπόδειξις, οὗ ἡ ἀρχή. πάλιν ἱπποδρομίαι καὶ πάλιν ὁ σύλλογος ἡμῖν ἐλλάτω (sic) γέγονεν.
Inc.: Ἐρώτησον τοίνυν τὸν ἐραιτικὸν (sic), Θεὸς δειλιᾷ . . .
fol. 128ᵛ desin.: . . . καὶ ἀναδύεται πάλιν ὡς ἄνθρωπος.
CPG 4320 Iohannes Chrys., *De consubstantiali*, PG 48, 765.48 ff.
Doctrina Patrum (chap. ΙΗ´), p. 119.4–9, VII.

104 Ἰωάννου ἐπισκόπου Κωνσταντινουπόλεως ἐν τῷ ξζ´ κεφαλαίῳ τοῦ εἰς τὸ κατὰ Ἰωάννην ὑπομνήματος.
Inc.: Οὐ λέγω ὅτι ἀπάλλαξόν με ἐκ τῆς ὥρας ταύτης . . .
desin.: . . . οὕτως οὐδὲ τὸ τῆς παρούσης ζωῆς ἐφίεσθαι.
CPG 4425 Iohannes Chrys., *In Iohannem homilia* 67, PG 59, 371.48 ff.
Doctrina Patrum (chap. ΙΗ´), p. 120.7–9, X.

105 Θεοφίλου ἐπισκόπου Ἀλεξανδρείας ἐκ τοῦ περὶ μετανοίας λόγου.
Inc.: Ὥσπερ τὸ πεινῆν καὶ τὸ διψῆν καὶ τὸ κοπιᾶν . . .
fol. 129 desin.: . . . τὸ μὲν πνεῦμα πρόθυμον, ἡ δὲ σὰρξ ἀσθενής.
CPG 2620 Theophilus Alexandrinus, *Sermo in fluxu sanguinis laborantem.*
Doctrina Patrum (chap. ΙΗ΄), p. 120.10–19, ΧΙ.

106 Κυρίλλου ἐκ τῆς πρὸς Νεστόριον β΄ ἐπιστολῆς.
Inc.: Ζωὴ γὰρ ὢν κατὰ φύσιν ὡς Θεός . . .
desin.: . . . ἀνθρώπου γεγονότος τε καὶ χρηματίσαντος.
CPG 5317 Cyrillus Alex., *Epist.* 17. *ACO* I,1,1, 37.29–38.3; *PG* 77, 113D.
Doctrina Patrum (chap. Κ΄), p. 124.14–15, ΙΙ. See also quotation **66**.

107 = **56** Τοῦ αὐτοῦ ἐκ τῆς πρὸς Σούκενσον α΄ ἐπιστολῆς.
Ἴσον γάρ ἐστιν εἰς ἀτοπίας—οὔτε ἡμεῖς οὕτω διακείμεθα.
Doctrina Patrum (chap. Κ΄), p. 124.16–18, ΙΙΙ.

108 Τοῦ αὐτοῦ ἐκ τοῦ κατὰ συνουσιαστῶν λόγου.
Inc.: ⟨Ν⟩αὶ μὴν καὶ ἐξ οὐρανοῦ καταβεβηκέναι λέγεται . . .
desin.: . . . καὶ δογματικῆς εὐτεκνίας (sic) ἐπιστήμονα.
CPG 5230 Cyrillus Alex., *Liber contra Synousiastas* (frag.), *PG* 76, 1429D.
Doctrina Patrum (chap. Κ΄), p. 125.3–9, V.

109 Ἀναστασίου ἐπισκόπου Ἀντιοχείας ἐκ τῶν πρὸς Σέργιον τὸν γραμματικόν·
Inc.: Κέκρυπται δὲ ταῖς ἀληθείαις ὑπὸ τῆς θείας φύσεως . . .
fol. 129ᵛ desin.: . . . ὅπερ πᾶσα παρίστησιν ἡ θεόπνευστος γραφή.
CPG 6957 Anastasius I Antiochenus, *Ad Sergium Grammaticum capita cl* (frag.), *PG* 89, 1285B–E (P **109–110** = frag. IV).
Doctrina Patrum (chap. Κ΄), pp. 125.10–126.12, VI.

110 Τοῦ αὐτοῦ
Inc.: Ἀλλ᾽ ἡ ἕνωσις μίαν ὑπέδειξεν ἡμῖν τὴν προσκύνησιν . . .
desin.: . . . καὶ ὅλον Θεὸν καὶ ὅλον ἄνθρωπον.
Doctrina Patrum (chap. Κ΄), p. 126.13–20, VII. See quotation **109**.

111 Ἐρώτησις ὀρθοδόξου·
Inc.: Λέγοντες δύο γεννήσεις ἐπὶ Χριστοῦ . . .
fol. 173ᵛ desin.: . . . οἱ ἅγιοι τελείως τὰ περὶ Θεοῦ ἐπίστανται.
CPG 7745 Anastasius Sinaita, *Hodegos*, ed. K.-H. Uthemann, *Anastasii Sinaitae Viae Dux*, CCSG 8 (Turnhout-Louvain, 1981). P, fols. 129ᵛ–173ᵛ = II,8,138–XIII,5,86 νομοθετεῖ; XIII,9,91–10,111; XIV,1,43 πρός–XV,96; XIX,1–XXIII,1,29, and XXIV, 22–98.
See also quotations **47, 194a–e, 239**.

112 Ἰουστίνου φιλοσόφου καὶ μάρτυρος ἐκ τοῦ περὶ τριάδος ι΄ λόγου κεφάλαιον δέκατον·
Inc.: Τότε δὲ τῶν οὐρανῶν οὐκ ἀποστάς . . .
fol. 174 desin.: . . . εἰς τὴν τοῦ ναοῦ διάπλασιν οὐσιώσας.
CPG 6218 Theodoretus Episc. Cyri, *Expositio rectae fidei*, ed. J. T. C. Otto, *Corpus apologetarum christianorum saeculi secundi*, IV (Jena, 1880), 34; *PG* 6, 1224C.
Doctrina Patrum (chap. ΚΑ΄), p. 134.1–3, V.

113 Ἀναστασίου ἐπισκόπου Ἀντιοχείας ἐκ τοῦ περὶ ἐνεργειῶν λόγου·
Inc.: Τῶν δύο φύσεων ἡ συνδρομή . . .
desin.: . . . ἧττον (sic) ἐν αἷς ἐστιν ὁ Χριστός.
CPG 6953 Anastasius I Antioch., *De operationibus*, PG 89, 1281C-D.
Doctrina Patrum (chap. ΚΑ΄), pp. 134.15–136.27, VIII (P = 134.15–135.22).

114 Κυρίλλου πρὸς Εὐλόγιον τὸν πρεσβύτερον·
Inc.: Ἐπιλαμβάνονταί τινες τῆς ἐκθέσεως, ἣν πεποίηνται . . .
fol. 174ᵛ desin.: . . . μίαν φύσιν τοῦ Θεοῦ λόγου σεσαρκωμένην.
CPG 5344 Cyrillus Alex., *Epist.* 44, *Commonitorium ad Eulogium presb.* ACO I,1,4,
35.4–14; *PG* 77, 224D.
Doctrina Patrum (chap. ΚΓ΄), p. 149.4–6, I. See also quotation **116**.

115 Τοῦ αὐτοῦ ἐκ τοῦ δευτέρου τόμου κατὰ τῶν Νεστορίου δυσφημιῶν.
Παῦσαι διαιρῶν τὰς φύσεις μετὰ τὴν ἕνωσιν.
Scholium: Ἰδοὺ τὸ διαιρεῖν ἐκώλυσε μετὰ τὴν ἕνωσιν, οὐ μὴν τὴν τούτων ἀνεῖλεν ὁμο-
λογίαν ὁ Κύριλλος.
CPG 5217 Cyrillus Alex., *Libri v contra Nestorium*. ACO I,1,6, 45.33; *PG* 76, 92C.
Doctrina Patrum (chap. ΚΓ΄), p. 149.9–12, III.

116 Πάλιν δὲ ὁ αὐτὸς ἐν τῇ πρὸς Εὐλόγιον ἐπιστολῇ· μετὰ τὸ καταγράψαι Νεστορίου
καὶ δεῖξαι αὐτὸν μόνῃ συναφείᾳ τῇ κατὰ τὴν ἀξίαν καὶ ὁμοτιμίαν τὴν ἕνωσιν πρεσβεύ-
οντα καὶ δύο υἱοὺς καὶ δύο Χριστοὺς κηρύττοντα ἐσάγει ἐπὶ λέξεως οὕτως ταῦτα·
Inc.: Οἱ δὲ ἐκ τῆς ἀνατολῆς . . .
desin.: . . . δυσὶ προσώποις ὡς ἑτέρῳ καὶ ἑτέρῳ.
CPG 5344 Cyrillus Alex., *Epist.* 44, *Commonitorium ad Eulogium presb.* ACO I,1,4, 36.22—
37.2; *PG* 77, 228A.
Doctrina Patrum (chap. ΚΓ΄), p. 149.12–17, IV. See quotation **114**.

117 = **62** Παμφίλου ἐπισκόπου Ἀβύδου πρὸς Ἰωάννην ἐπίσκοπον Ἀντιοχείας·
Inc.: Λέγοντες δὲ παθητὸν τουτέστι τὸν Χριστόν . . .
desin.: . . . καὶ θεότητα παθητήν, οὐ συκοφαντοῦμεν.
Doctrina Patrum (chap. Ζ΄), p. 48.9–14, IV.

118 Ἰωάννου ἐπισκόπου Κωνσταντινουπόλεως ἐκ τῆς πρὸς Φιλιππισίους ἑρμηνείας·
Inc.: Εἶπεν ὅτι ἡ μορφὴ τοῦ δούλου . . .
desin.: . . . ἀγγέλου ἔχειν μορφὴν πῶς οὖν ὁ υἱός.
CPG 4432 Iohannes Chrys., *In epistulam ad Philippenses argumentum et homiliae* 1–15,
PG 62, 223.6–15.

119 Anonymi
Sigla
P: Parisinus gr. 1115, fols. 174ᵛ–175
Ar: Londiniensis Musei Brit. Arundelianus 529, fol. 74ʳ⁻ᵛ

Γραφὴ καὶ μαρτυρίαι, ἅσπερ ἐξ ἁγίων καὶ ὀρθοδόξων πατέρων προέθεντο
τηλαυγῶς ἀποδεικνυούσας περὶ τῶν δύο φύσεων τοῦ ἑνὸς τῆς ἁγίας τριάδος.
Ὀρθοδοξίας ἐρασταὶ καὶ εὐσεβείας ζηλωταὶ τῇ τῶν θείων γραφῶν διδασκαλίᾳ
τὸν νοῦν εὖ μάλα ἐναιρήσωμεν· οἱ τῶν πατέρων μαθηταὶ καὶ τῶν ἀγγέλων μιμη-
5   ταὶ τὸν ἐκ Θεοῦ πατρὸς υἱὸν μονογενῆ Θεὸν λόγον καὶ ἄνθρωπον γεγονότα ἐν
πνεύματι καὶ ἀληθείᾳ προσκυνήσωμεν θάτεραν αὐτοῦ φύσιν μηδαμῶς ἀπαρ-

νούμενοι, εἴτε τὴν θείαν λέγω, εἴτε τὴν ἀνθρωπίνην, ὅπως μὴ τῶν ἀμφοτέρων
(fol. 175) ἐκπέσωμεν· εἰ δὲ δεδοίκαμεν ὑπομεῖναι τοῦτο, μᾶλλον δὲ εἰ ἐν ἐπι-
θυμίᾳ ἐσμὲν τοῦ ἐπιτυχεῖν τῆς μὲν τὴν κοινωνίαν τῆς δὲ (Ar. fol 74ᵛ) τὴν
10   σωτηρίαν, πῶς οὐκ ἀπάσης ἐν χρείᾳ καθεστήκαμεν νήψεώς τε καὶ προσοχῆς,
ὥστε διαδρᾶναι μὲν τὴν τῶν ἐναντίων ὑπόκρισιν, προσπελάσαι δὲ καὶ προσορ-
μισθῆναι τῇ τῶν ὀρθῶν δογμάτων ἀκριβείᾳ τε καὶ ἀληθείᾳ

1 Γραφὴ—2 τριάδος: Συμβουλία τῶν ἁγίων πατέρων Ar 4 ἐναιρήσωμεν: ἐνηρήσ. Ar 5
υἱὸν μονογενῆ: μονογενῆ υἱὸν Ar 10 ᾽ἀπάσης: ἀπὸ πάσης P

Locum non inveni.

120 Ἀποκάλυψις τοῦ πατρὸς ἡμῶν Γρηγορίου τοῦ Μεγάλου Νεοκαισαρείας ἐπισκόπου.
Inc.: Εἷς Θεὸς ἀρχὴ καὶ πατὴρ λόγου ζῶντος σοφίας ὑφεστώσης . . .
desin.: . . . ἀλλὰ ἄτρεπτος καὶ ἀναλλοίωτος ἡ αὐτὴ τριὰς ἀεί.
CPG 1764 Gregorius Thaumaturgus, *Confessio fidei. ACO* III, 3.2–13; *PG* 10, 983.
Doctrina Patrum (chap. ΛΖ΄), p. 284.1–22, II.

Post finem excerpti P add.:

Περὶ τῆς ἐν ᾅδη τοῦ Θεοῦ λόγου μετὰ τῆς ἡνωμένης αὐτῷ νοερᾶς ψυχῆς καθόδου
ὅπως οἱ θεόσοφοι ἡμῶν πατέρες ἐδίδαξαν.

Cf. *Doctrina Patrum* (chap. Ζ΄), p. 47.19–20.

121 = 64 Ἱππολύτου ἐπισκόπου Ῥώμης καὶ μάρτυρος·
Inc.: Διὰ τοῦτο "πυλωροὶ ᾅδου ἰδόντες σε ἔπτηξαν". . .
desin.: . . . καὶ μὴ γυμνῇ θεότητι.
Doctrina Patrum (chap. Ζ΄), pp. 53.14–54.5, XX.

122 Γρηγορίου ἐπισκόπου Νύσης ἐκ τοῦ εἰς τὸ Πάσχα λόγου·
Inc.: Ἐν τῷ καιρῷ τῆς κατὰ τὸ πάθος οἰκονομίας . . .
fol. 175ᵛ desin.: . . . ἐκ τῆς τῶν διαιρεθέντων ἑνώσεως.
CPG 3175 Gregorius Nyss., *De tridui inter mortem et resurrectionem domini nostri I. C.
spatio*, ed. E. Gebhardt, *Gregorii Nysseni Opera* IX. *Sermones* (Leiden, 1967), 293.21–
294.4; *PG* 46, 617A.
Doctrina Patrum (chap. Ζ΄), p. 54.6–7, XXI. See below, Appendix II, quotation **14***.

123 Κυρίλλου ἐκ τῆς (sic) πρὸς Θεοδόσιον τὸν βασιλέα προσφωνητικοῦ λόγου·
Inc.: Καὶ ἦν θαυμαστὸν ὅτι τὸ σῶμα μέν . . .
desin.: . . . ὁ τῆς ἐνανθρωπήσεως τρόπος.
CPG 5218 Cyrillus Alex., *Oratio ad Theodosium imp. de recta fide. ACO* I,1,1, 56.5–8/20–23;
PG 76, 1165A.
Doctrina Patrum (chap. Ζ΄), p. 54.7–8, XXII.

Post τρόπος add. P:

Πολλῶν δὲ ὄντων τῶν πανσόφως ὑπὸ τῶν θεοφόρων ἡμῶν πατέρων εἰρημένων
πρὸς δήλωσιν τῆς εὐσεβοῦς πίστεως καὶ τῆς εἰς ἕνα Θεόν, τὸν ἐν τρισὶν ὑποστάσεσι δοξαζόμενον καὶ προσκυνούμενον, ὁμολογίας, ἔτι γε μὴν καὶ περὶ τῆς
ἐνσάρκου οἰκονομίας τοῦ σωτῆρος ἡμῶν Χριστοῦ, τοῦ ἑνὸς τῆς ἁγίας τριάδος,
5   ἀρκεῖν ἡγοῦμαι τὰ παρατεθέντα τοῖς εὐπειθῶς καὶ φιλοθέως τούτων ἀκροω-

μένοις· ἱκανὰ γὰρ ταῦτα σαφῶς τοῖς ἀφιλερίστως καὶ μετὰ φόβου Θεοῦ (fol.
176) ἐντυγχάνουσι καὶ εὐσεβῶς καὶ φιλομαθῶς ζητοῦσι τῆς τε πανσέπτου τριάδος τὸ ὁμοούσιον καὶ τῆς τοῦ σωτῆρος ἡμῶν Χριστοῦ, τοῦ ἑνὸς τῆς ἁγίας τριάδος, φιλανθρώπου σαρκώσεως τὴν ἀληθῆ δόξαν· καὶ ὡς οὐ κατὰ συνουσίωσιν
10 ἢ φυρμὸν ἢ σύγχυσιν ἢ ἔκστασιν ἡ τῶν δύο φύσεων, (θεότητος λέγω καὶ ἀνθρωπότητος), καθ᾽ ὑπόστασιν γέγονεν ἕνωσις, ἀλλ᾽ ὅτι καὶ ἐν τῇ ἑνώσει καὶ μετὰ
τὴν ἕνωσιν μένουσι τὰ ἑνωθέντα τὴν φυσικὴν σώζοντα ἰδιότητα ἄτρεπτον, ἀναλλοίωτον, ἀδιάσπαστον, ἀδιαίρετον, ἀμέριστον. Ἀλλ᾽ ἵνα μὴ εἰς μῆκος τὸν
λόγον ἐκτείνωμεν, ἐνταῦθα πέρα⟨ς⟩ τοῖς λεγομένοις ἐπιθήσωμεν, σὺ δέ, ὦ τέ-
15 κνον, φιλοπόνῳ σπουδῇ καὶ πόθῳ θεογνωσίας, ἐπιμελῶς καὶ ἐπαγρύπνως τῇ
ἀναγνώσει πρόσεχε, τὸν φωτισμὸν ἄνωθεν ἐξαιτούμενος, ὅ⟨ς⟩ ἐκ τοῦ πατρὸς
τῶν φώτων, ἐξ οὗ πᾶσα δόσις ἀγαθὴ καὶ πᾶν δώρημα τέλειόν ἐστι καταβαῖνον
καὶ τοσοῦτον καταυγάζον τῶν φιλοθέων τὰς καρδίας, ὅσον ἡ πίστις χωρεῖ καὶ
τὸ ἡμέτερον ἔχει τῆς προθέσεως, ἤγουν τῆς εἰλικρινοῦς τῶν θείων λογίων ἐπι-
20 θυμίας.

124 Τοῦ μακαρίου Ἐφραὶμ εἰς τὸ ὅτε ἀνέβη ὁ Κύριος εἰς τὸ ὄρος καὶ μετεμορφώθη
ἔμπροσθεν τῶν μαθητῶν·
Inc.: Ἐκ τῆς χώρας θέρος καὶ χαρμοναί . . .
fol. 179ᵛ desin.: . . . καὶ μίαν δόξαν ἀναφέρει ἰσότητος ἡ ἐκκλησία τῷ πατρὶ καὶ τῷ υἱῷ
. . . ἀμήν.
CPG 3939 Ephraem Syrus, *Sermo in transfigurationem Domini et Dei salvatoris nostri I.*
C., ed. S. Assemani, *Patris nostri Ephraem Syri Opera omnia quae exstant etc.* (Rome, 1732–
46), 2, p. 41ᴅ–49.

125 Ἰωάννου ἐπισκόπου Κωνσταντινουπόλεως ἐκ τοῦ περὶ πίστεως λόγου.
Inc.: Πρῶτον οὖν ἔστιν ἁπάντων πίστις ἡ εἰς τὸν Θεόν . . .
desin.: . . . καὶ δοξαζομένη εἰς τοὺς αἰῶνας τῶν αἰώνων ἀμήν.
CPG 4206 Severianus Gabalensis, *De fide*, PG 60, 767–68.

126 Βασιλείου ἐπισκόπου Καισαρείας Καππαδοκίας ἐκ τῶν πρὸς Ἀμφιλόχιον κεφαλαίων ἀπὸ κεφαλαίου ιβ´ (sic).
fol. 180 Inc. Εἷς Θεὸς καὶ πατὴρ καὶ εἷς μονογενὴς υἱός . . .
fol. 180ᵛ desin.: . . . τῆς/ ὑπάρξεως ἀρρήτου φυλασσομένου.
CPG 2839 Basilius Caes., *De Spiritu Sancto*, ed. B. Pruche, *Saint-Esprit*, 404 par. 44.20–
408 par. 46.9; *PG* 32, 149ᴀ–152ʙ.
Doctrina Patrum (chap. Α´), p. 4.1–4, XI. See also below, Appendix II, quotation **25***.

127 Ἀμβροσίου ἐπισκόπου Μεδιολάνων ἐκ τῆς πρὸς Γρατιανὸν τὸν βασιλέα ἐπιστολῆς.
Inc.: Φυλάξωμεν τὴν ἕνωσιν (sic) τῆς θεότητος καὶ τῆς σαρκός . . .
desin.: . . . ἐν τῇ ἐμῇ οὐσίᾳ διαλέγεται.
CPL 150 Ambrosius Mediol., *De fide*, ed. O. Faller, *Sancti Ambrosii opera*, CSEL 78,
84.32–85.38; *PL* 16, 576ʙ.
Doctrina Patrum (chap. Β´), p. 15.1–10, XVI.

128 Τοῦ αὐτοῦ ἐκ τῆς ἑρμηνείας τοῦ θείου συμβόλου.
Inc.: Τοὺς δὲ λεγόντων (sic) ψιλὸν ἄνθρωπον τὸν Χριστόν . . .
desin.: . . . ἀναθεματίζει ἡ καθολικὴ καὶ ἀποστολικὴ ἐκκλησία.
CPL 153, Ambrosius Mediol., *Explanatio symboli ad initiandos*, PL 16, 849ᴀ.
Doctrina Patrum (chap. Β´), p. 15.11–21, XVII.

129 Τοῦ αὐτοῦ κατὰ Ἀπολλιναρίου.
Inc.: Ἀλλ᾽ ἐν ὅσῳ τούτους ἐλέγχομεν ἀνεφύησαν . . .
desin.: . . . μιᾶς φύσεως εἰπεῖν ἐπεχείρησαν.
CPL 152 Ambrosius Mediol., *De incarnationis dominicae sacramento*, ed. O. Faller, *CSEL*
79, 249.27–33; *PL* 16, 831A.
Doctrina Patrum (chap. Β´), p. 13.1–11, X.

130 Γρηγορίου ἐπισκόπου Να[ν]ζιανζοῦ ἐκ τῆς πρὸς Κληδόνιον ἐπιστολῆς·
Inc.: Φύσεις μὲν γὰρ δύο, Θεὸς καὶ ἄνθρωπος . . .
desin.: . . . ἀμφότερα ἐν τῇ συγκράσει.
CPG 3032 Gregorius Naz., *Epist.* 101, ed. P. Gallay, *Grégoire de Nazianze, Lettres théo-
logiques, SC* 208 (Paris, 1974), 44; *PG* 37, 180A.
Doctrina Patrum (chap. Β´), p. 11.6–7, I.

[Florilegium de Spiritu Sancto]

131 Τοῦ ἁγίου Ἐπιφανίου ἐπισκόπου Κύπρου ἐκ τοῦ λόγου τοῦ κατὰ Ἀρειανῶν.
Inc.: Παρελεύσομαι καὶ εἰς ἑτέρας λέξεις . . .
fol. 181 desin.: . . . ὑπαχθῆναι τῇ τοιαύτῃ εἰρωνίᾳ.
CPG 3745 Epiphanius Constantiensis, *Panarion*, ed. K. Holl, *Epiphanius, I. Ancoratus
und Panarion, GCS* 37 (Leipzig, 1933), 182.17–183.17.

Post εἰρωνίᾳ P add.:

> Ἐπιφάνιος οὗτος, φησίν, ὁ μέγας καὶ λαμπρὸς ὑποφήτης τοῦ πνεύματος, ὁ τὴν Κυ-
> πρίων νῆσον ἀσάλευτον θείαις θαυματουργίαις καὶ θειοτέραις (sic) δείξας διδάγ-
> μασι· καὶ αὖθις οὗτος τῆς τριάδος ζήλῳ φλεγόμενος τοῖς ὀρθοδόξως πιστεύουσιν
> ἔκραζε, διὸ ἡ τοῦ Θεοῦ ἐκκλησία πατέρα ἐν υἱῷ προσκυνεῖ υἱὸν ἐν πατρὶ σὺν ἁγίῳ
> ⟨πνεύματι;⟩, ᾧ ἡ δόξα καὶ τὸ κράτος καὶ ἡ τιμὴ καὶ προσκύνησις νῦν καὶ ἀεί.

Locum non inveni.

132 Not in *TLG*.
Ἐκ τοῦ κατὰ Εὐνομίου α´ τοῦ ἁγίου Βασιλείου·
> Χρὴ γινώσκειν ὅτι οὐκ οὐσία(ς) ἐστὶ σημαντικὸν τὸ πατρότης καὶ υἱότης καὶ ἐκπό-
> ρευσις, ἀλλὰ χαρακτηριστικὸν ἰδίωμα ἐφ᾽ ἑκάστης καὶ μιᾶς τῶν ὑποστάσεων.

Locum non inveni. Cf. Basilius Caes. *Adversus Eunomium libri v, PG* 29, 577.38–40:
Ὅθεν καὶ αἱ προσηγορίαι οὐχὶ τῶν οὐσιῶν εἰσι σημαντικαί, ἀλλὰ τῶν ἰδιοτήτων, αἳ τὸν
καθ᾽ ἕνα χαρακτηρίζουσιν.

133 Τοῦ ἁγίου Ἐπιφανίου ἐκ τοῦ Ἀγκυρωτοῦ τῆς ἕκτης ἐπιστολῆς τῆς γραφείσης εἰς
Πάμφιλον (3 extracts).
Inc.: Ὅτι εἷς ἡμῶν ἐστιν ὁ Θεός—(fol. 181ᵛ) ἐκ τοῦ υἱοῦ λαμβανόμενον. Καὶ μετὰ
βραχέα· Αὐτὸς γὰρ ὁ μονογενὴς λέγει—τῆς αὐτῆς θεότητος. Καὶ μετ᾽ ὀλίγα. Οὐδὲ
τὸ πνεῦμά τις οἶδεν εἰ μὴ ὁ πατὴρ καὶ ὁ υἱὸς παροῦ (sic) ἐκπορεύεται καὶ παρ᾽
οὗ λαμβάνει.
CPG 3744 Epiphanius Const., *Ancoratus*, ed. K. Holl, *Epiphanius, I. Ancoratus und
Panarion, GCS* 25 (Leipzig, 1915), 12.24–13.8; 15.3–6; 19.8 ff. See also quotations **134–
136, 138, 148.**

134 Τοῦ αὐτοῦ ἐκ τῆς αὐτῆς βίβλου καὶ τοῦ λόγου τοῦ περὶ τῶν δερματίνων χιτώνων (2 extracts).
Inc.: Περὶ τούτου ὁ Κύριος φησίν·—ἐκεῖνος μαρτυρήσει περὶ ἐμοῦ· καὶ αὖθις μετὰ βραχύ. Εἰ τοίνυν παρὰ τοῦ πατρός . . .
desin.: . . . ἐξ οὗ λαμβάνει καὶ παρ᾿ οὗ ἐκπορεύεται.
CPG 3744 Epiphanius Const., *Ancoratus, GCS* 25, 91.10–12/18–22.

135 Ἐκ τοῦ περὶ ἀναστάσεως λόγου.
Οὕτω δὲ πιστεύομεν αὐτῷ—καὶ τοῦ υἱοῦ λαμβανόμενον.
CPG 3744 Epiphanius Const., *Ancoratus, GCS* 25, 148.28–30.

136 Ἐκ τοῦ περὶ τῶν χιτώνων τῶν δερματίνων.
Τὸ δὲ πνεῦμα τὸ ἅγιον μόνον καλεῖται πατρὸς καὶ υἱοῦ, πνεῦμα ἀληθείας, πνεῦμα Θεοῦ καὶ πνεῦμα Χριστοῦ καὶ πνεῦμα χάριτος.
CPG 3744 Epiphanius Const., *Ancoratus, GCS* 25, 90.21–23.

137 Τοῦ ἐν ἁγίοις πατρὸς ἡμῶν Ἰωάννου τοῦ Χρυσοστόμου περὶ ἀκαταλήπτου λόγου·
Inc.: Ὅτι μὲν πανταχοῦ ἐστι Θεός . . .
desin.: . . . τὸ δὲ πῶς ἐξ αὐτοῦ οὐκ ἐπίσταμαι.
CPG 4318 Iohannes Chrys., *De incomprehensibili Dei natura homilia* 1, *PG* 48, 804.28–35.

138 Τοῦ ἁγίου Ἐπιφανίου ἐπισκόπου Κύπρου Κωνσταντίας ἐκ τῆς βίβλου, ἧς ἡ ἐπωνυμία Ἀγκυρωτός (2 extracts).
Inc.: Ἀλλ᾿ εἰ μὲν ἀμφότερα κατοικεῖ—τὸν ἐλθόντα πρός με. Καὶ μετὰ βραχέα. Ὅταν ἔλθῃ ὁ παράκλητος . . .
fol. 182 desin.: . . . ἐκ τοῦ υἱοῦ μόνου ὁδηγὸς ἀληθείας.
CPG 3744 Epiphanius Const., *Ancoratus, GCS* 25, 81.11–19, 91.10–25.

139 Ἰωάννου ἀρχιεπισκόπου Κωνσταντινουπόλεως τοῦ Χρυσοστόμου ἐκ τῆς ἑρμηνείας τοῦ κατὰ Ἰωάννην εὐαγγελίου λόγου, οὗ ἡ ἀρχή· Πάντα τὰ ἀγαθὰ τότε ἔχει τὸν μισθὸν ὅταν εἰς τέλος ἔλθῃ τὸ προσῆκον. Καὶ μετὰ βραχέα·
Inc.: Ἵνα οὖν μὴ ταῦτα ἐννοοῦντες θορυβοῦνται . . .
desin.: . . . περὶ ἀληθείας διαλεγόμενος ὅτι ἐγὼ πέμψω.
CPG 4425 Iohannes Chrys., *In Iohannem homiliae* 1–88, *PG* 59, 417.25–35.

140 Not in *TLG*.
Τοῦ αὐτοῦ ἐκ τοῦ λόγου τοῦ εἰς τὰ ἅγια Φῶτα·
Οὗτός ἐστιν ὁ υἱός μου ὁ ἀγαπητός, ὁ σὺν ἐμοὶ πέμψας ὑφ᾿ ἑαυτὸν τὸ πνεῦμα τὸ ἅγιον.
Locum non inveni (Iohannes Chrys.?). Also quotation **212**.

141 Τοῦ ἁγίου Μεθοδίου ἐπισκόπου Φιλίππων καὶ μάρτυρος ἐκ τοῦ περὶ ἁγνείας συμποσίου.
Inc.: Ἀτὰρ δὴ καὶ τὸ τῆς σοφίας νοερὸν πνεῦμα . . .
desin.: . . . καιρὸς ἤδη λέγειν τὰ περὶ παρθενίας.
CPG 1810 Methodius Olympius, *Convivium decem virginum*, ed. H. Musurillo, *Méthode d'Olympe. Le Banquet, SC* 95 (Paris, 1963), 179.10–15; ed. G. N. Bonwetsch, *Methodius, GCS* 27 (Leipzig, 1917), 71.2–6; *PG* 18, 121c10–124a3.

142 Τοῦ αὐτοῦ εἰς τὸ ῥητὸν τοῦ μδ΄ ψαλμοῦ· Ἐπενεχθήσονται τῷ βασιλεῖ παρθένοι—ἀγαλλιάσει. Ἑρμηνεία·
Inc.: Πάνυ προφανῶς ἐνθάδε λοιπὸν ἔοικεν . . .

desin.: . . . δορυφορουμένας τε καὶ παραπεμπομένας.
CPG 1810 Idem, ibid., *SC* 95, 196.4–11; *GCS* 27, 79.21–80.3; *PG* 18, 136c4–13.

143 Τοῦ αὐτοῦ ἑρμηνεία εἰς τὰς χιλίας σξ´ ἡμέρας·
fol. 182ᵛ Inc.: Τὰ γὰρ χίλια ἐν ἑκατὸν τάσσειν (sic) . . .
desin.: . . . τοῦτο καὶ τοῦ πατρὸς παρεκτικόν.
CPG 1810 Idem, ibid., *SC* 95, 228.25–31; *GCS* 27, 94.11–16, *PG* 18, 156a13–b5.

144 Προσφωνητικὸν παρὰ τῆς ἁγίας δ´ συνόδου πρὸς τὸν εὐσεβέστατον καὶ φιλόχριστον βασιλέα Μαρκιανόν, ὅτι οὐκ ἔνομόν (sic) τι κατὰ τῆς ἐν Νικαίᾳ πίστεως νῦν ὁ ἁγιώτατος ἀρχιεπίσκοπος τῆς μεγαλοπόλεως Ῥώμης Λέων ἐποιήσατο τὴν ἐπιστολὴν πρὸς τὸν ἐν ἁγίοις ἐπίσκοπον τῆς βασιλευούσης Κωνσταντινουπόλεως Φλαβιανόν, ἀλλὰ τοῖς ἁγίοις πατράσιν ἀκολουθῶν τοῖς μετὰ τῆς μεγάλης συνόδου τῶν ἐν Νικαίᾳ τὰς κατὰ καιρὸν ἀναφυείσας αἱρέσεις ἐλεγξάσης.
Inc.: Οἱ τῆς Ἀρείου σπορᾶς ἐν ἑαυτοῖς τὴν λύμην φυλάξαντες . . .
desin.: . . . τούτων ἔφοδον ἡμῖν ἀνέδειξε στρατηγούς.
CPG 9021 *Adlocutio ad Marcianum imp. aug. ACO* II,1,3, p. 111.22–31.

Post στρατηγοὺς add. P:

τοὺς τῆς εὐσεβείας ὑπασπιστάς, καθὼς καὶ πρώην ἐν τῇ ἁγίᾳ δευτέρᾳ συνόδῳ, τὸν ἁγιώτατον πατριάρχην Δάμασον, τὸν τρόπων καὶ θρόνου διάδοχον τῶν ἁγίων καὶ πανευφήμων ἀποστόλων γενάμενον καὶ καθεξῆς καὶ προπάροιθεν (sic) τοὺς θεοσόφους καὶ τρισμακαρίστους πατέρας ἡμῶν.

145 Τοῦ ἐν ἁγίοις πατρὸς ἡμῶν Βασιλείου ἀφοριστικαὶ ἔννοιαι περὶ τοῦ παναγίου πνεύματος τῇ τῶν γραφῶν ἀκολουθοῦσαι διδασκαλίᾳ· καὶ ὅτι δεσπότης τὸ πνεῦμα ἐκ τῶν πρὸς Ἀμφιλόχιον. Κεφάλαιον θ´·
Inc.: Ἤδη δὲ καὶ περὶ τοῦ ἁγίου πνεύματος . . .
fol. 183 desin.: . . . καὶ καθαρῶς ἁύλου καὶ ἀμεροῦς ὄνομά ἐστιν.
CPG 2839 Basilius Caes., *De Spiritu Sancto,* ed. B. Pruche, *Saint-Esprit,* 322.1–12; *PG* 32, 108a3–b1.

146 Τοῦ αὐτοῦ ἐκ τῶν κεφαλαίων τῶν πρὸς Ἀμφιλόχιον ὅτι καὶ ἐπὶ πατρὸς λέγεται τὸ δι᾽ οὗ καὶ ἐπὶ υἱοῦ τὸ ἐξ οὗ καὶ ἐπὶ τοῦ ἁγίου πνεύματος·
Inc.: Ὅτι οὔτε ὁ πατὴρ τὸ ἐξ οὗ . . .
desin.: . . . καὶ εἰς αὐτὸν τὰ πάντα.
CPG 2839 Idem, ibid., ed. Pruche, 272.2–17; *PG* 32, 77c14–80b5.

Post πάντα add. P:

αὐτῷ ἡ δόξα εἰς τοὺς αἰῶνας τῶν αἰώνων, ἀμήν.

147 Τοῦ αὐτοῦ πρὸς λέγοντας ὅτι πολλάκις γέγραπται περὶ υἱοῦ καὶ πατρός, περὶ δὲ τοῦ πνεύματος ἐν τῷ βαπτίσματι μόνον.
Inc.: Ἐὰν λέγῃ ὁ πατὴρ ἐν ταῖς ἐσχάταις ἡμέραις . . .
fol. 183ᵛ desin.: . . . ὁ υἱός, τοῦ πατρός εἰσι λόγια.
CPG 2837 Basilius Caesar., *Adversus Eunomium V, PG* 29, 761b–765c.

148 Ἔκθεσις πίστεως τοῦ ἁγίου Ἐπιφανίου ἐκ τῆς βίβλου τῆς ἐπονομαζομένης Ἀγκυρωτός.

Inc.: Πιστεύομεν εἰς ἕνα Θεόν . . .
desin.: . . . καὶ εἰς ζωὴν αἰώνιον, ἀμήν.
CPG 3744 Epiphanius Const., *Ancoratus, GCS* 25, 148.4–149.4.

149 Ἰστέον ὅτι ἐκπόρευσίς ἐστιν, ὥς φησιν (sic) οἱ θεοφόροι πατέρες, ἄχραντος (fol. 184) ἀκαταληψία, ὁμοίως καὶ ἀγεννησία πατρός, ἐκπόρευσις ὡσαύτως καὶ υἱοῦ γέννησις ὡσαύτως δὲ καὶ πνεύματος ἁγίου, καθώς φησιν ὁ θεηγόρος Γρηγόριος· εἰς Θεὸς καὶ πατήρ, εἰς ἓν αἴτιον υἱοῦ καὶ πνεύματος, ᾧ ἡ δόξα εἰς τοὺς αἰῶνας, ἀμήν.
Locum non inveni.

150

    Τοῦ ἁγίου Διονυσίου ἐκ τῆς πρὸς Τίτον ἐπιστολῆς.
    Χρὴ πάντα θεοπρεπῶς καὶ ὑπερφυῶς καὶ κατὰ θεωρίαν τὴν ἀκροτάτην ἐπὶ Θεοῦ νοεῖν, ἤγουν πρόσωπον καὶ ὀφθαλμούς, τὴν παμφαεστάτην καὶ ὑπερφαῆ καὶ παντοπτικὴν αὐτοῦ δύναμιν, καὶ εἶδος τὴν ἀνδρείαν· ὡσαύτως καὶ χεῖρας
5   καὶ τὴν πανδρακεστάτην (sic) δύναμιν· ἔτι δὲ καὶ τὰ ὑπερφυῆ καὶ ὑπερούσια χαρακτηριστικὰ ἰδιώματα, λέγω δὴ πατρὸς ἀνάρχου ἀγεννησίαν καὶ υἱοῦ, τοῦ συνανάρχου αὐτοῦ καὶ ἐνυποστάτου λόγου, σοφίας, καὶ δυνάμεως, ὑπερούσιον γέννησιν καὶ πνεύματος τοῦ παναγίου καὶ συναϊδίου πατρὸς καὶ υἱοῦ ταυτότητα καὶ θεότητα· ὡσαύτως καὶ τὴν ἐκ πατρὸς αὐτοῦ τοῦ παναγίου πνεύματος
10   ἐκπόρευσιν, ἐπίπνοιαν καὶ θεοπρεπῶς αὐτοῦ λαμβανομένην, ὥς φασί τινες, ⟨lacuna?⟩· ὑπερουσίαν (sic) γὰρ καὶ νοῦν καὶ λόγον πεφύκασιν, ὡς αὐτὸς ὁ κύριός φησιν· "οὐδεὶς ἔγνω τὸν πατέρα εἰ μὴ ὁ υἱός, ὡσαύτως δὲ καὶ τὸν υἱὸν οὐδεὶς ἔγνω εἰ μὴ ὁ πατήρ, ἀτὰρ δὴ καὶ τὸ πνεῦμα.

Locum non inveni in opere citato. See J. Paramelle, "Morceau égaré . . . ," 242–43

151 Τοῦ ἁγίου Βασιλείου ἐκ τῶν ἐπιστολῶν Γρηγορίῳ ἀδελφῷ περὶ διαφορᾶς οὐσίας καὶ ὑποστάσεως καὶ περὶ ἀγεννήτου καὶ γεννητοῦ καὶ ἐκπορευτοῦ, τουτέστι πατρὸς υἱοῦ καὶ ἁγίου πνεύματος.
Inc.: Ἐπειδὴ πολλοὶ τὸ κοινὸν τῆς οὐσίας—οὐσίαν ἢ ὑπόστασιν λέγειν· Καὶ μεθ᾽ ἕτερα.
    Ὅταν τοίνυν καὶ πρὸς ἐκείνην . . .
fol. 185ᵛ desin.: . . . τὰς γνωριστικὰς ἰδιότητας ἐπιλάμπειν ἑκάστῳ.
CPG 3196 Gregorius Nyss., *Ad Petrum fratrem de differentia essentiae et hypostaseos* = Ps.–Basilius Caes., *Epistula* 38, ed. Y. Courtonne, *Saint Basile, Lettres*, I (Paris, 1957), 81.1–4/84.12–89.49; *PG* 32, 325A3–7; 329B9–336B3.

152 Τοῦ ἁγίου Μαξίμου ἴσον ἐπιστολῆς πρὸς τὸν κύριν Μαρῖνον τὸν πρεσβύτερον τῆς Κύπρου.
Inc.: Νόμῳ θείῳ κατὰ Θεὸν εὐθηνούμενος (sic) θεοτίμητε πάτερ . . .
fol. 186 . . . προσδεομένοις καὶ χρήζουσιν. Καὶ μετὰ βραχέα. Τῶν τοῦ νῦν ἁγιωτάτου πάπα συνοδικῶν . . .
fol. 187 desin.: . . . τὸ δοκοῦν μεταλλεύειν οὐ καλῶς πειρωμένου.
CPG 7697.10 Maximus Confessor, *Opuscula theologica et polemica. Exemplum epistulae ad Marinum Cypri presbyterum, PG* 91, 133B–137C.

153 Τοῦ αὐτοῦ ἐκ τῆς ἐπιστολῆς τῆς ἐν Ῥώμῃ γραφείσης.
Inc.: Πάντα γὰρ τὰ πέρατα τῆς οἰκουμένης . . .
desin.: . . . ὀρθοδόξου θρησκείας μυστήριον.
CPG 7697.11 Maximus Confessor, *Ex epistula Romae scripta, PG* 91, 137C–140B.

154 Τοῦ αὐτοῦ.

(a) Inc.: Ἰστέον ὅτι ὑποστατικὴ ποιότης πατρὸς μὲν ἡ ἀγεννησία . . .
fol. 187ᵛ desin.: . . . ὡς οὐκ ἄσχετον οὐδὲ ἀνείδεον.

(b) Inc.: ἐπὶ γὰρ τῆς ἀγεννήτου καὶ ἀνάρχου φύσεως . . .
desin: . . . δύναιτ᾽ ἂν τὰ ὑπὲρ ἡμᾶς εἰκάζειν.

(a) Locum non inveni.

(b) *CPG* 7697.21 Maximus Confessor, *De qualitate, proprietate et differentia seu distinctione ad Theodorum presbyterum in Mazario*, *PG* 91, 249A5–10.

155 Τοῦ ἁγίου Κυρίλλου ἐκ τοῦ ἑορταστικοῦ λόγου.
Τὸ πνεῦμα τὸ ἅγιον ἐκπορεύεται μὲν ἐκ τοῦ πατρὸς χωρηγεῖται (sic) δὲ τῇ κτίσει διὰ τοῦ υἱοῦ.
CPG 5355 Cyrillus Alex., *Epistula* 55. *ACO* I,1,4, 60.23–24. See quotation **159**.

156 = **4A** Κυρίλλου ἐκ τοῦ λόγου τοῦ πρὸς τὰς βασιλίδας.
Inc.: Πιστεύομεν δὲ ὁμοίως καὶ εἰς τὸ πνεῦμα τὸ ἅγιον . . .
desin.: . . . ἡ ἁγία καὶ προσκυνουμένη τριάς.
CPG 5219 Cyrillus Alex., *Oratio ad Arcadiam et Marinam augustas de fide*. *ACO* I,1,5, 63.13–16; *PG* 76, 1204D9–1205A3.

157 Ἐκ τῶν (sic) προσφωνητικοῦ τοῦ πρὸς βασιλέα Θεοδόσιον τὸν μέγαν (2 fragments).
Inc.: Πρῶτον μὲν ὅτι τῆς πίστεως—ἀπὸ τῆς διανοίας ὑμῶν.// ἀπολύων γὰρ ἁμαρτιῶν τὸν αὐτῷ προσκείμενον . . .
fol. 188 desin.: . . . ζωοποιεῖσθαι λέγεται μεθ᾽ ἡμῶν.
CPG 5218 Cyrillus Alex., *Oratio ad Theodosium imp. de recta fide*, *ACO* I,1,1, 53.10–20/ 67.4–18; *PG* 76, 1157D11–1160A15/1188C12–1189A11.

Post ἡμῶν add. P:

> ἰδοὺ σαφῶς τὸ τοῦ Θεοῦ πνεῦμα, πνεῦμα λέγεται τοῦ Χριστοῦ· ἀλλ᾽ εἴπερ ἐστὶν ἄνθρωπος ἰδικῶς καὶ ἀνὰ μέρος κείμενος κατῳκηκότα μόνον τὸν τοῦ Θεοῦ λόγον ἔχων, πῶς αὐτοῦ τὸ θεῖον λέγεται πνεῦμα; ἀλλὰ μὴν ἴδιον αὐτοῦ τὸ πνεῦμά ἐστι, Θεὸς ἄρα καὶ οὐχ ἕτερος· οὐ γὰρ ἐν ἀνθρώπῳ γέγονεν ὁ τοῦ Θεοῦ
> 5 Θεὸς λόγος, ἀλλὰ γέγονεν ἄνθρωπος ἀληθῶς μετὰ τοῦ μεῖναι Θεός. οὕτω γὰρ νόει τό· "Χριστοῦ τὸ πνεῦμα ὑπάρχειν τοῦ πατρός"· ὥσπερ γὰρ ἕκαστος τῶν καθ᾽ ἡμᾶς ἐν ἰδίᾳ δυνάμει τὰ ἑαυτοῦ ἔργα πληροῖ, οὕτω καὶ ὁ Χριστός, ὡς ἰδίᾳ δυνάμει τῷ πνεύματι χρώμενος, ἐνεργεῖ τὰ παράδοξα θαυμάσια.

Locum non inveni.

158

(a) Χρὴ γινώσκειν ὅτι ἡ μὲν πρώτη ἁγία καὶ οἰκουμενικὴ σύνοδος γέγονεν ἐν Νικαίᾳ τιη΄ πατέρων ἐπὶ Σιλβέστρου τοῦ ἁγιωτάτου πάπα Ῥώμης· τινὲς δέ φασιν ἐπὶ Ἰουλιανοῦ καὶ Ἀλεξάνδρου Κωνσταντινουπόλεως, Μακαρίου καὶ Ἰουβεναλίου τῆς Θεουπόλεως καὶ Ἀλεξάνδρου Ἀλεξανδρείας.

Locum non inveni.

(a1) Ἡ ἔκθεσις πίστεως τῶν τιη΄ ἁγίων καὶ μακαρίων πατέρων τῶν ἐν Νικαίᾳ· α΄ σύνοδος.

Inc.: Πιστεύομεν εἰς ἕνα Θεὸν Πατέρα Παντοκράτορα . . .
desin.: . . . ἀναθεματίζει ἡ καθολικὴ καὶ ἀποστολικὴ ἐκκλησία.
CPG 8512 Concilium Oecumenicum Nicaenum, *Symbolum*, ed. G. L. Dossetti, *Il simbolo di Nicea e di Constantinopoli. Edizione critica*, Testi e ricerce di scienze religiose 2 (Rome, 1967), 66.

(b) Ἡ δὲ δευτέρα τῶν ἁγίων ρμ΄ γέγονεν (fol. 188ᵛ) ἐν Κωνσταντινουπόλει ἐπὶ Δαμάσου πάπα Ῥώμης, Νεκταρίου Κωνσταντινουπόλεως, Τιμοθέου Ἀλεξανδρείας, Μελετίου Ἀντιοχείας, Κυρίλλου Ἱεροσολύμων. Καὶ αὗται μὲν ἐκύρωσαν καὶ ἐβεβαίωσαν τὸ σύμβολον τῆς πίστεως.
In margine: Δευτέρα σύνοδος.
Ἔκθεσις πίστεως τῶν ἁγίων καὶ μακαρίων πατέρων τῶν ἐν Κωνσταντινουπόλει δευτέρας συνόδου· Πιστεύω εἰς ἕνα Θεὸν πατέρα παντοκράτορα.

(c) Ἡ δὲ τρίτη σύνοδος γέγονεν ἐπὶ τοῦ ἁγιωτάτου πάπα Κελεστίνου καὶ Κυρίλλου ἀρχιεπισκόπου Ἀλεξανδρείας.
In margine: σύνοδος τρίτη·
b–c loca non inveni.

(c1)   Ἡ ἐν Ἐφέσῳ τὸ πρῶτον ἐκ θείας συναθροισθεῖσα ἐπινεύσεως, διακοσίων μὲν πατέρων ἁγίων ἐγνώριζε τὸ πλήρωμα· ἧς ἡγεμόνες ἐτύγχανον οἱ ἁγιώτατοι τὴν μνήμην Κελεστῖνος ὁ τῆς Ῥωμαίων καὶ Κύριλλος ὁ τῆς Ἀλεξανδρέων ἁγιωτάτης τοῦ Θεοῦ μεγάλης ἐκκλησίας ἐτύγχανον· καταβαλούσης δὲ Νεστόριον καὶ
5   θεοτόκον παναληθῆ βεβαίως καὶ ἀσφαλῶς καὶ κυρίως καὶ ἀληθῶς τὴν πανάχραντον Θεοῦ μητέρα ἀνεκήρυξαν. οἷς ἑπόμενοι καὶ ἡμεῖς οἱ ἁμαρτωλοὶ ἴσως δοξάζομεν τὴν ὑπερένδοξον Χριστοῦ τοῦ Θεοῦ ἡμῶν μητέρα καὶ τῶν ἀχράντων δυνάμεων ἁγιωτέραν θεοτόκον καὶ πανάχραντον ἀειπάρθενον Μαρίαν καὶ ἁπάσης κτίσεως τιμιωτέραν ὁμολογοῦντες ψυχῇ, καρδίᾳ, καὶ στόματι, ὡς πρε-
10   σβεύουσαν ἀπαύστως ὑπὲρ τῶν ψυχῶν ἡμῶν.
Locum non inveni.

(d) Ὅρος τῆς ἁγίας καὶ οἰκουμενικῆς τετάρτης συνόδου πατέρων ἁγίων ἐν Χαλκηδόνι, οἷς ἦν ἀριθμὸς ἑπτὰ συνθέτους ἔχων δραμούσας εἰς ἑαυτὸν ἐννάδας.
In margine: σύνοδος δ΄
Locum non inveni.

(d1)
Inc.: Ἡ ἁγία καὶ οἰκουμενικὴ σύνοδος . . .
fol. 189 desin.: . . . καθολικῆς καὶ ἀποστολικῆς πίστεως.
CPG 9005 Concilium Oecumenicum Chalcedonense, *Gesta, Actio V. ACO* II,1,2, 126.8-127.8.

(d2) Τόμος τῆς ἐν Χαλκηδόνι τῶν χλ΄ πατέρων ἁγίας συνόδου·
Inc.: Ἡ ἁγία καὶ οἰκουμενικὴ σύνοδος εἶπεν· ἤρκει μὲν εἰς . . .
fol. 190 desin.: . . . ἢ λαϊκοὶ εἶεν ἀναθεματίζεσθαι αὐτούς.
CPG 9005 Concilium Oecum. Chalcedonense, *Gesta, Actio V. ACO* II,1,2, 128.15-130.11.

(d3) Inc.: ὁ τύπος καὶ ὅρος τῶν ἁγίων πατέρων ἀναγνωσθείς, ἐξεφωνήθη . . .
desin.: . . . αὕτη ἡ πίστις τὴν οἰκουμένην ἔσωσεν.
CPG 9007 Concilium Oecum. Chalcedonense, Gesta, Actio VI. ACO II,1,2, 155.6–12.

(d4) Λέοντος τοῦ ἁγιωτάτου, ἀποστολικοῦ καὶ οἰκουμενικοῦ πατριάρχου, πολλὰ τὰ ἔτη.
τῶν θεοτιμήτων καὶ πανευσεβῶν ἱερέων πολλὰ τὰ ἔτη. τῆς ἱερᾶς συγκλήτου πολλὰ
τὰ ἔτη. αὔξει ἡ πίστις τῶν Ῥωμαίων. στερεώσει ὁ Θεὸς τὸν ἰσαπόστολον καὶ διάδοχον τοῦ θρόνου τῶν ἀποστόλων πατριάρχην ἡμῶν.
Locum non inveni.

(d5)   ἐπειδὴ ἀρχῆθεν ἡ ἁγία καθολικὴ καὶ ἀποστολικὴ ἐκκλησία τοῦ Κυρίου ἡμῶν
          Ἰησοῦ Χριστοῦ ἀπ᾽ αὐτοῦ τοῦ σωτῆρος πρεσβεύειν παρείληφε καὶ ὁ τῶν μα-
          καρίων ἀποστόλων χορὸς φρονεῖν αὐτῇ παραδέδωκε καὶ πάντες οἱ μετ᾽ αὐτοὺς
          θεοκήρυκες ὑπὸ πνεύματος ἁγίου οἱ πατέρες ἐκήρυξαν καὶ ἡ τρισμακάριστος
      5   καὶ ἔνθεος τῶν ἐν Χαλκηδόνι συνειλεγμένων (cod. συνηλλεγμ.) θεοφόρων μυ-
          σταγωγῶν πατέρων πάνσεπτος σύνοδος μετὰ πασῶν τῶν ἁγίων συνόδων θεο-
          πνεύστοις φωναῖς ἀνεκήρυξε. καὶ ἡμεῖς πιστεύομεν καὶ ὁμολογοῦμεν καθὼς
          ἐξέθεντο καὶ ἐδίδαξαν τῆς εὐσεβείας τὸ μέγα καὶ πάνσεπτον τῆς σωτηρίας
          ἡμῶν μυστήριον.
Locum non inveni.

(e)   Ὅρος καὶ τύπος τῆς ἁγίας ε΄ συνόδου συγγραφεὶς ὑπὸ Πέτρου ἀρχιεπισκόπου
          Νικομηδείας καὶ καθεξῆς ἅπαντες οἱ τῷ ἁγίῳ πνεύματι συνηθροισμένοι·
          Ἐπὶ ταύταις δὲ ταῖς ἰσαρίθμοις τῶν ἁγίων καὶ θεολέκτων εὐαγγελίων καὶ
          πέμπτην ἄλλην (fol. 190ᵛ) ἁγίαν ὁμόφωνον μετὰ ταύτας συστᾶσαν οἰκουμε-
      5   νικὴν δεχόμεθα σύνοδον, τὴν ἐν τῇ βασιλίδι γεναμένην τῶν πόλεων, ἥτις κυροῖ
          μὲν τὴν ἐν Χαλκηδόνι περιώνυμον καὶ πάσας τὰς πρὸ αὐτῆς συνόδους, οὕτως
          διαγορευούσας τὴν ὀρθόδοξον πίστιν, καθὼς καὶ πᾶσαι αἱ ἅγιαι σύνοδοι.
Locum non inveni.

(e1)
Inc.: Πιστεύομεν εἰς ἕνα Θεὸν πατέρα παντοκράτορα . . .
desin.: . . . τριάδα μὲν κατὰ τὰς ὑποστάσεις, ἤγουν πρόσωπα.
CPG 9429.3 Concilium Oecumenicum Constantinopolitanum III, Gesta, Actio X, Libellus satisfactionis Petri episc. Nicomediae. ACO Ser. II, II,1, 390.26-392.6.

(e2)
Post πρόσωπα add. P:

          τοίνυν χρόνος πάνυ μακρὸς διελήλυθεν ἀφ᾽ οὗπερ οἱ πανευσεβεῖς καὶ θεοφόροι
          πατέρες θείᾳ βουλῇ καὶ θεσπίσματι τὴν λαμπρὰν ἐν Χαλκηδόνι σύνοδον ποιη-
          σάμενοι τὴν πίστιν ὑπὸ τουτωνὶ τῶν βελτίστων, ἤγουν τῶν πρὸ αὐτῶν, σαλευο-
          μένην ἐκράτυναν καὶ πάντων ἐγκρατεῖς δι᾽ εὐσέβειαν τῶν τῆς οἰκουμένης πε-
      5   ράτων γεγόνασιν. ὧν οὐκ ἄν ποτε κατεκράτησαν, εἰ μὴ Θεὸς ἦν ὁ ἀνίκητος, ὁ

καὶ τότε κρατύνας αὐτῶν τὸ συνέδριον καὶ εἰς ἔτι καὶ νῦν δι' αὐτῶν τὸν σωτήριον λόγον φθεγγόμενος.

Locum non inveni.

159 Τοῦ ἁγίου Κυρίλλου ἑρμηνεία εἰς τὸ ἅγιον σύμβολον τὸ ὑπὸ τῶν ἁγίων πατέρων γεγενημένον· Τοῖς ἀγαπητοῖς καὶ ποθεινοτάτοις Ἀναστασίῳ . . . Κύριλλος ἐν Χριστῷ χαίρειν. (5 fragments).
Inc.: Τὸ φιλομαθὲς καὶ φιλόπονον—(fol. 191) ὁρισάμενοι σύμβολον. Καὶ μεθ' ἕτερα. Γεγραφότα γὰρ οἶδα—(fol. 191ᵛ) εἰκόνος φθαρτοῦ ἀνθρώπου. Καὶ μεθ' ἕτερα. Ἑπόμεθα τοίνυν πανταχοῦ τοῖς ἱεροῖς γράμμασι—καὶ οὐκ ἔστι πάρεξ ἐμοῦ. Καὶ μεθ' ἕτερα. Ταῦτα φρονεῖ μεθ' ἡμῶν ὁ φιλόχριστος—λόγον καὶ τὰ ἑξῆς//οὐκοῦν ὡς . . .
fol. 192 desin.: . . . ὁ ἐνανθρωπήσας λόγος, δι' οὗ καὶ μεθ' οὗ τῷ Θεῷ καὶ πατρὶ τιμὴ . . . ἀμήν.
CPG 5355 Cyrillus Alex., *Epistula 55, Ad Anastasium, Alexandrum, Martinianum, Iohannem, Paregorium presb. et Maximum diac. ceterosque monachos Orientales. ACO* I,I, 4, 49.3–50.12; 51.16–32; 52.2–7; 60.11–34; 61.14–18; *PG* 77, 292A3–293A8, 296B4–D2, 316C3–320A4.

160 Κυρίλλου ἐπισκόπου. πρεσβυτέροις καὶ διακόνοις πατράσι μοναχῶν καὶ τοῖς σὺν ἡμῖν (sic) τὸν μονήρη βίον ἀσκοῦσι καὶ ἐν πίστει Θεοῦ ἱδρυμένοις ἐν Κυρίῳ χαίρειν. οὗ ἡ ἀρχή. Ἀφήκοντο (sic) μέν τινες κατὰ τὸ εἰωθός.
Inc.: Ἡμεῖς δέ, οἷς τὸ θεῖον εἰς νοῦν ἐνήστραψε φῶς . . .
desin.: . . . εἰς μίαν θεότητος ἑνοῦται φύσιν.
CPG 5301 Cyrillus Alex., *Epistula 1, Ad monachos Aegypti. ACO* I,1,1, 13.22–31; *PG* 77, 17B6–C6.

161 Κυρίλλου ἀρχιεπισκόπου Ἀλεξανδρείας πρὸς Νεστόριον τὸν αἱρετικόν. Τῷ εὐλαβεστάτῳ . . . ἐν Κυρίῳ χαίρειν. (5 fragments).
Inc.: Τοῦ σωτῆρος ἡμῶν λέγοντος ἐναργῶς—(fol. 192ᵛ) ἀλλὰ μάχαιραν καὶ τὰ ἑξῆς. (b) Ὑπετάξαμεν δὲ τούτοις ἡμῶν—καὶ εἰς τὸ ἅγιον πνεῦμα. Post πνεῦμα P add.: τὸ κύριον, τὸ ζωοποιοῦν τὸ ἐκ τοῦ πατρὸς ἐκπορευόμενον, τὸ σὺν πατρὶ καὶ υἱῷ συμπροσκυνούμενον καὶ συνδοξαζόμενον καὶ τὰ ἑξῆς. (c) Ἑπόμενοι δὲ πανταχῆ ταῖς—καὶ τὰ ἐν τῇ γῇ. Καὶ μεθ' ἕτερα. (d) Ἀλλ' ἕνα μόνον εἰδότες—τὸ ἴδιον ἑαυτῆς σῶμα. (e) ὅταν λέγῃ περὶ τοῦ πνεύματος . . .
fol. 194 desin.: . . . καὶ ζωοποιὸς ὡς Θεός, ἀνάθεμα ἔστω.
CPG 5317 Cyrillus Alex., *Epistula 17, Ad Nestorium. ACO* I,1,1, (a) 33.4–33.16; (b) 34.23–35.8; (c) 35.12–16; (d) 36.3–13; (e) 39.14–42.5; *PG* 77, 105C5–121D7. See also quotation **7A**.

162 Διονυσίου Ἀρεοπαγίτου ἐπισκόπου Ἀθηνῶν λόγου δευτέρου· περὶ ἡνωμένης καὶ διακεκριμ[μ]ένης θεολογίας καὶ τίς ἡ θεία ἕνωσις καὶ διαίρεσις. (2 fragments).
Inc.: Τὴν θεαρχικὴν ὅλην ὕπαρξιν—τῶν λογίων ὑμνεῖται. Καὶ μεθ' ἕτερα. ⟨Ῥ⟩ητέον ὡς αὐτός τε ὁ ἀγαθοφυής . . .
desin.: . . . οὕτως καὶ ὁ υἱὸς ζωοποιεῖ.
CPG 6602 Dionysius Areopagita, *De divinis nominibus*, ed. B. R. Suchla, *Corpus Dionysiacum*, I, 122.1–2; 122.14–123.8; *PG* 3, 636C1–3; 637A3–15.

163 Τοῦ ἁγίου Κυρίλλου ἐκ τῶν πράξεων καὶ εἰς τὸ ῥητὸν τοῦ κατὰ Ἰωάννην εὐαγγελίου ἐκ τῶν θησαυρῶν.

Inc.: Παρήγγειλαν (sic) αὐτοῖς ἀπὸ Ἱεροσολύμων. . .
fol. 195 desin.: . . . αὕτη τῆς ἐν πνεύματι λατρείας ἡ δύναμις.
CPG 5208 Cyrillus Alex., *Commentarii in Iohannem*, *PG* 74, 540B12–544A4.

164 Τοῦ ἐν ἁγίοις πατρὸς ἡμῶν Γρηγορίου τοῦ Νύσης ἐκ τῶν εἰς τὴν προσευχὴν τοῦ πάτερ ἡμῶν· ὁμιλία γ΄. (8 fragments).
Inc.: Ὁ τὴν εἰκόνα τῶν μελλόντων—ἀφαγνίζει τὸν εἰσιόντα.//ἐπειδὰν δὲ ἡ βασιλεία—συμμαχίαν ἐπιβοᾶται. Καὶ μετ᾽ ὀλίγα. Πῶς ἐστιν εἰς τὴν ὑποχείριον—οὐδὲ κτίσις ἐστίν. Καὶ μεθ᾽ ἕτερα. Ἐλθέτω τὸ πνεῦμά σου—ἡ αὐτὴ τούτων ἐστίν. Καὶ μεθ᾽ ἕτερα. Ὥστε τῷ πατρὶ κατὰ τὴν φύσιν—τριάδος ἡ φύσις. Καὶ μεθ᾽ ἕτερα. Ἴδιον τοῦ πατρὸς τὸ μή—(fol. 195ᵛ) οὔτε ἐστὶν οὔτε λέγεται. Καὶ μεθ᾽ ἕτερα. Ταύτης τοίνυν τῆς ἰδιότητος—τῆς ἀξίας νομίζουσιν. Καὶ μεθ᾽ ἕτερα. Εἰ οὖν φησιν ἀφίησι . . .
desin.: . . . οἱ τῇ ἰδίᾳ προσπολεμοῦντες ζωῇ.
CPG 3160 Gregorius Nyss., *De oratione dominica oratio III*, ed. J. F. Callahan, *Gregorii Nysseni opera* VII,2 (Leiden-New York-Cologne, 1992) 31.3–7; 39.12–17; 40.1–8; 40.13–41.7; 42.3–6; 42.14–43.6; 43.9–19; 44.3–7. *PG* 44 1148D4–8, 1157B10–C3, C12–D3, D9–1160A7, B12–C2.

165 Τοῦ ἁγίου Γρηγορίου Νύσης ἐκ τοῦ βίου τοῦ ἁγίου Γρηγορίου τοῦ θαυματουργοῦ.
Inc.: Ἀκοῦσαι γὰρ λέγεται—μεταστῆναι τῶν ὄψεων.// Ὡς (sic) Θεὸς καὶ πατὴρ λόγου . . .
desin.: . . . ἀλλ᾽ ἄτρεπτος καὶ ἀναλλοίωτος ἡ αὐτὴ τριὰς ἀεί.
CPG 3184 Gregorius Nyss., *De Vita Gregorii Thaumaturgi* (BHGa 715–715b), ed. G. Heil, *Gregorii Nysseni Opera* X,1, *Gregorii Nysseni Sermones* (Leiden-New York, 1990), 17.13–18; 17.24–19.5. *PG* 46, 912.29–36; 912.47–913.11.

Post ἀεὶ add. P:

Γρηγόριος οὗτός φησιν ὁ τῆς Νυσαέων ἐξοχώτατος πρόβολος.

166 Τοῦ αὐτοῦ περὶ λόγου Θεοῦ καὶ πνεύματος εἰς τὸ ψαλμικόν· Τῷ λόγῳ Κυρίου οἱ οὐρανοὶ ἐστερεώσαντο (fol. 196) καὶ τῷ πνεύματι τοῦ στόματος αὐτοῦ πᾶσα ἡ δύναμις αὐτῶν.
Inc.: Ἐπεὶ μὲν τῆς θείας φύσεως—μυστηρίου βαθύτητα.// Ὥσπερ δὲ τὸν λόγον ἐκ τῶν καθ᾽ ἡμᾶς—ἐν αὐτῇ φανεροῦσα.// Ἀλλ᾽ ἐπειδὴ καὶ ὁ τῆς εὐσεβείας λόγος . . .
desin.: . . . ἐν τῇ ἑνότητι τῆς φύσεως βλέπειν.
CPG 3150 Gregorius Nyss., *Oratio catechetica magna*, ed. J. H. Srawley, *The Catechetical Oration of Gregory of Nyssa* (Cambridge, 1903), 14.2–15.14; 13.5–14.1; 6.12–7.1. *PG* 45, 17A11–D1; 17A2–11; 13A2–4. See also quotations **176, 211.**

Post βλέπειν P add.:

διὰ τὸ προσήκειν τὰς ἰδιότητας ἀσυγχύτους φυλάσσειν ὅτι ἐπὶ τῆς τριάδος ἄλλος καὶ ἄλλος, ἵνα μὴ τὰς ὑποστάσεις συγχέωμεν, οὐκ ἄλλο δὲ καὶ ἄλλο· ἐν γὰρ τὰ τρία καὶ ταὐτὸν τῇ θεότητι.

167 Δαμάσου ἐπισκόπου Ῥώμης ὁμολογία τῆς καθολικῆς πίστεως ἀποσταλεῖσα πρὸς Παυλῖνον ἐπίσκοπον Θεσσαλονίκης· (sic)
Inc.: Ἐπειδὴ μετὰ τὴν ἐν Νικαίᾳ σύνοδον ἡ πλάνη ἀνέκυψεν . . .
fol. 197ᵛ desin.: . . . ἔχωμεν ἐν αὐτῷ τῷ ἀληθινῷ Θεῷ ἡμῶν.

CPL 1633 Damasus Papa, *Epist. IV* (ad Conc. Rom. a. 382 pertinet), Versio Graeca exstat apud Theodoretum Episc. Cyri, ed. L. Parmentier, *Theodoret Kirehengeschichte, GCS* 19 (Leipzig, 1911), 297.12–302.15; *PL* 13, 358–64.

Post ἡμῶν P add.:

> Δάμασος οὗτος ἦν ὁ τῆς καθ᾽ ὅλην τὴν οἰκουμένην καὶ ἀπὸ γῆς εἰς οὐρανοὺς διαλαμπούσης ἐκκλησίας τοῦ Θεοῦ, Πέτρου τοῦ κορυφαίου τῶν ἀποστόλων δεξάμενος τοῦ παμμεγίστου θρόνου τοὺς οἴακας ὑπὸ τοῦ μεγάλου ἀρχιερέως Χριστοῦ τοῦ Θεοῦ ἡμῶν.

168a, b Ἐκ τοῦ ἁγίου εὐαγγελίου κατὰ Ἰωάννην.

(a) Φησὶ γοῦν ὁ Κύριος ἡμῶν Ἰησοῦς Χριστός, ὅτι οὐδεὶς ἔγνω τὸν πατέρα εἰ μὴ ὁ υἱὸς καὶ τὸν υἱὸν εἰ μὴ ὁ πατὴρ καὶ τὸ πνεῦμα αὐτὸς ἀπεκάλυψεν. (Cf. Matth. 11.27).

(b) Καὶ πάλιν· ἐγὼ ἀπ᾽ ἐμαυτοῦ οὐ λαλῶ, ἀλλ᾽ ὁ πέμψας με πατήρ, αὐτὸς μαρτυρεῖ περὶ ἐμοῦ. (Cf. Ioh. 5.31/37).

169 Λίβελλος πληροφορίας πίστεως συνταγεὶς παρὰ Ἀγάθωνος τοῦ ἁγιωτάτου πατριάρχου Ῥώμης.

Inc.: Ἐπείπερ ἐπεζήτησεν ἡ ὑμετέρα θεσπέσιος καὶ τιμία . . .

fol. 198 desin.: . . . καὶ δύο φυσικὰς ἐνεργείας ὁμολογῶ.

CPG 9429.3 Concilium Oecumenicum Constantinopolitanum III, *Gesta, Actio X, Libellus satisfactionis Petri episc. Nicomediae. ACO Ser. II,* vol. II,1, 390.26–394.14.

170 In margine: Τοῦ ἁγίου Βασιλείου.

Φησὶ γοῦν ὁ θεῖος Βασίλειος ἐν εἰκοστῷ ἑβδόμῳ κεφαλαίῳ τὸ (sic) πρὸς Ἀμφιλόχιον περὶ τοῦ ἁγίου πνεύματος λόγῳ.

Inc.: Τῶν ἐκκλησία (sic) δογμάτων καὶ κηρυγμάτων . . .

fol. 198ᵛ desin.: . . . τὸ καιριώτατον ζημιούμενοι τὸ εὐαγγέλιον.

CPG 2839 Basilius Caes., *De Spiritu Sancto,* ed. B. Pruche, *Saint-Esprit,* 478 par. 66.1– 480 par. 66.9; *PG* 32, 188A5–B1.

171 Καὶ πάλιν ἐκ τῆς ἑρμηνείας τοῦ Νύσης τῆς ἐκ τοῦ ᾄσματος τῶν ᾀσμάτων· ἐμφερομένη μαρτυρία ἐκ τοῦ κατὰ Ἰωάννην εὐαγγελίου.

Inc.: Τὴν δόξαν ἣν ἔδωκάς μοι, φησίν, ἔδωκα αὐτοῖς . . .

desin.: . . . τὴν ἀνθρωπίνην φύσιν περιβαλλόμενος.

CPG 3158 Gregorius Nyss., *In Canticum canticorum homiliae XV,* ed. H. Langerbeck, *Gregorii Nysseni opera,* VI. *In Canticum Canticorum* (Leiden, 1962), 467.8–12; *PG* 44, 1117A11–B1.

172 Φωνὴ τοῦ ἀποστόλου ἐστὶν ἡ λέγουσα ὅτι ἐν αὐτῷ κατοικεῖ πᾶν τὸ πλήρωμα τῆς θεότητος σωματικῶς. Cf. idem, ibid., 391.4–5; *PG* 44, 1056B2–3.

173 Περὶ αἰτίου·

> Τὸ γὰρ αἴτιον τῷ ὄντι οὗ ἄνευ κατὰ τὸν φιλόσοφον, τὸ αἴτιον οὐκ ἂν ᾖ ποτέ τι δήποτε. αἴτιον εἴη τοῦ Θεοῦ ἄφατος δύναμις τῇ (sic) πάντα συνέχουσα καὶ πάντων ἰσχυροτέρα· αἰτία γάρ, φησί, καὶ πέρας ἐστί, τουτέστιν ἀρχὴ καὶ τέλος· ἐξαπέστειλεν ὁ Θεὸς τὸ πνεῦμα τοῦ υἱοῦ αὐτοῦ εἰς τὰς καρδίας ἡμῶν κρᾶζον
> 5 ἀββᾶ ὁ πατήρ.

2 εἴη sic cod. sed malim ἦ ἡ 4 ἐξαπέστειλεν—5 πατήρ: Gal. 4.6.
Locum non inveni.

174 Τοῦ ἁγίου Βασιλείου ἐκ τοῦ λόγου τῶν ἠθικῶν καὶ κατὰ Ἀρειανῶν καὶ Εὐνομιανῶν καὶ Σαβελλιανῶν.
Inc.: Ἐγὼ δὲ μετὰ πατρὸς οἶδα τὸ πνεῦμα . . .
desin.: . . . καὶ πατέρα κατὰ τὴν φύσιν ἑνότητος.
CPG 2869 Basilius Caes., *Contra Sabellianos et Arium et Anomaeos, PG* 31, 612B13–C9.

175 Τοῦ ἁγίου Κυρίλλου ἐκ τοῦ προσφωνητικοῦ λόγου τῆς ἐν Χαλκηδόνι συνόδου πρὸς τὸν βασιλέα Μαρκιανόν· ἐρρέθη καὶ ὑπὸ τῶν ἁγίων Φλαβιανοῦ καὶ Λέοντος καὶ Κελεστίνου.
Inc.: Ἀλλ᾽ ἐπειδὴ ἁπλῆν ἡ πίστις τηνικαῦτα τὴν διδασκαλίαν . . .
fol. 199 desin.: . . . τοῖς τῆς τριάδος συνηγόροις ἑάλωσαν.
CPG 9021 Cyrillus Alex., *Adlocutio ad Marcianum imp. aug. ACO* II,1,3, 111.20–29.

176 Τοῦ ἁγίου Γρηγορίου Νύσης ἐκ τοῦ κατηχητικοῦ λόγου·
Inc.: Τὸ γὰρ εἶναι λόγον Θεοῦ καὶ πνεῦμα Θεοῦ οὐσιωδῶς . . .
desin.: . . . τῷ πνεύματι τοῦ στόματος αὐτοῦ πᾶσα ἡ δύναμις αὐτῶν.
CPG 3150 Gregorius Nyss., *Oratio catechetica magna*, ed. J. H. Srawley, *The Catechetical Oration of Gregory of Nyssa* (Cambridge, 1903), 18.3–10; *PG* 45, 20B1–9. See also quotations **166, 211.**

177 ⟨Τοῦ αὐτοῦ⟩
Inc.: Οὐ λόγος οὖν ὑπάρχει ἀέρος τύπωσις σημαντική . . .
desin.: . . . ὃ παρὰ τοῦ πατρὸς ἐκπορεύεται.
CPG 3221 Gregorius Nyss., *Testimonia adversus Iudaeos, PG* 46, 193A4–10.

178 Τοῦ ἁγίου Κυρίλλου ἐκ τῆς πρὸς Ἰωάννην πατριάρχην Ἀλεξανδρείας (sic)·
Inc.: Κατ᾽ οὐδένα τρόπον σαλεύεσθαι παρά τινων . . .
desin.: . . . πνεῦμα Χριστοῦ οὐκ ἔχει, οὗτος οὐκ ἔστιν αὐτοῦ.
Iohannes Antiochiae est.
CPG 5339 Cyrillus Alex., *Epist.* 39, *Ad Iohannem Antiochenum. ACO* I,1,4, 19.20–20.3; *PG* 77, 180D7–181B1.

179   Τοῦ αὐτοῦ ἐκ τῆς ἑρμηνείας τῶν ιβ´ κεφαλαίων·
Ὁμολογοῦμεν οὖν ὁμοούσιον εἶναι τῷ πατρὶ τὸν υἱὸν καὶ τὸ πνεῦμα τὸ ἅγιον καὶ μίαν τὴν οὐσίαν τῆς τριάδος, τουτέστι μίαν θεότητα φυσικῶς, ⟨ἀγ⟩εννήτου μὲν ὄντος τοῦ πατρός, γεννηθέντος δὲ τοῦ υἱοῦ ἐκ πατρὸς ἀληθινῇ γεννήσει,
5   οὐ ποιήσει τῇ ἐκ βουλήσεως, τοῦ τε πνεύματος ἐκ τῆς οὐσίας τοῦ πατρός, δι᾽ υἱοῦ ἀϊδίως ἐκπεμφθέντος, ἁγιαστικοῦ τῆς ὅλης κτίσεως. εἷς Θεὸς καὶ πατήρ, ἡ θεότης ἡ μόνη. Θεὸς δὲ καὶ ὁ υἱός, εἰκὼν τῆς μιᾶς θεότητος ὤν, ἀληθὴς κατὰ γέννησιν καὶ φύσιν, ἣν ἐκ τοῦ πατρὸς ἔχει· κύριος εἷς υἱός, ὡσαύτως δὲ καὶ τὸ πνεῦμα τὴν τοῦ υἱοῦ κυριότητα διαπέμπον εἰς τὴν ἁγιαζομένην κτίσιν. ὁ
10   υἱὸς ἐπεδήμησε (fol.199ᵛ) κόσμῳ σάρκα ἐκ παρθένου λαβών, ἣν ἐπλήρωσεν ἁγίου πν⟨εύματος⟩ εἰς πάντων ἡμῶν ἁγιασμόν.

CPG 5223 Cyrillus Alex., *Explanatio xii capitulorum. ACO* I,1,5, 15–25.
Locum non inveni in opere citato.

180 Τοῦ αὐτοῦ ἐκ τῆς ἑρμηνείας τοῦ Εὐαγγελίου·

(a) Ὁ μὲν γὰρ Κύριος ἡμῶν—ὑπετόπησε γέννησιν.

(b) Καὶ πάλιν· Θεὸς ὁ πατήρ, τέλειον ὢν πρόσωπον, τέλειον ἔχει τόν λόγον ἐξ αὐτοῦ γεγεννημένον ἀληθῶς· τέλειον δὲ καὶ τὸ πνεῦμα τὸ ἅγιον ἐκ Θεοῦ δι' υἱοῦ χορη-γούμενον ἐν τοῖς υἱοθετουμένοις, ζῶν καὶ ζωοποι(οῦν), ἅγιον, ἁγιαστικὸν τῶν μετα-λαμβανόντων αὐτοῦ, οὐχ ὥσπερ πνοὴν ἐμπνευθεῖσαν (sic) ἀνυπόστατον, ἀλλ' ἐκ Θεοῦ ζῶσαν, διότι ἡ τριὰς προσκυνητή, δοξαστικὴ καὶ τιμία, καὶ σεβάσμιος τρι(άς?). ἐξ ἑαυτοῦ υἱοῦ δὲ ἐν πνεύματι δοξαζομένου, καθώς ἐστιν ἐκ πατρὸς φανερουμένων ἐν πνεύματι ἁγίῳ τοῖς ἁγιαζομένοις.

(c) ὅτι δὲ σεβασμία καὶ προσκυνητὴ ἡ ἁγία τριάς, μὴ χωριζομένη, μηδὲ ἀπαλλοτρι-ουμένη, τοῦτο διδάσκει ἡμᾶς Παῦλος ἐκ τῆς πρὸς Κορινθίους δευτέρας ἐπιστολῆς λέγων· "ἡ χάρις τοῦ Κυρίου ἡμῶν Ἰησοῦ Χριστοῦ καὶ ἡ ἀγάπη τοῦ Θεοῦ καὶ πατρὸς καὶ ἡ κοινωνία τοῦ ἁγίου καὶ ζωοποιοῦ αὐτοῦ πνεύματος εἴη μετὰ πάντων ὑμῶν, ἀμήν". (2 Cor 13.13)

(a) CPC 5208, Cyrillus Alex., Commentarii in Iohannem, PG 73, 244C3-13.
(b) Locum non inveni in opere citato.
(c) Locus scholium videtur esse quod non inveni.

181 Τοῦ ἁγίου Γρηγορίου τοῦ θεολόγου ἐκ τοῦ εἰς τὰ φῶτα α΄ λόγου· (3 fragments)
Inc.: Θεοῦ δὲ ὅταν εἴπω, ἑνὶ φωτί—ἤτουν θεότητος. Καὶ μεθ' ἕτερα. ἡμῖν δὲ εἷς Θεὸς πατήρ—μὴ φύσεις τεμνόντων. Καὶ μεθ' ἕτερα. πατὴρ ὁ πατὴρ καὶ ἄναρχος . . .
fol. 200 desin.: . . . κινουμένη καὶ μεταπίπτουσα.
CPG 3010.39 Gregorius Naz., Oratio 39, ed. C. Moreschini, Discours 38–41, 170 par. 11.12-172 par. 11.18; 172 par. 12.1-4; 174 par. 12.10-22; PG 36, 345C9-15, 348A9-12, B6–C4.

182 Τοῦ αὐτοῦ περὶ τοῦ ἁγίου πνεύματος·
Inc.: Ἢ ἀγέννητον πάντως ἢ γεννητόν· καὶ εἰ μὲν ἀγέννητον . . .
desin.: . . . οὔ τοι ἂν γένοιτο παραδοξότερον.
CPG 3010.31 Gregorius Naz., Oratio 31, ed. P. Gallay, Discours 27–31, 286, par. 7.2-9; PG 36, 140C2-8.

183 Τοῦ αὐτοῦ·
Inc.: Ποῦ γὰρ θήσεις τὸ ἐκπορευτόν . . .
desin.: . . . τῶν σῶν διαιρέσεων ἰσχυρότερος.
CPG 3010.31 Gregorius Naz., Oratio 31, ibid., 290, par. 8.6-15; PG 36, 141A15–B12.

184 Τοῦ αὐτοῦ·
Inc.: Τίς οὖν ἡ ἐκπόρευσις; εἰπὲ σὺ τὴν ἀγεννησίαν . . .
desin.: . . . τὰ ἐν ποσὶν εἰδέναι δυνάμενοι.
CPG 3010.31 Gregorius Naz., Oratio 31, ibid., 290, par. 8.16-20; PG 36, 141B13–C1.

185 Τοῦ αὐτοῦ· περὶ υἱοῦ·
Inc.: Διὰ τοῦτο μονὰς ἀπ' ἀρχῆς . . .
desin.: . . . ἀφελὼν πάντη τῶν ὁρωμένων.
CPG 3010.29 Gregorius Naz., Oratio 29, ibid., 180 par. 2.13-18; PG 36, 76B9-15.

186 Τοῦ αὐτοῦ·
Inc.: Διὰ τοῦτο ἐπὶ τῶν ἡμετέρων ὅρων . . .

desin.: . . . αὐτὸς ὁ Θεὸς καὶ λόγος.
CPG 3010.29 Gregorius Naz., *Oratio* 29, ibid., 180 par. 2.24–27; *PG* 36, 76c8–11.

187 Περὶ θεολογίας α΄· (3 fragments)
Inc.: ⟨Τ⟩ίνος γὰρ ἂν καὶ εἴη υἱός—οὐ συναλοιφομένων. Καὶ μεθ᾽ ἕτερα. αἱ δὲ ἰδιότητες, πατρὸς μέν—ἀϊδίου φωτός.// ἀκούεις γέννησιν . . .
fol. 200ᵛ desin.: . . . τί τὸ κινοῦν σε ἢ τί τὸ κινούμενον.
CPG 3010.20 Gregorius Naz., *Oratio* 20, ed. J. Mossay, *Discours 20–23*, 70 par. 6.21–par. 7.3; 72 par. 7.8–10; 78 par. 11.1–80 par. 11.6; *PG* 35, 1072c10–1073a3; 1073a9–12; 1077c1–7.

188 Τοῦ αὐτοῦ πρὸς Κληδόνιον κατὰ Ἀπολιναρίου·
Inc.: Ὅτι ἡμεῖς τῆς κατὰ Νίκαιαν πίστεως τῆς τῶν . . .
desin.: . . . καὶ τῆς καθολικῆς ἐκκλησίας.
CPG 3032 Gregorius Naz., *Epistula CII*, ed. P. Gallay, *Grégoire de Nazianze, Lettres théologiques*, *SC* 208 (Paris, 1974), 70–72; *PG* 37, 193c2–196a4.

189 Τοῦ αὐτοῦ περὶ θεολογίας·
Inc.: Οὐ παντός, ὦ οὗτοι, τὸ περὶ Θεοῦ φιλοσοφεῖν . . .
desin.: . . . ἀλλ᾽ ἔστι καὶ οἷς καὶ ἐφ᾽ ὅσον.
CPG 3010.27 Gregorius Naz., *Oratio* 27, ed. P. Gallay, *Discours 27–31*, 76 par. 3.1–4; *PG* 36, 13c12–d1.

190 Not in *TLG*
Τοῦ αὐτοῦ·

> Καὶ ὁ ἐπικαλούμενος ὀρθῶς τὸν Θεόν, ἐπικαλεῖται δι᾽ υἱοῦ, καὶ ὁ προσερχόμενος οἰκείως, διὰ Χριστοῦ προέρχεται· προσελθεῖν δὲ ἀδύνατον τῷ υἱῷ χωρὶς πνεύματος· τὸ πνεῦμα γὰρ ἡ ζωὴ καὶ ἡ ἁγία μόρφωσις τῶν ὅλων. καὶ τοῦτο ἐκπέμπων ὁ Θεὸς καὶ πατὴρ δι᾽ υἱοῦ τὴν κτίσιν ὁμοιοῖ πρὸς ἑαυτόν. εἰς οὖν
> 5 Θεὸς ὁ πατήρ, εἷς Θεὸς ὁ λόγος, ἓν πνεῦμα ζῶν ἡ ἁγιωσύνη τῶν ὅλων καὶ οὔτε Θεὸς ἕτερος ὡς πατήρ, οὔτε υἱὸς ἕτερος ὡς λόγος Θεοῦ, οὔτε πνεῦμα ἕτερον ὡς ἁγιαστικὸν καὶ ζωοποιὸν (sic).

Locum non inveni.

191 Τοῦ αὐτοῦ ἁγίου Γρηγορίου τοῦ Θεολόγου πρὸς Ἥρωνα τὸν φιλόσοφον·
Inc.: Ὁρίζου δὲ καὶ τὴν ἡμετέραν εὐσέβειαν—πατρὸς ἴδιον περιέλωμεν. καὶ πάλιν· Οὐ γὰρ ἐκ μεταμελείας ἡ θεότης . . .
fol. 201 desin.: . . . καὶ γινώσκεσθαι ὑπ᾽ ἀλλήλων.
CPG 3010.25 Gregorius Naz., *Oratio* 25, ed. J. Mossay, *Discours 24–26*, 192 par. 15.18–194 par. 15.29; 196 par. 16.20–198 par. 16.31; *PG* 35, 1220b3–c3; 1221b5–c3.

Post ἀλλήλων P add.:

> Πῶς τινες λέγουσιν ὅτι ἔκπεμψίς ἐστιν ἡ ἐκπόρευσις εἰπόντος τοῦ πατρὸς πρὸς τὸν ἐρωτήσαντα· τίς οὖν ἡ ἐκπόρευσις . . . οἱ μηδὲ τὰ ἐν ποσὶν εἰδέναι δυνάμενοι.

τίς οὖν ἡ—δυνάμενοι = quotation **184**.

192 ⟨Ἡ⟩? τοῦ ἁγίου Σωφρονίου ἀρχιεπισκόπου Ἱεροσολύμων πρὸς Σέργιον ἀπολογία·
Inc.: Πιστεύω τοίνυν, ὦ θεοτίμητοι,—(fol. 201ᵛ) κἂν ἐν τρισὶ δείκνυται ταῖς ὑποστάσεσιν. Καὶ μεθ᾽ ἕτερα. ὥσπερ οὖν ἕνα Θεὸν φρονεῖν ἐδιδάχθημεν—ἡ θεότης

κηρύττομεν. Καὶ μεθ᾽ ἕτερα. ἀριθμεῖται γοῦν ἡ παναγία τριάς—(fol. 202) καὶ ἐν-
τελῶς ὑπάρχουσα.// ἔστιν οὖν μετὰ τὸ εἶναι Θεός—κατὰ φύσιν καταγγέλλεται.//
τριὰς οὖν ἡ τριάς, οὐ τελεία μόνον—ἡ αὐτὴ παναγία τριάς.

Post τριὰς P add:

μηδεὶς δὲ πολυπραγμονείτω πῶς ὁ πατὴρ ἐγέννησε τὸν υἱὸν ἢ πῶς τὸ πανάγιον
πνεῦμα ἐκπορεύεται· τοῦτο γὰρ οὐδὲ αὗται αἱ ἅγιαι δυνάμεις γινώσκουσιν· ὥστε
οὖν ὁ πολυπραγμονῶν ἐκπίπτει τοῦ Θεοῦ. καὶ ταῦτα μὲν περὶ τῆς ὑπερουσίου καὶ
ὁμοουσίου καὶ ζωοποιοῦ τριάδος.// ταῦτα φρονεῖν καὶ πιστεύειν σοφώτατοι ἔκ τε
ἀποστολικῆς . . .

fol. 203 desin.: . . . Νεστορίῳ τῷ δυσσεβεῖ χαριζόμενος.
CPG 7635 Sophronius Hierosolymitanus, *Epistula Synodica ad Sergium CPolit.*, ACO
Ser. II, II,1, 418.6–420.5; 422.8–13; 424.4–426.22; 428.2–428.8; 428.15–428.19; 466.11–
470.17.
Cf. R. Riedinger, "Die Nachkommen der *Epistula Synodica.* . . . "

193 Ὅρος τῶν ἁγίων πατέρων τῆς ἁγίας συνόδου τῆς ἐν Χαλκηδόνι· τὴν τριάδα γοῦν τὴν
ἄκτιστον ἐν μονάδι θεότητι προσκυνεῖσθαι ἀεὶ θεσπίζομεν.
Inc.: Ἑπόμενοι τοίνυν τοῖς ἁγίοις πατράσιν ἕνα καὶ τόν . . .
desin.: . . . καὶ τὸ τῶν πατέρων ἡμῖν παραδέδωκε σύμβολον.
CPG 9005 Concilium Oecumenicum Chalcedonense, *Gesta, Actio V.* ACO II,1,2,
129.23–130.3.

fol. 203ᵛ **194**
(a) Πρόσωπα δὲ καὶ χαρακτῆρας—καὶ ἀπερίγραπτα. (b) Χρὴ γινώσκειν ὅτι τρεῖς
ὑποστατικαί εἰσιν—οὐδὲ γεννητὸν τὸ πνεῦμα τὸ ἅγιον. (c) Καὶ ὁμοούσιον μὲν τὸ
τῆς αὐτῆς οὐσίας καὶ ἐνεργείας ἀπαράλλακτος (sic) ὑπάρχων. (d) ὁμοούσιον δὲ λέγεται ὅτι ὁμοίαν οὐσίαν καὶ δύναμιν κέκτηται (e) ἡμιούσιον δέ τινες εἰρήκασι τὴν
σάρκα τὴν νεκρὰν ζωὴν (sic) κεχωρισμένην.
CPG 7745 Anastasius Sinaita, *Viae Dux* (*Hodegos*), ed. K.-H. Uthemann, CCSG 8: (a)
II,3.57 ff, (b) II,3.73–77, (c) II,5.21 ff, (d) II,5.24 ff, (e) II,5.34 ff. See also quotations **47,
111, 239.**

195 Τοῦ ἁγίου Γρηγορίου Νύσης·
Διατί μίαν θεότητα ἐπὶ πατρὸς καὶ υἱοῦ καὶ ἁγίου πνεύματος ὁμολογοῦντες, τρεῖς
Θεοὺς λέγειν ἀπαγορεύομεν; Ὅτι Θεὸς μὲν ὁ πατὴρ Θεὸς δὲ ὁ υἱὸς Θεὸς δὲ καὶ τὸ
πνεῦμα τὸ ἅγιον, εἷς δὲ ἐν τῷ αὐτῷ κηρύγματι ὁ Θεὸς διὰ τὸ μήτε φύσεως μήτε
ἐνεργείας θεωρεῖσθαι τὴν διαφορὰν τῇ θεότητι.

1 Διατί—2 Ὅτι, Θεὸς²—3 ἅγιον: typis expressa non inveni.

CPG 3139 Gregorius Nyss., *Ad Ablabium, quod non sint tres dei*, ed. F. Müller, *Gregorii
Nysseni opera dogmatica*, III,1 *Gregorii Nysseni opera dogmatica minora* (Leiden, 1958),
55.7–10; *PG* 45, 133A1–4. See quotation **201.**

196 Τοῦ αὐτοῦ·
Inc.: Αὐτὸ μὲν γὰρ τὸ θεῖον, ὅ, τί ποτε—τῷ κάτω βίῳ
Post βίῳ P add.:

ἄχραντον υἱὸν αὐτοῦ· καί, καθά φησιν ὁ ἀπόστολος, ἐξαπέστειλεν ὁ Θεὸς τὸν υἱὸν
αὐτοῦ γεννώμενον ἐκ γυναικός, γενόμενον ὑπὸ νόμον. quod non invenitur in textu

typis expresso. καὶ αὖθις· καὶ ἔσωσέ με διὰ τοῦ—περιήγαγε τάξιν. καὶ πάλιν·
ἐξαπέστειλεν γὰρ ὁ Θεὸς τὸ ἔλεος . . .

desin.: . . . τὴν ψυχήν μου ἐκ μέσου σκύμνων.

CPG 3155 Gregorius Nyss, In inscriptiones psalmorum, ed. J. McDonough, Gregorii Nysseni opera V, In inscriptiones Psalmorum, In sextum Psalmum, In Ecclesiasten (Leiden,
1962), 155.25–156.8; 156.8–11; 156.11–13; PG 44, 585C12–588A2.

197 Τοῦ ἁγίου Ἀμφιλοχίου ἐπισκόπου Ἰκονίου πρὸς Σέλευκον τὸν ἔγγονον Τραϊανοῦ
τοῦ στρατηλάτου·
Inc.: Πιστεύω εἰς ἕνα Θεὸν ἐν τρισὶ γνωριζόμενον . . .
fol. 204 desin.: . . . κατὰ τὴν ἐμὴν δύναμιν εἰρήσθω.
CPG 3245.15 Amphilochius Icon., Fragmenta, frag. xv (Epistula ad Seleucum), ed. C.
Datema, Amphilochii Opera, 263, 1; PG 39, 112B–D.

198   Ἑρμηνεία εἰς τό· ἐκ τοῦ ἐμοῦ λήψεται καὶ ἀναγγελεῖ ὑμῖν.
Πάλιν ἐν εἴδει φαίνεται πυροφλόγῳ·
ἴσως τὸ πῦρ ἐκεῖνο τῷ κόσμῳ φέρων (sic),
ὅπερ βαλεῖν ἔφησας ἐλθὼν ἐς χθόνα·
5   καὶ τοῦτο γὰρ προεῖπας ὡς ἐκ σοῦ λάβοι
καὶ τοῖς μαθηταῖς ἐκφράσοι σαφεστάτως
τῶν σῶν ἁπασῶν ἐντολῶν τὰς ἐκδόσεις.
ἡ τοῦ παρακλήτου τε καὶ ζωαρχίου
χάρις, τὸ πνεῦμα τῆς ἀληθείας, ὅπερ
10   καὶ τοῦ πατρὸς τὴν ἐκπόρευσιν ἀχρόνως
φέρειν ἔφησας αὐτὸ ἀψευδεστάτως.
σοῦ πνεῦμα θεῖον τὴν πανάχραντον χάριν
αἰτῶ πόρευμα πατρὸς εὐλογημένον,
ἄκτιστον, εὐκτὸν καὶ συνάναρχον πάλιν
15   υἱῷ τε καὶ Θεῷ πατρὶ τοῖς αἰωνίοις.

CPG 3245.13 Amphilochius Icon., Fragmenta, frag. xiii (In illud: De meo accipiet et annuntiabit vobis), PG 39, 109B–C; De genuinitate neganda vide C. Datema, Amphilochii
Opera, XXVI–XXVII.

199 Τοῦ ἁγίου Μεθοδίου ἐκ τῶν συμποσίων τῶν περὶ παρθενίας· περὶ μετανοίας.
Inc.: Κύριε δοξάζω σε, ὑμνῶ τὸ ὄνομά σου . . .
fol. 205 desin.: . . . ὑπνῶσαι πρὸς θάνατον, ὅτι σοὶ ἡ δόξα . . . ἀμήν.
Locum non inveni in opere citato.

200 Τοῦ ἁγίου Γρηγορίου τοῦ Θεολόγου· εὐχὴ ἐπὶ κοίτ⟨ης?⟩
Inc.: Σὲ καὶ νῦν εὐλογοῦμεν Χριστέ μου λόγε Θεοῦ . . .
fol. 205ᵛ desin.: . . . σοὶ Θεὲ προσλαλείτω τῷ πατρὶ καί . . . ἀμήν.
CPG 3034 Gregorius Naz., Carmina dogmatica (carmen 32, Hymnus Vespertinus), PG
37, 511A12–514A3.

201 Ἐκ τοῦ λόγου τοῦ πρὸς Ἀβλάβιον τοῦ ἁγίου Γρηγορίου Νύσης, διατί μίαν θεότητα
ἐπὶ πατρὸς καὶ υἱοῦ καὶ ἁγίου πνεύματος ὁμολογοῦντες τρεῖς Θεοὺς λέγειν παραι-
τούμεθα.
Inc.: Ὅταν τὸ ἀπαράλλακτον ὁμολογοῦντες τῆς φύσεως . . .
fol. 206 desin.: . . . ὀνομάτων μοναδικῶς ἐξαγγέλλεται.

CPG 3139 Gregorius Nyss., *Ad Ablabium, quod non sint tres dei*, ed. F. Müller, *Gregorii Nysseni opera dogmatica*, III,1 *Gregorii Nysseni opera dogmatica minora* (Leiden, 1958), 55.24–57.13; *PG* 45, 133β7–136α6. See quotation **195**.

202 Τοῦ Θεολόγου Γρηγορίου ἐκ τῶν ἐπῶν α΄ λόγου· (I, 1,2)
   (a) Υἱὲ Θεοῦ σοφίης βασιλεῦ λόγε ἀτρεκίη τε
   (b) εἰκὼν ἀρχετύποιο φύσις γεννήτορος ἴση
   (c) καὶ πνεῦμα ὅπερ ἐκ τοῦ πατρὸς πορεύεται
     τοῦ νοῦ φῶς τοῦ ἀνθρωπίνου.

   (a) Locum non inveni.
   (b) *CPG* 3036 Gregorius Naz., *Carmina de se ipso*, *PG* 37, 1017α8.
   (c) Locum non inveni.
   (d) Post ἀνθρωπίνου P add.:

> Ἰστέον ὅτι ὥσπερ Θεὸς ὁ πατήρ, Θεὸς ὁ υἱός, Θεὸς καὶ τὸ πνεῦμα τὸ ἅγιον, εἰς δὲ Θεὸς διὰ τὸ ἰσοδύναμον καὶ ἰσόθεον, οὕτως καὶ ἀρχὴ ὁ πατὴρ καὶ ἡ ἐκ τῆς ἀρχῆς ἀρχὴ καὶ ἐκ τοῦ φωτὸς φῶς, καθώς φησιν ὁ πολὺς ἐν θεολογίᾳ Γρηγόριος· ὁ υἱὸς καὶ σοφία καὶ λόγος καὶ δύναμις τοῦ Θεοῦ, ὥς φησιν ὁ προφήτης
> 5 Δαυίδ· ἐν τῷ φωτί σου Κύριε ὀψόμεθα φῶς· ὡσαύτως καὶ τὸ πανάγιον πνεῦμα· ἀλλ᾽ οὖν μία ἀρχὴ ἄναρχος ἐν ὑποστάσεσι τρισὶν ὁμοουσίοις κηρυττομένη· μοναρχίαν γάρ, φησί, σέβομεν, οὐχ ἣν ἓν περιγράφει πρόσωπον, ἀλλ᾽ ἣν φύσεως ὁμοτιμία συνίστησιν ἐν τρισὶν ὑποστάσεσι καὶ ἰδιώμασιν ἀδιαιρέτως προσκυνουμένη, εἰς Θεὸς ἐν ἀσυγχύτοις γνωριζόμενος, ᾧ ἡ δόξα καὶ τὸ κράτος εἰς
> 10 τοὺς αἰῶνας τῶν αἰώνων, ἀμήν.

  (d-I) 2 ἡ ἐκ τῆς—3 φῶς = *CPG* 3010.38, *Oratio 38*, ed. C. Moreschini, *Discours 38–41*, 132 par. 13.15–16; *PG* 36, 325β5.
  (d-II) 3 καθώς φησιν—6 κηρυττομένη, locum non inveni.
 (d-III) 7 μοναρχίαν—8 συνίστησιν = *CPG* 3010.29, *Oratio 29*, ed. P. Gallay, *Discours 27–31* (*Discours théologiques*), 178, par. 2.7–9, quod superest non inveni.

203 Εὐχὴ τοῦ ἁγίου Ἰωάννου τοῦ Χρυσοστόμου·
Inc.: Ὁ ἀγαθὸς καὶ φιλάνθρωπος Θεὸς ἐλέησον ἡμᾶς . . .
fol. 207 desin.: . . . ὁ σταυρωθεὶς ἐν σαρκὶ δι᾽ ἡμᾶς, ἐλέησον ἡμᾶς.
CPG 4741 Iohannes Chrys., *Deprecatio*, ed. M. Richard, "Témoins grecs des fragments XIII et XV de Méliton de Sardes," *Le Muséon* 85 (1972), 318–21.

204 Τοῦ ἁγίου Κλήμεντος ἐπισκόπου Ῥώμης μετὰ τὸν ἀπόστολον Πέτρον τοῦ ἀποστολικοῦ θρόνου ἡγησαμένου· εἰς τὸ ἅγιον πνεῦμα.
Inc.: Μακάριος ὁ κεκλεισμένους ὀφθαλμοὺς ἀνοίξας . . .
desin.: . . . τυποῦνται ἀληθείας τύπῳ χάριτος τελείας.
Clemens Romanus, *Fragmentum de Spiritu sancto* (not in *CPG*), *PG* 1, 460α1–β5.

205 Τοῦ ἁγίου Βασιλείου διάλεκτος πρὸς Ἀνόμοιον·
Inc.: Πεῦσις Ἀνομοίου· οὐκ ἔστιν οὖν διαφορὰ πατρὸς καί—(fol. 207ᵛ) ἐκπεπόρευται ἐκ πατρός.// Ἀνόμοιος· αὕτη ἐστὶν ἡ διαφορά; Ὀρθόδοξος· αὕτη. Καὶ μεθ᾽ ἕτερα· Ἀνόμοιος· δύο οὖν ἀγέννητα λέγεις . . .
desin.: . . . παρ᾽ οὗ καὶ ἐκπορεύεται.
CPG 2284 Athanasius Alex., *De s. trinitate dialogi v*, *PG* 28, 1120D1–10; 1121α8; 1145β10–C6.

206 Τοῦ ἁγίου Ἰωάννου τοῦ Χρυσοστόμου ἑρμηνεία τοῦ ἁγίου εὐαγγελίου· περὶ τοῦ ἁγίου συμβόλου.

Inc.: Οὐ λέγω ἦν ποτε ὅτε οὐκ ἦν ὁ πατήρ . . .

desin.: . . . αὐτῷ θαρρῶ τὴν ἐκ τῶν νεκρῶν ἐξανάστασιν.

CPG 4752 Iohannes Chrys., *Symbolum, PG* 39, 320 adn. 25 (320c6–D17); *CPG* 4587 Idem, *In illud: Simile est regnum caelorum patri familias, PG* 59, 584.17–49.

207 Τοῦ ἁγίου Ἐφραίμ.

Καὶ ἵνα μὴ εἴπωμεν ὑπ' ἀνάγκης γεγενεῖσθαι (sic) τὴν φυσικὴν γέννησιν τοῦ
υἱοῦ τοῦ Θεοῦ, τὸ ἅγιον πνεῦμα μὴ γεννηθὲν προῆλθεν ἐκ τῆς οὐσίας τοῦ πατρός, οὐχ ἡμιτελές, οὔτε ἐπιμιγές· οὐδὲ γὰρ πατὴρ μέν ἐστι, ποτὲ δὲ υἱός, ἀλλὰ
πνεῦμα ἅγιον τὸ πλήρωμα ἔχον τῆς ἀγαθότητος. ὅτι οὐ πάθει, οὐ χρόνῳ, οὐκ
5 ἀνάγκῃ, οὐ τρόπῳ, οὐκ αἰτίᾳ τινὶ πατὴρ τὸν υἱὸν ἐγέννησεν, ἀλλὰ φύσει ἀνάγ-
κη⟨ς⟩ ἐλευθέρα, ἣν συνιστᾷ διὰ τῆς ὑποστάσεως αὐτοῦ τὸ πνεῦμα τὸ ἅγιον ἐκ
τοῦ πατρὸς ἐκπορευόμενον καὶ δι' υἱοῦ διδόμενον. ὅτι θελήσας ὁ πατὴρ καὶ
ἄλλον κοινωνὸν προβάλλει, οὐχ οἷον ἔτεκεν, ἀλλὰ πνεῦμα ἅγιον ἐκ τῆς οὐσίας
αὐτοῦ συνέστησεν. οὐ πρὸ τοῦ υἱοῦ τὸ πνεῦμα προήγαγεν, ἵνα μὴ ἴδωμεν ὑπ'
10 ἀνάγκην τὸ θέλημα, ὅτι πῶς ἀπαθὴς ὢν ἐγέννησεν ἔχων ἀπόδειξιν τὸ πνεῦμα
τὸ ἅγιον· ὅτι μὴ γεννήσας κατ' αὐτὸν προήγαγεν, οὕτω καὶ γεννήˊσας, ἀπαθὴς
διέμεινεν.

Locum non inveni.

208
Sigla:
P: Parisinus graecus 1115, fols. 207ᵛ–208
V: Venetus Marcianus gr. 573, fol. 58ᵛ
Τοῦ αὐτοῦ·

Ἐρώτησις περὶ (om. P) πίστεως (om. P). Πῶς ἐστιν ἡ τριάς; Ἀπόκρισις· Ἡ
τριὰς ὁμοούσιος, τρισυπόστατος (τρεῖς ὑποστάσεις: V), μία δύναμις καὶ θεότης
πάντοτε ὁ πατήρ, πάντοτε ὁ υἱός, πάντοτε τὸ ἅγιον πνεῦμα (τὸ πν. τὸ ἅγ.: V).
εἰς Θεός ἐστιν ἐν τρισὶν ὑποστάσεσιν, ὡς θέλει καὶ ὡς βούλεται πανταχοῦ ὢν
5 ἓν νεῦμα, (P. fol. 208) ἓν θέλημα, μία βασιλεία ταῖς τρισὶν ὑποστάσεσιν, πατρὶ
καὶ (om. P) υἱῷ καὶ ἁγίῳ πνεύματι εἰς τοὺς αἰῶνας, ἀμήν.

Locum non inveni.

209 Τοῦ ἁγίου Βασιλείου κατὰ Εὐνομίου· (2 extracts).

Inc.: Καὶ ὁ μὲν Κύριος περὶ τοῦ παρακλήτου—εἰπεῖν περὶ τοῦ πνεύματος καὶ ταῦτα μὲν
οὕτως. Καὶ μεθ' ἕτερα. Καὶ νῦν μὲν πῶς οὐ φανερὸν ἔχει . . .

desin.: . . . παρὰ τοῦ πατρὸς καὶ (sic !!!) υἱοῦ ἐκπορεύεται.

CPG 2837 Basilius Caes., *Adversus Eunomium II, PG* 29, 649c3–652a6; 652b7–c1.

210 Τοῦ ἁγίου Καισαρείου πεῦσις προσαχθεῖσα ὑπὸ Κωνσταντίνου καὶ τῶν λοιπῶν·
(= Πεύσεις Β, Γ).

Inc.: Ἐπειδή τινας ἀλόγους καὶ βλασφήμους φωνὰς παρ' ἐνίων . . .

fol. 209 desin.: . . . φῶς, πῦρ, πνεῦμα αὐτῷ ἡ δόξα . . . ἀμήν.

CPG 7482 Ps.-Caesarius, *Quaestiones et responsiones, PG* 38, 857.14–864.4.

211 Τοῦ ἁγίου Γρηγορίου Νύσης ἐκ τοῦ κατηχητικοῦ λόγου (3 fragments).

Inc.: Πῶς τὸ αὐτὸ καὶ ἀριθμητόν ἐστι—εἰς θεότητας διαφόρους κατατεμνόμενον. Καὶ μεθ᾽ ἕτερα. Τῷ λόγῳ τοῦ Κυρίου—(fol. 209ᵛ) τοὺς ἀντιλέγοντας προσαρξόμεθα. Καὶ μεθ᾽ ἕτερα. Ἐπεὶ οὖν ἀγαθόν τι ὁ κόσμος ὁμολογεῖται . . .
fol. 210 desin.: . . . τὸν ἐξ ἐκείνου ὑφεστῶτα λόγον.
CPG 3150 Gregorius Nyss., Oratio catechetica magna, ed. J. H. Srawley, The Catechetical Oration of Gregory of Nyssa (Cambridge, 1903), 15.14–16.8; 18.8–20.6; 11.5–13.4; PG 45, 17D2–10, 20B6–D9, 16B5–D8.

Post λόγον P add.:

αὖθίς τε καὶ τὸ ἐξ αὐτοῦ ἐκπορευόμενον πνεῦμα ἅγιον καὶ δι᾽ υἱοῦ ἀποστελλόμενον.

212 Not in TLG
Τοῦ Ἰωάννου τοῦ Χρυσοστόμου ἐκ τοῦ λόγου τοῦ εἰς τὰ φῶτα· Οὗτός ἐστιν ὁ υἱός μου ὁ ἀγαπητὸς ὁ σὺν ἐμοὶ πέμψας ἐφ᾽ ἑαυτὸν τὸ πνεῦμα τὸ ἅγιον.
Locum non inveni. Also quotation **140**.

213 Not in TLG
Τοῦ αὐτοῦ εἰς τὸν ἐνενηκοστὸν ὄγδοον (?) ψαλμόν.
⟨Ὁ⟩ Κύριος ἐβασίλευσεν εὐπρέπειαν ἐνεδύσατο καὶ τὴν ἑαυτοῦ περιεβάλλετο δύναμιν· δύναμις δὲ καὶ εὐπρέπεια τοῦ υἱοῦ ὁ πατήρ, ὁ καὶ τὸ ἁγίασμα τοῦ πνεύματος τοῦ ἐκπορευομένου παρ᾽ αὐτοῦ τῷ ἰδίῳ οἴκῳ τῆς ἐκκλησίας ἐμπρέψαι παρασκευάσας.
Locum non inveni. 1 Ὁ—ἐνεδύσατο de psalmo xcii desumptum est.

214 Τοῦ ἁγίου Μαξίμου ἐκ τοῦ δευτέρου βιβλίου. Ἐρώτησις περὶ τῶν ζ᾽ ἐπαρυστρίδων·
Inc.: Καὶ ἐπαναπαύσεται ἐπ᾽ αὐτόν, φησί, πνεῦμα Θεοῦ . . .
desin.: . . . διὰ τοῦ υἱοῦ γεννηθέντος, ἀφράστως ἐκπορευόμενον.
CPG 7688 Maximus Confessor, Quaestiones ad Thalassium, PG 90, 672B8–C14.

215 Τοῦ ἁγίου Βασιλείου ὅτι τὸ ἀγέννητον καὶ γεννητὸν καὶ ἐκπορευτὸν ὑπάρξεώς τινός ἐστι δήλωσις καὶ οὐκ οὐσίας.
Inc.: Ἐρώτησις· ποίας κατηγορίας κατὰ φιλοσόφους . . .
fol. 210ᵛ desin.: . . . καὶ γεννητὸς καὶ οὐκ οὐσίας.
CPG 2837 Basilius Caes., Adversus Eunomium IV (= CPG 2571 Didymus Alex., De dogmatibus et contra Arianos), PG 29, 680D1–681A14.

216 Τοῦ αὐτοῦ.
Inc.: Ἐνῶ (sic) δὲ εἶπεν ὁ Κύριος ὅτι ἐγὼ ἐρωτήσω τὸν πατέρα . . .
desin.: . . . εἰς ἀπόδειξιν τοῦ ἁγίου πνεύματος συντελεῖ.
CPG 2837 Basilius Caes., Adversus Eunomium III, PG 29, 661B7–12.

217 Τοῦ αὐτοῦ.
Inc.: Ἐξαποστελεῖς τὸ πνεῦμά σου καὶ κτισθήσονται . . .
desin.: . . . τὸ συνέχον τὰ πάντα γνῶσιν ἔχει φωνῆς.
CPG 2837 Basilius Caes., Adversus Eunomium IV (= CPG 2571), PG 29, 713C12–716A4.

218 Τοῦ αὐτοῦ ὅτι δημιουργὸν τὸ πνεῦμα. (3 extracts).
Inc.: (a) Οἱ οὐρανοὶ διηγοῦνται—δύναμις ἁγιαστικὴ ἐνούσιος ἐνύπαρκτος. Καὶ μεθ᾽ ἕτερα. (b) Καὶ τὰ μὲν ὀνόματα τοιαῦτα—ἀρετὴν τελειώσεως λέγων. (c) ὑπ᾽ αὐτοῦ οὖν τοῦ Κυρίου . . .
desin.: . . . ἐκεῖνος ὑμᾶς διδάξει πάντα.

CPG 2837 Basilius Caes., *Adversus Eunomium:* (a) *Adv. Eunom. IV, PG* 29, 713B1-13, (b) *Adv. Eunom. III, PG* 29, 661B13–C8, (c) ibid., 664A8-11.

219 Τοῦ αὐτοῦ.

Inc.: Ἐγὼ δὲ εἰ μὲν πάντα διωριζόμην καταληπτά . . .

fol. 211 desin.: . . . καὶ ἕνα υἱὸν καὶ ἓν πνεῦμα ἅγιον.

CPG 2837 Basilius Caes., *Adversus Eunomium III, PG* 29, 668A4–D1.

Post ἅγιον P add.:

τὸ ἐκ τοῦ πατρὸς ἐκπορευόμενον καὶ ἐν υἱῷ ἀναπαυόμενον

220 Τοῦ αὐτοῦ.

Inc.: Ὅτι εὐσεβοῦς διανοίας ἐστὶ τὰ ἀποσιωπηθέντα . . .

desin.: . . . τῆς πρὸς πρόσωπον θεωρίας ἀξιωθῶμεν.

CPG 2837 Basilius Caes., *Adversus Eunomium III, PG* 29, 669C8-14.

221 Τοῦ αὐτοῦ.

Inc.: Ὅτι τὸ ἀγέννητον καὶ γεννητὸν καὶ ἐκπορευτὸν ὀνόματα οὐκ οὐσία—τί ὄνομα αὐτῷ φησὶν ἐγὼ εἰμι ὁ ὤν. Καὶ μεθ᾽ ἕτερα. ἄνθρωπόν τις εἰπὼν ἢ ξύλον ἢ λίθον, οὐσίαν— τὸ ἐκπορευτὸν δηλονότι.// Εἰ ὁ Θεὸς ἀγέννητος οὐσίᾳ . . .

fol. 211ᵛ desin.: . . . πρὸς ἐνέργειαν ὠφελιμώτερα.

CPG 2837 Basilius Caes., *Adversus Eunomium IV, PG* 29, 681C10–684A6, 684C5–9, 685A2–8.

Σχόλιον. Χρὴ γινώσκειν ὅτι τὸ ἀγέννητον καὶ τὸ γεννητὸν καὶ τὸ ἐκπορευτὸν οὐκ οὐσίας λέγομεν, ὀνόματα δὲ δηλοῦντα τὴν ἑκάστου αὐτῶν ὕπαρξιν.

222 Εἰς τὸ ὅτι εὐθὴς (sic) ὁ λόγος τοῦ Κυρίου καὶ πάντα τὰ ἔργα αὐτοῦ ἐν πίστει. (5 fragments).

(a) Εἰ τὰ ἔργα τοῦ Θεοῦ ἐν πίστει—ἐκ πατρὸς γέννησις. (P add.: καὶ τοῦ πνεύματος ἐκπόρευσις). Καὶ μεθ᾽ ἕτερα.

(b) Γεννᾷ Θεὸς οὐχ ὡς ἄνθρωπος—τὸ πνεῦμα καὶ οὐχ ἑτέρωθεν.

(c) Ὅτι οὐκ ἀπὸ ὁμωνυμίας ταυτότητος ἀλλὰ φύσεως θείας ἑνότης γνωρίζεται.

(d) Ὅτι δὲ ψυχῆς νόσημά ἐστι τὸ κακῶς καὶ περιέργως ζητεῖν ἐπὶ Θεοῦ καὶ μάλιστα μὲν μετὰ ἀπιστίας πᾶσι φανερῶν (sic).

(e) Τί δὲ ἐναντιοῦσαι τῇ καλῇ—ἀναλλοίωτος ἡ αὐτὴ τριὰς ἀεί.

CPG 2837 Basilius Caes.: (a) *Adversus Eunomium IV, PG* 29, 692D1-4, (b) idem, *Adversus Eunomium V, PG* 29, 736B2-8, (c) idem, *Adversus Eunomium V, PG* 29, 748C1-2, (d) idem, *Adversus Eunomium V, PG* 29, 752B6-8, (e) idem, *Adversus Eunomium V, PG* 29, 753A11–B3.

223 Ἐκ τοῦ λόγου ὅτι ὡς υἱὸς πρὸς πατέρα οὕτω πνεῦμα πρὸς υἱόν.

Inc.: Διὰ δὴ τοῦτο τὸ μὲν ἐκ Θεοῦ εἶναι τὸ πνεῦμα . . .

desin.: . . . ἐν δακτύλῳ Θεοῦ ἐκβάλλω τὰ δαιμόνια.

CPG 2837 Basilius Caes., *Adversus Eunomium V, PG* 29, 732A4-15; 733A11–B13.

224 Ἐκ τοῦ λόγου ὅτι καὶ ἄνευ τοῦ καλεῖσθαι υἱὸν τὸ πνεῦμα δῆλόν ἐστιν (fol. 212) ἐκ Θεοῦ ὑπάρχον· πῶς τὰ ἀνθρώπινα παραδείγματα προσαρμοστέον θεότητι καὶ οὐ καθαιρετέον.

Inc.: Οὐδὲ παρ' ἔλαττόν τι ἐξὸν (sic) μέλλομεν . . .
desin.: . . . ἐξ αὐτοῦ δὲ τὸ πνεῦμα καὶ οὐχ ἑτέρωθεν.
CPG 2837 Basilius Caes., Adversus Eunomium V, PG 29, 733c7–736b8.

225 Τοῦ ἐν ἁγίοις πατρὸς ἡμῶν Βασιλείου περὶ τοῦ παναγίου πνεύματος.
Inc.: Ἐνθυμηθῶμεν πᾶσα ψυχὴ ζητοῦσα περὶ τῶν θειοτέρων . . .
fol. 213 desin.: . . . κολλώμενος τῷ Κυρίῳ ἓν πνεῦμά ἐστιν, ᾧ ἡ δόξα . . . ἀμήν.
CPG 2837 Basilius Caes., Adversus Eunomium V, PG 29, 768b12–773b14.

226 Ὅτι ἀχώριστόν ἐστιν ἐπὶ πάσης ἐννοίας πατρὸς καὶ υἱοῦ τὸ ἅγιον πνεῦμα ἐπί τε τῆς τῶν ὄντων (sic) δημιουργίας καὶ ἐπὶ τῆς τῶν ἀνθρώπων οἰκονομίας καὶ ἐπὶ τῆς προσδοκουμένης (sic) κρίσεως. Καὶ μετὰ βραχέα.
Inc.: Τῷ λόγῳ Κυρίου οἱ οὐρανοὶ ἐστερεώθησαν καὶ τῷ . . .
fol. 213ᵛ desin.: . . . ἁγιασμὸς δὲ οὐκ ἄνευ πνεύματος.
CPG 2839 Basilius Caes., De Spiritu Sancto, ed. B. Pruche, Saint-Esprit, 374, 378 par. 38.29–380 par. 38.42; PG 32, 133a4–7; 136c3–d2.

227 Κεφαλαιώδης ἐπιδρομὴ τῆς πίστεως πῶς ἐν τῇ ὁμολογίᾳ τῶν τριῶν ὑποστάσεων τὸ εὐσεβὲς τῆς μοναρχίας δόγμα διατηροῦμεν, ἐν ᾧ καὶ οἱ (sic) κατ' αὐτῶν τὴν ὑπαρίθμησιν φασκόντων ἔλεγχος. In margine: κεφάλαιον ιη´.
Inc.: Πατέρα καὶ υἱὸν καὶ ἅγιον πνεῦμα παραδιδοὺς ὁ Κύριος—τῶν ὑποκειμένων ἐπινενόηται. Καὶ μεθ' ἕτερα. Καὶ οὐκ ἐντεῦθεν μόνον τῆς κατὰ τὴν φύσιν . . .
desin.: . . . τὴν τοῦ ὅθεν ἐκ πατρὸς προῆλθε.
CPG 2839 Basilius Caes., De Spiritu Sancto, ed. B. Pruche, Saint-Esprit, 402 par. 44.1–7; 408 par. 46.1–410 par. 46.20; PG 32, 148c9–d6, 152b1–c6.

Post προῆλθε P add.:
    καὶ δι' υἱοῦ πᾶσιν ἐκλάμπει τὴν τῆς θεότητος δύναμιν, ἐκ Θεοῦ καὶ πατρὸς τὴν ὑπόστασιν ἔχον, ξένῳ τρόπῳ ὑπάρξεως. quod non inveni.

228 i–xiii Ἐπανάληψις περὶ τῶν αὐτῶν.
(i) Τοῦ ἁγίου Βασιλείου ἐκ τοῦ πρὸς Σαβέλλιον λόγου τρίτου, ὅτι τὸ πνεῦμα τὸ ἅγιον οὐ κτῆμα Θεοῦ οὐδὲ κτίσμα καὶ ἐν τῷ τέλει τοῦ λόγου·
Inc.: Χριστὸς καὶ Κύριος ὀνομάζεται λέγοντος τοῦ—ἀλλ' εἰκὼν ὡς προείρηται. (P add.: καὶ χρῖσμα ἤδη καὶ δύναμις)// καὶ ἐν αὐτῷ τῷ κυρίῳ—πνεύματι ἁγίῳ καὶ δυνάμει (P add.: πεφηνώς).// πνεῦμα τῷ ζῶντι λόγῳ . . .
desin.: . . . νῦν ἀνακαίνωσιν καὶ τὴν συνδρομὴν (P add.: ἐμφύσημα).
CPG 2837 Basilius Caes., Adversus Eunomium V, PG 29, 725a15–b9; 725c1–2; 728d2–729a6.

(ii) Περὶ ἐμφυσήματος.
Inc.: ⟨Ἐξ⟩ετύπωσεν οὖν ἐμφυσήσας—ἡ τριὰς οὐκ ἐπιδέχεται// ὅτι οὔτε χωρὶς υἱοῦ . . .
desin.: . . . οὔτε υἱὸς χωρὶς πνεύματος.
Ibid., 729a6–15; 732a2–3.

(iii) Ἐκ τοῦ αὐτοῦ λόγου· ὅτι ὡς υἱὸς πρὸς πατέρα ἔχει, οὕτω πνεῦμα πρὸς υἱόν.
Inc.: Διὰ τοῦτο καὶ Θεοῦ μὲν λόγος ὁ υἱὸς ῥῆμα λέγεται . . .
desin.: . . . ῥῆμα υἱοῦ, διὰ τοῦ Θεοῦ.
Ibid., 732a4–9.

(iv) In margine: Μάχαιρα.

Inc.: Τὴν μάχαιράν φησι τοῦ πνεύματος, ὅ ἐστι . . .

desin.: . . . διὰ λόγου πάντα περιεργάζεται.

Ibid., 732A9–15.

(v) Τοῦ αὐτοῦ πρὸς τοὺς λέγοντας διατί μὴ καὶ τὸ πνεῦμα υἱὸς τοῦ υἱοῦ.

Inc.: Ὅτι οὐ διὰ τὸ μὴ εἶναι—ἢ κτίσμα κελεύεις νοεῖν. Καὶ μετ᾽ ὀλίγα. Ἐπεὶ οὖν ἄξιόν σοι φαίνεται—πῶς τὸ πνεῦμα θεότητος ἀλλότριον// διὰ δὴ τοῦτο, τὸ μὲν ἐκ Θεοῦ εἶναι . . .

desin.: . . . ἐλάβομεν καὶ τὸ διὰ υἱοῦ.

Ibid., 732B1–9; B13–C4; 733A11–14.

(vi) Περὶ υἱοῦ.

Inc.: Ὅτι ὁ νοῦς (sic) πεφηνέναι σαφὲς πεποίηκεν . . .

fol. 214ᵛ desin.: . . . υἱὸν δὲ τοῦ υἱοῦ προσαγορεῦσαι ἐφυλάξατο.

Ibid., 733A14–B3.

(vii) Τοῦ αὐτοῦ.

Inc.: Ὅτι καὶ ἄνευ τοῦ καλεῖσθαι υἱὸν τὸ πνεῦμα δηλονότι ἐκ Θεοῦ ὑπάρχει. Καὶ μεθ᾽ ἕτερα. Σὺ δὲ τοῖς ἀπίστοις ὁμοίως . . .

desin.: . . . ἐκφαίνει δὲ λόγον ἀληθῶς ἐξ αὐτοῦ.

Ibid., 736A5–B5.

(viii) Περὶ ἐκπέμψεως.

Inc.: Ἐκπέμπει πνεῦμα διὰ στόματος—ἀνθρωπικῶς ἢ σωματικῶς. Καὶ μεθ᾽ ἕτερα. υἱὸς Θεοῦ . . .

desin.: . . . πνεύματος ἁγίου χορηγὸς (P add. rubricis litt.: περὶ χορηγήσεως) εἰς ὑπό-στασιν καὶ μόρφωσιν κτήσεως (sic).

Ibid., 736B5–7; 736D1–3.

(ix) Περὶ ἐκπομπῆς.

Inc.: Ἐκπομπῇ γὰρ καὶ μεταδόσει πνεύματος τὰ γινόμενα γίνεται. Καὶ μεθ᾽ ἕτερα. Διόπερ καὶ ἑνὸς ὄντως (sic) τοῦ Θεοῦ—τὸ πνεῦμα ὑπ᾽ αὐτοῦ προσηγόρευται. Καὶ μεθ᾽ ἕτερα. Οὐκ ἂν δὲ Θεοῦ τὸ πνεῦμα μὴ ἔχων αὐτό—ἐν πατρὶ καὶ υἱῷ τὸ ἀχώριστον. Καὶ μεθ᾽ ἕτερα. Εἰ δὲ καὶ μὴ ὀνομάζων πνεῦμα . . .

fol. 215 desin.: . . . τό τε πατρὸς καὶ υἱοῦ καὶ ἁγίου πνεύματος.

Ibid., 737A1–2; 744C7–15; 745A13–B4; 745B12–748A10.

(x) Ὅτι οὐκ ἀπὸ ὁμωνυμίας ταυτότητος, ἀλλὰ φύσεως θείας ἑνότης γνωρίζεται = ibid., 748C1–2. In margine: Καὶ μετὰ γ᾽ φύλλα.

Inc.: Τί δὲ ἐναντιοῦτε (sic) τῇ καλῇ ταύτῃ πίστει . . .

desin.: . . . καὶ ῥῆμα καὶ πνεῦμα στόματος.

Ibid., 753A11–C1.

(xi) Καὶ μεθ᾽ ἕτερα δ᾽ φύλλα.

Inc.: Σειρὰ (σπεῖρα leg.) γάρ ἐστιν ἡ ἁγία τριὰς καὶ σεβάσμιος . . .

desin.: . . . εἴη μετὰ πάντων ὑμῶν.

Ibid., 760D4–761A10.

(xii) Καὶ ἀλλαχῇ περὶ τοῦ πνεύματος ὁ αὐτὸς ἐν τῷ τέλει τοῦ λόγου.

Inc.: Πνεῦμα δὲ Θεοῦ καὶ ἐξ αὐτοῦ πεφηνός . . .

desin.: . . . ὁ Θεὸς διὰ Ἰησοῦ Χριστοῦ.

CPG 2838 Basilius Caes., De Spiritu, PG 29, 772C11–13; D1–4.

Post Χριστοῦ P add.:

τοῦ Κυρίου ἡμῶν· Πνεῦμα ῥῆμα, δάκτυλος, πνοή, χριστός, κύριος, χρῖσμα, ἐμφύσημα, νοῦς Χριστοῦ, ἐκπόρευσις, ἔκπεμψις, ἀποστολή, πρόοδος, πρόχυσις, ἔκχυσις, ὕπαρξις, ἀπόρροια, ἀτμίς, ἀπαύγασμα, εἰκών, χαρακτήρ, ἔσοπτρον, (fol. 215ᵛ), πηγή, μετάδοσις, χορήγησις, ἐκπομπή, πεφηνός, ἐμπεφυκός, ὑπάρχον.

Locum non inveni.

229 Τοῦ ἁγίου Γρηγορίου τοῦ Θεολόγου περὶ πίστεως.

Ὁμολογοῦμεν πιστεύειν εἰς πατέρα υἱὸν καὶ ἅγιον πνεῦμα, τριάδα ὁμοούσιον, μίαν θεότητα, ἤτοι φύσιν καὶ οὐσίαν καὶ δύναμιν καὶ ἐξουσίαν ἐν τρισὶν ὑποστάσεσιν, ἤτοι προσώποις δοξάζοντες, εἰς ἃ βεβαπτίσμεθα καὶ οἷς πεπιστεύκα-
5 μεν καὶ οἷς συντετάγμεθα, τὰς μὲν ἰδιότητας χωρίζοντες, ἑνοῦντες δὲ τῇ θεότητι· μονάδα γὰρ ἐν τριάδι καὶ τριάδα ἐν μονάδι προσκυνουμένην, παράδοξον ἔχουσαν καὶ τὴν διαίρεσιν καὶ τὴν ἕνωσιν· μονάδα μὲν κατὰ τὸν τῆς οὐσίας ἤτουν θεότητος λόγον, τριάδα κατὰ τὰς ἰδιότητας, ἤγουν ὑποστάσεις, ἤτοι πρόσωπα· διαιρεῖται γὰρ ἀδιαιρέτως ἡ τριάς, ἵν᾿ οὕτως εἴπωμεν· ἐν γὰρ ἐν τρισὶν
10 ἡ θεότης καὶ τὰ τρία ἕν, τὰ ἐν οἷς ἡ θεότης, ἤ, τό τε ἀκριβέστερον εἰπεῖν, ἀεὶ θεότης Θεὸν ἕκαστον ἂν θεωρεῖται μόνον τοῦ νοῦ χωρίζοντος τὰ ἀχώριστα. Θεὸν τὰ τρία μετ᾿ ἀλλήλ⟨ων⟩ νοούμενα, τῷ αὐτῷ τῆς κινήσεως καὶ τῆς φύσεως [lacuna]. ἐπεὶ χ⟨ρὴ⟩ καὶ τὸν ἕνα Θεὸν ὁμολογεῖν καὶ τὰς τρεῖς ὑποστάσεις κηρύττειν, ἤγουν τὰ τρία πρόσωπα, ἑκάστην μετὰ τῆς ἰδιότητος. καὶ οὔτε τὴν
15 ἕνωσιν σύγχυσιν ἐργαζόμεθα κατὰ Σαβέλλιον, ἓν πρόσωπον τριώνυμον λέγοντες τὴν τριάδα, τὸν αὐτὸν πατέρα, υἱὸν καὶ πνεῦμα, οὔτε διαιροῦντες ἀλλοτριοῦμεν τῆς τοῦ Θεοῦ καὶ πατρὸς οὐσίας τὸν υἱὸν ἢ τὸ πνεῦμα τὸ ἅγιον κατὰ τὴν τοῦ Ἀρείου μανίαν εἰς τρεῖς διαφόρους οὐσίας κατατέμνοντες (cod.:–ας) τὴν θεότητα. Εἷς τοίνυν Θεός, ὁ πατήρ, ἐξ οὗ τὰ πάντα, καὶ εἷς Κύριος μονογενής,
20 δι᾿ οὗ τὰ πάντα, καὶ ἓν πνεῦμα ἅγιον, ἐν ᾧ τὰ πάντα.

Locum non inveni.

230
Sigla
P: Parisinus gr. 1115, fols. 215ᵛ–216
Vt: Athonensis Vatopedinus gr. 594, fol. 241ʳ⁻ᵛ
(a1) Διατί λέγεται λόγος καὶ δύναμις καὶ σοφία ὁ υἱὸς τοῦ Θεοῦ.

Λόγος λέγεται ὅτι οὕτως ἔχει πρὸς τὸν πατέρα αὐτοῦ οἰκείως καὶ συνημμένως, ὡς πρὸς νοῦν λόγος, μᾶλλον δὲ ὑπὲρ τοῦτο ἀσυγκρίτῳ ἑνώσει ἐνυπάρχων αὐτῷ ἀδιαστάτως, ἀσυγχύτως καὶ ἀχωρίστως καὶ διὰ τὸ ἀπαθὲς τῆς γεν-
5 νήσεως. ἐπεὶ καὶ ἐν ἡμῖν ὁ λόγος διὰ τὸ ἐξαγγελτικόν, ἤγουν τὸ ἀναγγεῖλαι αὐτὸν ἡμῖν τὸν πατέρα καὶ τὴν μεγάλην, κορυφαίαν βουλὴν καὶ τὴν ἄλλην ἅπασαν διδασκαλίαν αὐτοῦ καὶ ὅτι ὅρος ἐστὶ τῆς τοῦ πατρὸς γνώσεως ἡ γνῶσις τοῦ υἱοῦ καθὼς εἴρηται ὅτι· "ὁ ἑωρακὼς ἐμέ", ἤγουν νενοηκώς, "ἑώρακε τὸν πατέρα", τουτέστιν νενόηκεν. ἡ γὰρ τοῦ υἱοῦ γνῶσις, γνῶσίς ἐστι τοῦ πατρὸς
10 ἀπαράλλακτος· τοῦτο γὰρ ὁ πατήρ, ὅπερ ὁ υἱὸς καὶ οἷον δ᾿ ἂν ἀποδώσῃς λόγον περὶ (P, fol. 216) τῆς θεότητος τοῦ υἱοῦ, οὗτος ἀρκέσοι καὶ περὶ τῆς τοῦ πατρὸς

καὶ τοῦ ἁγίου πνεύματος καταλήψεως· ὁ γὰρ αὐτὸς λόγος ἀμφοτέροις ἄνευ τῆς
ὀνομασθείσης ἑκάστου τῶν ὑποστάσεων ἰδιότητος.

1 ὁ—Θεοῦ om. P   2 οὕτως:–οσ P αὐτοῦ om. Vt   3 ἀσυγκρίτῳ:–ως Vt   4 καὶ¹ om. Vt   5
τὸ²: τοῦ P   αὐτὸν— 6 πατέρα: ἡμῖν αὐτοῦ τὸν πατέρα P   8 ἤγουν νενοηκὼς om. P   9
γνῶσις¹ om. Vt   10 γὰρ om. Vt   11 ἀρκέσοι: ἀρκεῖ P   12   ἁγίου om. P

(a2)   Διατί δύναμις.
          Δύναμις δὲ ὅτι ὁ λόγος λόγῳ τὰ πάντα συνέστηκεν· ὅστις καὶ μέχρι τοῦ
          νῦν δείκνυται ἐν αὐτοῖς ἐμπρέπων ἁρμοδίως τὰ πάντα συνέχων καὶ τὴν τοῦ
          συνέχεσθαι αὐτὰ χορηγῶν δύναμιν καὶ λόγῳ κυβερνῶν καὶ διεξάγων αὐτά, καὶ
     5   τοὺς λόγους αὐτῶν ἐπιστάμενος μόνος (Vt, fol. 241ᵛ) αὐτός, ὡς παραγωγὸς
          αὐτῶν καὶ ποιητῆς μέχρι τῆς ὁρισθείσης στάσεως αὐτῶν, συγκρατῶν αὐτὰ καὶ
          μὴ ἐῶν φέρεσθαι ἄνευ τῆς αὐτοῦ νεύσεως. καὶ ὅτι "τὸ κράτος κατέλυσε τοῦ
          θανάτου ὡς δυνατὸς τὸν ἰσχυρὸν δήσας καὶ τὰ σκεύη αὐτοῦ διαρπάσας", ὡς
          αὐτὸς ἔφησεν, ἡμᾶς ἀφελόμενος ἐξ αὐτοῦ τάξας ἐκεῖνον ἐγκαταπαίζεσθαι ὑπὸ
     10   Χριστιανῶν καὶ τὰς δυνάμεις αὐτοῦ ἐκδιώκεσθαι. καὶ τοῦτο γὰρ ἔργον τῆς
          αὐτοῦ θεϊκῆς συγκαταβάσεως καὶ δυνάμεως.

1 Διατί δύναμις om. P   2 ὅστις: εἴτις codd.   3 post δείκνυται P add.: ἁρμοδίως   3 καί—
4 συνέχεσθαι om. P   5 λόγους om. Vt αὐτῶν: αὐτὸν Vt παραγωγὸς:–εὺς P   6   αὐτῶν om.
P   7 κατέλυσε: καταλύσας P 10 καὶ²—ἔργον om. Vt   11 συγκαταβάσεως καὶ om. Vt.

(a3)   Εἴρηται καὶ σοφία ὁ λόγος, ὡς ἐπιστήμη θείων καὶ ἀνθρωπίνων πραγμάτων, ὡς
          διδάσκων ἄνθρωπον γνῶσιν καὶ σοφίζων καὶ ὁδηγῶν, ὡς κατασκευάζων βουλὴν
          καὶ διαλύων στραγγαλιὰς καὶ συνδέσμους καὶ ἀναγγέλλων βαθέα, ὡς πάσης
          φρονήσεως καὶ ἐπιστήμης, ὡς πάσης γνώσεως καὶ δυνάμεως καὶ κυβερνήσεως
     5   καὶ ἀληθείας αἴτιος, τὴν πρώτην καὶ μεγάλην σοφίαν, τὸν πατέρα καὶ τὸ ἅγιον
          πνεῦμα σοφῶς ἀποκαλύψας καὶ διδάξας ἡμᾶς ὡς ἡμῖν μαθεῖν ὑπῆρξε δυνατόν.

1 ὁ: καὶ P   3 βαθέα: βαθεῖα codd.   5 ἅγιον om. P   6 σοφῶς om. P   μαθεῖν ὑπῆρξε: ὑπ.
μαθ. P.

a1–3 Loca non inveni.

Solus P, fol. 216ʳ⁻ᵛ
(b1)   Τί ἐστι δόγμα; Δόγμα ἐστὶν εὐσεβὲς ἀληθείας κράτος, ἢ τὸ πόνῳ ὁρισθὲν καὶ
          ὄντως οὕτως ἔχον, ἢ ζητήσεως ἀψευδοῦς διάγνωσις, ἢ ἐν λόγοις ἀπαλλαγὴ
          πλάνης. Δόγμα καθολικόν ἐστι γνώμη οἰκεία ἀβιάστως πᾶσι προτιθεμένη, ἢ
          καθ᾿ ἑτέρου ἀντίθεσις ἤγουν ἀνατροπή, ἢ ἰδιαιρέτως γνώμη, ἢ ἰδικῶς ὡρισμένη
     5   καὶ καθ᾿ ἑαυτὴν καὶ μόνον νοουμένη, ἢ ἡ κεχωρισμένη τῶν λοιπῶν δόξα καὶ
          ἰδίῳ ὅρῳ γνωριζομένη. Δόγμα ἐστὶν ὑπόληψις ἀνδρὸς βεβαία καὶ ἀληθὴς περὶ
          τῶν ζητουμένων ἐν φιλοσοφίᾳ, ἀμετάπτωτος ὑπὸ λόγου ὡς τὸ "ἡ ψυχὴ ἀθάνατός
          ἐστι". Δογματιστῆς ἐστι φρονήματος οἰκείου βεβαίωσις, ἢ καρπὸς λόγου εἰς
          Θεόν, ἢ εὐσέβεια εἰς Θεὸν καὶ βίος τούτῳ ῥυθμιζόμενος. Δόξα ἐστὶ δύναμις
     10   ψυχῆς, καθ᾿ ἣν ἄνευ αἰτίας γινώσκει τὰ πράγματα.

(b2)   Περὶ αἰτίου· αἴτιόν ἐστι τελικόν, δι᾿ ὃ γίνεται τὸ γινόμενον, οἷον ὡς πατὴρ τῶν

τέκνων καὶ οἱ τεχνῖται τῶν ἔργων· αἴτιόν ἐστι συνεργὸν ἐξ οὗ (P, fol. 216ᵛ)
ἐνυπάρχοντος γίνεται τὸ γινόμενον, οἷον ὡς χαλκὸς τοῦ ἀνδριάντος καὶ οἱ λί-
θοι τῆς οἰκίας καὶ ὅλως ἡ ὕλη τῶν σκευαστ(ῶν?), αἱ προτάσεις τοῦ συμπεράσ-
5 ματος καὶ τὰ μέρη τοῦ λόγου· πολλῶν γὰρ αἴτιον ἡ ὕλη.

(b3) Τί ἐστιν ὑπογραφὴ ὅρου· ὑπογραφή ἐστι ὁρισμὸς τυπώδης ἢ ὁρισμὸς ἀσθενὴς οἷον
ἄνθρωπός ἐστι ζῷον πολιτικόν.

b1 Locum non inveni. Sed tamen cf. 1 Τί—4 ἀνατροπὴ cum CPG 8042 Iohannes
Damasc., *Fragmenta philosophica e cod. Oxon. Bodl. T. 1. 6*, ed. B. Kotter, *Die Schriften des
Iohannes von Damaskos*, I (Berlin, 1969), 161.2-5
b2 Locum non inveni.
b3 Locum non inveni. Cf. CPG 8042, ibid., 161.12-14.

231 Τοῦ ἁγίου Μαξίμου περὶ κοινοῦ καὶ ἰδίου τουτέστιν οὐσίας καὶ ὑποστάσεως πρὸς
Κοσμᾶν θεοφιλέστατον διάκονον Ἀλεξανδρείας. Τῷ θεοφιλεστάτῳ . . . χαίρειν.
Inc.: Ἐπειδήπερ πολὺ ἡμῖν περὶ τῆς θείας σαρκώσεως—ὡς ἔχει τὸ ζῷον πρὸς τὸν δεῖνα
ἄνθρωπον. Καὶ μεθ᾽ ἕτερα. Οἱ δὲ ταὐτὸν λέγοντες οὐσίαν καὶ ὑπόστασιν—(fol. 217)
καὶ υἱὸν καὶ ἅγιον πνεῦμα ὑπολαμβάνουσιν. Καὶ πάλιν μετ᾽ ὀλίγα. Ἐπειδὴ χρὴ καὶ
τὸν ἕνα Θεὸν τηρεῖν . . .
fol. 217ᵛ desin.: . . . ταύτης τῆς ἐννοίας παντελῶς ἐκτραπέντας.
CPG 7699 Maximus Confessor, *Epistula xv*, cf. 7707.31, PG 91, 544C12–549A10.

232 Κατασκευὴ φυσικωτέρα παριστῶσα ὡς οὐδὲν τῶν ὄντων ἑτέρῳ ταύτόν ἐστιν κατ᾽
οὐσίαν καὶ ὑπόστασιν, διὰ τὸ μὴ ταὐτὸν εἶναι φύσιν καὶ ὑπόστασιν, ἀλλὰ τὰ μὲν κατ᾽
οὐσίαν ταὐτά, ταῖς ὑποστάσεσιν ἕτερα, τὰ δὲ ταὐτὰ καθ᾽ ὑπόστασιν, πάντως κατ᾽ οὐσίαν
ἕτερα.
Inc.: Εἰ δὲ ταὐτὸν μὲν οὐσία καὶ φύσις . . .
fol. 219 desin.: . . . τριάδος τοῦ Θεοῦ λόγου καθέστηκε λόγος.
CPG 7707.31 Idem, *Appendix ad epistulam xv ad Cosmam*, PG 91, 549A15–553C5.

233 Τοῦ ἁγίου Κυρίλλου.
Inc.: Καίτοι τὸ πνεῦμά ἐστι τὸ κατοικοῦν ἐν ἡμῖν . . .
desin.: . . . αὐτοῦ κατὰ φύσιν ἐστὶ καὶ διὰ τοῦτο Θεός.
CPG 5208 Cyrillus Alex., *Commentarii in Iohannem*, PG 73, 157C4-12.

234 Τοῦ ἁγίου Μαξίμου περὶ τῆς ἁγίας τριάδος.
Inc.: (a) Ἕν ἐστι τὸ ὑπεράναρχον—πάσης πασῶν γνώσεως ὑπέρκειται.
(b) Εἷς Θεός, ἑνὸς υἱοῦ γεννήτωρ—πνεύματος ἁγίου πηγή.
(c) Τὸ κατ᾽ οὐσίαν (fol. 219ᵛ) κυρίως ἀγαθόν ἐστι—καὶ ἔστι καὶ λέγεται.//
(d) Εἷς Θεός, ὅτι μία θεότης . . .
desin.: . . . ἡ αὐτὴ μονὰς καὶ τριάς.
Post τριάς PG add.: καὶ τὰ ἑξῆς, in P omnino habetur:

ὅλη μονὰς ἡ αὐτὴ καὶ ὅλη τριὰς ἡ αὐτή. μονὰς ὅλη κατὰ τὴν οὐσίαν ἡ αὐτὴ καὶ
τριὰς ὅλη κατὰ τὰς ὑποστάσεις ἡ αὐτή· πατὴρ γὰρ υἱὸς καὶ πνεῦμα ἅγιον ἡ
θεότης, ὅλη ἐν ὅλῳ τῷ πατρὶ ἡ αὐτὴ καὶ ὅλος ἐν ὅλῃ τῇ αὐτῇ ὁ πατήρ· καὶ ὅλη
ἐν ὅλῳ τῷ υἱῷ ἡ αὐτὴ καὶ ὅλος ἐν ὅλῃ τῇ αὐτῇ ὁ υἱός· καὶ ὅλη ἐν ὅλῳ τῷ ἁγίῳ
5 πνεύματι ἡ αὐτὴ καὶ ὅλον ἐν ὅλῃ τῇ αὐτῇ τὸ πνεῦμα τὸ ἅγιον. οὐ γὰρ ἐκ μέρους
ἡ θεότης ἐν τῷ πατρὶ ἢ ἐκ μέρους Θεὸς ὁ πατήρ, οὔτε ἐκ μέρους ἐν τῷ υἱῷ ἡ

θεότης ἢ ἐκ μέρους Θεὸς ὁ υἱός, οὔτε ἐκ μέρους ἐν τῷ ἁγίῳ πνεύματι ἡ θεότης
ἢ ἐκ μέρους Θεὸς τὸ πνεῦμα τὸ ἅγιον, οὔτε μεριστὴ ἡ θεότης, οὔτε ἀτελὴς Θεὸς
ὁ πατήρ, ὁ υἱός, ἢ τὸ πνεῦμα τὸ ἅγιον.

CPG 7695 Maximus Confessor, *Capita xv,* (a) *PG* 90, 1177A2-9; (b) 1180A4-8; (c) 1177A11-B3; (d) 1180A10-12.

235 Γρηγορίου τοῦ Θεολόγου ἐκ τοῦ λόγου τοῦ εἰς τὸ ῥητὸν τοῦ εὐαγγελίου.

Inc.: Ἔκτεμε τὴν Ἀρειανὴν ἀσέβειαν, ἔκτεμε τὴν Σαβελλίου . . .

desin.: . . . ὅταν προσώπων, ἀλλὰ μὴ θεότητος διαιρούμενα (sic).

CPG 3010.37 Gregorius Naz., *Oratio* 37, ed. C. Moreschini, *Discours 32–37,* 316 par. 22.8-13; *PG* 36, 308A11-B3. See also quotation **39**.

236 Τοῦ μακαρίου Κυρίλλου ἐπισκόπου Ἱεροσολύμων περὶ τῶν ἁγίων καὶ οἰκουμε-νικῶν συνόδων.

Inc.: Χρὴ γινώσκειν ὅτι ἐξ ἅγιαι καὶ οἰκουμενικαί εἰσι σύνοδοι . . .

fol. 221ᵛ desin.: . . . μέχρι τῆς καθαιρέσεως Νεστορίου γίνονται ἔτη υκη΄ τῷ δὲ Θεῷ ἡμῶν δόξα εἰς τοὺς αἰῶνας, ἀμήν.

Cf. ed. J. Munitiz, "The Manuscript of Justel's *Anonymi Tractatus de Synodis,*" *Byzantion* 47 (1977), 253–57.

237 Ἔκθεσις πίστεως τῶν ἁγίων τιη΄ πατέρων τῶν ἐν Νικαίᾳ καὶ διδασκαλία πάνυ θαυ-μαστὴ καὶ σωτήριος.

Inc.: Πιστεύομεν εἰς ἕνα Θεὸν πατέρα παντοκράτορα . . .

fol. 224ᵛ desin.: . . . αἱ ὁδηγοῦσαι εἰς τὴν αἰώνιον ζωὴν τοῦ Θεοῦ, αὐτῷ ἡ δόξα καί . . . ἀμήν.

CPG 2264 Athanasius Alex., *Syntagma ad Monachos, PG* 28, 836–45/ *CPG* 2298, *Didas-calia cccxviii patrum Nicaenorum, PG* 28, 1637–44/ *CPG* 2346 idem, *Epistula ad Mo-nachos,* "Une lettre grecque attribuée à s. Antoine," *Le Muséon* 55 (1942), 97–123.

See R. Riedinger and H. Thurn, "Die Didascalia CCCXVIII Patrum Nicaenorum und das Syntagma ad Monachos im Codex Parisinus Graecus 1115 (a. 1276)," *JÖB* 35 (1985), 75–92.

238 Ἀφρικανοῦ ἱστορίας.

Ἐν ἀρχῇ ἐποίησεν ὁ Θεὸς τὸν οὐρανὸν καὶ τὴν γῆν, τουτέστι τὸ πᾶν κατ' εἰδέαν ἢ ἀπὸ μέρους τῶν ἄκρων, εἴ τι ἕτερον διὰ τούτων σημαίνεται. α΄ Πρώτη μὲν ἡμέρα τὸ φῶς, ὃ ἐκάλεσεν ἡμέραν. β΄ Δευτέρα δὲ (fol. 225) στερέωμα πρὸς
5 διάκρισιν ὕδατος, οὐρανὸν ἐπονομάσας. γ΄ Τρίτη δὲ ἦν γῆς φανέρωσις, καὶ θα-λάσσης σύνοδοι. δ΄ Τετάρτη φωστῆρες. ε΄ Πέμπτη ἐξ ὑδάτων ψυχαὶ νηκτῶν (cod.: ψυκτῶν) τε καὶ ἀερίων. στ΄ Ἕκτη τε ἐκ τῆς γῆς ζῷα, ἄνθρωπος κατ' εἰκόνα Θεοῦ, τὸ χοϊκὸν ἀπὸ γῆς πλασθείς, καθ' ὁμοίωσιν δὲ ἐμψυχωμένος, ἢ ὅτι τὸ μὲν κατ' εἰκόνα προσδοὺς (cod.: προσδεύς), τὸ δὲ καθ' ὁμοίωσιν προσδο-
10 κᾶται.

CPG 1690 Iulius (Sextus) Africanus, *Chronographiae,* fragmentum supra primum edi-tum est.

239 Ἀναστασίου μοναχοῦ τοῦ ἁγίου ὄρους τοῦ Σινᾶ ἔκθεσις ἐν ἐπιτομῇ περὶ πίστεως.

Inc.: Ἰστέον καὶ μὴ ἀγνοητέον ὅτι οὐ δεῖ ἡμᾶς ἀβασανίστως . . .

fol. 226ᵛ desin.: . . . καὶ ἐν ἑτέροις εἰρήκαμεν, τῷ δὲ Χριστῷ καὶ Θεῷ ἡμῶν ἡ δόξα . . . ἀμήν.

CPG 7745 Anastasius Sinaita, *Viae Dux (Hodegos), CCSG* 8, I, 2.1–137. See also quotations **47, 109, 194a–e.**

240 Τοῦ ἁγίου Γρηγορίου Νύσης περὶ Τριάδος καὶ ὅτι τρεῖς ὑποστάσεις καὶ μία θεότης.
Inc.: Ἐκ τοῦ καθ᾽ ἡμᾶς ἐστι γνῶναι καὶ τὰ περὶ ἡμᾶς . . .
desin.: . . . τὸν νοῦν ἔχειν καὶ λόγον καὶ πνεῦμα.
CPG 1781 Gregorius Thaumaturgus, *De deitate et tribus personis,* ed. C. P. Caspari, "Nogle nye kirkehistoriske Anecdota II. Et Gregorius Thaumaturgus tillagt Fragment," *Theologisk Tidsskrift for den evangelisk-lutherske Kirche i Norge,* ser. 2, 8 (1882), 53–59. See also Appendix II, quot. 4*.

241 Ἱππολύτου Θηβαίου ἐκ τοῦ χρονικοῦ αὐτοῦ συντάγματος.
Inc.: Ἀπὸ τῆς ἐνανθρωπήσεως τοῦ Χριστοῦ μέχρι τῆς τῶν μάγων . . .
fol. 228 desin.: . . . Ἀγγαίου, ἀδελφοῦ Ζαχαρίου τοῦ ἱερέως.
Ed F. Diekamp, *Hippolytos von Theben, TU* (Münster, 1898), 1–10.6.

242   Περὶ τῶν γ´ ἡμερῶν τῆς ἀναστάσεως τοῦ Χριστοῦ.
Τὰς τρεῖς ἡμέρας καὶ τὰς τρεῖς νύκτας, ἃς ἐποίησεν ὁ Χριστὸς ἐν τῇ καρδίᾳ
τῆς γῆς, οὕτως ἀριθμήσεις· ἐγένετο μετὰ τὴν ἕκτην ὥραν ἐν ᾗ τέθνηκεν ὁ Κύριος Ἰησοῦς Χριστὸς σκότος καὶ μετὰ τὸ σκότος τὸ κρατῆσαν ἕως ὥρας θ´ τὸ
5   λοιπὸν τῆς παρασκευῆς, ἡμέρα μία. τὸ τοῦ σαββάτου νυχθήμερον ὁλόκληρον,
δευτέρα ἡμέρα, ἡ δὲ "ὀψὲ σαββάτου" ὡς ὁ Ματθαῖος εἶπε, "τῇ ἐπιφωσκούσῃ
εἰς μίαν σαββάτων", καὶ ἐν τούτῳ γὰρ ἐδήλωσε τῆς ἡμέρας ἐπικειμένης, ἔδει
φωτίζεσθαι τὴν νύκτα ἀλλ᾽ οὐχὶ τὴν ἡμέραν, τῆς νυκτὸς καταλαμβανούσης
αὐτὴν σκοτοῦσθαι ὑπὸ τῆς ἄκρας νυκτός, τρίτη γέγονεν ἡμέρα, ἐν ᾗ κατὰ τὴν
10   πρόρησιν αὐτοῦ ὁ Κύριος ἡμῶν ἀνέστη. ὁ δὲ λέγων ἀπὸ τὸ γενόμενον ἀπὸ ἔκτης
ὥρας μέχρι ἐννάτης σκότος εἰς νύκτα λαμβανόμενον τρεῖς ἡμέρας καὶ τρεῖς
νύκτας γεγονέναι, μέρη (cod.: μέρει) μὲν κἀκεῖνος ἡμερῶν ⟨καὶ⟩ οὐ τελείας
λέγει· τὴν γὰρ παρασκευὴν διελών, τὸ μὲν μέχρι ὥρας ἕκτης ὡς ⟨ἐν⟩τελῆ
(cod.:–λεῖ μίαν ἐκτίθεται, τὸ δὲ ἀπὸ ὥρας θ´ ὡς δευτέραν (cod.:–ας) καὶ
15   ποτέρα[ν] τούτων ἐστὶ παρασκευή, ἢ ποῖον τὸ σάββατον; οὐ γὰρ δεῖ· δύο ἐφεξῆς
ἡμέραι γίνονται παρασκευαὶ ἢ δύο σάββατα· καὶ μίαν μὲν τὴν ἀληθῆ νύκτα
οἶδεν, ἑτέραν δὲ τὴν οὐκ οὖσαν προστίθησι· πάθος γὰρ τεράστιον καὶ πένθος
ὥσπερ τῆς ἡμέρας ἐκείνης γέγονε τὸ σκότος μόνον, οὐκ ἐγκαλυψαμένου καὶ
μεγαλορρημονήσαντος ἐπὶ τοῖς γενομένοις τοῦ ἡλίου· νὺξ δὲ οὐκ ἦν ἐναρίθ-
20   μιος. εἰ δὲ ξένη καὶ περιττὴ λέγοιτο νύξ, ἀσέληνος ἦν καὶ ἀνάστερος καὶ διὰ
τοῦτο ταῖς ἄλλαις νυξὶν οὐ συγκαταψηφίζεται. εἰ δὲ μετὰ τὴν παρασκευήν ἐστι
τὸ σάββατον καὶ μετὰ τοῦτο ἡ μία τῶν σαββάτων πεπλήρωτο, δηλονότι μέχρι
τῆς ἕκτης ὥρας τότε ἡ παρασκευή· ἀπὸ δὲ τῆς θ´ ὥρας, ἦλθε τὸ σάββατον καὶ
ἡ μία τὸ σάββατον γέγονε τὸ σάβ⟨β⟩ατον καὶ ἡ μία τῶν σαββάτων εἰς δευτέραν
25   ὑπεβιβάσθη. καὶ πῶς ἔτι αὐτὴν κυριακὴν ἑορτάζομεν; συνεχέθη γὰρ δηλονότι
τῶν ἡμερῶν ὁ ἀριθμὸς παρεμπεσούσης (cod.: παραπεμπούσης) τῆς ἐμβολίμου
(fol. 228ᵛ) ἡμέρας· οὐχ οὕτως δὲ προεφήτευσε Ζαχαρίας, "ἐν ἐκείνῃ", γάρ
φησι, "τῇ ἡμέρᾳ οὐκ ἔσται φῶς καὶ ψῦχος καὶ παγετός· ἔσται μίαν ἡμέραν, καὶ
ἡ ἡμέρα ἐκείνη γνωστὴ τῷ Κυρίῳ καὶ οὐχ ἡμέρα καὶ οὐ νὺξ καὶ οὐ(?) πρὸς
30   ἑσπέραν ἔσται".

Locum non inveni.

243 Τοῦ ἁγίου Ἐπιφανίου ἐπισκόπου Κύπρου περὶ τῶν προφητῶν, πῶς ἐκοιμήθησαν καὶ
ποῦ κεῖνται.

Inc.: Νάθαν (sic) ὁ προφήτης ἐγένετο ἐν ἡμέραις Δαυίδ . . .
fol. 233 desin.: . . . ὀνομάτων Ἰσραήλ, ὧν οὐκ ἐμνημονεύσαμεν.
CPG 3777 Epiphanius Const., De prophetarum vita et obitu, recensio prior, ed. Th. Schermann, Prophetarum Vitae fabulosae, indices apostolorum discipulorumque domini Dorotheo,
Epiphanio, Hippolyto aliisque vindicatae, Bibliotheca Teubneriana 223 (Leipzig, 1907),
4–25; PG 43, 393–414.

fol. 233ᵛ **244**
(a) Τοῦ αὐτοῦ περὶ τῶν ἁγίων ἀποστόλων, ποῦ ἕκαστος αὐτῶν ἐκήρυξε καὶ πῶς καὶ ποῦ
ἐτελεύτησαν καὶ τὰ ἅγια αὐτῶν σώματα ποῦ κεῖνται καὶ ἐν ποίοις τόποις.
Inc.: Σίμων Πέτρος ὁ τῶν ἀποστόλων κορυφαῖος . . .
fol. 234ᵛ desin.: . . . ἐπίσκοπος Θηβῶν ἐκεῖ ἀπέθανε καὶ ἐτάφη.
CPG 3780 Epiphanius Const., Index apostolorum, ed. Schermann, Prophetarum vitae
fabulosae, 107.14–117.4.

(b) Inc.: . . . Ἡρωδιανὸς καὶ αὐτὸς πρὸς Ῥωμαίους ἐπίσκοπος . . .
fol. 235 desin.: . . . σὺν αὐτῷ ἀπετμήθησαν ὑπὸ Νέρωνος.
CPG 3781 Epiphanius Const., Index discipulorum, ed. Schermann, ibid., 121.7–126.10.

(c) I   Εἰσὶ τὰ ὀνόματα τῶν γονέων τῶν ιβ´ ἀποστόλων—τὸν Κανανίτην, ζηλωτὴν
          ἐκάλεσεν.
      II Περὶ τοῦ Μελχισεδέκ. Καὶ γὰρ παρά τισι τοῦ Μελχισεδὲκ ὁ πατὴρ καὶ ἡ μήτηρ
          ἐμφέρεται, οὐχὶ δὲ κατὰ τὰς ῥητὰς γραφὰς καὶ [lacuna iv litt.] εἰπεῖν δέ ἐστιν
          Ἡρακλᾶν καλεῖσθαι αὐτοῦ τὸν πατέρα, μητέρα δὲ καὶ Ἀσταρώθ τὴν δὲ καὶ Ἀ-
          στερίαν. Περὶ τοῦ Δανιήλ. Ὁμοίως τε εὑρήκαμεν καὶ τοῦ Δανιὴλ τὸν πατέρα
          Σαβαάν τινα καλούμενον. Περὶ τοῦ Ἠλία. Ἠλίας ὁ Θεσβίτης, ἀδελφὸς γέγονεν
          Ἰωδαὲ τοῦ ἱερέως, ἐξ Ἰουδαίων ⟨εὐ?⟩δήλων καὶ αὐτὸς ὑπάρχων, υἱὸς δὲ τοῦ
          Ἀχιβαάμ. Περὶ τῶν τριῶν παίδων. ⟨Κα⟩ῦσιν (cod.:–σει) δὲ τῶν τριῶν παίδων,
          Σεδράχ, Μισάχ, Ἀβδεναγώ, οὔτε ἐν ἀποκρύφοις, οὔτε ἐν παραδόσεσιν εὕρα-
          μεν. ἆρα κἀκεῖνοι οἱ παῖδες, Σεδρὰχ λέγω, φαντασιάσωσιν ἡμᾶς λογίζεσθαι ἃ
          μὴ χρὴ καὶ ὑπέρογκα θαυμάζειν ὑπὲρ τὸ μέτρον ἑκάστης ὑποθέσεως, ἀλλὰ
          μὴ γένοιτο.

c–I Textus anonymus de apostolorum parentibus, ed. Schermann, ibid., 203.1–204.7
c–II Locum non inveni.

245 Κανὼν περὶ τοῦ μὴ δεῖν τὸν ἱερέα β´ λειτουργίας ποιεῖν.
Inc.: ⟨Ὁ⟩ ὀρθὸς λόγος καὶ ἡ ἀκριβὴς τῶν πραγμάτων κατανόησις . . .
fol. 235ᵛ desin.: . . . ἐπεὶ καὶ ὁ Χριστὸς ὁ ἀληθινὸς ἱερεύς . . .
Ed. J. Hergenröther, Monumenta Graeca ad Photium pertinentia (Regensburg, 1869), 11.

fols. 235ᵛ–283ᵛ:

Florilegium adversus Iconoclastas (see Appendix II).

fol. 283ᵛ **246** Ἐπιστολὴ τοῦ ἁγίου Βασιλείου ἐπισκόπου Καισαρείας Καππαδοκ[ε]ίας
πρὸς τὸν ἐν ἁγίοις Ἀμφιλόχιον, ἐπίσκοπον τοῦ Ἰκονίου· περὶ κανόνων.
Inc.: Ἀνοήτῳ, φησίν, ἐπερωτήσαντι σοφία λογισθήσεται . . .
fol. 287ᵛ desin.: . . . καὶ αὐτόθεν εὑρήσεις τὴν λύσιν τοῦ ζητήματος.

CPG 2900 Basilius Caes., *Epistula CLXXXVIII*, ed. Y. Courtonne, *Saint Basile, Lettres,* II (Paris, 1961), 120–31; *PG* 32, 664в–684в12.

247 Καὶ ὅσα ἐπιτίμια.
Inc.: Εἴ τις ὑγιαίνων τῷ σώματι ἀμελοίη τῶν προσευχῶν . . .
desin.: . . . ἀφοριζέσθω ὁμοίως ἑβδομάδα μίαν.
CPG 2897.1 Basilius Caes., *Poenae in monachos delinquentes* (Epitimia 24), *PG* 31, 1305c1–1308c1.

fol. 288 **248** Ἐπιστολὴ τοῦ ἁγίου Γρηγορίου ἐπισκόπου Νύσης εἰς τὸν ἐν ἁγίοις Λητόϊον ἐπίσκοπον Μελιτινῆς.
Inc.: ⟨Ἐ⟩ν καὶ τοῦτο τῶν εἰς τὴν ἁγίαν ἑορτὴν συντελούντων . . .
fol. 292 desin.: . . . κἄν τι μικρότερον τῆς σῆς μεγαλοφυῖας εἴη.
CPG 3148 Gregorius Nyss., *Epistula canonica ad Letoium, PG* 45, 221в1–236c4.

249: see **250** Ὅπως χρὴ διαδέχεσθαι τοὺς ἀπὸ αἱρέσεως μετερχομένους ἐν τῇ ἁγίᾳ καθολικῇ καὶ ἀποστολικῇ ἐκκλησίᾳ.
Inc.: Ἀρειανοὺς μὲν καὶ Μακεδονιανοὺς πνευματομάχους . . .
fol. 293 desin.: . . . προστίθεσθαι τῇ ἀληθείᾳ ὡς Ἕλληνας δεχόμεθα.
PG 100, 1317–21.

250 Ὅπως δεῖ ἀναθεματίζειν ἐγγράφως τοὺς ἀπὸ Μανιχαίων προσερχομένους τῇ ἁγίᾳ τοῦ Θεοῦ ἐκκλησίᾳ.
Inc.: Ἀνάθεμα Μάνεντι ἤτοι Μανιχαίῳ, τῷ καὶ Κουβρίκῳ . . .
fol. 293ᵛ desin.: . . . καὶ ἡμῖν τοῦ αὐτοῦ ὑπάρχοντος.
PG 100, 1321в–23в. Cf. G. Ficker, "Eine Sammlung von Abschwörungsformeln," *ZKG* 27 (1906), 443–64.

251   ἐκ τοῦ Πηλουσιώτου ἐρώτησις· τί ἐστιν εἰ ὁ ὀφθαλμός σου σκανδαλίζει σε ἔκβαλε αὐτὸν καὶ τὰ ἑξῆς; Ἀπόκρισις. Εἴτε τῶν ἐμφανῶν ἀνθρώπων, εἴτε τῶν ὑποδεεστέρων σκανδαλίζει σε εἰς τὴν κατὰ Θεὸν πίστιν, εἴτε τῶν προσγενῶν, ἀπόστησον αὐτὸν ἀπὸ σοῦ ἢ ἀπόστα ἀπ᾽ αὐτοῦ.

Locum non inveni.

252 Τοῦ ἁγίου Ἰωάννου τοῦ Χρυσοστόμου ἐκ τῆς πρὸς Ἑβραίους ἐπιστολῆς.
Inc.: Πείθεσθε τοῖς ἡγουμένοις ὑμῶν καὶ ὑπείκε[ι]τε αὐτοῖς—εἰ δὲ βίου ἕνεκεν, μὴ περιεργάζου.// τῶν μὲν ἠθῶν ἕνεκα . . .
desin.: . . . περὶ βίου ἐστὶν οὐ περὶ πίστεως.
CPG 4440 Iohannes Chrys., *In epistulam ad Hebraeos argumentum et homilia 34, PG* 63, 231d5–10; 232в6–12.

253 *Testimonia* varia excerpta de V.T. (adversus Iudaeos?).

          (α) περὶ τοῦ βαπτίζεσθαι.
fol. 294 (β) ὅτι τὰ ἔθνη μέλλουσιν ἐπιστρέφειν πρὸς Κύριον προσκαλούμενα.
fol. 294ᵛ (γ) ὅτι τὰς ἑορτὰς καὶ τὰς θυσίας ἀποστρέφεται ὁ Θεὸς τῶν Ἰουδαίων.
fol. 295 (δ) ὅτι τοὺς Ἰουδαίους ἁμαρτάνοντας καὶ μὴ ἐμμένοντας ἐν τῷ νόμῳ ἀ-πωθεῖται.
fol. 298 (ε) ὅτι Χριστὸς ὁ Θεός.
fol. 298ᵛ (στ) ὅτι ὁ λόγος υἱὸς τοῦ Θεοῦ.
          (ζ) ὅτι πνεῦμα ὁ υἱὸς τοῦ Θεοῦ.

(η) ὅτι δύναμις καὶ σοφία τοῦ Θεοῦ ὁ Χριστός.

(θ) ὅτι οὐ κτιστὸν τὸ πνεῦμα ἀλλ' ἐκ τοῦ πατρός.

(ι) ὅτι κτίστης ὁ λόγος.

fol. 299 (ια) ὅτι Κύριος ὁ Χριστός.

(ιβ) ὅτι φῶς ὁ Χριστός.

(ιγ) περὶ τῆς ἐνανθρωπήσεως.

(ιδ) περὶ ὁδοῦ ἐπαινετῆς.

fol. 299ᵛ (ιε) ὅτι ἤμελλε (sic) πάσχειν.

(ιστ) περὶ τοῦ σημείου τοῦ σταυροῦ.

fol. 300 (ιζ) ὅτι οἱ προφῆται ὀνομαστὸν Χριστὸν ἐκύρησον (sic) ἐρχόμενον.

fol. 302 (ιη) ὅτι διὰ τὰς ἁμαρτίας ἡμῶν ἀπέθανεν ἵνα ἁγιασθῶμεν.

254 Τοῦ ἁγίου Ἀθανασίου ἐκ τῶν πρὸς αὐτὸν ἐρωτήσεων.

Inc.: Τῷ εὐαγγελίῳ μὴ πιστεύοντας Ἕλληνας καὶ τὰς θείας . . .

fol. 302ᵛ desin.: . . . καὶ ἀνίατα πάθη θεραπεύσει.

CPG 2257 Athanasius Alex., *Quaestiones ad Antiochum ducem, Qu. cxxxvi, PG* 28, 681D7–684C7.

255 Ἐρώτησις Χριστιανῶν τε καὶ Ἰουδαίων Χριστὸν ὁμολογούντων, ἀμφιβαλλόντων δὲ τῶν Ἰουδαίων καὶ λεγόντων οὔπω αὐτὸν ἐληλυθέναι, ἀλλὰ μέλλει ἔρχεσθαι. πῶς αὐτοὺς πεῖσαι ὀφείλωμεν ὅτι καὶ Θεός ἐστιν ὁ Χριστὸς καὶ ὅτι ἦλθε καὶ ὅτι ἀληθής ἐστι καὶ οὐ πλάνος, ὡς αὐτοὶ νομίζουσιν.

Inc.: Ὅτι μὲν Θεὸς καὶ Κύριος ὁ Χριστός ἐστιν οἱ προφῆται . . .

fol. 306 desin.: . . . ὁ γὰρ υἱὸς τοῦ Θεοῦ ἐρχόμενος ἀνελεῖ αὐτὸν τῷ πνεύματι τοῦ στόματος αὐτοῦ· ὅτι αὐτῷ ἡ δόξα . . . ἀμήν.

CPG 2257 Athanasius Alex., *Quaestiones ad Antiochum ducem, Qu. cxxxvii, PG* 28, 684C8–700.

fol. 306ᵛ Colophon:

Τὸ παρὸν βιβλίον ἐγράφη διὰ χειρὸς ἐμοῦ Λέοντος τοῦ Κιννάμου, τελειωθὲν σὺν Θεῷ, μηνὶ Μαρτίῳ ιδ´ ἰνδ(ικτιῶνος) δ´, ἡμέρᾳ ἑβδόμῃ, ἔτους ͵ϛψπδ´ ἐπὶ τῆς βασιλείας τῶν εὐσεβεστάτων καὶ πιστοτάτων καὶ ἐκ Θεοῦ ἐστεμμένων μεγάλων βασιλέων ἡμῶν, τοῦ τε κυροῦ Μιχαὴλ Δούκα Ἀγγέλου Κομνηνοῦ τοῦ Παλαιολόγου καὶ νέου Κωνσταντίνου, καὶ Θεοδώρας τῆς εὐσεβεστάτης αὐγούστης, καὶ τοῦ κυροῦ Ἀνδρονίκου Κομνηνοῦ τοῦ Παλαιολόγου, καὶ Ἄννης τῆς εὐσεβεστάτης αὐγούστης, καὶ ἐναπετέθη ἐν τῇ βασιλικῇ βιβλιοθήκῃ· μετεγράφη δὲ ἀπὸ βιβλίου εὑρεθέντος ἐν τῇ παλαιᾷ βιβλιοθήκῃ τῆς ἁγίας ἐκκλησίας τῆς πρεσβυτέρας Ῥώμης, ὅπερ βιβλίον ἐγράφη καὶ αὐτὸ ἐν ἔτει ͵ϛσξζ´, ὡς ἀριθμεῖσθαι τοὺς χρόνους τοῦ τοιούτου βιβλίου ἄχρι τοῦ παρόντος ιζ´ πρὸς τοῖς πεντακοσίοις. Ἔχει δὲ τὸ παρὸν βιβλίον τετράδια γεγραμμένα μη´ καὶ φύλλα τπα´, καὶ τετράδια ἄγραφα β´.

3. Additional Part of the Manuscript
(14th–15th cent., fols. 307–314ᵛ)

fol. 307 **12A** Κυρίλλου πρὸς Θεόγνωστον καὶ Χαρμόσυνον πρεσβυτέρους καὶ Λεόντιον διάκονον διάγοντας ἐν Κωνσταντινουπόλει καὶ τὰς ἀποκρίσεις αὐτοῦ ποιουμένους. Κύριλλος Θεογνώστῳ . . . χαίρειν.

Inc.: Περὶ πάντων γράφομεν τῶν πραγμάτων . . .

desin.: . . . τῇ πίστει τῇ ἐκτεθείσῃ παρὰ τῶν ἁγίων ἡμῶν πατέρων.
CPG 5337 [8861] Cyrillus Alex., *Epistula 37, Ad Theognostum et Charmosynum presb. et Leontium diac. ACO* I,1,7, 154; *PG* 77, 168–69.

13A Ἐπιστολὴ Ἰωάννου ἐπισκόπου Ἀντιοχείας πρὸς Κύριλλον. Τῷ δεσπότῃ μου . . . χαίρειν.
Inc.: Ἀπειλήφαμεν ἀλλήλους, δέσποτα . . .
fol. 307ᵛ desin.: . . . σὺν σοὶ ἀδελφότητα πλεῖστα προσαγορεύομεν.
CPG 6311 [8852] Iohannes I Antioch., *Ep. ad Cyrillum Alex. ACO* I,1,7, 155; *PG* 77, 248–50.

fol. 308 **14A** Ἐκ τῆς βίβλου τῆς συντεθείσης παρὰ κυροῦ Ματθαίου ἱερομονάχου κατὰ Λατίνων. αἱ διὰ τοῦ υἱοῦ λέγουσαι τὸ ἅγιον πνεῦμα ῥήσεις, παρὰ τῶν ἁγίων πατέρων.
Inc.: Οὐ δέον δὲ κἀκείνας οἶμαι παραλιπεῖν . . .
fol. 314ᵛ desin.: . . . τὸ γὰρ πῶς, οὐδὲ ἀγγέλοις ἐννοεῖν δέδοται.
Ineditum.

APPENDIX II

List of Contents of Folios 235ᵛ–283ᵛ of Parisinus Graecus 1115 (Iconophile Florilegium)

Abbreviations
A = Acts of the seventh ecumenical council (Nicaea II), Mansi, XII–XIII
Dam. = Iohannes Damascenus, ed. Kotter, *Schriften III*
M = Mosquensis Hist. Mus. 265 (numbers refer to App. III)
V = Venetus Marc. gr. 573 (numbers refer to App. IV)

fol. 235ᵛ **1*** Διάλογος στηλιτευτικὸς γενάμενος περὶ πιστῶν καὶ ὀρθοδόξων καὶ πόθον καὶ ζῆλον Θεοῦ ἐχόντων πρὸς ἔλεγχον τῶν ἐναντίων τῆς πίστεως καὶ τῆς διδασκαλίας τῶν ἁγίων καὶ ὀρθοδόξων πατέρων.
Inc.: Ναβουθὲ ὁ Ἰσραηλίτης ἵνα μὴ τὸν πατρῷον ἀμπελῶνα . . .
fol. 239 desin.: . . . σὺν τῷ ἀνάρχῳ αὐτοῦ πατρὶ καὶ τῷ ζῳοποιῷ αὐτοῦ πνεύματι, νῦν καὶ ἀεί . . . ἀμήν.
CPG 8121 Iohannes Hierosolym.(?), *Adversus Iconoclastas*, *PG* 96, 1347–61 = *PG* 109, 499–516.

2* Συνοδικὸν Ἰωάννου ἀρχιεπισκόπου Ἱεροσολύμων στηλιτεῦον τοὺς κατὰ τὴν ἄοικον καὶ ἀκέφαλον ψευδώνυμον ἑβδόμην σύνοδον.
Inc.: Πιστεύω εἰς ἕνα Θεὸν πατέρα παντοκράτορα . . .
fol. 245ᵛ desin.: . . . συνόδων καὶ μὴ μετὰ τῆς ἀκεφάλου ταύτης.
CPG 8114 Iohannes Hierosolym., *De sacris imaginibus contra Constantinum Caballinum*, *PG* 95, 309–44.
M **7ᴹ**.

3* Τοῦ ἁγίου Γερμανοῦ.
Inc.: Τὴν καλὴν παραθήκην φυλάττοντες τῶν πανευφήμων . . .
fol. 246 desin.: . . . Θεοῦ ἀπολαύοντας παντοίας θαυματουργίας.
CPG 8005 Germanus I CPolitanus, *Confessio fidei de imaginibus*, ed. Darrouzès, "Deux textes inédits du Patriarche Germain," 9–11.
M **12ᴹ**.

4* Τοῦ ἁγίου Γρηγορίου Νύσης. Περὶ τριάδος, ὅτι ὁμοούσιος καὶ ὅτι τρεῖς ὑποστάσεις καὶ μία θεότης.
Inc.: Ἐκ τοῦ καθ᾽ ἡμᾶς ἐστι γνῶναι καὶ τὰ ὑπὲρ ἡμῶν ἡμᾶς . . .
desin.: . . . ἐν τῷ τὸν νοῦν ἔχειν καὶ λόγον καὶ πνεῦμα.
CPG 1781 Gregorius Thaumaturgus, *De deitate et tribus personis*. See Appendix I, quotation **240**, fol. 226ᵛ.

5* Τοῦ αὐτοῦ ἐκ τοῦ γ´ λόγου τοῦ εἰς προσευχὴν τοῦ εὐαγγελίου.

Inc.: Ὧν γὰρ ἡ ἐνέργεια μία τούτων καὶ ἡ δύναμις . . .
fol. 246ᵛ desin.: . . . καὶ ἐνέργειαν διαφορὰν ἐξευρίσκομεν.
CPG 3160 Gregorius Nyss., De oratione dominica orationes v, ed. J. F. Callahan, Gregorii
Nysseni opera VII,2 (Leiden-New York-Cologne, 1992), 41.6–10; PG 44, 1160A.
Doctrina Patrum (chap. IB), p. 76.8–10, XVI.

6* Τοῦ αὐτοῦ ἐκ τῆς προσευχῆς (sic) Εὐστάθιον ἐπιστολῆς περὶ τῆς ἁγίας τριάδος.
Inc.: Ἐὰν ἴδωμεν διαφερούσας τὰς ἐνεργείας . . .
desin.: . . . τῆς φύσεως συλλογίζεσθαι.
CPG 3137 Gregorius Nyss., Ad Eustathium de sancta trinitate, ed. F. Müller, Gregorii
Nysseni opera, III,1 (Leiden, 1958), 11.4–15; PG 32, 692D–695A.
Doctrina Patrum (chap. IB), p. 76.16–19, XVIII.

7* Τοῦ αὐτοῦ ἐκ τοῦ κατὰ Ἀπολιναρίου λόγου.
Inc.: Ὁ γὰρ εἰπὼν ὅτι μὴ τὸ ἐμόν . . .
desin.: . . . διὰ τὴν κοινωνίαν τῆς φύσεως.
CPG 3144 Gregorius Nyss., Antirrheticus adversus Apollinarium, ed. F. Müller, ibid.,
181.23–27; PG 45, 1196A.
Doctrina Patrum (chap. IZ), p. 116.1–3, IV.

8* Ἀμβροσίου ἐπισκόπου Μεδιολάνων ἐκ τῆς πρὸς Γρατιανὸν τὸν βασιλέα ἐπιστολῆς.
Inc.: Καὶ γὰρ ἑκατέρας μετέχει . . .
desin.: . . . υἱὸς ἀνθρώπου λέγεται (sic) ὁ παθών.
CPL 150 Ambrosius Mediol., De fide II 7, 58, ed. O. Faller, Sancti Ambrosii opera, CSEL
78, 76.46–49; PL 16, 571B (Viae Dux, CCSG 8, X.2, 5, 52–56).
Doctrina Patrum (chap. H), p. 56.13–17, VII.

9* Εἰρηναίου ἐπισκόπου Λουγδόνων τῆς Γαλλίας· κατὰ Βαλεντίνου.
Inc.: Ὥσπερ γὰρ ἡ κιβωτὸς κεχρυσωμένη . . .
desin.: . . . τὸ περιφανὲς τῶν φύσεων ἀποδειχθῇ.
CPG 1315.3 Irenaeus Lugdunensis, Fragmenta varia graeca = Frag. 8. Est Hippolyti
Commentarii in Reges (cf. CPG 1881.2), PG 7, 1233A (Viae Dux, CCSG 8, X.1, 2.185–90).

10* Ἀμφιλοχίου ἐπισκόπου Ἰκονίου ἐκ τῆς πρὸς Σελεύκιον (sic) ἐπιστολῆς.
Inc.: Ἐὰν εἴπωσιν ὡς μιᾶς οὐσίας . . .
desin.: . . . ἢ γὰρ ἀπαθὲς ὅλον ἢ παθητόν.
CPG 3245.15 Amphilochius Icon., Fragmentum xv (f) (epistula ad Seleucum), ed. C. Datema, Amphilochii Opera, 263.2; PG 39, 113C.

11* Πρόκλου ἀρχιεπισκόπου Κωνσταντινουπόλεως ἐκ τῆς ὁμιλίας τῆς ῥηθείσης ἐν
Πουλχεριάναις μετὰ τὸ γενέθλιον.
Μορφή, μορφὴν προσέλαβε καὶ ἡ τριὰς οὐκ ἐπλεόνασεν εἰς τετράδα, δύο φύσεων
ἕνωσις καὶ ἑνὸς υἱοῦ τόκος, λόγου καὶ σαρκὸς ἀσύγχυτος ἕνωσις.
CPG 5802 Proclus Const., Homilia III. De incarnatione Domini (BHG 1914d), PG 65,
705D–706A.

12* Τοῦ αὐτοῦ ἐν τῇ τεσσαρακοστῇ.
Inc.: Οὗτος γὰρ ἀληθὴς Θεὸς καὶ ἀψευδὴς ἄνθρωπος . . .
fol. 247 desin.: . . . κἂν Ἕλληνες διασπαράττονται.
CPG 5822 Proclus Const., Homilia XXIII. De dogmate incarnationis, PG 65, 842C.
Doctrina Patrum (chap. Z), pp. 48.15–49.6, V.

13* Ἰωάννου ἀρχιεπισκόπου Κωνσταντινουπόλεως ἐκ τῆς πρὸς Καισάρειον μονάζοντα ἐπιστολῆς.
Inc.: Ἀγαπητὲ εἰς τὸ προκείμενον ἐπανέλθωμεν . . .
desin.: . . . τῆς σῆς ἀγάπης θαυμάσιε.
CPG 4530 Iohannes Chrys., *Epistula ad Caesarium, PG* 52, 760.
Doctrina Patrum (chap. B), p. 19.10–24, XXVIII.

14* Γρηγορίου ἐπισκόπου Νύσης ἐκ τοῦ εἰς τὸ Πάσχα λόγου.
Inc.: Ἐν τῷ καιρῷ τῆς κατὰ τὸ πάθος οἰκονομίας . . .
fol. 247ᵛ desin.: . . . τῶν/ διαιρεθέντων ἑνώσεως.
CPG 3175 Gregorius Nyss., *De tridui inter mortem et resurrectionem Domini nostri I.C. spatio,* ed. E. Gebhardt, *Gregorii Nysseni opera* IX (Leiden, 1967), 293.8–294.4; *PG* 46, 617A.
Doctrina Patrum (chap. Z), p. 54.6–7, XXI.

15* Τοῦ ἁγίου Βασιλείου ἐπισκόπου Καισαρείας Καππαδοκείας. Μαρτυρίαι περὶ τῶν ἐν τοῖς ἁγίοις οἴκοις εἰκόνων.
Inc.: Πρότερον μὲν τῶν ἁγίων οἱ θάνατοι, καὶ μετὰ βραχέα· ἀνάστητέ μοι . . .
desin.: . . . καὶ ὁ τῶν παλαισμάτων ἀγωνοθέτης Χριστός.
CPG 2861 Basilius Caesariensis, *In Barlaam martyrem,* (*BHG* 223) *PG* 31, 489A–B.
A XIII 80B–D; Dam. I 34; II 30; III 46.
V **24.**

16* Τοῦ αὐτοῦ ἐκ τοῦ λόγου τοῦ εἰς τοὺς τεσσαράκοντα μάρτυρας.
Inc.: Δεῦρο οὖν εἰς μέσον αὐτοὺς ἀγαγόντες διὰ τῆς . . .
desin.: . . . ταῦτα γραφικὴ σιωπῇ διὰ τῆς μιμήσεως δείκνυσιν.
CPG 2863 Basilius Caes., *In XL martyres Sebastenses, PG* 31, 508D–509A; Thümmel, *Frühgeschichte,* 287.
A XII 1014E; 1066D–E/ XIII 277B–C; 300C.
Dam. I 44, 46; II 40, 43; III 106.
Doctrina Patrum (chap. ME), p. 329.12–13, XIII.
M **53ᴹ**; V **23.**

17* Τοῦ αὐτοῦ ἐκ τῆς ἐπιστολῆς τῆς πρὸς Ἰουλιανὸν τὸν βασιλέα καὶ παραβάτην.
Inc.: Κατὰ τὴν θεόθεν ἐπικεκληρωμένην ἡμῖν ἀμώμητον . . .
desin.: . . . πάσαις ταῖς ἐκκλησίαις ἡμῶν τούτων ἀνιστορουμένων.
CPG 2900 Basilius Caes., *Epistula 360,* ed. Y. Courtonne, *Saint Basile, Lettres,* III (Paris, 1966), 200; *PG* 32, 1100B.
A XII 1066C–D/ XIII 72E–73A.
M **14ᴹ.**

18* Τοῦ αὐτοῦ ἐκ τοῦ λόγου τοῦ περὶ ὀργῆς.
Inc.: Τῷ ὄντι φύσιν τῆς εἰκόνος ἐστί . . .
desin.: . . . δεικνύουσα τὴν ὁμοίωσιν.
CPG 2859 Basilius Caes., *De fide, PG* 31, 468A–B.
V **7.**

fol. 248 **19*** Τοῦ αὐτοῦ ἐκ τοῦ λόγου τοῦ κατὰ Σαβελλιανῶν καὶ Ἀρείου καὶ τῶν Ἀνομοίων.

Inc.: Μάχεται Ἰουδαϊσμὸς Ἑλληνισμῷ καὶ ἀμφότεροι Χριστιανισμῷ. Καὶ μεθ᾽ ἕτερα· ἀλλ᾽ ὁ τῆς ἀληθείας λόγος . . .
desin.: . . . τὴν τιμὴν ἐβεβαίωσε διὰ τῆς τούτου ὁμολογίας.
CPG 2869 Basilius Caes., Contra Sabellianos et Arium et Anomaeos, PG 31, 605D–608A.
A XIII 72A-B; Dam. I 48; II 44 in scholio.

20* Ἑλλαδίου τοῦ μαθητοῦ αὐτοῦ καὶ διαδόχου τῆς ἱεραρχίας αὐτοῦ ἐκ τοῦ βίου αὐτοῦ.
Inc.: Παρειστήκει ὁ ἅγιος Βασίλειος τῇ τῆς δεσποίνης εἰκόνι . . .
desin.: . . . μετ᾽ οὐ πολὺ δὲ τὸ δόρυ ἠ[γ]μαγμένον κατέχοντα.
Dam. I 60; II 56; III 53.
V 25.

21* Τοῦ ἁγίου Γρηγορίου τοῦ Θεολόγου ἐκ τῶν ἐπῶν, περὶ ἀρετῆς λόγου καὶ εἰς Πολέμωνα.
Inc.: Θεὸν τὸν πάντων αἴτιον πρῶτον καλῶ· οὐδ᾽ ὁ Πολέμων . . .
desin.: . . . καὶ τοῦτο πολλοῖς οἶδα τῶν λαλουμένων.
CPG 3035 Gregorius Naz., Carmina moralia 1–40, PG 37, 737–38; Thümmel, Frühgeschichte, 290–91.
A XIII 13B–C; Dam. III 109.
V 9.

22* Τοῦ αὐτοῦ ἐκ τῶν αὐτῶν ἐπῶν τοῦ εἰς ἐπισκόπου λόγου.
Ζωγράφος ἐστὶν ἄριστος, ὃς ἐν πινακέεσσι χαράσσει μορφὰς ἀτρεκέας ἔμπνοα δερκομένας.
CPG 3036 Gregorius Naz., Carmina de se ipso 1–99, PG 37, 1262A.
V 26a.

23*: see **21*** Τοῦ αὐτοῦ περὶ παρθενίας λόγου.
Εἰκόνα μὲν γράψ᾽ ἕν (sic) τις ἀπ᾽ εἰκόνος ἀντὶ χερείων καὶ πλάστης ἐτύπωσε ἐοικότα πλάσματα μορφαῖς.
CPG 3035 Gregorius Naz., Carmina moralia, PG 37, 558A.
V 27.

24* Τοῦ αὐτοῦ ἐκ τοῦ δευτέρου λόγου τοῦ περὶ υἱοῦ.
Inc.: Οἱ τὰς μορφὰς γράφοντες καὶ τὰ γράμματα—κἀκεῖθεν χειραγωγουμένους.//εἰκόνος . . .
desin.: . . . τοῦ ἀρχετύπου καὶ οὗ λέγεται.
CPG 3010.30 Gregorius Naz., Oratio 30, ed. Gallay, Discours 27–31, 246 par. 11.15–17; 268 par. 20.23–24; PG 36, 116C15–117A1; 129B7–8.
Dam. III 64.
Doctrina Patrum (chap. ME), p. 326.23–25, III.
V 26.

25* ⟨Βασιλείου Καισαρείας⟩
Inc.: ⟨ . . . ⟩ λέγεται καὶ ἡ τοῦ βασιλέως εἰκών . . .
fol. 248ᵛ desin.: . . . τῆς ὑπάρξεως ἀρρήτου φυλασσομένου.
CPG 2839 Basilius Caes., De Spiritu Sancto, ed. Pruche, Saint-Esprit, 406 par. 45.15–408 par. 46.9; PG 32, 149B–152B.
A. XIII 69D–E; Dam. I 35; II 31; III 48.

Doctrina Patrum (chap. A), p. 4.1–4, XI; (chap. ME), p. 329.14–16, XIV.
V 8.

26* Ἰγνατίου ἀρχιεπισκόπου Ἀντιοχείας καὶ μάρτυρος ἐκ τῆς πρὸς Φιλιππισίους.
Inc.: Εἷς πατὴρ καὶ εἷς υἱὸς καὶ εἷς παράκλητος . . .
desin.: . . . ἀληθῶς καὶ ηὐξήθη, ἀληθῶς ἔφαγε καὶ ἔπιεν.
CPG 1026 Ignatius Antioch., *Epistulae interpolatae et epistulae suppositiciae*, ed. F. X. Funk–F. Diekamp, *Patres Apostolici* II (Tübingen 1913), 146.17–150.1; *PG* 5, 921B–924A.

27* Γρηγορίου ἐπισκόπου Ναζιανζοῦ ἐκ τοῦ περὶ βαπτίσματος,
Inc.: Ἐπὶ πᾶσι καὶ πρὸ πάντων φύλασσέ μοι . . .
fol. 249 desin.: . . . μετρῆσαι τὸ φῶς ἐνιζόμενον.
CPG 3010.40 Gregorius Naz., *Oratio* 40, ed. Moreschini, *Discours 38–41*, 292 par. 41.1–294 par. 41.24; *PG* 36, 417A–C (cf. *Doctrina Patrum*, p. 189.13–16).

Post διάφοροι P add.:

Ὅτι ὧν ἡ ἐνέργεια μία τούτων καὶ ἡ οὐσία μία καὶ ἡ βούλησις μία, καὶ ὧν αἱ φύσεις διάφοροι, τούτων καὶ αἱ ἐνέργειαι διάφοροι. Ἐξ ὧν συνάγεται τὸ μίαν εἶναι τῆς παναγίας Τριάδος τὴν οὐσίαν, πρὸς ἀνατροπὴν τῆς Ἀρείου καὶ Εὐνομίου κακοδοξίας, οἵτινες τὸ ὁμοούσιον ἀρνούμενοι τὸ ἀνόμοιον ἐπὶ τῶν τριῶν πρεσβεύουσιν ὑποστάσεων.

28* Κυρίλλου ἀρχιεπισκόπου Ἀλεξανδρείας ἐκ τοῦ αʹ βιβλίου τῶν θησαυρῶν (in marg.: κεφάλαιον ιδʹ).
Inc.: Τὰ ἑτερογενῆ τε καὶ ἑτεροφυῆ . . .
desin.: . . . ἀποδώσει τὴν ἐνέργειαν.
CPG 5215 Cyrillus Alex., *Thesaurus de sancta et consubstantiali Trinitate*, PG 75, 241B.
Doctrina Patrum (chap. IB), p. 74.1–3, II.
(*Viae Dux*, CCSG 8, VIII. 1.62–63).

29* Τοῦ αὐτοῦ ἐκ τοῦ δευτέρου βιβλίου τῶν θησαυρῶν κεφ. λβʹ.
Inc.: Ὅτι τὰ κατὰ φύσιν τῆς ἀλλήλων . . .
desin.: . . . πρὸς ἐμφέρειαν οὐσιώδη καλῶς ἀπηκριβωμένος.
CPG 5215 Cyrillus Alex., *Thesaurus*, PG 75, 557A2–14.

30* Τοῦ αὐτοῦ ἐκ τοῦ δευτέρου βιβλίου τοῦ εἰς τὸ κατὰ Ἰωάννην.
fol. 249ᵛ Inc.: Ἐνεργήσει γὰρ ὁμοίως τά . . .
desin.: . . . ἐνεργείας τρόπος οὐχ ὁ αὐτός.
CPG 5208 Cyrillus Alex., *Commentarii in Iohannem*, PG 73, 349C.
Doctrina Patrum (chap. IB), p. 74.8–10, V.

31* Τοῦ αὐτοῦ ἐκ τοῦ αʹ βιβλίου τῶν θησαυρῶν, κεφ. ιʹ.
Inc.: Τὰ τὴν αὐτὴν ἐνέργειαν ἔχοντα . . .
desin.: . . . τὸ ἀλλήλοις κατὰ πάντα προσεοικέναι.
CPG 5215 Cyrillus Alex., *Thesaurus*, PG 75, 105A.
Doctrina Patrum (chap. IB), p. 73.23–24, I. See also quotation **28***.

32* Τοῦ αὐτοῦ ἐκ τοῦ γʹ λόγου πρὸς Ἑρμείαν.
Inc.: Φύσεις γὰρ ἀλλήλαις εἰς διαφοράν . . .

desin.: . . . κατ᾽ ἐνέργειαν οὐχ ὁμοίως ἔχειν.
CPG 5216 Cyrillus Alex., *De sancta trinitate dialogi vii, PG* 75, 797D.
Doctrina Patrum (chap. IB), p. 74.11–12, VI.

33* Τοῦ ἁγίου Βασιλείου ἐπισκόπου Καισαρείας ἐκ τῆς πρὸς Ἀμφιλόχιον ἀποκρίσεως.
In marg.: κεφάλαιον η´.
Inc.: Ὁ ἑωρακὼς ἐμὲ ἑώρακε τὸν πατέρα . . .
desin.: . . . τῷ πατρὶ καὶ υἱῷ θεωρεῖται.
CPG 2839 Basilius Caes., *De Spiritu Sancto,* ed. Pruche, *Saint-Esprit,* 318 par. 21.1–5;
PG 32, 105B.
Doctrina Patrum (chap. IZ), p. 115.18–20, III.

34* Τοῦ αὐτοῦ ἐκ τοῦ γ´ λόγου κατὰ Εὐνομίου.
Inc.: Εἰ πάντα ἐνεργεῖ Θεός—εἶναι δεῖ καὶ τὰς ἐνεργείας. Καὶ μετὰ βραχέα. πῶς ἑτερό-
της οὐσίας . . .
desin.: . . . ταυτότης ἐνεργείας εὑρίσκεται;
CPG 2837 Basilius Caes., *Adv. Eunomium libri v, PG* 29, 717B; 721A.
Doctrina Patrum (chap. IB), p. 75.18–19, XIII (= Εἰ—ἐνεργείας).

35* Τοῦ αὐτοῦ ἐκ τῆς εἰς τὸν α´ ψαλμὸν ὁμιλίας.
Inc.: Διατί, φησίν, ὁ προφήτης ἄνδρα . . .
desin.: . . . τούτων αἱ ἐνέργειαι αἱ αὐταί.
CPG 2836 Basilius Caes., *Homiliae super psalmos, PG* 29, 216D.
Doctrina Patrum (chap. IB), p. 76.6–7, XV.

36* Τοῦ ἁγίου Γρηγορίου ἐπισκόπου Ναζιανζοῦ ἐκ τοῦ περὶ θεολογίας σχεδιασθέντος
λόγου α´.
Inc.: Τηρεῖτο (sic) δ᾽ ἂν ὡς ὁ ἐμὸς λόγος, εἷς μὲν Θεός . . .
fol. 250 desin.: . . . καὶ βούλημα καὶ τὴν τῆς οὐσίας ταυτότητα.
CPG 3010.20 Gregorius Naz., *Oratio* 20, ed. Mossay, *Discours 20–30,* 70 par. 7.1–5; *PG*
35, 1073A.
Doctrina Patrum (chap. A), p. 3.11–18, X.

37* Τοῦ αὐτοῦ περὶ υἱοῦ λόγου β´.
Inc.: Ἐπειδὴ δὲ ὡς παρὰ τοῦ προλαβόντος . . .
desin.: . . . μία θεότης οὕτω καὶ βούλησις.
CPG 3010.30 Gregorius Naz., *Oratio* 30, ed. Gallay, *Discours 27–31,* 250 par. 12.13–20;
PG 36, 117D–120A.
Doctrina Patrum (chap. IZ), p. 115.10–12, I.

38* Τοῦ αὐτοῦ ἐκ τῆς πρὸς Κληδόνιον ἐπιστολῆς.
Inc.: Φύσεις μὲν γὰρ δύο . . .
desin.: . . . ἀμφότερα ἐν τῇ συγκράσει.
CPG 3032 Gregorius Naz., *Epistulae,* ed. P. Gallay, *Grégoire de Nazianze, Lettres théo-
logiques, SC* 208 (Paris, 1974), 44.19–21; *PG* 37, 180A.
Doctrina Patrum (chap. B), p. 11.6–7, I. Also quotation **130.**

39* Τοῦ αὐτοῦ ἐκ τοῦ λόγου τοῦ εἰς τὰ θεοφάνια.
Inc.: Ἀπεστάλη μέν, ἀλλ᾽ ὡς ἄνθρωπος . . .
desin.: . . . νόμῳ ἀνθρωπείου σώματος.

CPG 3010.38 Gregorius Naz., *Oratio* 38, ed. Moreschini, *Discours 38–41*, 358 par. 15.1–3; *PG* 36, 328C.
Doctrina Patrum (chap. Z), p. 52.1–3, X.

Post σώματος P add.:

> ἀπώχρει (sic) ταῦτα πρὸς τὸ δεῖξαι σαφῶς ὅτι, ὥσπερ μία τῆς ἁγίας Τριάδος ἡ οὐσία, οὕτω καὶ μία δύναμις καὶ μία ἐνέργεια καὶ μία βούλησις· οὐ γὰρ σκοπὸς ἡμῖν πρὸς μῆκος τὸν λόγον ἐκτεῖναι, ἀλλὰ διὰ βραχέων τοὺς ἐντυγχάνοντας πρὸς τὴν τῶν ἱερῶν τῆς ἐκκλησίας διδασκάλων εὐσεβῆ παράδοσιν· [lacuna]
> 5 εἰρήσεται δὲ λοιπὸν καὶ περὶ τῆς θείας ἐνανθρωπήσεως, ἤγουν τῆς κατὰ σάρκα τοῦ Θεοῦ λόγου οἰκονομίας καὶ ὅπως δεῖ περὶ τῆς ἑνώσεως δοξάζειν, καὶ ὅτι ἐκ δύο φύσεων καὶ ἐν δύο φύσεσιν ὁ Κύριος ἡμῶν Ἰησοῦς ὁ Χριστὸς ὑπὸ τῶν θεοπνεύστων τῆς ἀποστολικῆς ἐκκλησίας διδασκάλων κηρύττεται ἀδιαιρέτως καὶ ἀδιασπάστως, ἀτρέπτως τε καὶ ἀσυγχύτως.

40* Κυρίλλου ἐπισκόπου Ἀλεξανδρείας· ἐκ τοῦ προσφωνητικοῦ πρὸς Θεοδόσιον τὸν βασιλέα λόγου.
Inc.: Τὸν Θεοῦ μεσίτην— (fol. 250ᵛ) ἐν πολλοῖς ἀδελφοῖς. Καὶ μετ᾽ ὀλίγα· Γεγένηται γὰρ κατ᾽ ἀλήθειαν—παραδόξως συναδόμενος (sic). Καὶ μεθ᾽ ἕτερα· Πανταχόθεν οὖν ἄρα . . .
desin.: . . . καὶ οὐ φύσεως παρατροπή.
CPG 5218 Cyrillus Alex., *Oratio ad Theodosium imp. de recta fide. ACO* I,1,1, 52.19–28; 57.14–18; 72.15–23; *PG* 76, 1157A, 1168B, 1200B.
Doctrina Patrum (chap. Z), pp. 47.21–48.4, I–III.

41* Τοῦ αὐτοῦ ἐκ τῆς πρὸς Σουκένσον α΄ ἐπιστολῆς.
Inc.: Ὅταν οὖν ἐννοοῦμεν τοῦτο . . .
fol. 251 desin.: . . . ἰδίαν ἐποιήσατο σάρκα.
Sequitur scholium: Σημειωτέον ὅτι ἐνταῦθα—καὶ ἀδιαιρέτους ἐσήμανεν. = *Doctrina Patrum*, p. 16.3–9.
CPG 5345 Cyrillus Alex., *Epistula* 45, *Ad Successum episc. Diocaesareae. ACO* I,1,6, 153.20–154.11; *PG* 77, 232D.
Doctrina Patrum (chap. B), p. 16.1–2, XIX.

42* Τοῦ αὐτοῦ ἐκ τῆς β΄ πρὸς Σουκένσον ἐπιστολῆς.
Inc.: Εἰ μὲν γὰρ μίαν εἰπόντες—ῥάβδον ἑαυτοῖς ὑποστήσαντες. Καὶ μετ᾽ ὀλίγα. Ὀρθότατα δὲ καὶ πάνυ συνετῶς . . .
desin.: . . . ἡ αὐτοῦ γὰρ πέπονθε σάρξ.
Scholium: Σημειωτέον· Καὶ νῦν—δύο εἶναι φύσεις. (= *Doctrina Patrum*, p. 17.2–6).
CPG 5346 Cyrillus Alex., *Epist.* 46, *Ad Successum. ACO* I,1,6, 160.19–24; 161.4–8; *PG* 77, 244A,B.
Doctrina Patrum (chap. B), pp. 16.10–17.8, XX, XXI.

43* Τοῦ ἁγίου Γρηγορίου ἐπισκόπου Νύσης ἐκ τοῦ περὶ θεότητος λόγου καὶ εἰς τὸν Ἀβραάμ.
Inc. Οἷόν τι πάσχουσι πρὸς τοὺς πολυανθεῖς τῶν λειμόνων (sic). Καὶ μεθ᾽ ἕτερα· εἶδον πολλάκις ἐπὶ γραφῆς . . .
desin.: . . . περιηγμένας ἔχων εἰς τοὐπίσω τὰς χεῖρας.
CPG 3192 Gregorius Nyss., *De deitate Filii et Spiritus Sancti, PG* 46, 572C.

A XII 1066b/ XIII 9c–d; 117a. Dam. I 52; II 48; III 50.
Doctrina Patrum (chap. ME), p. 328.27–31, X.

44* Τοῦ αὐτοῦ ἐκ τῆς ἑρμηνείας τοῦ ᾄσματος τῶν ἀσμάτων.
Inc.: Κατὰ τὴν ζωγραφικὴν ἐπιστήμην, ὕλη πάντως ἐστί . . .
desin.: . . . ὃ διὰ τῶν χρωμάτων ὁ τεχνίτης ἀνέδειξεν.
CPG 3158 Gregorius Nyss., *Hom. xv, In Canticum canticorum*, ed. H. Langerbeck, *Gregorii Nysseni opera vi* (Leiden, 1960), 28.7–17; *PG* 44, 776a.
A XII 1066b–c.
M 42ᴹ.

45* Τοῦ αὐτοῦ ἐκ τοῦ α´ πρὸς Εὐνόμιον λόγου.
Inc. (a) Ἐν τῇ τῶν ὁμοίων συμφωνίᾳ—ἀγούσης τὸ ὅμοιον θεωρεῖται. (b) οὐδὲ γὰρ δυνατόν ἐστιν—τοῦ ὁρατοῦ φαινόμενον. (P add.: ἐν ἄλλῳ δὲ ὁ κατὰ ἀλήθειαν (fol. 251ᵛ) ἄνθρωπος καὶ ἐν ἄλλῳ ἡ εἰκὼν φαίνεται) (c) καὶ ἄνθρωπος ὀνομάζεται ὁ διὰ τῆς μιμήσεως . . .
desin.: . . . τὸ ὁμοίωμα, ἀλλὰ τὸ ἀρχέτυπον τοῦ ὁμοιώματος.
CPG 3135 Gregorius Nyss., *Contra Eunomium libri*, ed. W. Jaeger, *Gregorii Nysseni opera*, I,1 (Leiden, 1960): (a) 180.1–3, (b) 180.9–10, (c) cf. 79.15–18.

46* Τοῦ αὐτοῦ ἐκ τοῦ ἀναπληρωματικοῦ κεφαλαίου.
Inc.: Κατὰ τὴν συνήθειαν οἱ τὰς εἰκόνας τῶν . . .
desin.: . . . καὶ λέγεται κατὰ συνήθειαν καὶ ἡ εἰκὼν βασιλεύς.
CPG 3154 Gregorius Nyss., *De opificio hominis*, *PG* 44, 136c5–11.
Dam. I 49; II 45.
M 54ᴹ.

47* Τοῦ αὐτοῦ ἐκ τοῦ ε´ κεφαλαίου τοῦ ἀναπληρωματικοῦ.
Inc.: Τὰς ἀνθρωπίνας μορφὰς διὰ χρωμάτων τινῶν . . .
desin.: . . . ὡς ἂν διενεχθῇ πρὸς τὸ ὁμοίωμα.
CPG 3154 Gregorius Nyss., *De opificio hominis*, *PG* 44, 137a5–10.
Dam. I 50; II 46.
M 55ᴹ.

48* Τοῦ αὐτοῦ ἐκ τοῦ ιϛ´ κεφ. τοῦ ἀναπληρωματικοῦ
Τὸν ἐπὶ τοῦ χαλκοῦ χαρακτῆρα Καίσαρα λέγει τὸ εὐαγγέλιον, δι᾽ οὗ μανθάνομεν κατὰ μὲν τὸ σχῆμα τὴν ὁμοίωσιν εἶναι τοῦ μεμορφωμένου πρὸς Καίσαρα, ἐν δὲ τῷ ὑποκειμένῳ τὴν διαφορὰν ἔχει.
CPG 3154 Gregorius Nyss., *De opificio hominis*, *PG* 44, 184a.

49* Τοῦ ἁγίου Γρηγορίου τοῦ Θαυματουργοῦ ἐκ τῆς ἑρμηνείας τῆς σοφίας Σολομῶντος.
Οἱ οὖν ἐναγεῖς καὶ ἀκάθαρτοι αἱρετικοί, μὴ ὁμολογοῦντες ὁμοούσιον τῷ πατρὶ τὸν υἱόν, οὐδὲ τὴν ἐν εἰκόνι γραφὴν αὐτοῦ τοῦ σαρκωθέντος Θεοῦ λόγου προσκυνεῖν θέλουσι· καὶ ἔστωσαν ἀνάθεμα καὶ τῆς τῶν Χριστιανῶν πίστεως ἀλλότριοι.
Locum non inveni.
V 22.

50* Τοῦ αὐτοῦ ὅρος συνοδικός.
Οἱ μὴ προσκυνοῦντες τὸν σταυρὸν τὸν τίμιον τοῦ Κυρίου Ἰησοῦ Χριστοῦ καὶ τὴν ἁγίαν ἐν εἰκόνι μορφὴν αὐτοῦ κατασπαζόμενοι ὡς Θεοῦ σαρκωθέντος καὶ οὐχ ὡς ἀνθρώπου ψιλοῦ, ἔστωσαν ἀνάθεμα.

Locum non inveni.
V **6.**

51* Τοῦ ἁγίου Γρηγορίου Νύσης ἐκ τοῦ λόγου τοῦ εἰς τὸ μακάριοι οἱ πτωχοί.
'Επὶ τῆς σωματικῆς εὐμορφίας τὸ μὲν πρωτότυπον κάλλος ἐν τῷ ζῶντί τε καὶ ὑφεστῶτι προσώπῳ ἐστί, δευτέρα δὲ ἡ μετὰ τοῦτο τὸ κατὰ μίμησιν τῆς εἰκόνος δεικνύμενον.
CPG 3161 Gregorius Nyss., *Orationes viii de beatitudinibus*, ed. J. F. Callahan, *Gregorii Nysseni opera* VII,2 (Leiden-New York-Köln, 1992), 80.23–26; *PG* 44, 1197B.
V **11.**

52* Τοῦ αὐτοῦ· ἐκ τῆς αὐτοῦ ἑρμηνείας.
Εἶδον ἐγὼ ἐν τοίχῳ πολλάκις γραφέντα θαύματα καὶ φοβοῦντα τὸ τῆς πείρας ἀ-γνοοῦντας, τῇ πείρᾳ τε τῆς βασάνου τὸ ἀφόρητον δεικνῦντας (sic)· οἶδε γὰρ καὶ γραφὴ σιωπῶσα λαλεῖν καὶ τὰ μέγιστα ὠφελεῖν.
Solum οἶδε—ὠφελεῖν desumptum de opere "De Sancto Theodoro" (*CPG* 3183, Gregorius Nyss., *De Sancto Theodoro*, ed. J. P. Cavarnos, *Gregorii Nysseni opera* X,1, 63.12–13; *PG* 46, 737D) est. Quod superest non inveni.
M **51ᴹ**; V **12.**

53* Τοῦ ἁγίου Ἰωάννου τοῦ Χρυσοστόμου ἐκ τοῦ λόγου εἰς Μελέτιον ἐπίσκοπον Ἀντιοχείας καὶ εἰς τὴν σπουδὴν τῶν συνελθόντων.
Inc.: Πανταχοῦ τῆς ἱερᾶς ταύτης ἀγέλης περιφέρω τοὺς ὀφθαλμούς. Καὶ μετὰ βραχέα· Καὶ ἦν εὐσεβείας διδασκαλία . . .
fol. 252 desin.: . . . τῆς ἀποδημίας ἔχειν τὴν παραμυθίαν.
CPG 4345 Iohannes Chrys., *De S. Meletio Antiocheno*, *PG* 50, 516A–B.
A XIII 8c–d. Dam. II 62.
M **26ᴹ**; V **10.**

54* Τοῦ αὐτοῦ ἐκ τοῦ λόγου τοῦ εἰς τὸν νιπτῆρα.
Inc.: Πάντα ἐγένοντο διὰ δόξαν Θεοῦ χρῆσιν δὲ ἡμετέραν . . .
desin.: . . . ἀλλὰ τὸν οὐράνιον χαρακτῆρα αἰδεῖται.
CPG 4216 Severianus Gabalensis, *Homilia de lotione pedum*, ed. A. Wenger, "Une homélie inédite de Sévérien de Gabala sur le lavement des pieds," *REB* 25 (1967), 226, 8.
A XII 1067A/XIII 68D–E. Dam. III 122.
M **41ᴹ**.

55* Τοῦ αὐτοῦ ἐκ τοῦ λόγου ὅτι παλαιᾶς καὶ καινῆς διαθήκης εἷς ὁ νομοθέτης καὶ εἰς τὸ ἔνδυμα τοῦ ἱερέως.
Inc.: Τῆς Χριστοῦ βασιλείας τὸ εὐαγγέλιον προκηρύττουσιν μὲν οἱ προφῆται. Καὶ μεθ' ἕτερα· ἐγὼ καὶ τὴν κηρόχυτον . . .
desin.: . . . Κύριε ἐν τῇ πόλει σου τὴν εἰκόνα αὐτῶν ἐξουδενώσεις.
CPG 4192 Severianus Gabalensis, *Homilia de legislatore*, *PG* 56, 407D.
A XIII 9A; 300D; 324C.
Dam. II 60; III 105.
M **24ᴹ**; V **30.**

56* Not in *TLG*.
Τοῦ αὐτοῦ εἰς τὴν τεσσαρακοστὴν καὶ περὶ μετανοίας.
Πολλὰς πολλάκις εἶδον εἰκόνας καὶ γραφέας ἐθεασάμην χρώμασι τὴν ἀλήθειαν μι-

μουμένους καὶ χειρὶ καὶ τέχνη διασύροντας ἅπερ ἡ φύσις ἤγαγε, τουτέστιν ἡ ἀ-
λήθεια.
Locum non inveni.
M 40ᴹ; V 31.

57* Τοῦ αὐτοῦ ἐκ τοῦ λόγου τοῦ εἰς τὴν γέννησιν τοῦ Κυρίου, οὗ ἡ ἀρχή· μυστήριον.
Inc.: Ἐπειδὴ γὰρ καταλιπόντες αὐτὸν οἱ ἄνθρωποι . . .
desin.: . . . λανθανόντως δὲ εἰς ἑαυτὸν λατρείαν ἀπενέγκηται.
CPG 4560 Iohannes Chrys., *In natalem Christi diem, PG* 56, 394.2–6.

58* Τοῦ αὐτοῦ ἐκ τῆς ἑρμηνείας τοῦ κατὰ Ἰωάννην εὐαγγελίου.
Inc.: ⟨Ὁ⟩ διὰ τῶν χαραγμάτων τῶν λευκῶν . . .
desin.: . . . τύπος καὶ ἡ εἰκὼν οὐκ ἀλλότριον τῆς ἀληθείας.
CPG 4425 Iohannes Chrys., *In Iohannem homiliae* 1–88, *PG* 59, 93.5–10.
V 29.

Post ἀληθείας P add.:

οὐκ οἶδας ὅτι, ἐὰν εἰκόνα τοῦ βασιλέως ὑβρίσῃς, εἰς τὸ πρωτότυπον τῆς ἀξίας φέρει
τὴν ὕβριν; οὐκ οἶδας ὅτι ἐὰν τὴν εἰκόνα τὴν ἀπὸ ξύλων κατασύρῃς, οὐχ ὡς εἰς
ἄψυχον ξύλον τολμήσας κρίνει, ἀλλ᾽ ὡς κατὰ βασιλέως· εἰκὼν γὰρ βασιλέως φέρει
τὴν ἑαυτῆς [lacuna] πρὸς τὸν βασιλέα.

Cf. Appendix III, **25ᴹ/ 39ᴹ**; App. IV, **41.**

59* Τοῦ αὐτοῦ ἐκ τῆς ἑρμηνείας τῆς πρὸς Ἑβραίους ἐπιστολῆς.
Inc.: Καὶ πῶς ἡ εἰκὼν τοῦ δευτέρου τὸ πρῶτον ὁ Μελχισεδέκ . . .
fol. 252ᵛ desin.: . . . καὶ τὴν νέαν τῶν πραγμάτων τύπον.
Dam. I 53; II 49; III 51. B. Kotter locum non invenit.

60* Ἐκ τοῦ βίου τοῦ ἁγίου Ἰωάννου Χρυσοστόμου·
Inc.: Ἠγάπα δὲ ὁ μακάριος Ἰωάννης—ἄγαν. Καὶ μετ᾽ ὀλίγα. Ἦν δὲ καὶ τὸ ἐκτύπωμα—
αὐτῷ ὁμιλῶν. Καὶ μεθ᾽ ἕτερα. Ὡς δὲ ἐπαύσατο ὁ Πρόκλος . . .
desin.: . . . ὅμοιός ἐστι τούτῳ, ὡς δὲ ὑπολαμβάνω καὶ αὐτός ἐστιν.
CPG 7979 Georgius Alex., *Vita s. Iohannis Chrysostomi (BHG* 873), ed. F. Halkin, *Douze
récits byzantins sur Saint Jean Chrysostome,* SubsHag 60 (Brussels, 1977), 142, 147.
Dam. I 61; II 57; III 54.
Doctrina Patrum (chap. ME), p. 330.1–12, XVI.
V 32.

61* Τοῦ ἁγίου Κυρίλλου Ἀλεξανδρείας· ἐκ τοῦ εἰς τὸν Ματθαῖον ἁγίου εὐαγγελίου.

Ζωγραφεῖ γὰρ ἡ πίστις τὸν ἐν μορφῇ Θεοῦ ὑπάρχοντα λόγον, ὃς τῆς ζωῆς ἡμῶν
λύτρωσις προσηνέχθη τῷ Θεῷ, τὴν καθ᾽ ἡμᾶς ὁμοίωσιν ὑποδὺς καὶ γενόμενος
ἄνθρωπος. Καὶ μετ᾽ ὀλίγα· Εἰκόνων ἡμῖν ἀποπληροῦσι χρείαν αἱ παραβολαί,
τὴν δύναμιν τῶν σημαινομένων, οἱονεί πως καὶ ὀφθαλμῶν παρενθέσεις (sic)
5 καὶ ἀφῇ χειρὸς ὑποβάλουσαι καὶ τὰ ἐν ἰσχναῖς ἐννοίαις ἀφανῶς ἔχοντα τὴν
θεωρίαν.

CPG 5206 Cyrillus Alex., *Commentarii in Matthaeum*. Fragmentum non invenitur apud J. Reuss, *Matthäus-Kommentare aus der griechischen Kirche, TU* 61 (Berlin, 1957), 153–269.

A XII 1067в.

62* Τοῦ αὐτοῦ ἐκ τῆς ἐπιστολῆς τῆς πρὸς Ἀκάκιον ἐπίσκοπον Σκυθοπόλεως περὶ τοῦ ἀποπομπαίου.

Inc.: Τοῖς παρὰ τῆς σῆς ὁσιότητος—ἥσθην ἄγαν. Καὶ μεθ᾽ ἕτερα. Φαμὲν οὖν ὅτι σκιὰ καί—ἀπαστράψει κάλλος. Καὶ μεθ᾽ ἕτερα. Γέγραπται τοίνυν—ἐπείραζε τὸν Ἀβραάμ. Καὶ μετέπειτα. ἀναστὰς δὲ τῷ πρωί—Ἰσαὰκ τὸν υἱὸν αὐτοῦ. Καὶ μεθ᾽ ἕ-τερα. Καὶ εἶπεν Ἀβραάμ—ἀναστρέψωμεν πρὸς ὑμᾶς. Καὶ μετ᾽ ὀλίγα. Καὶ ᾠκοδόμη-σεν ἐκεῖ Ἀβραάμ . . .

fol. 253 desin.: . . . ἐνὶ κατιδεῖν αὐτὸν ἄπαντα δρῶντα τὰ εἰρημένα.

CPG 5341 Cyrillus Alex., (*Ep.* 41), *ad Acacium episcopum Scythopolis*. *ACO* I,1,4, 40.3; 47.21–24; 47.30–31/35–36; 48.3–5; 48.7–22. *PG* 77, 217A, 220A–B. Cf. Thümmel, *Frühgeschichte*, 311.

A XIII 12в–13а.

63* Τοῦ αὐτοῦ ἐκ τοῦ λόγου τοῦ εἰς μάρτυρας.

Πάλιν μαρτυρικῆς ἀνδραγαθίας τὰ γνωρίσματα λάμπουσιν· εἶδον κατὰ τοῖχον γραφῆς ἐναθλοῦσαν τοῖς σκάμμασι κόρην καὶ οὐκ ἀδακρυτὶ τὴν θέαν κατώπτευσα· ταῦτα δέ μοι προὐξένησεν ἡ ἐντοιχογραφὴ (sic) διὰ χρωματουργίας τὴν ἀνδρίαν ὑφη-γουμένη τῆς μάρτυρος.

Locum non inveni. Cf. Thümmel, *Frühgeschichte*, 311.

M 50ᴹ; V 1.

64* Τοῦ αὐτοῦ ἐκ τοῦ ε´ βιβλίου πρὸς Ἑρμείαν.

Εἰκόνι μὲν πρὸς τὸ ἀκριβῶς ἀρχέτυπον, ἀρχετύπῳ δὲ αὖ πρὸς ἐμφερεστάτην εἰκόνα τὸ διαλλάττον οὐδέν, κατά γέ φημι τῷ ἐν ὁμοίῳ τε καὶ ὡς ἐν εἴδει ταὐτόν.

CPG 5216 Cyrillus Alex., *De sancta Trinitate dialogi vii*, *PG* 75, 944D6–10.

V 2.

65* Τοῦ αὐτοῦ ἐκ τῶν θησαυρῶν, τοῦ στ´ κεφαλαίου·

Πᾶν ὅπερ καθ᾽ ὁμοίωσιν γένοιτό τινος, ἀπολείπεται πάντως τῆς πρὸς τὸ πρωτότυπον ἰσότητος, τῆς δὲ ἐκείνου δόξης ἐστὶ δεύτερον, φέρει δ᾽ οὖν ὅμως τὴν ὁμοίωσιν τοῦ πρωτοτύπου.

CPG 5215 Cyrillus Alex., *Thesaurus*, *PG* 75, 76D.

V 3.

66* Τοῦ αὐτοῦ ἐκ τοῦ κατὰ αἱρετικῶν τῶν κατ᾽ Αἴγυπτον ἐπισκόπων.

Inc.: Περὶ Γεωργίου τοῦ ἀσεβοῦς, τοῦ γεωργήσαντος . . .

desin.: . . . πάντας ἀγχόνη παρέδωκεν.

Locum non inveni. Cf. Melioranskij, *Georgij*, XXVIII (M 1ᴹ)

V 4.

67* Τοῦ αὐτοῦ ἐκ τῶν θησαυρῶν ιβ´ κεφαλαίου.

Inc.: Ὥσπερ ἄν τις εἰς εἰκόνα διαγεγραμμένην ἄριστα βλέποι . . .

fol. 253ᵛ desin.: . . . καὶ τὸ τῆς γραφῆς ἐν ἐκείνῳ σῴζεται.

CPG 5215 Cyrillus Alex., *Thesaurus*, *PG* 75, 184D–185A.

V 28.

68* Τοῦ ἁγίου Ἀθανασίου περὶ τῆς ἐνανθρωπήσεως τοῦ Κυρίου.
Inc.: Ἱκανῶς μὲν ἐκ πολλῶν ὀλίγα λαβόντες ἐγράψαμεν. Ἔπειτα καὶ ταῦτα τὰ ἐν ξύλοις . . .
desin.: . . . οὐ καταβάλλεται, ἀλλ᾽ ἐν αὐτῇ συνιστορεῖται.
CPG 2091 Athanasius Alex., *Oratio de incarnatione Verbi*, ed. Ch. Kannengiesser, *Sur l'incarnation du Verbe*, SC 199 (Paris, 1973), 1.1 (p. 256.1–2); 14.1 (p. 314.1–4). *PG* 25, 96; 120c.
A XII 1067c.
Doctrina Patrum (chap. ΜΕ), p. 327.7–8, VII.

69* Τοῦ αὐτοῦ ἐκ τοῦ κατὰ Ἀρειανῶν.
Inc.: Ἐν τῇ εἰκόνι τοῦ βασιλέως τὸ εἶδος καὶ ἡ μορφή ἐστι . . .
desin.: . . . ἡ γὰρ ἐκείνου μορφὴ καὶ τὸ εἶδός ἐστιν ἡ εἰκών.
CPG 2093 Athanasius Alex., *Orationes contra Arianos iii*, *PG* 26, 332A–B.
A XII 69B–C; 273A. Dam. III 114.14–24.
M **52**^M; V **21.**

70* Τοῦ αὐτοῦ ἐκ τῆς πρὸς Ἀντίοχον Δοῦκα διαλέξεως καὶ ἐρωτήσεως, κεφάλαιον ρλζ΄.
Inc.: Τοῦ Θεοῦ διὰ τῶν προφητῶν ἐπιτρέποντος μὴ προσκυνεῖν . . .
fol. 254 desin.: . . . προσκυνοῦμεν καὶ ἀσπαζόμεθα οἱ πιστοί.
CPG 2257 Athanasius Alex., *Quaestiones ad Antiochum ducem*, ed. Thümmel, *Frühgeschichte*, 354–55; *PG* 28, 621A.
Dam. III 59.
Doctrina Patrum (chap. ΜΕ), pp. 327.9–328.23, VIII.

71* Τοῦ αὐτοῦ·
Inc.: Δεῦρο ἄρατε τοὺς ὀφθαλμοὺς τῆς διανοίας ὑμῶν . . .
fol. 254ᵛ desin.: . . . τὸ θαῦμα τοῦτο ἐν Βηρυτῷ τῇ πόλει γέγονεν.
CPG 2262 Ps.-Athanasius Alex., *Narratio de cruce seu imagine Berytensi*, *PG* 28, 805–12 (*BHG* 780–788b).
A XIII 24E–32A.
M **10**^M.

72* Ἐκ τοῦ βίου τοῦ ἁγίου ἱερομάρτυρος Παγκρατίου.
Inc.: Καί φησιν ὁ μακάριος Πέτρος, ὁ ἀπόστολος· τέκνον . . .
desin.: . . . τῶν παρ᾽ ἡμῶν εἰς αὐτοὺς κηρυχθέντων.
BHG 1410, 1400a. Evagrius ep., *Vita et passio Pancratii ap. ep. Tauromenii*, ed. H. Usener, *Kleine Schriften*, IV (Berlin-Leipzig, 1913), 418.

73* Παμφίλου ἱερομάρτυρος ἐκ τῆς ἐν Ἀντιοχείᾳ τῶν ἀποστόλων γενομένης συνόδου, τουτέστιν ἐκ τῶν συνοδικῶν κεφαλαίων τοῦ τετάρτου.
Inc.: Πρὸς τὸ μηκέτι πλανᾶσθαι εἰς εἴδωλα τοὺς σῳζομένους . . .
desin.: . . . μηδὲ ὁμοιοῦσθαι Ἰουδαίοις καὶ Ἕλλησιν.
Ed. F. X. Funk, *Didascalia et Constitutiones Apostolorum*, II (Paderborn, 1906), 144–46.
A XII 1018c.
M **37**^M; V **5.**

74* Ὑπατίου ἀρχιεπισκόπου Ἐφέσου ἐκ τῶν περὶ Ἰουλιανὸν ἐπ᾽ Ἀτραμυτίου συμμικτῶν ζητημάτων βιβλίου α΄ κεφ. ε΄· περὶ τῶν ἐν τοῖς ἁγίοις οἴκοις.

Inc.: Παρακινεῖν δὲ αὖθις, φῇς, τὴν θείαν παράδοσιν . . .

fol. 255ᵛ desin.: . . . καθόλου τὸ θεῖον ἢ ταὐτόν, ἢ ἴσον, ἢ ὅμοιον.

CPG 6806 Hypatius Ephesinus, *Quaestiones miscellaneae* (*fragmentum*), ed. F. Diekamp, *Analecta Patristica*, OCA 117 (Rome, 1938), 127–29. Cf. Thümmel, *Frühgeschichte*, 320–21.

75* Τοῦ ἁγίου Διονυσίου, ἐπισκόπου Ἀθηνῶν, ἐκ τοῦ λόγου τοῦ περὶ τελετῆς μύρου.

Inc.: Καθάπερ ἐπὶ τῶν αἰσθητῶν εἰκόνων . . .

desin.: . . . παρὰ τὸ τῆς οὐσίας διάφορον.

CPG 6601 Ps.-Dionysius Areopag., *De ecclesiastica hierarchia,* ed. Heil and Ritter, *Corpus Dionysiacum*, II, 96.5–9; *PG* 3, 473B–C.

Doctrina Patrum (chap. ME), p. 327.4–6, VI.

V 20.

76* Τοῦ αὐτοῦ ἐκ τῆς (sic) περὶ οὐρανίου ἱεραρχίας λόγου. (8 fragments).

Inc.: (a) Ὅτι μὲν εἰκότως προβέβληνται—καὶ ὑπερφυῶν θεαμάτων. καὶ αὖθις. (b) οὖν ἐκ πάντων—ἑτεροίως ἀπονενέμηται. (c) καὶ ἔστιν οὐκ ἀπᾳδούσας—(fol. 256) αἰσθητῶν ἰδιοτήτων ὁριζομένων. (d) οὐδὲν οὖν ἄτοπον—ὁμοιοτήτων ἀπαλλάττουσι (sic). (e) καὶ τῶν εἰς ἡμᾶς δέ—ἀγγέλων ὄργανα. (f) καὶ ὅλως οὐκ ⟨ἂν⟩ ἀπορήσειεν—ἀφανέσι τὰ φαινόμενα. (g) ἀρκεῖ δὲ τοῖς ἐχέφροσι—ὁμότροπον διασάφησιν. (h) ἔστι δὲ οὐ πᾶς ἱερός . . .

desin.: . . . ἐπεοικὼς καὶ ἀπεμφαίνων (sic) πλαττόμενος.

CPG 6600 Ps.-Dionysius Areopag., *De coelesti hierarchia,* ed. Heil and Ritter, *Corpus Dionysiacum*, II, 11: (a) 11.11–16; (b) 13.24–14.3; (c) 15.1–7; (d) 16.5–7; (e) 55.12–13; (f) 55.16–17; (g) 58.4–6; (h) 11.19–12.4. *PG* 3: (a) 140A7–14; (b) 141C5–9; (c) 144B8–C4; (d) 145A13–15; (3) 333C1–2; (f) 333C6–8; (g) 337C1–4; (h) 140B3–C4.

Frag. (a) = Dam. I 11.5–10; III 21.7–13.

V 20.

77* Τοῦ αὐτοῦ ἐκ τοῦ περὶ τῆς ἐκκλησιαστικῆς ἱεραρχίας λόγου. (2 fragments).

Inc.: (a) Ἡμεῖς οὖν αἰσθηταῖς εἰκόσι ἐπὶ τὰς θείας, ὡς δυνατόν, ἀναγόμεθα θεωρίας. (b) οἱ γὰρ πρῶτοι τῶν τῆς καθ' ἡμᾶς . . .

desin.: . . . κατὰ τοὺς ἱεροὺς ἡμῶν ἐδοῦσαν (sic) θεσμούς.

CPG 6601 Ps.-Dionysius Areopag., *De ecclesiastica hierarchia,* ed. Heil and Ritter, *Corpus Dionysiacum*, II, 65.14–15; 67.16–23, *PG* 3: (a) 373B2–3; (b) 376C10–D10.

Frag. (a) = Dam. I 32; II 28; III 44.

V 20.

78* Τοῦ αὐτοῦ ἐκ τῶν πρὸς Τιμόθεον κεφάλαιον βʹ ὅτι πρεπόντως τὰ θεῖα καὶ οὐράνια καὶ διὰ τῶν ἀνομοίων συμβόλων ἐμφαίνονται.

Inc.: Χρὴ τοιγαροῦν, ὡς οἶμαι, πρῶτον ἐκθέσθαι . . .

fol. 258 desin.: . . . εἶναι τὴν ἱεραρχίαν οἰόμεθα καὶ τὰ ἑξῆς.

CPG 6600 Ps.-Dionysius Areopag., *De coelesti hierarchia,* ed. Heil and Ritter, *Corpus Dionysiacum*, II, 9.16–16.16. *PG* 3, 136D1–145B12.

79* Τοῦ αὐτοῦ ἐκ τῆς περὶ οὐρανίου ἱεραρχίας. (2 fragments).

Inc.: Τίνες αἱ μορφωτικαί—(fol. 258ᵛ) ἀναλυτικῶς ἀνακάμπτωμεν. Καὶ μετ' ὀλίγα· ἀρκτέον δὲ τοῦ λόγου . . .

fol. 261 desin.: . . . τυπωτικαῖς φαντασίαις καὶ τὰ ἑξῆς.

CPG 6600 Ps.-Dionysius Areopag., *De coelesti hierarchia,* ed. Heil and Ritter, *Corpus*

Dionysiacum, II, 50.13 (cf. app. crit. 10 ff)–51.1; 51.22–59.7. *PG* 3, 325D1–328A7; 328D1–340B5.

80* Τοῦ αὐτοῦ ἐκ τοῦ περὶ ἐκκλησιαστικῆς ἱεραρχίας.
Ἀλλ᾽ αἱ μὲν αἱ περὶ ἡμᾶς οὐσίαι καὶ τάξεις, ὧν ἤδη μνήμην ἱερὰν ἐποιησάμην, ἀσώματοί τέ εἰσι καὶ νοητὴ καὶ ὑπερκόσμιός ἐστιν ἡ κατ᾽ αὐτὰς ἱεραρχία.
CPG 6601 Ps.-Dionysius Areopag., *De ecclesiastica hierarchia*, ed. Heil and Ritter, *Corpus Dionysiacum*, II, 65.7–10. *PG* 3, 373A7–9.
Dam. I 32, II 28; III 44.

81* Τοῦ ἁγίου Ἀναστασίου ἐπισκόπου Θεουπόλεως ἐπιστολὴ πρός τινας σχολαστικοὺς (sic), δι᾽ ἧς ἀπεκρίνατο πρὸς αὐτὸν πρὸς τὴν ἐνεχθεῖσαν παρ᾽ αὐτοῦ ἀπορίαν.
Inc.: Εἰ τῷ μόνον ἐπερωτήσαντι σοφίαν σοφία λογισθήσεται. Καὶ μεθ᾽ ἕτερα· Καὶ μηδεὶς προσκοπτέτω τῇ τῆς προσκυνήσεως . . .
desin.: . . . μήπω τῆς ἔνδον ἀναγνώσεως πεῖραν εἰληφώς.
CPG 6954 Anastasius I Antioch., *Epistula ad scholasticum* (*frag.*), *PG* 89, 1408A.
A XIII 56A–B.

82* Τοῦ αὐτοῦ ἐκ τῆς πρὸς Συμεῶνα, ἐπίσκοπον Βοστρῶν περιέχουσα περὶ Σαββάτου.
Inc.: Ὥσπερ ἀπόντος βασιλέως ἡ εἰκὼν αὐτοῦ . . .
desin.: . . . εἰς αὐτὸν ἐκεῖνον, οὗ ὁ τύπος, ἀναφέρει τὴν ὕβριν.
CPG 6955 Anastasius I Antioch., *Ad Symeonem Bostrensem* (*frag.*), *PG* 89, 1405 A6–B2.
A XIII 56E–57A. Dam. II 66; III 127.
V **13.**

83* Εὐσταθίου ἐπισκόπου Ἀντιοχείας ἐκ τοῦ λόγου τοῦ εἰς τὴν Σαμαρεῖτιν·
Ἡμεῖς οὖν ἀνακεκαλυμμένῳ προσώπῳ τὴν τοῦ Κυρίου ἐνοπτριζόμεθα παναγίαν σάρκα διὰ τῆς ἐν εἰκόνι μορφῆς· τὸ γοῦν τῆς ψυχῆς ὄμμα ἀθόλωτον ἔχοντες πρὸς τὸ [τῆς] πρωτότυπον καὶ τῆς εἰκόνος μόρφωμα προσβλέποντες δοξάζωμεν (sic) τὸ τῆς εἰκόνος ἀρχέτυπον.
CPG 3365 Eustathius Antioch., *In Samaritanum*, ed. M. Spanneut, *Recherches sur les écrits d'Eustathe d'Antioche avec une édition nouvelle des fragments dogmatiques et exégétiques* (Lille, 1948), 121 (frag. 74).
V **14.**

84* Sigla
P: Parisinus gr. 1115
V: Venetus Marc. gr. 573, fols. 5ᵛ–6

    Ἰωσίππου τοῦ ἁγιωτάτου ἐπισκόπου Νικομηδείας ἐκ τοῦ λόγου τοῦ ἐν τοῖς διωγμοῖς.
    Τοὺς ὑπὲρ Χριστοῦ χριστοπρεπῶς διαλάμψαντας καὶ τελείαν τὴν πρὸς αὐτὸν ἐνδειξαμένους ἀγάπην καὶ κατὰ τὸ⟨ν⟩ ἕως σαρκὸς καὶ αἵματος (P fol. 261ᵛ)
5 δι᾽ ὑπομονῆς διαπρέψαντας ⟨ἀγῶνα⟩, παντοίαις προσήκει γεραίρειν τιμαῖς· οὐ μόνον γὰρ τὸ ἀκούειν αὐτῶν τοὺς ἄθλους καὶ ζηλοῦν καλόν, ἀλλὰ καὶ οἱ χρωματικοῖς αὐτοὺς ἀπομορφωσάμενοι τύποις ὑ(V fol. 6)πογραμμὸν τῆς ἐκείνων ἀνδρείας αὐτοὺς ἑαυτοῖς καὶ τοῖς μετ᾽ αὐτοὺς περιέστησαν.

---

4 κατὰ τὸ⟨ν⟩ ἕως: κατὰτομὴ V, κατὰ τὸ ἕως P

Locum non inveni.

85* Τοῦ ἁγίου Ἀμβροσίου ἀρχιεπισκόπου Μεδιολάνων πρὸς Γρατιανὸν τὸν βασιλέα ἐκ τοῦ τρίτου βιβλίου, κεφάλαιον θ´.

Τί γὰρ μήποτε καὶ τὴν θεότητα καὶ τὴν σάρκα αὐτοῦ προσκυνοῦντες μερίζωμεν τὸν Χριστόν, ἢ ὅτε ἐν αὐτῷ τὴν θείαν εἰκόνα καὶ τὸν σταυρὸν προσκυνοῦμεν μερίζομεν αὐτόν; μὴ γένοιτο.

CPL 152 Ambrosius Mediol., *De incarnationis dominicae sacramento, PL* 16, 873ʙ (*CSEL* 79, chap. 7, 75.125–27).

A XII 1067ᴄ–ᴅ. Dam. III 116.

86* Τοῦ ἁγίου Ἐπιφανίου·

Μὴ γὰρ βασιλεὺς ἔχων εἰκόνα δύο βασιλεῖς εἰσιν; ἀλλ᾽ ὁ βασιλεὺς εἷς ἐστι καὶ μετὰ τῆς εἰκόνος. Τοῦ αὐτοῦ· καὶ γὰρ καὶ οἱ βασιλεῖς διὰ τὸ ἔχειν εἰκόνας οὐ δύο εἰσὶ βασιλεῖς, ἀλλὰ βασιλεὺς εἷς σὺν τῇ εἰκόνι.

CPG 3745 Epiphanius Const., *Panarion* (*Adversus haereses*), ed. K. Holl, *Panarion, GCS* 37 (Leipzig, 1933), 12.10–11.

A XII 1067ᴅ.

87* Βασιλείου ἐπισκόπου Σελευκείας ἐκ τῶν θαυμάτων τῆς πρωτομάρτυρος τοῦ Χριστοῦ Θέκλας εἰς τὸν Μυρσεῶνα.

Inc.: Συνέβη κατ᾽ ἐκεῖνον τὸν καιρὸν τὸν ἱερέα . . .

fol. 262 desin.: . . . εἰς τὸ μεταγραφῆναι τοῖς βηληθεῖσιν (sic).

CPG 6675 Basilius Seleuciensis, *De vita et miraculis s. Theclae libri ii* (*BHG* 1718n), ed. G. Dagron, *Vie et miracles de s. Thècle*, SubsHag 62 (Brussels, 1978), Appendix, 416.24– 417.56.

V **36.**

88* Ἐκ τοῦ βίου τοῦ ἁγίου Δοσιθέου μαθητοῦ τοῦ ἁγίου Δωροθέου.

Inc.: Ἦν δὲ οὗτος Διλικίνου (sic) στρατηλάτου διάγων—ἁγίους τόπους. Καὶ μετ᾽ ὀλίγα. Ὡς οὖν ἦλθον . . .

desin.: . . . ἀλλ᾽ ἐγένετο ἀφανής, ἦν γὰρ ἡ ἁγία θεοτόκος.

CPG 7360 Dorotheus Gazaeus, *Vita s. Dosithei* (*BHG* 2117–2119), ed. L. Regnault and J. de Préville, *Dorothée de Gaza, Oeuvres spirituelles, SC* 92 (Paris, 1963), 124 par. 3.1– 126 par. 3.53.

89* Τοῦ ἁγίου Μεθοδίου ἐπισκόπου Πατάρων καὶ μάρτυρος ἐκ τοῦ β´ ἀντιρρητικοῦ λόγου περὶ ἀναστάσεως οὗ ἡ ἀρχή· Ἴδωμεν δὴ οὖν, ἃ τὸ πρῶτον εἰς τὸν ἀπόστολον προήχθημεν εἰπεῖν.

Inc.: Αὐτίκα γοῦν τῶν τῇδε βασιλέων αἱ εἰκόνες . . .

desin.: . . . κρίνεται, ἀλλ᾽ ὡς εἰς αὐτὸν ἀσεβήσας τὸν βασιλέα.

CPG 1812 Methodius Olympius, *De resurrectione*, ed. G. N. Bonwetsch, *Methodius, GCS* 27 (Leipzig, 1917), 379.9–16.

PG 18, 289ᴀ–ʙ; Dam. III 138.

90* Σεβηριανοῦ Γαβάλων ἐκ τοῦ εἰς τὰ ἐγκαίνια τοῦ σταυροῦ.

Inc.: Πῶς οὖν ἡ εἰκὼν τοῦ ἐπικαταράτου ἤνεγκε τῷ λαῷ . . .

fol. 262ᵛ desin.: . . . εἰς αὐτὸν μὴ ἀπώληται, ἀλλ᾽ ἔχῃ ζωὴν αἰώνιον.

CPG 4270 Severianus Gabalensis, *Oratio in dedicationem pretiosae et vivificae crucis*, ed.

J. Zellinger, *Studien zu Severian von Gabala* (Münster, 1926), p. 134.12–36; *PG* 56, 499, 501–3. Cf. Thümmel, *Frühgeschichte*, 330–31.

Dam. I 58; II 54; III 52.

91* Τοῦ ἁγίου Κυρίλλου ἀρχιεπισκόπου Ἱεροσολύμων· ἐκ τοῦ τῆς β΄ κατηχήσεως.

Inc.: Δεινὸν ἡ ἁμαρτία καὶ νόσῳ χαλεπωτάτη ψυχῆς ἡ παρανομία. Καὶ μεθ᾽ ἕτερα· τίνα γὰρ ὑπόνοιαν ἔχει περί . . .

desin.: . . . τὸ ἱλαστήριον τῆς κιβωτοῦ, ὧν ἀνὰ μέσον ἐλάλει Κύριος.

CPG 3585.2 Cyrillus Hierosolym., *Catecheses ad illuminandos* 1–18, ed. W. K. Reischl and J. Rupp, *Cyrilli Hierosolymorum archiepiscopi opera*, I (Munich, 1848), 60; *PG* 33, 421B.

A XIII 160A–B.

Doctrina Patrum (chap. ME), p. 330.13–15, XVIII.

92* Ἐκ τῶν κινηθέντων δογμάτων μεταξὺ τοῦ ἐν ἁγίοις Μαξίμου καὶ Θεοδοσίου ἐπισκόπου Καισαρείας τῆς Βιθυνίας καὶ τῶν σὺν αὐτῷ.

Inc.: Τὰ κεκηρυγμένα περὶ τῆς ἀμωμήτου ἡμῶν τῶν Χριστιανῶν πίστεως. Καὶ μεθ᾽ ἕτερα· Μάξιμος εἶπε· Δεσπόται ἐπὰν ἔδοξε—ἐπιβεβαιώσει (sic) τῶν λαληθέντων. Καὶ μετὰ βραχύ. Στραφεὶς τοίνυν πρὸς τὸν ἐπίσκοπον . . .

desin.: . . . καὶ τῆς αὐτὸν τεκούσης παναγίας ἀειπαρθένου Μαρίας.

CPG 7735 Anastasius Apocrisiarius, *Acta in primo exsilio seu dialogus Maximi cum Theodosio ep. Caesareae in Bith.* (*BHG* 1233), *PG* 90, 136D; 156A9–B4; 164.

A XIII 37E–40B. Dam. II 65; III 131.

M **38**ᴹ; V **34.**

93* Κωνσταντίνου διακόνου καὶ χαρτοφύλακος τῆς ἁγιωτάτης ἐκκλησίας Κωνσταντινουπόλεως ἐκ τοῦ ἐγκωμίου τοῦ εἰς πάντας τοὺς ἁγίους τοὺς κατὰ τὴν οἰκουμένην μάρτυρας.

Inc.: Εἶτα οἴεσθαι (sic), ὦ οὗτοι, ἔφησαν—(fol. 263) τὸ σὰρξ φανῆναι σχηματισάμενος. Καὶ μετ᾽ ὀλίγα. Τοιγαροῦν ἐν ᾗ παρεδείχθη μορφῇ . . .

fol. 263ᵛ desin.: . . . καὶ σχήματα κατὰ τὸ δοκοῦν διαγλύφοντες.

CPG 7403 Constantinus Diaconus et Chartophylax CPolitanus, *Laudatio omnium martyrum* (*BHG* 1191), *PG* 88, 496D6–497D7; 500A12–B2. Cf. Thümmel, *Frühgheschichte*, 325–26.

A XIII 185A–188A.

94* Ἐκ τῶν κανόνων τῶν συνελθόντων πατέρων ἐν τῇ ἕκτῃ συνόδῳ· κανὼν πγ΄ (sic)·

Inc.: Ἔν τισι τῶν σεπτῶν εἰκόνων γραφαῖς, ἀμνὸς τῷ δακτύλῳ . . .

desin.: . . . καὶ τῆς ἐντεῦθεν γενομένης τῷ κόσμῳ ἀπολυτρώσεως.

CPG 9444 Concilium Trullanum a. 692, quinisextum dictum, canon 82, Mansi XI, 977E–980B.

A XIII 40E–41A; 220C–E/XII 1079A–C; 1123E–1126A. Dam. III 137.

M **49**ᴹ; V **38.**

95* Στεφάνου τοῦ ἁγιωτάτου ἐπισκόπου Βοστρῶν· περὶ ἁγίων εἰκόνων.

Inc.: Περὶ δὲ τῶν εἰκόνων τῶν ἁγίων θαρροῦμεν . . .

fol. 264 desin.: . . . ἡμῶν καὶ εὐχαριστίας προσφέρειν τῷ Θεῷ.

CPG 7790 Stephanus Bostrensis, *Contra Iudaeos fragmenta*, ed. Alexakis, "Stephen of Bostra," 51–55.

A XII 1067D–1070D. Dam. III 73, 72.
V **35**.

96* Τοῦ ἁγίου Ἱερωνύμου πρεσβυτέρου Ἱεροσολύμων·
Inc.: Καὶ γὰρ ὡς συνεχώρησε ὁ Θεὸς προσκυνεῖν . . .
desin.: . . . καὶ προσκυνεῖν καὶ δεῖξαι τὸ ἔργον ἡμῶν.
CPG 7817 Hieronymus Hierosolym. Theologus Graecus, *De effectu baptismati, PG* 40,
865C–D (= *Dialogus de cruce*).
A XII 1070E. Dam. III 125.
M **16ᴹ**; V **50**.

97* Τοῦ ἁγίου Συμεῶνος τοῦ εἰς τὸ Θαυμαστὸν ὄρος ἐκ τῆς ἐπιστολῆς τῆς πεμφθείσης
πρὸς τὸν βασιλέα Ἰουστιανὸν (sic).
Inc.: Οἱ πανευσεβεῖς καὶ καλλίνικοι ὑμῶν νόμοι . . .
fol. 264ᵛ desin.: . . . μηδεμία εἰς αὐτοὺς γένηται φιλανθρωπία.
CPG 7366 Symeon Stylita Iunior, *Epistula ad Iustinum iuniorem, PG* 86.2, 3217C–D.
A XIII 161A–B (Dam. III 126 = *PG* 86.2, 3220).
M **1ᴹ**; V **33**.

98* Ἀντιπάτρου ἐπισκόπου Βοστρῶν ἐκ τοῦ λόγου τοῦ εἰς τὴν αἱμόρρουν.
Inc.: Ὅτι μὲν πρώτη Ἰουδαίων κλῆσις ἐδίδαξεν ἡ γραφή . . .
desin.: . . . τοῦ δὲ πλούτου τὰ λειπόμενα προσενέγκασα τῷ Χριστῷ.
CPG 6683 Antipater Bostrensis, *Homilia in mulierem quae fluxum sanguinis passa est*
(*fragmentum*), *PG* 85, 1793C–D.
A XIII 13D–E.

99* Τοῦ μακαρίου Ἀστερίου ἐπισκόπου Ἀμασείας ἔκφρασις εἰς Εὐφημίαν τὴν μάρτυρα.
Inc.: Πρώην, ὦ ἄνδρες, Δημοσθένην εἶχον ἐν χερσὶ τὸν δεινόν . . .
fol 265ᵛ desin.: . . . εἰ μὴ πολὺ κατόπιν τῆς ἐξηγήσεως ἤλθομεν.
CPG 3260.1 Asterius Amasenus, *Homiliae i–xiv, PG* 40, 333–37 (= *homilia xi, BHG*
623–623a), ed. C. Datema, *Asterius of Amasea, Homilies I–XIV, Text, Introduction, and
Notes* (Leiden, 1970), 153–55.
A XIII 16A–17D; 308A–309B.

100* Θεοδώρου ἀναγνώστου Κωνσταντινουπόλεως· περὶ τῆς ἐκκλησιαστικῆς ἱστορίας.
Inc.: Ζωγράφος τις τὴν εἰκόνα τοῦ δεσπότου γράφων . . .
desin.: . . . καὶ παρ᾽ αὐτὰ τῆς ἰάσεως ἔτυχεν.
CPG 7503 Theodorus Anagnostes, *Historia ecclesiastica* (*fragmenta*), ed. G. Ch. Han-
sen, *Theodorus Anagnostes, Kirchengeschichte, GCS* 54 (Berlin, 1971), 107–8; *PG* 86,
220C–221A.
Dam. III 130.
M **19ᴹ**; V **37**.

101* Ἰωάννου ἐπισκόπου Θεσσαλονίκης ἐκ τοῦ λόγου.
Inc.: Μέχρι τότε πειράζων τὸν Κύριον ἡμῶν καὶ Θεὸν Ἰησοῦν, τὸν Χριστὸν προσεκαρτέρησεν ὁ ἐχθρὸς εἰς τὴν ἔρημον. Καὶ μετ᾽ ὀλίγα· Ἕλλην εἶπεν· ὑμεῖς οὖν ἐν ταῖς
ἐκκλησίαις . . .
fol. 266 desin.: . . . ἀπεστάλησαν ὑπὸ τοῦ μόνου Θεοῦ γεγένηνται.
CPG 7923 Iohannes I Thessalonicensis, *Sermo* (*fragmentum de imaginibus*). Cf. Thümmel, *Frühgeschichte, 327–28.*

A XIII 164c–165c.

102* Ἐκ τῆς διαλέξεως Ἰουδαίου τε καὶ Χριστιανοῦ.
Inc.: Ὁ Ἰουδαῖος λέγει· ἐπείσθην εἰς πάντας . . .
fol. 266ᵛ desin.: . . . ὁμοίωμα μὴ ποιῆσαι ὁμοίωμα ἐποίησεν;
A XIII 165ε–168c. Cf. Thümmel, *Frühgeschichte*, 361–62.

103* Λεοντίου ἐπισκόπου Νεαπόλεως, τῆς Κυπρίων νήσου, ἐκ τοῦ ε΄ λόγου ὑπὲρ τῆς Χριστιανῶν ἀπολογίας καὶ κατὰ Ἰουδαίων καὶ περὶ τῶν ἁγίων εἰκόνων.
Inc.: Φέρε δὴ λοιπὸν περὶ τῶν σεπτογράφων εἰκόνων . . .
fol. 269ᵛ desin.: . . . καὶ τοὺς χαρακτῆρας τῶν ἁγίων αὐτοῦ, ὅτι αὐτῷ πρέπει δόξα . . . ἀμήν.
CPG 7885.1 Leontius Neapolitanus, *Contra Iudaeos orationes v* (*fragmenta*), ed. Déroche, "L'*Apologie contre les Juifs* de Léontios de Néapolis," 66–72; *PG* 93, 1597ʙ–1609.
A XIII 44ᴀ–53c. Dam. I 54, 56; III 84, 86–89.
M **2ᴹ**.

104* Ἐκ τῆς δεήσεως τῶν μοναχῶν καὶ κληρικῶν Ἀντιοχείας κατὰ Σεβήρου πρὸς τὴν ε΄ σύνοδον.
fol. 270 Inc.: Οὐ μὴν οὐδὲ αὐτῶν ἐφείσατο τῶν ἁγίων θυσιαστηρίων . . .
desin.: . . . ἐν εἴδει περιστερᾶς σχηματίζεσθαι τὸ ἅγιον Πνεῦμα.
CPG 9329.6 Synodus Constantinopolitana (a. 536), *Actio V, Preces clericorum et monachorum Antiochiae ad Iohannem CPolitanum et Synodum* (cf. *CPG* 9202 nota). *ACO* III, 60.35–61.3.
A XIII 181ε–184ᴀ.
M **46ᴹ**.

105* Ἐκ τῆς ἐκκλησιαστικῆς ἱστορίας Σωζομενοῦ τόμου ε΄.
Inc.: Ἐμοὶ δὲ τῶν ἐπὶ Ἰουλιανοῦ συμβάντων . . .
desin.: . . . τῶν ἐν τῇ καθ᾽ ἡμᾶς οἰκουμένῃ ἐμπύρων (sic).
CPG 6030 Sozomenus, *Historia ecclesiastica*, ed. J. Bidez and G. C. Hansen, *Sozomenus Kirchengeschichte, GCS* 50 (Berlin, 1960), 227.24–228.11; *PG* 67, 1280ʙ–c.

106* Ἐκ τῆς ἐκκλησιαστικῆς ἱστορίας Εὐαγρίου ἐκ τοῦ δ΄ λόγου.
Inc.: Μετὰ γὰρ τὸ προσβαλεῖν τῇ πόλει τὸν Χοσρόην . . .
fol. 270ᵛ desin.: . . . με⟨τε⟩δίδοσαν ἅπαντα τοῦ πυρὸς ἀμφινεμομένου.
CPG 7500 Evagrius Scholasticus, *Historia ecclesiastica*, ed. J. Bidez and L. Parmentier, *Evagrius. The Ecclesiastical History*, 2nd ed. (Amsterdam, 1964), 174.15–175.17; *PG* 86, 2748ᴀ–2749ᴀ.
A XIII 189ε–192c.

107* Τοῦ ὁσίου πατρὸς ἡμῶν Σωφρονίου ἐπισκόπου Ἱεροσολύμων ἐκ τοῦ ἐγκωμίου τοῦ εἰς τοὺς ἁγίους Κῦρον καὶ Ἰωάννην.
Inc.: Ἄλλοι μὲν ἄλλως τοὺς ἁγίους τιμάτωσαν, πολυμερῶς . . .
desin.: . . . τοὺς ἐραστὰς ἀμείβεσθαι τοῖς δώροις εἰώθασιν.
CPG 7645 Sophronius Hierosolym., *Laudes in ss. Cyrum et Iohannem* (*BHG* 475–476), *PG* 87.3, 3388ᴀ.
A XIII 57ʙ–ᴅ.
V **15**.

108* Καὶ μεθ' ἕτερα· ἀπὸ θαύματος.
Inc.: Ἀλεξάνδρειαν Αἰγύπτου καὶ Λιβύων ἀκούω μητρόπολιν. Καὶ μεθ' ἕτερα· ἐλθόντες οὖν εἰς νεών τινα . . .
fol. 271 desin.: . . . τὴν νόσον ἀπέθετο καὶ τὴν ῥῶσιν ἀπέλαβεν.
CPG 7646 Sophronius Hierosolym., *Narratio miraculorum ss. Cyri et Iohannis (BHG* 478), PG 87, 3557D–3560D.
A XIII 57D–60B. Dam. III 132.

109* Ἐκ τῶν θαυμάτων τῶν ἁγίων Κοσμᾶ καὶ Δαμιανοῦ τῶν Ἀναργύρων.
Inc.: Ἕτερός τις ἀνὴρ ἐπιεικὴς σφόδρα, σύριγγα ἐσχηκώς . . .
fol. 271ᵛ desin.: . . . οὗτός ἐστι, βοηθήσατε αὐτῷ διὰ τάχους.
BHG 389 *Cosmas et Damianus, Miraculum 30*, ed. L. Deubner, *Kosmas und Damian* (Leipzig-Berlin, 1907), 173.1–174.26.
A XIII 64B–D.

110* Ἐκ τῶν αὐτῶν θαυμάτων περὶ τῆς γυναικὸς Κωνσταντίνου τοῦ ἐν Λαοδικείᾳ.
Inc.: Συνέβη τινὰ ἄνδρα ἐν στρατείᾳ ἐξεταζόμενον . . .
fol. 272 desin.: . . . διήγουν (sic) οἱ ἅγιοι κατὰ τὴν αὐτῶν φωνήν.
BHG 387 *Cosmas et Damianus, Miraculum 13*, ed. Deubner, *Kosmas und Damian*, 132.1–134.37.
A XIII 64E–65D.

111* Ἐκ τῶν αὐτῶν περὶ τῆς γυναικὸς τῆς ἐχούσης τὴν(?) στρόφον·
Inc.: Καλῶς ὁ σοφώτατος Παῦλος, ὁ στύλος καὶ διδάσκαλος . . .
desin.: . . . προσγενομένην αὐτῇ ἐν τῷ τοιούτῳ σχήματι θεραπείαν.
BHG 387, *Miraculum 15*, ed. Deubner, *Kosmas und Damian*, 137.1–138.27.
A XIII 68A–D.

112* Θεοδωρήτου ἐπισκόπου Κύπρου (sic) ἐκ τῆς φιλοθέου ἱστορίας ἐκ τοῦ βιβλίου Συμεῶνος τοῦ στυλίτου.
Συμεώνην τὸν πάνυ, τὸ μέγα θαῦμα τῆς οἰκουμένης. Φασὶ γὰρ οὕτως ἐν Ῥώμῃ τῇ μεγίστῃ πολυθρύλλητον γενέσθαι τὸν ἄνδρα, ὡς ἐν ἅπασι τοῖς τῶν ἐργαστηρίων προπυλαίοις εἰκόνας αὐτῷ βραχείας ἀναστῆσαι, φυλακήν τινα καὶ ἀσφάλειαν ἐντεῦθεν πορίζοντα.
CPG 6221 Theodoretus Episc. Cyri, *Historia religiosa (BHG* 1439–1440), ed. P. Canivet and A. Leroy-Molinghen, *Théodoret de Cyr, L'histoire des moines de Syrie*, I, SC 234 (Paris, 1977), 159.1; 182.19–22; *PG* 82, 1473A.
A XIII 73B. Dam. III 55.

113* Ἐκ τοῦ βιβλίου τοῦ ὁσίου πατρὸς ἡμῶν Συμεῶνος τοῦ ἐν τῷ Θαυμαστῷ ὄρει κεφάλαιον ριη'· περὶ τῆς γυναικὸς τῆς ἐν Ῥωσοπόλει ἀτεκνούσης καὶ βιαίω κατεχομένης δαίμονι, ἥτις ἰαθεῖσα καὶ παιδοποιήσασα εἰκόνα τῷ (fol. 272ᵛ) δικαίῳ ἀνέθετο ἐν τῷ οἴκῳ αὐτῆς, ἥτις μεγάλως ἐθαυματούργει.
Inc.: Γυνή τις ἦν ἐν Ῥωσοπόλει τῆς Κιλικίας, Θεοτέκνα . . .
fol. 273 desin.: . . . τὸ γεγονὸς εἰς αὐτὴν παράδοξον.
CPG 7369, *Vita Symeonis Stylitae iunioris (BHG* 1689), ed. P. Van den Ven, *La vie ancienne de S. Syméon Stylite le Jeune (521–592)*, I, II, SubsHag 32.1, 2 (Brussels, 1962–70), 96–98 (= 118).
A XIII 73B–76C.

114* Ἕτερον θαῦμα τοῦ ὁσίου πατρὸς ἡμῶν Συμεών.

Inc.: Συνέβη δὲ ἐν ταῖς ἡμέραις ἐκείναις ἄνδρα τινά . . .

desin.: . . . προσκυνοῦντες μετὰ προσευχῆς τῇ εἰκόνι, ἐχώρουν.

Ed. van den Ven, *La vie ancienne*, 139–41 (= 158).

A XIII 76D–77B. Dam. III 92,

115* Φωτεινοῦ τοῦ θεοφιλεστάτου πρεσβυτέρου καὶ ἐκκλησιεκδίκου τῆς ἁγιωτάτης ἐκκλησίας Κωνσταντινουπόλεως· (fol. 273ᵛ) ἐκ τοῦ βίου τοῦ ἐν ἁγίοις πατρὸς ἡμῶν Ἰωάννου τοῦ νηστευτοῦ ἐπισκόπου γενομένου τῆς αὐτῆς πόλεως.

Inc.: Ἕτι μηδὲ τοῦτο λάθοι τὸ θαῦμα· μὴ δὲ χωροῦμεν . . .

fol. 275 desin.: . . . τοῦτο μὲν οὖν τὸ πέρας τῆς ὑποθέσεως.

CPG 7971 Photinus CPolitanus, *Vita Iohannis Ieiunatoris (fragmentum)* (*BHG* 893).

A XIII 80D–85C.

116* Ἐκ τοῦ βίου τῆς ὁσίας Μαρίας τῆς Αἰγυπτίας.

Inc.: Μυστήριον βασιλέως κρύπτειν καλόν. Καὶ μεθ᾽ ἕτερα. Κλαίουσα δὲ ὁρῶ τοῦ τόπου . . .

fol. 275ᵛ desin.: . . . τῆς αὐλῆς τοῦ ναοῦ καὶ συντόνως ἐβάδιζον.

CPG 7675 Sophronius Hierosolym., *Vita Mariae Aegyptiacae* (*BHG* 1042), *PG* 87, 3713B–3716A.

A XIII 85D–89A. Dam. III 135.

117* Ἐκ τοῦ μαρτυρίου τοῦ ἁγίου Προκοπίου.

Inc.: Κατὰ τοὺς καιροὺς ἐκείνους ἐβασίλευε Διοκλητιανὸς ὁ τύραννος. Καὶ μεθ᾽ ἕτερα· καὶ προσκαλεσάμενος κρυφίως—Κύριε τὸ θέλημά σου. Καὶ μετ᾽ ὀλίγα. Ὁ δὲ Μάρκος οὐκ . . .

desin.: . . . καὶ ἐπορεύθη τὴν ὁδὸν αὐτοῦ χαίρων.

BHG 1577 *Passio S. Procopii,* ed. Papadopoulos-Kerameus, *Analecta Hierosolymitikes Stachyologias,* V (St. Petersburg, 1898), 1.1–2; 5.23–29; 6.10–27.

A XIII 89A–D.

118* Ἐκ τοῦ βίου τοῦ ὁσίου πατρὸς ἡμῶν Θεοδώρου ἀρχιμανδρίτου τῆς μονῆς τῶν Συκεῶν. (2 fragments).

fol. 276 Inc.: Εὐλογητὸς ὁ Θεὸς καὶ πατὴρ τοῦ Κυρίου ἡμῶν Ἰησοῦ Χριστοῦ. Καὶ μεθ᾽ ἕτερα· ἐγένετο θανατικόν—τοῦ πόνου ὑγιὴς ἐγένετο. Καὶ μετὰ βραχύ· μιμήσασθαι τοίνυν θέλων τὸν Δαβίδ . . .

desin.: . . . εὐκόλως καὶ εὐμαθῶς ἀπεστήθιζε τὸ ψαλτήριον.

CPG 7973 Georgius Syceota, *Vita Theodori Syceotae* (*BHG* 1748), ed. A.-J. Festugière, *Vie de Théodore de Sykéon,* I, *Texte grec;* II, *Traduction, commentaire et appendice,* SubsHag 48 (Brussels, 1970), 8.1–10; 13.1–15.

A XIII 89E–92B.

119* Ἐκ τοῦ μαρτυρίου τοῦ ἁγίου Ἀναστασίου τοῦ Πέρσου.

Inc.: Ὁ μονογενὴς υἱὸς καὶ λόγος τοῦ Θεοῦ δι᾽ οὗ τὰ πάντα ἐγένετο. Καὶ μεθ᾽ ἕτερα· ὅμως σὺν αὐτῷ ἀπίει (sic) . . .

desin.: . . . κἀκεῖσε τοῦ ἁγίου ἀξιωθῆναι βαπτίσματος.

BHG 84, *Vita et martyrium Anastasii Persae,* ed. B. Flusin, *Saint Anastase le Perse et l'histoire de la Palestine au début du VIIᵉ siècle,* I (Paris, 1992), 51 par. 9.4–10.

A XIII 21A–C.

120* Ἐκ τῶν θαυμάτων τοῦ αὐτοῦ ἁγίου μάρτυρος τοῦ Χριστοῦ Ἀναστασίου.
Inc.: Θαυμάτων διήγησιν προβαλλέσθαι βούλομαι. Καὶ μετ᾽ ὀλίγα. Φέρε δὴ καὶ τὰ ἐν
  Καισαρείᾳ τῆς Παλαιστίνης . . .
fol. 277 desin.: . . . δοξάζουσα τὸν Θεὸν καὶ μεγαλαυχοῦσα τὸν μάρτυρα.
BHG 89g, Miracula x Anastasii Persae, ed. Flusin, Saint Anastase, 117.1; 131.1–133.45.
A XIII 21c–24c.

121* Ἐκ τοῦ Λειμωναρίου.
Inc.: Διηγήσαντο ἡμῖν οἱ αὐτοὶ πατέρες λέγοντες . . .
desin.: . . . καὶ ἐπίομεν καὶ ἐδοξάσαμεν τῷ Θεῷ ἡμῶν, ἀμήν.
CPG 7376 Iohannes Moschus, Pratum Spirituale (BHG 1442), PG 87.3, 2940a–b.
A XIII 193d–e.
M 22ᴹ.

122* Ἐκ τοῦ αὐτοῦ Λειμωναρίου.
Inc.: Διηγήσατο ἡμῖν Διονύσιος, ὁ πρεσβύτερος . . .
fol. 277ᵛ desin.: . . . οὔτε ἐξ ἐρήμου φοιτῶν εἰς τὸ σπήλαιον.
PG 87.3, 3052a–d.
A XIII 193e–196c.

123* Ἐκ τοῦ αὐτοῦ Λειμωναρίου.
Inc.: Ἔλεγόν τινες τῶν γερόντων, ὅτι ἦν τις ἐγκλειστός . . .
desin.: . . . μετὰ τῆς ἰδίας αὐτοῦ μητρὸς ἐν τῇ εἰκόνι.
PG 87.3, 2900b–d.
A XIII 193a–c; 60d–61b. Dam. I 64; II 67; III 13.
M 48ᴹ.

124* Ἐκ τοῦ βίου τοῦ ἐν ἁγίοις Σιλβέστρου πάπα Ῥώμης.
Inc.: Αὐτὴ τοίνυν τῇ νυκτὶ ὀπτασίαν ὁρᾷ ὁ βασιλεύς—ὄρει κρυπτόμενον. Καὶ μεθ᾽ ἕτερα.
  Ταῦτα ἀκούσας ὁ βασιλεύς . . .
desin.: . . . ἐγὼ εἰ μὴ ἐπίστευον, οὐκ ἂν πρὸς σὲ ἔπεμπον.
BHG 1628–30, Vita Silvestri, ed. F. Combefis, Illustrium Christianorum martyrum lecti
triumphi (Paris, 1660), 276.4–15; 278.15–279.16.
A XII 1058c–1059c.
M 36ᴹ.

fol. 278 **125*** Ἐκ τῆς δεήσεως τῶν ἐν Παλαιστίνῃ μοναχῶν καὶ κληρικῶν ἐπισκόπων
πρὸς Ἀγαπητὸν πάπαν Ῥώμης.
Inc.: Οἱ ἀπὸ τῆς μανίας Διοσκόρου καὶ Εὐτυχέως καταγόμενοι . . .
desin.: . . . ὅπου γε τῆς ἐν σινδόνι γραφῆς ἀψύχου οὐκ ἐφείσατο.
CPG 9325.3 Synodus Constantinopolitana (a. 536), Actio I, Libellus monachorum ad
Agapetum. ACO III, 137.8–31.

126* Διάλογος Μόσχου μοναχοῦ καὶ ἐγκλειστοῦ πρός τινα περὶ εἰκόνων ἁγίων.
Inc.: Μετὰ πολλὴν δὲ τὴν διάλεξιν ἔφη πρὸς ὃν διελέγετο . . .
fol. 280 desin.: . . . ὁ δὲ ἔφη· ἐγώ σε καὶ περὶ τούτων πληροφορῶ.
Ineditum. See Alexakis, "An Early Iconophile Text . . . ," DOP 52, 1998.

127* Ἐκ τῆς ἐξόδου τῶν υἱῶν Ἰσραήλ.
Καὶ εἶπε Κύριος—(fol. 280ᵛ) πρὸς τοὺς υἱοὺς Ἰσραήλ.
Exodus 25.16–21.
A XIII 4D–E; XII 1063B.

128* Ἐκ τῶν ἀριθμῶν.
Αὕτη ἡ ἐγκαίνισις τοῦ θυσιαστηρίου—καὶ ἐλάλει πρὸς αὐτόν.
Numeri 7:88–90.
A XIII 5A.

129* Ἐκ τοῦ προφήτου Ἰεζεκιήλ.
Καὶ εἰσήγαγέ με εἰς τὸν ναόν—εὖρος τοῦ ἐλάμ. Καὶ μεθ᾽ ἕτερα. Καὶ ὁ οἶκος καὶ τὰ πλησίον—τοῦ φατνώματος τὰ Χερουβίμ.
Ezechiel 41:1/16–20.
A XIII 5A–B.

130* Ἐκ τῆς πρὸς Ἑβραίους ἐπιστολῆς Παύλου·
Εἶχε μὲν οὖν καὶ ἡ πρώτη—κατασκιάζοντα τὸ ἱλαστήριον.
Ad Hebraeos 9.1–5.
A XIII 5C. Dam. I 22.29–39.

131* Ἰωάννου τοῦ εὐλαβεστάτου Ἱεροσολυμίτου μοναχοῦ διήγησις.
Inc.: Βούλομαι ἐγὼ ὁ μέτριος καὶ πάντων ἔσχατος ἀποδεῖξαι . . .
fol. 281ᵛ desin.: . . . ἐπίχειρα τῆς ψευδομαντείας αὐτοῦ κομισαμένῳ.
PG 109, 517–20.
A XIII 197A–200B.

132* Ἐκ τῆς πρὸς Γαλάτας ἐπιστολῆς.
Ὦ ἀνόητοι Γαλάται—προεγράφη ἐν ὑμῖν σταυρούμενος.
Ad Galatas 3.1.
M 1ᴹ.

133* Ἐπιστολὴ Γρηγορίου τοῦ ἁγιωτάτου πάπα Ῥώμης πρὸς Γερμανὸν πατριάρχην Κωνσταντινουπόλεως.
Inc.: Ποία καὶ τίς θυμηδία τὴν ἐμὴν οὕτως οἶδεν εὐφραίνειν . . .
fol. 283ᵛ desin.: . . . ἁγιώτατε καὶ πᾶσι τοῖς Χριστιανοῖς πο⟨θη⟩τέ.
CPG 8006 *Epistula Gregorii Papae ad Germanum CPolitanum, PG* 98, 148–156B.
A XIII 92C–100A.

Post ποθητέ P add.:

Ἀνάθεμα τοῖς αἱρετικοῖς Θεοδοσίῳ τῷ ψευδωνύμῳ ἐπισκόπῳ Ἐφέσου, Σισσινίῳ, τῷ ἐπίκλην Παστιλλᾷ, Βασιλείῳ τῷ κακεμφάτῳ Τρικακκάβῳ, Ἰωάννῃ Νικομηδείας καὶ Κωνσταντίνῳ Νακολασίας.

A XIII 400A–B.

APPENDIX III

List of Contents of the Iconophile Florilegium of Mosquensis Historici Musei 265 (Vladimir 197) (M) (fols. 142–241)

Abbreviations

A = Acts of Nicaea II, Mansi, XII–XIII
Dam. = Kotter, *Schriften III*
P = Parisinus gr. 1115 (numbers refer to App. II)
V = Venetus Marcianus gr. 573 (numbers refer to App. IV)

fol. 142 **1ᴹ** Νουθεσία γέρωντος (sic) περὶ τῶν ἁγίων εἰκόνων·
Inc.: Γεώργιος ὀνόματι καθήμενος ἐν ὄρη (sic) τῶν Ἐλαιῶν . . .
fol. 171ᵛ desin.: . . . καὶ Θεὸς ἡμῶν ἐλεήσει πάντας τοὺς ὀρθοδόξους.
Ed. Melioranskij, *Georgij*, V–XXXIX; also Misides, *Ἡ παρουσία τῆς Ἐκκλησίας Κύπρου*, 153–92.

2ᴹ Λεωντίου (sic) ἐπισκόπου Νεαπόλεως τῆς Κύπρου λόγος περὶ τῶν ἁγίων εἰκόνων. (In marg. super.: Ἀντιβολῆ (sic) Χριστιανοῦ μετὰ Ἰουδαίου καὶ αἱρετικοῦ).
Inc.: Φέρε δεὶ (sic) λοιπὸν περὶ τῶν σεπτογράφων . . .
fol. 177 desin.: . . . τῶν ἁγίων αὐτοῦ, ὅτι αὐτῷ πρέπει δόξα . . . ἀμήν.
P 103*.

fol. 177ᵛ **3ᴹ** Τοῦ ἁγίου Γρηγορίου, ἐπισκόπου Νύσης· εἰς τὴν εὕρεσιν τῆς ἁγίας, ἀχράντου, ἀχειροποιήτου Καμουλιανῶν, ἀναδειχθείσεις (sic) μὲν ἐν τοῖς χρόνοις ⟨Δ⟩ιοκλητιανοῦ βασιλέως τῇ μακαρίᾳ Βαάσσῃ, φανερωθείσεις (sic) δὲ ἐν τοῖς χρόνοις Θεοδοσίου τοῦ πιστοῦ βασιλέως διὰ τοῦ προλεχθέντος ⟨ . . . ⟩ίου ἀνδρός.
Inc.: Ὁ Κύριος ἡμῶν Ἰησοῦς Χριστός, ὁ ἀληθινὸς ἡμῶν Θεός, . . .
fol. 182ᵛ desin.: . . . εἰς τοὺς αἰῶνας τῶν αἰώνων, ἀμήν.
CPG 3224 Gregorius Nyss., *Inventio imaginis in Camulianis* (*BHG* 790), ed. B. Melioranskij, *Commentationes Nikitinianae* (St. Petersburg, 1901), 321–27; also E. von Dobschütz, *Christusbilder, TU* 18 (Leipzig, 1899), pp. 12**–18**.

4ᴹ Ἰωάννου ταπεινοῦ μοναχοῦ Δαμασκηνοῦ πρὸς τοὺς ἀντιλέγοντας τῶν εἰκόνων.
Inc.: Δῶτε (sic) συγγνώμην αἰτοῦντι δεσπόται μου . . .
fol. 191ᵛ desin.: . . . κατὰ τὴν ἡμετέραν λατρείαν ἐκείνης χάριν ἐγένετο. Αὐτῷ ἡ δόξα εἰς τοὺς αἰῶνας τῶν αἰώνων, ἀμήν.
CPG 8045 Iohannes Damascenus, *Orationes de imaginibus tres*, Dam. II 1–10; 14–23 (cf. *Schriften III*, p. 36).

5ᴹ fol. 192 Τοῦ αὐτοῦ πρὸς τοὺς καταλέγοντας τῶν εἰκόνων.
Inc.: Πολλῶν τοίνυν ἀνέκαθεν ἱερέων τε καὶ βασιλέων . . .

desin.: . . . ἔξωθεν γέλωτα καὶ ἄθρυσμα (sic) γίνεσθε (sic).
Dam. II 69.1–10.

6ᴹ Τοῦ αὐτοῦ.
Inc.: Γινωσκέτω οὖν πᾶς ἄνθρωπος, ὁ τὴν εἰκόνα . . .
desin.: . . . τιμῶνται καὶ δοξάζωνται ὁ δὲ διάβολος καταισχύνεται.
Dam. II 11.1–24.

fol. 192ᵛ **7ᴹ** Ἰωάννου μοναχοῦ Ἱεροσολύμων συνοδικὸν στηλιτεύων (sic) τοὺς κατὰ τὴν ἄοικον καὶ ἀκέφαλον εὐδαίμωνα (sic) ἑβδόμην σύνοδον.
Inc.: Πιστεύω εἰς ἕνα Θεὸν πατέρα παντοκράτορα . . .
fol. 199 desin.: . . . καὶ μὴ μετὰ τῆς ἀκεφάλου· ὅτι πρέπει τῆς ἁγίας τριάδος ἡ δύναμις . . . ἀμήν.
P 2*.

fol. 199ᵛ **8ᴹ** Γρηγορίου (sic) πάπα Ῥώμης· ἐπιστολὴ γραφῆσα (sic) πρὸς Λέωντα (sic) τὸν βασιλέα περὶ τῶν σεπτῶν εἰκόνων.
Inc.: Τὰ γράμματα τῆς ὑμετέρας θεοφρουρήτου βασιλείας . . .
fol. 208ᵛ desin.: . . . τὴν εἰρήνην δωρήσεται τῇ ἁγίᾳ αὐτοῦ ἐκκλησίᾳ εἰς τοὺς αἰῶνας τῶν αἰώνων, ἀμήν.
BHG 1387d, *Gregorii papae II epistulae ad Leonem Isaurum imp.*, ed. Gouillard, "Origines," 277–97.
A XII 959A–974B.

fol. 209 **9ᴹ** Τοῦ αὐτοῦ Γρηγωρίου πάπα πρὸς Λέωντα (sic) τὸν βασιλέα ἐπιστολὴ δευτέρα.
Inc.: Τὰ γράμματα τῆς ὑμετέρας θεοφρουρήτου βασιλείας . . .
fol. 212ᵛ desin.: . . . παράσχῃ πάσῃ τῇ οἰκουμένῃ εἰς τοὺς αἰῶνας, ἀμήν.
BHG 1387d, ed. Gouillard, "Origines," 299–305.
A XII, 975B–982B.

fol. 213 **10ᴹ** Λόγος τοῦ ἐν ἁγίοις πατρὸς ἡμῶν Ἀθανασίου, ἀρχιεπισκόπου Ἀλεξανδρείας περὶ τῆς εἰκόνος (sic) τοῦ Κυρίου ἡμῶν Ἰησοῦ Χριστοῦ, τοῦ γεναμένου θαύματος ἐν Βηρυτῷ τῇ πόλει.
Inc.: Ἄρατε τοὺς ὀφθαλμοὺς τῆς διανοίας ὑμῶν . . .
fol. 217 desin.: . . . καὶ δοξάσωμεν τὴν αὐτοῦ ἀγαθώτητα (sic) τοῦ ἀληθεινοῦ (sic) υἱοῦ τοῦ Θεοῦ τοῦ ζῶντος· αὐτῷ γὰρ πρέπει δόξα . . . ἀμήν.
P 71*.

11ᴹ Τιμοθέου πρεσβυτέρου τῆς ἁγιωτάτης ἐκκλησίας Κωνσταντινουπόλεως πρὸς Ἰωάννην πρεσβύτερον τῆς αὐτῆς ἁγιωτάτης ἐκκλησίας περὶ διαφορᾶς τῶν προσερχομένων τῇ ἁγιωτάτῃ ἡμῶν πίστει.
Inc.: Τρεῖς τάξεις εὑρίσκομεν τῶν προσερχομένων τῇ ἁγίᾳ καθολικῇ ἐκκλησίᾳ, θεοφιλέστατε συλλειτουργὲ (sic) Ἰωάννῃ καὶ πάντων ἐμοί . . .
fol. 217ᵛ desin.: . . . ὅπερ ἑρμηνεύεται πασσαλορυγχεῖται.
CPG 7016 Timotheus Presbyter CPolitanus, *De iis qui ad ecclesiam accedunt*, ed. V. Beneševič, *Syntagma XIV titulorum sine scholiis secundum versionem palaeo-slovenicam, adiecto textu graeco* (St. Petersburg, 1906–7), 707–9, *PG* 86, 12–16A4.

fol. 218 **12ᴹ** Τοῦ μακαρίου Γερμανοῦ πατριάρχου Κωνσταντινουπόλεως λόγος περὶ τῶν πανσέπτων καὶ ἁγίων εἰκόνων.

Inc.: Τὴν καλὴν παρακαταθήκην φυλάττωντες (sic) . . .
fol. 219 desin.: . . . Θεοῦ ἡμῶν ἀπολαύοντες παντοίας θαυματουργίας.
P 3*.

13ᴹ Τοῦ αὐτοῦ ἐπιστολὴ πρὸς τὸν ἐπίσκοπον Συνάδων.
Inc.: Ἐπιστολὴν τῆς ὑμετέρας θεοφιλίας ἀποδέδωκεν ἡμῖν . . .
fol. 223 desin.: . . . τὴν ὑπὲρ ἔχουσαν (sic) πάντα νοῦν εἰρήνην.
CPG 8002 Germanus I CPolitanus, Epistula ad Iohannem episcopum Synadensem, PG
98, 156–61.
A XII 100ʙ–105ᴀ.

14ᴹ Ἐπιστολὴ τοῦ ὁσίου πατρὸς ἡμῶν Βασιλείου πρὸς Ἰουλιανὸν τὸν παραβάτην.
Inc.: Κατὰ τὴν θεόθεν ἐπικεκληρομένην (sic) ἡμῶν ἀμώμητον . . .
fol. 223ᵛ desin.: . . . ταῖς ἐκκλησίαις ἡμῶν τούτων ἀνιστορουμένων.
P 17* (M⟩P).

15ᴹ Εὐσεβίου τοῦ Παμφίλου ἐκ τῆς ἐκκλησιαστικῆς ἱστορίας.
Inc.: Ἀστέριός τις μνημονεύεται τῶν ἐπαξίας (sic) . . .
fol. 225 desin.: . . . καὶ εἰς ἡμᾶς σῴζονται καὶ ἀποσῴζουσιν σέβας.
CPG 3495 Eusebius Caes., Historia ecclesiastica, ed. E. Schwartz, Eusebius Werke, II,
1–3, Die Kirchengeschichte, GCS 9.2 (Leipzig, 1906), 670.10–674.6; PG 20, 677ʙ–681ᴀ.
Dam. III 69 (M⟩Dam.).

16ᴹ Τοῦ ἁγίου Ἱερονύμου (sic) πρεσβυτέρου Ἱεροσολύμων.
Inc.: Χάριν τούτου συνεχώρησεν ὁ Θεὸς παντὶ ἔθνη (sic) . . .
desin.: . . . καὶ δικνύειν (sic) τὴν διάθεσιν ἡμῶν τὴν πρὸς αὐτούς.
P 96*.

17ᴹ Τοῦ ἁγίου Σωφρονίου ἐπισκόπου Ἱεροσολύμων· περὶ τοῦ βίου τοῦ Λατόμου.
Inc.: Καὶ κάθημαι ἔμπροσθεν τοῦ πυλῶνος, ὡς ὅτε . . .
fol. 225ᵛ desin.: . . . ἰδοὺ θόρυβος πολὺς ἤρχετο καὶ τὰ λοιπά.
CPG 7363 Daniel Scetiota, Narrationes, ed. M. L. Clugnet, "Vie et récits de l'abbé
Daniel de Scété," ROC 5 (1900), 258.24–259.2.
Dam. III 134 (M⟩Damι).

18ᴹ Τοῦ ἁγίου Διονυσίου τοῦ Ἀρεοπαγίτου· ἐκ τοῦ πρώτου αὐτοῦ λόγου.
Inc.: Διὸ τὴν ὁσιωτάτην ἡμῶν ἱεραρχίαν, ἡ τελετάρχης . . .
desin.: . . . τῇ κατ᾽ αὐτῶν ὑλαίᾳ χειραγωγίᾳ χρήσοιτο.
CPG 6600 Ps.-Dionysius Areopag., De coelesti hierarchia, ed. Heil and Ritter, Corpus
Dionysiacum, II, 8.14–21; PG 3, 121ᴄ–ᴅ (cf. Hadrianum, 32–33; Acta Conc. Rom. a. 731,
n. 8).

19ᴹ Ἐκ τῆς ἐκκλησιαστικῆς ἱστορίας Θεοδώρου ἀναγνώστου Κωνσταντινουπόλεως.
Inc.: Ζωγράφος τις τὴν εἰκόνα τοῦ δεσπότου . . .
fol. 226 desin.: . . . τῆς ἰάσεως ἔτυχεν. Χάριτι αὐτοῦ τοῦ . . . ἀμήν.
P 100*; V 37.

20ᴹ Ἐκ τοῦ βίου τῆς ὁσίας Εὐπραξίας.
Inc.: Λέγει οὖν ἡ Εὐπραξία τῇ διακόνῳ· ὧδε μένω . . .
fol. 226ᵛ desin.: . . . συντάσσομαι καὶ οὐκέτι ἀπέρχομαι ἐντεῦθεν.
BHG 631, Vita Eupraxiae in Thebaide, AASS Mart. II, 729ᴄ.

Dam. III 136.

21ᴹ Τοῦ ὁσίου πατρὸς ἡμῶν Γερμανοῦ πατριάρχου Κωνσταντινουπόλεως ἐκ τοῦ λόγου τοῦ ⟨εἰς?⟩ τὸν ἀποκλισμὸν (sic) περὶ τοῦ Σουλεημᾶ⟨ν⟩.
Inc.: Ὅ τε γὰρ Σουλεημᾶν ὑπεκρίνατο τὸ γλυκὺ δέλεαρ . . .
desin.: . . . διωκούσης τὸν δόλιον. Τῷ δὲ οὕτως εὐδοκήσαντι ἀλη(fol. 227)θεινῷ (sic) Θεῷ . . . χάρις . . . ἀμήν.
Ed. Darrouzès, "Deux textes inédits du Patriarche Germain," 11–13.

22ᴹ Ἐκ τοῦ παραδεισίου ἐξήγησις.
Διηγήσαντο ἡμῖν οἱ ἅγιοι—ἐπίωμεν καὶ ἐδοξάσαμεν τὸν Θεόν.
P 121*.

23ᴹ Ἐκ τῶν αὐτῶν λειμώνων.
Inc.: Ἐν Ἀντιοχίᾳ τῇ μεγάλῃ διακονίαι πολλαί εἰσιν . . .
fol. 228 desin.: . . . καὶ πάντες δὲ οἱ ἀκούσαντες ἐδόξασαν τὸν Θεόν.
CPG 7376 Iohannes Moschus, *Pratum spirituale,* ed. Nissen, "Unbekannte Erzählungen aus dem Pratum Spirituale," 367.24–368.24.
V 51 (M⟩V).

Post Θεόν M add.:

> Ταῦτα δὲ εἴρηται ὅπως μὴ ἐκκακήσωμεν ἀγαθοποιοῦντες· ἀψευδὴς γὰρ ὁ λέγων "ὁ ἐλεῶν πτωχὸν δανείζει Θεῷ"· καὶ πάλιν ὁ αὐτὸς Κύριος "μακάριοι οἱ ἐλεήμονες, ὅτι αὐτοὶ ἐλεηθήσονται", οὗτινος μακαρισμοῦ ἀξιωθείημεν ἐν Χριστῷ Ἰησοῦ τῷ Κυρίῳ ἡμῶν, ᾧ ἡ δόξα καὶ τὸ κράτος εἰς τοὺς αἰῶνας τῶν
> 5 αἰώνων, ἀμήν. Χριστὸς δῴη χάριν τοῖς ἐμοῖς πόνοις.

fol. 228ᵛ **24ᴹ** Τοῦ ἁγίου Ἰωάννου τοῦ Χρυσοστόμου ἐκ τοῦ λόγου ὅτι παλαιᾶς καὶ καινῆς διαθήκης εἷς ὁ νομοθέτης καὶ εἰς τὸ ἔνδυμα τοῦ ἱερέως.
Ἐγὼ καὶ τὴν κηρόχυτον—τὴν εἰκόνα αὐτῶν ἐξουδενώσεις.
P 55*; V 30 (P⟩M).

25ᴹ Τοῦ αὐτοῦ ἐκ τῆς ἑρμηνείας τῆς παραβολῆς τοῦ σπόρου.
Inc.: Ἔνδυμα βασιλικὸν ἐὰν ὑβρίσῃς, οὐ τὸν ἐνδεδυμένον . . .
desin.: . . . τὴν ἑαυτῆς ὕβριν εἰς τὸν βασιλέα ἄγει.
CPG 4209 Severianus Gabalensis, *De sigillis sermo,* PG 63, 544.7–15.
A XII 1066ᴇ–1067ᴀ. Dam. II 61.
P 58* (additamentum); V 29 (additamentum), **44.**

26ᴹ Τοῦ αὐτοῦ ἐκ τῆς ἐπιστολῆς τῆς πρὸς Μελέτιον ἐπίσκοπον.
Καὶ ἦν εὐλαβείας διδασκαλία—(fol. 229) ἀποδημίας ἔχειν παραμυθίαν.
P 53*; V 10 (P⟩M).

27ᴹ Τοῦ αὐτοῦ ἐκ τοῦ περὶ παρθενίας λόγου.
Inc.: Πολλοὶ τῆς ἱεροσύνης (sic) ἦρξαν χρήμασιν . . .
desin.: . . . μὴ ἐκ τοῦ παραδείγματος ἐσοφρονίσθησαν (sic).
CPG 4313 Iohannes Chrys., *De virginitate,* ed. H. Musurillo and B. Grillet, *Jean Chrysostome. La virginité,* SC 125 (Paris, 1966), 24.24–28.

fol. 229ᵛ **28ᴹ** Τοῦ μακαρίου Γερμανοῦ χρήσης. (sic).
Inc.: Ὑπὲρ πάντα δὲ προνοητέον ἡμῖν, ὅπερ μου . . .

desin.: . . . ὡς τῆς ἀληθείας οὐκ οὔσης παρ᾽ αὐτοῖς.
CPG 8004 Germanus I Const., *Epistula ad Thomam episcopum Claudiopoleos*, PG 98, 184D–185A1.
A XIII 124D7–E6.

29ᴹ Ἐκ τῶν διαταγῶν τῶν ἀποστόλων.
Inc.: Τοὺς ἀθέους αἱρεσιῶτας ἀμετανοήτως ἔχωντας (sic) . . .
desin.: . . . μήτε προσευχαῖς κοινονῆσαι (sic) αὐτοῖς.
CPG 1730 *Constitutiones Apostolorum*, ed. F. X. Funk, *Didascalia et Constitutiones apostolorum*, I (Paderborn, 1905), VI, 18.1 (= p. 341.14–17).

30ᴹ Τοῦ ἁγίου Ἰγνατίου.
Inc.: Εἴ τις ἐν ἀλλοτρίᾳ γνώμῃ . . .
desin.: . . . μὴ συναπόλλεσθε αὐτοῖς.
CPG 1026 Ignatius Antioch., *Epistulae interpolatae et epistulae suppositiciae* (= recens. longior), *Ep. ad Philadelphienses*, ed. F. X. Funk and F. Diekamp, *Patres Apostolici*, II (Tübingen, 1913), p. 172, lines 17–20; PG 5, 821A13–B2.

fol. 230   **31ᴹ** Ἐκ τῆς ἁγίας οἰκουμενικῆς ε΄ συνόδου.
Inc.: Ἀλλ᾽ ἰδέναι (sic) κατὰ τὴν εὐαγγελικήν τε καὶ ἀποστολικήν . . .
desin.: . . . τοῖς ἔργοις αὐτοῦ τοῖς πονηροῖς.
CPG 9329.10 Synodus Constantinopolitana (a. 536), *Gesta, Actio V, Sententia synodi*. ACO III, 111.20–23.

31aᴹ Ἐκ τῆς ἁγίας ἕκτης συνόδου.
Ὅτι οὐ δεῖ παρὰ τῶν Ἰουδαίων ἢ αἱρετικῶν τὰ πεμπώμενα (sic) ἑορταστικὰ λαμβάνειν, οὐδὲ συνεορτάζειν αὐτοῖς.
Locum non inveni (cf. CPG 9444 Concilium Oecumenicum in Trullo, *Canones cii*. Canon xi, Mansi XI 945E).

32ᴹ: see **30ᴹ** Τοῦ ἁγίου Ἰγνατίου ἐκ τῆς πρὸς τοὺς Σμυρναίους ἐπιστολῆς.
Inc.: Τί γὰρ ὠφελεῖ εἰ ἐμὲ ἐπαινεῖ τις, τὸν δὲ Κύριόν μου . . .
desin.: . . . γένοιτό μοι αὐτῶν μνημονεύειν ⟨32a⟩ (fol. 233) μέχρις ἂν μετανοήσωσιν.
CPG 1026 Ignatius Antioch., *Ep. ad Smyrnaeos*, ed. Funk and Diekamp, *Patres Apostolici*, II, p. 196, lines 1–5; PG 5, 845C4–848A6.

32aᴹ ⟨Ἰωάννου Δαμασκηνοῦ⟩
fol. 230 Inc.: ἐν μὲν γὰρ τῷ εὐαγγελίῳ καὶ Θεός, καὶ ἄγγελος . . .
fol. 233 desin.: . . . ὕλης δημιουργόν, τὸν ὕλην δι᾽ ἐμὲ γενάμενον.
Dam. II 10.8–14.14. See quotation **4ᴹ**.

33ᴹ Τοῦ αὐτοῦ ἁγίου.
Inc.: Τοὺς μισοῦντας οὖν τὸν Θεὸν μισεῖν χρή· . . .
desin.: . . . μετάνοιαν παρακαλεῖν ἐὰν (sic) ἆρα θέλωσιν.
CPG 1026 Ignatius Antioch., *Epistula ad Philadelphienses*, ed. Funk and Diekamp, *Patres Apostolici*, II, p. 172, line 21–p. 174, line 3; PG 5, 821B4–10.

fol. 233ᵛ   **34ᴹ** Ἅγιος Γρηγόριος·
Οὐδέποτε ἴδων εἰκόνας ἁγίων καὶ γραφὰς καὶ ἄνευ δακροίων παρῆλθων (sic) ἐκεῖθεν· οἶδεν γὰρ καὶ γραφὴ σιωπῶσα τὰ μέγιστα ὠφελεῖν. καὶ πάλιν ὁ ἅγιος Βασίλειος

τί εἶχεν ἀνάγκην τοσοῦτον κόπον καταβαλέσθε εἰς Κεσάριαν (sic) ἵνα ἱστορήσει τὴν εἰκόνα τοῦ Χριστοῦ;
Fragmentum de tractatu *Adversus Const. Caballinum* desumptum est; *PG* 95, 321D3–7.
P 2*; M 7ᴹ.

35ᴹ Ἐκ τῆς ἐκθέσεως τοῦ ἁγίου Ἀναστασίου πατριάρχου Θεουπόλεως, ἐξήγησης (sic) περὶ τῶν ἐν Περσίδη (sic) πραχθέντων περὶ τῶν μάγων διηγουμένων.
Inc.: Ἡμεῖς δὲ εἴπαμεν αὐτῇ· μῆτερ μητέρων, ἅπαντες . . .
fol. 234 desin.: . . . ὡς ἔδη (sic) ἤλθομεν ἐν ᾧ τόπῳ κατελύσαμεν.
CPG 6968 Anastasius I Antioch., *De gestis in Perside*, ed. E. Bratke, *Das sogenannte Religionsgespräch am Hof der Sassaniden*, *TU* 19.3 (Leipzig, 1899), 17.16–18.17; *PG* 10, 108A5–C2. *BHG* 806 (App. II 13), *De gestis in Perside narratio Africani immo Aphroditiani.*

36ᴹ Ἐκ τοῦ βίου τοῦ ἁγίου Σιλβέστρου πάπα Ῥώμης μαρτυρίαι.
Inc.: Ὁ δὲ ἅγιος Σίλβεστρος ἀποκρινόμενος ἔφη· εἰρήνη . . .
fol. 235 desin.: . . . τύχης τῶν σῶν τραυμάτων τὴν ὑγίαν (sic).
Ed. F. Combefis, *Illustrium Christi martyrum lecti triumphi* (Paris, 1660), 277.14–279.8.
P 124*.

37ᴹ Παμφίλου ἱερομάρτυρος· ἐκ τῆς ἐν Ἀντιωχίᾳ (sic) γεναμένης συνόδου ὑπὸ τῶν ἀποστόλων, κεφάλαιον τέταρτον.
Inc.: Τοῦ μηκέτι πλανᾶσθαι εἰς τὰ εἴδωλα τοὺς σῳζομένους . . .
desin.: . . . πλανᾶσθαι εἰς εἴδωλα, μηδὲ ὁμοιοῦσθαι Ἰουδαίοις.
P 73*; V 5.

38ᴹ Μαξίμου φιλοσόφου καὶ ὁμολογητοῦ ἐκ τῶν περὶ αὐτὸν πεπραγμένων μεταξὺ αὐτοῦ τε καὶ Θεοδοσίου ἐπισκόπου.
Inc.: Καὶ ἐπὶ τούτοις ἀνέστησαν πάντες μετὰ χαρᾶς . . .
desin.: . . . αὐτῶν χεῖρας ἐπὶ βεβαιώσει τῶν λαληθέντων.
P 92*; V 34 (V⟩A⟩P⟩M).

39ᴹ = 25ᴹ Τοῦ Χρυσοστόμου εἰς τὴν παραβολὴν τοῦ σπόρου.
Ἔνδυμα βασιλικὸν ἐὰν ὑβρίσης—(fol. 235ᵛ) εἰς τὸν βασιλέα ἐνάγη.

fol. 235ᵛ 40ᴹ Τοῦ αὐτοῦ ἐκ τοῦ λόγου τῆς τεσσαρακοστῆς.
Πολλὰς πολλάκις εἶδον εἰκόνας—τουτέστιν ἡ ἀλήθεια.
P 56*; V 31 (persimile).

41ᴹ Τοῦ αὐτοῦ ἐκ τοῦ λόγου τοῦ εἰς τὸν νηπτῆρα. (sic).
Πάντα οὖν ἐγένοντο—τὸν οὐράνιον χαρακτῆρα αἰδεῖται.
P 54* (persimile).

fol. 236 42ᴹ Τοῦ ἁγίου Ἰωάννου τοῦ Χρυσοστόμου· ἐκ τῆς ἑρμηνείας τοῦ ᾄσματος τῶν ᾀσμάτων.
Ὥσπερ δὲ κατὰ τὴν γραφικήν—ὁ τεχνίτης ἀνέδειξεν.
P 44*.

43ᴹ Τοῦ ἁγίου Γρηγορίου τοῦ Θεολόγου ἐκ τοῦ κατὰ Ἰουλιανὸν λόγου.
Inc.: Νόμος ἐστὶν βασιλεικὸς (sic) οὐκ οἴδαμεν εἰ καί . . .
fol. 237 desin.: . . . κλέπτειν τὰς ἐγχειρήσεις τὰ προκείμενα.

CPG 3010.4 Gregorius Naz., *Oratio 4, Oratio I contra Iulianum,* ed. Bernardi, *Discours 4–5 contre Julien,* 202 par. 80.1–206 par. 81.27; *PG* 35, 605в10–608с5.
V 46.

44ᴹ Τοῦ Χρυσοστόμου ἐκ τοῦ λόγου περὶ τῆς καταστροφῆς τῶν ἀνδριάντων.
Inc.: Ταῦτα προλέγων ταῦτα ἐξέβη νῦν—στήσωμεν δίκην. καὶ πάλιν. οὐκ ἀρκεῖ εἰς ἀπολογίαν—(fol. 237ᵛ) καὶ ὕβρεις γινομένας. καὶ πάλιν. νῦν εὔκαιρον ἀναβοῆσαι . . .
desin.: . . . διὰ τὴν προσηγορίαν ἀεὶ δεῖ τιμῆς ἀπολαύειν.
CPG 4330 Iohannes Chrys., *Ad populum Antiochenum, hom. ii, PG* 49, 38.20–24; 38.48–58; 57.9–15.

45ᴹ Ἰωάννου ἐπισκόπου Γαβαλῶν (sic) ἐκ τοῦ κατὰ Σεβῆρον λόγου.
Inc.: Οὐδὲ γὰρ τὴν τῶν ἀγγέλων τιμὴν ἀλώβητον εἴασε . . .
desin.: . . . καὶ ταύτην διαιρεῖν καὶ ἐπ᾽ ἄλλους κινεῖν.
CPG 7525 Iohannes Gabalensis, *Vita Severi Antiocheni* (frag.).
A XIII 184в–с.

46ᴹ Ἐκ τῆς δεήσεως τῶν μοναχῶν καὶ κληρικῶν Ἀντιοχείας κατὰ Σεβήρου πρὸς τὴν πέμπτην σύνοδον.
Οὐ μὴν οὐδὲ αὐτῶν ἐφείσατο—(fol. 238) ὀνομάζεσθαι τὸ ἅγιον πνεῦμα.
P 104* (persimile).

fol. 238   **47ᴹ** Ἐκ τοῦ μαρτυρίου τοῦ ἁγίου Γρηγορίου Ἀρμενίας.
Inc.: Καὶ ἐπειδὴ ἠγάπησαν ἄνθρωποι σέβειν τάς . . .
desin.: . . . καὶ τὴν ἐπάνω ἀνθρωπόμορφον εἰκόνα.
CPG 7547.2 Agathangelus, *Historia Armeniae, Versio Graeca* (*BHG* 712), ed. G. Lafontaine, *La version grecque ancienne du livre arménien d'Agathange,* Publications de l'Institut Orientaliste de Louvain 7 (Louvain-la-Neuve, 1973), 202, 34.1–13.

fol. 238ᵛ **48ᴹ** Ἐξήγησις ἐκ τοῦ παραδεισίου.
Inc.: Ὁ ἀββᾶς Θεόδωρος ὁ Ἐλιώτης διηγήσατο ἡμῖν . . .
fol. 239 desin.: . . . σοῦ δὲ τοῦ λοιποῦ οὐ μὴ ἀκούσω.
P 123* (M)P).

49ᴹ Ἐκ τῆς ἁγίας οἰκουμενικῆς ἕκτης συνόδου.
Ἔν τισι τῶν σεπτῶν εἰκόνων—τῷ κόσμῳ ἀπολυτρώσεως.
P 94*; V 38.

fol. 239ᵛ **50ᴹ** Κυρίλλου ἀρχιεπισκόπου Ἀλεξανδρείας εἰς τὴν ὁσίαν μάρτυρα.
Πάλιν μαρτυρικῆς ἀνδραγαθίας—ὑφηγουμένην τῆς μάρτυρος.
P 63*; V 1 (persimile).

51ᴹ Τοῦ ἁγίου Γρηγορίου τοῦ Νύσης· εἰς τὸν ἅγιον μάρτυρα Βασιλίσκον.
Τὰ μὲν περὶ τῆς τοῦ ἀνδρὸς ὑπομονῆς, ὅσα περὶ διηγήσεως ἴσμεν (sic) ταῦτα, ἅτινα καὶ ἐγὼ ἐν τύχω (sic) πολλάκις ἰδὼν (sic) γραφέντα καὶ φοβοῦντα πρὸ τῆς πείρας τοὺς ἀγνοοῦντας τῇ πείρα τὰς βασάνους τὸ ἀφόριτον (sic)· καὶ μετ᾽ ὀλίγα· οἶδεν γὰρ καὶ γραφὴ σιωπῶσα τὰ μέγιστα ὀφελεῖν (sic).
P 52*; V 12, locum non inveni.

52ᴹ Τοῦ ἁγίου Ἀθανασίου, ἀρχιεπισκόπου Ἀλεξανδρείας ἐκ τοῦ τετάρτου λόγου κατὰ Ἀρειανῶν.
Inc.: Ὁ γὰρ οὕτως [lacuna] ὅτι ἕν εἰσιν ὁ υἱὸς καὶ ὁ πατήρ . . .

fol. 240 desin.: . . . ἡ γὰρ ἐκείνου μορφὴ καὶ τὸ εἶδός ἐστιν ἡ εἰκών.
P **69***; V **21** (Dam.)M⟩A⟩P).

53^M Τοῦ ἁγίου Βασιλείου ἐκ τοῦ λόγου εἰς τοὺς τεσσαράκοντα μάρτυρας.
Ἐπεὶ καὶ πολέμων ἀνδραγαθήματα—διὰ μιμήσεως δείκνυσιν.
P **16***; V **23** (P⟩M).

54^M Τοῦ ἁγίου Γρηγορίου Νύσης ἐκ τοῦ ἀναπληρωματικοῦ τουτέστιν τοῦ περὶ τῆς κατασκευῆς τοῦ ἀνθρώπου.
Ὥσπερ κατὰ τὴν ἀνθρωπίνην—(fol. 240ᵛ) τῆς ἀξίας τοῦ ὀνόματος.
P **46***, (M⟩P).
M = Dam. I 49; II 45.

55^M Τοῦ αὐτοῦ.
Inc.: Τὸ δὲ θεῖον κάλλος οὐ σχήματί τινι μορφῆς . . .
desin.: . . . μετενεχθείη πρὸς τὸ ὁμοίωμα.
P **47*** (M⟩P).
Dam. I 50; II 46.

Post ὁμοίωμα M add.:

Ὅρα ὡς τὸ μὲν θεῖον κάλλος—ὡς Θεοῦ σεσαρκωμένου εἰκών.

Quod est scholium Iohannis Damasceni: Dam. I 51; II 47.

fol. 241 **56**^M Τοῦ ἐν ἁγίοις πατρὸς ἡμῶν Ἀνδρέου ἐπισκόπου.
Inc.: Ὅτι οὐδὲν ἀκανόνιστον παρὰ Χριστιανοῖς πρῶτον . . .
desin.: . . . ἑορακέναι τὰς τοιαύτας εἰκόνας.
CPG 8193 Andreas Cretensis, *De sanctarum imaginum veneratione, PG* 97, 1301–4
(*BHG* 1125) (*Recensio*).

List of Contents of the Iconophile Florilegium of Venetus
Marcianus Graecus 573 (V) (fols. 2–26)

Abbreviations

Dam. = Kotter, *Schriften III*
 P = Parisinus gr. 1115 (numbers refer to App. II)
 M = Mosquensis Hist. Mus. 265 (numbers refer to App. III)

fol. 2 Μαρτυρίαι τῶν ἁγίων καὶ θεοσόφων πατέρων εἰς τὰς πανσέπτους καὶ ἱερὰς εἰκόνας.

1 Ἔφη τοίνυν ὁ τρισμακάριος ἀληθῶς καὶ διαβόητος εἰς εὐσέβειαν Κύριλλος, ὁ γεγονὼς
κατὰ καιροὺς τῆς Ἀλεξανδρέων ἐκκλησίας ἐπίσκοπος ἐν τῷ λόγῳ τῷ εἰς μάρτυρας.
Πάλιν μαρτυρικῆς ἀνδραγαθείας—ὑφηγουμένη τῆς μάρτυρος.
P **63***; M **50**ᴹ.

2 Τοῦ ἁγίου Κυρίλλου ἐκ τοῦ πέμπτου βιβλίου τῶν πρὸς Ἑρμείαν.
Εἰκόνι μὲν πρὸς τὸ ἀκριβῶς—ὡς ἐν εἴδει ταὐτόν.
P **64*** (persimile).

3 Τοῦ αὐτοῦ ἐκ τῆς βίβλου τοῦ (fol. 2ᵛ) θησαυροῦ τοῦ ἕκτου κεφαλαίου.
Πᾶν ὅπερ καθ᾿ ὁμοίωσιν—τὴν ὁμοίωσιν τοῦ πρωτοτύπου.
P **65*** (persimile).

4 Τοῦ αὐτοῦ ἐκ τοῦ δευτέρου λόγου τοῦ κατὰ τῶν αἱρετικῶν τῶν κατ᾿ Αἴγυπτον
ἐπισκόπων.
Περὶ Γεωργίου τοῦ ἀσεβοῦς—(fol. 3) ἀγχόνῃ παρέδωκεν.
P **66*** (persimile); M **1**ᴹ.

5 Παμφίλου ἱερομάρτυρος ἐκ τῆς ἐν Ἀντιοχείᾳ τῶν ἀποστόλων γεναμένης συνόδου
τουτέστιν ἐκ τῶν συνοδικῶν κεφαλαίων τοῦ τετάρτου.
Πρὸς τὸ μηκέτι ἀποπλανᾶσθαι—ὁμοιοῦσθαι Ἰουδαίοις καὶ ἔθνεσιν.
P **73*** (P om. v vocabula); M **37**ᴹ.

6 Τοῦ ἁγιωτάτου Γρηγορίου τοῦ Θαυματουργοῦ ὅρος συνοδικός.
Οἱ μὴ προσκυνοῦντες—ἔστωσαν ἀνάθεμα.
P **50*** (persimile).

7 Βασιλείου τοῦ ἁγιωτάτου ἐπισκόπου Καισαρείας Καππαδοκίας ἐκ τοῦ λόγου τοῦ
περὶ ὀργῆς.
fol. 3ᵛ Τῷ ὄντι φησὶν (sic) τῆς εἰκόνος—δεικνύουσα τὴν ὁμοίωσιν.
P **18*** (persimile).

8 Τοῦ αὐτοῦ ἐκ τοῦ πρὸς Ἀμφιλόχιον περὶ ἁγίου πνεύματος κεφαλαίου ιη΄.
Inc.: Βασιλεὺς λέγεται καὶ ἡ τοῦ βασιλέως εἰκὼν καὶ οὐ . . .
desin.: . . . ἐν τῇ κοινωνίᾳ τῆς θεότητός ἐστιν ἡ ἕνωσις.
P **25*** (P⟩V = Dam.).

9 Γρηγορίου τοῦ Θεολόγου· ἐκ τοῦ περὶ ἀρετῆς καὶ εἰς Πολέμωνα λόγου.
Inc.: Οὐδ᾽ ὁ Πολέμων ἐμοί γε σιγηθήσεται· . . .
fol. 4 desin.: . . . καὶ τοῦτο πολλοῖς οἶδα τῶν λαλουμένων.
P **21*** (P⟩V).

10 Τοῦ ἐν ἁγίοις πατρὸς ἡμῶν Ἰωάννου τοῦ Χρυσοστόμου ἐκ τοῦ λόγου τοῦ πρὸς Μελέτιον ἐπίσκοπον Ἀντιοχείας καὶ μάρτυρα, ἐν ᾧ καὶ εἰς τὴν σπουδὴν τῶν συνελθόντων.
Inc.: Ὅπερ οὖν ἐπ᾽ ὀνόματι αὐτοῦ ἐποιήσατε, τοῦτο . . .
fol. 4ᵛ desin.: . . . διπλῆν τινα τῆς ἀποδημίας ἔχειν παραμυθίαν.
P **53***; M **26**ᴹ (P⟩M⟩V).

11 Τοῦ ἁγίου Γρηγορίου Νύσης ἐκ τοῦ λόγου τοῦ εἰς τὸ μακάριοι οἱ πτωχοὶ τῷ πνεύματι.
Ἐπὶ τῆς σωματικῆς εὐμορφίας—τῆς εἰκόνος δεικνύμενον.
P **51*** (persimile).

12 Φάσκει τε αὐτὸς καὶ ἐν ἑτέρῳ χωρίῳ.
Εἶδον ἐγὼ ἐν τοίχῳ—καὶ τὰ μέγιστα ὠφελεῖν.
P **52*** (verbatim); M **51**ᴹ.

13 Ἀναστασίου τοῦ ἁγιωτάτου ἐπισκόπου Θεουπόλεως ἐπιστολὴ πρὸς Συμεὼν ἐπίσκοπον Βόστρης περιέχουσα περὶ Σαββάτου.
Ὥσπερ ἀπόντος βασιλέως—(fol. 5) ἀναφέρει τὴν ὕβριν.
P **82*** (persimile).

14 Εὐσταθίου τοῦ ἁγιωτάτου ἐπισκόπου Ἀντιοχείας ἐκ τοῦ λόγου τοῦ εἰς τὴν Σαμαρεῖτιν.
Ἡμεῖς οὖν ἀνακεκαλυμμένῳ προσώπῳ—τὸ τῆς εἰκόνος ἀρχέτυπον.
P **83*** (persimile).

15 Σωφρονίου τοῦ ἁγιωτάτου ἐπισκόπου Ἰεροσολύμων ἐκ τοῦ ἐγκωμίου τοῦ εἰς Κῦρον καὶ Ἰωάννην τοὺς μάρτυρας.
fol. 5ᵛ Inc.: Ἄλλοι μὲν ἄλλως τοὺς ἁγίους τιμάτωσαν . . .
desin.: . . . ἐπὶ τὴν τῶν μαρτύρων τιμὴν ἀμιλλάσθωσαν (sic).
P **107*** (P⟩V).

16 Ἰωσσίππου τοῦ ἁγιωτάτου ἐπισκόπου Νικομηδείας ἐκ τοῦ λόγου τοῦ ἐν τοῖς διωγμοῖς.
Inc.: Τοὺς ὑπὲρ Χριστοῦ χριστοπρεπῶς διαλάμψαντας . . .
fol. 6 desin.: . . . καὶ τοῖς μετ᾽ αὐτοὺς περιέστησαν.
P **84*** (persimile).

Post περιέστησαν V add.:

Προσπαρέλκουσαν (sic) οὖν βεβαίωσιν αὐτῶν τῶν ἁγίων εἰκόνων καὶ ἐπισφράγησιν τῶν ἐμαυτοῦ λόγων καὶ ἑτέρων ὁσίων πατέρων ἰάμβια εὑρημένα ἐν ἐκκλησίαις ἐνθήσομαι.

17 Τοῦ ἁγιωτάτου Γερμανοῦ ἐπισκόπου Κωνσταντινουπόλεως, ἐπίγραμμα εἰς τὴν τοῦ Σωτῆρος εἰκόνα γραφέν.

Ὁ τὰς νοητὰς καὶ θεατὰς οὐσίας ἐξεικονίζων ὡς Θεὸς κατ' οὐσίαν, τὸ ῥευστὸν ἡμῶν προσλαβὼν τῆς εἰκόνος, ἀνθρωπομόρφως εἰκονίζεται εἰκόνι.

Ed. I. B. Pitra, *Iuris Ecclesiastici Graecorum Historia et Monumenta*, II (Rome, 1868), 365.

18 Ταρασίου τοῦ μακαριωτάτου ἐπισκόπου Κωνσταντινουπόλεως, ἐπίγραμμα εἰς τὸν ἀπεικονισμὸν τῆς σταυρώσεως.

Ἐλευθερώσας πάντας εἰδώλων πλάνης στηλογραφεῖται Χριστὸς ἐσταυρωμένος.

Ed. Pitra, ibid.

19 Νικηφόρου τοῦ ὁσιωτάτου ἐπισκόπου Κωνσταντινουπόλεως, ἐπίγραμμα εἰς τὸν τῶν ἁγίων εἰκόνων ἀνάγραπτον διάκοσμον·

fol. 6ᵛ Τύπους θεωρῶν ἐνθέων μυστηρίων, τρόπους νόησον ἐγγράφους σωτηρίους, ἐν οἷς τὰ σεπτὰ τῆς κενώσεως λόγου σοφῶς ἀθροοῦνται καὶ νοοῦνται προσφόρως.

Ed. Pitra, ibid.

Post προσφόρως V add.:

Οὗτοι μὲν οἱ Χριστομάκαρες καὶ Χριστομέτοχοι πατέρες καὶ τῆς κρυφίας ἐπιπνοίας ὑποφῆται τὰς τιμιωτάτας εἰκόνας σωτηρίοις τύποις ἀνασκεψάμενοι καὶ παραδώσαντες ὡς ἱερὰ σύμβολα τῶν ἀληθῶν ἀποφάσεων καὶ ὡς φαινόμενα μιμήματα τῶν ἀφανῶν ὑποστάσεων τιμᾶσθαι παρεκελεύσαντο.

20 Τοῦ ἁγίου Διονυσίου τοῦ Ἀρεοπαγίτου, μαρτυρίαι εἰς τὰς αὐτὰς ἁγίας καὶ ἱερὰς εἰκόνας. Ἔφη τοίνυν ὁ τρισμακάριος ἀληθῶς καὶ διαβόητος εἰς εὐσέβειαν Διονύσιος, ὁ κατὰ καιροὺς γεγονὼς τῆς Ἀθηναίων ἐκκλησίας πρόεδρος ἐν τῷ λόγῳ τῷ περὶ τελετῆς τοῦ μύρου.

Inc.: Καθάπερ ἐπὶ τῶν αἰσθητῶν εἰκόνων εἰ πρὸς τό . . .

fol. 8ᵛ desin.: . . . κατὰ τοὺς ἱεροὺς ἡμῶν ἔδωσαν θεσμούς.

P **75*–77***.

21 Ἀθανασίου τοῦ ἁγιωτάτου ἀρχιεπισκόπου Ἀλεξανδρείας ἐκ τοῦ λόγου τοῦ κατὰ Ἀρειανῶν.

Ἐν τῇ εἰκόνι τοῦ βασιλέως—ὁ ἐν τῇ εἰκόνι γεγραμμένος.

P **69***; M **52ᴹ** (Dam⟩M⟩A⟩P⟩V).

22 Τοῦ ἁγιωτάτου Γρηγορίου ⟨ . . ⟩ τοῦ Θαυματουργοῦ ἐκ τῆς ἑρμηνείας τῆς σοφίας Σολομῶντος.

Οἱ οὖν ἐναγεῖς καὶ ἀκάθαρτοι—(fol. 9) πίστεως ἀλλότριοι.

P **49*** (persimile).

23 Τοῦ ἁγίου Βασιλείου ἐκ τοῦ λόγου τοῦ εἰς τοὺς τεσσαράκοντα μάρτυρας.

Δεῦρο οὖν εἰς μέσον αὐτούς—διὰ τῆς μιμήσεως δείκνυσιν.

P **16*** (persimile); M **53ᴹ**.

24 Τοῦ αὐτοῦ ἐκ τοῦ εἰς Βαρλαὰμ τὸν μάρτυρα.

fol. 9ᵛ Ἀνάστητέ μοι ὦ λαμπροί—ἀγωνοθέτης Θεός.

P **15*** (variis lectionibus).

25 Ἑλλαδίου τοῦ μαθητοῦ αὐτοῦ καὶ διαδόχου τῆς ἱεραρχίας αὐτοῦ ἐκ τοῦ βίου αὐτοῦ.
Παρειστήκει ὁ ἅγιος Βασίλειος—(fol. 10) ἠμαγμένον κατέχοντα.
P **20*** (persimile).

26 Γρηγορίου τοῦ Θεολόγου ἐκ τοῦ δευτέρου λόγου τοῦ περὶ υἱοῦ.
Οἱ τὰς μορφὰς γράφοντες—τοῦ ἀρχετύπου καὶ οὗ λέγεται.
P **24*** (persimile).

26a Τοῦ αὐτοῦ ἐκ τῶν ἐπῶν τοῦ εἰς ἐπισκόπου λόγου.
Ζωγράφος ἐστίν—ἔμπνοα δερκομένας.
P **22*** (verbatim).

27 Τοῦ αὐτοῦ ἐκ τοῦ περὶ παρθενίας λόγου.
Εἰκόνα μὲν ἔγραψέν τις—πλάσματα μορφαῖς.
P **23*** (persimile).

fol. 10ᵛ **28** Κυρίλλου τοῦ ἁγιωτάτου ἀρχιεπισκόπου Ἀλεξανδρείας ἐκ τοῦ βιβλίου τοῦ
θησαυροῦ δωδεκάτου κεφαλαίου.
Ὥσπερ ἄν τις εἰς εἰκόνα—εἶδος ἐν ἐκείνῳ σῴζεται.
P **67*** (persimile).

29 Τοῦ ἁγίου Ἰωάννου τοῦ Χρυσοστόμου ἐκ τῆς ἑρμηνείας τοῦ κατὰ Ἰωάννην εὐαγ-
γελίου.
Ὁ διὰ τῶν χαραγμάτων—(fol. 11) οὐκ ἀλλότριον τῆς ἀληθείας.
Post ἀληθείας V add.: οὐκ οἶδας—βασιλέα quod est additamentum in P **58***.

30 Τοῦ αὐτοῦ ἐκ τοῦ λόγου τοῦ ὅτι παλαιᾶς καὶ νέας διαθήκης εἷς ὁ νομοθέτης.
Ἐγὼ καὶ τὴν κηρόχυτον γραφήν—(fol. 11ᵛ) αὐτῶν ἐξουδενώσεις.
P **55*** (V om. Inc.); M **24ᴹ**.

31 Τοῦ αὐτοῦ ἐκ τοῦ λόγου τοῦ εἰς τὴν ἁγίαν τεσσαρακοστὴν καὶ περὶ μετανοίας.
Πολλὰς πολλάκις εἶδον—τουτέστιν ἡ ἀλήθεια.
P **56*** (persimile); M **40ᴹ**.

32 Ἐκ τοῦ βίου τοῦ αὐτοῦ ἁγίου Ἰωάννου τοῦ Χρυσοστόμου.
Ἠγάπα ὁ μακάριος Ἰωάννης—τῆς θεωρίας αὐτῷ ὁμιλῶν.
P **60*** (P⟩V).

fol. 12 **33** Συμεὼν τοῦ στηλίτου τοῦ ἐν τῷ Θαυμαστῷ ὄρει ἐκ τῆς ἐπιστολῆς τῆς πεμ-
φθείσης πρὸς τὸν βασιλέα Ἰουστῖνον.
Οἱ πανευσεβεῖς τῶν καλλινίκων ὑμῶν—γένηται φιλανθρωπία.
P **97*** (persimile).

34 Ἐκ τοῦ τόμου τῶν κινηθέντων δογμάτων μεταξὺ τοῦ ἐν ἁγίοις Μαξίμου καὶ Θεοδοσίου ἐπισκόπου Καισαρείας τῆς Βιθυνίας.
Inc.: Ἀνέστησαν οὖν μετὰ φόβου καὶ δακρύων . . .
fol. 12ᵛ desin.: . . . ἐπὶ τῷ βασιλεῖ τὴν αἰτίαν παρέπεμψεν.
P **92***; M **38ᴹ** (V om. Inc. textus P).

35 Στεφάνου τοῦ ἁγιωτάτου ἐπισκόπου Βωστρῶν (sic) περὶ εἰκόνων τῶν ἁγίων.
Inc.: Περὶ δὲ τῶν εἰκόνων τῶν ἁγίων θαρροῦμεν . . .
fol. 14 desin.: . . . οἱ ἅγιοι ὑπὲρ ἡμῶν τὸ θεῖον ἐξιλεοῦνται.
P **95***.

36 Βασιλείου ἐπισκόπου Σελευκείας ἐκ τῶν θαυμάτων τῆς ἁγίας πρωτομάρτυρος Θέκλης.
Inc.: Συνέβη κατ᾽ ἐκεῖνον τὸν καιρὸν ἱερέα τῶν Ἑλλήνων . . .
fol. 15 desin.: . . . εἰς τὸ μεταγράψαι τοῖς βουληθεῖσιν.
P **87*** (V om. partes quasdam textus P).

37 Θεοδώρου ἀναγνώστου Κωνσταντινουπόλεως ἐκ τῆς ἐκκλησιαστικῆς ἱστορίας.
Ζωγράφος τις τὴν εἰκόνα—(fol. 15ᵛ) τῆς ἰάσεως ἔτυχεν.
P **100*** (persimile); M **19ᴹ**.

38 Τῆς ἁγίας καὶ οἰκουμενικῆς ἕκτης συνόδου.
Ἔν τισι τῶν σεπτῶν εἰκόνων—(fol. 16) τοῦ κόσμου ἀπολυτρώσεως.
P **94*** (persimile); M **49ᴹ**.

Κεφαλαίων ἔκθεσις δηλούντων ὅτι ἀεὶ ἦσαν εἰκόνες, ὥσπερ ἐπὶ τῆς παλαιᾶς οὕτω δὴ καὶ ἐν πάσῃ τῇ νέᾳ.

39 Τοῦ ἁγίου Βασιλείου ἐκ τῶν ἀσκητικῶν.
Inc.: Ὥσπερ γὰρ οἱ πλείονες ζωγράφοι εἰ ἑνὸς προσώπου . . .
fol. 16ᵛ desin.: . . . τοῦ βίου χαρακτὴρ ἐπιλάμψει.
CPG 2883 Basilius Caes., *Prologus iv (Sermo asceticus) (Ascetico magno* praemissus), *PG* 31, 884B3–13.

40 Τοῦ ἁγίου Βασιλείου ἐπιστολὴ πρὸς Γρηγόριον τὸν Θεολόγον.
Ἐν ταύταις γὰρ καὶ τῶν πράξεων—ἔργων πρόκεινται. Καὶ μετ᾽ ὀλίγον· καὶ πανταχοῦ ὥσπερ—μεταθεῖναι φιλοτέχνημα.
CPG 2900 Basilius Caes., *Epistulae*, ed. Y. Courtonne, *S. Basile, Lettres*, I (Paris, 1957), 8 par. 3.2–6; 9 par. 3.28–31; *PG* 32, 228B11–C3; 229A8–12.

41 Τοῦ αὐτοῦ ἐκ τοῦ περὶ τριάδος λόγου.
Ἀδύνατον γὰρ ἰδεῖν τήν—ἀποχωρίσαι τὸ φῶς. Καὶ μετὰ βραχέα· διὰ δὲ τοῦ χαρακτῆρος—(fol. 17) σφραγὶς ἀναγόμεθα.
CPG 2839 Basilius Caes., *De Spiritu Sancto*, ed. B. Pruche, *Saint-Esprit*, 476 par. 64.16–19; 22–23. *PG* 32, 185BC.

42 Τοῦ αὐτοῦ ἐκ τῆς ὁμιλίας τῆς ῥηθείσης ἐν Λακίζοις.
Inc.: Ἐπειδὴ εἶδεν τὸν ἄνθρωπον κατ᾽ εἰκόνα καὶ ὁμοίωσιν . . .
fol. 17ᵛ desin.: . . . τοῦ θεομάχου εἶναι τὸν πονηρόν.
CPG 2912 Basilius Caes., *Homilia dicta in Lacisis*, *PG* 31, 1456C3–D7.
Dam. III 56; I 48; II 44 *sch.*
Doctrina Patrum (chap. ME), p. 329.4–11, XII.

43 Not in *TLG*.
Ἰωάννου τοῦ Χρυσοστόμου·
    Πρῶτον ὁ ἄνθρωπος ἔλαβεν εἰκόνα νεκρὰν καὶ τότε εἰκόνα ζῶσαν καὶ ζῶντα χαρακτῆρα.
Locum non inveni.

44 Τοῦ αὐτοῦ εἰς τὴν παραβολὴν τοῦ σπόρου.
Ἔνδυμα βασιλικὸν ἐὰν ὑβρίσῃς—εἰς τὸν βασιλέα ἀνάγει.
M **25ᴹ, 39ᴹ** (persimile).

45 Not in *TLG*.

Τοῦ αὐτοῦ ἐκ τοῦ λόγου τοῦ περὶ νηστείας ἐν τῇ α΄ ἡμέρᾳ τῆς Μ΄.

Σάλπιγγος πολεμικῆς ἠχησάσης. καὶ μετ᾽ ὀλίγον· φρίττουσιν γοῦν τοὺς νηστεύοντας δαίμονες ὡς εἰκόνας (fol. 18) μαρτύρων ἀναιμάκτων ὁρῶντες· ἐχθρὰ γὰρ αὐτοῖς τῆς νηστείας ἡ φύσις.

Locum non inveni.

46 Τοῦ ἁγίου Γρηγορίου τοῦ Θεολόγου ἐκ τοῦ κατὰ Ἰουλιανοῦ στηλιτευτικοῦ.

Inc.: Νόμος ἐστὶν βασιλικός, οὐκ οἶδα μὲν εἰ καὶ πᾶσι . . .

desin.: . . . αὐτοῖς ἀπληστότερόν τε καὶ τελεώτερον.

M **43**ᴹ (M⟨V⟩). (V = *PG* 35, 605ʙ10–ᴄ9).

47 Τοῦ ἁγίου Γρηγορίου Νύσης ἐκ τοῦ λόγου τοῦ εἰς τὸν πρωτομάρτυρα Στέφανον.

Inc.: Οὕτω γὰρ ἂν ὁ τῆς εἰκόνος διασωθείη λόγος . . .

fol. 18ᵛ desin.: . . . διὰ τῶν οἰκείων τῇ εἰκόνι χαρακτηρίζεται.

CPG 3186 Gregorius Nyss., *Encomium in s. Stephanum protomartyrem i*, ed. O. Lendle, Gregorii Nysseni Sermones Pars II, in *Gregorii Nysseni Opera* X,1 (Leiden-New York-Kopenhagen-Köln, 1990), 93.16-94.3; PG 46, 720ᴅ.

Doctrina Patrum (chap. ME), p. 329.1–3, XI (persimile).

48 Ἴσον κελεύσεως Ἡρακλείου βασιλέως πρὸς Ἰωάννην πάπαν Ῥώμης·

Inc.: Σημαίνομεν τῇ μακαριότητι ὑμῶν, ὡς ἐν τῷ εὐαγεῖ . . .

fol. 19 desin.: . . . τοῦ αὐτοῦ δὲ καὶ τὰ παθήματα.

Cf. F. Dölger, *Regesten*, I (Munich-Berlin, 1924), 25, n. 215.

49 Θεοδώρου Ἀντιοχέως ἐκ τῆς ἑρμηνείας τῆς κτίσεως, λόγου γ΄.

Inc.: Εἴ τις βασιλεὺς πόλιν τινὰ μεγίστην . . .

fol. 21 desin.: . . . τοῦ οὗπερ μίμημα φέρει μόνον.

CPG 3827 Theodorus Mopsuestenus, *Fragmenta in Genesim*, ed. Petit, "L'homme créé 'à l'image' de Dieu," 274–80.

50 Τοῦ ἁγίου Ἱερωνύμου ἐπισκόπου Ἱεροσολύμων.

Χάριν τούτου συνεχώρησεν ὁ Θεός—διάθεσιν ἡμῶν τὴν πρὸς αὐτόν.

P **96*** (persimile); M **16**ᴹ.

51 Τοῦ ἁγίου Σωφρονίου ἐκ τοῦ Λειμωναρίου.

fol. 21ᵛ Inc.: Ἐν Ἀντιοχ⟨ε⟩ίᾳ τῇ μεγάλῃ—ἕκαστος ἔχρῃζεν. Καὶ μετ᾽ ὀλίγον. Ἦλθέν τις ἀδελφός—λόγον ποιούμενος λέγει αὐτῷ. Καὶ μεθ᾽ ἕτερα. Ὁρᾷ ἑαυτὸν ὁ τῆς διακονίας . . .

fol. 22 desin.: . . . ἐμοὶ ἔνδυμα γέγονεν.

M **23**ᴹ.

52 Τοῦ ἁγίου Νείλου πρὸς Ἡλιόδωρον Σελεντιάριον ἐπιστολὴ ΣΟΖ΄.

Inc.: Διὰ τῶν κατὰ τόπον καὶ τόπον διαφόροις χρόνοις . . .

fol. 23ᵛ desin.: . . . μνήμης τῶν μακαρίστων μαρτύρων λαμβάνοντι.

CPG 6043 Nilus Ancyranus, *Epistulae*, PG 79, 580–81; Mansi, XIII 32ᴄ–33ᴄ.

53   Περὶ ἀχειροποιήτων εἰκόνων·

Διὰ δὲ τὸν τῆς ἀρχαιότητος λόγον ἤγουν ὅτι ἐν τῷ γεννηθῆναι Χριστόν, εἶτα ἐν τῷ θαυματουργεῖν φιλανθρώπως πρὸ τοῦ σταυροῦ καὶ τῆς ἀναλήψεως καὶ ἀπὸ τούτων τὰ ἐπὶ τῶν ἀποστόλων γενάμενα ἱστορητέον καὶ ταῦτα τά τε ἐν
5   ἀχειροποιήτοις καὶ ἐν χειροποιήτοις ἀνατεθειμένα εἰς τιμὴν καὶ προσκύνησιν

(fol. 24). Α΄. Ἡ ἐν Ἐδέσσῃ ἀπ᾽ αὐτοῦ Χριστοῦ δοθεῖσα τῷ ζωγράφῳ τοῦ Αὐγάρου τῷ ζωγραφεῖν ἐκ πίστεως αὐτὸν δοκιμάζοντι, καθὰ ἐγγράφως ἔχομεν.

Β΄. Ἡ ἑτοιμασία τῆς αἱμόρρου Βερονίκης τοῦ ῥάκκους· ἣν εἰκόνα ὁ ἀποδεχόμενος τὰς προθέσεις Κύριος ἀχειροκμήτως ἐγγράψαι εὐδόκησεν. Καὶ αὕτη ἐ-
10 στὶν ἐν Ῥώμῃ μετὰ ἐγγράφου λόγου ἀπὸ Τιβερίου τῶν ἡμερῶν εὑρεθεῖσα διὰ πολλῆς ἐκζητήσεως δοθεῖσα αὐτοῖς, ἤγουν μετὰ ἕνα ἢ δύο χρόνους τῆς τοῦ δεσπότου Χριστοῦ ἀναλήψεως, ἢ καὶ νοσοῦντα τὸν αὐτὸν βασιλέα ἰάσατο.

Γ΄. Ἡ ἐν Καμουλιανοῖς τῆς Καισαρείας ἀχειροποίητος τοῦ δεσπότου εἰκών, ἣν ἐξηγεῖται ὁ Νύσης Γρηγόριος ὑπάρχειν ἐν κιδάρει καθαρᾷ.
15 Δ΄. Ἡ ἐν τῇ τῆς Τραστιβέρεως ἐκκλησίᾳ ἐν Ῥώμῃ προσκυνουμένη καὶ σεβομένη ἀχειροποίητος ἀληθῶς, ἥντινά φασιν ὅτι ἑνὶ τῶν μαρτύρων προευτρεπιζομένῳ τῷ οἴκῳ αὐτὴ ἡ δέσποινα προλαβοῦσα σὺν τῷ ἐγκολπίῳ υἱῷ καὶ Θεῷ ἑαυτὴν καθυ(fol. 24ᵛ)πέδειξεν ἀχειρόγραπτα, καὶ τὸν τοῦ οἴκου εὐτρεπισμὸν ἑαυτῇ κατεκτήσατο οὐ χειροπρακτήσασα, ἄπαγε, ἀλλὰ δεσποτικῶς καὶ ἐντιμο-
20 δούλως ποιήσασα· τιμὴν γὰρ ἡγεῖται καὶ δοῦλος ὅταν ὁ δεσπότης αἱρήσεται οἰκῆσαι τὸ τούτου ἀληθῶς καταγώγιον.

Ε΄. Ἡ ἐν Λύδδῃ ἀχειροποίητος πρὸς τῇ πορφυρᾷ πλακὶ τῆς δεσποίνης ἡμῶν τῆς ὑπεραγίας Θεοτόκου· καὶ τοῦτο ἐγγράφῳ λόγῳ μαρτυρουμένη ὅπως Χριστιανῶν καὶ Ἰουδαίων περὶ τοῦ οἴκου μαχομένων, θείως κινηθέντι τῷ κατ᾽ ἐκεῖνο
25 καιροῦ ἄρχοντι ἐπὶ κρίματος γέγονεν, ἵνα μετὰ τεσσαρακοντήμερον προσευχήν, οὗ δ᾽ ἂν μέρους φανείη τι ἐν τῷ οἴκῳ σημεῖον, τούτου δῆλον ὅτι ἀποκληρωθείη ὁ οἶκος. Καὶ μηδενὸς μὲν τῶν Ἰουδαίων ὑποδειχθέντος, τῆς δὲ ὑπεραγίας δεσποίνης ἡμῶν τοῦ χαρακτῆρος ἀχειρογράφως ἐν τῷ κεκλῆσθαι ἐκτυπωθέντος ἐν τῷ πρὸς δυσμὰς τῆς ἐκκλησίας τοίχῳ πρὸς τῇ πορφυρᾷ, ὡς
30 εἴρηται, πλακί, (fol. 25) γέγονεν ἔργον ὁ τοῦ κρίματος λόγος καὶ Χριστιανοὶ τὸ ἀνάκτορον παρειλήφασιν αὐτῆς τῆς ἰδίας αὐτῶν αἰσχύνης σὺν τῇ δυνάμει τῆς ἀχειρογράπτου εἰκόνος τῆς παρθένου ἐκδιωκούσης τοὺς ἀντιθέους Ἑβραίους. Οὐ γὰρ μόνον ὅτι τὸ κρίμα οὕτως ἐτέτακτο πεφεύγεσαν, ἀλλ᾽ ὅτι καὶ ἰδόντες τὸ τοιοῦτον θεῖον σημεῖον ἑαυτοὺς ἐξῶθουν, "φύγωμεν", λέγοντες,
35 "τῆς γὰρ μητρὸς τοῦ Θεοῦ αὐτῶν, ὥς φασιν, τὸ ἐκτύπωμα, ἰδού, πέφανται".

Στ΄. Ἡ ἐν Γεθσημανῇ ἐν κίονί τινι ὡς βενέτῳ ἐξ ἀληθοῦς παραδόσεως καὶ ἀεννάου θαυματουργίας ἀχειροποίητος προσκυνουμένη.

Ζ΄. Ἡ ἐν Ἀλεξανδρείᾳ τιμωμένη παραδόξως ἐληλυθυῖα τὴν βεβαίωσιν τῆς προσκυνήσεως λαβοῦσα ἀξίως τῷ πρωτοτύπῳ καὶ θεουργῶς ἐνεργουμένη
40 Χριστῷ καὶ τὴν τούτου ἐπὶ θαλάσσης πεζοπορίαν μιμησαμένη, τρισὶν ἡμέραις καὶ τοσαύταις προπυρσευομένη τοῖς ὁρῶσι νυξὶν καὶ τὴν (fol. 25ᵛ) ἑαυτῆς παράδειξιν ἐμποιοῦσα μέχρις ἂν καταφανὴς τοῖς πᾶσιν γενομένη, αὐτῷ τῷ πάπᾳ προσκυνήσαντι ταῖς χερσὶν αὐτοῦ καὶ τῷ δήμῳ φέρουσα ἑαυτὴν ἐμπαρέθετο.

Η΄. Ἡ ἐν Ῥώμῃ ἀχειρόγραπτος τῆς ὑπεραγίας Θεοτόκου εἰκών, ἣν ὅτε ἡ νόσος
45 ἐπικωμᾶν πέφυκεν πάσαις πόλεσιν, ἤγουν ἐν τῇ τοῦ αὐγούστου ὥρᾳ κατὰ τὴν κοίμησιν τῆς δεσποίνης, πανδημεὶ ἐκπομπεύοντες καὶ ὑποτιθέντες ἑαυτοὺς καὶ προσκυνοῦντες πάσης ψυχικῆς καὶ σωματικῆς ἀλεξιφάρμακον νόσου οἱ Ῥωμεῖς περιφέρουσιν.

Θ΄. Ἡ ἐκ χαλκοῦ θερμελάτου καὶ ἐκ μέρους χρυσοῦ καὶ ἀργύρου, ἀλλ᾽ οὐκ
50 ἀχειροποίητος, αὐτῆς ἐκείνης τῆς ῥηθείσης αἱμόρρου κατὰ αἴτησιν τὴν πρὸς Ἡρώδην συγχωρηθείσης διὰ δεήσεως τῆς πρὸς αὐτὸν γενέσθαι. Καὶ αὐτῆς διὰ διαφόρων μαρτύρων δεικνυμένης· ὅτι τε δεκτὴ Θεῷ διὰ τῆς ἐν αὐτῇ ἀνα(fol. 26)φυούσης παντακέστορος βοτάνης ὡς Θεόδωρος καὶ Ἰωάννης ἱστοροῦσιν καὶ ὡς αὐτὸς ὁ Χρυσόστομος καὶ Ἀστέριος Ἀμασ(ε)ίας, ὃν καὶ εἰσάγει ὁ εἷς τῶν

55 ἱστορούντων περὶ τούτου· ὅτι δι᾽ εὐχῆς οὗτος Ἀστέριος ἐν αὐτῇ ἐκείνῃ τῇ Πα-
    νεάδι λοιμικὴν φθορὰν τοῦ λαοῦ ἔστησεν. Καὶ οὗτος δὲ ὁ μακάριος Ἀστέ-
    ριος μέχρις τῶν χρόνων Μαξιμίνου λέγει αὐτὴν εἶναι· οὗ ζηλοτυποῦντος,
    φησίν, τοῦ Μαξιμίνου ἐν τῷ ἀγάλματι τὸν Χριστόν, καθεῖλεν τὸ ξόανον μόνον,
    οὐ τὴν μνήμην τῶν γεγραμμένων.

33 πεφεύγεσαν:–ωσαν cod. 45 τῇ: τῷ cod. ὥρᾳ: ὥραν cod. 52 δεκτὴ: δεκτέα cod.
54 ὂν: ὦν cod.

Locum non inveni.

Addendum
Contents of the Iconophile Florilegium of Nicetas of Medicion

Vaticanus gr. 511,fols. 66ᵛ–68ᵛ.

    1 = P **72***
    2 = P **132***
    3 = P **76***
    4 = P **70***
    5 = P **69***
    6 = P **15***
    7 = P **25***
    8 = P **17***
    9 = M **47**ᴹ
   10 = P **50***
   11 = P **21***

12
fol. 67ᵛ Καὶ πάλιν (= Γρηγορίου τοῦ Θεολόγου).
    Εἴπερ ἀγγελικὸν λαμπροφορία καὶ φαιδρότης ὅταν τυποῦνται σωματικῶς, σύμβολον
    οἶμαι τοῦτο τῆς κατὰ φύσιν αὐτῶν καθαρότητος.
CPG 3010.25 Gregorius Naz., *Oratio 25*, ed. Mossay, *Discours 24–26*, 158 par. 2.10-12;
PG 35, 1200.17-20.

   13 = P **43***
   14 = P **52***
   15 = P **55***
   16 = M **25**ᴹ
   17 = P **56***
   18 = P **53***
   19 = P **60***
   20 = P **86***
   21 = P **66***
   22 = P **63***

23 = Dam. I 55 II 51
24 = P **82***
25 = P **95***
26 = P **97***
27 = P **94***

Concordance of Appendices II–IV and Other Iconophile Florilegia

Abbreviations

A = Acts of the seventh ecumenical council, Mansi XII (= 12), XIII (= 13)
D = *Doctrina Patrum*
Dam. = Kotter, *Schriften III* (Florilegia I, II, III, = 1, 2, 3)
M = Mosquensis Hist. Mus. 265 (numbers refer to App. III)
N = Vaticanus gr. 511 (numbers refer to App. IV addendum)
P = Parisinus gr. 1115 (numbers refer to App. II)
R = Roman Councils of 731, 769 (list on pp. 39–40)
S = scholium
V = Venetus Marcianus gr. 573 (numbers refer to App. IV)

P	M	V	N	R	D	Dam.	A
1							
2	7						
3	12						
4							
5					12.16		
6					12.18		
7					17.4		
8					8.7		
9							
10							
11							
12					7.5		
13					2.28		
14					7.21		
15		24	6			1.34/2.30/3.46	13.80B–D
16	53	23		18	45.13	1.44, 46/3.47,106	12.1014,66/13.277,300

P	M	V	N	R	D	Dam.	A
17	14		8	17			12.1066/13.72E–73A
18		7					
19						1.48/2.44S	13.72A–B
20		25				1.60/2.56/3.53	
21		9	11			3.109	13.13B–C
22		26a					
23		27					
24		26			45.3	3.64	
25		8	7		45.14	1.35/2.31/3.48	12.1146A/13.69D–E
26							
27							
28					12.2		
29							
30					12.5		
31					12.1		
32					12.6		
33					17.3		
34					12.13		
35					12.15		
36					1.10		
37					17.1		
38					2.1		
39+S					7.10		
40					7.1–3		
41+S					2.19		
42					2.20–21		
43			13	15	45.10	1.52/2.48/3.50	12.1066B/13.9C–D, 117A
44	42			16			12.1066B–C
45							
46	54					1.49/2.45	

P	M	V	N	R	D	Dam.	A
47	55					1.50/2.46	
48							
49		22					
50		6	10				
51		11					
52	51	12	14				
53	26	10	18			2.62	13.8B–D
54	41			13		3.122	12.1067A/13.68D–E
55	24	30	15			2.60/3.105	13.9A, 300D, 324C
56	40	31	17				
57							
58		29					
59						1.53/2.49/3.51	
60		32	19		45.16,17	1.61/2.57/3.54	
61				20			12.1067B
62							13.12B–13A
63	50	1	22				
64		2					
65		3					
66	(1)	4	21				
67		28		9			
68				21	45.7		12.1067C
69	52	21	5			3.114	13.69A–C, 273A
70			4	6	45.8	3.59	
71	10						13.24E–32A
72			1				
73	37	5					12.1018C
74							
75		20			45.6		
76		20	3			1.11/3.21	
77		20				1.32/2.28/3.44	

P	M	V	N	R	D	Dam.	A
78							
79							
80						1.32(2–4)	
81							13.56A–B
82		13	24			2.66/3.127	13.56E–57A, 273A
83		14					
84		16					
85			22			3.116	12.1067C–D
86			20	23			12.1067D
87		36					
88							
89						3.138	
90						1.58/2.54/3.52	
91				45.18			13.160A–B
92	38	34				2.65/3.131	13.37E–40B
93							13.185A–188A
94	49	38	27			3.137	12.1079A–C/13.40E–41A
95		35	25	24		3.72,73	12.1067D–1070D
96	16	50		25		3.125	12.1070E
97	(1)	33	26				13.161A–B
98							13.13D–E
99							13.16A–17D, 308A–309B
100	19	37				3.130	
101							13.164C–165C
102							13.165E–168C
103	2					3.84,86–89/ 1.54,56	13.44A–53C
104	46			12			13.181E–184A
105							
106							13.189E–192C
107		15					13.57B–D
108						3.132	13.57D–60B

P	M	V	N	R	D	Dam.	A
109							13.64B–D
110							13.64E–65D
111							13.68A–D
112						3.55	13.73B
113							13.73B–76C
114						3.92	13.76D–77B
115							13.80D–85C
116						3.135	13.85D–89A
117							13.89A–D
118							13.89E–92B
119							13.21A–C
120							13.21C–24C
121	22						13.193D–E
122							13.193E–196C
123	48					1.64/2.67/3.13	13.193A–C, 60D–61B
124	36						12.1058C–1059C
125							
126							
127			1				12.1063B/13.4D–E
128							13.5A
129							13.5A–B
130						2.22	13.5C
131							13.197A–200B
132	(1)		2				
133							13.92C–100A
	3						
	4					2.1–10, 14–23	
	5					1.66/2.69	
	6					2.11	
	8						12.959A–974B
	9						12.975B–982A

P	M	V	N	R	D	Dam.	A
	11						
	13						13.100A–105A
	15					3.69	
	17					3.134	
	18		8				
	20					3.136	
	21						
	23	51					
58ad	25	44	16	19		2.61	12.1066E–1067A
	27						
	28						13.124D7–E6
	29						
	30						
	31						
	31a						
	32						
	32a					2.10–14	
	33						
	34						
	35						
	43	46					
	44						
	45						13.184B–C
	47		9				
	56						
		17					
		18					
		19					
		39					
		40					
		41					

P	M	V	N	R	D	Dam.	A
		42			45.12	1.48S/3.56	
		43					
		45					
		47			45.11		
		48					
		49					
		52					13.32c–33c
		53					
			12				
			23			1.55/2.51	
				2			
				3			
				4			
				5			
				7	45.4	3.43	
				10			
				11			
				14			
					45.1	3.61	
					45.2	3.62	
					45.5		
					45.9		13.309d
					45.12	3.56,57	
					45.15	3.58	
						1.28/2.24	
						1.30/2.26	
						1.37/2.33	
						1.39/2.35	
						1.40/2.36	
						1.42/2.38	
						2.63	

P	M	V	N	R	D	Dam.	A
						2.64	
						3.60, 63, 65–68	
						3.70, 71, 74–83	
						3.85, 90, 91–104	
						3.107, 108	
						3.110–13, 115	
						3.117–21, 123–4	
						3.126–29, 133	

Possible Stemma of Iconophile Florilegia

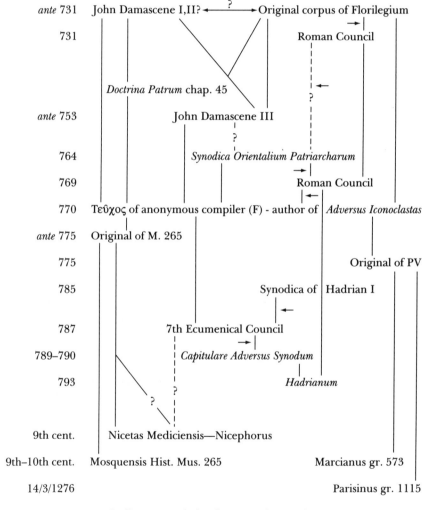

ante 731   John Damascene I,II? ←——?——→ Original corpus of Florilegium

731   Roman Council

Doctrina Patrum chap. 45

ante 753   John Damascene III

764   *Synodica Orientalium Patriarcharum*

769   Roman Council

770   Τεῦχος of anonymous compiler (F) - author of | *Adversus Iconoclastas*

ante 775   Original of M. 265

775   Original of PV

785   Synodica of | Hadrian I

787   7th Ecumenical Council

789–790   *Capitulare Adversus Synodum*

793   *Hadrianum*

9th cent.   Nicetas Mediciensis—Nicephorus

9th–10th cent.   Mosquensis Hist. Mus. 265   Marcianus gr. 573

14/3/1276   Parisinus gr. 1115

→   Indicates translation from Greek to Latin
←   Indicates translation from Latin to Greek

ADDENDA

Page 33, note 150
For a number of different problems related to the correspondence of Nilus of Ankyra, see A. Cameron, "The Authenticity of the Letters of St Nilus of Ancyra," *Greek, Roman, and Byzantine Studies* 17 (1976), 181–96.

Pages 37–38 and 83–84
For the Greek sources of the *Hadrianum*, see now A. Alexakis, "The Source of the Greek Patristic Quotations in the *Hadrianum* (*JE 2483*) of Pope Hadrian I," *AHC* 26 (1994), 14–30.

Pages 49 and 110ff
The problem of the authorship of the various recensions of *Adversus Constantinum Caballinum* is thoroughly examined now by M.-F. Auzépy in very convincing terms. According to her, the earliest version of this work can possibly be identified with a synodal letter written in 730 by John, patriarch of Jerusalem. This version was subsequently reworked before 769 in Rome into a dialogue. A further expansion of the text that took place between 785 and 787 gave the long version that is published in *PG*. A little later the same text is attributed by the author of the *Vita Stephani Iunioris* to St. John of Damascus. See M.-F. Auzépy, "L'Adversus Constantinum Caballinum et Jean de Jérusalem," *Byzantinoslavica* 56 (1995), 323–38, esp. 337–38.

Pages 53–54 and 312: Matthew Blastares *Contra Latinos*
For more on this late work, see L. Burgmann, M.-Th. Fögen, A. Schmink, and D. Simon, *Repertorium der Handschriften des byzantinischen Rechts, I: Die Handschriften des weltlichen Rechts* (Nr. 1–327) (Frankfurt am Main, 1995), 45, 78, 176, 266.

Page 82, note 141
For the contacts between Rome and the empire of Nicaea before 1261, see now J.-S. Langdon, "Byzantium in Anatolian Exile: Imperial Vicegerency Reaffirmed during Byzantino-Papal Discussions at Nicaea and Nymphaion, 1234," *Byzantinische Forschungen* 20 (1994), 197–233.

Page 85, note 161
Another early version of "Abschwörungsforlmeln" has been published by S. N. C. Lieu, "An Early Byzantine Formula for the Renunciation of Manichaeism," *Jahrbuch für Antike und Christentum* 26 (1983), 154–218.

Pages 207 and 333: Διάλογος Μόσχου μοναχοῦ καὶ ἐγκλειστοῦ . . .
An edition, translation, detailed commentary, and extensive discussion of this fragment is forthcoming: A. Alexakis, "An Early 'Iconophile' Text: The *Dialogue of the Monk and Recluse Moschos concerning the Holy Icons*," *DOP* 52 (1998).

Page 230, note 10
E. A. Sophocles, *Greek Lexicon of the Roman and Byzantine Periods* (New York, 1900); H. G. Liddell, R. Scott, and H. S. Jones, *A Greek-English Lexicon* (Oxford, 1968).

Page 231: Michigan Papyri XIII

For this primary source, see R. A. Coles, *Reports of Proceedings in Papyri* (Brussels, 1966); P. J. Sijpesteijn, ed., *Michigan Papyri XIII,* nos. 660–661; L. MacCoull, "The Aphrodito Murder Mystery," *Journal of Juristic Papyrology* 20 (1990), 103–7; J. G. Keenan, "The Aphrodito Murder Mystery: Return to the Scene of the Crime," *Bulletin of the American Society of Papyrologists* 32 (1995), 57–63. I wish to thank Dr. L. MacCoull for these references.

BIBLIOGRAPHY

1. Sources

A. Manuscript Sources
Moscow:
Mosquensis Historici Musei 265 (Vladimir 197), fols. 142–241, containing the Νουθεσία γέροντος and an Iconophile florilegium

Paris:
Parisinus graecus 1115
Parisinus graecus 1250, fols. 173–332, containing the Ἔλεγχος καὶ ἀνατροπὴ of Nicephorus I
Parisinus Coislinianus graecus 93, fols. 1–159, containing the Ἔλεγχος καὶ ἀνατροπὴ of Nicephorus I

Rome:
Vaticanus graecus 511, fols. 66ᵛ–68ᵛ, containing the Ἐκλογὴ περὶ τῆς τῶν ἁγίων εἰκόνων προσκυνήσεως of Nicetas of Medicion
Vaticanus graecus 836, containing the acts of the seventh ecumenical council

Venice:
Venetus Marcianus graecus 573, fols. 2–26, containing an Iconophile florilegium

For other manuscripts less frequently cited, see the Index of Manuscripts.

B. Other Sources

Acta Concilii Florentini. Ed. J. Gill, Concilium Florentinum, Series B: *Quae Supersunt Auctorum Graecorum Concilii Florentini,* Pars I, vol. V, fasc. 1–2. Rome, 1953.

Acta et Miracula Anastasii Persae. Ed. B. Flusin, *Saint Anastase le Perse et l'histoire de la Palestine au début du VIIᵉ siècle,* 2 vols. Paris, 1992.

Acta Iohannis. Ed. E. Junod and J. D. Kaestli, *Acta Iohannis,* CCSA 1. Turnhout, 1983.

Agathangelus. *Historia Armeniae, Versio Graeca (BHG* 712), ed. G. Lafontaine, *La version grecque ancienne du livre Arménien d'Agathange,* Publications de l'Institut Orientaliste de Louvain 7. Louvain-la-Neuve, 1973.

Agathias. *Agathiae Historiarum Libri Quinque,* ed. R. Keydell, *CFHB* 1. Berlin, 1967.

Amphilochius Iconiensis. *Opera,* ed. C. Datema, *Amphilochii Iconiensis Opera, CCSG* 3. Turnhout-Louvain, 1978.

Anastasius I Antiochenus. *De Gestis in Perside (BHG* 806, App. II 13, *De gestis in Perside Narratio Africani immo Aphroditiani),* ed. E. Bratke, *Das sogenannte ReligionsGespräch am Hof der Sassaniden, TU* 19.3. Leipzig, 1899.

Anastasius Sinaita. *Viae Dux,* ed. K.-H. Uthemann, *Anastasii Sinaitae Viae Dux, CCSG* 8. Turnhout-Louvain, 1981.

———. *Disputatio adversus Iudaeos, PG* 89, 1203 ff.

Athanasius Alexandrinus. *Oratio de Incarnatione Verbi,* ed. Ch. Kannengiesser, *Sur l'incarnation du Verbe, SC* 199. Paris, 1973.

Basilius Caesariensis. *De Spiritu Sancto,* ed. B. Pruche, *Basile de Césarée. Traité du Saint-Esprit. Texte grec, introduction et traduction, SC* 17bis. Paris, 1968.

———. *Epistulae,* ed. Y. Courtonne, *Saint Basile, Lettres,* I–III. Paris, 1957–66.

Basilius Seleuciensis. *De Vita et Miraculis S. Theclae Libri ii (BHG* 1718n), ed. G. Dagron, *Vie et miracles de s. Thècle,* SubsHag 62. Brussels, 1978.

Codex Carolinus. Ed. W. Gundlach, *MGH, Epistolae* III, *Epistolae Merowingici et Karolini Aevi,* I. Berlin, 1892, pp. 469–657.

Collectio Avellana, Epistulae Imperatorum, Pontificum, Aliorum inde ab a. 367 usque ad a. 553. Ed. O. Günter, *CSEL* 35. Bonn, 1895–98.

Concilium Romanum 769. Mensis Aprilis die 12–14. Ed. A. Werminghoff, *MGH, Concilia* II.1, *Karolini Aevi* I.1. Hanover-Leipzig, 1904–8, pp. 74–92.

Cyrillus Alexandrinus. *Commentarii in Matthaeum,* ed. J. Reuss, *Matthäus-Kommentare aus der griechischen Kirche, TU* 62, V. Reihe, Bd. 6. Berlin, 1957, pp. 153–69.

Cyrillus Hierosolymitanus. *Catecheses ad Illuminandos,* ed. W. K. Reischl, *Cyrilli Hierosolymorum Archiepiscopi Opera quae Supersunt Omnia.* Munich, 1848.

Daniel Scetiota. *Narrationes,* ed. M. L. Clugnet, "Vie et récits de l'abbé Daniel de Scété." *ROC* 5 (1900), 49–73; 254–71; 370–91; *ROC* 6 (1901), 56–87.

Dorotheus Gazaeus. *Vita s. Dosithei (BHG* 2117–2119), ed. L. Regnault and J. de Préville, *Dorothée de Gaza, Oeuvres spirituelles, SC* 92. Paris, 1963.

Ephraem Syrus. *Sermo in Transfigurationem Domini et Dei Salvatoris Nostri I. C.,* ed. S. Assemani, *Patris Nostri Ephraem Syri Opera Omnia quae Exstant etc.* Rome, 1732–46, G. 2, 41D–49.

Epiphanius Constantiensis. *Ancoratus, Panarion,* ed. K. Holl, *Epiphanius,* I. *Ancoratus und Panarion, GCS* 25, 31, 37. Leipzig, 1915, 1922, 1933.

———. *De prophetarum Vita et Obitu,* ed. Th. Schermann, *Prophet. Vitae Fabulosae,* Teubner 223. Leipzig, 1907.

———. *Index Apostolorum,* ed. Th. Schermann, ibid., pp. 107–17.

Epitoma Libri VIII Constitutionum Apostolorum seu Constitutiones per Hippolytum. Ed. F. X. Funk, *Didascalia et Constitutiones Apostolorum,* II. Paderborn, 1905; repr. Turin, 1962.

Eusebius Caesariensis. *Historia Ecclesiastica,* ed. E. Schwartz, *Eusebius Werke,* II, 1–3, *Die Kirchengeschichte, GCS* 9.2. Leipzig, 1906.

Eustathius Antiochenus. *In Samaritanam,* ed. M. Spanneut, *Recherches sur les écrits d'Eustathe d'Antioche avec une édition nouvelle des fragments dogmatiques et exégétiques.* Lille, 1948.

Evagrius Scholasticus. *Historia Ecclesiastica,* ed. J. Bidez and L. Parmentier, *Evagrius. The Ecclesiastical History,* 2nd ed. Amsterdam, 1964.

Georgius Alexandrinus. *Vita S. Iohannis Chrysostomi (BHG* 873), ed. F. Halkin, *Douze récits byzantins sur Saint Jean Chrysostome,* SubsHag 60. Brussels, 1977, pp. 69 ff.

Georgius Syceota. *Vita Theodori Syceotae (BHG* 1748), ed. A.-J. Festugière, *Vie de Théodore de Sykeon.* I: *Texte grec.* II: *Traduction, commentaire et appendice,* SubsHag 48. Brussels, 1970.

Georgius Syncellus. *Ecloga Chronographica,* ed. A. Mosshammer, *Georgii Syncelli Ecloga Chronographica.* Leipzig, 1984.

Gregorius Nazianzenus. *Epistulae CI, CII*, ed. P. Gallay and M. Jourjon, *Grégoire de Nazianze, Lettres théologiques*, SC 208. Paris, 1974.

———. *Oratio 4 (Oratio I contra Iulianum)*, ed. J. Bernardi, *Grégoire de Nazianze, Discours 4–5 contre Julien*, SC 309. Paris, 1983, pp. 86–292.

———. *Oratio 20 (De Dogmate et Constitutione Episcoporum)*, ed. J. Mossay, *Grégoire de Nazianze, Discours 20–23*, SC 270. Paris, 1980, pp. 56–84.

———. *Oratio 25 (In Laudem Heronis Philosophi)*, ed. J. Mossay, *Grégoire de Nazianze, Discours 24–26*, SC 284. Paris, 1981, pp. 156–204.

———. *Oratio 29 (Theologica III de Filio I)*; *Oratio 30 (Theologica IV de Filio II)*; *Oratio 31 (Theologica V de Spiritu Sancto)*, ed. P. Gallay and M. Jourjon, *Grégoire de Nazianze, Discours 27–31 (Discours théologiques)*, SC 250. Paris, 1978, pp. 176–342.

———. *Oratio 37 (In Dictum Evangelii: Cum Consumasset Jesus Hos Sermones)*, ed. C. Moreschini, *Grégoire de Nazianze, Discours 32–37*, SC 318. Paris, 1985, pp. 270–318.

———. *Oratio 38 (In Theophania)*; *Oratio 39 (In Sancta Lumina)*; *Oratio 40 (In Sancto Baptismate)*, ed. C. Moreschini, *Grégoire de Nazianze, Discours 38–41*, SC 358. Paris, 1990, pp. 104–310.

———. *Oratio 43 (In Laudem Basilii Magni)*, ed. J. Bernardi, *Grégoire de Nazianze, Discours 42–43*, SC 384. Paris, 1992, pp. 116–306.

Gregorius Nyssenus. *Ad Ablabium, quod non sint tres dei; Ad Eustathium de Sancta Trinitate*, ed. F. Müller, *Gregorii Nysseni Opera*, III,1. *Gregorii Nysseni Opera Dogmatica Minora*. Leiden, 1958, pp. 35–57; 1–16.

———. *Contra Eunomium Lib. v*, ed. W. Jaeger, *Gregorii Nysseni Opera* I,1, *Contra Eunomium Libri*. Leiden, 1960.

———. *De Oratione Dominica III; Orationes viii de Beatitudinibus*, ed. J. F. Callahan, *Gregorii Nysseni Opera* VII,2. *De Oratione Dominica; De Beatitudinibus*. Leiden-New York-Cologne, 1992, pp. 31–44.

———. *De Sancto Theodoro*, ed. J. P. Cavarnos, *Gregorii Nysseni Opera* X,1. *Gregorii Nysseni Sermones*, II. Leiden-New York, 1990, pp. 61–71.

———. *De Tridui inter Mortem et Resurrectionem Domini Nostri I.C. Spatio*, ed. E. Gebhardt, *Gregorii Nysseni Opera*, IX. *Sermones*, I. Leiden, 1967, pp. 273–306.

———. *In Canticum Canticorum Homiliae xv*, ed. H. Langerbeck, *Gregorii Nysseni Opera*, VI. *Gregorii Nysseni In Canticum Canticorum*. Leiden, 1962.

———. *In Inscriptiones Psalmorum*, ed. J. McDonough and P. Alexander, *Gregorii Nysseni Opera*, V. *In Inscriptiones Psalmorum; In Sextum Psalmum; In Ecclesiasten Homiliae*. Leiden, 1962, pp. 24–175.

———. *Inventio Imaginis in Camulianis (BHG 791)*, ed. B. Melioranskij, *Commentationes Nikitinianae*. St. Petersburg, 1901, pp. 321–27.

———. *Oratio Catechetica Magna*, ed. J. H. Srawley, *The Catechetical Oration of Gregory of Nyssa*, Cambridge Patristic Texts 2. Cambridge, 1903.

———. *De Vita Gregorii Thaumaturgi*, ed. G. Heil, *Gregorii Nyssen: Opera*, x, 1. *Gregorii Nysseni Sermones*. Leiden-New York, 1990, pp. 3–57.

Hadrianus I Papa. *Hadrianum*, ed. K. Hampe, *MGH, Epistulae 5, Karolini Aevi 3*. Berlin, 1899, pp. 5–57.

Hippolytus Romanus. *Fragmenta*, ed. H. Achelis, *Hyppolyt's kleinere exegetische und homilitische Schriften*, GCS 1,2. Leipzig, 1987.

Hippolytus Thebanus. Σύνταγμα Χρονικόν, ed. F. Diekamp, *Hippolytos von Theben, Texte und Untersuchungen.* Münster, 1898.

Hypatius Ephesinus. *Quaestiones Miscellaneae* (fragmentum), ed. F. Diekamp, *Analecta Patristica, OCA* 117. Rome, 1938, pp. 127–29.

Ignatius Antiochenus. *Epistulae Interpolatae et Epistulae Suppositiciae* (= recensio longior), ed. F. X. Funk and F. Diekamp, *Patres Apostolici,* II. Tübingen, 1913.

Iohannes Chrysostomus. *Deprecatio,* ed. M. Richard, "Témoins grecs des fragments XIII et XV de Méliton de Sardes." *Le Muséon* 85 (1972), 318–21.

Iohannes Damascenus. *Contra Imaginum Calumniatores Orationes Tres,* ed. B. Kotter, *Die Schriften des Johannes von Damaskos,* vol. III, *PTS* 17. Berlin-New York, 1975.

———. *Fragmenta Philosophica e Cod. Oxon. Bodl. T. 1. 6,* ed. B. Kotter, *Die Schriften des Johannes von Damaskos,* vol. I, *PTS* 7. Berlin, 1969.

Libellus Synodalis Parisiensis (825. Nov. 1). Ed. A. Werminghoff, *MGH, Concilia,* II.2, *Aevi Karolini* 1,2. Hannover-Leipzig, 1908, pp. 473–551.

Liber Pontificalis. Ed. L. Duchesne, 2 vols. Paris, 1886–92.

Libri Carolini sive Caroli Magni Capitulare de Imaginibus. Ed. H. Bastgen, *MGH, Legum Sectio* III, *Concilia,* II, *Supplementum.* Hannover-Leipzig, 1924.

Mansi, J. D. *Sacrorum Conciliorum Nova et Amplissima Collectio,* 31 vols. Florence-Venice, 1759–98.

Marcus Eugenicus. *Testimonia a Marco Ephesio Collecta,* ed. L. Petit, *Marci Eugenici Metropolitae Ephesi: Opera anti-Unionistica,* Concilium Florentinum Series A: Documenta et Scriptores, vol. X, fasc. 2. Rome, 1977.

Methodius Olympius. *Convivium Decem Virginum,* ed. H. Musurillo and V. H. Debidour, *Méthode d'Olympe. Le Banquet, SC* 95. Paris, 1963. Older edition by G. N. Bonwetsch, *Methodius, GCS* 27. Leipzig, 1917.

Michael VIII imp. Letter to Pope Clement IV (Jan.–Feb. 1267), ed. N. Festa, "Lettera inedita dell'Imperatore Michele VIII." *Bessarione* 4.6 (1899–1900), 45–57.

Miracula SS. Cosmae et Damiani (*BHG* 387). Ed. L. Deubner, *Kosmas und Damian.* Leipzig-Berlin, 1907.

Nicephorus I. *Contra Eusebium et Epiphanidem,* ed. J. B. Pitra, *Spicilegium Solesmense Complectens Sanctorum Patrum Scriptorumque Ecclesiasticorum Anecdota hactenus Opera etc.* Paris, 1852–58, I 371–503, IV 292–380.

———. *Apologeticus Minor pro Sacris Imaginibus. PG* 100, 833–50.

Nicolaus Cotron(i)ensis. *Liber de Fide Trinitatis, ex Diversis Auctoritatibus Sanctorum Graecorum Confectus Contra Grecos (Libellus),* ed. H. F. Dondaine, *Sancti Thomae de Aquino Opera Omnia Iussu Leonis XIII P.M. Edita.* Rome, 1969, appendix.

Georgius Pachymeres. *De Michaele et Andronico Palaeologis,* ed. A. Failler, *Georges Pachymérès, Relations historiques, CFHB* 24. 1,2. Paris, 1984.

Paschalis I. Letter to Leo V on Image Worship, ed. G. Mercati, "La lettera di Pasquale I a Leone V sul culto delle sacre imagini," *ST* 5. (Rome, 1901), pp. 227–35.

Passio S. Procopii (*BHG* 1577). Ed Papadopoulos-Kerameus, Ἀνάλεκτα Ἱεροσολυμιτικῆς Σταχυολογίας, V. St. Petersburg, 1898, pp. 5 ff.

Philo Historiographus. *Fragmenta,* ed. G. Mercati, "Un preteso scritto di san Pietro vescovo d'Alessandria e martire sulla bestemmia e Filone l'istoriografo," *Opere minori*, II, *ST* 77. (Vatican City, 1937), pp. 437–38.

Photius. *Bibliotheca*, ed. R. Henry, *Photius, Bibliothèque*. Paris, 1959 ff.

Pseudo-Dionysius Areopagita. *De Divinus Nominibus*, ed. B. R. Suchla, *Corpus Dionysiacum*, I. *Pseudo-Dionysius Areopagita De divinis nominibus*, *PTS* 33. Berlin-New York, 1990.

———. *De Coelesti Hierarchia; De Ecclesiastica Hierarchia; De Mystica Theologia; Epistulae*, ed. G. Heil and A. M. Ritter, *Corpus Dionysiacum*, II, *PTS* 36. Berlin-New York, 1991.

Scriptor Incertus. Ed. F. Iadevaia, *Scriptor Incertus*. Messina, 1987.

Severianus Gabalensis. *Homilia de Lotione Pedum*, ed. A. Wenger, "Une homélie inédite de Sévérien de Gabala sur le lavement des pieds." *REB* 25 (1967), 219–35.

Socrates Scholasticus. *Historia Ecclesiastica*. PG 67, 33–841.

Sozomenus. *Historia Ecclesiastica*, ed. J. Bidez and G. C. Hansen, *Sozomenus Kirchengeschichte*, *GCS* 50. Berlin, 1960.

Theodoretus episc. Cyri. *Eranistes*, ed. G. H. Ettlinger, *Theodoret of Cyrus, Eranistes*. Oxford, 1975.

———. *Historia Religiosa*, ed. P. Canivet and A. Leroy-Molinghen, *Théodoret de Cyr. L'histoire des moines de Syrie*, 2 vols. Paris, 1975–77.

Theodorus Anagnostes. *Historia Ecclesiastica* (fragmenta), ed. G. Ch. Hansen, *Theodorus Anagnostes, Kirchengeschichte*, *GCS* 54. Berlin, 1971.

Theodorus II Laskaris. Θεοδώρου Βασιλέως τοῦ Λάσκαρι· Λόγος ἀπολογητικὸς πρὸς ἐπίσκοπον Κοτρώνης κατὰ Λατίνων περὶ Ἁγίου Πνεύματος, ed. H. B. Swete, *Theodorus Laskaris Junior: De Processione Spiritus Sancti Oratio Apologetica*. London, 1875.

Theodorus Studita. *Epistulae*, ed. G. Fatouros, *Theodori Studitae Epistulae*, *CFHB* 31 1,2. Berlin-New York, 1992.

Theophanes. *Chronographia*, ed. C. de Boor. Leipzig, 1883–85.

Thomas de Aquino. *Contra Errores Graecorum*, ed. H. F. Dondaine, *Sancti Thomae de Aquino Opera Omnia Iussu Leonis XIII P.M. Edita*, vol. 40. *Contra Errores Graecorum*. Rome, 1969.

Timotheus Presbyter Constantinopolitanus. *De iis qui ad Ecclesiam accedunt*, ed. V. Beneševič, *Syntagma XIV Titulorum sine Scholiis secundum Versionem Palaeoslovenicam, Adiecto Textu Graeco*. St. Petersburg, 1906–7, pp. 707–38.

Trophies of Damascus. Ed. G. Bardy, *PO* 15.2. Paris, 1920.

Vita Eupraxiae (*BHG* 631). *AASS, Mart. II*, 727–35.

Vita Martini Papae (*BHG* 2259). Ed. P. Peeters, "Une Vie grecque du pape S. Martin I." *AB* 51 (1933), 225–62.

Vita et Martyrium S. Anastasii Persae. Ed. B. Flusin, *Saint Anastase le Perse et l'histoire de la Palestine au début du VIIe siècle*, 2 vols. Paris, 1992.

Vita Nicephori Patriarchae Constantinopolitani by Ignatius Diaconus (*BHG* 1335). Ed. C. de Boor, *Nicephori Archiepiscopi Constantinopolitani Opuscula Historica*. Leipzig, 1880, pp. 139–217.

Vita Nicetae Mediciensis by Theosterictus (*BHG* 1341). *AASS, Aprilis*, xviii–xxvii.

Vita Pancratii (*BHG* 1410a,b,n). Ed. H. Usener, *Kleine Schriften*, IV. Berlin-Leipzig, 1913, pp. 418–21. For full edition, see C. J. Stallman, *The Life of St. Pancratius of Taormina*. Oxford University, D.Phil. thesis, 1986.

Vita Silvestri (BHG 1628–30). Ed. F. Combefis, *Illustrium Christi Martyrum Lecti Triumphi.* Paris, 1660, pp. 258–336.

*Vita Symeonis Stylitae Iunioris (BHG*ª 1689). Ed. P. van den Ven, *La vie ancienne de S. Syméon Stylite le Jeune (521–592),* 2 vols. SubsHag 32.1,2. Brussels, 1962–70.

Vita Tarasii by Ignatius Diaconus *(BHG* 1698). Ed. I. A. Heikel, *Acta Societatis Scientarum Fennicae* 17 (1891), 391–439.

For the critical editions of other works that have been anthologized in Parisinus gr. 1115, and the Iconophile Florilegia of codd. P, V, M, see Appendices I–IV

2. Secondary Literature

Abramowski, L. "The Controversy over Diodore and Theodore in the Interim between the Two Councils of Ephesus." In *Formula and Context: Studies in Early Christian Thought,* Variorum. Hampshire, 1992; originally published in German in *ZKG* 67 (1955–56), 252–87.

Adler, W. *Time Immemorial,* DOS 26. Washington, D.C., 1989.

De Aldama, J. A. *El Simbolo Toledano I,* Analecta Gregoriana 7. Rome, 1934.

Alexakis, A. "Some Remarks on the Colophon of the Codex *Parisinus Graecus* 1115." *Revue d'histoire des textes* 22 (1992), 131–43.

———. "Stephen of Bostra: *Fragmenta contra Iudaeos (CPG* 7790): A New Edition," *JÖB* 43 (1993), 45–60.

———. "A Florilegium in the Life of Nicetas of Medicion and a Letter of Theodore the Studite." *DOP* 48 (1994), 179–98.

Alexander, P. "Hypatius of Ephesus, a Note on Image Worship in the Sixth Century." *HTR* 45 (1951), 177–84.

———. "The Iconoclastic Council of St. Sophia (815) and Its Definition." *DOP* 7 (1953), 35–66.

———. "Church Councils and Patristic Authority: The Iconoclastic Councils of Hiereia (754) and St. Sophia (815)." *HSCPh* 63 (1958), 493–505.

———. *The Patriarch Nicephorus of Constantinople: Ecclesiastical Policy and Image Worship in the Byzantine Empire.* Oxford, 1958.

Amman, E. "Julius (Sextus) Africanus." *DTC* 8 (1925), cols. 1920–23.

Anastos, M. "The Ethical Theory of Images Formulated by the Iconoclasts in 754 and 815." *DOP* 8 (1954), 151–60.

Astruc, C., et al. *Les manuscrits grecs datés des XIII et XIV siècles conservés dans les bibliothèques publiques de France,* I (XIIIᵉ s.). Paris, 1989.

Atsalos, B. *La terminologie du livre-manuscrit à l'époque byzantine,* ΕΛΛΗΝΙΚΑ, ΠΑΡΑΡΤΗΜΑ 21. Thessalonike, 1971.

Auzépy, M.-F. "La place des moines à Nicée II (787)." *Byzantion* 58 (1988), 5–21.

Bardy, G. "Faux et fraudes littéraires dans l'antiquité chrétienne." *RHE* 32 (1936), 7–23, 275–302.

Batiffol, P. "Librairies byzantines à Rome." *Mélanges d'archéologie et d'histoire* 8 (1888), 297–308.

Beck, H.-G. *Kirche und theologische Literatur im byzantinischen Reich.* Munich, 1959.

Belting, H., and G. Cavallo. *Die Bibel des Niketas (Ein Werk der höfischen Buchkunst in Byzanz und sein antikes Vorbild).* Wiesbaden, 1979.

Beneševič, V. N. *Kanoničeskij Sbornik XIV Titulov.* St. Petersburg, 1905.

———. "Monumenta Vaticana ad Ius Canonicum Pertinentia." *Studi byzantini* 2 (1927), 127–86.

Böhringer, L. "Zwei Fragmenta der römischen Synode von 769 im Codex London British Library, Add. 16413." In *Aus Archiven und Bibliotheken (Festschrift für Raymund Kottje zum 65. Geburtstag),* ed. H. Mordek. Frankfurt, 1992, pp. 93–105.

Bracke, R. *Ad Sancti Maximi Vitam.* Louvain, 1980.

Brock, S. "An Early Syriac Life of Maximus the Confessor." *AB* 91 (1973), 299–346.

Browning, R. "Recentiores non Deteriores." *Bulletin of the Institute of Classical Studies of the University of London* 7 (1960), 11–21; repr. in *Griechische Kodikologie und Textüberlieferung,* ed. D. Harlfinger. Darmstadt, 1980, pp. 259–75.

Caspar, E. "Die Lateransynode von 649." *ZKG* 51 (1932), 75–137.

———. *Geschichte des Papsttums,* vol. II. Tübingen, 1933.

Cavallera, F. "Les fragments de Saint Amphiloque dans l'Hodegos et le Tome Dogmatique d'Anastasius le Sinaïte." *RHE* 8 (1907), 473–97.

Chadwick, H. "Florilegium." *RAC* 7 (1969), cols. 1131–60.

Chrestou, P. "Testimonia Neglected by the Seventh Ecumenical Council." *AHC* 20 (1988), 251–57.

Chrysos, E. Ἡ Ἐκκλησιαστικὴ πολιτικὴ τοῦ Ἰουστινιανοῦ. Thessalonike, 1969.

———. "Νεώτεραι Ἔρευναι περὶ Ἀναστασίων Σιναϊτῶν." *KΛHPONOMIA* 1 (1969), 121–43.

———. "Die Akten des Konzils von Konstantinopel I (381)." In *Romanitas—Christianitas: Untersuchungen zur Geschichte und Literatur der römischen Kaiserzeit (Festschrift Johannes Straub).* Berlin, 1982, pp. 426–35.

———. "Konzilsakten und Konzilsprotokolle vom 4. bis 7. Jahrhundert." *AHC* 15 (1983), 30–40.

Conte, P. *Regesto delle lettere dei Papi del secolo VIII, Saggi.* Milan, 1984.

———. *Il Sinodo Lateranense dell'ottobre 649.* Vatican City, 1989.

Crabbe, A. "The Invitation List to the Council of Ephesus and Metropolitan Hierarchy in the Fifth Century." *JTS* 32.2 (1981), 369–400.

Dagron, G. "Byzance et l'Union." In *1274 Année charnière, mutations et continuités,* Colloques Internationaux du CNRS 558. Paris, 1977, pp. 191–202.

Darrouzès, J. *Recherches sur les ὀφφίκια de l'Église byzantine,* Archives de l'Orient Chrétien 11. Paris, 1970.

———. "Deux textes inédits du Patriarche Germain." *REB* 45 (1987), 5–13.

Davis, R. *The Lives of the Eighth-Century Popes (Liber Pontificalis),* Liverpool, 1992.

Der Nersessian, S. "Une apologie des images du septième siècle." *Byzantion* 17 (1945), 58–87.

Déroche, V. "L'authenticité de l'Apologie contre les Juifs' de Léontios de Neapolis." *BCH* 110 (1986), 655–69.

———. "L'*Apologie contre les Juifs* de Léontios de Neapolis." *TM* 12 (1994), 45–104.

Devreesse, R. "La vie de S. Maxime le Confesseur et ses recensions." *AB* 46 (1928), 7–49.

———. "Par quelles voies nous sont parvenus les commentaires de Théodore de Mopsueste?" *RBibl* 39 (1929), 362–77.

———. "Le florilège de Léonce de Byzance." *RevSR* 10 (1930), 545–76.

————. *Codices Vaticani Graeci, Codd. 330–603.* Vatican City, 1937.

————. *Essai sur Théodore de Mopsueste, ST* 141. Vatican City, 1948.

————. *Introduction à l'étude des manuscrits grecs.* Paris, 1954.

Diekamp, F. *Doctrina Patrum de Incarnatione Verbi. Ein griechisches Florilegium aus der Wende des siebenten und achten Jahrhunderts.* Münster, 1907; reedited with additions by E. Chrysos and B. Phanourgakis, Münster, 1981.

Dobroklonskij, A. *Prepodobnyj Feodor, ispovednik i igumen studijskij,* I/II. Odessa, 1913–14.

Dobschütz, E. von. *Christusbilder. Untersuchungen zur christlichen Legende, TU,* N.F. 3, parts 1–4. Leipzig, 1899.

Dolbeau, F. "Une liste ancienne d'Apôtres et de Disciples, traduite du grec par Moïse de Bergame." *AB* 104 (1986), 299–314.

Dölger, F. *Constantin der Grosse und Seine Zeit.* Freiburg, 1913.

————. *Corpus der griechischen Urkunden des Mittelalters und der Neueren Zeit.* Reihe A: *Regesten.* Abt. 1: *Regesten der Kaiserurkunden des oströmischen Reiches.* I. Teil: *Regesten von 565–1025.* Munich-Berlin, 1924.

Dondaine, A. "Nicolas de Cotrone et les sources du Contra Errores Graecorum de saint Thomas." *Divus Thomas* 28 (1950), 313–40.

Dossetti, G. *Il Simbolo di Nicea e di Constantinopoli.* Rome, 1967.

Dvornik, F. "Emperors, Popes and General Councils." *DOP* 6 (1951), 1–23.

Ehrle, F. *Historia Bibliothecae Romanorum Pontificum.* Rome, 1890.

Eustratiades, S., and Arcadios Vatopedinos. *Catalogue of the Greek Manuscripts in the Library of the Monastery of Vatopedi on Mount Athos,* Harvard Theological Studies. Cambridge, Mass., 1924.

Festa, N. "Ancora la lettera di Michele Paleologo a Clemente IV." *Bessarione* 4–6 (1899–1900), 531 ff.

Ficker, G. "Eine Sammlung von Abschwörungsformeln." *ZKG* 27 (1906), 443–64.

Fonkič, B. L., and F. B. Poljakov, *Grečeskie rykopisi sinodalnoj biblioteki.* Moscow, 1993.

————. "Paläographische Grundlagen der Datierung des Kölner Mani-Kodex." *BZ* 83 (1990), 22–30.

Forshall, J. *Catalôgue of Manuscripts in the British Museum, New Series, Vol. I, Part I. The Arundel Manuscripts.* London, 1834.

Franchi, A. *Il Concilio II di Lione (1274) secondo la Ordinario Concilii Generalis Lugdunensis.* Rome, 1965.

Freeman, A. "Carolingian Orthodoxy and the Fate of the Libri Carolini." *Viator* 16 (1985), 65–108.

Gamillscheg, E., and D. Harlfinger. *Repertorium der griechischen Kopisten 800–1600,* Veröffentlichungen der Kommission für Byzantinistik, Band III, 2. Teil, Handschriften aus Bibliotheken Frankreichs. Vienna, 1989.

Geanakoplos, D. J. *Emperor Michael Palaeologus and the West (1258–1282).* Cambridge, Mass., 1959.

de Ghellinck, J. *Patristique et moyen âge,* vol. II. Brussels-Paris, 1947.

Gero, S. "The Libri Carolini and the Image Controversy." *GOTR* 18 (1973), 7–24.

————. *Byzantine Iconoclasm during the Reign of Leo III: With Particular Attention to the Oriental Sources, CSCO* 346, Subsidia 41. Louvain, 1973.

————. "Hypatius of Ephesus on the Cult of Images." In *Christianity, Judaism and*

Other Greco-Roman Cults: Studies for Morton Smith at Sixty, ed. J. Neusner, Part II. Leiden, 1975, pp. 208–16.

———. *Byzantine Iconoclasm during the Reign of Constantine V: With Particular Attention to the Oriental Sources, CSCO* 384, Subsidia 52. Louvain, 1977.

———. "The True Image of Christ: Eusebius' Letter to Constantia Reconsidered." *JTS* 32 (1981), 460–70.

Giannelli, C. *Codices Vaticani Graeci, Codd. 1684–1744.* Vatican City, 1961.

Gouillard, J. "Aux origines de l'Iconoclasme: Le témoignage de Grégoire II?" *TM* 3 (1968), 243–307.

Granić, B. "Der Inhalt der Subscriptionen in den datierten griechischen Handschriften des 11., 12., und 13. Jahrhunderts." *Byzantion* 1 (1924), 251–72.

Grillmeier, A. *Jesus der Christus im Glauben der Kirche,* vol. 2.1. Freiburg-Basel-Vienna, 1985.

Grotz, H. "Beobachtungen zu den zwei Briefen Papst Gregors II. an Kaiser Leo III." *Archivum Historiae Pontificiae* 18 (1980), 9–40.

———. "Weitere Beobachtungen zu den zwei Briefen Papst Gregors II. an Kaiser Leo III." *Archivum Historiae Pontificiae* 24 (1986), 365–75.

———. "Die früheste römische Stellungsnahme gegen den Bildersturm (Eine These, die es zu beweisen gilt)." *AHC* 20 (1988), 150–61.

Grumel, V. *La chronologie. Traité d'études byzantines,* vol. I. Paris, 1958.

———. *Les regestes des Actes du Patriarchat de Constantinople,* vol. I, fasc. 2–3, 2nd ed. revised by J. Darrouzès. Paris, 1989.

Hartmann, W. *Die Synoden der Karolingenzeit im Frankreich und in Italien.* In *Konziliengeschichte,* ed. W. Brandmüller, Reihe A: Darstellungen 6. Paderborn, 1989.

Hefele, C. J., and H. Leclercq. *Histoire des conciles.* Paris, 1907 ff.

Hennephof, H. *Textus Byzantinos ad Iconomachiam Pertinentes.* Leiden, 1969.

Hergenröther, J. *Monumenta Graeca ad Photium Pertinentia.* Regensburg, 1869.

Holl, K. *Die Schriften des Epiphanius gegen die Bilderverehrung,* Gesammelte Aufsätze zur Kirchengeschichte II,2. Tübingen, 1928. Originally published in *Sitzungsberichte der Königlichen Preussischen Akademie der Wissenschaften,* Phil.-hist. Kl. 35 (1916), 828–68.

Hussey, J. M. *The Orthodox Church in the Byzantine Empire.* Oxford, 1986.

Jaffé, P. *Regesta Pontificum Romanorum ab Condita Ecclesia ad Annum post Christum Natum MCXCVIII,* 2nd ed. by G. Wattenbach. Leipzig, 1885–88.

Jugie, M. "Origine de la controverse sur l'addition du *Filioque* au Symbole." *RSPhTh* 28 (1939), 369–85.

Kazhdan, A. "'Constantine Imaginaire' Byzantine Legends of the Ninth Century about Constantine the Great." *Byzantion* 57 (1987), 196–250.

———. "Do We Need a New History of Byzantine Law?" *JÖB* 39 (1989), 1–28.

Kazhdan, A., and H. Maguire. "Byzantine Hagiographical Texts as Sources on Art." *DOP* 45 (1991), 1–22.

Kelly, J. N. D., *Early Christian Creeds.* London, 1960.

———. *The Athanasian Creed.* New York-Evanston, 1964.

———. *The Oxford Dictionary of Popes,* Oxford, 1986.

Kitzinger, E. "The Cult of Images in the Age before Iconoclasm." *DOP* 8 (1954), 83–150.

Kotzabassi, S. "Der Kopist des Geschichtswerkes von Dukas." In *Symbolae Berolinenses für Dieter Harlfinger,* ed. F. Berger, Ch. Brockmann, et al. Amsterdam, 1993, pp. 307–23.

Ladner, G. B. "The Concept of the Image in the Greek Fathers and the Byzantine Iconoclastic Controversy." *DOP* 7 (1953), 3–34.

Laurent, V., and J. Darrouzès. *Dossier grec de l'union de Lyon (1273–1277),* Archives de l'Orient Chrétien 16. Paris, 1976.

Lemerle, P. *Le premier humanisme byzantin.* Paris, 1971.

Loenertz, R.-J. "Autour du traité de Fr. Barthélemy de Constantinople contre les Grecs." *Archivum Fratrum Praedicatorum* 6 (1936), 361–71.

———. "Notes d'histoire et de chronologie Byzantines." *REB* 20 (1962), 171–80.

Madoz, J. "¿Una nueva redacción de los textos seudo-patristicos sobre el Primado en Jacobo de Viterbo?" *Gregorianum* 17 (1936), 562–83.

Manaphes, K. Αἱ ἐν Κωνσταντινουπόλει βιβλιοθῆκαι. αὐτοκρατορικαὶ καὶ πατριαρχικὴ καὶ περὶ τῶν ἐν αὐταῖς χειρογράφων μέχρι τῆς ἁλώσεως *(1453),* Μελέτη Φιλολογική. Athens, 1972.

Mango, C. "La culture grecque et l'Occident au VIIIᵉ siècle," *Settimane di Studio del Centro Italiano di Studi sull'alto Medioevo 20* (Spoleto, 1973), 683–721.

———. "The Availability of Books in the Byzantine Empire, A.D. 750–850." In *Byzantine Books and Bookmen: A Dumbarton Oaks Colloquium.* Washington, D.C., 1975, pp. 29–45.

———. "L'origine de la minuscule." In *Colloques Internationaux du C.N.R.S.,* no. 559, *La paléographie grecque et byzantine.* Paris, 1977, pp. 175–80.

———. *The Art of the Byzantine Empire 312–1453.* Toronto, 1986.

Martini, A., and D. Bassi. *Catalogus Codicum Graecorum Bibliothecae Ambrosianae,* vol. I. Milan, 1906.

May, G. "Das Lehrverfahren gegen Eutyches im November des Jahres 448." *AHC* 21 (1989), 1–61.

Melioranskij, B. M. *Georgij Kiprianin i Ioann Ierusalimlianin, dva maloizviestnych bortsa za pravoslavie v VIII viekie.* St. Petersburg, 1901.

Melloni, A. "L'Opus Caroli Regis contra Synodum' o 'Libri Carolini'." *Studi medievali,* ser. 3, 29.2 (1988), 873–86.

Mercati, G. "Un preteso scritto di san Pietro vescovo d'Alessandria e martire sulla bestemmia e Filone l'istoriografo." In *Opere minori,* II, *ST* 77 (1937), 426–39.

Meunier, B. "Cyrille d'Alexandrie au Concile de Florence." *AHC* 21 (1989), 147–74.

Meyendorff, J. *Christ in Eastern Christian Thought.* Washington, D.C., 1969.

Michels, H. "Zur Echtheit der Briefe Papst Gregors II. an Kaiser Leon III." *ZKG* 99 (1988), 376–91.

Mioni, E. *Bibliothecae Divi Marci Venetiarum Codices Graeci Manuscripti,* vol. II. Rome, 1981.

———. *Introduzione alla paleographia greca.* Padova, 1973.

Misides, A. Ἡ παρουσία τῆς Ἐκκλησίας Κύπρου εἰς τὸν ἀγῶνα ὑπὲρ τῶν εἰκόνων. Leukosia, 1989.

de Montfaucon, B. *Palaeographia Graeca.* Paris, 1708.

Munitiz, J. "Synoptic Greek Accounts of the Seventh Council." *REB* 32 (1974), 147–86.

————. "The Manuscript of Justel's *Anonymi Tractatus de Synodis.*" *Byzantion* 47 (1977), 239–57.

————. "Le *Parisinus Graecus 1115:* Description et arrière-plan historique." *Scriptorium* 36 (1982), 51–67.

Murphy, F. X., and P. Sherwood. *Constantinople II et Constantinople III,* vol. III of *Histoire des Conciles Oecuméniques.* Paris, 1974.

Murray, Sr. M. Charles. "Art and the Early Church." *JTS* 28 (1977), 305–45.

Nicol, D. M. "The Greeks and the Union of the Churches: The Preliminaries to the Second Council of Lyons, 1261–1274." In *Medieval Studies Presented to Aubrey Gwynn, S. J.,* ed. J. A. Watt, J. B. Morall, and F. X. Martin. Dublin, 1961, pp. 454–80.

————. "The Byzantine Reaction to the Second Council of Lyons, 1274." In *Councils and Assemblies,* ed. G. J. Cuming and D. Baker. Cambridge, 1971, pp. 113–46.

Nissen, Th. "Unbekannte Erzählungen aus dem Pratum Spirituale." *BZ* 38 (1938), 351–76.

Noble, T. F. X. "The Declining Knowledge of Greek in Eighth- and Ninth-Century Papal Rome." *BZ* 78 (1985), 56–62.

————. *The Republic of St. Peter, The Birth of the Papal State 680–825.* Philadelphia, 1984.

Noret, J. "Le palimpseste 'Parisinus gr. 443'." *AB* 88 (1970), 141–52.

Omont, H. *Inventaire sommaire des manuscrits grecs de la Bibliothèque Nationale et des autres bibliothèques de Paris et des départements, I, III.* Paris, 1886, 1888.

————. *Fac-similes des manuscrits grecs datés de la Bibliothèque Nationale du IXe au XIVe siècle.* Paris, 1891.

Orlandis, J., and D. Ramos-Lissón. *Die Synoden auf der Iberischen Halbinsel bis zum Einbruch des Islam (711).* In *Konziliengeschichte,* ed. W. Brandmüller, Reihe A: Darstellungen. Paderborn, 1981.

Ostrogorsky, G. *Studien zur Geschichte des byzantinischen Bilderstreits,* Historische Untersuchungen 5. Breslau, 1929.

————. "Les débuts de la querelle des images." In *Mélanges Charles Diehl,* I. Paris, 1930, pp. 235–55.

————. *History of the Byzantine State.* Oxford, 1980.

Ouspensky, L. *Theology of the Icon,* 2 vols., trans. A. Gythiel and E. Meyendorff. Crestwood, N.Y., 1992. 2 vols.

Ouspensky, P., and V. Beneševič. *Catalogus Codicum Manuscriptorum Graecorum qui in Monasterio Sanctae Catharinae in Monte Sina Asservantur,* vol. I. St. Petersburg, 1911–18.

Paramelle, J. "Morceau égaré du *Corpus Dionysiacum* ou Pseudo-pseudo-Denys? Fragment grec d'une *Lettre à Tite* inconnue." In *Denys l'Areopagite et sa posterité en Orient et en Occident,* Actes du Colloque, 21-24 septembre 1994, ed. Y. de Andia. Paris, 1996, pp. 237–266.

Patacsi, G. "Le Hieromoine Hierothée, théologien du Saint-Esprit." *ΚΛΗΡΟΝΟΜΙΑ* 13 (1981), 299–330.

Pattenden, Ph. "The Text of the *Pratum Spirituale.*" *JTS* 26 (1975), 38–54.

Pelikan, J. *The Spirit of Eastern Christendom (600–1700). The Christian Tradition: A History of the Development of Doctrine,* vol. II. Chicago, 1974.

Perria, L. "Il *Vat. gr.* 2200. Note codicologiche e paleografiche." *Rivista di studi bizantini e neoellenici,* N.S. 20–21 (1983–84), 25–68.

Petit, F. "L'homme créé 'à l'image' de Dieu: Quelques fragments grecs inédits de Théodore de Mopsueste." *Le Muséon* 100 (1987), 269–81.

Pierres, J. S. *Maximus Confessor, Princeps Apologetarum Synodi Lateranensis.* Diss. Pont. Univ. Greg. Rome, 1940.

Podskalsky, G. "Orthodoxe und Westliche Theologie." *JÖB* 31.2 (1981), 513–27.

le Quien, M. *Oriens Christianus in Quatuor Patriarchatus Digestus.* Paris, 1740.

Ramos-Lissón, D. "Die Synodalen Ursprünge des 'Filioque' im römisch-westgotischen Hispanien." *AHC* 16 (1984), 286–99.

Ravegnani, G. *Le bibliotheche del Monastero di San Giorgio Maggiore.* Florence, 1986.

Rees, S. "The *De Sectis:* A Treatise Attributed to Leontius of Byzantium." *JTS* 40 (1939), 346–60.

Reynolds, L. D., and N. G. Wilson. *Scribes and Scholars: A Guide to the Transmission of Greek and Latin Literature,* 2nd ed. London, 1975.

Richard, M. "La tradition des fragments du traité Περὶ τῆς ἐνανθρωπήσεως de Théodore de Mopsueste." *Le Muséon* 56 (1943), 55–75.

———. "Les traités de Cyrille d'Alexandrie contre Diodore et Théodore et les fragments dogmatiques de Diodore de Tarse." In *Mélanges Felix Grat,* I. Paris, 1946, pp. 99–116.

———. "Notes sur les florilèges dogmatiques du Vᵉ et du VIᵉ siècle." In *Actes du VIᵉ Congrès International d'Études Byzantines,* I. Paris, 1950, pp. 307–18.

———. "Les florilèges diphysites du Vᵉ et du VIᵉ siècle." In *Das Konzil von Chalkedon, Geschichte und Gegenwart,* ed. A. Grillmeier and H. Bacht. Wurzburg, 1951, pp. 721–48.

———. "Florilèges spirituels grecs." *DSp* 5. Paris, 1962–64, cols. 475–512.

Riedinger, R. "Grammatiker-Gelehrsamkeit in den Akten der Lateransynode von 649." *JÖB* 25 (1976), 57–61.

———. "Aus den Akten der Lateransynode von 649." *BZ* 69 (1976), 17–38.

———. "Griechische Konzilsakten auf dem Wege ins lateinische Mittelalter." *AHC* 9 (1977), 252–87.

———. *Lateinische Übersetzungen griechischer Häretikertexte des siebenten Jahrhunderts,* SBWien 352. Vienna, 1979.

———. "Zwei Briefe aus den Akten der Lateransynode von 649." *JÖB* 29 (1980), 37–59.

———. "Sprachschichten in der lateinischen Übersetzung der Lateranakten von 649." *ZKG* 92 (1981), 180–202.

———. "Die Lateransynode von 649 und Maximos der Bekenner." In *Maximus Confessor, Actes du Symposium sur Maxime le Confesseur,* Fribourg, 2–5 septembre 1980, ed. F. Heinzer and C. von Schönborn. Fribourg, 1982, pp. 111–21.

———. "Die *Epistula Synodica* des Sophronios von Jerusalem in Codex Paris. BN gr. 1115." *BYZANTIAKA* 2 (1982), 145–54.

———. "Die Nachkommen der Epistula Synodica des Sophronios von Jerusalem (a. 634; CPG 7635)." *Römische historische Mitteilungen* 26 (1984), 91–106.

———. "Der *Tomus* des Papstes Damasus (CPL 1633) in Codex Paris. gr. 1115." *Byzantion* 54 (1984), 634–37.

———. "Die Lateranakten von 649, ein Werk der Byzantiner um Maximos Homologetes." *Byzantina* 13.1 (= *Dorema eis I. Karayannopoulon*) (1985), 519–34.

———. *Der Codex Vindobonensis 418, seine Vorlage und seine Schreiber.* Steenbrugge, 1989.

Riedinger, R., and H. Thurn. "Die Didascalia CCCXVIII Patrum Nicaenorum und das Syntagma ad Monachos im Codex Parisinus Graecus 1115." *JÖB* 35 (1985), 75–92.

Roberg, B. *Die Union zwischen der griechischen und der lateinischen Kirche auf dem II. Konzil von Lyon* (1274). Bonn, 1964.

de Rossi, I. B. *De Origine Historia Indicibus Scrinii et Bibliothecae Sedis Apostolicae.* In H. Stevenson, *Codices Palatini Latini Bibliothecae Vaticanae.* Rome, 1886.

Routh, M. J. *Reliquiae Sacrae,* vol. II. Oxford, 1846.

Sambin, P. "Il vescovo Cotronese Niccolò da Durazzo e un inventario di suoi codici latini e greci (1276)." In *Note e discussioni erudite a cura di Augusto Campana,* vol. III. Rome, 1954.

Sansterre, J. M. *Les moines grecs à Rome aux époques byzantine et carolingienne (milieux du VIᵉ siècle–fin du XIᵉ siècle),* fasc. 1–2. Brussels, 1983.

Schäferdiek, K. *Die Kirche in den Reichen der Westgoten und Sueven bis zur Errichtung der westgotischen katholischen Staatskirche,* Arbeiten zur Kirchengeschichte 39. Berlin, 1967.

Schermann, Th. "Die Geschichte der dogmatischen Florilegien vom V.–VIII. Jahrhundert." *TU* 28.1. Leipzig, 1904.

———. "Propheten- und Apostellegenden nebst Jüngerkatalogen des Dorotheus und verwandter Text." *TU* 31.3. Leipzig, 1907.

Schönborn, Chr. von. *L'icône du Christ,* 3rd ed. Paris, 1986.

Schwartz, E. *Codex Vaticanus Graecus 1431,* AbhMünchPhilos.-hist.Kl. Munich, 1927.

———. *Der Prozeß des Eutyches,* SBMünchPhilos.-hist.Kl., Abt. 5. Munich, 1929.

———. *Drei dogmatische Schriften Iustinians,* AbhMünchPhilos.-hist.Kl., N.F. 18. Munich, 1939.

Serruys, D. "Anastasiana." École Française de Rome, *Mélanges d'archéologie et d'histoire* 22 (1902), 157–207.

———. "Les Actes du concile iconoclaste de l'an 815." École Française de Rome, *Mélanges d'archéologie et d'histoire* 23 (1903), 345–51.

Ševčenko, I. "The Search for the Past in Byzantium around the Year 800." *DOP* 46 (1992), *Homo Byzantinus: Papers in Honor of Alexander Kazhdan,* ed. A. Cutler and S. Franklin, pp. 279–93.

Sherwood, P. *An Annotated Date-List of the Works of Maximus the Confessor,* Studia Anselmiana 30. Rome, 1952.

———. *St. Maximus the Confessor (The Ascetic Life, the Four Centuries on Charity).* London, 1955.

Simonetti, M. "La processione dello Spirito Santo secondo i Padri Greci." *Aevum* 26 (1952), 33–41.

———. "La processione dello Spirito Santo nei Padri Latini." *Maia* 7 (1955), 308–24.

Sinkewicz, R. E. "The *Solutions* Addressed to George Lapithes by Barlaam the Calabrian and Their Philosophical Context." *Medieval Studies* 43 (1981), 151–217.

Spagnolo, A., and C. H. Turner. "A Fragment of an Unknown Latin Version of the Apostolic Constitutions." *JTS* 13 (1912), 492–512.

Speck, P. *Artabasdos. Der rechtgläubige Vorkämpfer der göttlichen Lehre,* ΠΟΙΚΙΛΑ ΒΥΖΑΝΤΙΝΑ 2. Bonn, 1981.

———. "ΓΡΑΦΑΙΣ Η ΓΛΥΦΑΙΣ. Zu dem Fragment des Hypatios von Ephesos über die Bilder"; and "Zu dem Dialog mit einem Juden des Leontios von Neapolis." ΠΟΙΚΙΛΑ ΒΥΖΑΝΤΙΝΑ 4, Varia 1. Bonn, 1984, pp. 211–72.

————. "Eine Interpolation in den Bilderreden des Johannes von Damaskos." *BZ* 82 (1989), 114–17.

————. *Ich bin's nicht, Kaiser Konstantin ist es gewesen,* ΠΟΙΚΙΛΑ ΒΥΖΑΝΤΙΝΑ 10. Bonn, 1990.

————. "Schweinefleisch und Bilderkult. Zur Bilderdebatte in den sogennanten Judendialogen." In *To Hellenikon: Studies in Honor of Speros Vryonis.* New York, 1993, pp. 367–83.

Speyer, W. *Die literarische Fälschung im heidnischen und christlichen Altertum. Ein Versuch ihrer Deutung.* Munich, 1971.

Stallman, C. J. *The Life of St. Pancratius of Taormina,* D.Phil. thesis. Oxford University, 1986.

Stein, D. *Der Beginn des byzantinischen Bilderstreites und seine Entwicklung bis in die 40er Jahre des 8. Jahrhunderts.* Munich, 1980.

von den Steinen, W. "Entstehungsgeschichte der Libri Carolini." *Quellen und Forschungen aus italienischen Archiven und Bibliotheken* 21 (1929–30), 1–93.

Sullivan, F. *The Christology of Theodore of Mopsuestia,* Analecta Gregoriana 82. Rome, 1956, pp. 35–159.

Swete, H. B. *On the History of the Doctrine of the Procession of the Holy Spirit from the Apostolic Age to the Death of Charlemagne.* Cambridge, 1876.

Tăutu, A. *Acta Urbani IV, Clementis IV et Gregorii X.* Vatican City, 1953.

Tetz, M. "Zum Streit zwischen Orthodoxie und Häresie an der Wende zum 4. und 5. Jahrhunderts." *Evangelische Theologie* 20 (1961), 354–68.

Thümmel, H. "Neilos von Ankyra über die Bilder." *BZ* 71 (1978), 10–21.

————. *Die Frühgeschichte der ostkirchlichen Bilderlehre, Texte und Untersuchungen zur Zeit vor dem Bilderstreit, TU* 139. Berlin, 1992.

Troianos, S. Ἡ ἐκκλησιαστικὴ δικονομία μέχρι τοῦ θανάτου τοῦ Ἰουστινιανοῦ. Athens, 1964.

————. Ἡ ἐκκλησιαστικὴ διαδικασία μεταξὺ 565 καὶ 1204. Athens, 1969.

Turner, C. H. "An Arian Sermon from a MS in the Chapter Library of Verona." *JTS* 13 (1912), 19–21.

————. "A Primitive Edition of the Apostolic Constitutions and Canons: An Early List of Apostles and Disciples." *JTS* 15 (1913–14), 53–65.

Turyn, A. *Dated Greek Manuscripts of the Thirteenth and Fourteenth Centuries in the Libraries of Great Britain,* DOS 17. Washington, D.C., 1980.

Uthemann, K.-H. "Ein Beitrag zur Geschichte der Union des Konzils von Lyon (1274). Bemerkungen zum Codex Parisinus gr. 1115 (Med. Reg. 2951)." *AHC* 13 (1981), 27–49.

Vailhé, P. S. "Saint Michel le Syncelle et les deux frères Grapti." *ROC* 6 (1901), 313–32.

Vasiliev, A. A. "The Iconoclastic Edict of the Caliph Yazid II, A.D. 721." *DOP* 9–10 (1955–56), 25–47.

Van den Ven, P. "La patristique et l'hagiographie au concile de Nicée de 787." *Byzantion* 25–27 (1955–57), 235–62.

Vives, J., T. M. Martinez, and G. Martinez Diez. *Concilios visigóticos e hispano-romanos,* España Cristiana, Textos 1. Barcelona-Madrid, 1963.

Vladimir (Archimandrite). *Sistematičeskoe opisanie rykopisej Moskovskoj Sinodalnoj (Patriaršei) biblioteki,* vol. I. Moscow, 1894.

Vogel, M., and V. Gardthausen. *Griechische Paläographie*, 2 vols. Leipzig, 1911–13.

Vosté, J. M. "L'oeuvre exégétique de Théodore de Mopsueste au IIe concile de Constantinople." *RBibl* 38 (1929), 382–95.

Waegeman, M. "The Text Tradition of the Treatise *De Sectis* (Ps. Leontius Byzantinus)." *L'antiquité classique* 45 (1976), 190–96.

Wallach, L. *Diplomatic Studies in Latin and Greek Documents from the Carolingian Age.* Ithaca-London, 1977.

West, M. L. *Textual Criticism and Editorial Technique.* Stuttgart, 1973.

Winkelmann, F. "Die Quellen zur Erforschung des monenergetisch-monotheletischen Streites." *Klio* 69 (1987), 515–59.

Wright, W. *Catalogue of Syriac Manuscripts in the British Museum,* vol. II. London, 1871.

Zellinger, J. *Studien zu Severian von Gabala,* Münsterische Beiträge zur Theologie 8. Münster, 1926.

Zettl, E. *Die Bestätigung des V. Ökumenischen Konzils durch Papst Vigilius,* Untersuchungen über die Echtheit der Briefe *Scandala* und *Aetius* (JK 936.937), Antiquitas Reihe I, Abhandlungen zur alten Geschichte, Bd. 20. Bonn, 1974.

abbot, 18, 31 n. 144, 163, 193, 194, 204–5
Acephaloi, 192
acts. *See* conciliar minutes
Albania, 237
Alexandria, 55, 168, 194, 231
anagnostes, 3
anathematization, 11, 23, 29, 36, 86, 93, 99, 209–10, 255
post mortem, 13, 15, 56
ἀναφοραί, 16, 229
angels, 173, 214, 247
Anomoians, 149
Antioch (Θεούπολις), 55, 115, 172–74, 192, 197
apograph, 55 n. 55, 101, 169
of the archetype of Paris. gr. 1115, 259–60
of the τεῦχος of 770, 108, 170, 224
apostles, 4, 5, 55 n. 55, 66, 88, 96, 102, 130, 146–47, 172
Arabic numbers, 44
archetype (original)
of the acts of Nicaea II, 140–41
of the *Doctrina Patrum*, 61, 65, 68–71
of the *Libellus* (Greek original), 239, 247
of Paris. gr. 1115 (and, for the Iconophile florilegium, of Mosquensis Hist. M. 265 and Venetus Marc. gr. 573), 1, 2, 43, 44, 47–48, 50–51, 53, 55 n. 55, 57, 58 n. 65, 61, 68–71, 83, 84 n. 157, 98 n. 23, 101–3, 104 n. 40, 105–8, 114, 119, 125, 133–34, 136, 137, 140, 141, 150–51, 155, 157, 173, 175, 180, 182, 188, 191, 197, 201, 208–9, 212–13, 215, 216, 217, 234–60 passim
an official document, 254–55
updating of, 255–56

archidiaconus, 12, 15 n. 60
archimandrite, 61 n. 75
archipresbyterus, 224 n. 185
Arians/Arianism, 3, 74, 168–69
Armenians, 34 n. 155, 104 n. 41, 136 n. 105
ἀρχεῖα (ἐν Βυζαντίῳ), 230
officers of, 230
ἀχειροποίητον(α), 97
azyma, 235

baptism, 98
bishops (ἐπίσκοπος), 14, 20, 22, 56, 61 n. 73, 96, 128, 130, 142, 165, 180, 181, 227, 230, 258
Cypriot, 30 n. 142, 231
Iconoclast, 50
pro-Latin, 54
signatures of, 101
suffragan, 51
Western, 73
books (codices, βίβλοι, βιβλίον, κωδίκιον), 2, 5 n. 16, 6 n. 18, 8, 18, 22–23, 25–26, 29, 30, 34–35, 42, 85, 103 n. 39, 118, 135–36, 142, 146, 151, 163, 164, 171, 188, 189, 191–93, 195, 200, 204, 205, 215, 222, 227–28, 231–33, 243, 249–50, 252–54, 258, 260. *See also* manuscripts
destroyed by the Iconoclasts, 193, 205, 215
Greek, 257–58, 260
Byzantines, 48, 82, 168, 237, 238

canons, 5, 15, 39, 41 n. 182, 52, 85, 89–91, 101, 182, 230, 255
chancery (imperial), 45
Christian Church, 4, 95 n. 16, 96, 231, 238
Eastern (Orthodox), 75, 236, 238
Western (Catholic), 224 n. 186, 234–36, 251 n. 35, 254

primacy of, 82, 235, 238–39, 247

Christians, 113, 119, 120, 145–48, 149, 189, 191, 209, 210, 215, 220, 232, 244
  Eastern (Orthodox), 3, 5, 80
  Western (Catholic), 75, 80
christology, 92 n. 1, 99
churches, 75, 102, 106 n. 45, 142, 145, 146, 200–201
  of Cosmas and Damian (Constantinople), 196
  of St. Sophia, 31
clerics, 2, 11, 34 n. 154, 192, 219, 227, 237, 257
colophon
  of codex Taurinensis gr. B.I.2, 48 n. 27
  of Paris. gr. 1115, 1, 45–50, 84, 85, 108, 252, 254, 256–57
    credibility of, 47–51, 72, 85, 257
    dates of, 47–50, 108, 170, 254–55
  "wandering," 48, 253
conciliar minutes, 1, 6 n. 19, 11, 15 n. 61, 16, 19, 41–42, 93, 136–226 passim, 227, 232–33, 235, 250 n. 32, 257, 258
conciliar proceedings/procedure, 3, 6, 9–10, 12, 14, 16–17, 18, 19, 21, 22, 23, 33, 41, 136, 151, 222, 227, 228–29, 231
Constantia (Salamis on Cyprus), 61 n. 73, 227
Constantinople, 21, 22 n. 97, 25 n. 108, 29, 31 n. 142, 44, 72, 76, 85 n. 158, 108, 109, 151, 153, 196, 209, 224, 225, 239–40, 243, 249, 251, 258, 260 n. 29
  Arab siege of, 209
correspondence, 8, 13, 51, 55, 57, 85 n. 158, 109 n. 53, 176, 223, 238
  papal, 257, 258
councils and synods, 1, 3, 42, 86, 136, 209, 230. See also, ecumenical councils

Apostolic synod in Antioch, 172
Council of Ferrara-Florence (1438–39), 54, 76, 81–82, 249 n. 28
Council of Lyons (1274), 50, 82 n. 141, 85 n. 158, 236 n. 8, 249 n. 28, 251, 254
Lateran Council (649), 1, 6 n. 18, 16–21, 24, 27, 31, 41, 51, 52, 56, 230, 258
  "stage managed," 12, 14, 16, 20–21, 41–42, 164, 189, 192–94, 222, 228–30
Synod of Braga III (675), 75
Synod of Constantinople (448), 55, 216; (536), 38, 119, 192, 219; at St. Sophia, Iconoclastic (815), 31, 42, 226, 232
Synod of Ephesus (449) ("Robber" Council), 8, 9, 55
Synod of Fréjus (796), 72
Synod of Gentilly (767), 76 n. 122
Synod of Hiereia (754), 3 n. 6, 31–37, 93, 95, 97, 111, 163, 210, 225, 228
Synod of Jerusalem (764), 3, 208–10
Synod of Paris (825), 138, 139
Synod of Rome (731), 3, 116–20, 121 n. 81, 122, 136, 139, 148, 156, 165, 176–77, 184, 208, 211, 213, 228; Lateran (769), 3, 116–17, 119, 136, 139, 156, 165, 176–77, 210, 228
Synod of Toledo III (589), 74–75; IV (633), 75; VI (638), 75; VIII (653), 75; XII (681), 75; XVI (693), 75
cross, 98, 104, 106 n. 42, 180, 184–85
  the Holy Cross, 201
  veneration of, 104, 106 n. 42, 117, 175, 184–85
Croton (Cotrone), 236–37
crucifixion, 87, 95
curia, 51, 237, 254

Damascus, 115
Daphne (in Syria), 192
deposition (of a bishop), 26

diaconus (deacon), 11 n. 42, 15 n. 61, 121, 193
dogma, 3–4, 9, 31, 36, 37, 41, 48, 52, 75, 77, 85, 86, 96, 223, 230, 250, 251
  Catholic, 74, 234, 238–39
  Orthodox, 230, 238
dossier, 253, 259, 260 n. 29
dyothelete, 26, 31. *See also* florilegium
Dyrrachium (Durrazo), 237

East, 115, 176, 225
ecumenical councils, 5, 23, 78, 112, 120, 230, 247–48, 259 n. 26
  Council of Nicaea I (1st, 325), 240, 244
  Council of Constantinople I (2nd, 381), 6 n. 19, 17, 85, 244
  Council of Ephesus (3d, 431), 1, 6–8, 15, 17, 23, 44, 52–54, 244
  Council of Chalcedon (4th, 451), 1, 8–10, 15, 17, 22 n. 92, 23, 36, 42, 44, 52, 55, 244
  Council of Constantinople II (5th, 553), 1, 3–5, 10–18, 21, 23, 38, 44, 52, 54–56, 229–30
  Council of Constantinople III (6th, 680/1), 1–2, 6, 21–31, 38, 42, 44, 52, 57, 86, 112, 231–33
  Council in Trullo (Quinisextum), 38, 101, 182–83, 219, 223
  Council of Nicaea II (7th, 787), 1–3, 21, 36–38, 42, 44, 49–50, 93, 110, 114 n. 72, 120, 136, 137, 150–51, 157, 182, 188, 191, 209, 210, 213, 215, 219, 222–24, 228, 229 n. 6, 230, 232–33
  as trials, 229–31
    minutes of, 229
editio conciliorum Romana, 138–39, 141, 200
ekphrasis, 153, 156, 187–88
emperor (βασιλεύς), 104–5, 111, 118–19, 131, 152, 168–70, 174, 177–80, 231, 236, 239
  Byzantine, 235–36
  of Nicaea, 236–37
eras

Alexandrian, 48, 108, 170, 255
Byzantine, 47, 49 n. 33, 257
chiliastic, 49 n. 33
ἐρωταποκρίσεις, 57–58
epigrams, 106 n. 45, 259
Europe
  Northern, 109 n. 55
  Western, 73–75, 115, 225, 238
    "inner West," 109 n. 55
excommunication, 56
exemplar, 44, 52, 53, 54, 94, 101, 108, 151, 166, 170, 206, 212–14, 217, 220, 241, 250

fabrication, 76, 122
falsification of texts, 5, 6, 17, 22, 33, 38, 99, 222, 229
  of the colophon of Paris. gr. 1115, 48
  of conciliar acts, 23–24
fathers (authors), 200, 210, 227, 231, 238, 244, 252
  Greek (Oriental), 4, 6, 8 n. 29, 9, 13 nn. 49 and 51, 17, 23, 27 n. 121, 33, 49, 53, 55, 73 n. 99, 76–79, 81, 83, 92, 96, 98, 99, 103, 116, 120, 234–35, 239, 247–48, 260
  Latin, 4, 9, 14, 16, 18 n. 75, 27 n. 121, 38, 73 n. 99, 76–79, 83, 96, 98, 99, 103, 116, 135, 238–39, 247–49, 251, 254, 255
florilegium/a (anthologies, quotations, *testimonia,* χρήσεις, φωναί), 61, 67, 68, 70, 96–97, 118, 135–37, 200, 231–33
  of Albinus of Milan, 250 n. 33
  conciliar, 3, 8, 42, 51
    of the Council of Chalcedon, 8–10, 229 n. 4
    of the Council of Constantinople II, 11
    of the Council of Constantinople III, 21–29, 231, 258
    of the Council of Ephesus, 2, 6–8, 42
  dyothelete, 2, 17–18, 24, 26 n. 119, 27, 29, 42, 231

heretical, 26 n. 119, 36, 230
on the Holy Spirit (*Filioque*),
    procession of, 54, 57, 71–85, 119,
    244, 247, 256, 260
    pro-Latin, 82, 84, 247
Iconoclastic, 31–37, 99, 230 n. 7,
    233 n. 16
Iconophile, 2–3, 36, 38, 103 n. 39,
    119, 120, 124, 130, 210, 226,
    228, 232, 260
        of the *Doctrina Patrum,* 107,
            116–17, 123–25, 133
        of John of Damascus, 114–17,
            123–37, 142–226 passim,
            228
        of the Lateran Council, 2, 4 n.
            10, 6 n. 18, 17–18, 24, 27,
            29, 42, 258
        of Mosquensis Hist. M. 265,
            40, 100–105, 108–226
            passim
        of Nicetas of Medicion, 103–6,
            222, 225
        of Paris. gr. 1115, 2, 40, 42,
            43–44, 48 n. 24, 49, 52,
            58–60, 69, 85, 92–226 pas-
            sim, 250 and n. 31, 252,
            254, 259
        of the Roman Synods of 731
            and 769, 37–42, 116–22,
            124, 133, 134
        of the seventh ecumenical
            council (787), 137–222
            passim
        of the year 770, 98–108, 114
            n. 72, 134–36, 172, 194,
            200, 215–17, 228
        of Venetus Marc. gr. 573, 40,
            100, 106–7, 116–226
            passim
    monothelete, 2, 17, 18, 24, 29, 42
    of Macarius of Antioch (monothe-
        lete), 25–26
    Nestorian, 7–8
    of Nicholas of Cotrone (*Libellus*),
        234–53
    orthodox, 229

patristic, 1, 4, 5, 232
prepared in advance, 2, 11–12, 14,
    16
of the Synod of Hiereia, 31–35
of the Synod of St. Sophia, 34–35
of the *Synodica rectae fidei* of the Ori-
    ental patriarchs, 38
textual accuracy, 4 n. 11, 231
of Theodore of Mopsuestia, 11–12
of Theodore of Pharan, 17, 30
Franks, 109 n. 55
Fratres Minores, 237

hagiography, 93, 225
handwriting, 44, 45 (*see also,* script)
Hellenism/es, 149, 172
Herakleia of Pontos, 250 n. 34, 251
heresy, 22, 41 n. 182, 96, 112, 229–30
    formal disavowals of, 85
heretics, 4, 5, 11, 13, 15, 17, 18, 31,
    107 n. 49, 209, 232
Hiereia, palace of, 95, 98
Holy Scripture, 4–5, 32 n. 146, 37, 41
    n. 181, 44, 58, 85, 86, 93, 98, 113,
    116, 120, 122, 163, 166, 187, 207–8,
    219, 238–39, 247–48, 251–52
Holy Spirit, 52, 77, 152, 236, 238, 246
    Filioque, 49, 50, 54, 72–85, 234–36,
        241, 246 and n. 25, 247, 251 n.
        35
        introduction of *Filioque* in
            Spain, 73–75
    Filioque controversy, 48, 54, 72, 84
        n. 158
    in the form of a dove, 192
    procession of, 38, 49, 71, 72–75, 77–
        81, 83–84, 235–36, 240–41, 251
        n. 35
        only from the Father, 236

Iconoclasm, 36, 48 n. 24, 92 n. 1, 94,
    96, 103, 119, 135, 140, 193, 209,
    213, 222, 225–26
    in Byzantine territories, 209
    in Syria, 49, 208
Iconoclastic
    committees, 34–36, 233 n. 16

delegates, 76 n. 122
theology, 36, 113, 136, 226
writings, 31, 115 n. 73
Iconoclasts, 35, 36, 50, 95–99, 123 n.
    87, 191, 210
Iconophiles, 31 n. 145, 36, 103, 120,
    135, 193, 222
    bishops, 76 n. 122
    quotations/works, 37–38, 50, 97,
        100, 103, 113, 115 n. 73, 116,
        119, 120, 121, 123 n. 87, 135,
        136 n. 105, 173, 182, 222–23,
        227, 229, 232–33, 234
iconophobic, 32
idolatry, 131
idols, 96, 111–12
images/icons, 105, 124 n. 88, 128, 142,
    152, 154, 164, 166–67, 182, 197,
    201, 224 n.186
    Abraham, sacrifice of, 121 n. 81,
        153
    ἀχειροποίητοι, 106 n. 44
    of angels, 130, 163, 173
    of the apostles, 98, 102, 146, 190,
        210
    of Basiliscus, the martyr, 223–24
    of Christ, 102–4, 106 n. 42, 132,
        146, 170–71, 172, 175, 180, 189–
        90, 210
        ἀχειροποίητος of Camouliana,
            106 n. 44, 193
        ἀχειροποίητος of Edessa, 109
            n. 53
        as lamb, 101, 182–83
        with Virgin Mary, 205–7
    of the emperor, 104, 118–19, 130,
        152, 158–61, 168–70, 174, 177–
        78, 211–12
    veneration of the image, 174
    issuing blood, 171
    of John the Baptist, 101, 182–83
    kissing image, 133
    of martyrs, 98, 102, 105, 146, 190
    of prophets, 102, 146
    of saint(s), 98, 117, 184–85, 190,
        191, 210
    of Symeon the Stylite, 196, 197

    miraculous image of, 197
    veneration (worship) of, 3, 37, 38,
        50, 92, 93, 96–99, 112, 117, 120,
        123, 128, 146, 160, 171, 175,
        176, 184–86, 189–90, 206, 214–
        17, 224 n. 186, 232
    of the Virgin Mary, 98, 102, 132–33,
        146, 179–80, 200, 210
incarnation, 22 n. 97, 49 n. 33, 59 n.
    68, 63, 64 n. 79, 65, 68, 96, 99, 102,
    146, 164, 166, 176, 189–90
indiction, 46, 49 n. 33, 94, 95, 254
"indulgenza," 251
interpolations, 99, 101, 106, 108, 109
    n. 53, 113, 121 n. 82, 136, 151, 166,
    176 n. 145, 184, 209, 210, 215–16,
    253, 255
interpreters, 238
Italy, 196
    North, 45 n. 16

Jerusalem, 115, 136, 192
Jews, 62–63, 90, 93, 171, 172, 184–85,
    187, 189–91, 215, 220
    conversion to Christianity, 171
    soothsayer, 140
    veneration of Cherubins, 184–85
Judaism, 149
judicial system, 229
    Continental, 229–30
    British, 229
jury, 229, 230

καινοφωνίαι, 5, 22
καινοτομίαι, 18
κομψεία (δικαστηρίων), 230
konzilsakten, 229 n. 4
konzilsprotokolle, 229 n. 4

language, 109 n. 53, 237
    Greek, 19, 56, 77, 95, 108, 116, 117,
        119, 121, 134, 138, 155, 212,
        235, 237, 239–40, 257
    Latin, 19, 28, 51, 77, 135, 193, 212,
        237
Lateran palace, 20, 257

Latins/Romans, 77, 78, 109 n. 53, 193, 231, 233, 236, 249 n. 28
anti-Latin, 49, 50, 52, 55, 72, 81, 249
Mark of Ephesus, 81
pro-Latin, 54, 234, 249
legates
of the Oriental patriarchs, 49, 208
papal, 22, 23, 25, 26, 29, 82, 146, 224, 231, 258
lemma (title), 9, 28, 33, 61, 62, 78, 84, 85, 89–90, 119, 128, 129, 131–33, 141, 142, 152, 157, 163, 171, 187, 194, 212, 215, 222, 241, 259 n. 27
library, 253
of the Basilica of St. Peter, 256, 257
of Boniface VIII, 257
imperial (in Constantinople), 27 n. 119, 46, 50, 249
Lateran, 20, 46, 257 and n. 11, 258–60
of Nicholas of Cotrone, 253
papal, 20, 46, 121, 250 and n. 33, 256–58, 260
patriarchal (in Constantinople), 23, 26, 27 n. 119, 29, 30, 205, 215, 225, 260 n. 29
San Giorgio Maggiore in Venice, 253
Vatican, 157, 200
liturgy, 75, 89–91

majuscule (uncial), 44, 103, 188, 250, 252
manuscripts (codices), 12, 22, 23, 36, 43, 45, 46, 49, 52, 53, 55 n. 51, 68, 70, 74, 77, 85, 86 n. 165, 88, 89–91, 98, 100–102, 110, 113, 114 n. 70, 123 n. 87, 128, 138–40, 142, 149, 150, 151, 157–58, 163, 191, 200, 222, 224–25, 228, 232, 243, 246, 247–48, 254, 256, 258
collection of, 17, 22, 23, 25, 26, 29 n. 132, 30, 42, 61 n. 71, 139, 141, 215, 224, 228
Greek, 251–53
group of Karahissar, 45
Latin, 235, 253

marginal notes (marginalia), 44, 45, 56–57, 77, 95, 210, 242, 255 and n. 5, 256
mutilated, 46, 53–54, 123, 150, 247, 249
martyrium, 193, 202–3
martyrs, 56, 102, 105, 146, 180–81, 201
Middle Ages, 243
minuscule, 44, 100–101, 103, 145, 194, 250, 252
Latin, 250 n. 31
miracles, 170, 171, 194, 195–99, 203
monasteries
of St. Andrew of Nesiou, 163
of Baion, 26 n. 115, 31 n. 144
of Chenolakkou, 188
of Dionysiou, Mt. Athos, 45 n. 14
of "eremitani," Padua, 251–52
Greek monasteries in Rome, 22
of Hormisdas, 194
of Hyakinthos, 193
of Maximinou, 205
of San Giorgio Maggiore in Venice, 251–53
of St. Sabbas in Rome, 224 n. 186
of Studios, 5 n. 16, 223
of Syceon, 201
monks, 18, 19–20, 24, 110, 164, 188, 192, 193, 219, 222, 227–28
Byzantine monks, 51
Greek monks in Rome, 250 n. 31, 257, 259
monophysites, 88
monotheletes, 16, 17, 20, 22, 23, 26, 31, 72. See also florilegium
creed, 23, 25
patriarch, 76
writings, 30–31
Monotheletism, 21, 22, 23, 25

Nicaea, 225
Nicholas of Cotrone, testament of, 251–53
nomokanon, 90
notarius, 11 n. 42, 15 n. 61
Novatian church, 3

οἰκουμένη, 104, 180, 230
ὁμοούσιος(ν), 69, 79
operation (ἐνέργεια), 18, 22 n. 97, 25

Padua, 251–53
pagans (Ἕλληνες), 93, 97
Palestine, 98, 115, 119
paper, 44, 47, 252
  Oriental, 44
  Western, 44
papyrus (χάρτης), 101, 182, 232
paragraphs, 101, 110 n. 59, 113, 114
  n. 71, 115, 172, 235 n. 3
parchment, 44, 252
patriarchs, 175
  of Constantinople, 22, 76, 123 n.
    87, 131 n. 102, 223, 233 n. 16
  Oriental, 49, 135, 173, 225
patristic authority, 3–4, 24, 26, 37, 119,
  120, 223–26, 235, 247–48, 251 n. 35
patristic writings, 3–5, 8 n. 27, 9, 18,
  36, 93, 96, 97, 113, 119, 120, 121,
  249 n. 28, 254, 258–59
πιττάκιον (sheet of paper), 33, 34
  n. 159, 228–29
popes, 73, 75–76, 121, 231, 238, 250
Porphyreon, 186
priests (presbyters, ἱερεύς), 18, 22, 56,
  76, 89–90, 96
primicerius notariorum, 8, 12, 15, 42
prophets, 87, 102, 117, 146, 163
prostration, 132–33
πρόσωπον (person), 62–63
purgatorium, 235, 247

quires (τετράδιον, τετράδες, quaterni), 5
  n. 16, 7, 23, 44–46, 53, 54, 252–53

Ravenna, capture of, 109 nn. 53 and
  55
Rhosopolis in Cilicia, 197–98
Romans. See Latins
Rome, 19, 20 n. 87, 29, 38, 51–52, 61
  n. 73, 62, 73, 75, 76 n. 122, 85, 98
  n. 23, 109 n. 53, 114–16, 119, 120,
  135, 136, 162, 163, 168, 176, 192,

196, 209, 225, 231, 234, 236, 250
  n. 31, 255, 257, 259–60
rubrica, 56–57, 242–43

Sabellians, 149
sacellarius, 121
Sancta Synodus (ἁγία σύνοδος), 15–16,
  26 n. 116
Senate (Rome), 229 n. 4
scholium(a), 61, 68–71, 77, 86, 106,
  123, 129, 134, 149, 200
scribal errors, 44, 47, 48, 98 n. 23, 109
  n. 53, 128, 131, 137–38, 142, 144–
  46, 149–51, 155, 160, 166, 169,
  181–82, 186, 188, 189, 193, 201,
  250, 252
scribe (copyist), 5 n. 16, 44, 54, 61, 70,
  134, 137, 144, 148, 169, 171, 173,
  187, 212–14, 217, 260
  scribe L, 45
  scribe X1, 53–54
scrinium (papal), 20, 135, 257–60
script, 45, 53, 137, 252
secretaries, 214, 215, 227–28, 233
Σεπτέτον, 109 n. 53
statues (bronze), 104–5
stemma, 88 n. 172, 110, 141, 151, 184,
  260
subdiaconus, 121
συλλαβή, 109 n. 53
Syria, 115

τεῦχος (of 770), 98, 108, 119, 146, 151,
  152, 165, 170, 178, 188, 216, 217,
  221–22, 225
  Oriental version of, 115
textual criticism, 6, 22, 31, 106 n. 44
Theopaschitism, 62
Three Chapters, 15, 36, 56
translations
  de verbo ad verbum, 235
  into Greek, 18 n. 76, 24 n. 108, 28,
    51, 104 n. 40, 138, 144 n. 124,
    167–68, 176, 177–78, 183–85,
    216–18, 223, 234, 251, 254, 255
    n. 4
  into Hebrew, 88

into Latin, 10, 12 n. 43, 18, 19, 20,
    38, 76, 84, 88–89, 116–19, 134,
    138–40, 142, 144 n. 124, 148,
    155, 157, 160, 162, 165, 168,
    173, 176, 177, 184–85, 187, 189,
    195, 200, 202, 203, 208, 211–13,
    216–20, 232, 234–37, 241–43,
    246, 250 and n. 32, 251
into Syriac, 88
translators, 147–48, 155, 156, 165, 168,
    212, 235
transmission of texts, 5, 27, 51, 88–91,
    114 n. 69, 115, 133, 134, 139, 140,
    143, 148, 160, 162, 163, 170, 178,
    191, 193, 195, 200, 203, 215, 224,
    228, 259

union of churches, 238–39
    anti-unionists, 50, 249

pro-unionists, 81, 254
    policy, 249
ὑπόστασις, 62–63, 68, 69

Venice, 251–53
Visigoths, 74

will (θέλημα), 18, 22 n. 97, 25, 231
worship of woods, 104

ὕπατος, 179–80

φύσις (nature), 59 n. 68, 62–63, 65, 66,
    99

χειροποίητον (α), 97. See also
    images/icons
    veneration of, 113, 117, 120,
        184–85
χριστιανοκατήγοροι, 50, 208

INDEX OF PROPER NAMES

Abraham, 153

Acacius of Melitene, 6

Acacius of Scythopolis, 165

Aetios, deacon, 15 n. 61

Agathangelos, 104 n. 41, 223

Agathias, historian, 229

Agathon, Pope (678–681), 5 n. 14, 22–25, 238, 248, 258

Albinus of Milan, 250 n. 33

Ambrose of Milan, 4, 9, 16, 18 n. 75, 27 n. 121, 73 n. 99, 83 n. 153, 127, 175–77, 218, 239, 247–48

Amphilochius of Iconium, 9, 78, 83 n. 150

Anastasius Apocrisiarius, 21 n. 88, 127, 178, 220

Anastasius Bibliothecarius, 76, 138, 159–62, 164, 166, 167, 184, 185, 189, 196, 200, 213, 225, 250 n. 32, 255

Anastasius of Antioch, 27 n. 121, 93, 127, 173–74, 220, 221

Anastasius the Persian, St., 202–3, 220, 225

Anastasius the Sinaite, 52, 57, 254

Andronicus Camaterus; 72 n. 93

Andronicus II Palaeologus, Emperor (1282–1328), 46, 249

Anna, wife of Andronicus II Palaeologus, 46

Anthimus of Trebizond, monothelete, 29 n. 130

Antiochus, dux, 116–17

Antiochus of Ptolemais, 9 nn. 33 and 34

Antipater of Bostra, 187, 220

Arcadius of Cyprus, 197

Aristotle, 258

Arius, 69, 149

Asterius of Amasea, 187, 220

Athanasius I of Alexandria, 4, 9, 27 n. 121, 33, 73 n. 99, 83 n. 153, 85, 92, 166–71, 218, 220, 231, 239, 248

Atticus of Constantinople, 9 n. 32

Augustine of Hippo, 4, 14, 16, 18 n. 75, 27 n. 121, 38, 73, 83 n. 153, 214, 239, 247–49

Avitus of Vienne, 73

Barlaam, martyr, 142–43, 220

Basiliscus, martyr, 223–24

Basil of Caesarea, 4, 5 n. 17, 6 n. 20, 9, 17, 27 n. 121, 33, 49, 50, 73 n. 99, 78, 83 n. 153, 85, 92, 109 n. 55, 120, 127–28, 142–49, 151, 215, 218, 220–21, 223, 239, 241, 248

Basil of Pisidia, Iconoclast bishop, 209, 334

Boethius, 74

Boniface, St. (8th c.), 109 n. 55

Boniface VIII, Pope (1294–1303), 257

Calonymus, deacon and *notarius*, 11 n. 42

Capreolus of Carthage, 7

Cassiodorus, 74

Celestine I, Pope (422–432), 6, 238, 248

Charles the Great/Charlemagne, 3 n. 7, 37–38, 83

Chosroes II, king of the Persians, 193

Cinnamus, Leo. *See* Leo Cinnamus

Constans II, Emperor (641–668), 17 n. 71, 21

Constantine, deacon and *chartophylax* of St. Sophia, 180–81, 220

Constantine, deacon and *notarius*, 200

Constantine, Pope (708–715), 121

Constantine Meliteniotes, 72 n. 93

Constantine of Constantia (Cyprus), 174, 227

Constantine of Nakolia, Iconoclast, 209, 221 n. 179, 334

Constantine I, Emperor (324–337), 46, 62–63, 207

Constantine II of Constantinople (754–766), 47

Constantine IV, Emperor (668–685), 22–25, 258

Constantine V, Emperor (741–775), 31–32, 34, 36, 76 n. 122, 110, 225

Constantine VI, Emperor (780–797), 39, 138 n. 114, 224 n. 186, 255

Cosmas, deacon and *skeuophylax* (?), 193

Cosmas and Damian, Sts., 194–95, 220

Cosmas of Alexandria (8th c.), 38 n. 174

Cosmas of Epiphania, Iconoclast, 50

Cyril of Alexandria, 4, 6, 8 n. 29, 9, 13 nn. 49 and 51, 17, 23, 27 n. 121, 33, 49, 53, 55, 73 n. 99, 76–79, 81, 83 n. 153, 92, 164–66, 218, 220, 223, 239, 247, 248

Cyril of Jerusalem, 85–86, 93, 123, 178, 220, 239, 248

Cyrus and John, Sts., 194, 220, 225

Cyrus of Alexandria, 16, 17, 22, 30

Damasus I, Pope (366–384), 238, 248

Daniel of Scete, 133

Demosthenes, 187

Demosthenes, patricius (?), 21 n. 88

Deusdedit of Calaris, 28 n. 125, 41 n. 181

Didymus the Blind, 73 n. 99

Diocletian, Emperor, 201

Diodorus, *primicerius notariorum*, 12, 15

Dionysius Areopagite. *See* Pseudo-Dionysius Areopagite

Dioskoros of Alexandria, 10, 22 n. 92, 55

Domnus of Antioch, 55

Domnus I, Pope (676–678), 22

Ephraim of Antioch, 27 n. 121

Ephraim the Syrian, 61 n. 73, 65–66, 78

Epiphanius of Constantia/Salamis, 27 n. 121, 78, 87–88, 177, 216, 218, 240

Euagrius, church historian, 192–93, 220

Eucherius of Lyon, 73

Eulogius, *latomus,* 133

Eunomius, 69

Euphemia, martyr, 187

Eusebius of Caesarea, 33, 83 n. 153

Eustathius, abbot of Maximinou, 204–5

Eutyches, archimandrite in Constantinople and monophysite, 8, 15 n. 61

Faustus of Riez, 73

Felix I, Pope (269–274), 7

Forty Martyrs of Sebasteia, 143, 220

Fulgentius of Ruspe, 73, 239, 248–49

Gabriel, the archangel, 66

Gennadius of Marseilles, 73

Gennadius I of Constantinople (458–471), 131 n. 102

George, monk and collaborator of Macarius of Antioch, 24

George, Roman presbyter, 22

George Metochites, 72 n. 93

George of Cyprus, 36 n. 169

George of Syceon, 201, 220

George Pachymeres, 236 n. 8, 249 n. 28

George Synkellus, 86–87

George I of Constantinople (679–686), 22–25

Germanus I of Constantinople, 36 n. 169, 50, 93, 106, 108, 119–22, 163, 209, 213–14, 219, 220, 221 n. 179

Gregory, abbot of the monastery of Hormisdas, 194

Gregory, abbot of the monastery of Hyakinthos, 193

Gregory of Nazianzus, 4, 6 n. 20, 9, 13, 17, 27 n. 121, 33, 78, 83 n. 153, 92, 120, 149–50, 153, 221, 223, 239, 248

Gregory of Neocaesarea, 33, 92, 120, 240

Gregory of Nyssa, 4, 6 n. 20, 7, 9, 27 n. 121, 33, 78, 83 n. 153, 85, 92, 120,

127, 152–55, 218, 219, 221, 223–24, 239, 240, 248

Gregory of Pesinus, 172

Gregory the Illuminator of Armenia, 104, 223

Gregory I the Great, Pope (590–604), 38, 83 n. 153, 239, 247–49, 250 n. 33

Gregory II, Pope (715–731), 37 n. 171, 93, 108–9, 119–22, 136 n. 105, 163, 209, 220

Gregory III, Pope (731–741), 37 n. 171, 109 n. 55

Hadrian I, Pope (772–795), 3 n. 7, 37–39, 83–84, 109 n. 53, 138, 143, 155, 168, 191, 207, 216, 217, 224, 239, 248, 255

Heliodorus, silentiarius, 213

Helladius, disciple of Basil of Caesarea, 128

Heraclius I, Emperor (610–641), 17

Hesychius of Jerusalem, 13 n. 49

Hieronymus, presbyter of Jerusalem, 184–85, 217, 218, 239, 247–49

Hilary of Poitiers, 4, 18 n. 75, 73 n. 99, 83 n. 153, 239, 247–48

Hippolytus of Thebes, 87

Honorius I, Pope (625–638), 30

Hormisdas, Pope, (514–523), 73–74

Hypatius of Ephesus, 93, 222–23

Ibas of Edessa, 15

Ignatius of Antioch, 107 n. 49

Innocent IV, Pope (1243–54), 237

Irene, Empress (797–802), 39, 138 n. 114, 224 n. 186, 255

Isidorus of Pelusium, 61 n. 73

Iubal, Jew, 62–63

Jacob of Edessa, monophysite, 88

John, patriarch of Jerusalem (8th c.), 47, 49, 94

John, Roman deacon, 22

John, the apostle, 33 n. 151

John, the evangelist, 240

John Chrysostom of Constantinople

(398–404), 4, 9, 27 n. 121, 33, 36, 65, 66, 78, 92, 110, 109 n. 55, 120, 127, 136, 154, 156–57, 163, 210, 218–21, 239, 243, 246, 248

John Moschos, 55, 203, 220–21

John of Antioch, 55

John of Aversa, 237

John of Damascus (7th–8th c.), 2, 36 n. 169, 39 n. 177, 94, 96, 101, 106, 110, 113–18, 121 n. 81, 123–36, 142–43, 151, 162, 163, 166, 179–80, 207, 213, 216, 217, 221, 225, 227–28, 233, 252

John of Gabala, 214, 220

John of Jerusalem, delegate of the Oriental patriarchs to Nicaea II, 49–50, 99, 139–40, 173, 208–9, 216–17, 233, 255

John of Montenero, 81 n. 139

John of Nicomedia, Iconoclast, 209, 334

John of Scythopolis, 27 n. 121

John of Synada, 213

John of Thessalonica, 188–89, 215, 220

John II Kappadokes of Constantinople (518–520), 192, 219

John IV the Faster of Constantinople (582–595), 199–200, 220

John VI Kantakouzenos, Emperor (1347–1354), 45 n. 14

John VII the Grammarian of Constantinople (834–843), 34

John XI Beccus of Constantinople (1275–1282), 72 n. 93, 249 n. 28

Julian, Emperor (361–363), 145–48

Julianus Pomerius, priest in Arles, 73

Julius Sextus Africanus, 86–87

Justin, martyr, 27 n. 121

Justin I, Emperor (518–527), 74 n. 105

Justin II, Emperor (565–578), 186–87

Justinian I, Emperor (527–565), 10–14, 23, 27, 36

Justinian II, Emperor (685–695/705–711), 86, 122

Leo Cinnamus/Kinnamos, 44–47, 50–51, 53, 55, 57, 61, 70, 77, 84 n. 157,

85, 103, 128, 130, 131, 137–38,
142–44, 149, 151, 153, 155, 166,
177, 181–82, 186–89, 193–94,
201–3, 206, 210, 217, 220, 241–43,
246 n. 25, 249–50, 252, 254–55, 257
Leo I the Great, Pope (440–461), 4,
8–9, 18 n. 75, 27 n. 121, 55, 73, 83
n. 153, 239, 248
Leo II, Pope (682–683?) 239, 248
Leo III Isaurian, Emperor (717–741),
108–9, 119–20, 140, 225
Leo V the Armenian, Emperor, (813–
820), 34, 36
Leontius of Neapolis (Cyprus), 106,
127, 190–91, 220
Leontius of Neapolis (Italy), 18
Leontius Scholasticus/Byzantius
(Ps.-Leontius) 52, 57
Lykomedes, 33 n. 151

Macarius of Antioch, 22–26, 29–31, 41
n. 182
Macrobius of Seleukeia, 23
Marinus, priest of Cyprus, 76–78
Maris, the Persian, 15
Marius Victorinus, 73 n. 99
Mark of Ephesus, 81 nn. 139 and 140
Martin I, Pope (649–655), 6 n. 18, 16–
21, 41 n. 181, 72, 76, 258
Mary, Virgin, 66, 98, 102, 132–33, 146,
179–80, 200
Mary of Egypt, 200–201, 220
Maslama/Masalmas, Arab general, 209
Matthew Blastares, 53–54
Maur of Croton, 237
Maximus of Aquileia, 19 n. 77, 41 n.
181
Maximus the Confessor, 18–21, 76–79,
85 nn. 158, 159, 178–80
Meletius of Antioch, 156–57, 219
Menas of Constantinople (536–552), 23
Methodius Olympius, 78, 83 n. 150,
129–30
Methodius I of Constantinople (843–
847), 256
Metrophanes of Smyrna, 249 n. 28
Michael VIII Palaeologus, Emperor

(1261–1282), 46, 50–51, 237 n. 12,
238–40, 248–51, 254–55
Moschos, monk and recluse, 207, 333

Nabuchadnesar, 178
Nectarius I of Constantinople (381–
397), 3
Nestorius of Constantinople (428–431),
6, 7 n. 21
Nicephorus Blemmydes, 72 n. 93
Nicephorus I of Constantinople (806–
815), 31–35, 91, 99, 106, 123 n. 87,
223–25, 233
Nicetas, abbot of Medicion, 103–7, 114
n. 69, 222–23, 225
Nicholas of Cotrone, 234–53, 255
Nicholas of Cyzicus, 189
Nicholas II Chrysoberges of Constanti-
nople (979–991), 90
Nicholas III Grammatikos of Constanti-
nople (1084–1111), 90
Nilus of Ankyra, 33, 213, 214, 220, 221
n. 179

Olympiodorus, eparchus, 33, 221 n.
179
Olympius, exarch of Ravenna, 21
Omar II/Umar, Arab ruler (715–720),
209
Origen of Alexandria, 56, 73 n. 99

Pamphilus, martyr, 172
Pancratios of Taormina, 103–4, 223,
225
Paschal I, Pope (817–824), 255 n. 4
Pastor of Palencia, 74
Paul, the apostle, 90, 207
Paul I, Pope (757–767), 37 n. 171, 258
Paul V, Pope (1605–1621), 138
Paul II of Constantinople (641–654),
17, 22, 30
Paul of Antioch, monothelete, 29 n.
130
Paulinus of Aquileia, 72
Pepin the Short, 258
Peter, *primicerius notariorum,* 8 n. 27
Peter, Roman presbyter and abbot of

the monastery of St. Sabbas, 191–
92, 224 n. 186
Peter, Roman presbyter, 191–92, 224
Peter, the apostle, 55 n. 55, 90, 103,
207
Peter of Alexandria, 7 n. 20
Peter of Constantinople (655–666), 22,
30
Peter of Nicomedia, 171
Phosterius, archimandrite, 61 n. 73
Photeinos, prebyter and defensor of St.
Sophia, 199
Photius I of Constantinople (858–867/
878–886), 49–50, 72, 85 n. 158, 87,
89–91
Polemon, St., 149–50
Proclus of Constantinople (434–447),
4, 9
Procopius, martyr, 201, 220
Pseudo-Athanasius of Alexandria, 57
Pseudo-Dionysius Areopagite, 17, 78,
93, 106, 125, 127, 135, 233, 258
Pseudo-Julius, Pope, 7
Pyrrhus of Constantinople (638–641,
655), 16, 22, 30

Rabbulas of Edessa, 13 n. 49
Reccared, king of the Visigoths, 74

Serantapechos/
Tessarakontapechys(chos),
Sarantapechys, Serantapicus, 140
Sergius of Constantinople (610–638),
16, 17, 22, 30
Sergius I, Pope (687–701), 121
Severian of Gabala, 157, 210–12, 246
Severus of Antioch, 29 n. 130, 192, 214
Sextilianus of Tunis, 14
Silvester I, Pope (314–335), 61 n. 73,
62–64, 207, 238, 248
Sissinius, Novatian *anagnostes* and
bishop, 3
Sissinius Pastillas, Iconoclast bishop of
Perge, 99, 109 n. 55, 209, 334
Socrates, church historian, 3 n. 8
Sophronius of Jerusalem, 30, 51–52,

71, 78, 83 n. 153, 132, 194, 200,
204, 206, 220
Sozomen, church historian, 3 n. 8
Stephen, monk and *bibliophylax,* 193,
204–5
Stephen, monk and assistant/disciple(?)
of Macarius of Antioch, 22
Stephen of Bostra, 93 n. 6, 183–84,
218
Stephen II/III, Pope (752–757), 37 n.
171
Stephen III/IV, Pope (768–772), 37 n.
171, 210 n. 164
Symeon of Bostra, 173–74
Symeon the Younger Stylite, 185–86,
196–97, 217, 220

Tarasius I of Constantinople (784–
806), 21, 83, 106, 196, 205, 224–25,
227, 255
Tertullian, 73 n. 99
Thara, Pharisee, 63
Themistius, deacon of Alexandria, 17
Theodora, wife of Justinian I, 23
Theodora, wife of Michael VIII, 46
Theodore, abbot of Studios, 5 n. 16,
222–23, 225
Theodore, archimandrite of Syceon,
201, 220
Theodore, Roman presbyter, 22
Theodore, subdeacon, 194
Theodore of Antioch (8th c.), 38 n. 174
Theodore of Bostra, monothelete, 29
n. 130
Theodore of Jerusalem (8th c.), 38 n.
174
Theodore of Mopsuestia, 11–15, 56
Theodore of Myra, 33
Theodore of Pharan, 17, 22, 30
Theodore of Tyana, 13 n. 51
Theodore I, Pope (642–649), 19, 51,
76
Theodore II Laskaris, emperor of Ni-
caea (1254–1258), 236–37, 237 n.
12, 239, 250–51
Theodoret of Cyrus, 9–10, 14–15, 196,
220

Theodosius, abbot of St. Andrew of
    Nesiou, 163–64
Theodosius of Alexandria, 24 n. 108
Theodosius of Amorium, 33
Theodosius of Caesarea in Bithynia,
    179–80
Theodosius of Catane, 142
Theodosius of Ephesus, Iconoclast, 99,
    209, 210, 334
Theodosius I, Emperor (379–395), 3,
    13 n. 49
Theodotus of Ancyra, 6
Theophanes, abbot of Baion, 26 n.
    115, 31 n. 144
Theophilus of Alexandria, 4, 7
Theophylactus, *primicerius notariorum,*
    20
Theosebes, monk(?) (8th c.), 110, 115
Theosterictus, monk of Medicion(?),
    103 n. 37
Thomas, monk of Chenolakkos, 188
Thomas Aquinas, 234, 250–51

Thomas of Claudiopolis, Iconoclast,
    121 n. 82, 221 n. 179
Timotheus, disciple of Apollinaris of
    Laodiceia, 7
Turibius of Astorga, 74 nn. 104 and
    110

Umar. *See* Omar II
Urban IV, Pope (1261–1264), 234, 239,
    249–51

Victor of Carthage, 51
Victricius of Rouen, 74
Vigilius, Pope (537–555), 10, 12 n. 43,
    15, 23
Vrthanes Kherthog, 104 n. 41, 136 n.
    105

Yazid II, Arab ruler (720–724), 209

Zacharias, Pope (741–752), 37 n. 171,
    121 n. 82

INDEX OF WORKS CITED[1]

Agathangelus
  CPG 7545.2   *Historia Armeniae, Versio Graeca (BHG* 712)   **104,** 136 n. 105, 341,
                350

Agathias Scholasticus
              Historiarum libri quinque   230 n. 11

Agatho, Papa
  CPG 9417   *Epistula Synodica ad Constantinum IV imp.*   5 n. 14, 24, 231, 248,
                258, 270

Alcimus Avitus ep. Viennensis
  CPL 990   *Dialogi cum Gundobado rege vel librorum contra Arrianos relliquiae*   73
                n. 102

Ambrosius ep. Mediolanensis
  CPL 150   *De fide*   6 n. 20, 9 n. 35, 16 n. 67, 28 n. 124, 218, 248, 273, 275–
                76, 282, 314
  CPL 152   *De incarnationis dominicae sacramento*   40, 116, 126, **175–77,** 248,
                255, 273, 283, 327
  CPL 153   *Explanatio symboli ad initiandos*   248, 282
  CPL 160   *Epistula supposititia II*   39
              Expositio fidei (frag.) = Pseudo-Ambrosius   248, 273

Amphilochius Iconiensis
  CPG   *Fragmentum iii* (e libro deperdito *De generationi domini secundum*
  3245.3b, c   *carnem*)   7 n. 24
  CPG 3245.6   *Fragmentum vi* (Περὶ τῆς ἡμέρας καὶ ὥρας)   277
  CPG 3245.8   *Fragmentum viii* (ex illo: *Iesus autem proficiebat sapientia*)   277
  CPG 3245.12   *Fragmentum xii* (ex *Oratione in illud: Quia pater maior me est*)   9
                n. 35
  CPG 3245.13   *Fragmentum xiii* (in illud: *De meo accipiet et annuntiabit vobis*)
                83 n. 150, **297**
  CPG 3245.15   *Fragmentum xv* (*epistula ad Seleucum*)   **65,** 69, 71, 83 n. 150, 271,
                272, 274, 275, 297, 314
  CPG 3252   *Encomium s. Basilii magni*   32

Anastasiana Incertae Originis
  CPG 7781   *Doctrina Patrum*   44, 52, 55 n. 55, 58–71, 78, 99, 107, **116–17,**
                118, 123–25, 130, 133–35, 152, 153, 168, 178, 246, 256,
                259, 271–83, 313–20

---

[1] Bold page numbers indicate citations of the relevant work (or part thereof) in Greek or Latin.

Anastasius I Antiochenus
   CPG 6953   *De operationibus*   280
   CPG 6954   *Epistula ad scholasticum* (frag.)   93, **173,** 220, 227 n. 1, 326
   CPG 6955   *Ad Symeonem Bostrensem* (frag.)   93, 106 n. 44, 126, **173–75,** 221,
                227 n. 1, 326, 344, 351
   CPG 6957   *Ad Sergium Grammaticum capita cl* (frag.)   279
   CPG 6968   *De gestis in Perside* (*BHG* 806)   340

Anastasius Apocrisiarius
   CPG 7735   *Acta in primo exsilio seu dialogus Maximi cum Theodosio ep. Caesareae*
                in Bithynia (*BHG* 1233)   100 nn. 30 and 32, 107 n. 47,
                126, **178–80,** 221, 328, 340, 346
   CPG 7736   *Relatio motionis inter Maximum et principes*   21 n. 88

Anastasius Sinaita
   CPG 7745   *Viae Dux* (*Hodegos*)   43 n. 1, 44, 52, 55 n. 51, 57–58, 69 n. 86,
                254, 260 n. 29, 270–71, 279, 296, 307–8

Andreas Cretensis
   CPG 8193   *De sanctarum imaginum veneratione* (*BHG* 1125)   342

Andronicus Camaterus
              Testimonia   72 n. 93

Antiochus ep. Ptolemaidis
   CPG 4296 n.   *Homilia de nativitate* (frag.)   10 n. 35

Antipater Bostrensis
   CPG 6683   *Homilia in mulierem quae fluxum sanguinis passa est* (frag.)   **187,** 220,
                329

Apollinaris Laodicenus
   CPG 3656   *Contra Diodorum ad Heraclium*   29 n. 128

Asterius Amasenus
   CPG 3260.1   *Homiliae i–xiv, Homilia de divite et Lazaro*   35
   CPG 3260.1   *Homiliae i–xiv, Relatio in Euphemiam martyrem*   **187–88,** 220, 225
                n. 187, 329

Athanasius Alexandrinus
   CPG 2090   *Oratio contra Gentes*   32
   CPG 2091   *Oratio de incarnatione Verbi*   40, 92, 116, 124 n. 89, 125, **166–68,**
                218, 255, 324
   CPG 2093   *Orationes contra Arianos iii*   6 n. 20, 9 n. 35, 24 n. 108, 92, 100
                nn. 30 and 33, 107 n. 47, 126, **168–70,** 220, 227 n. 1,
                277, 324, 341–42, 345, 350
   CPG 2095   *Epistula ad Epictetum*   6 n. 20, 274
   CPG 2098   *Epistula ad Adelphium*   32
   CPG 2161   *Homilia in illud: nunc anima mea turbata est*   30 n. 142, 231
   CPG 2264   *Syntagma ad Monachos*   52, 307
   CPG 2284   *De sancta trinitate dialogi v*   298

CPG 2298   *Didascalia cccxviii patrum Nicaenorum*   52, 307

CPG 2346   *Epistula ad Monachos* (spuria)   52, 307

              See also Pseudo-Athanasius Alexandrinus

Atticus CPolitanus

CPG 5650   *Homilia in nativitatem*   7 n. 24

CPG 5655   *Epistula ad Eupsychium*   9 n. 32, 10 n. 35

CPG 5657   *Fragmentum*   7 n. 24

Augustinus ep. Hipponensis

CPL 262   *Epistula* 140   16 n. 67

              Epistula 185, *De correctione Donatistarum liber*   14 n. 52

CPL 326   *Contra Iulianum Pelag.* (frag.)   26 n. 115, 27 n. 122

CPL 334   *Epistula ad Catholicos de secta Donatistarum*   14 n. 52

CPL 335   *Contra Cresconium*   14 n. 52

CPL 702   *Contra sermonem Arianorum*   16 n. 67

              Locus non repertus   40, 116, 214

Barlaam Calabrus

              Dogma Latinorum   52, 261

Basilius Caesariensis

CPG 2836   *Homiliae super psalmos*   318

CPG 2837   *Adversus Eunomium I*   9 n. 35

              Adversus Eunomium II   **81,** 82, 241–43, 299

              Adversus Eunomium III   241–43, 300–301

CPG 2571   *Adversus Eunomium IV* (= Didymus Alexandrinus)   241–43, 300–301, 318

              Adversus Eunomium V   241–43, 247 n. 27, 285, 301–3

              Adversus Eunomium (non inventum in opere citato)   78, 275, **283**

CPG 2838   *De Spiritu*   242–43, 303–4

CPG 2839   *De Spiritu Sancto*   5 n. 17, 6 n. 20, 50, 82, 92, 113 n. 66, 121, 124 n. 92, 126, 151, 220, 227 n. 1, 282, 285, 292, 302, 316, 318, 344, 347, 350

CPG 2845   *De ieiunio, homilia i*   275

CPG 2859   *De fide*   92, 315, 343

CPG 2861   *In Barlaam martyrem*   92, 124 n. 87, 126, **141–43,** 220, 227 n. 1, 315, 345, 350

CPG 2863   *In XL martyres Sebastenses*   40, 92, 100 n. 30, 106 n. 44, 113 n. 66, 116, 124 n. 92, 125, 126, **143–45,** 218, 221, 315, 342, 345

CPG 2869   *Contra Sabellianos et Arium et Anomaeos*   92, 126, **149,** 220, 227 n. 1, 247 n. 27, 293, 315–16

CPG 2883   *Prologus iv* (*Sermo asceticus, Ascetico magno* praemissus)   347

CPG 2897.1   *Poenae in monachos delinquentes* (Epitimia 24)   310

CPG 2900   *Epistula* 38 (*see* Gregorius Nyssenus *CPG* 3196)

              Epistula 188, *ad Amphilochium*   259, 309–10

              Epistula 214   272

              Epistula 244   14 n. 52

	Epistula 360 40, 92, 100 nn. 30 and 33, **102–3,** 114 n. 72, 116, **145–49,** 218, 220, 227 n. 1, 315, 337, 350
	Epistula I ad Gregorium Nazianzenum 32, 347
CPG 2911	*Enarratio in prophetam Isaiam* 124 n. 91
CPG 2912	*Homilia dicta in Lacisis* 107, 124 n. 91, 126, **131,** 347
	Ad Iohannem Antiochenum in *Doctrina Patrum* (= *Pamphilus ep. Abydi?*) 273, 280

Basilius Seleuciensis
| CPG 6675 | *De vita et miraculis s. Theclae libri ii.* (*BHG* 1718n)   93 n. 3, 327, 347 |
| | *Fragmentum ignotum*   35 |

Beda Venerabilis
| CPL 1375 | *Historia ecclesiastica gentis Anglorum*   257 n. 11 |

Biblica
Exodus	20:4 32 n. 147
	25:1–22 39, 93 n. 4, 116, 207–8, 219, 334
Numeri	7:88–90 93 n. 4, 207, 219, 334
	21:8–9 39, 116
Deuteron.	4:12/5:8 32 n. 147
Regum I	1:1–4.18 269
Regum III	6:23/6:32 39, 116
Psalmi	92:1 300
Ezechiel	41:1/16–20 93 n. 4, 207, 219, 334
Matthaeus	11:27 292
Iohannes	1:18/4.24/5.37/20.29 32 n. 147
	5:31/37 292
	14:28 9 n. 55
Ad Romanos	1:23, 25/10:17 32 n. 147
Ad Corinthios II	5:16–17 32 n. 147
	13:13 294
Ad Galatas	3:1 100 n. 30, 114 n. 72, 334, 350
	‘4:1 292–93
Ad Hebraeos	9:1–5 93 n. 4, 126, 207–8, 219, 334

Boethius
| CPL 890.1 | *Quomodo Trinitas unus Deus ac non tres dii*   74 n. 106 |

Cassiodorus
| CPL 900 | *Commenta psalterii*   74 n. 106 |

Clemens Romanus
| | *Fragmentum de Spiritu sancto*   298 |

Constantinus Diaconus et Chartophylax CPolitanus
| CPG 7403 | *Laudatio omnium martyrum* (*BHG* 1191)   **180–82,** 220, 328 |

Constantinus Meliteniotes
    De processione   72 n. 93

Constantinus V, Imperator
    Πεύσεις   31 n. 145, 33, 34

Cyprianus ep. Carthaginensis
    CPL 47   *De opere et eleemosynis*   6 n. 20

Cyrillus Alexandrinus
    CPG 5206   *Commentarii in Matthaeum*   26, 40, 92, 116, **164–65,** 218, 278,
                            322–23
    CPG 5208   *Commentarii in Iohannem*   27 n. 122, 53, 54, 76, 77, **79,** 247 n. 27,
                            248, 263, 272, 277, 278, 290–91, 294, 306, 317
                    Locus non inventus in opere citato   294
    CPG 5215   *Thesaurus de sancta et consubstant. Trinitate*   24 n. 108, 28 n. 125,
                            40, 69, 71, 92, 106 n. 44, 116, **118–19,** 124 n. 91, 277–
                            78, 317, **323,** 343, 346
    CPG 5216   *De sancta trinitate dialogi vii*   92, 106 n. 44, 317–18, **323,** 343
    CPG 5217   *Libri v contra Nestorium*   280
    CPG 5218   *Oratio ad Theodosium imp. de recta fide*   27 n. 123, 67–68, **81,** 124
                            n. 91, 261, 281, 287, 319
    CPG 5219   *Oratio ad Arcadiam et Marinam aug. de fide*   **79,** 261, 276, 287
    CPG 5220   *Oratio ad Pulcheriam et Eudociam augustas de fide*   8, 262
    CPG 5221   *Apologia xii capitulorum contra Orientales*   8
    CPG 5222   *Apologia xii anathematismorum contra Theodoretum*   262
    CPG 5223   *Explanatio xii capitulorum*   247 n. 27, 262
                    Locus non inventus in opere citato   **293**
    CPG 5229   *Libri contra Diodorum et Theodorum* (frag.)   13 n. 49, 14 n. 52
    CPG 5230.2   *Liber contra Synousiastas* (frag.)   14 n. 52, 279
    CPG 5231   *De dogmatum solutione*   52, 57–58, 271
    CPG 5233h   *Contra Iulianum imp.*   27 n. 122
    CPG 5247   *Homilia iii. De Paulo Emeseno*   248, 263
    [8847]
    CPG 5301   *Epistula 1, Ad monachos Aegypti*   290
    CPG 5304   *Epistula 4, Ad Nestorium*   10 n. 35, 273, 274
    CPG 5317   *Epistula 17, Ad Nestorium*   77, 82, 247 n. 27, 262, 273, 279, 290
    CPG 5337   *Epistula 37, Ad Theognostum et Charmosynum presb. et Leontium*
    [8861]   *diac.*   312
    CPG 5339   *Epistula 39, Ad Iohannem Antiochenum (de pace)*   10 n. 35, 84
    [8448]   n. 155, 239, 248, 264, 293
    CPG 5341   *Epistula 41, Ad Acacium ep. Scythopolis*   92, **165–66,** 220, 323
    CPG 5344   *Epistula 44, Commonitorium ad Eulogium presb.*   280
    CPG 5345   *Epistula 45, Ad Successum episc. Diocaesareae*   10 n. 35, 272, 279,
                            319
    CPG 5346   *Epistula 46, Ad Successum episc. Diocaesareae*   271, 319
    CPG 5355   *Epistula 55, Ad Anastasium, Alexandrum , . . . ceterosque monachos*
                            Orientales   13 n. 49, 14 n. 52, 247 n. 27, 287, 290

CPG 5367   *Epistula 67, Ad Iohannem et synodum Antiochenum*   14 n. 52
CPG 5368   *Epistula 68, Ad Acacium Melitenum*   13 n. 49
CPG 5369   *Epistula 69, Ad Acacium Melitenum*   14 n. 52
CPG 5370   *Epistula 70, Ad Lamponem presb. Alexandrinum*   13 n. 49
CPG 5371   *Epistula 71, Ad Theodosium imperatorem*   14 n. 52
CPG 5372   *Epistula 72, Ad Proclum CPolitanum*   14 n. 52
CPG 5374   *Epistula 74, Ad Rabbulam Edessenum*   13 n. 49
               Sermo in martyres (non inveni)   92, 100 nn. 30 and 31, **105**, 107
                    n. 47, 114 n. 72, **323**, 341, 343, 351
               Sermo c. haereticos in Aegypto (non inveni)   92, 100 n. 30, 114
                    n. 72, 323, 343, 350
               Commentarii in Epistulam ad Hebraeos in *Doctrina Patrum*   277

Cyrillus Hierosolymitanus
CPG 3585.2   *Catecheses ad illuminandos* 1–18,   93, 123, 124 n. 89, 125, **178,**
                    220, 328
CPG 3590   *Homilia aquae in vinum conversae* (frag.)   276
               Tractatus de sex Synodis (= Anonymous)   85–86, 307

Damasus, Papa
CPL 1633   *Tomus Damasi*   51, 291- 92

Daniel Scetiota
CPG 7363   *Narrationes* (*BHG* 618)   **132–33,** 337

Dionysius Areopagita. *See* Pseudo-Dionysius Areopagita

Dorotheus Gazaeus
CPG 7360   *Vita s. Dosithei* (*BHG* 2117–19)   93 n. 3, 327

Ephraem Antiochenus
CPG 6902   *Apologia concilii Chalcedon.* (frag.)   27 n. 122

Ephraem Syrus
CPG 3939   *Sermo in transfigurationem Domini et Dei s.n.I.C.*   **65–66,** 71, 282
               Loca non inventa   **299**

Epiphanius Constantiensis
CPG 3744   *Ancoratus*   **79, 80, 240–41,** 283–86
CPG 3745   *Panarion (Adversus haereses)*   28 n. 126, 40, 64 n. 79, **104,** 116,
                    176 n. 145, **177–78,** 216, 218, 247 n. 27, 275, 283–84,
                    327, 350
CPG 3749   *Tractatus contra eos qui imagines faciunt* (frag.)   35
CPG 3750   *Epistula ad Theodosium imp.* (frag.)   35
CPG 3751   *Testamentum ad cives* (frag.)   32
CPG 3754   *Epistula ad Iohannem Hierosolymitanum*   35
CPG 3777   *De prophetarum vita et obitu, recensio prior*   87–89, 308–9
CPG 3780   *Index apostolorum*   88–89, 91, 309
CPG 3781   *Index discipulorum*   88–89, 309

Eucherius ep. Lugdunensis
CPL 489   *Instructionum ad Salonium l. ii*   73 n. 101

Eusebius Caesariensis
    CPG 3495   *Historia ecclesiastica*   84, **132,** 337
    CPG 3503   *Epistula ad Constantiam Augustam* (frag.)   33

Eusebius Dorylaeus
    CPG 5941   *Libellus ad Flavianum episc. Const. et Synodum*   248, 264
    [8904.1]

Eustathius Antiochenus
    CPG 3365   *In Samaritanum*   106 n. 44, **326,** 344

Eutychius CPolitanus
    CPG 6937   *Epistula ad Vigilium papam*   10, 248, 267

Evagrius Scholasticus
    CPG 7500   *Historia ecclesiastica*   93 n. 7, **192–93,** 220, 330

Faustus ep. Reiensis
    CPL 962   *De Spiritu Sancto*   73 n. 101

Flavianus CPolitanus
    CPG 5933   *Epistula ad Leonem papam*   246, 264
    [8914]
    CPG 5934   *Epistula ad Theodosium imp.*   248, 264
    CPG 5935   *Epistula ad Leonem papam*   248, 264
    [8915]

Flavianus I Antiochenus
    CPG 3435.6   *Fragmentum ex homilia in Theophania*   10 n. 35

Fulgentius ep. Ruspensis
    CPL 826   *De fide ad Petrum*   73 n. 102

Galla Placidia
    CPG [8960]   *Epistula ad Pulcheriam augustam*   248, 265–66

Gelasius Caesariensis
                Fragmentum in *Doctrina Patrum*   272, 276

Gennadius ep. Massiliensis
    CPL 958   *Liber sive diffinitio ecclesiastic. dogmatum*   40, 116
    CPL 958a   *Libri ecclesiasticorum dogmatum*   73 n. 101

Georgius Alexandrinus
    CPL 7979   *Vita s. Iohannis Chrysostomi*   92, 124 n. 92, 125, 126, 322, 346, 350

Georgius Metochites
                Antirrhesis   72 n. 93
                Historia Dogmatica   72 n. 93

Georgius Pachymeres
                De Michaele VIII Palaeologo   236 n. 8, 249 n. 28

Georgius Syceota
    CPG 7973   *Vita Theodori Syceotae* (*BHG* 1748)   93 n. 3, **201–2,** 220, 332

Georgius Syncellus
     Ecloga Chronographica   86–87

Germanus I CPolitanus
   CPG 8002   *Epistula ad Iohannem episcopum Synadensem*   50, **213,** 220, 337
   CPG 8003   *Epistula ad Constantinum ep. Nacoliae*   50, 214
   CPG 8004   *Epistula ad Thomam ep. Claudiopoleos*   50, 121 n. 82, 214, 338–39
   CPG 8005   *Confessio fidei de imaginibus*   100 nn. 30 and 31, 313, 336–37
                     Epigramma in imaginem Salvatoris   137, 255, 259, **345**
                     Sermo (frag.)   338

Gregorius Nazianzenus
   CPG 3010.4   *Oratio 4, Contra Iulianum I*   340–41, 348
   CPG 3010.12   *Oratio 12, Ad patrem*   24 n. 108, 28 n. 126
   CPG 3010.20   *Oratio 20, De dogmate et constitutione episcoporum*   295, 318
   CPG 3010.21   *Oratio 21, In laudem Athanasii*   52, 269
   CPG 3010.25   *Oratio 25, In laudem Heronis Philosophi*   295, 350
   CPG 3010.27   *Oratio 27, Theologica I*   295
   CPG 3010.29   *Oratio 29, Theologica III*   294–95, 298
   CPG 3010.30   *Oratio 30, Theologica IV*   9 n. 35, 92, 106 n. 44, **124–25,** 126, 316,
                     318, 346
   CPG 3010.31   *Oratio 31, Theologica V*   247 n. 27, 294
   CPG 3010.37   *Oratio 37, In Matthaeum*   52, 269, 307
   CPG 3010.38   *Oratio 38, In Theophania*   70, 124 n. 88, 134, 298, 318–19
   CPG 3010.39   *Oratio 39, In sancta lumina*   84, 294
   CPG 3010.40   *Oratio 40, In sanctum baptisma*   69, 71, 317
   CPG 3010.43   *Oratio 43, In laudem Basilii Magni*   52, 269
   CPG 3010.45   *Oratio 45, In sanctum Pascha*   40, 116, 119
   CPG 3032   *Epistulae*   6 n. 20, 9 n. 35, 13 n. 51
                     Epistula 101   283, 318
                     Epistula 102   82, 295
   CPG 3034   *Carmina dogmatica* 1–38 (*carmen 32, Hymnus Vespertinus*)   297
   CPG 3035   *Carmina moralia* 1–40   32, 92, 106 n. 44, 126, **149–51,** 221, 316,
                     344, 346, 350
   CPG 3036   *Carmina de se ipso* 1–99   92, 298, 316, 346
                     De fide (non inventum)   **304**
                     Loca non inventa   295, 298

Gregorius Nyssenus
   CPG 3135   *Contra Eunomium libri*   27 nn. 122 and 123, 92, 272–73, 276, 320
   CPG 3136   *Refutatio confessionis Eunomii*   24 n. 108
   CPG 3137/   *Epistula 189,6, ad Eustathium de s. trinitate*   28 n. 127, 314
     2900
   CPG 3139   *Ad Ablabium, quod non sint tres dei.*   296–98
   CPG 3143   *Ad Theophilum adversus Apollinaristas*   14 n. 52
   CPG 3144   *Antirrheticus adversus Apollinarium*   24 n. 108, 314
   CPG 3148   *Epistula canonica ad Letoium*   310
   CPG 3150   *Oratio catechetica magna*   291, 293, 300

CPG 3154   *De opificio hominis*   27 n. 122, 92, 100 nn. 30 and 33, 126, **128–29,** 320, 342

CPG 3155   *In inscriptiones psalmorum*   297

CPG 3158   *In Canticum canticorum, hom. XV*   40, 92, 100 n. 30, 116, **154–56,** 218, 292, 320, 344

CPG 3160   *De oratione dominica orationes V*   82, 247 n. 27, 291, 314

CPG 3161   *Orationes viii de beatitudinibus*   6 n. 20, 7, 92, 106 n. 44, **321,** 344

CPG 3167   *Epistula ad Theophilum*   13 n. 49

CPG 3175   *De tridui inter mortem et resurrectionem d.n.I.C. spatio*   35, 67, 281, 315

CPG 3183   *De sancto Theodoro*   92, 100 n. 30, 106 n. 44, 113 n. 66, 114 n. 72, 223–**24, 321, 341,** 344, 350

CPG 3184   *De Vita Gregorii Thaumaturgi*   **79–80,** 82, 84, **240,** 247 n. 27, 291

CPG 3186   *Encomium in s. Stephanum protomartyrem i*   107, 124 n. 90, 348

CPG 3192   *De deitate Filii et Spiritus Sancti*   40, 92, 116, 121 n. 81, 122, 124 n. 92, 125, 126, **152–53,** 155–56, 219, 221, 319–20, 350

CPG 3196   *Ad Petrum fratrem de differentia essentiae et hypostaseos*   151, 247 n. 27, 286

CPG 3215   *Homilia I, De creatione hominis*   35

CPG 3221   *Testimonia adversus Iudaeos*   293

CPG 3224   *Inventio imaginis in Camulianis* (*BHG* 790)   106 n. 44, 335

Gregorius Thaumaturgus

CPG 1764   *Confessio fidei*   281

CPG 1781   *De deitate et tribus personis*   69, 71, 308, 313

         Interpretatio Sapientiae Solomontis (non inveni)   92, 100 n. 44, 120, **320,** 345

         Definitio synodalis (non inveni)   92, 106 n. 44, 120, **320–21,** 343, 350

Gregorius I, Papa

CPL 1714   *Registrum epistularum* 9.147,41, *ep. ad Secundinum*   39, 116

Gregorius II, Papa

JE 2180   *Epistula I ad Leonem Isaurum imp.* (*BHG* 1387d)   108–10, 119–23, 336

JE 2181/CPG 8006   *Epistula Gregorii Papae ad Germanum CPolitanum*   93, 108, 119–22, 163, **209–10,** 220, 334

JE 2182   *Epistula II ad Leonem Isaurum imp.* (*BHG* 1387d)   108–10, 119–23, 336

Hadrianus I, Papa

JE 2448   *Epistula Synodica*   39–40, 109 n. 53, 138 n. 114, 143, **145, 147–49, 153, 155, 157–62, 164–68, 175–78, 184–85, 207,** 214, 216–19

JE 2449   *Epistula ad Tarasium CPolitanum*   255

JE 2483   *Hadrianum*   3 n. 7, 37–40, 83–84, 109 n. 53, 116–19, 135, 138, **157, 159, 161–62, 211–13,** 260

Heraclius, Imperator
           Iussio (fragmentum ineditum)   348

Hesychius Hierosolymitanus
   CPG 6582   *Historia ecclesiastica* (frag.)   13 n. 49

Hieronymus Hierosolymitanus, Theologus Graecus
   CPG 7817   *De effectu baptismati (Dialogus de cruce)*   40, 100 n. 30, 107 n. 47,
                        116, 126, **184–85,** 217, 218, 255, 329, 337, 348

Hilarius, Papa
   CPG [8950]   *Epistula Hilarii diaconi (postea papae) ad Pulcheriam augustam* 248,
                     265

Hilarius Pictaviensis
   CPL 433   *De Trinitate*   24 n. 108

Hippolytus Romanus
   CPG 1895   *Frag. iii, De Paschate*   67, 273, 281
    nota (b)

Hippolytus Thebanus
           Syntagma   87, 308

Hormisdas, Papa
   CPL 1683   *Epistula LXXIX ad Iustinum imp.*   74 n. 105

Hypatius Ephesinus
   CPG 6806   *Quaestiones miscellaneae* (frag.)   93, 324–25

Ibas Edessenus
   CPG 6500   *Epistula Ibae ad Marim Persam*   15

Ignatius Antiochenus
   CPG 1026   *Epistulae interpolatae et ep. suppositiciae*   69, 71, 317, 339

Iohannes, monachus Hierosolymitanus
           Narratio   49–50, 99, **139–40, 208–9,** 216, 233, 255, 334

Iohannes Chrysostomus
   CPG 4313   *De virginitate*   338
   CPG 4318   *De incomprehensibili Dei natura homilia 1*   284
   CPG 4320   *De consubstantiali*   24 n. 108, 27 n. 122, 278
   CPG 4330   *Ad populum Antiochenum, hom. ii*   341
   CPG 4345   *De S. Meletio Antiocheno*   36, 92, 100 nn. 30 and 32, 106 n. 47,
                     126, **156–57,** 219, 321, 338, 344, 350
   CPG 4369   *In illud: pater, si possibile est, transeat . . .*   26 n. 115, 27 n. 122
   CPG 4415   *In Psalmum 145*   32
   CPG 4424   *In Matthaeum homiliae 1–90*   10 n. 35, 27 n. 122
   CPG 4425   *In Iohannem homiliae 1–88*   10 n. 35, 92, 247 n. 27, 278, 284, 322,
                     346
   CPG 4432   *In epistulam ad Philippenses argumentum et homiliae 1–15*   65, 71,
                     280

CPG 4440   *In epistulam ad Hebraeos argumentum et homilia* 34   310
CPG 4510   *In Sanctum Romanum homilia* 2   35
CPG 4530   *Epistula ad Caesarium*   271, 315
CPG 4560   *In natalem Christi diem*   92, 322
CPG 4587   *In illud: Simile est regnum caelorum patri familias*   299
CPG 4741   *Deprecatio*   298
CPG 4752   *Symbolum*   299
                In Abraham (Locum non inveni)   35
                In Psalmum xcviii (non inveni)   **300**
                In epistulam ad Hebraeos (non inveni)   92, 126, **129,** 322
                In quadragesimam de penitentia (non inveni)   92, **105,** 106 n. 44,
                    107 n. 47, 113 n. 66, **321–22,** 340, 346, 350
                In sancta lumina (non inveni)   78, **243,** 247 n. 27, **284, 300**
                In viduam in *Doctrina Patrum*   275
                Fragmentum ignotum   347
                In ieiunium quadragesimae (non inveni)   348
                See also: Severianus Gabalensis and Pseudo-Iohannes Chrys.

Iohannes Damascenus
CPG 8042   *Fragmenta philosophica e cod. Oxon. Bodl. Auct. T. 1. 6*   **305–6**
CPG 8045   *Orationes de imaginibus tres*   96, **97** n. 18, 101, 106 **n. 42,** 107,
                    113–18, 121 n. 81, 123–36, 141–43, **143–45, 149–53,**
                    156–64, 168–70, 173–76, 179–80, 182–85, 190–92, 194,
                    196–97, 199–201, 204–7, 210–13, 219, 221, 255 n. 4,
                    335–36, 339, 342, 351
CPG 8056   *Sacra parallela*   58
CPG 8087.8   *De unione*   52, 53, 261
CPG 8114   *De sacris imaginibus contra Constantinum Caballinum (Adversus Const.*
                    Cab./ Synodicon Iohannis Hierosolymitani?)   47, 49, 100
                    nn. 30 and 33, 101, **110–16,** 253, 313, 336, 339–40
CPG 8121   *Adversus Iconoclastas*   49, **93–99,** 108, 115, **189–90,** 225, 253, 313

Iohannes Gabalensis
CPG 7525   *Vita Severi Antiocheni* (frag.),   **214,** 220, 341

Iohannes Moschus
CPG 7376   *Pratum Spirituale (BHG* 1442)   55, 56, 93 n. 3, 100 nn. 30 and 31,
                    107, 126, 127, **203–7,** 215, 220–21, 227 n. 1, 228, 248,
                    267, 333, 338, 341, 348

Iohannes Thessalonicensis
CPG 7923   *Sermo (fragmentum de imaginibus)*   93, **188–89,** 191, 220, 329–30

Iohannes Veccus
                Epigraphae   72 n. 93, 249 n. 28

Iohannes I Antiochenus
CPG 6310   *Epistula ad Cyrillum Alex. de pace*   248, 263
    [8851]

CPG 6311   *Epistula ad Cyrillum Alex.*   312
[8852]

Iosephus ep. Nicomedeae
                Sermo in persecutiones (fragmentum ineditum)   106 n. 44, 123
                    n. 87, **326–27,** 344

Irenaeus Lugdunensis
    CPG 1315.3   *Fragmenta varia graeca, frag.* 8 (= Hippolytus, *Commentarii in
                    Reges*)   69, 71, 259, 314

Isidorus Pelusiota
    CPG 5557   *Epistularum lib. I*   **64,** 71, 274–75
                Fragmentum ignotum   **310**

Iulianus Pomerius, presbyter Arelatensis
    CPL 998   *De vita contemplativa*   73 n. 101

Iulius Sextus Africanus
    CPG 1690   *Chronographiae*   **86–87, 307**

Iuris Pseudo-Apostolici Collectiones
    CPG 1730   *Constitutiones Apostolorum*   339
                Constitutiones Apostolorum (non inventum in opere citato)   35
                Didascalia et Constitutiones Apostolorum   100 n. 30, 107 n. 47, 324,
                    340, 343

Iuris Pseudo-Apostolici opera singula
    CPG 1741   *Epitoma libri VIII Constitutionum apostolorum seu Constitutiones per
                    Hippolytum*   52, **269**

Iustinianus I, Imperator
    CPG 6879   *Epistula dogmatica ad Zoilum*   27
    CPG 6882   *Epistula contra tria capitula*   14 n. 54
    CPG 6885   *Confessio fidei*   14 n. 54
    CPG 6887   *Epistula ad Synodum de Theodoro Mopsuesteno*   10
                Adversus Nestorianos et Acephalos   27

Leo I, Papa
    CPG [8911]/   *Epistula ad Faustum presbyterum*   248, 264
    CPL 1656
    CPG [8922]   *Epistula ad Flavianum CPolitanum (Tomus)*   8, 10 n. 35, 24 n. 108,
                    27 n. 122, 55, 83, 248, 267, 272, 274
    CPG [8923]   *Epistula ad Theodosium augustum*   248, 265
    CPG [8924]   *Epistula ad Pulcheriam augustam*   248, 265
    CPG [8926]   *Epistula ad Faustum et Martinum presbyteros et reliquos archimandri-
                    tas*   248, 265
    CPG [8927]   *Epistula ad synodum quae apud Ephesum convenit*   248, 265
    CPG [8929]   *Epistula ad Iulianum episc. Coi*   248, 264
    CPG [8948]   *Epistula Leonis papae et sanctae synodi ad Theodosium augustum*   248,
                    265

CPG [8949]   *Epistula Leonis et sanctae synodi ad Pulcheriam augustam*   248, 265
CPG [8954]   *Epistula ad clerum CPolitanum*   248, 266
CPG [8955]   *Epistula ad Faustum, Martinum, Petrum, Emmanuelem presb. et*
                    archim.   248, 266
CPG [8993]   *Epistula ad concilium Chalcedonense (synodum Nicaeae constitu-*
                    tam)   248, 267
CPL 1656   *Epistula 15 ad Turibium Astor.*   74 n. 104
             Epistula 165,6 ad Leonem imp.   28 nn. 124 and 126
             Epistula 165,8 ad Leonem imp.   28
CPL 1657   *Sermo LXXVI*   74 n. 104

Leontius Neapolitanus
   CPG 7885.1   *Contra Iudaeos orationes v* (frag.)   93, 100 n. 30, 121, 126, **190–92,**
                    220, 330, 335
                Fragmentum ignotum   35

Leontius Scholasticus (Pseudo-Leontius)
   CPG 6823   *Liber de sectis*   52, 57, 270

Macarius Antiochenus
   CPG 7625   *Confessio fidei*   25

Marcus Eugenicus Metropolita Ephesi
             Testimonia a Marco Ephesio collecta   81 n. 140

Martinus I, Papa
   CPG 9398.2   *Allocutio*   16

Matthaeus Vlastares
             Contra Latinos   53, 312

Maurus ep. Ravennae
   CPG 9398.3/   *Epistula ad Martinum*   16
   CPL 1169

Maximus Confessor
   CPG 7688   *Quaestiones ad Thalassium*   82, 247 n. 27, 300
   CPG 7695   *Capita xv*   306–7
   CPG 7697.10 *Opuscula theologica et polemica, Ep. ad Marinum Cypri presby-*
                    terum   30 n. 139, **76–77,** 82, 286
   CPG 7697.11 *Epistula Romae scripta*   82, 247 n. 27, 286
   CPG 7697.15 *Spiritualis tomus ac dogmaticus*   4 n. 13, 19
   CPG 7697.21 *De qualitate, proprietate et differentia seu distinctione ad Theodorum*
                    presbyterum in Mazario   287
   CPG 7699   *Epistula xv*   306
   CPG 7705   *Ambiguorum Liber*   276
   CPG 7707.31 *Appendix ad epistulam xv ad Cosmam*   306
             Loca non inventa   287

Menas CPolitanus
   CPG 6931   *Libellus professionis*   23

Methodius Olympius
CPG 1810   *Convivium decem virginum*   83 n. 150, 284–85
             Fragmentum non inventum in opere citato   297
CPG 1812   *De resurrectione*   126, **129–30,** 327

Michael VIII Palaeologus, Imp.
             Epistula ad Urbanum IV Papam   **238–40,** 248, 251 n. 35

Nestorius CPolitanus
CPG 5690   *Sermo I*   7 n. 21
CPG 5691   *Sermo II*   7 n. 21
CPG 5692   *Sermo III*   7 n. 21
CPG 5694   *Sermo V*   7 n. 21
CPG 5697   *Sermo VIII*   7 n. 21
CPG 5698   *Sermo IX*   7 n. 21
CPG 5699   *Sermo X*   7 n. 21
CPG 5700   *Sermo XI*   7 n. 21
CPG 5703   *Sermo XIV*   7 n. 21
CPG 5704   *Sermo XV*   7 n. 21
CPG 5705   *Sermo XVI*   7 n. 21

Nicephorus Blemmydes
             Sermones   72 n. 93

Nicephorus CPolitanus
             Adversus Epiphanidem   31 n. 145
             Antirrheticus I   31 n. 145
             Antirrheticus II   31 n. 145
             Apologeticus minor pro sacris imaginibus   **232**
             Contra Eusebium   31 n. 145, 33 n. 153, 223 n. 184
             Epigramma in imagines   137, 255, 259, **345**
             Refutatio et eversio   32 n. 145, 34 n. 154, 35 n. 165, 99, 123 n.
                 223–24,

Nicolaus Cotronensis
             Liber de Fide Trinitatis (Libellus)   234–39, **240–51,** 260

Nilus Ancyranus
CPG 6043   *Epistula ad Olympiodorum eparchum*   33, 34 n. 159, 214
             Epistula ad Heliodorum selentiarium   213, 220, 348

Paschalis I, Papa
             Epistula ad Leonem V imp.   255 n. 4

Pastor ep. Gallaeciae
CPL 559   *Libellus in modum symboli*   74 n. 110

Paulus CPolitanus
CPG 7620   *Epistula ad Theodorum papam*   17 n. 71
CPG 7621   *Typus*   17 n. 71

Paulus Emesenus
    CPG 6365   *Homilia I de nativitate Alexandriae habita*   248, 263
    [8847]
    CPG 6366   *Homilia II de nativitate Alexandriae habita*   **64,** 71, 248, 263, 274
    [8847]
    CPG 6367   *Homilia III de pace Alexandriae habita*   248, 263
    [8847]

Petrus Alexandrinus
    CPG   *De deitate* (frag.)   6 n. 20
    1635.1.2.3

Philo historiographus
    CPG 7512   *Historia ecclesiastica* (frag.)   52, 56, 269–70

Phosterius presbyter et archimandrita
                    Interpretatio Symboli   64, 71, 275

Photinus CPolitanus
    CPG 7971   *Vita Iohannis Ieiunatoris* (frag.)   93 n. 3, **199–200,** 220, 332

Photius CPolitanus
                    Κανὼν περὶ τοῦ μὴ δεῖν τὸν ἱερέα β΄ λειτουργίας ποιεῖν   49, **89–**
                         91, 255, 309
                    Bibliotheca   87

Proclus CPolitanus
    CPG 5802   *Homilia III, de incarnatione Domini*   69, 71, **314**
    CPG 5822   *Homilia XXIII, de dogmate incarnationis*   314
    CPG 5897   *Ep. 2, Tomus ad Armenios*   13 n. 49, 14 n. 52
    CPG 5900   *Ep. 3, Ad Iohannem Antiochenum*   14 n. 52, 248, **268–69**
                    Fragmentum non repertum   10 n. 35

Pseudo-Athanasius Alex.
    CPG 2231   *De incarnatione contra Apollinarium libri ii*   26 n. 115, 27 n. 122,
                         272, 274, 277
    CPG 2240   *Testimonia e scriptura (De communi essentia patris et filii et spiritus san-*
                         cti)   52, 57–58, 271
    CPG 2257   *Quaestiones ad Antiochum ducem*   39, 92, **116–17,** 124 n. 92, 125,
                         126, 311, 324, 350
    CPG 2262   *Narratio de cruce seu imagine Berytensi*   92, 100 nn. 30 and 33,
                         170–72, 217, 220, 324, 336
    CPG 2806   *De incarnatione et contra Arianos* (Marcellus Ancyranus)   26, 278

Pseudo-Caesarius
    CPG 7482   *Quaestiones et responsiones*   299

Pseudo-Dionysius Areopagita
    CPG 6600   *De coelesti hierarchia*   39, 93, 106, 114 n. 72, 116, 118, 124 n. 89,
                         125, 126, 129, 325–26, 337, 345, 350

CPG 6601   *De ecclesiastica hierarchia*   93, 106, 118, 124 n. 88, 125, 126, 129,
                 325–26, 345
CPG 6602   *De divinis nominibus*   26 n. 115, 290
CPG 6607   *Ep. 4, Ad Gaium monachum*   17, 276
CPG 6613   *Ep. 10, Ad Iohannem theologum*   39, 116, 124 n. 93, 118
                 Epistula ad Titum (inedita)   **286**

Pseudo-Iohannes Chrysostomus
CPG 4574   *Sermo in S. Thomam apostolum*   28 n. 126

Pseudo-Iustinus (= Theodoretus ep. Cyri)
CPG 6218   *Expositio rectae fidei*   28 n. 125, 279

Rabbulas Edessenus
CPG 6494   *Epistula ad Cyrillum Alex.* (frag.)   13 n. 49

Scripta Apollinaristica Incerta
CPG 3741.2   *Fragmentum 186*   6 n. 20, 7

Sergius CPolitanus
CPG 7605   *Epistula ad Cyrum Alexandrinum*   17

Severianus Gabalensis
CPG 4192   *Homilia de legislatore* (= Pseudo-Iohannes Chrysostomus)   92,
                 100 nn. 30–32,107 n. 47, 121, 126, 321, 338, 346, 350
CPG 4206   *De fide* (= Pseudo-Iohannes Chrysostomus)   **65–67,** 71, **245–46,**
                 247 n. 27, 282
CPG 4209   *De sigillis sermo* (= Pseudo-Iohannes Chrysostomus, *De parabola
                 seminis*)   40, **104–5,** 107, 116, 126, 136, **211–13,** 218,
                 322, 338, 346, 348, 350
CPG 4213   *In pretiosam et vivificam crucem*   136 n. 105
CPG 4216   *Homilia de lotione pedum* (= Pseudo-Iohannes Chrysostomus,
                 Sermo in quinta feria paschae)   39 n. 176, 40, 92, 100 nn.
                 30 and 31, 113 n. 66, 114 n. 72, 116, 126, **157–62,** 219–
                 21, 227 n. 1, 321, 340
CPG 4270   *In dedicationem pretiosae et vivificae crucis*   126, **130–31,** 327–28

Socrates Scholasticus
CPG 6028   *Historia ecclesiastica*   3 n. 8, 121

Sophronius Hierosolymitanus
CPG 7635   *Epistula Synodica ad Sergium CPolitanum*   30, 51–52, 57, 71, 83,
                 259, 270, 296
CPG 7645   *Laudes in ss. Cyrum et Iohannem* (*BHG* 476)   93 n. 3, 126, **194,** 220,
                 227 n. 1, 330, 344
CPG 7646   *Narratio miraculorum ss. Cyri et Iohannis* (*BHG* 478)   93 n. 3, **194,**
                 220, 227 n. 1, 331
CPG 7675   *Vita Mariae Aegyptiacae* (*BHG* 1042)   93 n. 3, 126, **200–201,** 220,
                 332

Sozomenus
CPG 6030   *Historia ecclesiastica*   3 n. 8, 93 n. 7, 330

Stephanus Bostrensis
    CPG 7790   *Contra Iudaeos fragmenta*   40, 93 n. 6, 97, 116, 121,122, 126, 218,
             255, 328, 347, 350

Symeon Stylita Iunior
    CPG 7366   *Epistula ad Iustinum Iuniorem*   100 n. 30, 114 n. 72, **185–87,** 217,
             220, 329, 346, 351
    CPG 7369   *Vita Symeonis Stylitae Iunioris (BHG* 1689)   93 n. 3, 126, **197–99,**
             220, 227 n. 1, 331–32

Tarasius CPolitanus
             Epigramma in imaginem crucifixionis   137, 255, 259, **345**

Themistius, diaconus Alexandrinus
    CPG 7285   *Antirrheticus contra tomum Theodosii* (frag.)   29 n. 129

Theodoretus ep. Cyri
    CPG 6214   *Impugnatio xii anathematismorum Cyrilli*   14 n. 56
    CPG 6215   *Libri V contra Cyrillum*   15 n. 58
    CPG 6217   *Eranistes*   9–10 n. 35
    CPG 6220   *Pro Diodoro et Theodoro*   13 n. 49
    CPG 6221   *Historia religiosa (BHG* 1439–1440)   93 n. 3, 126, **196–97,** 220,
             227 n. 1, **331**
    CPG 6226   *Ex sermone Chalcedone contra Cyrillum habito*   14 n. 56
    CPG 6227   *Ex alio sermone ibidem contra Cyrillum habito*   14 n. 56
    CPG 6228   *Ex sermone ibidem, cum essent abituri, habito*   14 n. 56
    CPG 6229   *Ex allocutione Antiochiae dicta*   14 n. 56
    CPG 6230   *Ex alia allocutione ibidem dicta*   14 n. 56
    CPG 6240   *Ep. 16, Ad Irenaeum digamum*   13 n. 49
    CPG 6255   *Ep. 162, Ad Andream Samosatenum*   14 n. 56
    CPG 6266   *Ep. 171, Ad Iohannem Antiochenum*   14 n. 56, 261
    CPG 6270   *Ep. 172, Ad Nestorium*   14 n. 56
    CPG 6276   *Epistula ad eos qui in Euphratesia . . . et Cilicia vitam monasticam
             degunt*   14 n. 56
    CPG 6287   *Ep. 180, Ad Iohannem Antiochenum cum mortuus esset Cyrillus*   14
             n. 56
             See also Pseudo-Iustinus

Theodorus Anagnostes
    CPG 7503   *Historia ecclesiastica* (frag.)   100 nn. 30 and 33, 106 n. 44, 126,
             131, 329, 337, 347

Theodorus Mopsuestenus
    CPG 3827   *Fragmenta in Genesim*   11 n. 40, 348
    CPG 3833   *Expositio in Psalmos*   11 n. 40
    CPG 3834   *Commentarius in XII prophetas minores*   11 n. 40
    CPG 3835   *Fragmenta in Iob*   11 n. 40
    CPG 3837   *Fragmenta in Canticum*   11 n. 40
    CPG 3840   *Fragmenta in Matthaeum*   11 n. 40
    CPG 3842   *Fragmenta in Lucam*   11 n. 40

CPG 3843	*Commentarii in Iohannem*	11 n. 40
CPG 3844	*Frag. in Actus Apostolorum*	11 n. 40
CPG 3848	*Frag. in epistulam ad Hebraeos*	11 n. 40
CPG 3852	*Homiliae catecheticae* (*Lib. ad baptizandos*)	11 n. 40
CPG 3856.2a	*De incarnatione* (frag.)	11 n. 40
CPG 3858	*Contra Apollinarium*	11 n. 40
CPG 3871g	*Expositio Symboli*	11 n. 40

Theodorus Pharanitanus
CPG 7601	*Sermo ad Sergium*	17 n. 69, 30 n. 139
CPG 7602	*De interpretationibus*	17 n. 69, 30 n. 139

Theodorus Studita
> *Poenae monasteriales*   5 n. 16
> *Antirrheticus II*   223 n. 183
> *Refutatio poem. Iconomach.*   223 n. 183
> *Epistulae*   223 n. 183

Theodorus II Laskaris
> Λόγος ἀπολογητικὸς πρὸς ἐπίσκοπον Κοτρώνης κατὰ Λατίνων περὶ τοῦ Ἁγίου Πνεύματος   **236,** 237, 251 **n. 35**

Theodosius Alexandrinus
CPG 7133	*Tomus ad Theodoram aug.* (frag.)	24 n. 108, 29 n. 129

Theodotus Ancyranus
CPG 6133	*Fragmentum contra imagines*	32

Theophanes Confessor
> *Chronographia*   94

Theophilus Alexandrinus
CPG 2582	*Epistulae festales, ep. V*	6 n. 20, 7
CPG 2583	*Epistulae festales, ep. VI*	6 n. 20, 7
CPG 2605	*Epistula ad Porphyrium ep. Antiochenum*	13 n. 49
CPG 2620	*Sermo in fluxu sanguinis laborantem*	279

Theosebes (monachus?)
> Νουθεσία γέροντος περὶ τῶν ἁγίων εἰκόνων   100, **110–16, 146–48,** 183, 187, 219, 335

Thomas de Aquino
> *Contra errores Graecorum*   234–35

Timotheus Apollinarista
CPG 3726	*Epistula ad Prosdocium*	6 n. 20, 7

Timotheus Presbyter CPolitanus
CPG 7016	*De iis qui ad ecclesiam accedunt*	336

Victricius ep. Rotomagensis
CPL 481	*De laude sanctorum*	74 n. 108

Vigilius, Papa
   CPG [9336]   *Epistula ad Iustinianum imp.* item *ad Theodoram*   23 n. 101
   JK 920
   CPG [9350]   *Epistula ad Eutychium CPolitanum*   10, 248, 267
   JK 932
   CPG [9363]   *Constitutum*   12 n. 43
   JK 935
   CPG [9364]   *Epistula ii ad Eutychium CPolitanum*   48 n. 26, 54, 248, 268
   JK 936
   CPG [9365]   *Ex epistula adversus Tria Capitula* (constitutum II)   48 n. 26, 54
   JK 937

Xystus Papa
   CPG [8792]   *Epistula Xysti papae ad Cyrillum Alexandrinum*   262
   CPG [8793]   *Epistula (ad episcopos Aegyptios)*   262

CONCILIA

Concilium I oecumenicum, Nicaenum a. 325
   CPG 8512   *Symbolum*   7, 17, 83, 244–45, 251 n. 35, **288**
   CPG 8513   *Canones*   232

Concilium II oecumenicum, CPolitanum I a. 381
   CPG 8599   *Symbolum*   17, 72, 74–75, 98, 235

Concilium Toledanum a. 400
             Regula fidei   74

Concilium III oecumenicum, Ephesinum a. 431
   CPG 8675.8   *Gesta, Actio I, Symbolum apud Ephesum* (= Cyrilli Anathematismi,
   [8644]   *CPG* 5317)   17
   CPG 8675.9   *Gesta, Actio I*   6–7
   CPG 8721   *Gesta, Actio VI*   6–8
   CPG 8760   *Sacra qua Synodus dissolvitur, Cyrillo et Memnone restitutis*   262

Concilium Ephesinum a. 449 ("latrocinium")
   CPG [8910] ff   *Epistulae ad synodum spectantes ante gesta scriptae*   55

Concilium IV oecumenicum, Chalcedonense a. 451
   CPG 8982   *Epistula Marciani imperatoris et Valentiniani iii ad (Leonem episc.*
                 Romae et) Anatolium episc. CPolis   248, 266
   CPG 8997   *Epistula Pulcheriae augustae ad Strategium consularem Bithyniae*   248,
                 266
   CPG 8998   *Epistula Marciani et Valentiniani ad concilium Nicaeae Chalcedonem*
                 transferendum   248, 266
   CPG 8999   *Epistula eorundem ad idem concilium*   248, 266
   CPG 9000   *Gesta, Actio I*   9, 22 n. 92
   CPG 9001   *Gesta, Actio II*   244–45
   CPG 9002   *Gesta, Actio III*   9, 244–45, 248, 267
   CPG 9005   *Gesta, Actio V, Definitio*   17, 244–45, 288, 296

CPG 9007   *Gesta, Actio VI*   244–45, 289
CPG 9021   *Adlocutio ad Marcianum imp. aug.*   8–10, 285, 293

Synodus CPolitana a. 536
    CPG 9325.3   *Gesta, Actio I, Libellus monachorum ad Agapetum*   93 n. 8, 333
    CPG 9329.6   *Gesta, Actio V, Preces clericorum et monachorum Antiochiae ad Iohannem*
                           CPolitanum et synodum   40, 93 n. 8, 100 n. 30, 114 n. 72,
                           116, 119, 135, **192,** 219, 330, 341
    CPG 9329.10   *Gesta, Actio V, Sententia synodi*   339

Synodus Mopsuestena a. 550
    CPG 9340   *Gesta*   14 n. 52

Concilium V oecumenicum, CPolitanum II a. 553
    CPG 9355   *Gesta, Actio I*   10
    CPG 9356   *Gesta, Actio II*   10
    CPG 9357   *Gesta, Actio III*   **4 n. 9,** 18
    CPG 9358   *Gesta, Actio IV*   11–12
    CPG 9359   *Gesta, Actio V*   12–14
    CPG 9360   *Gesta, Actio VI*   15
    CPG 9361   *Gesta, Actio VII*   15
    CPG   *Gesta, Actio VIII, Sententia Synodica*   15, 17, 248, 267–68
    9362.1.2
    CPG [9364]   *Epistula ii Vigilii ad Eutychium CPolitanum*   48 n. 26, 54, 248, 268

Concilium Toledanum III a. 589
              Anathemata   74–75

Concilium Lateranense a. 649
    CPG [9395]   *Ep. Probi et universorum episcoporum concilii proconsularis ad Paulum*
    9399.6   *ep. CPolitanum*   16 n. 67
    CPG [9396]   *Ep. Victoris ep. Carthaginensis ad Theodorum papam*   51, 56, 248,
    9399.7   269
    CPG 9398   *Secretarius I*   16
    CPG 9399   *Secretarius II*   16 nn. 66 and 67, 17, 229
    CPG 9399.2   *Libellus abbatum . . . et monachorum graecorum*   18 n. 76
    CPG 9400   *Secretarius III*   17
    CPG 9401   *Secretarius IV*   17
    CPG 9402.1   *Secretarius V*   4 nn. 9 and 10, 6 n. 18, 17–18
    CPG 9402.5   *Canones xx*   19

Concilium VI oecumenicum, CPolitanum III a. 680–81
    CPG 9416   *Sacra Constantini IV imp. ad Domnum papam*   22
    CPG 9417   *Ep. Synodica Agathonis ad Constantinum IV imp.*   5 n. 14, 24, 231,
                           248, 258, 270
    CPG 9418   *Ep. Agathonis et synodi ad Constantinum IV imp.*   24, 248, 270
    CPG 9419   *Sacra Constantini IV imp. ad Georgium CPolitanum*   22
    CPG 9420   *Gesta, Actio I*   22–23, 229
    CPG 9421   *Gesta, Actio II*   23
    CPG 9422   *Gesta, Actio III*   23–24

CPG 9423   *Gesta, Actio IV*   24
CPG 9424   *Gesta, Actio V*   25
CPG 9425   *Gesta, Actio VI*   25
CPG 9426   *Gesta, Actio VII*   25
CPG 9427   *Gesta, Actio VIII*   5 n. 15, 25–26, 270
CPG 9428   *Gesta, Actio IX*   26
CPG 9429   *Gesta, Actio X*   26–30
CPG 9429.3   *Libellus satisfactionis Petri episc. Nicomediae*   52, 57, 289, 292
CPG 9430   *Gesta, Actio XI*   30
CPG 9431   *Gesta, Actio XII*   30
CPG 9432   *Gesta, Actio XIII*   30
CPG 9433   *Gesta, Actio XIV*   23–24, 30 n. 142
CPG 9437   *Gesta, Actio XVIII*   30–31

Concilium Trullanum a. 692, quinisextum dictum
    CPG 9444   *Canon* 11   339
               Canon 82   93 n. 8, 100 nn. 30 and 31, **101,** 107 n. 44, 113 n. 66, 114 n. 72, 121, 126, **182–83,** 219, 223, 328, 341, 347, 351

Concilium Romanum a. 731
         Gesta   37–41, 228
         Florilegium   39–40, 121 n. 81, 122, 133, 134, 135, 138–39, 148, 156, 176–77, 208, **211–13,** 233

Synodus CPolitana, Hieriae a. 754
         Horos   31–34, 36 nn. 168 and 169, 99, 134 n. 103, 163, 188, 225 n. 187, 230 n. 7
         Florilegium Iconoclasticum   32–34, 230 n. 7

Synodus Hierosolymitana a. 764 (?)
         Acta   208–9, 210
         Synodica rectae fidei (a. 764/5)   38–39, 135, 225

Concilium Romanum (Lateranense) a. 769
         Gesta   37–41, 210, 228
         Florilegium   39–40, 121 n. 81, 133, 138–39, 176–77, 233
         Synodica rectae fidei Orientalium Patr.   38–39, 135, 225

Concilium VII oecumenicum, Nicaenum II a. 787
         Gesta, Actio I   **172,** 232
         Gesta, Actio II   **143–44,** 153, **154–57, 158–62, 166–68, 175–78, 183–84, 207, 210–13**
         Gesta, Actio III   **145–49**
         Gesta, Actio IV   33 n. 150, 50, **142–43, 145–49, 150–53, 156–64, 168–75, 179–80, 182–83, 187–88, 190–92, 194–210, 213–14,** 219, 227 n. 1, 228
         Gesta, Actio V   33 n. 151, **178, 181–82, 186–90, 192–93, 203–9, 214,** 219, 228
         Gesta, Actio VI   32 nn. 145, 146, and 147, 36 n. 169, 134 n. 103,

143–45, 149, 163–66, 168–70, 174–75, 182–83, 187–88, 210–13, 225 n. 187
Gesta, Actio VII   93, 99, **209,** 255

Synodus CPolitana, S. Sophia celebrata a. 815
Horos   32 n. 145, 34
Florilegium Iconoclasticum   32 n. 145, 35–36, 232

Synodus Parisina a. 825
Libellus Synodalis   138–40, **145–49, 155–56, 158–62, 165, 167, 177–78, 183–84, 211–13**

Concilium Ferrarense-Florentinum a. 1438–39
Gesta   54, 76, **80,** 81 n. 139, 249 n. 28

MISCELLANEA

Anonyma
1. Γραφὴ καὶ μαρτυρίαι . . . (Locum non inveni)   65–66, 71, **280–81**
2. Διάλογος Μόσχου μοναχοῦ καὶ ἐγκλειστοῦ πρός τινα περὶ εἰκόνων ἁγίων (ineditum)   207, 333
3. Διατί λέγεται λόγος καὶ δύναμις καὶ σοφία . . . (non inveni)   78, **304–6.**
4. Disputatio Iudaei et Christiani   93, 97 n. 21, **189–90,** 220, 330
5. Formae abrogationis haereticorum   310
6. Περὶ αἰτίου· τὸ γὰρ αἴτιον . . . (non inveni)   78, **292–93**
7. Περὶ ἀχειροποιήτων εἰκόνων (ineditum)   100 n. 44, **349–50**
8. Περὶ τοῦ Μελχισεδὲκ (ineditum)   **309**
9. Περὶ τῶν γ΄ ἡμερῶν τῆς ἀναστάσεως τοῦ Χριστοῦ (ineditum)   87, **308**
10. Textus anonymus de apostolorum parentibus   88, 309
11. Tractatus de Synodis   **244–45,** 247 n. 27, 248, **287–90**

Carolingia varia
Capitulare adversus Synodum pro sacrarum imaginum erectione   37, 138, 187
Codex Carolinus   258
Libri Carolini   37 n. 172, 138, **158–62, 165, 167**

Liber Pontificalis   **121–22, 210,** 258
Scriptor Incertus de Leone Armeno   33 n. 149, 34–35

VITAE SANCTORUM

Acta Apocrypha Iohannis   33, 139
Vita Basilii Caesariensis (Helladio auctore)   92, 106 n. 44, **126–27,** 316, 346
Vita Martini Papae (Syriace)   20 n. 87
BHG 84   Vita et martyrium Anastasii Persae   93 n. 3, **202–3,** 220, 332

BHG 89g   *Miracula x Anastasii Persae*   93 n. 3, **203,** 220, 333

BHG 387   *Cosmas et Damianus, Miracula x*   93 n. 3, **194–96,** 220, 227 n. 1, 331

BHG 389   *Cosmas et Damianus, Miraculum 30*   93 n. 3, **194–96,** 220, 227 n. 1, 331

BHG 631   *Vita Eupraxiae in Thebaide*   **133,** 337

BHG 1341   Theosterictus monachus, *Vita Nicetae Mediciensis*   103 n. 37

BHG 1410– 1400a   Evagrius ep. *Vita et passio Pancratii ap. ep. Tauromenii*   92, 93 n. 3, **103–4,** 223, 324, 350

BHG 1577   *Passio S. Procopii*   93 n. 3, **201,** 220, 332

BHG 1628– 1630   *Vita Silvestri*   93 n. 3, 100–101, 207, 333, 340

BHG 1634 ff   *Acta Silvestri*   **62–64,** 71, 248, 271–72

BHG 2259   *Vita Martini Papae*   20 n. **87,** 21 **n. 89**

INDEX OF MANUSCRIPTS CITED

Greek

Athos (Mount)
Athonensis Dionysiou 175 (3709): 142 n. 123, 149, 221 n. 180
Athonensis Dochiariou 78: 167
Athonensis Laurae B 26: 45
Athonensis Vatopedinus 507 (alias *594*): 58 n. 67, 123 n. 87, 304–305

Breslau
Breslauensis graecus 437: 139–40

Brussels
Bruxellensis 11376: 86 n. 163

Chicago
Chicaginiensis Bibliothecae Universitatis graecus 965: 45

Florence
Laurentianus graecus VI 12: 80 n. 138

Iena
Jenensis mscr. Bose 1: 80 n. 138

London
Londiniensis Arundelianus 529 (= Brittanici Musei Add. 10445): 53, 55 n. 55, 56–57,
    58 n. 65, 66, 259 n. 27, 260, 280–81
Londiniensis Brittanici Musei, Add. 36821: 256 n. 9

Madrid
Scorialensis graecus 449 (Ψ. II. 14): 139–40
Scorialensis graecus 463 (Ψ. III. 8): 128

Milan
Ambrosianus graecus 21 (A 84 sup.): 183–84
Ambrosianus graecus E 49–50: 258 n. 23
Mediolanensis Bibliothecae Nationalis Brerae AF. IX. 31: 90
Mediolanensis Bibliothecae Nationalis Brerae AF. X. 47: 139

Moscow
Mosquensis Historici Musei graecus 265 (Vladimir 197): 40, 100–226 passim, 260 n. 29
Mosquensis Historici Musei graecus 398 (Vladimir 315): 90–91
Mosquensis Historici Musei graecus 443 (Vladimir 232): 58 n. 65

Munich
Monacensis graecus 380: 89 n. 181, 90

Naples
Neapolitanus graecus 54 (II B 16): 129 n. 100, 142 n. 123, 211 n. 165, 221 n. 180
Neapolitanus graecus 75 (II C 7): 90–91

Oxford
Oxoniensis Bodleianus graecus, Auctarium T 16 (olim Miscellaneus 184): 58 n. 67, 71, 123, 306
Oxoniensis Bodleianus graecus, Roe 22: 45
Oxoniensis Bodleianus graecus, Roe 28: 110 n. 59

Paris
Parisinus graecus 582: 158–59
Parisinus graecus 767: 110 n. 59
Parisinus graecus 1115: passim
Parisinus graecus 1144: 58 n. 67
Parisinus graecus 1250: 32 n.145, 35 n. 165, 223–24
Parisinus graecus 1470: 256
Parisinus Coislinianus graecus 93: 32 n. 145, 35 n. 165, 124 n. 87, 223

St. Petersburg
Petropolitanus Bibliothecae Publicae graecus 105: 45

Sinai (Mount, Monastery of St. Catherine)
Sinaiticus graecus 1109: 91
Sinaiticus graecus 1117: 90
Sinaiticus graecus 1121: 90

Turin
Taurinensis graecus Bibliothecae Nationalis B.I.2: 48 n. 27
Taurinensis graecus Bibliothecae Nationalis 110 (B II 9): 139, 140, 203 n. 157

Vatican City
Vaticanus graecus 430: 89 n. 181, 90
Vaticanus graecus 511: 103–6, 350–51
Vaticanus graecus 640: 90
Vaticanus graecus 660: 139–40
Vaticanus graecus 828: 89 n. 181, 90
Vaticanus graecus 834: 139–40
Vaticanus graecus 835: 139
Vaticanus graecus 836: 137–41, 200, 232
Vaticanus graecus 1119: 89 n. 181, 90
Vaticanus graecus 1150: 89 n. 181, 90
Vaticanus graecus 1181: 137–41
Vaticanus graecus 1255: 158–59
Vaticanus graecus 1431: 8 n. 31
Vaticanus graecus 1455: 27
Vaticanus graecus 1506: 88
Vaticanus graecus 1666: 258 n. 23
Vaticanus graecus 1702: 58 n. 65, 260 n. 29
Vaticanus graecus 2013: 158–59

Vaticanus graecus 2200: 58 n. 67, 71 n. 90.
Vaticanus graecus 2220: 260 n. 29
Vaticanus Ottobonianus graecus 14: 158–59
Vaticanus Ottobonianus graecus 27: 158–59, 191
Vaticanus Ottobonianus graecus 85: 158–59
Vaticanus Pii II graecus 23: 158–59

Venice
Venetus Marcianus graecus 166: 139–40, 191, 203 n. 157
Venetus Marcianus graecus 573: 40, 100–226 passim, 260 n. 29

Vienna
Vindobonensis Historicus graecus 7: 90–91
Vindobonensis Historicus graecus 27: 139–40
Vindobonensis Historicus graecus 127: 260 n. 29
Vindobonensis Theologicus graecus 10: 110 n. 59
Vindobonensis Theologicus graecus 77: 89
Vindobonensis Theologicus graecus 190: 260 n. 29

Latin

London
Londiniensis Bibliothecae Brittanicae Add. 16413: 38 n. 173, 39 n. 178, 116–17

Vatican City
Vaticanus latinus 808: 235–36
Vaticanus Ottobonianus latinus 3057: 250 n. 33

Verona
Verona Chapter Library ms. LI: 88 n. 174, 91

Syriac

London
Londiniensis Bibliothecae Brittanicae Add. 12172: 88 n. 172

INDEX OF MODERN AUTHORS

Abramowski, L., 13 n. 50
Achelis, H., 273
Adler, W., 87 n. 168
Aldama, J. A. de, 74 n. 110, 75 n. 114
Alexakis, A., 183, 216–17, 222–23 nn. 181 and 182, 328, 333
Alexander, P., 32 n. 145, 34–36, 99 n. 24, 188 n. 151, 226, 233 n. 16
Anastos, M., 36 n. 168, 226
Arcadios Vatopedinos, 123 n. 87
Assemani, S., 282
Astruck, Ch., 43 n. 5
Atsalos, B., 98 n. 22

Bacht, H., 1 n. 1
Baker, D., 249 n. 28
Bardy, G., 22 n. 93, 273
Bastgen, H., 138 n. 116
Batiffol, P., 48 n. 24, 229 n. 4, 256
Beck, H. G., 49 nn. 32 and 33, 103 n. 36, 123 n. 86, 125 n. 96, 225 n. 187, 236 n. 8
Belting, H., 48 n. 27
Beneševič, V. N., 89 n. 180, 90 n. 183, 230 n. 9, 336
Bernardi, J., 269, 341
Bidez, J., 192, 330
Böhringer, L., 38 n. 173, 39 n. 178, 116–17
Bonwetsch, N., 130 n. 101, 284, 327
Bracke, R., 178 n. 148
Brandmüller, W., 74 n. 109
Bratke, E., 340
Brock, S., 20 n. 87
Browning, R., 48 n. 23

Callahan, J. F., 291, 314, 321
Canart, P., 45 n. 12, 256 n. 9
Canivet, P., 196, 331
Caspar, E., 16 n. 64, 18 n. 77, 121 n. 82

Caspari, C. P., 308
Cavallera, F., 47 n. 23
Cavallo, G., 48 n. 27
Cavarnos, J. P., 321
Chadwick, H., 1 n. 1
Chrestou, P., 48 n. 24, 124 n. 87
Chrysos, E., 6 n. 19, 10 n. 36, 11 n. 41, 12 n. 43, 13 n. 50, 14 n. 55, 15 n. 61, 48 n. 23, 95 n. 17, 229 n. 4
Clugnet, M. L., 337
Coleti, N., 237 n. 9
Combefis, F., 1 n. 1, 43 n. 2, 62 n. 76, 76, 94, 97 n. 20, 110 n. 59, 254, 272, 333, 339
Conte, P., 20 n. 87, 109 n. 53
Courtonne, Y., 145, 272, 286, 310, 315, 347
Cuming, G. J., 249 n. 28

Dagron, G., 237 n. 8, 327
Darrouzès, J., 15 n. 59, 101 n. 35, 114 n. 70, 313, 338
Datema, C., 187–88, 274, 277, 297, 314, 329
Davis, R., 122, 210 n. 164, 224 n. 186
Delehaye, H., 88 n. 171
der Nersessian, S., 104 n. 41, 136 n. 105
Déroche, V., 62 n. 75, 106 n. 42, 139 n. 118, 190–92, 225 n. 188, 330
Deubner, L., 194–96, 331
Devreesse, R., 11 n. 41, 20 n. 87, 43 n. 2, 48 n. 24, 71 n. 92, 82, 103 n. 38
Diekamp, F., 48 n. 25, 58–62, 64–71, 87 n. 169, 123 n. 87, 271, 308, 317, 325, 339
Dobschütz, E. von, 335
Dolbeau, F., 89 n. 176
Dölger, F. J., 62 n. 76, 348
Dondaine, A., 236 n. 8, 237 n. 12, 239 n. 16, 250 n. 33

Dondaine, H. F., 234 n. 1, 235 n. 2, 243–44
Dossetti, G., 74 n. 112, 288
Duchesne, L., 121
Dvornik, F., 229 n. 4

Eustratiades, S., 123 n. 87

Failler, A., 236 n. 8, 249 n. 28, 314
Faller, O., 273, 282
Festa, N., 237 n. 8
Festugière, A. J., 201–2, 332–33
Ficker, G., 85 n. 161, 310
Flusin, B., 202–3, 332
Fonkič, B. L., 100 nn. 27 and 28
Franchi, A., 82 n. 141
Freeman, A., 37 nn. 170 and 172
Funk, F. X., 90 n. 182, 172, 269, 317, 324, 339

Gallandius, A., 188
Gallay, P., 283, 294–95, 298, 316, 318
Gamillscheg, E., 44 n. 7
Gardthausen, V., 48 n. 24
Geanakoplos, D. J., 236 n. 8
Gebhardt, E., 281, 315
Gellinck, J. de, 1 n. 1
Gero, S., 31 n. 145, 32 nn. 146 and 148, 37 n. 172, 48 n. 24, 93 n. 2, 104 n. 41, 110 nn. 56 and 57, 125 n. 96, 137 n. 108, 140 n. 120, 208 n. 161
Giannelli, C., 260 n. 29
Gill, J., 54 n. 50, 76 n. 126, 81 n. 139, 82 n. 142
Gouillard, J., 48 n. 24, 100 n. 28, 108 n. 51, 120–21, 209–10 n. 163, 336
Granić, B., 48 n. 23
Grillet, B., 338
Grillmeier, A., 1 n. 1, 8 n. 5
Grotz, H., 108–9
Grumel, V., 89 n. 179, 94 n. 10, 121 n. 82, 254 n. 3
Günter, O., 12 n. 43
Gythiel, A., 92 n. 1

Halkin, F., 322
Hampe, K., 118
Hansen, G. Ch., 329, 330

Harduin, J., 141, 200
Harlfinger, D., 44 n. 7, 48 n. 23
Hartmann, W., 37 n. 171
Hefele, C., 1 n. 1, 3 n. 8
Heikel, I. A., 225 n. 187
Heil, G., 276, 291, 325–26, 337
Hennephof, H., 31 n. 145
Henry, R., 87 n. 168
Hergenröther, J., 89 n. 181, 309
Holl, K., 35 nn. 165 and 166, 177, 275, 283, 327
Hunger, H., 260 n. 29
Hussey, J., 72 n. 96, 75–76, 249 n. 29, 254 n. 2

Iadevaia, F., 33 n. 149, 34 n. 156

Jaeger, W., 276, 320
Junod, E., 138 n. 113, 139

Kaestli, J. D., 138 n. 113, 139
Kannengieser, Ch., 166, 324
Kazhdan, A., 62 n. 76, 104 n. 41
Kelly, J. N. D., 73 n. 99, 74 n. 112, 75 n. 121, 76 n. 122, 109 n. 55
Kitzinger, E., 93 n. 2
Kotter, B., 100 n. 28, 101, 107 n. 48, 113 nn. 64 and 65, 117, 125 n. 95, 128, 129 nn. 99 and 100, 144 n. 125, 211 n. 165, 306, 322
Kotzabassi, S., 45 n. 16, 53 n. 47
Kresten, O., 260 n. 29
Kurtz, E., 100 n. 27
Kydell, R., 230 n. 11

Lafontaine, G., 341
Lampe, G. W. H., 230 n. 10
Langerbeck, H., 154–55, 292, 320
Leclercq, H., 1 n. 1, 3 n. 8
Lendle, O., 348
Le Quien, M., 48 n. 24
Leroy-Molinghen, A., 196, 331
Lilla, S., 260 n. 29
Loenertz, R. J., 236 n. 8

Maguire, H., 104 n. 41
Mango, C., 20 n. 85, 33 n. 149, 34 n. 156, 45 n. 18, 48 n. 27, 137 n. 108, 164 n. 140, 250 n. 31, 259

Martin, F. X., 236 n. 8
McDonough, J., 297
Melioranskij, B. M., 48 n. 27, 49 n. 37, 100 n. 27, 101 n. 34, 110–12, 114, 115 n. 74, 146 n. 128, 208 n. 162, 209, 216 n. 169, 323, 335
Melloni, A., 37 n. 172
Mercati, G., 56 n. 60, 183, 255 n. 4, 269
Meunier, B., 249 n. 28
Meyendorff, E., 92 n. 1
Meyendorff, J., 92 n. 1
Michels, H., 108–9
Mioni, E., 106 n. 43, 259
Misides, A., 110 n. 56, 335
Montfaucon, B. de, 45 n. 18, 47 n. 22, 48
Moreschini, C., 269, 294, 298, 307, 317, 319
Morral, J. B., 236 n. 8
Mossay, J., 269, 295, 318, 350
Mosshammer, A., 87 n. 166
Müller, F., 296, 298, 314
Munitiz, J., 43–46, 48 n. 24, 50–51, 53 n. 46, 54, 84 n. 158, 85 n. 162, 86 n. 163, 106 n. 44, 244, 252 n. 40, 307
Murphy, F. X., 19 n. 77, 22 n. 94
Murray, s. A. Ch., 32 n. 146
Musurillo, H., 284, 338

Neusner, J., 93 n. 2
Nicol, D. M., 236 n. 8
Nissen, Th., 338
Noble, T. F. X., 109 n. 55
Noret, J., 110 n. 57

Oikonomides, N., 45 n. 14
Omont, H., 43 n. 5
Orlandis, J., 74–75
Ostrogorsky, G., 31–32 n. 145, 33, 35 nn. 165 and 167, 121 n. 82
Ouspensky, L., 92 n. 1

Papadopoulos-Kerameus, A., 201, 332
Paramelle, J., 84 n. 158, 286
Parmentier L., 192, 292, 330
Patacsi, G., 237 n. 8
Pattenden, Ph., 204 n. 158

Peeters, P., 20 n. 87, 21 n. 89
Pelikan, J., 4 n. 12, 72 n. 97, 73 n. 99, 80 n. 136, 92 n. 1
Petit, L., 81 n. 140, 348
Phanourgakis, B., 124 n. 87
Pierres, J., 19 n. 82
Pinard, J., 106 n. 44, 252 n. 40
Pitra, I., 345
Podskalsky, G., 237 n. 8
Poljakov, F. B., 100 nn. 27 and 28
Préville, J. de, 327
Pruche, B., 151, 282, 285, 292, 302, 316, 318, 347

Ramos-Lissón, D., 73 n. 99, 74–75
Ravegnani, G., 253 n. 42
Regnault, L., 327
Reischl, W. K., 178, 328
Reuss, J., 164 n. 141, 323
Richard, M., 1 n. 1, 3 nn. 5 and 8, 4 n. 11, 5 n. 17, 8 n. 31, 11 n. 41, 12 n. 44, 298
Riedinger, R., 16–21, 22 n. 94, 23 n. 103, 27 n. 120, 29 n. 131, 31 n. 142, 41 n. 181, 44 n. 8, 51–52, 71 nn. 90 and 91, 85 n. 160, 252 n. 39, 258–59, 296, 307
Ritter, A. M., 276, 325–26, 337
Roberg, B., 82 n. 141, 236 n. 8, 237 n. 11
Rossi, I. B. de, 257–58 nn. 10 and 15–17
Routh, M. J., 87 n. 166
Rupp, J., 328

Sambin, P., 237 n. 8, 251
Sansterre, J. M., 18 n. 76, 19 n. 81, 20 n. 84, 26 n. 119, 27 n. 120, 48 n. 27, 115 n. 75, 122 n. 83, 231 n. 14, 255 n. 4, 256 n. 9, 257–59
Schäferdiek, K., 75 n. 112
Schermann, Th., 47 n. 23, 88–89, 309
Schieffer, R., 1 n. 2
Schönborn, Ch. von, 92 n. 1
Schwartz, E., 8 n. 30, 14 n. 54, 45 n. 17, 48 n. 23, 53–54, 55 nn. 52 and 54, 77, 337
Serruys, D., 32 n. 145, 123 n. 87

Setton, K. M., 236 n. 8

Ševčenko, I., 87 n. 167

Sherwood, P., 19 n. 77, 22 n. 94, 76 nn. 124 and 129, 85 n. 159

Simonetti, M., 73 n. 99

Sinkewicz, R. E., 261

Spagnolo, A., 88 n. 174

Spanneut, M., 326

Speck, P., 94–95, 98 n. 23, 99, 110 n. 59, 115 n. 73, 121 n. 82, 125 n. 97

Speyer, W., 5 n. 15, 205 n. 159

Srawley, J. H., 291, 293, 300

Stallman, C. J., 99 n. 26

Stein, D., 121 n. 82, 125 n. 97

Steinen, W. von den, 177 n. 146

Stevenson, H., 257 n. 10

Straub, J., 48 n. 23, 56 n. 56

Suchla, R. B., 290

Sullivan, F., 11 n. 41, 12 nn. 44 and 45

Swete, H. B., 72–76, 236 n. 6

Tăutu, A., 239 nn. 13–15, 249, 251

Tetz, M., 5 n. 17

Thümmel, H. G., 32 n. 148, 39 n. 150, 315, 316, 323, 324, 328, 329, 330

Thurn, H., 44 n. 8, 51 n. 41, 52 n. 45, 307

Treadgold, W., 109 n. 55

Troianos, S., 229 nn. 3 and 5

Turner, C. H., 88 nn. 174 and 175

Turyn, A., 45 n.13

Ughelli, F., 237 n. 9

Usener, H., 324

Uthemann, K. H., 43 n. 1, 45–52, 54–55, 58 n. 65, 69 n. 86, 71–72, 82, 89, 100 n. 27, 137 nn. 108 and 109, 215–17, 271, 279, 296

Van den Ven, P., 1 n. 1, 2 n. 4, 138 n. 111, 145 n. 127, 150, 197–99, 331, 332

Vives, J., 74 n. 111, 75 nn. 113, 115, 117

Vladimir (Archimandrite), 100 nn. 27 and 28

Vogel, M., 48 n. 24

Vosté, J. M., 11 n. 41

Waegeman, M., 57 n. 61

Wallach, L., 39 n. 177, 40 n. 179, 138 nn. 112 and 117, 144 n. 124, 155 n. 133, 157, 160, 162, 163, 164 n. 141, 167–68, 176, 177, 205, 212, 214 n. 168

Watt, J. A., 236 n. 8

Wenger, A., 157–58, 160, 162, 321

Werminghoff, A., 38 n. 173, 39 n. 175, 138 n. 115, 177 n. 146

West, M. L., 145 n. 126

Winkelmann, F., 29 n. 131

Zettl, E., 48 n. 26, 55 n. 51, 56 nn. 57 and 59, 253